FIVE EASY
DECADES

FIVE EASY DECADES

How Jack Nicholson
Became the Biggest Movie Star
in Modern Times

DENNIS McDOUGAL

WILEY

John Wiley & Sons, Inc.

For Carl Albert McDougal (1920–2005)

My father, my teacher, my confessor, my compadre.
Leader of the band all the way to the end of the line.

Published by John Wiley & Sons, Inc., Hoboken, New Jersey
Published simultaneously in Canada

Design and composition by Navta Associates, Inc.

For general information about our other products and services, please contact our Customer Care Department within the United States at (800) 762-2974, outside the United States at (317) 572-3993 or fax (317) 572-4002.

Wiley also publishes its books in a variety of electronic formats. Some content that appears in print may not be available in electronic books. For more information about Wiley products, visit our web site at www.wiley.com.

Library of Congress Cataloging-in-Publication Data:
McDougal, Dennis.
    Five easy decades : how Jack Nicholson became the biggest movie star in modern times / Dennis McDougal.
        p. cm.
    Includes bibliographical references and index.
    ISBN 978-1-62045-658-3

    1. Nicholson, Jack. 2. Motion picture actors and actresses—United States—Biography. I. Title.
    PN2287.N5M36 2008
    791.4302'8092—dc22
    [B]   2007012089

Printed in the United States of America

10 9 8 7 6 5 4 3 2

CONTENTS

PREFACE

I began *Five Easy Decades* several years ago as an homage to the American film actor who seemed to express the very essence of what it meant to be a man of his time. Jack Nicholson was the guy who got away with everything: he lived as he chose, slept with whoever caught his fancy, ingested all manner of controlled substances, earned millions as a movie star, and still won accolades and public approval, despite his guilty grin. Like most fans, I admired him, even envied him. His presence in a movie pretty much guaranteed that I'd be standing in line at the box office on a Saturday night.

Tracking Jack through fifty years of showbiz, from the death of the studio system to the dawn of the digital age, turned out to be an exercise in tracking Hollywood itself. Whither went tinseltown, Jack was one step ahead, from counterculture to comic book heroes, from boomer malaise to indie films, and always Jack cashed in on the back end, boosting his stock higher than that of any other Hollywood plutocrat.

I saw all of his movies, not just the standouts like *Chinatown*, *Batman*, or *Five Easy Pieces*, and my respect for him only increased. Jack's development, depth, and range began to unfold for me in a different way. Few of his fans have ever seen *The King of Marvin Gardens*, *The Passenger*, *Ironweed*, or *The Pledge*, but they should. Even abject failures such as *The Fortune* and *The Border* rise to Jack's disciplined level of the Method whenever he's onscreen, and the earliest pre–*Easy Rider* films, from *The Cry Baby Killer* to *Psych-Out*, show how he used his years as a Roger Corman disciple to hone his screen craft into a mesmerizing instrument. No matter what, Jack always tried to give the performance of his life.

As I dug deep into the Nicholson legend, however, I couldn't help but judge him in a different way. It turns out he didn't get laid, stoned, and rich with impunity. He did not come through unscathed, nor did many of the people he got close to—at least, his version of closeness. The ghosts of a past he never came to terms with always constrained intimacy. Few, if any, people ever really got to know Jack, despite the locker room camaraderie among his entourage and his crazy bid for sexual validation by seducing all women all the time.

I wanted Jack's cooperation and tried to get past the layers of protection he's built around himself, but Patrick McGilligan—my friend and fellow Hollywood historian who wrote his own well-received Jack biography in the early 1990s—correctly predicted that I would fail.

Just as Jack has never agreed to a TV interview, he has never cooperated with a biographer, though a dozen or more books have been published about him over the last thirty years. Questions over which he has no control and cameras not purposely placed to show him at his best are anathema. Jack prefers the occasional magazine Q&A or quickie newspaper interview, usually granted in conjunction with the release of his latest movie. If a still photographer comes along for the ride, Jack has final call on when and how the camera is used. Candid shots of Jack Nicholson are almost never candid.

For better or worse, I took the snub in stride. My career has always been about digging, because usually those I write about—from mafiosi to moguls—would prefer to remain unknown, even if they appear to operate out in the open. Such is the terrain we have come to know as Hollywood. If stars routinely came clean, Army Archerd, Liz Smith, *People* magazine, Page Six, *Entertainment Tonight*, and half the British press corps would be out of a job. It's called showbiz because stars put on a show, even when they are not acting. Getting to who they really are is never an easy task.

Besides, it became clear to me early on that even in the longest and most probing interviews, Jack prefers to be seen at a remove; he remains an icon glimpsed through a glass darkly because that's the way he likes it. When questions cut too close, he either dodges them like the expert that he is, or, in a few rare instances, he calls a curt end to the discussion altogether. How would I be any different?

Fortunately, he and his friends and associates have left a long paper trail extending back to the 1960s, and while not very revealing in isolation, when pieced together these thousands of Jack documents begin to form a picture of the real John Joseph Nicholson Jr. who came to Hollywood in 1954 and stayed for good.

On this foundation I built a story based on court documents, property records, birth and death certificates, scores of books and unpublished manuscripts, and hundreds of hours in the stacks of the Academy of Motion Picture Arts and Sciences Margaret Herrick Library; the British Film Institute; the Billy Rose Library of the New York Public Library; the American Film Institute's Louis B. Mayer Library; the film libraries of UCLA, USC, and the University of Wisconsin; the National Archives in College Park, Maryland; the California State Archives in Sacramento; the Los Angeles City and County libraries; the Long Beach Library; the Pitkin County Library in Aspen, Colorado; and the Monmouth County Library in Manasquan, New Jersey.

Add dozens of interviews with friends, associates, and family members whom Jack either didn't know or forgot long ago, and a portrait began to emerge of a troubled man who nevertheless remained true to his art, reliably sniffing out the roles that defined the zeitgeist and scored at the box office.

Witness *The Departed*, Jack's most recent triumph and the Best Picture Oscar winner for 2006. Almost forty years after *Easy Rider*, there he stood at the Academy Awards, chunkier, bald, but still wearing his trademark shades as he handed out the gold to Best Director Martin Scorsese. Though Jack didn't win an award—didn't even add his pivotal role as the gangster Frank Costello to the pantheon of a dozen memorable film characters previously honored with Oscar nominations—there wasn't a soul on or off the stage who didn't credit Jack as the glue that held *The Departed* together. Matt Damon and Leo DiCaprio may have been the nominal leads, and Mark Wahlberg may have received the Best Supporting Actor nomination, but it was Jack Nicholson who lured jaded film fans away from their TVs, iPods, and computer screens. During an era of declining interest in that most traditional of American art forms, the movies, crowds returned in droves to theaters for an old-fashioned Scorsese shoot-'em-up because they wanted one more dose of Nicholson.

To me, Jack stands alone among his generation of actors as a star who continues to shine. Robert Redford's all but retired. Al Pacino's become a wild-eyed caricature of a character actor. Dustin Hoffman and Robert DeNiro are reduced to *alter cocker* comedy roles. Even Jack's old cruising partner Warren Beatty has faded from public view. Jack and Clint Eastwood have endured, but Eastwood did it behind the camera more than he did in front.

Jack's peers ended up parodying themselves. While Jack is always unmistakably Jack, he's avoided typecasting by shifting with the tide. He made career decisions that no other star made, and it kept him at the culture's leading edge for more than a generation.

But the cost has been steep. Jack came close with Anjelica Huston and Rebecca Broussard but never found his soul mate. A family tree cursed with alcoholism, cancer, and early death haunts and harrows him even now, though it does serve as a deep emotional well from which to draw the mesmerizing characters Jack has captured on film. It's hard to pinpoint where he got mired in perpetual adolescence, but the mystery of his illegitimate birth had to have something to do with it.

He never knew his father, and his mother, grandmother, and aunt all lied about his murky beginnings way past the time that they ought to have set the record straight. Perhaps all that *Chinatown*esque confusion ("I'm your mother [slap]. I'm your sister [slap]. I'm your mother *and* your sister!") set him on the path toward his own paternal profligacy. By most counts, he's a father six times over—the first one legitimate and all the others out of wedlock. There are two other possibles whom those closest to Jack whisper about, including one young man who lives with handicaps brought on by his actress mother's drug abuse. That would bring the number of Jack progeny to eight, but these are among the closely held secrets he has generally succeeded in keeping from his fans. He's opened his checkbook to all his children, if not to their mothers. That's more than his own father did. But generosity of spirit remains a separate matter. Jack can giveth, but Jack can also taketh away.

A reader's note: This book is rife with footnotes—observations, sidelights, and bits of information that did not fit neatly into the narrative but seemed to me to add depth and texture to the story. If they daunt, skipping past them is no detriment, but they remain for the illumination and entertainment of those who want to spend more time getting to know Jack

"He has taken on the mien of a gangster-king who knows he can do pretty much as he wants to do, oddly like Sinatra," one of Jack's oldest friends told me. "But as Jack must know, a part of the public romanticizes that very kind of thing; for example, the melodramatic loneliness which sets in all the more towards the end, à la Sinatra."

When it comes to those closest to him, Jack is loyal and demands loyalty in return—a simple enough interpretation of the Golden Rule, if it didn't carry the codicil that he also demands servitude. Bad or critical news is delivered seldom or never, and those beholden to him get an opportunity to cross him only once. With the speed and ice of a feudal lord, Jack severs relationships like an enemy's head when he is displeased. Nobody gets a second chance.

But is it right to hold a star to a higher standard? We do so with politicians because we believe that private morality is a way of gauging public trust. With an actor, we want to trust that he is emotionally honest, a true reflection of the times and a conduit through whom we can experience our own shortcomings and triumphs. In this way Jack is a true artist, a true reflection of the last five decades. Never mind his perpetual erection, his temper tantrums, his potty mouth and pot head. We still want Jack's autograph. It's for our kid sister.

His Hollywood odyssey took him from actor to star to superstar to icon in a very short time, and his challenge then became to hold on tightly to the rights and privileges that America accords its demigods. Avoiding career pitfalls, Jack calculated his public and played the game accordingly. He gave them a character they could love or hate from the gut, and they forgave his trespasses. As the Joker or George Hanson, Garrett Breedlove or J. J. Gittes, Jack is worshipped to this day. To those who know him only through his movies, he's nothing less than a national treasure.

Throughout the writing of this book, everyone wanted to know: What is Jack Nicholson *really* like?

I always dodged the question. I would not say because I could not say. I can dissect Jack the human being, with all the frailties and failings to which we all are heir, but that's no answer. Like the rest of us, he doesn't sum up nicely in a punchline or the last reel of one of his movies. For that alone, I hold him in the same regard I hold Sinatra.

I don't know that I'd have ever befriended the Chairman of the Board, but no one before or since has ever captured the regret of closing time more eloquently.

Similarly, no one before or since has ever defined the twentieth-century American man's alienation, disillusion, and triumph on the screen in quite so true and entertaining a fashion as Jack. I can say without hesitation that like Sinatra, he's an artist. And what is art? Well, Jack's contemporary Bob Dylan once defined it as "the perpetual motion of illusion." "The highest purpose of art is to inspire," Dylan said. "What else can you do? What else can you do for anyone but inspire them?"

For better or worse, Jack inspires. What else can he do?

PROLOGUE

OR FIFTY YEARS, JACK NICHOLSON HAS CREATED A PUBLIC persona the director Richard Rush described as "the cool man that we all grew up knowing was the one we had to be." Many men wanted to be like him; women frequently just wanted him. He has been a role model, an artist, a ganja pioneer, a basketball fanatic, a master of the Method, a clown, a collector, a lothario, an icon, and a cipher who *appears* absolutely frank and open for all the world to see, yet remains soberly resolute, brooding, cagily reflective, and manipulative—even dangerous in his more helpless moments of desperate introspection: as moody as the family cat who warns away tots with a baring of teeth and a twitch of the tail.

The actor-producer Michael Douglas, who hired Jack to star in *One Flew over the Cuckoo's Nest*, called him "the only actor more comfortable in front of the camera than in real life." Off the screen, Jack can be magnanimous one moment and petty the next. He toys with others' dreams like a tabby with a mouse, yet weeps the worst when he dooms those dreams and the dreamer dies. He is at once grandiose and mean-spirited, generous and cheap, eloquent and muddled, wicked and wise. He surrounds himself with sycophants and opulence while decrying the lot of the common man, and he never misses a chance to bed the uncommon woman.

Jack's life story parallels that of the modern entertainment industry—from MGM to MySpace and from Universal to YouTube. With today's lightning-swift shifts from cinema multiplex to MTV to the uncharted frontiers of the World Wide Web, Jack is one of the last of the old-time movie stars. He learned early to dodge the bullet of scandal and to market himself as a brand name, all the while maintaining his independence from the Hollywood machine. While the Tom Cruise generation became corporate franchises and mini-conglomerates unto themselves, Jack remained Jack—and yet it was his greed that helped to hasten the twilight of the stars.

"There are stars who have made bigger pictures, but there's no one who is as known around the world as he is, who still connects with teenagers," said his old friend Robert Evans, the producer of such films as *Chinatown* and *The Two Jakes*. "Every kid knows him. Jack stands alone. He's an original. He's not playing anybody. That's who he is."

Steeped in matinees and movie lore, Jack has always been ambivalent—even a little prehistoric—about advancing technology. Television and computers, and their newfangled cousin the Internet, may have triumphed, but the anachronistic Jack defiantly continues to stand tall, Ray-Bans in one hand, a buggy whip in the other.

Though his iconic days may be numbered, Jack cannot be discounted. He has turned in both near-perfect performances and dazzling duds in his long, enviable career. Nothing he has ever done, on or off the screen, is easily dismissed. "Not everyone may like the films, but they're not a waste of two hours of your time," he once told an interviewer.

Jack has never willingly lowered his standards or his guard, and he continues to be honored by his peers and celebrated by his fans, decade after decade, as an exemplar of all that is right and true, quirky, frequently dark, and a little twisted in the modern American male. A star with all the trappings, his concerns with creature comforts and celluloid immortality frequently trump friends and family. He can be icy, mean-spirited, and as empathetic as a reptile. But his roles consistently reflect the tumultuous times in which we live.

It's too bad Jack Nicholson isn't in charge of the movie industry instead of Rupert Murdoch, Sumner Redstone, or the bland corporate mandarins who have homogenized Time Warner, Sony, and General Electric into conveyor belts heaped with crap. Jack would never spend $100 million on a *Waterworld* or another *Alexander*, or release the horror of *Gigli* on an unsuspecting nation. Jack would *never* intentionally force-feed homogenous digitized dung to his fellow Americans. But then, Jack never aspired to run the show; his fatal flaw has been that he was happy just to chart the course and go along for the ride. As long as he reaped the steepest rewards the harvest would bear, he didn't mind much what seeds the studios sowed.

A full generation ago, Jack told the *Village Voice* in his familiar singsong drawl, "I'm a New Jersey person, a suburban personality. I don't exude aristocracy or intellectualism. But I try to give the common men that I play some extraordinary facet." One would be hard-pressed to get such a declaration from today's cookie-cutter stars. Despite the skyrocketing cost of admission (in summer 2007, $10 a head for a first-run ticket to *Pirates of the Caribbean*; $5 extra for a medium-size popcorn), there is little in twenty-first-century American cinema that qualifies as "extraordinary," and all of us are the lesser for it. As the *New York Times* film critic Tony Scott observed, "What we want from movies is not just distraction, diversion or passing amusement. We want satisfaction."

For half a century, Jack Nicholson has satisfied. Even on those rare occasions when he works from a bad script, he never phones in a "not bad" performance. Whether he's way over the top in *Mars Attacks!* (1996) or under the radar in *Blood and Wine* (1996), Jack delivers each and every time.

He throws off his own vanity "with both hands," as he puts it, and demands more from a screenplay than the words on the page. Exercising his hubris to the hilt, Jack preciously suggested in a 1986 interview that every modern actor should aspire to become "the *littérateur* of his era." And yet, even as he approached his seventieth birthday, he continued to live up to his own charge. Comic and sinister, he was the best part of Martin Scorsese's 2006 organized crime romp, *The Departed*.

According to Jack, as mass media exalted movie stars to unprecedented influence, actors could anticipate and shape the times in which they lived. As much as or even more than authors—and certainly more than politicians—film actors were in a position to influence history simply by paying laserlike attention to the roles they chose and the manner in which they interpreted them. "Nicholson's performance puts quotation marks around the character; it recalls *every* character in a similar situation that the spectator has *ever* seen," observed the film scholar Dennis Bingham.

Jack doesn't just chew scenery or hit his mark. He knows his character, precisely fitting himself into the emotional jigsaw puzzle of a film and frequently into the larger world outside the movie theater. He submerges backstory like an iceberg. The part the audience sees on the screen is just the electrified tip.

Stanley Kubrick recognized this quality the first time he saw *Easy Rider* (1969). Jack, Kubrick said, brought a kind of intelligence to the screen that cannot be taught. "There is James Cagney, Spencer Tracy, Humphrey Bogart, and Henry Fonda," declared the director Mike Nichols. "After that, who is there but Jack Nicholson?"

Jack has been venerated by the Academy of Motion Pictures Arts and Sciences with twelve nominations and more acting Oscars (three) than any other male actor in Hollywood history.[1] In 1994, he was the first of his generation honored by the American Film Institute for Lifetime Achievement, and seven years later, in 2001, he was named a Kennedy Center honoree. In 2004, when the former Kansas congressman Dan Glickman succeeded Jack Valenti as president of the Motion Picture Association of America (MPAA), the first person he declared he wanted to meet in his new role as Hollywood's Washington czar was Jack Nicholson.

Jack's influence extends far beyond the screen. No standup comic alive dares take the stage without a Jack impression tucked away. David Letterman owes Jack his deadpan acidity, and Howard Stern owes him his faux vulgarity. Jack-in-the-Box apes him to sell hamburgers, and he's more familiar to Los Angeles Lakers fans than are most of the players. His widely known mannerisms (flexing brows, sneering drawl, killer smile) and signature indoor sunglasses are required parts of a star's uniform. For nearly fifty years, Jack has been a lightning rod for the Next Big Thing in Hollywood and the standard-bearer of American celebrity.

"Celebrities, in fact, have inherited much of the glamour and sexiness that used to attach itself to the aristocracy," observed the *New York Times*'s Charles McGrath. "But if the margins have shifted, and if fame, for example, now counts for more than breeding, what persists is the great American theme of longing, of wanting something more, or other than what you were born with—the wish not to rise in class so much as merely to become classy."

Despite his bourgeois roots, Jack Nicholson has devoted a lifetime to being perceived as classy: he's the Gatsby of Mulholland Drive. More than 150 years ago, the French nobleman Alexis de Tocqueville paid his famous visit to the new nation and concluded that America was a place "where boundaries of class seem just elusive and permeable enough to sustain both the fear of falling and dream of escape."

Jack Nicholson fell out of New Jersey and escaped to Hollywood.

BOOK I

AUSPICIOUS BEGINNINGS

1937–1968

1

ON APRIL 22, 1937, THE PURPORTED DAY ON WHICH JOHN JOSEPH Nicholson Jr. arrived in this world, "They Can't Take That Away from Me" crawled up radio's hit parade on its way to becoming a pop standard. A stubborn elegy to lost love, the song could have been Jack Nicholson's personal anthem: from the tenderest age, Jack had it all taken away, beginning with his own birthright.

At a moment in history when talking pictures were hitting their stride and newspapers hyped Louis B. Mayer as the highest-salaried man in America, RKO handpicked for airplay the breakout single from the soundtrack of the movie musical *Shall We Dance*, Fred Astaire's seventh tap-fest with Ginger Rogers.[1]

But Jack wasn't destined to be a Broadway dandy like Astaire. Even more than with other actors, the remarkable facts of Jack's life are so mired with the fictions—both deliberate and unintentional— that just getting him into focus is a rigorous yet hypnotic exercise.

To begin to fathom Jack Nicholson, we must first understand that no one ever gave him a damned thing. Born a bastard, he arrived without a pedigree, but he was never told the whole truth about his parents until the guilty parties were all in their graves. Jack earned, negotiated, lifted, salvaged, seduced, maximized, wheedled, and hustled everything he ever had, and then fought like hell just to hold on.

As to his birth, "alleged" and "supposed" have become permanent attachments. He has no birth certificate. He has no father. His birth father certainly wasn't the amiable alcoholic John Joseph Nicholson Sr., who died after a lifelong ballet with the bottle just one year after Jack's high school graduation. John Sr. may have taken the boy for egg creams at the neighborhood pub or to ball games on those rare occasions when he was sober. He may even have given Jack some brandy-flavored fatherly advice from time to time. But John Sr. was not the man who sired Jack.

Any description of Jack Nicholson's paternity remains murky at best. The official biography says that Jack was born at home on Sixth Street in Neptune City, New Jersey, but it's far more likely he was born under an assumed name at St. Vincent's, a Roman Catholic charity hospital operated by the Sisters of Mercy on Manhattan's Lower West Side.[2] There is no accurate record of the birth date. In 1943, when Jack was baptized at the Church of the Ascension in nearby Bradley Beach, his family told the priest that he was born in 1938, not 1937.

Much later, it would be revealed that his older sister June was his real mother. His grandmother, who had adopted the role of mom, never let on any differently to her boy Jack. He grew up knowing Mrs. Ethel May Nicholson as "Mud" (short for "Mudder"). Even after Ethel May died in January 1970, Jack claimed that he didn't learn the maternal truth until four years later—an assertion disputed by some of his oldest acquaintances, who maintain that he knew much earlier but played the story for maximum publicity.

As the legend goes, a journalist dug deep into the public record for a *Time* magazine cover story and concluded that Mudder—Neptune's premier home hairdresser throughout the 1940s—was not Jack's mother at all. His real mother had been his "sister" June. But by the time Jack learned the truth, June, too, was gone—dead of cancer at age forty-four on July 31, 1963. Only his other sister, Lorraine, survived to confirm the tale, and confirm it she did, although even she professed to be ignorant as to who Jack's true father might be.

Jack grew up during the 1940s in Neptune City, located on the New Jersey shore about an hour's drive south of Manhattan. Neptune's nearest moderate-size neighbor, Asbury Park, would nurture Danny DeVito and Bruce Springsteen and the E Street Band for the next generation, but during Jack's youth, the biggest celebrity from the Jersey Shore was Bud Abbott, of the comedy team Abbott and Costello. Jack came to know the duo only from his trips to the Saturday matinee at the Palace Theater in nearby Bradley Beach. He had no obvious brushes with celebrities while growing up, even though June most likely wound up pregnant with him as an indirect result of her own show-business aspirations.

Jack's true father was likely one of two leading contenders, both minor vaudevillians who performed at summer festivals and church bazaars along the Jersey Shore. They shared June's passion to somehow sing and dance their way into the big time, just as Fred Astaire and Ginger Rogers had.

Eddie King (née Kirschfield) was a Latvian musician who illegally immigrated to the United States in 1925 and passed himself off as a bandleader, a vocalist, a drama coach, a gymnast, and a dance instructor. He opened a dance studio at 702 Cookman Avenue in the early thirties, and June was among his first pupils. Pert, leggy, and barely beyond puberty, redheaded June became King's leading prodigy and partner, performing with him at theaters, fairs, and amateur talent shows all over north Jersey. For a while, they paired for a local Saturday morning radio show called *Eddie King and His Radio Kiddies.* When June dropped out of school in 1934 to perform professionally, she continued to appear onstage with Eddie while also striking out on her own as a model, a singer, and a chorus girl.

After singing and dancing from New York to Florida over the next two years, June made the acquaintance of Jack's other likely paternal candidate. Don Rose (née Furcillo) was a local barber's son who aspired to sing out front for a big band, as Bing Crosby or Frank Sinatra did. He fell for June during the summer of 1936, when she was preparing to take her act on the road once more, to Dallas and Miami Beach. Like Eddie King, Don Rose was nearly ten years older than June, but unlike the bachelor King, Rose was married with a young son. He was separated from his wife at the time, awaiting an annulment. An indiscriminate young woman, June was taken in by his attentions.

In the decades that followed, Rose laid claim to siring Jack Nicholson, while Eddie King—who bore a striking resemblance to the future film star—did not. But whether Jack's father was King-Kirschfield, Rose-Furcillo, or someone else, the one certainty was that June Nicholson had become pregnant by the autumn of 1936.

Unplanned pregnancy was nothing new among the Nicholsons. June's parents had their own shotgun wedding in 1918. Ethel May gave birth to June just three months after becoming Mrs. John Joseph Nicholson. But June's prospects for a face-saving quickie marriage were not so rosy. Immigration authorities caught up with Kirschfield in 1937 and shipped him off to Ellis Island for deportation to his native Latvia, and Furcillo never came through with the promised divorce. Thus, months shy of her eighteenth birthday, June had two choices: having either an abortion or an illegitimate child.

While Jack has rarely championed political causes, he does have a strong personal position against abortion.[3] Had some earlier *Roe v. Wade*–like decision given a desperate movie star–wannabe named June Nicholson the right to choose, her son has little doubt today which option she would have taken.

In an early interview, Jack explained his position this way: "As an illegitimate child born in 1937, during the Depression, to a broken lower-middle-class family, you are a candidate for . . . " He paused to gather his thoughts. "You're an automatic abortion with most people today," he concluded.[4]

In the early months of 1937, June disappeared from Neptune City. No one knew where she went, but rumor had it she was staying with a cousin in New York. A postcard she mailed to a friend just weeks before Jack was born gave a return address of 225 E. 40th Street.

In the spring, while Fred Astaire was crooning "They Can't Take That Away from Me" to Ginger Rogers in movie houses all across America, June Nicholson gave birth to a baby boy. Although New York City birth records list no child with the last name of Nicholson, King, Kirschfield, Furcillo, or Rose born on April 22, 1937, there is an entry for a John J. Wilson who was born in Manhattan on that day. At the time, June used the stage name "June Nilson," and the neighbor family then closest to Mud and her girls in Neptune City was named Wilson.

Ethel May Nicholson stood by following the birth, not as a doting forty-year-old grandmother, but as a new mother in name and in fact, for all legal and practical purposes. "My mother's intimate friends, her card group, knew June was pregnant," recalled Lorraine, who was just fourteen at the time. "One of them told me that they did that thing where they all put their hands on top of each other and swear to secrecy."

June eventually moved on, marrying and starting a new family in another state. She never acknowledged Jack as anything other than a younger brother and never addressed the question of his paternity. But Ethel May became Mud—the central guiding force in Jack's young life.

At birth he'd been set on a course in search of his father, and that would become the primary, as well as primal, theme of his life—as haunting as a Joseph Campbell backstory, as harrowing as any Jedi tale. Long before Jack learned the truth, he seemed to know that his was an upbringing steeped in denial.

"I never really had a father around the house, because my mother and father were separated before I was born," Jack told a journalist in 1974, a few months before he allegedly discovered who his real mother was. "My mother and my sisters and brother-in-law were in the house, so I guess he [the brother-in-law] was kind of like my father figure. It's hard to say. I always had a very adult dialogue with all of my family, because I think I established an early communication on a person-to-person level."

The man Jack grew up believing to be his father was the amiable drunk John Joseph Nicholson Sr.—a red-haired, bespectacled Irishman with an artistic bent and a dapper flair for fashion, from his jaunty hat all the way down to a flashy pair of brown-and-white patent leather shoes.[5] "A quiet, melancholy, tragic figure—a very soft man," though never angry or cruel, as Jack remembered him. During the early 1930s, John Joseph made a living decorating department-store windows and painting signs.

But ends never quite met during the Depression. Ethel May took it upon herself to bolster the family's income by answering a newspaper ad to purchase a permanent-wave machine that included a how-to cosmetology course. She opened a home beauty parlor that catered to factory girls—a niche that hadn't been filled by the local salons owned and operated by men.[6] Unlike her male counterparts, Mud worked nights and on Sundays. "No man will give a woman an equal break in business," she used to lament.

As Mud's business grew, her husband's tapered off to nothing. Jack recalled Mud driving the old man to drink, but whether the drinking led to unemployment, or vice versa, by the time Jack came along, John Joseph Sr. and his wife quarreled often, chiefly over money.

The final blowout took place when Jack was about four years old. Sometimes Jack remembers John Joseph Sr. packing up and leaving of his own volition; at others, he recalls Ethel May forcing the old man to get out of the house and all of their lives. Regardless of the circumstances, the result was the same. Jack's "father" left to live with his own mother in another part of town. He sometimes got sober, washed dishes for a spell at Mom's Kitchen diner on South Main, then slid back into drink again, usually at the Chateau Lounge up in Asbury Park. Most Sunday mornings, Mud found him passed out on her front steps. "He got drunk on apricot brandy after the firehouse baseball game one year and never stopped drinking," Ethel May told Jack when he was old enough to understand. "Never, never, never."

John Joseph Sr. occasionally sobered up long enough to return to

Ethel May's for short visits and to take Jack downtown for a soda or an occasional ball game. "I remember the first outing I ever went on alone with him was up to the Polo Grounds," recalled Jack. "I saw Mel Ott hit a home run. I saw Bill Nicholson, my namesake, park one. It was the Giants and the Cubs. We were both Yankee fans, but they weren't in town."

For most of Jack's young life, though, he had no father. As the former *Time* magazine film critic Jay Cocks put it, Jack's father "drifted in and out after that, dwelling somewhere just on the edge of Nicholson's consciousness, like a phantom who could tell a secret, if you could only catch him."

Raised by women, Jack marveled at how he had managed to escape drowning in all that estrogen: "My mother ran a beauty parlor in a bedroom of our house, and I was surrounded by women and hair dryers. Under such circumstances, it's a miracle that I didn't turn out to be a fag."

The household that John Joseph Sr. left behind consisted of Jack, Ethel May, and her two grown daughters, June and Lorraine— survivors all. "Here was Mud, and she carried everybody on her back like a tiny little elephant, and it didn't seem to faze her," Jack recalled. "She marched right through it. These were strong women—made their own way in a period of time when it just wasn't done that much. They were my early loves and my early adversaries, those backyard-intellectual Irish German women."

Sixty years after his birth, Jack told the film critic David Thomson, "They wanted me. And I was raised in a household of women so I was not repressed by a dominant male figure. They always encouraged me. They said, 'We don't really care what you do, just make sure that you don't lie to us and that you tell us where you are.' And if I was anywhere they didn't want me to be, they let me know about it."

Though it took Jack a while to come to grips with the fundamental dishonesty of his birth, he maintained that this elaborate deceit had no lingering effect on his attitudes toward women. "Many people have asked me, 'Isn't there some resentment about the deceptiveness of women?' Well, I didn't need them [his mother, his grandmother, and his aunt] to find *that* out. When you think about it, I'm sure it caused them a lot of problems and soul-searching."

Two months after Jack's birth, June hit the road again in pursuit of her elusive stardom: Philadelphia, Miami, Chicago—wherever she could find work as a hoofer during the dying days of vaudeville. By 1944, at the ripe old age of twenty-five, she had retired from the stage and drifted north to Ohio, where she took a job at a Cleveland airfield. She snagged a divorced test pilot named Murray "Bob" Hawley with Connecticut blue blood in his veins. They married in Hawley's hometown of Ann Arbor, Michigan, and had a son and a daughter before migrating to Stony Brook in Southampton, New York, where they lived the good life during the last part of the decade. During school vacations, June imported Jack and gave him a taste of the Gatsby existence into which she had married.

But Hawley eventually abandoned June for another woman, just as he had his first wife and children back in Michigan. Broken in heart and spirit, June, in her late twenties, revisited New Jersey, her family, and her kid "brother," filled with bitter advice about showbiz, false love, and single motherhood. She vowed never to fall for another man again.

In the earliest days of World War II, June's counsel was as absent from Jack's young life as June herself was. Most of the time, Jack was just another Jersey kid, knocking around a Jersey neighborhood, and by default, Lorraine became Jack's surrogate mother. "When I registered Jack for kindergarten, he didn't even have a birth certificate," Lorraine recalled. "But since the secretary was a friend of mine, she never mentioned it, so I didn't. I just said, 'Oh, I'll bring it in later.'"

In June's absence, "'Rain" fed him, diapered him, and kept him out from under the customers' feet at Ethel May's hair salon. Lorraine, following her marriage to George W. "Shorty" Smith in the autumn of 1940, even supplied Jack with the closest candidate he would ever have to an adult male role model. "I had Shorty," he said. "I had Smith around. He was married to Lorraine. That, believe me, is as good a father as anybody's ever going to get or need. I can be as hard on my family or friends as anybody—I'm fairly objective—but there's nobody much that's impressed me as much as Shorty."

Squat, gruff Shorty Smith had been forced to learn to dance at Eddie King's studio when June was King's star pupil. He played football in high school and worked as a brakeman for Conrail after he married Lorraine, but even for a union man, jobs were spotty during the early 1940s. He joined the Merchant Marine during the war, and

Lorraine continued to live with Ethel May until the Smiths could afford their own place a few miles north in Asbury Park.

Like John Joseph Sr., Shorty enjoyed his gin—as illustrated by his large, red nose. But unlike the man whom Jack believed to be his father, Shorty came home from the bar every night. He "sat around all day with his shirt off and bullshitted," yet Jack credits him and his drinking buddy Ray Kramer[7] with demonstrating the nuances of masculine behavior: everything from lifting the toilet seat and standing to pee to an early and profound appreciation for a well-executed double play. "Shorty just had a grasp—innate, not a conscious ability—about life," said Jack, adding, "I hope I've got it."

He was always a bright boy, this restless young John Nicholson Jr., with chubby cheeks, ears that stuck out from the sides of his head, and oddly feral eyes. "I think I knew the power of my smile by the time I was five or six," he said. "Once I started looking at myself, though, I thought, 'I've got to keep my lips closed. Otherwise, I look like an inebriated chipmunk.'"

Inventive, glib, and a charmer, he also had a temper. For one interviewer, Lorraine recalled that Jack "could get so mad he could hardly talk." He turned tantrums into performance, stomping around the house, slamming doors, and belting the wall, all the while barking mild curses, calculated to raise eyebrows but seldom alarm: "For cripes' sakes!"

"They always said I thought I was smarter than they were, over and over again," said Jack. "And of course, I did! And I loved entertaining them on this level."

Once the trauma of kicking John Sr. out of the house had passed, Jack's childhood evolved uneventfully. According to Jack's own recollections, his was "a very sort of non-puritanical, non-Kiwanis, middle-class upbringing. My mother was an independent businesswoman. She didn't have tremendous scope in her thinking: she didn't want to run the town or the area. My family was always big into honesty—not too much punishment."

One spanking he remembered came after a visit to the grocery store. He was sent for bread and milk and came home instead with *Submariner*, *The Human Torch*, *Captain Marvel*, and *Batman*. The worst part was that Mud kept the comics. "To me back then, the cartoon was like Shakespeare blown up," said Jack.

He collected baseball cards, along with comic books, and played

Little League baseball. Joe DiMaggio was his idol for a while. From the cradle on, he was a cutup and a performer. In fourth grade he spent as much time in the corner by the blackboard as Bart Simpson does, bringing down the house by powdering his face with chalk dust and miming behind the teacher's back.

During a junior high school variety show, he once led a conga line, lip-synching to a Sinatra record. His eighth-grade teacher, Virginia Doyle, recalled that Jack "was always the first to volunteer for any variety show." And yet, "at bottom, he was the most serious of boys," she added. "He was very unhappy, disappointed by his father, and with the hilarity of all the pranks, I always felt they were to cover up some sadness."

"He was quite scholarly in his own sense: a maverick," said Alan "Hoop" Keith, a classmate who grew up with Jack and remained close throughout their lives. "He tended to play it down a little bit, even then."

"He would read something so damn fast," recalled Bernard "Dutch" Nichols, another Jersey pal. "That's what amazed me about him."

Never mind that Jack preferred DC comic superheroes to Dickens or Twain. Even better than Batman or Captain America were the movies. Early on, before his reluctant intellectualism began to show, Jack was as captivated by cinema as his chums were. They all grew up at the height of the matinee era, when cartoons and at least one cliffhanger serial sandwiched a double feature each Saturday afternoon at the Palace Theater. The price of admission was nine cents. "Neptune was a helluva place for a man to fall in love with John Ford," Jack later observed.

Like every kid in America, Jack was hooked on cowboy serials, but Hopalong Cassidy, Red Ryder, Gene Autry, and Roy Rogers played second fiddle to feature films like *My Friend Flicka* (1943)[8] and *Thunderhead* (1945). "I got insane over *Thunderhead*, which was the sequel to *My Friend Flicka*," he recalled. "I mean, me and my two guys—my mom kept a box of pennies and I used to reach in there and take a handful and we went every day. That picture got me. I always loved movies."

He told another interviewer that he sat through *The Babe Ruth Story* (1948) five times. He followed Preston Foster into high adventure. After a rousing horse opera or a blood 'n guts war movie, Jack and pals often adjourned to the nearby woods and staged another hour or two of Western shoot-'em-ups, or they hit Bradley Beach like hellbent Marines storming Normandy. In movies, action mattered the most, the gorier the better.

"I even remember the movies I never saw but heard about from other kids, like *Thirty Seconds over Tokyo* [1944]," recalled Jack. "All I had to hear was that they cut off a guy's hands with his black gloves on, and that image stuck with me forever."

Jack's was the last generation to come of age without the full impact of TV's influence. Though Ethel Nicholson was among the first on her block to buy a television set,[9] by the time Jack was a teenager he was far more interested in pop jazz and jukeboxes than *I Love Lucy* or *The Milton Berle Show.* "I've had a consistent attachment to pop music since I was a kid," he recalled.

Pals like Ken Kenney, the son of a saloon pianist and one of Jack's early best friends, holed up in Jack's room, where the two of them cranked up Stan Kenton, Harry James, or Louis Bellson records as high as the volume could go. "My generation, class of '50 to '54, we brought rock and roll to the world," Jack boasted. "My age group brought this banging noise; we're the original juvenile-delinquent rock and rollers. We brought percussion and ended melody."

In Jack's grammar school and junior high years, it was radio—not television or rock and roll music—that fed imaginations. Jack's family listened to the radio comedy of *Fibber McGee* and *Amos 'n Andy*, the spooky drama of *Lights Out* and *Gangbusters*, play-by-play big league baseball, boxing, football,[10] and the adventures of another Jack: *Jack Armstrong, All-American Boy.*

Jack Armstrong was everything Jack Nicholson was not. Except for those rare occasions when the radio star stopped in at fictitious Hudson High to pick up a football trophy or his straight-A report card, the brilliant, handsome, athletic Jack Armstrong and his pals Billy and Betty Fairfield trotted the globe for fifteen minutes each day, joining the Fairfields' Uncle Jim on high adventure in some exotic locale: Egypt, Africa, Easter Island, India. Forerunners of the Scooby-Doo gang, Armstrong and the intrepid Fairfields stalked Arizona cattle rustlers, found a lost Eskimo tribe near the Arctic Circle, busted up a counterfeiting ring, and scoured the Amazon for an ancient Incan city, among other far-flung exploits.[11]

By contrast, the Neptune City limits circumscribed Jack's pedestrian childhood. Cattle rustlers and counterfeiters never made it to the Jersey Shore. Beyond his radio fantasies or Saturday matinees, Jack was defined by central New Jersey's own unique system of social caste. While nominally a melting pot showcase of American democracy, the townships along the shore were as rigidly striated as any European ghetto. Patricians and plebes, blacks and whites, Irish and Italians, Catholics and Jews rarely mixed, and even tiny hamlets had their right and wrong sides of the tracks.[12]

By 1945, Mud's business thrived, and she was able to move her family from their single-story bungalow on Sixth Street to a two-story corner house in a tonier part of working-class Neptune, less than half a block from the Shark River lagoon. Each morning Jack walked seven blocks from their new place at 2 Steiner Avenue to Theodore Roosevelt Elementary, where a higher class of students attended. There, Jack made his stage debut at age ten, singing "Managua Nicaragua" during a talent show, although Mud deadpanned years later that Jack actually broke into showbiz portraying a carrot in the "Good Eating Habits" pageant.

When Jack was ready for high school, the family moved once more—this time, two miles farther south to old-money Spring Lake, Jersey's so-called Irish Riviera, where Ethel May set up her beauty parlor in a rambling duplex at 505 Mercer Avenue, across the street from Potter Park and half a block from the railway station. Jack recalled Mud's profit hovering around $5,000 a year—a healthy living during the postwar years. Business was brisk, and for her whip-smart young Jack, Mrs. Nicholson had her eye on nearby Manasquan High. The school drew students from the "snobby little town" of Sea Girt, as Jack's classmate Gail Dawson described her neighborhood, home to the nouveau riche who settled there during the war.

When Jack entered Manasquan High in 1950, he masked his Neptune roots by demonstrating that he was bright enough to skip a grade, even though his immaturity still shone. He might have been as smart as any high school freshman, but he still had the baby fat that had plagued him since kindergarten, as well as a high nasal soprano that had a long way to drop to become his adult baritone growl. Among the older and better-heeled Manasquan students, who all had their own nicknames, Jack's was "Chubs." "I've been overweight since I was four years old," he said. For the next ten years, he answered gibes with his fists, but "the first time I got my ass kicked, that was all over." From junior high onward, he substituted sarcasm for brawling.

"Jack could do the 'dozens' better than anybody in school," said his classmate Jon Epaminondas. A nasty adolescent put-down contest in which boys try to out-trash one another's mother, the "dirty dozens," or simply the "dozens," was Jack's secret weapon. Until he reached his full five feet, nine inches, and pals switched his nickname to "Nick," the munchkin Jack could stiletto bullies with a snide jibe.

Yet Jack's squirt stature handicapped any would-be athleticism. He moved up from Little League to American Legion baseball during summer vacation, but when he joined the high school football team as a freshman, he wound up becoming its equipment manager. The following school year he managed the basketball team but seldom got to play—allegedly because he and the coach didn't get along. One of his oft-told high school tales involved a feisty bit of vandalism. Jack claimed to have taken a Louisville slugger to the equipment room of a rival team following a bitter game and gotten himself banned from sports. "It became a matter of record, but I'm not sure it actually happened," said Hoop Keith, who added, "He wanted to be an athlete, was probably frustrated about not having been a little bigger, a little taller, maybe even a little older at the time. He was always the youngest in the group. He was accepted as part of the group. You didn't have to be an athlete to hang around with us."

Despite his frustration, Jack laid claim to basketball as his favorite spectator sport. Over the years, he loved to weave his own personal theories about basketball's fast-break action, which seemed to reflect the frenetic pace of postwar America. As the culture shed its interest in plodding, feudalistic football rituals and baseball's endless statistics, Jack made sure he was already sitting courtside, indulging himself in what he called the "night comedy" of the NBA.

"It was Bob Cousy's heyday," observed Dutch Nichols, who, along with Jack, Hoop, and the other members of the basketball squad, worshipped the Boston Celtics. But glory on the court remained as elusive for Jack as it had been on the football field or the baseball diamond. A competent player but never quite up to varsity standards, Jack had to live the life of a jock vicariously, writing about sports for the school newspaper, *The Blue and Gray*. He found power in the pen. The Manasquan yearbook, the *Treasure Chest*, described "jolly and good-natured Nick" as an "enthusiastic writer of those English compositions."

"I always wrote my way out of trouble in school," Jack recalled. "I had to stay after class every day my sophomore year and they would assign you to write a thousand-word essay story, and I'd write thousands of words. By the time I knew no one would be reading I'd slip in all sorts of mean comments about the people who ran the school."

Jack's teachers were ambivalent about him. By his own count, Jack was suspended three times: once for swearing, once for smoking, and once for vandalizing a rival school's scoreboard. Jack's Latin teacher, Ruth Walsh, made him sit up front just because he *looked* like a troublemaker. Miss Belting, Manasquan's spinster English teacher, warred with him, and long after Jack had become a star, she scoffed to a whole new generation of Manasquan undergrads that Jack "always had a big mouth and he's *still* got a big mouth."

Most of Jack's peers loved him, though. Although his talent for bringing fantasy to life on stage was not immediately apparent, Jack went from being freshman class clown to best actor as a senior. "Jack didn't get involved in plays until his junior year," recalled Epaminondas.

Jack's role in *Out of the Frying Pan*—a 1941 farce about young actors who stage a murder to win the attention of a successful Broadway producer—was minor, but Jack soaked up the applause and signed on again with the drama department the following year. This time he was the standout.

The playwright-screenwriter John Patrick (*Teahouse of the August Moon, High Society, Some Came Running*) wrote *The Curious Savage* in 1950 for the silent screen star Lillian Gish, but by the time the play moved Off-Off-Off Broadway to Manasquan High three years later, it was Sandra Hawes who landed the title role. "Jack was one of the crazies in the insane asylum," recalled Hawes, who is now Mrs. Sandra Frederick. "That was just natural for him."

The widow Savage, committed by her stepchildren to a sanitarium, conspires to get out of the loony bin with her fellow inmates, including a "pink, plump, and cherubic" idiot savant named Hannibal—a part tailor-made for Jack. On the page, Hannibal simply spouts statistics and catches throwaway lines, but in Jack's crazed hands, the supporting role became a study in obsessive-compulsive hilarity. He carried around a violin on stage, sawing two (and only two) notes between punch lines, and wound up stealing the show. In fellow cast member Donna Newton's yearbook, he urged her to remember "the rebellion we staged" the night Mrs. Savage and her fellow nutcases took over the asylum.

Jack's Hannibal also cemented Jack's place in Manasquan's social hierarchy. Voted by the senior class "Best Actress" to Jack's "Best Actor," Sandra Hawes was a Sea Girt princess who dared to ignore class distinctions when it came to Jack, as did most of her peers. "He was part of the 'in' crowd even though he never really had any love life to speak of," said Hawes. "He would hang around with the most popular girls in high school, and he was a part of whatever they did. He was probably the only one who didn't have to have a girlfriend to be part of that crowd all the time, because he was fun to be with. He was a kidder, a joker, always cutting up."

By default, wit had to be Jack's way of winning women. In addition to being younger, shorter, and a product of the working class compared to most of his peers, Jack had acne[13] ("I was presented the Pimple Award and every other kind of gross-out award in my youth," he told an interviewer) and no car. He either took the bus or spent hours hitchhiking, teaching himself to juggle by the side of the road while he waited for rides.

What was worse, Mud had instructed Jack to act like a gentleman. When Nancy Smith's steady dumped her just before the 1953 senior prom, Jack asked her to go with him, even though he was still only a junior. The following year Gail Dawson accompanied him to their prom and wore flats so she wouldn't tower over her date. They may have slow danced to "Blue Velvet," but Jack never made a move on her.

There was also the matter of money. Jack cut lawns, then caddied at the Spring Lake Golf Club or the Manasquan Country Club when he was a little older. As a junior, he became an usher at the Rivoli Theater in Belmar, where he got to see films like *Serpent of the Nile* (1953)—one of Jack's all-time favorite bad movies—for free. Ushering paid better than his previous jobs had, but never enough to finance much of a social life. While his peers were making plans for college, Jack still couldn't afford his first car.

Nevertheless, in the fall his classmates elected him vice president of their 157-member graduating class. He was listed as one of Manasquan's "Big Wheels" in the *Treasure Chest* at the end of his senior year and voted both class pessimist and class optimist. "I'm just a well-rounded personality," he deadpanned.

On May 24, 1954, three weeks before graduation, Ethel May filed a Delayed Report of Birth with the New Jersey State Health Department so that Jack could get his driver's license. Giving her maiden name, Ethel Rhoads, she listed herself and John Joseph Nicholson as Jack's parents and claimed that their son, John Joseph Nicholson Jr., had been born at the family home on 1410 Sixth Avenue in Neptune City, New Jersey, on April 22, 1937. It was a solid-enough lie to last another twenty years.

Jack took a summer job as a lifeguard at Bradley Beach to earn some extra cash. In his red trunks and skullcap, with a zinc oxide smear across the bridge of his nose, he cut a heroic if somewhat insolent figure sitting in his lifeguard's tower. "I was like death itself, guarding those people," he recalled.

Jack was no longer "Chubs" but a trim, fit "Nick" Nicholson who reveled in the looks cast his way by scantily clad women and adoring children. Jack Armstrong no longer had a thing on Jack Nicholson.

Two incidents that summer found their way into dozens of later interviews and became permanent threads in the suspect tapestry that Jack wove about his own beginnings. During his lifeguard stint, he claimed to have run into the actor Cesar Romero on the beach one day.[14] His first real exchange with a movie star went something like this:

Jack: "What's it like making movies out there in Hollywood?"

Romero: "Hollywood is the lousiest town in the world, when you're not working."

The second incident cast Jack in the role of hero. He rowed against huge waves kicked up by an offshore storm to rescue several swimmers caught in a riptide. In some accounts, he saved five; in others, a half dozen. He admitted to puking his guts out afterward, but the result was triumph: the shrimp who couldn't make the basketball team had made the grade as a bona fide lifesaver.

New Jersey is hard on its heroes, though. Jack's brother-in-law Shorty Smith had once been the Shore's first all-state football player, but Jack saw him reduced to a featherbedding brakeman who spent more time in taverns than in railyards. And there was Jack's father, John Joseph Sr., who sank to the bottom of a bottle, never to emerge.

By summer's end, Jack had an offer to escape, if just for a month or two. A year earlier, the newly divorced June Nicholson Hawley and her two children had moved to Los Angeles, where she landed a full-time job as a secretary at an aircraft plant. She invited Jack to come out for a visit before starting college. It was a big deal. Except for a few weekend visits to New York and the senior class trip to Washington, D.C., Jack had never traveled much outside the state.

At the time, Lorraine sold perfumes and foundation creams behind the cosmetics counter at Steinbach's, Asbury Park's oldest department store, and she seemed to understand that this was how it would be forever. She and Shorty had three kids of their own and had already blown any chance of rising much higher in the hidebound caste system of the Jersey Shore.

Before Jack left for California, Lorraine took her kid brother aside and told him, "Look, Jack, you're gifted. But if you stay around here, you'll always just be Jack Nicholson. Everybody will know everything about you, and no matter how good you are you'll be a big fish in a little pond. But if you take a shot and get out of town, you might feel differently. You could at least be a fish in a big pond."

As summer ended, Jack took off for Los Angeles.

"Nobody knew he was going out there until he was gone," recalled his classmate Jon Epaminondas.

2

IN SEPTEMBER 1954, JACK MOVED INTO HIS SISTER JUNE'S apartment in the Los Angeles suburb of Inglewood. The Pacific sun shone daily, while every night there was a party going on—if a restless young man knew where to look. Southern California felt like home, and Jack's monthlong vacation stretched into a lifetime. "In New York, you have to make $50 a week to keep from freezing to death," he once observed, "but in California you can sleep on the ground."

Mud wanted her boy to get serious and come back to New Jersey, and June agreed: with two kids plus happy Jack, her tiny apartment seemed like it might explode. But L.A. grew on Jack. Palm trees. Convertibles. Sunglasses. An abundance of deeply tanned, coconut-scented women who had no idea he was once known as Chubs.

In the autumn, New Jersey's Bradley Beach closed up shop, but the California coastal towns from Palos Verdes to Santa Monica remained wide open for business. Venice had a boardwalk just like Asbury Park's, but no one battened down the hatches or put up storm windows, because there *was* no winter in Southern California. Jack wasn't about to leave.

June's place was within walking distance of Hollywood Park, where Jack could play the ponies. Back in Jersey, he claimed to have purchased his first car with winnings from the Monmouth Park Racetrack, but he had to leave that dirt brown '47 Studebaker behind when he emigrated west. He was once more a pedestrian.

One evening after dinner, as Jack told the story, June got fed up with Jack's shiftlessness and told him to get the hell out. "I had about three dollars in my pocket," Jack recalled.

He decided to check out Hollywood Boulevard and made the mistake of setting out on foot across the Baldwin Hills. Who could blame him? The Hollywood sign shimmered in the autumn heat, unobstructed against the backdrop of the Santa Monica Mountains and near enough to reach out and touch. Jack hiked as far as La Brea and Sunset before he realized why everyone drives in L.A. The round trip was almost thirty heel-blistering miles. Upon his return, the pitched battles with his sister resumed. "We used to have incredible fights," Jack said about June. "She projected all her fears onto me. By the end of her life, she was a total conservative. And she saw me as a bum."

When Jack began to consider a movie career, his sister's advice boiled down to a single, bitter contraction: "Don't." Jack ignored her and went right to the top. While working part time in a toy store, he applied for a job at Metro-Goldwyn-Mayer (MGM), the largest, richest, and most powerful film factory in town. Then he waited.

Television's erosion of the movie business had been considerable in the first half of the decade. Average ticket prices doubled to 50 cents by 1954, while weekly movie house attendance dipped to 49 million—less than half the number of people who had attended regularly during the 1940s. But the studios remained optimistic. More than two hundred stars were still under contract, and the major studios, including MGM, released 427 films that year, adding gimmicks like 3-D, Cinerama, and Cinemascope to lure Americans away from their TV sets.[1] "When I first started working at MGM, they wouldn't shoot TV shows on the lot because it was seen as competition to film," Jack recalled. "They wouldn't even let their cameramen own TV sets—it was a stipulation in their contracts."

It wasn't all bad at the local Bijou. The year Jack arrived was the year Elia Kazan cast his next star, James Dean, in *East of Eden* (1955) and cemented Marlon Brando's place in Hollywood history by directing Brando to an Oscar as the ex-boxer Terry Malloy in *On the Waterfront* (1954). Jack told his friends he admired Sinatra, James Dean, Henry Fonda, and Montgomery Clift, but it was Brando he wanted to become. "I must have seen every performance of *On the Waterfront*—twice a night," recalled Jack. "You just couldn't take your eyes off the guy. He was spellbinding."

So was Sinatra. Following his Oscar-winning comeback in *From Here to Eternity* (1953), Sinatra hypnotized Jack in *The Man with the Golden Arm* (1955) and infected him with a lifelong addiction to hats—a further addition to Jack's growing wardrobe.[2] His nickname for Sinatra was "the Rag," in deference to the singer's fashion sense.

Despite tough times, MGM could still afford to hire experienced supernovae like Brando and Sinatra by filling its employment ranks with cheap, eager young gofers like the toothy young Jack Nicholson. Just as Jack was about to accept defeat, tuck his tail between his legs, and take the Southern Pacific back to Neptune, MGM hired him at $30 a week to become low man on the cartoon division's totem pole. "I did everything there," he recalled. "Mail boy, production, punching and stacking the papers, keeping the cartoonists happy with supplies."

He moved out of June's place and into his own postage stamp–size apartment above a garage just a few blocks from MGM's Culver City headquarters. Jack started out each day requisitioning No. 2 pencils, racing around the studio on a bicycle delivering mail, running bets for the animators to the studio bookie, and finishing up by answering fan mail for the cartoon cat-and-mouse team Tom and Jerry. For the next two years, he immersed himself in all things Hollywood. He saw as many stars as he wanted and learned everyone's first name, from executives to grunts. "I had crushes on Grace Kelly, on Rita Moreno . . . ," Jack recalled.

He also lived on a shoestring. He and his roommate, another MGM gofer named Roger "Storeroom" Anderson, lunched at Romero's coffee shop on Wilshire, where the lasagna was cheaper and more authentic and came in larger portions than those served in the MGM commissary. Whenever they got the urge, Jack and Roger sneaked into rehearsals and studied the lighting, the direction, and the camera work on MGM's soundstages. Jack wandered at will through Andy Hardy's neighborhood, Sherwood Forest, and the streets of Laredo on the studio's legendary back lot. He made himself indispensable with the jocks in the cartoon division. He bowled or positioned himself as guard on the department basketball team. He played outfield for the softball league and golfed nine holes at the El Rancho course on summer evenings in preparation for MGM's annual company tournament in nearby Fox Hills.

"He liked to tease and aggravate, needle and razz," the *Tom & Jerry* animator Erv Spence recalled. "He'd needle me. I'd get riled up, and that's what he wanted. Then that big grin would come out."

Jack was having a good time but still owned no car and earned little money. When the animator Oliver "Lefty" Callahan offered Jack his old '49 Chevy for $400, Jack had to wire home to New Jersey for cash.

Despite constant penny-pinching, Jack wore his hair in a well-trimmed flattop with "the most perfect duck's ass you've ever seen," according to his high school classmate Jon Epaminondas. "Brylcreem was my best friend," Jack recalled.

He kept up with fashion: button-down shirts, white bucks, khakis, and pegged trousers. Instead of baseball cards, he now collected colognes, record albums, and, of course, hats. He would remain a collector throughout his life, rarely throwing things away.

When Epaminondas came out to California for a visit, he found Jack living with Storeroom Roger. The three of them spruced up one night and went trolling at the Hollywood Palladium, but they were so broke they had to pool their money so they could buy a single gray plastic comb from a men's room vending machine. It must have done the trick because all three were making headway on the dance floor until a panicky Jack signaled his buddies into a huddle.

"We've gotta get out of here!" he whispered. "I've *got* to get to the men's room."

"What happened?" asked Epaminondas.

"I was dancing with this girl," said Jack, rolling his eyes. "She was dancing so damn close to me and I got so damn excited that I exploded in my pants."[3]

Jack couldn't be blamed if he felt as if he'd arrived in the Promised Land. On New Year's Day, while his friends back in New Jersey were freezing, he watched floral floats and gorgeous women glide down Pasadena's Colorado Boulevard during the Tournament of Roses parade. In the summer of 1955, he witnessed Disneyland open amid the orange groves of Anaheim.

Nineteen fifty-five was also the year James Dean threatened Brando's primacy as the country's favorite antihero, blazing across the screen in *East of Eden* (1955).[4] He didn't replace Brando as Jack's idol, but he came close. According to one account, Jack almost met Dean in the flesh at the Hollywood home of the flamboyant actor cum California bohemian Samson DeBrier.

The year Jack Nicholson first discovered his own future was the year his father's ended. John Joseph Nicholson Sr. drank himself to death on July 24, 1955. Lorraine and Shorty nursed him through his colon cancer and the heart disease that killed him, although no one doubted alcohol was the real culprit. He was fifty-seven. Jack didn't attend his memorial. "I was living in Los Angeles at the time," said Jack, "and the financial aspects of the trip made it prohibitive—or at least gave me a reason for it to be pro-hibitive—and I didn't particularly want to fly east just to go to the funeral."

Another death that year had far more immediate impact. On September 30, 1955, James Dean roared into eternity in his brand new silver Porsche Spyder. Following a head-on collision just north of Paso Robles, Dean died at twenty-four of a broken neck. His final cryptic words were "He's got to see us."

Jack and his peers did get to see James Dean in *East of Eden*, but in the months that followed his death, Dean's two remaining films, especially *Rebel without a Cause*, confirmed his legend. He would come to influence Jack and his entire generation. "We were a very rebellious generation," said the producer Harry Gittes, one of Jack's oldest and closest friends.[5] "I loved *Rebel without a Cause*, but I still don't know what they were rebelling against."

Jack was then in the nascent stages of creating his own legend, and one of his oft-quoted chestnuts in years to come involved an improb-able chance meeting in the elevator one day shortly after James Dean's death. The venerable MGM producer Joe Pasternak (*Destry Rides Again, Please Don't Eat the Daisies*) studied Jack's face between floors. As the doors slid open and Jack was about to exit, Pasternak said, "You ever thought of acting?"

Jack answered, "No," and got off at the animation department.

An hour later, the cartoon division chief Bill Hanna called Jack into his office.

"Did Joe Pasternak ask you if you wanted to be an actor?" Hanna demanded.

"Yeah," said Jack.

"Well, what did you say?"

"No."

"Jack, let me ask you a question: Do you want to be a goddamn office boy all your life?"

No, he didn't. A screen test was arranged, and, by May 1956, Jack's career looked as if it was about to take off. During the month after Pasternak watched the test, Jack came back down to earth. He had a great smile, a wiry physique, and sly bedroom eyes, but no training beyond his high school drama club. Besides, he had an insufferable Jersey twang. Pasternak suggested a voice coach.

On Hanna's recommendation, Jack signed up for classes with then up-and-coming character actor Joe Flynn, who told Jack that Pasternak was nuts.[6] Jack's voice might annoy some, but it was distinctive in a profession where distinction was everything. "I want to say one thing to you, Jack, that's very important," said Flynn. "Everyone you meet in this business is going to try to get you to take voice lessons. Don't do it."

On the strength of Flynn's recommendation, Jack joined a repertory theater: West Hollywood's Players Ring.[7] Jack claimed a walk-on role in *Tea and Sympathy*, and from July to September 1956, he debuted on the professional stage for $14 a week. "There were three other guys in the production: Michael Landon, Edd Byrnes, and Robert Fuller," he recalled. "When the show was over, they all got jobs in their own TV series—but I just lay around, still 'preparing.'"[8]

Little breaks did begin to come his way. Family and friends back home in New Jersey witnessed Jack's progress from afar when, on September 2, 1956, the *Asbury Park Press* reported that "Jack Nicholson, 19, formerly of Spring Lake, will have a TV role tomorrow afternoon in 'Drama,' a *Matinee Theatre* presentation on WNBT, Ch. 4. The program is scheduled from 3:00 to 3:30 p.m. The *Matinee Theatre* program will emanate from Hollywood."[9]

Although Jack began to get a few gigs, he didn't quit his day job until his day job quit him. In the closing days of 1956, the MGM animation production chief Fred Quimby called all 110 employees together to quash growing rumors that the ailing studio was getting out of the cartoon business. "Don't worry," Quimby reassured his troops. "This place is like the Rock of Gibraltar." Two weeks later, MGM folded the cartoon division in a cost-cutting move and laid off everyone, including Jack.

Over the next several years, Jack learned what it meant to be a hit-or-miss Hollywood actor. He paid his $25 to join the Screen Actors Guild and $15 dues to the American Federation of Television and Radio Actors, then had his photo composite made. He wedged his buzz-cut mug into the "young leading men" category of the Academy Players Directory, alongside such contemporaries as Warren Beatty, Dennis Hopper, Dean Stockwell, and Robert Blake. He read the trades and went on cattle calls at Revue or Four Star, picking up whatever TV work he could.

Jack complained that he and Walter Matthau were blackballed from Warner Bros. because they had "bad deportment"—a term no one ever defined. Once Jack claimed he had gotten kicked out of a filming of *M Squad*, but, at the first opportunity, he padded his résumé with the credit. He'd made the transformation from honest office boy to bona fide low-level Hollywood actor.

One former New Jersey classmate stationed in Panama recalled seeing Jack's face in a military training film around that time. Jack got hired on TV's *Divorce Court*, sometimes appearing as a petitioner and sometimes as a respondent, but always walking away with a paycheck that he had to stretch until the next job. "You had to act elated if you won, depressed if you lost," explained John Herman Shaner, another East Coast refugee and *Divorce Court* regular who met Jack in acting class.

Jack took whatever he could get in order to remain in the game, paying his way as he paid his dues. It was during this lean period that he met Jeff Corey. "My first acting teacher, Jeff Corey, used to say that all art really can only be a stimulating point of departure," Jack said. "You can't change the world, but you can make the world think."

Luana Anders, another MGM gofer, and Jud Taylor, an actor who befriended Jack during his Players Ring period, introduced Jack to

Corey's classes.[10] The widely respected coach began teaching in the early 1950s as a quiet answer to the red-baiting smears of the House Un-American Activities Committee. Corey had been a New York stage actor who had embraced communism during the 1940s, while the USSR was an American ally. His promising career in TV and film (*The Killers, Brute Force*) was cut short after he appeared before congressmen investigating the red menace in Hollywood. When he refused to name names, his Actor's Lab was "red baited out of existence," Corey recalled, "and one of the charges put up was that the lab did the plays of O'Casey, Chekhov, and Shaw. That was just a reflection of the idiocy of the times."

Out of business but loath to give up his family's L.A. lifestyle, the bushy-browed, hawk-nosed thespian managed for a while as a construction worker at $14 a day. Then he began to teach aspiring young actors in the garage of his Chermoya Avenue home, and he godfathered much of the talent that dominated Hollywood for the rest of the century. His alumni ranged from James Dean to Carol Burnett and included, among many others, the screenwriters Carole Eastman and Robert Towne, the directors Irvin Kershner and Tony Bill, and a host of actors—Richard Chamberlain, Millie Perkins, Robert Blake, Pat Boone, Jane Fonda, Dean Stockwell, Anthony Perkins, and Sally Kellerman.

When Jack first showed up, Corey sided more with Pasternak than with Joe Flynn on Jack's need for voice lessons. "I was never sure about Jack's way of talking," he said. "You could always hear his larynx rattle. It turned out to be a very good kind of laid-back quality in Jack, and he's made good use of it."

According to Corey, "Jack was a very agreeable kid," despite his contrary nature. Jack remembered Corey as less admiring in class, claiming that Jack's performances lacked poetry. Corey challenged Jack as "physically leaden." A typical exchange, Jack told one interviewer, went something like this:

"Jocko, there's absolutely nothing happened," Corey complained after Jack did a scene. "What are you doing? Why are you in class? You're not doing anything. I don't see any work."

"Well, Jeff," Jack replied, "let me ask you something. Do you think it's possible that I'm doing something and you're not seeing it?"

Jack and Robert Blake[11] were among Corey's hungriest students, both arriving early for his Tuesday and Thursday evening classes[12] and conning Corey into a game of three-wall handball in the court behind the house. Corey provided a sense of family by exposing them to his own domestic life with his wife and three daughters.

"Robert and Jack both came from working-class backgrounds in New Jersey," said Corey. "They used to come into our house, where the only available john was, and look through the French doors into our dining room. They were astonished: *that family sits and eats together!* Which was outside of their experience."

In Corey's classes Jack met his first serious girlfriend. "He saw me in class and decided we should go out," said Georgiana Carter, a petite blond Southern California native with strict Catholic parents. They remained ambivalent over her drift toward theater, as well as her taste in boyfriends. "Initially, he was very persistent," Georgiana remembered about Jack. "I liked him a lot, and pretty soon I couldn't do without him. He was a year younger than I. He was very boyish and had a very soft look about him, which he lost somewhere along the line."

Soon enough, Jack and Georgiana were showing up at Corey's classes hand in hand. As word of Corey's coaching spread, his classes outgrew his garage and expanded to a warehouse at Western and Fernwood, which was converted to a theater by his students. The Store Theater, renamed the Fernwood, was a true repertory, with Corey's students literally building the stage on which they performed. The only thing they all had in common was that they were broke. "We didn't have a penny," recalled Jack. "We used to go out and steal lumber from lumberyards at night. We stole the toilets out of gas stations. Lighting, boards, everything, we ripped off one way or another."

Jack continued to absorb as he performed, directing and producing while he expanded his circle of friends, many of whom would remain within his entourage for decades thereafter. When the time was right, Jeff Corey got Jack his first movie audition. "Jeff recommended me," said Jack. "I read for it just like every other actor in town. I screamed and yelled—I know I gave the loudest reading, if not the best. And when I got the part I thought, 'This is it! I'm made for this profession.' Then I didn't work [again] for a year."

3

I N THE SPRING OF 1958, THE *ASBURY PARK PRESS* REPORTED
that favorite son Jack Nicholson, "who played leads in Manasquan
High School stage productions a few years ago, is taking dramatics
more seriously in Hollywood and today Jack starred in his first screen
try, the teenage thriller [*The*] *Cry Baby Killer.*"

As Jack recalled his proud moment, he virtually resurrected James
Dean: "I thought: 'Two months in the business and I got the lead in
a movie. I'm a *star!*'"

Only he wasn't.

Based on an actual Inglewood, California, café holdup, *The Cry
Baby Killer* (1958) was "ripped from the headlines" by the B-movie
actor turned screenwriter Leo Gordon and the B-movie script doctor
Melvin Levy. In the real-life holdup, a teen gunman knocked over a
cash register and held hostages, while the Los Angeles television station KTTV went live with the siege and eventual surrender—a forerunner of the Eyewitness News Team's penchant for turning disaster,
crime, and car chases into entertainment.

In the Gordon-Levy script, Jack's misunderstood character is
driven to violence by two thugs who move in on his girlfriend at a
drive-in and beat him into submission. He evens the score with a couple of pistol shots, weeping each time he kills someone, then holes up
in the restaurant with hostages until he's shot by police.

The *Hollywood Reporter*'s Jack Moffitt called *The Cry Baby Killer*
"screen journalism." *Variety*'s critic concurred: "The carnival atmosphere of the gathering crowd, morbid and ghoulish approach of television in its coverage of the event, and the contrast of life continuing
in the shadow of the horror, are intelligently presented."

But these same critics panned Jack's performance.[1] *Variety* concluded that "Young Nicholson is handicapped by having a character
of only one dimension to portray."

"He was very serious about his work," recalled Mitzi McCall, who
had a bit part in the film. "I mean, there wasn't any horsing around on
the set where he was concerned. He was dedicated even in a cocka-
mamie B movie."

Jack recalled the six-day shoot as "a blinding haze": "I was completely into it. I used everything religiously that I had ever learned in class. I was constantly preparing and writing all over my script; it was a mess with notes and everything. Then I saw it and I thought it was terrible."

So did the audience, which "went berserk" with boos and catcalls during a Hollywood preview, according to Jack. He slunk from the theater. McCall recalled seeing him at the Hollywood unemployment office every Wednesday for months thereafter.

Only one other name among *The Cry Baby Killer*'s credits is still recognized today.[2] The executive producer Roger Corman cranked out the feature for American International Pictures (AIP) at a cost of $7,000. By contrast, Jack's entire annual income was $1,400.[3] Even more so than MGM, AIP depended on starving young hopefuls like Jack to boost its bottom line. AIP made movies for nearly nothing, so any cash at the box office was gravy. Still, *The Cry Baby Killer*'s hostile reception gave it the smell of a definite loser.[4] It turned a profit only when AIP sold it to television.

Incorporated the same year that Jack came to California, AIP was originally the American Releasing Corporation until its two founders, the attorney Samuel Arkoff and the former B-film salesman James Nicholson (no relation to Jack), changed the name two years later. AIP pledged to deliver low-budget youth exploitation films dedicated to winning profits, not Oscars, and Corman was their leading profiteer.

By 1957, AIP had become synonymous with teen angst, fear, and lust. Its mainstay was cheap horror created in the tradition (but with nowhere near the budget) of Universal Pictures during the 1930s and early 1940s, when Dracula, Frankenstein, the Wolfman, and the Mummy carried the studio. By the 1950s, Universal hit the nadir of its venerable history and was reduced to producing a trickle of B-Westerns, an occasional romance, or bland heehaw comedies. Universal's "stars" during the Eisenhower era were Ma and Pa Kettle and Francis the Talking Mule.

Universal wasn't the only victim of television, which took its toll among the majors. RKO, the home of Fred and Ginger, became the first to sell its film library to TV and, soon thereafter, the first to fold. In 1957, the B-movie factory Republic Pictures, which produced the

Western serials that had thrilled young Jack back in Neptune, also quit the big screen. It concentrated on producing for TV until that also became too competitive. Like RKO, Republic shut its doors forever five years later, in 1962.

In a myopic drive to produce high-end features that TV could not duplicate, dinosaurs like Warner Bros. and MGM dumped their second-tier "B" production units, just as they had their cartoon divisions, enlarging the gaping hole in the market left by the end of RKO and Republic. Filling that vacuum with sci-fi horror, AIP moved on to other teen fodder. Unlike the hidebound moguls who were driving their mainstream studios toward extinction, AIP had no qualms about asking its target audience what it wanted to see, becoming the first studio to poll teens, develop focus groups, and distribute marketing questionnaires. Standing traditional filmmaking on its head, AIP began with an outrageous title suggested by one of its teen respondents—*The Brain Snatchers*, for example. AIP chief James Nicholson then followed up with an eye-popping poster of bloody gray matter oozing through the bony fingers of a creepy, long-nailed claw, which became a tool to raise capital to hire a producer, a director, and actors. Tedious details such as writing a script came last.

Corman met Jack in Jeff Corey's classes. He'd enrolled to learn something about the Method and to recruit hungry talent who'd work for nothing in future AIP spectaculars. Jack was the perfect candidate, as well as Corman's match. "Nicholson was feisty," said the Corman biographer and ex-employee Beverly Gray. "He was not scared of Roger. He wanted to be actor, writer, do it all, and he had the chutzpah for it."

When they weren't mugging for the camera, Corman's wide-eyed stars and starlets were editing, rewriting scenes, or repairing the roof of Corman's house. As often as possible, Corman shot on location without paying for permits. If he had to use a soundstage, he either recycled used sets or threw one together in hours. Retakes were verboten. He preferred to use old footage from previous AIP epics instead of spending extra on shooting new film.

"Roger thought if you were smart enough, you could grow into doing anything," said Gray. "It was a helluva lot of fun. The whole merry bunch of them got to go off to cheap, exotic places all over the globe to shoot movies. And Jack Nicholson became part of that game."

. . .

Jack took the fizzle of *The Cry Baby Killer* stoically. At least he hadn't missed his first shot at stardom while still cooling his heels in Neptune. Being of draft age during the earliest years of the Vietnam War, he joined the Air National Guard and put in several weeks of boot camp in Texas, followed by training a couple days a month with an airfield crash crew at Van Nuys Airport. "That was the great rich kids' draft dodge," Jack remembered. "We were all draft dodgers. We didn't want to be there."

Even his stint in the military was more Hollywood than New Jersey: sons of producers and writers and even the lead singer of the Four Preps were in his drill unit.

Two men whose futures would intertwine with Jack's were the screenwriter Walon Green (*The Wild Bunch*, *Sorcerer*) and an entry-level talent agency employee named Sandy Bresler. Like Jack's friends in Corey's acting workshop, both young men captured Jack's imagination and his fealty. While they were too junior and inexperienced to help him up the industry ladder at the time, Jack made note of their skills and called on them later. Green co-wrote the screenplay for *The Border* (1982)—one of Jack's most understated and underrated performances—and went on to produce episodes of TV's *Law & Order* for the series creator Dick Wolf.

The son of an Oscar-winning MGM producer, Bresler had easy access to studio film libraries and cemented his friendship with Jack by selling his old cars to Jack cheap and showing up at his house from time to time with a projector and prints of seldom-seen movies. During Jack's post–*Easy Rider* career, Bresler became his sole and ceaseless agent—a rarity in the duplicitous world of Hollywood, where agents, publicists, and managers are as dispensable as parking valets and promises.

While serving his country as a weekend warrior, Jack led a double life as a civilian: struggling actor during the day and beat intellectual after dark. In the mornings he put on a coat and tie and hit the auditions, looking like a clean-cut frat boy in search of his first real job. At night he haunted coffee houses and avant-garde hangouts,

His roommate Dale Wilbourne said that Jack had "one foot in both sides. He wasn't as adventurous as some of the rest of us were. He had a sense of the panorama of things. There is sitting up late and talking about wonderful esoteric things, and there's also the rent."

John Herman Shaner, who had also enrolled in Jeff Corey's class, misunderstood Jack's surface conformism, fastidious grooming, and Protestant work ethic when they first met. "It wasn't until later, the mid-60s, that I realized this guy is totally untraditional."

Mud phased out her beauty shop in the late fifties and followed Jack to Hollywood, moving into a duplex with June and her two youngsters at 6045 Whitsett Avenue in North Hollywood. Meanwhile, June had taken on a new job at J. C. Penney. She didn't date, and her social life consisted of cards and wine with a local Catholic priest each Friday night. Lorraine and Shorty came to L.A. for visits, but mostly June and Mud were on their own.

The Nicholson women invited Jack to dinner every Sunday, fussing over him the way they used to back in New Jersey and cooking for the young prince while Jack kicked back and read the Sunday paper. Wilbourne remembered Mud as "a lady with a compulsion to please, almost like a Jewish mother."

Shaner concurred. Once, when Jack brought him by for Thanksgiving dinner, Mud took Shaner aside in the kitchen. "Jack told me you were working," she whispered. It was true. Shaner had hit a lucky streak with small roles in several TV series, including *Man with a Camera* and *The Walter Winchell File*. Jack hadn't been so fortunate, and yet he preferred to play Monopoly or watch movies on TV during the day instead of getting a "regular" job.

"I'm worried about Jack," Mud said. "I don't know if he's got the temperament for the business. He's got a wonderful mind. He's good at arithmetic. He'd make a wonderful accountant. Do you think he's going to be successful as an actor?"

Though a third her age, Shaner draped an arm over Mud's shoulders and said, "Mrs. Nicholson, Jack is terrific. He's great. He's going to be a big star."

Shaner didn't believe a word of what he told her. Jack tried too hard, for one thing. His first agent, Fred Katz, died around the same time that MGM shut down its cartoon division, and Jack signed with Byron Griffith, his girlfriend Georgiana's agent, as well as the representative for Connie Stevens and Dennis Hopper. "We were all mad and crazy to act and we were constantly underemployed—all of us," said Shaner.

In the wake of *The Cry Baby Killer*, Jack moved into a sparsely furnished Craftsman bungalow near Fountain and Gardner Avenues in the seedy heart of Hollywood, sharing the rent with Wilbourne and David Robbins, a photographer. Jack had an immediate impact on his roomies."Jack turned me on to the *Saturday Review*," said Wilbourne. "He got it on a regular basis. He was reading a lot of stuff. Camus. Sartre. *The Children of Sanchez.*"

The bungalow became a quasi–college dorm, with Jack following Henry David Thoreau's advice about serious reading: Thomas Mann, Henry Miller, James Joyce, Alan Ginsberg, and Jack Kerouac. Without the aid of a university's required-reading list, Jack took on the study of both classics and au courant titles and kept himself abreast of political and philosophical shifts in the culture.

On his bedroom walls, he put up posters of W. C. Fields peeking over a poker hand and an exasperated Humphrey Bogart in a scene from *The Petrified Forest* (1936), sitting on the running board of a car in the middle of the desert.[5] An early folkie, Jack brought his hi-fi and substantial record collection to Fountain Avenue. It included recordings by Odetta, and later, in the mid-sixties, it grew to include the first Rolling Stones albums and a very young Bob Dylan. "He thought Bob Dylan was the greatest thing that ever happened," said Shaner.

Jack frequently stayed home Friday nights and read about Michelangelo and French academic painting. He finagled high-end illustrated art books on Picasso and his contemporaries. Though Jack was poor, he was already looking into collecting, paintings by James Strombotne being among his first acquisitions. A Pomona College graduate who had a studio in Pasadena, Strombotne had his first major show in Beverly Hills in 1958, and over the years, Jack continued to buy his work, acquiring more than twenty canvases.[6]

"Jack liked the energy of art, and being around stuff that was evolving," said Wilbourne. Jack's mother also aspired to be an artist. Beginning with paint-by-numbers kits, Mud branched out to produce her own creations, some that she styled after Picasso. Half a century later, they remained a sentimental part of Jack's collection.

In 1959, Jack moved on from Corey's classes to those taught by the young New York stage actor Martin Landau. Unlike Corey, with his low-key explication of the Method, Landau was fresh out of Manhattan's famous Actors Studio and favored the "sense memory" approach to acting. "How a character hides his feelings tells us who he is," said Landau. "No one shows their feelings. I mean, anger—the clenching of the teeth, the gripping of the hand is holding back anger; that's not anger. Bad actors run to all that crap.

"In a well-written script, the dialogue, what characters say to each other, is what a character is willing to reveal and share with someone else. The 90 percent he isn't saying is what I do for a living."

Using exercises first developed by Lee Strasberg, Landau relied upon improvisation.[7] Like Strasberg, he counseled the "private moment" as a freeing technique: spontaneous stage activity that an actor would normally do only in private, such as getting naked, masturbating, or passing gas. Landau's friend James Dean boasted of just such a private moment during the filming of *East of Eden*, when he unzipped and urinated in front of cast and crew to loosen himself up before a big scene.

Wilbourne recalled one exercise in which Jack lay on the stage and played a stomach to Wilbourne's mouth. They made up dialogue as they worked through their indigestion. In another exercise, an actor would stand on stage and chant "Happy Birthday" or some other ditty, one syllable at a time, making eye contact with each face in the audience while concentrating on his body tension.

"It was Marty's idea that if you can find a way of being aware of where your tension is, then you find a way to let it out, rather than sublimate it," said Wilbourne.

"I sang 'Three Blind Mice' for two years in his class," Jack recalled in a 1985 interview, during which he extolled the technique for its unerring location of "heinie tension." Jack maintained that a tight ass would always get in an actor's way of fully assuming a role.

In the summer of 1959, Roger Corman not only gave Jack a second chance at a James Dean–like rebel role but he cast him opposite his real-life sweetheart, Georgiana Carter. Corman shot the teen-angst drag-strip saga *The Wild Ride* (1960) (aka *Velocity*) on a budget of $12,000 on location along the banks of the Delta River and at a racetrack in Sonoma County. Cast and crew scrimped every cent in true Corman style. They drove up from L.A. on their own and lived together à la summer camp in a hot, crowded rental across the bay from San Francisco. Actors were a negligible part of Corman's filmmaking process.

"Roger told me the secret of doing a film in one or two weeks is you hire a good director, the best cameraman you can, the best soundperson you can get, then just shoot it," said Harvey Berman, then a college instructor and a part-time actor whom Corman drafted to direct.[8] Jack and Georgiana each earned $200 a week, but most of Berman's students and other locals who appeared with them in the film worked for nothing.

"If there was anything about Jack that struck me, it was that he was terribly intense about succeeding," said Berman. "He really wanted everything to work. He wanted to know every motivation for every moment in order to make it truthful. He wanted every relationship laid out."

Berman couldn't have cared less about motivation. He had twenty setups a day, a paper-thin budget, and an impossible two-week delivery deadline.[9] From the first day, Jack gave him fits. Before they switched on the cameras, Jack had to know how his character related to the actor cast as his best pal and rival for Georgiana's affections.

"Do you think I'm *really* drawn to him?" Jack demanded.

"What?" said Berman.

"Do you think maybe I really have a homosexual desire for him?"

"No."

"Well, it would explain our tightness together."

"No, these are kids," Berman said. "Kids have that tightness. You're both fighting over the same girl. I don't think you're both fighting over the same girl because you're in love with each other. That's carrying it a little bit too far."

While not as big a stinker as *The Cry Baby Killer*, *The Wild Ride* did not turn out to be Jack's big breakthrough, either. As a sneering young drag racer bent on shaming his girl and destroying his best friend, he whined less and muted his hammy histrionics. But unlike the faint moralism that crept into the final frames of *The Cry Baby Killer* or *Rebel without a Cause*, the pointless script of *The Wild Ride* led Jack and the rest of the cast nowhere. Following a short run in drive-ins, the second-billed dud disappeared, and the only lasting partnership that emerged from the experience was that of Jack and the fledgling director Monte Hellman.

Yet another Corey-Landau student, Hellman got his first assignment to direct a film from Corman, after which he was asked to co-produce and edit *The Wild Ride*.[10] "I think Jack really seemed like more than an actor," said Hellman. "He had such diverse interests.

He was obviously very bright and had an overall way of looking at things, as opposed to just a myopic vision of his own particular part in something."

Hellman told Jack that he, too, should think about directing and writing. Two other Corey-Landau classmates who cemented their friendships with Jack around that time had already begun writing: Carole Eastman, a thin, ethereal ex-dancer-model whose mother worked as a secretary to Bing Crosby and whose father had once been a grip for Warner Bros.; and Robert Towne, the tall, brooding son of a San Pedro real estate developer. Through her darting almond eyes, Eastman radiated timid irony, while Towne was stand-offish, looking askance at everyone except Jack, who nicknamed him "Beaner" and briefly roomed with him. They shared the conviction that they would someday inherit the movie industry, if not the earth.

A Claremont College graduate who fancied himself an intellectual, Towne embraced Camus and began analysis with the celebrated Beverly Hills Freudian disciple Martin Grotjahn while still in his twenties.[11] Waxing philosophical decades later, Jack parroted Towne's grandiosity, referring to *The Myth of Sisyphus* almost as if both of them were still sitting at their corner table in the Unicorn café, sipping espresso: "The actor is Camus's ideal existential hero, because if life is absurd, and the idea is to live a more vital life, therefore the man who lives more lives is in a better position than the guy who lives just one."

Jack did have more lives to live after *The Wild Ride*. He got the part of a villain in *Too Soon to Love* (1960), another low-budget independent directed by Richard Rush (*The Stunt Man, Getting Straight*), but with a larger budget than most AIP quickies. Rush's sole directing credit up to that time had been a single television show, but *Too Soon to Love* was that rarest of late 1950s film assignments: a modest independent that did not bear Corman's stingy fingerprints. While far from big budget, the pseudo *Romeo and Juliet* story was a genuine feature. "It was an exploitation film made for about $50,000, which we were pretty successful with," recalled Rush, who helped to produce *Too Soon to Love*, in addition to directing it. "We sold it to Universal for $250,000, and it hit at just that magic time when the critics had invented the 'New Wave.'"

Retitled *High School Honeymoon* and *Teenage Lovers* for European audiences, *Too Soon to Love* was "the first of the American New Wave" because it tapped into taboos such as teen pregnancy, according to Rush. It was also Francis Ford Coppola's first writing assignment, although, according to Rush, it turned out "he had more youth than discipline." Rush, with the novelist László Görög, turned Coppola's effusive prose into a workable shooting script, and they took the writing credit for themselves.

Mildly successful at the drive-ins and overseas, *Too Soon to Love* marked yet another entry in Jack's acting résumé, but his biggest credit yet was at a little shop right around the corner.

Two years before Roger Corman shot his cult classic *The Little Shop of Horrors* (1960), the science fiction author Arthur C. Clarke published "The Reluctant Orchid," a tongue-in-cheek short story about a botanist who discovers a carnivorous orchid and feeds it the domineering aunt he despises. Although the Corman screenwriter Chuck Griffith may have been influenced by Clarke, there is little doubt that his twisted and venerable vision of the feckless Skid Row storekeeper Seymour Krelboyne and his ravenous talking plant Audrey was uniquely his own.

"This was *the* low-budget production of all time," recalled Jack. In just two days[12] and on a budget of $27,000, Corman shot *The Little Shop of Horrors*, the second in an AIP trilogy of black comedies[13] that masqueraded at the box office as horror films. So tight was the budget that when Jack auditioned, Corman made him scale the fence at Chaplin Studios, rather than pay a security guard to open the gate. Corman parsed out scenes only to actors who appeared in them so that he wouldn't have to pay to print extra scripts.

"I was in a sequence which was 13 pages long: six and a half pages before I came in and six and a half afterwards," said Jack. He played opposite his old friend John Shaner, and when the two of them showed up to get their scripts, Corman handed Jack the last six pages and Shaner the first. He ripped the remaining page in two and handed half to each actor. "That was it," said Jack. "That's all we knew about it. I didn't know what the picture was or anything like that. I did make Shaner let me read his half of the page."

Jack had no need to know because his scene wasn't crucial to the plot of *The Little Shop of Horrors*. In a more efficient, story-driven movie, Jack might have wound up on the cutting-room floor, but because Corman hated to waste anything, the giddy masochist Wilbur Force became the first in a long line of memorable Nicholson characters who now populate film history with catch lines etched into America's collective consciousness. "No Novocain," says Wilbur. "It dulls the senses."

"He did it verbatim from the script, but added all that juicy business on his own," said the screenwriter Griffith. "Roger rarely gave detailed directions. He assumed the actors were the experts on that. Luckily, in Jack's case, it was true."

Like Harvey Berman, Monte Hellman, and all the other naifs Corman hired at various times to direct his movies, he cared most about getting something—anything—on film as soon as possible and moving on. When Jack showed up on the set dressed as a geek, with his hair slicked down like Alfalfa in an *Our Gang* comedy, there was no quibble over wardrobe. Corman zipped through his entire sequence, from setup and rehearsal through final take, in an hour and ten minutes. As the cameras rolled, Jack burbled a "Goody, goody!" over the prospect of having a tooth yanked out, then sat in a dentist's chair as the actor Jonathan Haze leaped on his chest wielding a drill and a scalpel. "There was this dental machine, which was expensive," Jack recalled. "Roger would never pay a valid rental on it. Obviously, he borrowed it from his dentist."

As Haze and Jack wrestled, the machine tipped and a panicky Corman leaped to catch it, bobbling into camera range and ruining the shot. "And that was it," said Jack. "We never finished the scene."

But what was shot stayed in the picture, and long after Corman forgot his momentary fear of busting up expensive dental equipment, he never forgot the scene that Jack turned into the real beginning of his own Hollywood legend.

"The scene developed into an improvised duel between the dentist's drill and a scalpel, but in the middle of the scene they got so wild they knocked over the dentist's chair," Corman recalled in his version of events. "I turned to the prop man and asked how long it would take to set up the chair. He said half an hour, so we didn't reshoot. That's how the scene ends in the film, with the collapse of the dentist's chair. And everybody on the set just died laughing."

Little Shop led Jack to the prize role of Weary Reilly, the neighborhood bully in United Artists' *Studs Lonigan* (1960) and Jack's proudest acting achievement for several years thereafter.

Now somewhat dated, *Studs Lonigan* compressed into 103 minutes the classic James T. Farrell trilogy about the short, tragic life of an Irish working-class kid in Depression-era Chicago. Studs falls victim to booze, racism, greed, and petty crime, and Weary Reilly helps to trip him up on his way down. Shot in black and white but on a big studio budget, the period piece gave Jack his first real chance to show range and Method—all those techniques he learned from Jeff Corey and Martin Landau. Jack maintained that he landed the part because he was "the only actor in Hollywood with the stamina and energy to read [Farrell's] 700-page trilogy."

Though audiences did not stay away in the same numbers they did with *The Cry Baby Killer* or *The Wild Ride*, *Studs Lonigan* failed at the box office. It became a classic Hollywood casualty, faintly praised by critics as "artsy but unsatisfactory," while ending a short run in theaters as a commercial bomb. Like his co-stars Frank Gorshin and Christopher Knight, who played the title role, Jack got good reviews, but few people across the country saw the film—yet another abject lesson in Jack's long apprenticeship: just because it's good doesn't mean people will pay to watch.

Offscreen, Jack suffered his reverses as well. He and Georgiana had advanced their love life despite her father's strict Catholicism, but the closer Georgiana grew to Jack's family, the more distance he seemed to put between them. "The feeling I got was that she was feeling neglected, not getting enough attention," said Wilbourne. "Jack, even in those days, always had his buddies. The ladies I met that he was with were always in competition with his pals."

Things came to a head when Georgiana pushed too hard. "We broke up because we had an argument about getting married," she said. "I was stunned to hear that he didn't want to. Before that, I always thought that was some kind of mutual understanding. I always thought we would be [married]. Somewhere along the line I had the notion that maybe that might happen. He said no—absolutely no. I said, Well, let's not see one another, and we didn't for a while. I was just working. He said there was someone else and he couldn't do two relationships at once. I was very upset."

As years passed, Georgiana watched Jack evolve and deepen as an actor, and she was never surprised at his eventual success. "I think Jack was very centered, always," she said. "He used to tell me I had rabbit ears, and that was something he didn't have at all."

By "rabbit ears," Jack meant that Georgiana worried too much about others' opinions. Early on in their relationship, he had warned her of the crippling effects of critics and advised her to remain focused and to refuse defeat. "I think everyone has doubts in the dark of night, especially trying to do something in a place like Hollywood," she said, "but I don't think Jack ever had the same kind of gnawing insecurity most people do."

4

FOLLOWING THE RELEASE OF *THE LITTLE SHOP OF HORRORS* and *Studs Lonigan*, Jack enjoyed a split second in the limelight before lapsing back into the now-familiar anonymity. His few weeks' work was followed by months of unemployment. "I actually had a very good time just living in California," he mused. "Maybe I was aggravated because I only worked 30 days a year or something like that, but on the other hand, I had 330 days off."

Daily Variety called 1961 "one of the darkest years" in American film history. In a sagacious bit of industry analysis, the *New York Times*'s Murray Schumach deconstructed moguls' declining fortunes in a lengthy study that blamed stars such as Debbie Reynolds, Cary Grant, Doris Day, and Frank Sinatra, whose personal production companies indiscriminately called the shots.

Celebrities and their managers had usurped studio power, carrying salary demands and production profligacy to dizzying new heights. In debacles yet to come—notably, MGM's *Mutiny on the Bounty* (1962)[1] and Fox's *Cleopatra* (1963)[2]—the costs shot so high and the movies tanked so badly that they dragged their studios down with them. Even Jack and his peers indirectly felt *Cleopatra*'s sting when Martin Landau shut down his acting workshop to study Italian and leap on the Fox gravy train as Rufio, the trusted lieutenant of Marc Antony (Richard Burton).

While Jack had done Westerns on TV, *The Broken Land* (1961) was his first appearance in a big-screen Western. During one of his extended periods of unemployment, he learned horseback riding at the Griffith Park stables—a skill that won him the part over Burt Reynolds. Jack was cast as Will Brocious, a bad-luck hombre given to folksy wisdom and a fast gun.

Barely an hour long and more thinly plotted than any early *Gunsmoke* episode, *The Broken Land* was released on the bottom half of a drive-in double bill beneath the inscrutable tag line "This is the story of the insurgents!"[3] Even Jack believed he could have written a better script.

Shortly after *The Broken Land* wrapped, Robert Lippert gave Jack that chance. Lippert commissioned Jack and his newest roommate, Don Devlin, another Jeff Corey alumnus, to pitch a political suspense thriller set in Puerto Rico.[4]

With *Anatomy of a Psycho* (1961), Devlin switched from acting to screenwriting and agreed to coauthor *Thunder Island* (1963). Despite the double-billed screenwriting credit (Jack's first), it was Devlin's facility with structure and dialogue that made *Thunder Island* a surprisingly well-crafted B-movie.

"Jack only became a so-called professional writer out of desperation," recalled *Thunder Island's* producer-director Jack Leewood. The co-writers earned $1,250 for their efforts, but Leewood didn't invite them to Puerto Rico for the actual filming. After all, they were only the writers.

Thunder Island's story of a quirky American hit man hired to assassinate a former Caribbean dictator resonated with the headlines of the day. When the sixty-five-minute feature premiered a year later, the *Hollywood Reporter* concluded, "The theme obviously has current interest, but considering the volatile nature of Latin American politics, when doesn't it?"

During the Bay of Pigs invasion back in April 1961, the Air National Guard had briefly activated Jack's unit, which went on alert again during the subsequent Cuban missile crisis. Castro was on Jack's mind, and if politics and current events sneaked into his screenplay, it would not be the last time politics made its way into his films. "I haven't been happy with America politically since Jack Kennedy's first campaign," he recalled a dozen years later.[5]

Among the first to embrace the challenge of John F. Kennedy's

New Frontier, Jack was also among the first to be disillusioned, and while he rarely advertised his political leanings, he didn't seem to mind injecting his opinions into his films, as long as they didn't interfere with his characters or the stories.

Jack moved in with Sandra Knight, Robert Blake's ex-girlfriend[6] and another of Martin Landau's regulars. The honey-haired blonde so resembled Jack's ex that several of his acquaintances mistook her for Georgiana. The actor Bruce Dern remembered her switching to long black hair, which complemented the stern, druidic facial features of a coffeehouse regular.

"Sandra was beautiful and very voluptuous," said Helena Kallianiotes, a belly dancer who worked at the Intersection, a Greek nightclub in Hollywood.[7] Part of Jack's growing collection of eclectic pals during the 1960s, Helena remained in his entourage for the next forty years. "Big bosoms and lots of hair," Helena observed. "[Sandra] and Jack kind of looked alike—had the same nose."

Like Jack, Sandra got started by acting in school plays, but her father was a studio cop and that connection helped land her a job working alongside her future husband when she was just fourteen. "He was working as a messenger boy at MGM and I was working as a messenger girl," Sandra recalled. "Jack was much older than I was, and I just thought he was so cute."

Her father's connections continued to click, and Sandra won her first movie part at seventeen, the same year she graduated from Venice High. Debuting as Robert Mitchum's girlfriend in the moonshine thriller *Thunder Road* (1958), she segued into the recurring role of ravished ingénue, beginning with *Frankenstein's Daughter* (1958).

By the time Sandra left Blake for Jack, she and Jack were bound together by mutual friends and a dedication to the art of filmmaking. And there was the additional shared allure of altered states. For years, Jack had generally shunned booze for grass. An early cannabis convert, he frequently lit up in Jeff Corey's driveway before heading into class. Despite Jack's herbal devotion, it wasn't until he started seeing Sandra that he first dropped acid.

Since the very year Jack arrived in California, the Beverly Hills psychiatrist Oscar Janiger had been soliciting volunteers in an ongoing psychosocial experiment with lysergic acid diethylamide—LSD. An early disciple of the Swiss biochemist Albert Hoffman, who discovered LSD, "Dr. Oz" Janiger prescribed the drug to about a thousand subjects in the 1950s and 1960s, including Aldous Huxley, Cary Grant, Anaïs Nin, Andre Previn, John Huston, and Rita Moreno. For twenty dollars a hit, Janiger offered to guide subjects who showed an interest in unlocking their creative consciousness through a hallucinogenic daydream known in the psychedelic sixties as a "trip."

Jack got wind of Dr. Oz and two of his disciples, Mortimer Hartman and Arthur Chandler, through other actors who'd survived the psychedelic experience, and, on May 29, 1962, with Sandra's approval, he showed up at their office for an exploration of his innermost being. He listed his occupation as actor, popped his first 150 micrograms, and spent the next five hours down a rabbit hole.

"I hallucinated a lot, primarily because of the way the therapist structured it," Jack recalled. "He put a blindfold on me, which makes you much more introspective, gives you more dreamlike imagery. Imagine what acid is like when you know nothing about it. You think it's going to be like getting stoned on grass, which I had done. But all of your conceptual reality gets jerked away, and there are things in your mind that have in no way been suggested to you."

Jack saw God, reexperienced his birth, felt his body dissolve, and watched sap scream through the veins of the leaves in trees. He developed a queasy stomach, which he described to his therapist as "a kind of fluttering in my genital area." When his crotch grew cold and more uncomfortable, panic set in. "At one point, I came back to consciousness screaming at the top of my lungs 'til I had no more breath to exhale," Jack recalled. "I thought I'd have to try to remedy this genital discomfort myself by cutting my cock off."

When Jack talked about this particular episode in follow-up sessions, his psychiatrist told him that the urge to self-mutilate related to fears of homosexuality. "It was really a kind of paranoia," recalled Jack. "The drug just aggravated it."

Besides raising Jack's castration consciousness, the drug also raised the nettlesome issue of his birth, years before he professed to know the truth about Mud and June. "I became conscious of very early emotions about not being wanted—feeling that I was a problem to my family as an infant," said Jack.

He ascribed his unease to Mud's frustration at having to raise him as a single mother. "Some of that must have been communicated," he rationalized. "Realizing that made me understand in psychological terms a certain kind of relationship that I have with the female sex—one of dependence upon them, wanting to please them because my survival depended on it."

Three weeks after his first acid trip, Jack and Sandra were married. "I got married on a Friday because on Wednesday Sandra said she wanted to.[8] And I didn't have a reason not to," he said. "While the ceremony was going on, that part of me that, at night, half believes in God, was looking upwards and saying, 'Now remember I'm very young and this doesn't mean I'm not never going to touch another woman.'"

In a radical departure from the rigid Irish Catholicism of Jack's youth, he and Sandra took their vows before a Unitarian minister from Canoga Park, while two more Landau regulars bore witness: the best man Harry Dean Stanton and the maid of honor Millie Perkins. The doe-eyed starlet from *The Diary of Anne Frank* (1959), Perkins was Sandra's oldest Hollywood friend, while Stanton was a "Porsche-driving, troubled night person," according to Jack. Raised on a Kentucky tobacco farm, he was a dedicated and lifelong smoker whom Jack nicknamed "Snap" because Stanton resembled the wan, skeletal member of the comic trio that advertised Kellogg's Rice Krispies. The wedding was on Sunday, June 17, 1962. Sandra was twenty-two; Jack had just turned twenty-five.

As with Georgiana, Jack saw Sandra not only as his soul mate but also as his leading lady. She had just finished costarring as another ravished ingénue in *Terror at Black Falls* (1962), a low-budget Western, followed by a role in *Tower of London* (1962), a Corman-ized version of *Richard III* ("Mother England meets Father Terror!"), in which Sandra played a courtesan.

When Jack landed the role of Peter Lorre's doofus son in *The Raven* (1963), it made sense to be on the lookout for another ravished ingénue part, but the TV actress Olive Sturgess had already snagged the role. The eternally frugal Corman saw yet another opportunity for a two-for-one shoot, though, and the newlywed Nicholsons became prime beneficiaries of his latest scam: a cheapie tagged onto the more respectable production based on Edgar Allen Poe's ghostly elegy to love and death.

Corman shot *The Terror* (1963) back-to-back with *The Raven*, doubling up on dramatic exteriors in Big Sur as well as gloomy interiors in the same haunted castle soundstage in L.A. that he rented for both pictures. The pennywise Corman also hired the aging horror star Boris Karloff to play a bogeyman in both films, but one movie was a fully authorized $350,000 union shoot, the other a seat-of-the-pants production. The resulting two horrorfests could not have been more horrifyingly dissimilar.

The Raven was a well-conceived, clever spoof of Poe's classic poem, written by the scare meister Richard Matheson (*The Incredible Shrinking Man*, *Duel*, *The Omega Man*), while the overwrought melodrama *The Terror* was tossed together as they went along. The Corman scenarists Leo Gordon (*The Cry Baby Killer*) and Jack Hill stood by helplessly as they saw their work dissolve into a hasty Corman mélange of bad acting, bad direction, and rinky-dink animation.

Asked a decade later to name the worst of his early films, Jack didn't hesitate: "*The Terror* embarrasses me as much as anything."

The Raven, on the other hand, was a romp. Cast as Rexford Bedlo, the foppish son of the fumbling necromancer Dr. Adolphus Bedlo (Peter Lorre), Jack struck just the proper discordant note. Despite a glut of puns and pratfalls, and scant direction from Corman, he played it deadpan among the cast of horror veterans. "It was too many funny people in one movie," said Jack. "The kind of direction you get is: 'You can't be as funny as they are.' That's the interpretation of the role from Roger."

Lorre and Jack played off each other like Laurel and Hardy. In a getup that looked like a swishy Robin Hood hand-me-down, Jack crept through Karloff's castle, always leading with his nose. He never quite saved his warlock-turned-raven father (Lorre) and never quite got the girl (Sturgess), yet somehow finished out the story back at the castle of Karloff's archrival, the faux-foul Dr. Erasmus Craven (Vincent Price).

But not without a monstrous dry cleaning bill: "One other thing I remember about *The Raven*" Jack said, "was that the raven we used shit endlessly over everybody and everything."[9]

Jack learned from his elders, paying close attention to Karloff's script notations and Price's elocution. Lorre adopted a fatherly role with Jack off camera and offered a bit of advice: "If you want to last in this business, you'd better be frugal." Lorre knew whereof he spoke. He'd gone from flush to bankrupt during his long film career, and he worked until his death two years later at age fifty-nine—not because he wanted to, but because he had to.

Jack took Lorre's words to heart and never strayed beyond his budget. Even when he was stone broke, he kept a savings account and had the discipline not to dip into it. Twenty years hence, he would be able to tell the journalist Nancy Collins with absolute confidence: "I still, to this day, have never borrowed a nickel from anybody and never felt like I couldn't take care of myself."[10]

With *The Raven* wrapped in October 1962, Lorre and Price went home, but Corman still had Karloff under contract.[11] He also had two more days of paid-up use of the haunted castle set and his regular rag-tag gang of movie wannabes who would work for next to nothing. "Jack came in and we shot for those two days," said Corman. "All I had was a script for those two days, and then I shut down. That portion of the film was union, and the rest of the picture was made nonunion."

Because Corman was a Directors Guild of America member, he couldn't direct the nonunion *The Terror* without the threat of guild expulsion, so he hired young and hungry nonguild directors to guide his actors through the rest of the nonunion (that is, dirt cheap) shoot.

"Jack would appear every now and then whenever we needed him," Corman recalled. The screenwriter Jack Hill's UCLA classmate Francis Ford Coppola directed the first three or four days, followed by Monte Hellman, and then two other Corman pals. "Finally at the end of it there was still one day left to finish, and by that time I'd run out of friends of mine who were directors who'd come around for a day, and Jack said, 'Well, I'm as good as these guys; I'll direct it.'"

But Jack's first turn as a director didn't help. *The Terror* remained terrible, beginning with Sandra—glamorous with chestnut hair, green eyes, and flowing low-cut dresses but unconvincing and zombielike as the seventeenth-century Baroness Von Lepp. The only real emotion Sandra showed onscreen was during her make-out sessions with her real-life husband. A faint Valley girl accent cast doubt on the Germanic origins of the mysterious Helene Von Lepp, who feared she might wind up "day-ud" by the baron's "ha-yund."

Jack did little better, delivering lines with a flat, familiar Jersey twang.[12] From the ill-advised opening sequence, when he trudged into the Pacific in his Napoleonic uniform on Coppola's orders, his performance went from bad to worse. "I almost drowned out there in the ocean," complained Jack. "I was supposed to go out into the water to find Helene. This was Francis's idea. I went out into that big fucking arch up there in Big Sur. This is wintertime and there's no stunt doubling."

After a wave slammed him to the ocean floor, Jack experienced a "split second of panic because I was out a ways already. I came flying out of there and just threw that fucking costume off while I ran, freezing to death."

But the Nicholsons did come away from *The Terror* with one major dividend: during their eleven-day, no-expenses-paid trip to Big Sur, Sandra got pregnant.

Months later, after Corman had come up with enough cash to film *The Terror* finale, Sandra and Karloff flailed in a flooding dungeon and the force of the water flushed her brassiere up and out of her dress. Stifling his laughter, Jack hoisted his very pregnant wife out of the soup and struggled to carry her up the dungeon steps. "I mean, this was my fucking wife and it looked so hysterically goofy," said Jack. "I had a great time. Paid the rent. They don't make movies like *The Terror* anymore."

One day in the spring of 1963, Georgiana Carter's phone rang. It was Jack. No, he wasn't calling about getting back together; it was about his sister. "June and I had a falling out over something stupid and hadn't stayed in touch," Georgiana recalled. "And he told me she was really very sick . . . pretty bad, and would I go see her?"

What Georgiana saw lying in a hospital bed on North Vermont Avenue was a skeletal reminder of the robust redhead who used to drive her to J. C. Penney's each morning, regaling her with tall tales of her dancing days when she briefly rubbed elbows with Lucky Luciano as an Earl Carroll showgirl or played straight woman to the rising young comedian Pinky Lee. At forty-four, June Frances Hawley had contracted cervical and breast cancer, and it spread quickly. Within six months, she dropped from 120 to 80 pounds. It was a slow, painful passing, with a profound effect on all who knew her, but especially on Jack, who remained edgy speaking about the ravages of cancer decades later.

"I got a job in Mexico when June was dying," he recalled. "First time with a studio, a lot of weeks. Sandra was pregnant with Jennifer, and June was in a terminal state. She looked me right in the eye and

said, 'Shall I wait?' In other words, 'Shall I try and fight this through?'
And I said no."

Jack left June's side, and, in a magazine interview Lorraine gave
years later, she told what happened next: "When the door of the elevator closed, Jack slumped to the floor, sobbing hysterically."

During the final week of July, Jack flew to Acapulco to begin work
for Warner Bros. on *Ensign Pulver* (1964), his first big-budget film.
He hadn't yet learned the truth about his relationship to his older sister, although he sensed they were cut from the same cloth, more basic
than brother and sister. "June and I had so much in common. We both
fight hard," he said, still in the present tense more than twenty years
after her death.

But just how much in common, he claimed he didn't discover until
long after there was nothing more to say, or anyone to say it to. On
July 31, 1963, June died at Cedars of Lebanon Hospital, purportedly
taking her secret to the grave. She was buried at the San Fernando
Mission near Glendale, still Catholic but no longer a Jersey girl.[13] She
hadn't made it *in* Hollywood, but she made it *to* Hollywood, and, like
her unacknowledged son, she opted to stay.

"She had a lot of talent, and it was never recognized," said John
Herman Shaner. "The thing that remains with me is not that it was a
misspent life, but an unfulfilled life."

June's death certificate listed her as "widowed," although the late
Murray "Bob" Hawley had divorced her and abandoned their two
children, Pamela Ruth and Murray Jr., years earlier.[14] Bob remarried,
moved to Canada, and started yet another family. Murray Jr. was nineteen, married, and in the navy by the time his mother died, but Mud
stayed on to look after Pam, who'd dropped out of high school in the
tenth grade to attend beauty school.

A little more than a month later, Jack returned from Guadalajara,
and, on September 13, 1963, Sandra gave birth to a six-pound,
eleven-ounce girl. She had June's Irish red hair and blue eyes, but
they named her Jennifer Lorraine.

Except as a paid vacation on the Mexican Riviera, *Ensign Pulver*
turned out to be a bust. A bland sequel to the filmed version of
Mister Roberts (1954), Josh Logan's bittersweet Broadway play about
World War II navy life, *Ensign Pulver* reeked of the stagy desperation
of its creator.

Logan embodied old Hollywood. He had studied in Moscow with Stanislavski in the 1930s, directed the young Henry Fonda and James Stewart in Cape Cod summer stock before any of them ever saw a camera, and bridged the gap between Broadway and Hollywood by directing film versions of *Picnic* (1955), *Bus Stop* (1956), *South Pacific* (1957), and *Sayonara* (1958).

But the 1960s were another era, and Logan was slipping. United Artists had just released the director Richard Lester's *A Hard Day's Night* (1964) in more countries more rapidly than any film in history. If the Beatles were not proof enough that the times were changing, the growing popularity of antiheroes like Sean Connery's James Bond and Peter Sellers's Inspector Jacques Clouseau should have been fair warning. Boomer audiences couldn't have cared less about Logan's overproduced theatrics and lame, lowbrow comedy. Still, Warner Bros. gave the Broadway impresario a fat budget to write, produce, and direct *Ensign Pulver*, which its own baby-faced star, Robert Walker Jr., later tried to disown. "I was embarrassed by *Ensign Pulver*," Walker said in a 1992 interview. "I'm *still* embarrassed by *Ensign Pulver*."

Upon reporting for duty aboard an ancient naval cargo vessel anchored in Acapulco Bay, Jack meant to attach himself to Logan's hip. He'd learned the value of networking in his acting classes and during his after-hours café schmoozing, but Corman and Lippert showed him the next step: the importance of apprenticeship. If an actor wanted to graduate from cattle calls, he had to learn from the studio veterans who'd invested years working behind the camera.

The actor Larry Hagman, whose first major studio film was also *Ensign Pulver*, recalled, "Once shooting began, [Jack] emerged as an off-screen ringleader among the cast of up-and-comers that included me, James Farentino, James Coco, and Peter Marshall."

The day before principal photography began, Logan assembled the cast and lectured them on his creative process. "If we ever saw him sitting alone, he told us we were not to disturb him," said Hagman. "If he was by himself, he explained, he was thinking about the film, lining up shots, or, as he put it, 'creating,' and he did not want to be bothered."

The first day of shooting in the tropical sun, the actors obeyed. Even the brash and inquisitive Jack kept his distance. Logan was "creating." He nodded off and baked for hours in his director's chair, and still no one approached. Only after the director was hauled off in a gurney to his hotel room to recover from second-degree burns did the cast learn the bipolar truth: Logan was on lithium.

Jack knew a thing or two about the effects of drugs. In fact, he turned on with most of the cast, but not with mind-numbing pharmaceuticals. When he saw Hagman knocking back piña coladas like soda pop, Jack suggested an alternative.

"Hag, you drink too much," he said.

"I don't think it's a problem," said Hagman, who eventually lost his liver to booze.

"Neither do I," said Jack. "I just think you ought to try something else."

"Like what?"

"A little grass. I'll go out and get some."

While Hagman showed the same reluctance that other cast members did when first tempted by devil weed, Jack could be persuasive. He scored some Acapulco gold in town, and soon the cast was lighting up in Jack's hotel room. Years before Cheech and Chong demonstrated the comic effects of toking between takes, Jack "pulverized" the cast members of *Ensign Pulver*, who were alternately manic or mellow onscreen but rarely funny. "Jesus Christ, this stuff is fantastic," remarked Hagman. "I've never had anything like it in my entire life!"

Jack was more circumspect in his own drug use when he was around Logan. Once the director had recovered from his burns, a sobered Jack turned on his powers of persuasion. When Logan was on his lithium, he spoke of his young protégé as "an entrepreneur, tummler, and an inspiration" but had no idea Jack was also the cast's cannabis connection.

At Jack's suggestion, Logan cast Millie Perkins as *Ensign Pulver's* female lead. Scenes from *The Walking Dead* (1936), a Karloff movie, were incorporated into *Ensign Pulver* as *Young Dr. Jekyll Meets Frankenstein*, the captain's (Burl Ives) favorite at movie call. At times, Logan anointed wisecracking Jack as his uncredited "assistant producer"; at others, he leaned on Jack, telling him that he photographed badly, couldn't act, and had no business being in front of the camera. Jack's response: "I'm going to try harder."

Nevertheless, not much of Jack remained in the final cut. Except for two or three hammy lines shouted in shipboard crowd scenes, his scenes wound up on the cutting-room floor. His name wasn't even among the opening credits.

Hagman, on the other hand, got priority billing on the strength of his mother's (Mary Martin) friendship with Logan, while Robert Walker Jr. landed *Ensign Pulver's* title role because of his lineage.[15] Just twenty-four, Walker had minor roles in two previous films, but he was the son of the 1940s matinee idol Robert Walker and the actress Jennifer Jones, who had divorced the elder Walker to marry the über producer David O. Selznick. "Jack used to weep over the fact that he didn't have that pedigree," said the screenwriter Charles Eastman, Carole Eastman's brother.

It wasn't the first time Jack competed with the nepotism that frequently underlies Hollywood flops, but *Pulver* did give him entrée into the hedonistic world of Hollywood royalty. "I remember he drove this little Karmann Ghia convertible around with a torn top," recalled Walker, who became a fan of Jack's. "You just loved to hang out with him. This guy was so charming, and there was such a wonderful edge to his personality."

Unlike the Nicholsons, who still resided near Plummer Park on the Hollywood flatlands in an ancient rented bungalow, both Walker and Hagman lived like grandees in brand-new beach houses at the exclusive Malibu Colony, where parties happened at the drop of a wine cork any night of the week. Jack and Sandra were now regulars on the list of invitees and stopped by often. Jack showed off Jennifer to the young, rich heirs of Hollywood's matinee era before handing her over to her barefoot mother. "He called me Ona, which was short for On-a-[Teething] Biscuit," Jennifer recalled. "And that name stuck with me until I went to school."

Jack's new friends knew that he and his young family were poor, but it didn't matter to them. "Weekends, there'd be sixty people over at the house," said Walker. "Two cases of Lafite Rothschild, 1959, every weekend. Or Mouton Rothschild—burgundy or cabernet, $300 a case, a couple cases a week. My wife would cook wonderful meals."

By now an enthusiastic weed booster, Hagman began to harvest from his own "marijuana tree" and share the wealth at bacchanals, wearing a caftan or the occasional chicken costume to encourage the spirit of happy insanity. Frisbees, volleyballs, and rock and roll filled the air on weekends. Hagman took on the nickname "the Mad Monk of Malibu" and donned a gorilla suit most Sundays to lead a parade of stoned inebriates along the beach, much to the horror of older residents.

The actress Merle Oberon was one of those older residents. She moved out and the French director Roger Vadim and his fiancée, Jane Fonda, moved in, renting Oberon's beach house for $200 a month. Fonda began to compete with all the other parties by staging more upscale literary chatfests, luring attendees with her homemade crème brûlée. Her brother, Peter, his writer pal Terry Southern, and Vadim's close friend the French actor Christian Marquand[16] were among those who split their time between the beach bashes and Jane's *très sérieux* salons.

"One came across writers, artists, singers, and film people, many of whom were not yet famous," recalled Vadim. "People like Jack Nicholson, Larry Hagman, John Phillips[17] of the Mamas and Papas, Mia Farrow, Jacqueline Bisset, and Bob Towne, among many others, were our friends and neighbors."

In a nondescript building across the street from MGM, no guards protected Lippert Productions from the entreaties of unemployed actors in search of screen time. As a Twentieth Century Fox stepchild on the verge of becoming an orphan, Lippert operated beneath the Fox umbrella but far outside the studio gates.[18] Anyone could walk in, and Jack did—often. He sweet-talked his way past the receptionist so he could hone his networking skills on a young producer who kept him working through some of the leanest years of his career. "It was the era of pretty guys," recalled Fred Roos, Jack's target inside the Lippert organization. "His face and look was anything but."

Though no Troy Donahue, Tab Hunter, or Rock Hudson, Jack still impressed Roos as intense and dedicated. When they'd first met four years earlier, Roos was a junior agent at the Music Corporation of America (MCA), where he represented Don Devlin's actress wife, Pilar Seurat. But following MCA's merger with Universal Studios in 1962, Roos hired on at Lippert as a story analyst. He moved up to junior producer, where he helped Devlin and Jack land their *Thunder Island* gig.

In the interim, Jack had returned to acting while Devlin switched to producing, winning a Best Documentary Oscar in 1963.[19] Devlin felt that he'd graduated from the cheesy Lippert-Corman phase of his career, so Jack had to find a new writing partner, and he did so in the person of his old acquaintance Monte Hellman.

Like Jack, Hellman had befriended Roos and also dropped by Lippert Productions on occasion, looking for work. The pair's persistence paid off in the winter of 1964, when Lippert announced plans to make a couple of B adventure films in the Philippines. *Thunder Island* had turned out so well that Roos gave Jack a crack at solo screenwriting, this time a murder mystery set in the Far East.

"It's a role that he wrote for himself, and there's a lot of Jack in it," said Hellman. "He plays a kind of psychological criminal."

In back-to-back productions, Roos hired Hellman to direct and gave him a $160,000 budget to film Jack's screenplay *Flight to Fury* (1964), along with a war film, *Back Door to Hell* (1964). Jack was to act in both movies, as well as write *Flight to Fury*, for a salary of $400 a week. Another Corey graduate, John Hackett, wrote and acted with Jack in *Back Door to Hell*.

In March 1964, Hellman, his actress wife, his child, and both actor-screenwriters set off for Manila on the SS *Chusan*. With stops in Hawaii, Hong Kong, and Japan, the entire voyage took twenty-eight days, but it was far cheaper than international airfare, which was then regarded as luxury travel. Jack and Hackett used their shipboard time to work on their scripts: Jack wrote in longhand, while Hackett banged away on a typewriter seven or eight hours each day, all the way to Luzon.

Hackett's rewrite of one of Lippert's existing screenplays was a straightforward combat flick, centering on three soldiers sent undercover to the Philippines to knock out a Japanese communication center just prior to General McArthur's 1944 invasion. Killed in combat near the end of *Back Door to Hell*, Jack's character is both a glib "grab bag of trivia" and an unlikely New Jersey intellectual capable of translating English to fluent Japanese. Hackett might have taken writing credit, but the wry use of the term *funabulist* (tightrope walker) as he crosses a Philippine river by rope is pure Nicholson.

Jack's script for *Flight to Fury* was original, contemporary, and far more perverse than *Back Door to Hell*: idiosyncrasy had become compulsive. As his character, the jewel thief Jay Wickham, tries to lay his hands on a cache of stolen diamonds, he knocks off other members of the cast until there's only one rival left. The film ends with Wickham tossing the diamonds into a river and shooting himself. Hellman and Roos both saw *Flight to Fury* as a tongue-in-cheek homage to the offbeat John Huston caper film *Beat the Devil* (1953).[20]

Back in L.A., Robert Lippert watched the rushes and declared *Flight to Fury* an outrageous waste of his money. He wanted action, not clever nouvelle vague repartee, and ordered most of Jack's wiseass dialogue and send-ups of clichéd characters cut in a futile attempt to salvage a routine adventure story. The result was unreleaseable. Bolstered with stock combat footage[21] and a staccato bongo-and-rattle soundtrack, *Back Door to Hell* played on the bottom half of a double bill with *Hush . . . Hush, Sweet Charlotte* (1964) later that year, but *Flight to Fury* was so butchered it didn't even get a theater run.

Years later, after Jack had become successful and Lippert had long retired, Jack tried to buy back *Flight to Fury* in an apparent effort to restore his original vision, according to Jack Leewood, but nothing ever came of it. "Nobody wanted to see it, even in drive-ins," Leewood said.

Ten years of Hollywood hard knocks had not yet beaten all of the youthful enthusiasm out of Jack, even if incipient cynicism crept into his work. Following *Flight to Fury*, he threw himself deeper into writing. When he couldn't get an acting gig, he hired himself out as a researcher, working uncredited on close to a dozen films or TV shows. "I was under the pressure of being a family man with a daughter, and one day I accepted a job to act in a movie in the daytime and I was writing a movie at night and I'm back in my little corner and my beloved wife, Sandra, walked in on what was, unbeknownst to her, this *maniac*," Jack recalled. "I remember being at my desk and telling her, 'Even if you don't *hear* me typing, it doesn't mean I'm not *writing*. This *is* writing . . .' I remember that total animus."

Teaming with Hellman, Jack began to develop *Epitaph* for Corman in 1962 shortly after he and Sandra married. An autobiographical study of a struggling actor torn between his career and a woman whose pregnancy forces the then taboo question of abortion,[22] at one point the ninety-six-page screenplay was titled *To Hold the Mirror*. Jack wrote the lead for himself, while Millie Perkins was to have been his love interest. Scenes marking the disintegrating relationship between the protagonists—the struggling actor Josh and his actress girlfriend Lois—reflected the opening rifts in Jack and Sandra's own marriage, with anger and Jack's adultery unraveling their bond.

Cast against the backdrop of the Sunset Strip, Josh and his male friends go to auditions, acting classes, beat hangouts, all-night diners, and parties in *Epitaph*. Meanwhile, Lois undergoes an abortion, tries to pursue her own career, and has a brief, unsatisfying fling with another actress as Josh drifts away. Interspersed throughout the script are snippets from *Studs Lonigan*, *The Terror*, and other films in which Jack or Sandra or both had acted. In the end, Jack's character, Josh, climaxes a raucous Hollywood party scene with a one-night stand, while Lois lies awake at home, knowing she has lost him.

"When we came back from the Philippines we went to Roger and said, 'Okay, we're ready to do *Epitaph*,'" said Hellman. "He said that in the time that had elapsed, he had changed his mind. He didn't want to do that. It was too European, too arty. The subject of abortion was too difficult for American audiences."

Always keenly commercial, Corman suggested that Jack and Monte whip up a couple of Westerns instead, "with plenty of tomahawks and a lot of ketchup." He had a $75,000 budget for one film but, following his two-for-one logic, promised not quite twice as much if they came up with a second movie. As seasoned Cormanistas, the writing team now had enough cachet to draft a set of scenes and then make up the rest as they went along, but as producing partners, Jack and Hellman decided to apply a little discipline to the two projects and make a couple of *très original* nouvelle vague Westerns right under Corman's nose.

While Jack plotted one of the scripts, he and Hellman hired Carole Eastman to write the other.[23] In January 1965, the pair started to collaborate in a second-floor office of the Writer's Building in Beverly Hills.

"I didn't know then that Jack thrives on a certain amount of distraction when he writes," Carole recalled, "and as one who reaches for her six-shooter if she hears a pin drop on the next block, it wasn't the most auspicious of circumstances that we started, at his suggestion, to work in the same room."

While Jack whipped through his own script, Eastman struggled. Periodically, he'd chortle, drop his pen, and read from his notepad. "Jack's like the little kid who sneaks up behind you, pushes you in the mud, and then innocently says, 'What'd *I* do?'" she recalled. Carole agonized over each word while Jack thundered through. He whistled; she chewed her lip.

"What's wrong, Speed?" he taunted.

"Nothing's wrong. I'm just thinking."

"Okay, then let me read you what *I've* written," he'd say, taking great pleasure in sticking it to his slower, more pensive partner. After a spirited reading, he'd ask, "What do you think of *that*?"

By day's end, Jack had a pile of scenes and Carole had "a series of red polka dots on a Kleenex from the blood on my nether lip." The next day and all the days thereafter she remained at home in Hermosa Beach to work on her script.

Yet, over time, it was Eastman's screen effort, inspired by a Jack London short story, that came to be perceived as the standout. She described *The Shooting* (1965) as "Roy Rogers meets *Last Year at Marienbad*," an old Republic Western serial influenced by "French, Italian, and Japanese importations that awakened an almost religious awe and fervor in oneself."

An odd, spare experiment in revenge melodrama, *The Shooting* reeked of European influence in its utter lack of backstory and "Huh?" climax, designed far more for postcinema argument than for audience satisfaction.

As Eastman's script opens, Millie Perkins rides into a remote encampment in the Utah desert and hires a bounty hunter, played by her real-life boyfriend, Warren Oates.[24] With a deadpan expression, she all but orders Oates to escort her to a town several days away by horseback. Accompanied by his simple-minded sidekick, played by Will Hutchins, Oates agrees without ever questioning Perkins about her reasons for making such a trip.

In fact, under Hellman's stark direction, none of the actors display much emotion. Instead, they all move through their roles like stylized Kabuki figures with screen personalities as deep as a bottle cap.

Halfway across the desert, and halfway through the film, Jack appears out of nowhere as Millie Perkins's hired gun—again, with no explanation as to why she might need such a preening thug or how he might fit into her entourage. After hamming it up in several sneering scenes, Jack kills Hutchins with no apparent provocation, and Oates retaliates by breaking Jack's gun hand.

Meanwhile, Perkins discovers a fresh set of hoofprints in the desert and takes off, followed by Oates. They dismount at the base of a mountain and Oates pursues her on foot up the slope. Halfway up, Perkins raises her pistol to shoot at a man higher in the rocks up ahead—a renegade who (blink, blink, rub the eyes) seems to be *Warren Oates*.

Only in the closing frames, as the renegade shoots down Perkins and the second Warren Oates in slow motion, do the unanswered questions at the film's beginning start to make murky sense.[25] Though the movie never spells it out, the backstory the audience is somehow supposed to absorb through osmosis is that Oates had a twin brother who murdered Millie Perkins's husband and child. That is why she hired Jack and posed as a damsel in distress to get Oates to lead her to his evil twin.

Jack, who stole the movie as the nasty gun-slinging Billy Spears, also coproduced *The Shooting*, which he dubbed "a McLuhan mystery."[26] *Ride in the Whirlwind* (1965), on the other hand, was "an existential western."

His third and best screenwriting effort, *Ride in the Whirlwind* had as little backstory as *The Shooting* did, but here backstory seemed far less essential to the plot: three riders stumble upon a nest of stage-coach robbers and are mistaken as thieves by pursuing vigilantes. One of the trio is gunned down, while the two survivors—Jack and Cameron Mitchell—get away. The vigilantes string up two of the actual outlaws—Harry Dean Stanton and Rupert Crosse—neither of whom utters a word about Jack and Mitchell's innocence.

Meanwhile, the two survivors are cornered in a box canyon, holed up in a farmhouse with a pair of aging settlers and their grown daughter, Millie Perkins. All the while protesting their innocence, Jack and Mitchell are driven to shoot Perkins's father, take the settlers' horses, and try to outrun a posse. The movie ends with the mortally wounded Mitchell holding off pursuers as Jack escapes on horseback.

While not so vague or austere as *The Shooting*, *Ride in the Whirlwind* remained true to a half-century of horse opera conventions, while striking a new and far more radical note about the nature of frontier justice. A Manichean tradition of right and wrong had descended from the earliest Hollywood Westerns, with noble lawmen battling the forces of cattle-rustling and gun-toting evil, personified by brutes clad in black hats. The *High Noon* axiom of good trumping evil still prevailed well into the 1960s in TV's *Gunsmoke*, *Have Gun Will Travel*, *Bonanza*, and a host of puerile Warner Bros. series, including *Maverick*, *Cheyenne*, and *Bronco Lane*.

But *Ride in the Whirlwind* became one of the first in a wave of ambivalent Westerns that challenged the clarity of Western stereotypes. From *The Wild Bunch* (1969) and *Butch Cassidy and the*

Sundance Kid (1969) to many of Clint Eastwood's shoot-'em-ups, culminating in *Unforgiven* (1992), white and black hats began blurring to gray. Any demarcation between good and evil all but vanished.

Jack maintained that he was influenced by Albert Camus's essay *The Myth of Sisyphus*, with its bleak existentialist metaphor of all mankind pushing a boulder up a hill, day after day, only to have it roll back down, over and over, ad infinitum. Jack's *Ride in the Whirlwind* costar Cameron Mitchell even saw elements of anti-McCarthyism in Jack's script: the vigilantes assumed a "guilt by association," just as the House Un-American Activities Committee had once assumed that anyone acquainted with a communist must be a "fellow traveler."

By mid-decade, peace and prosperity seemed to settle on Hollywood. Instead of trying to destroy the networks, studios learned to coexist, supplying much of TV's programming, while joining CBS, ABC, and NBC in presenting a united front during labor negotiations.[27]

Universal Studios, swallowed in a controversial 1962 buyout by the rapacious talent agency MCA, led the way in the brave new Hollywood. Formulaic television programming rolled off studio assembly lines like Model Ts. TV had all but erased the venerable B-movie staple. Double features faded from theaters and drive-ins. Paying customers got to see only one movie at a time.

And yet the fewer films Hollywood produced, the worse these seemed to become. Even bad features remained star-driven, regardless of the stars' acting quality. Elvis Presley had sunk to the level of *Harum Scarum* (1965),[28] while venerated masters like James Stewart and Brian Donlevy were being tossed together with the likes of Fabian (*Dear Brigitte* [1965]) or Annette Funicello (*How to Stuff a Wild Bikini* [1965]), in a feeble effort to appeal to both young and old.

Hollywood still offered little to boomers beyond James Bond and beach blanket bingo. The "youth market," which old-line film executives did not recognize as the bulk of America's moviegoers, now outnumbered their elders two to one. According to the Census Bureau, as the nation's population approached 200 million, 63 percent were under thirty-five. Their combined annual income of $281 billion should have been incentive enough to make movies targeted at them, but the studios kept catering to their parents' generation.

Bad movies for older audiences aside, Hollywood's fortunes appeared to have found a new equilibrium. *Diversification, merger,* and *vertical integration* became the industry's buzzwords. While average weekly attendance at the nation's theaters continued to decline (down to an all-time low of 17,800 by 1967), ticket prices kept climbing (up to $1.20 the same year), and studios learned to absorb their losses by investing in the obvious (TV production, pop music, amusement parks) and not-so-obvious (gift store chains, real estate, savings and loans, hotels, and so on). By the year of *The Graduate* (1967),[29] when old Hollywood finally discovered the youth market, annual box office receipts topped $1 billion for the first time.

Overall, times got to be so good that the guilds and most trade unions still managed a 10 percent salary hike, despite the new studio-network negotiating juggernaut. At the same time that studio fortunes were shifting, the writers, actors, and directors guilds, along with the Teamsters and the International Association of Theatrical and Stage Employees, grew fatter and more exclusive. The Screen Actors Guild (SAG) and AFTRA didn't even have to threaten a strike to improve pay and perks.

But actors like Jack who operated outside the system still eked out a living. His total take for *The Shooting* and *Ride in the Whirlwind* was $5,000. "What was interesting was he was ready to quit when I met him," said Cameron Mitchell. "I really encouraged him not to."

Mitchell tried in vain to get the executive producer of *High Chaparral* to hire Jack. "This kid is smart," Mitchell pleaded. "This kid knows how to write and produce. We should hire him as our producer."

In the winter of 1966, Jack convinced the show runners at *Dr. Kildare* to hire him as a running character for four episodes, and later that year, he appeared uncredited as a crew member on the short-lived *Voyage to the Bottom of the Sea*. But at a time when CBS was paying James Arness $1.8 million a year to star in fifty-four episodes of *Gunsmoke*, Jack still earned guild minimum with no guarantee he'd ever land a long-running role. He saw no future in TV, and TV saw no future in him. "The television stuff I did was all shit," he proclaimed years later, long after vowing he'd never make another appearance in the medium as an actor, and certainly not as a guest on a talk show.

Jack continued to put his faith in film, not so much as an actor but as a producer and a writer. After *Epitaph* and *Ride in the Whirlwind*, he began work on another spec script he called *Love and Money*, based on a growing national interest in flower children and psychedelics. He also studied the process of turning raw footage into a movie over the six months during which Hellman edited *The Shooting* and *Ride in the Whirlwind*.

Upon presenting Corman rough cuts, Hellman heard: "There's no Indians. Where are the Indians?"

But even Corman had to admit he was impressed with Hellman's results, though he presumed most domestic distributors wouldn't agree. The nouvelle vague Westerns were still way too hazy for American audiences. Corman sold the U.S. rights to the Walter Reade Organization, which, in turn, tried to peddle both films to TV with scant success. Years passed before art-house audiences got a glimpse of either movie.

Corman guessed that he'd fare far better in France and sanctioned Hellman's plan to send Jack to the 1966 Cannes Film Festival with both "thinking man's Westerns," as the two films came to be dubbed. Corman hoped that he'd find a European distributor and develop a following among the more sophisticated audiences on the other side of the Atlantic.

Accompanied on the trip by his old pal Don Devlin, Jack sneaked the movies aboard the plane in hatboxes so he wouldn't have to pay import duties. Once he cleared customs, he felt as if he was home. Unlike U.S. audiences, the film nerds of Cannes and Paris worshipped Roger Corman as much as they did Jerry Lewis, and they seemed to know most of the movies in which Jack had appeared.[30] They paid particular homage to Jack's masochistic comic turn in *The Little Shop of Horrors*. While not exactly a star, Jack was no longer in the uncomfortable position of always having to explain what movies he'd appeared in.

Cannes was also the hub of European filmmaking, and, while still little known to most Americans in 1966, the then seventeen-year-old festival was an annual convention for every up-and-coming director on the continent. In addition to developing a taste for Gallic culture, Jack furthered his cinematic education and established long-term friendships with such future colleagues as Milos Forman, Bernardo Bertolucci, and Tony Richardson. "I liked his movies, was able to get them seen, and I think probably helped Jack in making some deals," Richardson recalled.

Even after the festival ended and Devlin flew home, Jack stayed on in Paris through much of the summer, crashing at the apartment of the French film distributor and producer Pierre Cottrell and living a bohemian existence until his welcome wore thin and the $750 he'd brought with him for his trip slipped away. "For some reason everybody took a liking to him and they would not charge anything when he went to nightclubs," said Cottrell. "He was always politicking."

On the practical side, Jack's visit had turned out to be pretty much a bust. He and Devlin arrived too late to enter the films in the festival competition, and exhibitors who did screen the films and showed any interest in buying them were prevented from putting *The Shooting* or *Ride in the Whirlwind* in theaters because of a legal dispute over foreign distribution rights. After the litigation was settled and the movies were shown, they were every bit the cult hits Corman guessed they would be, but none of that happened until two years later, in 1968.

In the summer of 1966, Jack returned home to Sandra and Hollywood, broke and empty-handed. "There was not much happening for him in the States. I think it was really a dead time for him," said Cottrell, adding, "He was very insecure. He didn't get secure until much, much later. There had been too many years in which he had not clicked; he felt maybe it would not happen for him."

Corman, on the other hand, finally clicked big-time. After years of making two-bit AIP quickies, he was hired by Twentieth Century Fox to direct his first big-budget studio release, *The St. Valentine's Day Massacre* (1967), a minute-by-minute documentary-style reconstruction of the events leading to the most infamous gangland slaughter of the Roaring Twenties.

Corman wanted Jack to be a part of it, but despite their excitement, they were about to get an abject lesson in the featherbedding profligacy that had eaten away at Hollywood from the inside since the twilight of the studio system.

Used to AIP's shoestring budgets, Corman found ways to cut costs from day one. He turned the Von Trapp mansion from *The Sound of Music* (1965) into Al Capone's house. The fin de siècle New York storefronts under construction for *Hello Dolly!* (1969) became the streets of 1929 Chicago. When he needed a bar for one of Capone's brothels, Corman borrowed it from the set for *The Sand Pebbles* (1966).

Instead of praise for his creative cost cutting, Corman found that he couldn't even cast his own picture without prior approval. He wanted the hefty Orson Welles as Al Capone but got rail-thin Jason Robards Jr. instead because his Fox overseers didn't like Welles's prickly reputation. The revered creator of *Citizen Kane* was labeled the kind of meddlesome actor who took over once the cameras rolled. Fox wanted a malleable star and a cast of sheep.

Corman's troubles didn't end there. Studio executives retained veto power all the way down the list. They even nixed Corman's choice of Jack as one of the featured gangsters. Fox already had someone else under contract whom they ordered Corman to use. "Don't give us problems," he was warned.

After Corman broke the news to Jack, he offered a consolation prize in the form of a supporting role. It would have put Jack in front of the cameras for two of the seven weeks of production and given him a chance to show his stuff, but Jack surprised Corman when he learned that the director was also considering Bruce Dern. Jack asked for an even smaller role: the silent driver of a getaway car.

"Jack, you don't want a nothing one-line part," said Corman.

"Roger, forget that it's one line," said Jack. "I want the seven weeks' work."

As Corman had laid out the production schedule, the getaway driver had to be on the set the first and last week of production. Even though there was nothing for Jack to do in between, he knew that SAG rules required the studio to pay him at least $375 a week for all seven weeks.[31] If Jack had learned nothing else during his first decade in Hollywood, he knew how to exploit loopholes. He never passed up a chance to stick it to the bean counters. "The first time I ever heard the term 'per diem' was from Jack," said his friend John Hackett. "I had to ask what that meant. Jack *always* got the per diem."

Given the studio's overall mismanagement, Jack's contract was one instance of featherbedding that Corman didn't mind accommodating. He brought *The St. Valentine's Day Massacre* in on schedule and $200,000 under budget, but his frugality with the studio's money never showed up on Fox's doctored books. "It wasn't that they were out to get me, but they had a multimillion-dollar overhead, which they had to spread around to whatever was shooting," said Corman. Thus, when the director called on the Teamsters to move lumber from one side of the set to the other, he got five to do what one could have done. Jack wasn't the only union member who sat idle through most of the production and still collected a paycheck.

In the finished film, Jack is even more invisible than he was in *Ensign Pulver*. His single speech is a smartass commentary on the oil that Capone's killers used to rub down their Tommy guns. "It's garlic," Jack says. "The bullets don't kill ya. Ya die of blood poisoning."

But neither the punchline nor Corman's frugal ways could save *The St. Valentine's Day Massacre*. Despite solid reviews, the voiceover drone influenced by TV's *The Untouchables* and the plodding, minute-by-minute documentary style didn't work on the big screen. Even the violent climax depicting the savage slaughter of seven of Capone's enemies didn't excite audiences. Though it was far more graphic than any previous gangster film and foreshadowed the bloody ending of *Bonnie and Clyde* (1968), *The St. Valentine's Day Massacre* flopped.

The autumn of 1966 devolved into winter, and the Nicholsons' marriage grew rockier. Their shouting matches led to another mutual acid trip—this time under the supervision of a marriage counselor Jack later characterized as "something of a charlatan."

"This therapist didn't really understand LSD," Jack recalled. "He had never taken it himself. He gave it to Sandra first, in conjunction with a five-hour therapeutic session, but he gave her the maximum dosage. At one point, she looked at me and saw a demon, a totally demonic figure. For whatever reason, either because it's true about me, or because of her own grasping at something, it was pretty bad."

Sandra could live with penny-pinching and constant struggle, but she couldn't live with the devil. Fortunes change in Hollywood, though, and often in a split second. That same winter, the brakes began to grind on his Karmann Ghia. "The brakes were so bad, he was getting worried for [Sandra's] safety," said John Hackett. "I said, 'Well, fix them,' and he said, 'I don't have the money to fix them.' I said, 'Do it yourself' and he said, 'I don't know *how* to do-it-yourself.'"

Hackett agreed to help. While he was under the car, the phone rang and Jack went inside. He came out chortling, the patented Jack grin riding from ear to ear. He'd gotten two jobs at once—one to write *The Trip* (1967) and the other to co-star in *Rebel Rousers* (1970). For weeks thereafter, he became the chief object of envy among the Corey alumni. "He went into the house poor and came out, in our eyes, rich," said Hackett.

5

ALL BIKER FILMS TRACE THEIR ROOTS TO *THE WILD ONE*, Marlon Brando's 1954 tour de Harley, which was based on the July 4, 1947, takeover of the isolated California coastal town of Hollister, about a hundred miles south of San Francisco. An article in *Harper's* January 1951 issue[1] by the author Frank Rooney, "The Cyclists' Raid," struck a note with the maverick producer Stanley Kramer, who hired the graylisted screenwriters John Paxton (*Crossfire, On the Beach*) and Ben Maddow (*The Unforgiven, Asphalt Jungle*) to turn the story into a script.

Brando, still riding the crest of his star-making role as Stanley Kowalski in *A Streetcar Named Desire*, loved the screenplay until Columbia Studios censored much of the violence. After he soured on the sanitized version, Brando honored his contract but still got in his digs. Instructed to narrate a prologue, he sneered the speech in a sappy Southern accent. His contempt for studio overlords had the unintended effect of underscoring the contempt of his character, the gang leader Johnny Strabler, for just about everything.

"What're you rebelling against, Johnny?" asks the small-town waitress portrayed by the ingénue Mary Murphy.

"Whaddya got?" asks Brando.

Later in the film, Murphy delivers a good girl's lament that resonated for an entire generation: "I wish I was going someplace. I wish you were going someplace. We could go together."

While panned by many critics, *The Wild One* found its audience in the restless postwar prerock teen culture and influenced every antihero who came after, from Elvis to the Fonz to the Ramones, and, in film, a generation of young rebels leading to the likes of Sean Penn and Johnny Depp. But the original was Brando, and, for the rest of his life, he would remain something of an acting god to Jack. "I was in high school back in the '50s when he came into the game, and I watched him change the rules," Jack wrote in the summer of 2004, on the occasion of the eighty-year-old actor's passing. Published as a eulogy in *Rolling Stone*, Jack's appreciative tribute left little doubt of the debt he felt he owed.

By 1966, Brando[2] was long gone from biker films, but the genre had supplanted horse opera as melodrama for the young and the restless. As the "chopper" film actor Jeremy Slate told *Cinema* magazine, "The contemporary motorbike picture is a blending of the two basic elements of the true Western: the lone hero against the world, moving with the speed of a tuned-up Harley—and speed is what is needed to keep the kids coming back. They've had it with horses."

Roger Corman and AIP began their own biker franchise with *The Wild Angels* (1966), a crucible for the coming revolution in American film. Starring Peter Fonda and Nancy Sinatra, two second-generation Hollywood brats with bankable names, *The Wild Angels* also became the training ground for several other careers.[3] The New York University film student Peter Bogdanovich made his Hollywood debut as Corman's assistant, while Richard Rush, who had directed Jack six years earlier in *Too Soon to Love*, took a credit as properties manager. Roger Corman directed, Monte Hellman edited, and *The Little Shop of Horrors*'s Chuck Griffith wrote the screenplay. Though Jack wasn't in the film, Corman credited him with streamlining the title from *All the Fallen Angels* to *The Wild Angels*. Jack "always had a knack for titles and campaigns," said Corman.

Pointless and prurient, *The Wild Angels* opened the 1966 Venice Film Festival and eventually astonished the major studios by pulling in more than $10 million. Hollywood's bandwagon instinct to cash in on another's success rather than create something new took immediate hold. Within months, a half dozen *Wild Angels* clones were in production, and Jack was riding with them, beginning with *Rebel Rousers*. "I helped get *Rebel Rousers* made and I made sure Jack was in it," said Bruce Dern, cast in the starring role of outlaw leader.

"That was the worst thing I ever made," understated the director Martin B. Cohen,[4] Dern's manager and a Broadway transplant who knew something about bad movie making, having just finished *Blood of Dracula's Castle* (1968) and *Nightmare in Wax* (1969)[5] in the months leading up to *Rebel Rousers*. Distributors agreed with his final assessment: the saga of a middle-aged couple (Cameron Mitchell and Diane Ladd) clashing with outlaw bikers, led by Jack and Dern, went unreleased for three years. It got a theatrical run only after Jack hit his star stride in the wake of *Easy Rider*.

No sooner did he finish *Rebel Rousers* than Jack mounted up again for three and a half weeks in Oakland and Bakersfield, this time as a costar of the much better *Hell's Angels on Wheels* (1967). The producer Joe Solomon, king of the cycle flicks,[6] tapped the much-in-demand Richard Rush to direct. While no studio would hire Rush, he got regular offers to crank out another $150,000 independent quickie. "At that time, I had the somewhat dubious reputation of being the best of the two-dollar hookers," Rush recalled.

The National Catholic Office for Motion Pictures gave *Hell's Angels on Wheels* a "C" for Condemned: "Trash is the word for this exploitation of sex and brutality for their own sake. Theater owners who book this film are patently guilty of complete social irresponsibility to their communities, especially to the young."

Though hardly sexy or violent by twenty-first-century standards, *Hell's Angels on Wheels* did have plenty to condemn: László Kovács's artsy travelogue cinematography (which would work so well in *Easy Rider*) juxtaposed against slugfests and the sappy theme song, "Moving but Going Nowhere"; unprovocative dance sequences that looked as if they'd been lifted from a *Laugh-In* skit; and stagy fights reminiscent of the Sharks versus the Jets in *West Side Story* (1961), complete with borrowed riffs from Leonard Bernstein's orchestration.

It was during *Hell's Angels on Wheels* that Jack developed "that shit-eating grin, which is a defensive way of looking at the world," said Rush. "When you don't know what's happening, or when you're hurt, you cockily grin your way through."

But *Variety* saw Jack's smile less kindly. The reviewer slammed Jack's Poet as "the non-conforming non-conformist made up mostly of variations on a grin."

Nevertheless, *Hell's Angels on Wheels* took in $6 million at the box office, provoking those eternal Hollywood constants, ego and greed. The movie generated two lawsuits: Sabrina Scharf demanded $1 million in damages for reducing the type size of her name in the credits beneath the far larger names of Adam Roarke and Jack Nicholson, and two of Joe Solomon's backers claimed they'd been cheated out of their share of the film's profits.

. . .

Jack's five-year marriage fizzled just before the Summer of Love. He moved out of the Hollywood flatlands on April Fool's Day 1967 and moved in with Robert Towne. "But that only lasted one day," said Jack. "I don't think either of us was particularly easy to live with."

Next, Jack bunked with his best man. Harry Dean Stanton had also recently divorced. Jack denied that his marriage flamed out. He simply said it ended: "It wasn't fulfilling what I wanted it to do. I was working day and night, and I couldn't take the arguments. They bored me."

Jack's friends saw past his stoicism. During *Rebel Rousers*, Bruce Dern watched him move between uncontrollable weeping one moment to dead-on professionalism the next.

As the mother of his daughter and the lifelong recipient of Jack's goodwill, Sandra remained mum on the reasons he left, though she did charge him with "extreme cruelty" and called for a mutual restraining order when the divorce became final sixteen months later.[7] In the decades to come, she'd back up Jack's story that they simply drifted apart.

During the filming of *Hell's Angels on Wheels*, he'd taken up with Mireille "Mimi" Machu, the gyrating, high-stepping blonde who appeared in one of the bar fight scenes. Mimi went by the screen name I. J. Jefferson and approximated a willowy flower child, although she'd already had a fling with (and an illegitimate child by) the pop star Sonny Bono three years earlier. Richard Rush called her "a girl who blushed, not because she was shy, but because it was part of her nature. She was not a girl who was easy to shock. Her emotions were on the surface."

Not so with Sandra. She presented a dreamy, more sedate public image. Behind closed doors, though, she could be as tempestuous as she was ethereal. "They were *fiery*," Helena Kallianiotes recalled of Sandra and Jack as a couple.

Their split was not a simple matter of adultery or Sandra's nagging insecurity versus Jack's explosive temper. They broke up over sex, drugs, and rock 'n' roll; they broke up over Jack's obsession with success; and they broke up over God. "The probable cause was that she became stimulated in a mystical area, and I couldn't get with that," said Jack.

In the waning days of the marriage, Sandra found solace in meditation and the homilies of Jiddu Krishnamurti,[8] urging Jack to join her in pilgrimages to the Indian yogi's U.S. headquarters near the town of Ojai.[9] "What I noticed when I first saw Krishnamurti speak was he and Bob Dylan appeared onstage the exact same way," Jack recalled. "They were just kind of there—no flourish, no nothing. What Krishnamurti says could be reduced to 'live in the now.' It's a phrase we hear endlessly, but in fact it's the point." Encouraged by his best man, Harry Dean Stanton, another Krishnamurti convert,[10] Jack made a genuine effort, but in the end, he preferred ganja to gurus.

"Sandra got turned on to religion," recalled Kallianiotes. "She fell in love with God and Jack couldn't compete."[11]

In the Laurel Canyon bachelor pad on Skyline Drive where he retreated with Stanton, Jack kept Spartan quarters: a bed, a desk, and a record player. Stanton had lived there a couple of years and still hadn't unpacked his boxes. Jack smoked weed and wrote screenplays, calculating that his future now lay behind the camera. At the time, he characterized himself less as an actor than "kind of a journeyman troublemaker." "Jack didn't want to be a star," said his fellow actor Henry Jaglom. "Jack wanted to be a director."

He learned from his mentors Corman, Hellman, and Rush that the path he now chose was far more circuitous and uncertain than the path to stardom. Fraught with obstacles and the potential for far more mean-spirited criticism than acting, directing began with a typewriter and an original vision.

"Being stoned has helped me creatively in writing," Jack observed. "It relaxes you and makes you a little more content to be in a room all by yourself. It's easier to entertain yourself mentally. It produces a lot of shit, too. Most writers have more trouble writing than coming up with quality stuff."

On weekends, he blew off steam at round after round of parties. "Orgies in the strictest definition," recalled Jack. "There were a lot of rooms in my house, and people could take their private little trips."

Just a mile off busy Sunset Boulevard and beyond the neon heart of Hollywood, rustic Laurel Canyon had become the mecca of L.A.'s sixties counterculture. Residents cultivated weed in the woods and threw rent parties on the weekends. Timothy Leary dropped in and turned on among the faithful whenever he happened to be in the neighborhood. The director Hal Ashby, another cannabis devotee, lived nearby. The Beatles and the Stones made pilgrimages when they came to town, and at one time or another the Doors, the Byrds, and Buffalo Springfield had all lived farther up the winding canyon road from Jack and Harry's place. Among his new neighbors, Jack could count Carole King, Frank Zappa, Judy Collins, David Crosby, Joni Mitchell, Graham Nash, Stephen Stills, Alice Cooper, Leonard Cohen, Neil Young,[12] Cass Elliott, Jackson Browne, and the inscrutable pop music czar Lou Adler, who turned many a rebel rocker into a recording star at the same time that he joined Jack's growing entourage of fast and loyal pals.

"I thought of it as a crap game, but Jack was way ahead of the rest of us in understanding the workings of Hollywood," said Adam Roarke. "Jack always had a five-year plan," said Harry Gittes, the gap-toothed ad executive with a vague resemblance to Bruce Dern, who'd fallen in with the Nicholson crowd. "He always knew where he was going and how he was going to get there."

It had become abundantly clear that Jack wasn't going to get there via the tube. By 1967, his contempt for TV and its minions had become mutual. "I got him something on *Guns of Will Sonnett* and Aaron Spelling got mad at me," said Fred Roos, who had moved on from Lippert Productions to become a TV casting director.[13] "He yelled at me after seeing his work, like I was bringing some weirdo into his midst."

Roos also landed Jack his final sitcom appearance in an episode of *The Andy Griffith Show*. Shot during the summer and aired on October 23, 1967, "Aunt Bee, the Juror" featured Jack as the defendant with the innocent hazel eyes, who Aunt Bee doesn't believe looks like a criminal. She hangs the jury, Jack goes free, and the real thief is captured in the courtroom before the commercial break. Just a year earlier, Jack had played a different role—the father of a foundling left on the courthouse steps—in another *Andy Griffith* episode, titled "Opie Finds a Baby." The only comfort Jack could take in his truncated TV career was that, year to year, no one—including the producers—seemed to remember anything in which he'd ever appeared.

In the dozen years since he'd landed in L.A., Jack's adopted home-town had undergone as sure and subtle a renaissance as had the kid from Neptune. The genteel Sunset Strip of late forties supper clubs like Mocambo, Ciro's, and the Trocadero had become the province of head rock night spots like Gazzari's, Pandora's Box, and the Whisky a Go Go.[14] The kitschy Hollywood Boulevard Walk of Fame had expanded by more than two thousand stars over eighteen city blocks since the Hollywood Chamber of Commerce unveiled the first eight brass-and-terrazzo stars in 1958.[15] Five years later, Universal premiered its popular studio tram tours.

For studios, it was the era of the merger. MCA-Universal was the one major that thrived. The rest fell like dying sequoias. Gulf & Western Corporation swallowed Paramount in 1966. Transamerica took over United Artists the following year. Seven Arts Ltd. paid Jack Warner, the last of the founding moguls, $84 million for Warner Bros. in 1967, only to sell off the studio two years later to Kinney National. Even MGM would soon be in play, briefly falling into the hands of the Seagrams chairman Edgar Bronfman before the airline magnate Kirk Kerkorian took over and began dismantling the studio in 1969.

But boardroom musical chairs still hadn't changed old-style film output. For every moderately budgeted *Bonnie and Clyde* (1967)[16] or *The Graduate* (1967) that featured young unknowns and targeted boomers, the studios still produced dozens of big-budget, big-star clunkers, from *Thoroughly Modern Millie* (1967) to *A Countess from Hong Kong* (1967).[17] "The absurd thing was that they were finding out about that time that the entire movie audience is a youth audience," said Richard Rush.

In June 1967, the same month that Sandra and Jack separated, the Beatles released *Sgt. Pepper's Lonely Hearts Club Band* and Roger Corman began filming *The Trip*—the story of a burned-out TV commercial director who drops acid because he's wracked with guilt over his pending divorce.

In Jack's unedited screenplay, the director saves himself through a night of sex and psychedelics and everyone—his wife, his girlfriend, and the TV ad director himself—lives more or less happily ever after his acid trip. Awakening the next morning, his girlfriend turns to him and asks if he has found any insight following a night of freaking and fucking. The protagonist ends the movie with a line straight out of *Gone with the Wind*: "I'll think about it tomorrow."

"I don't believe it," a weepy Peter Fonda told his wife, so moved was he when he first read Jack's script. *The Trip* ranked with the best of Fellini, he said. "I don't believe that I'm really going to have a chance; that I get to be in this movie. This is going to be the greatest film ever made in America."

While flattered, Jack had fewer illusions. He knew what happened to a screenplay between casting and completion. In the weeks leading up to production, he had watched Roger Corman hack away the pages that called for expensive special effects. Making movies on the cheap had become so ingrained in Corman's pennywise methods that scrimping was an unbreakable habit. To save a few extra dollars, he sacrificed quality, continuity, and whole chunks of storyline.

The butchering didn't end there. When AIP's Sam Arkoff got Corman's final cut later that summer, he added a disclaimer denouncing drug use at the front of the film and shattered the upbeat ending with a Fonda freeze frame, cracked like his reflection in a busted mirror. Even a rebel studio like AIP would not risk an endorsement of LSD. Arkoff further demeaned the hallucinogen in AIP's own ad copy as "a Lovely Sort of Death."

In the end, "The picture was very McLuhanesque. It was about the juxtaposition of reality," Jack told an interviewer. "The theory was to show how quickly things move." He consoled himself further by eulogizing, "It was the best movie Roger ever made, and that's something."

Turning on was the one thing *The Trip*'s star, the producer-director, and the screenwriter all had in common. Even Corman, who described himself as the squarest of squares, made a point of dropping acid in the Big Sur wilderness near Monterey just before filming began. He spent a day tripping with his face in the dirt and came away believing in the drug's mind-expanding efficacy, but it didn't expand his budget.

Fonda first learned about LSD in 1963 from a London physician who treated him for manic depression, although he didn't take the hallucinogen until two years later in the summer of 1965, after he'd lost a friend to suicide and needed something to "help me understand my mind." Fonda became as big an LSD advocate as Corman and costar Dennis Hopper, who played Fonda's drug dealer and father confessor in *The Trip*.[18]

Jack, of course, had done acid several times and incorporated his experiences into *The Trip*. "Jack used an ingenious editorial style to bombard the mind of the audience and still keep a story line running," Fonda declared.

Jack wrote a part for himself as Fonda's guide through the psychedelic wilderness, but Corman awarded Bruce Dern the role instead, having lost faith in Jack's screen charisma. Although Jack was Dern's acting equal, other directors wouldn't hire him, and Corman joined their ranks. He began to think of Jack less as an actor and more as a writer. Dern concurred. "The original script that he wrote for *The Trip* was just sensational," Dern said.

And Corman's timing in producing the movie seemed impeccable. To drum up mainstream interest, he invited the media to a preproduction body-painting session at Hollywood's Brave New World nightclub, knowing full well that a photo op featuring near-naked flower children getting breasts, butts, and bellies painted in Day-Glo would be irresistible to local TV. Further whetting the public appetite, *Playboy* did a full-color spread, featuring nipples and airbrushed crotch shots, which were then verboten in *Time* and *Newsweek*.[19]

The Trip opened in L.A. the following August 1967.[20] The U.S. response was mild curiosity, but Corman's epic suffered howls and condemnation from the British and the Catholics. The British Board of Film Classification feared that the movie glorified LSD and banned it until 2003,[21] when a board spokeswoman proclaimed "The film is now so outdated that it is highly unlikely to influence anyone. We are more concerned with other drugs now." What was more, she opined, Fonda's "acting is terrible. To be perfectly frank, the film is dreadful. There are lots of scenes of Peter Fonda walking around the countryside marveling at the clouds."

At the time of the release, a handful of critics saw beyond the hype over drugs, sanitized sex, strobing, and subliminal editing. Jack's underlying story turned out to be a far more heavy-handed soap opera, based on his personal sins. In lieu of seeking absolution from a priest at Our Lady of Providence back in Neptune City, *The Trip* became Jack's confessional.

The *New Yorker*'s Penelope Gilliatt had a field day with Fonda's sad-sack character, who resists divorcing his wife (Susan Strasberg, who looks very much like Sandra Knight) at the same time that he's lusting after his girlfriend (Salli Sachse, who behaves very much like Mimi Machu), all the while wading through dream sequences heavy on medieval Bergmanesque symbolism: "a merry-go-round, a few cathedral furnishings, an electric chair that has a touch of the hair dryer about it."

Nonetheless, at least some moviegoers could still be fooled part of the time. *The Trip* earned more than $6 million at the box office and played to standing-room-only crowds at the 1968 Cannes Film Festival. It went on to become one of the more lucrative of Roger Corman's hundreds of cheap but profitable films and led to Jack's next project: the flower power peace, love, and drug epic *Psych-Out* (1968).

"I had been in Reichian therapy and so was Jack," said his *Psych-Out* costar Susan Strasberg. "Reich was a brilliant man with complex theories, far ahead of their time, about the bio-energy of the body. And I remember Jack distilling it down to: 'You fuck better.'"

One of Freud's more promising disciples, Dr. Wilhelm Reich had been dead ten years by the time Jack discovered him, embraced his teachings, and turned the Austrian psychiatrist into one of the guiding lights of his life and career. By the time Jack starred in *Psych-Out*, Reich was entrenched in his belief system.

Following World War I, Reich had spawned an offshoot of psychoanalysis that traced all neuroses, dysfunction, and even malignant tumors to a lousy sex life. Controversy dogged the Vienna-educated physician most of his life, but it heated to scorching after he immigrated to the United States at the outset of World War II. Reich's contention that frequent orgasms kept men and women mentally, physically, and emotionally fit turned out to be as popular an idea during the uptight Truman and Eisenhower administrations as Dr. Alfred Kinsey's revelations that Americans liked adultery: half the country was titillated, while the other half was appalled. At the rise of McCarthyism, the onetime communist Dr. Reich was ripe for a witch hunt in 1947.[22]

While Reich was never convicted of anything more heinous than contempt of court,[23] he stood accused of quackery for maintaining that Orgone, a sexually based life force similar to Freud's libido, could be captured like electricity and used to help patients overcome a host of mental and physical maladies, including cancer. After his contentious ten-year stalemate with the Food and Drug Administration over his radical theories, the sixty-year-old psychiatrist succumbed to heart failure on November 3, 1957, while he was serving a two-year federal prison term.

"He was a great man," said Harry Dean Stanton. "Died in jail, of course, but he's the one who talked about the life-negative and live-positive principles. He called it 'the Emotional Plague': the terror of being responsible for yourself. . . . I was just as terrified as the next guy for much of my life, but the more you face that terror, the better it gets. Terror's nothing but energy. Tremendous energy, sure, but you can face it. It makes you healthier, happier."

Jack became a Reich devotee in the late sixties for the same reasons he dabbled in Krishnamurti and LSD: to get to the core of his creativity. In conversations with Strasberg during the filming of *Psych-Out*, Jack admitted that his "volatile field of energy" made him hard to live with. He called himself "an existential romantic" pursuing life, liberty, and orgasmic release. When his therapist insisted that he be analyzed in the nude, Jack stripped. "It didn't take any rationalization," Jack said, maintaining that he got immediate results. As a result of Reich, "I don't falsify sensuality," Jack declared.

But neither was he just another horn-dog hedonist. Jack's evolving beliefs still left plenty of room for monogamous intimacy. "You can feel the difference when you make love and there's love there, and when you make love and there's not love there," he said. "I'm not a Victorian, but a fact's a fact."

These fundamental distinctions between making love and having sex allowed Jack to pursue differing relationships with different women.[24] He proudly bore the predatory mantle his coffeehouse pals once bestowed upon him—"the Great Seducer"—but offered up a very different side to many of the women in his life. From his earliest Hollywood years, Jack had surrounded himself with a bevy of women who remained friends. Helena Kallianiotes, Luana Anders, Lynn Bernay, Sally Kellerman, Carole Eastman, and Carol Kane were among his closest, most protective, and staunchest supporters, but none became notches on his bedpost. They were what his pal Bruce Dern called "dames": women who took risks and in the process earned male respect. "If they dance particularly well, they become great dames," he said.

Kellerman, who was thirty pounds overweight when she and Jack first became friends, used to binge with him on potato chips and ice cream while she shared her sniffling blues over her latest lost love. "Jack was the funniest man in the world and always available when I needed him—a true friend," she said.

"I have always felt like a sister," said Bernay, another Corey graduate who remained close to Jack. There were women he counted as equals and there were women after whom he lusted, and how he differentiated between the two touched off heated arguments over just how much—or how little—Jack respected women. "Mostly, they stay with Jack because he has incredible charisma," said Bernay. "It's utterly charming. It's playful, delicious. It's seductive as hell. How the hell can you resist it?"

Fresh from her role as Peter Fonda's wife in *The Trip*, Strasberg fell into the friend category.[25] Even though she resembled Sandra and had much in common with Jack and got naked with him for a love scene in *Psych-Out*, the most they shared was mutual embarrassment beneath the klieg lights as a jealous Mimi Machu hovered nearby.

"When we did our love scene, I was wearing a minidress and Jack wore his jeans and boots," Strasberg recalled. "I asked him if he could take his boots off. Peter Fonda had played his [role] in the nude in *The Trip*. Neither one of us wanted to show our thighs, but I had to."

Jack simulated sex for the role, but Mimi was not appeased, according to Strasberg. Again assuming her screen name, I. J. Jefferson, Mimi evened the score in her role as the flirtatious Pandora, hopping into a coffin with Adam Roarke during one of her own *Psych-Out* scenes.

In addition to writing *Psych-Out*, Jack had packaged the movie for himself and was determined not to lose the lead to Roarke, Bruce Dern, or some other actor. He finished the screenplay in May 1967, after Strasberg finished filming *The Trip*. Then titled *Love Is a Four Letter Word*, Jack's script underwent a name change when the producer and *American Bandstand* host Dick Clark opted instead for *The Love Children*. After AIP's Sam Arkoff objected that it sounded like a movie about illegitimate children, Clark switched names again.

Psych-Out was Clark's nod to *Psycho* (1960), which had terrific audience name recognition even though Alfred Hitchcock's horror classic bore no resemblance to Jack's screenplay. Because it was Clark's first feature film, he became a hands-on producer and took a keen interest in the day-to-day operation. With his sharp commercial eye, he became one of the first producers to use a movie score to promote pop acts—in the case of *Psych-Out*, the acid rock bands Strawberry Alarm Clock and the Seeds. At the same time, Clark paid attention to every dollar detail, down to the product placement of Dr Pepper cans.

After Clark passed the script on to the veteran TV writer Betty Ulius for a complete rewrite, whatever was left of Jack's story vanished, too. He got no writing credit but did accept the consolation prize: the starring role of Stoney, a ponytailed lead guitarist for the fictive rock group Mumbly Jim.

Shot over twenty-two days in and around Haight-Ashbury, *Psych-Out* was another Richard Rush–AIP quickie, this time exploiting a deaf flower child (Strasberg) in search of her long-lost hippie brother, played by Dern. As Strasberg's ambivalent lover, Jack helps her find the drugged-out Dern, only to lose him as he dies in a building fire. As in *Hell's Angels on Wheels*, Jack is left behind to comfort the shrieking ingénue.

During filming, Rush again called on Sonny Barger, but this time not for his technical assistance. After panhandlers pulled knives on the cast and crew, Rush hired the Angels to patrol the shoot. The Summer of Love had ended by the time Rush's cameras rolled in October 1967, and Clark observed that a "tougher element" had taken over the Haight. By the time *Psych-Out* was released in March 1968, peace, love, and understanding had given way to paranoia, lust, and heroin. In the pages of *Variety*, Clark predicted that hippies would soon fade across America, not just in San Francisco.

Nevertheless, in the first widely read tribute to Jack in more than a decade of his acting, the *Los Angeles Times*'s Kevin Thomas praised him as "an exciting off-beat personality that continues to impress with each new appearance." Jack had given his character complexity and nuance as the charming, oversexed opportunist Stoney, with one eye glazed over on weed while the other was fixed on capturing a recording contract for Mumbly Jim. One critic pegged Stoney as "a prodigious womanizer and closet nine-to-fiver"—a description that worked well for Jack himself.

Jack felt good to be working again as an actor, but he continued to suffer disappointments. He was perfect for the role of the hustling husband who pimps Mia Farrow to Satan in *Rosemary's Baby* (1968), but the director Roman Polanski nixed him as too sinister to portray the clean-cut, duplicitous Guy Woodhouse—a part that went instead to the far more sinister-looking John Cassavetes.

It was Jack's success as a writer, not his acting, that kept him moving up the food chain. As the tumultuous year 1967 wound to a close,

Fred Roos introduced Jack to a young novelist who looked like a sure fit with Jack's *The Trip* and *Psych-Out* sensibility.

Drive, He Said was Jeremy Larner's first novel, and though it was written five years earlier, before drugs and Vietnam fomented the youth revolution, its antiwar focus seemed suited to the campus unrest of the era. What was more, its hero was the basketball star Jack had always longed to be. Jack might have preferred to write the screenplay for *Catcher in the Rye*—he even conspired once with Henry Jaglom to get the film rights[26]—but after he read *Drive, He Said* and met Larner in the flesh, adapting the novel for the screen and delivering another furtive blow against the Establishment became his back-burner obsession.

Larner, a journalist who came to L.A. to cover the 1968 Rose Bowl for the *Saturday Evening Post*, asked Jack whether he'd like to come along and watch USC face off against Indiana while they discussed *Drive, He Said*. Jack gave him a nod and his best sneer. Larner remembered Jack as likable but brash during the game, lecturing on O. J. Simpson's broken-field running style in one breath while explaining how movies were made in the other. Jack boasted that he was about to launch his biggest project to date, involving the stars of the hit TV sitcom *The Monkees*, and he felt quite full of himself. He struck Larner as bright and driven but not happy. "I remember thinking even then that he's a charming guy, but there was something peculiar about him I didn't understand," said Larner. "It was hard to tell him anything about sports, for example. He knew it all, though it was pretty clear he hadn't played."

The Trojans beat Indiana 14–3, Jack bade adieu, and Larner finished his *Post* assignment. He carried on through the rest of 1968 by writing speeches for Senator Eugene McCarthy's quixotic presidential bid, hearing nothing further from Jack. And yet, while nothing immediate came of Jack's promise to turn *Drive, He Said* into a movie, Larner didn't discount him as just another Hollywood blowhard.

"One of the very tricky things about dealing with Jack is that he handles himself very well to his own advantage, especially for somebody who, in some respects, is self-destructive," said Larner. "He manipulates you very well. He means to, but he doesn't mean to. And obviously it's highly imperfect because I don't think of him as a happy guy—but he's a successful guy. The bottom line is he enjoys his triumphs, and he enjoys many things about life. But to me, he never seems to be happy."

A few months before Jack met Larner, he cemented another life-long partnership. Over time, both Jack and the director Bob Rafelson honed the story of their chance meeting at a Hollywood foreign film screening, although neither can recall what movie they saw or where they saw it.[27] All either remembers was that the film had subtitles and they were the only two people in the house who stood to applaud when it was over. As the audience shuffled out, Jack and Rafelson agreed to meet for coffee, found themselves finishing each other's sentences, and presto, one of the great director-actor marriages was consummated. "We're like Colossus," pontificated Jack. "We bestride two worlds—art and industry—which should get us a big pain from the stretch."

When the time came to make Jack's Monkees movie, Rafelson knew just where to turn.

Both Rafelson and Jeremy Larner represented a new type of Nicholson acquaintance. Each was well bred and Eastern educated; came from stable, literate, middle-class stock; and could know nothing about the visceral hunger of a New Jersey outrider born a bastard at the fringe of poverty.

Rafelson, showing as much facility with self-mythologizing as Jack did, approximated his own rough-and-tumble blue-collar background in his résumé. Despite growing up solvent in Manhattan with strong early ties to the upper echelons of Hollywood,[28] Rafelson claimed to have knocked around as a drummer in a jazz band, an itinerant Mexican folksinger, a rodeo rider, a crewman on an ocean liner, and an army deejay before enrolling as a philosophy student at Dartmouth. In truth, he had graduated first to advertising in New York and then became a TV story editor for the producer David Susskind. In 1962, Rafelson migrated west with a half-baked idea for a television series centered around a rock band. "If I couldn't be a rock 'n' roll singer," he mused, "I wanted as a filmmaker to create a rock 'n' roll group."

Working first at MCA-Universal's Revue Productions before moving on to ABC, Desilu, and Columbia's Screen Gems television production division, Rafelson developed TV pilots (*The Wackiest Ship in the Army, The Greatest Show on Earth*) but found no takers for his rock band idea. It had to wait until he teamed up with an old acquaintance from his salad days in New York: a Rafelson contemporary destined to become another rung on Jack's ladder to success.

Rafelson might have had his toe in the business as the nephew of one of its great screenwriters, but Bert Schneider had been steeped in Hollywood from birth. The middle son of the Columbia Studios' chairman Abe Schneider wanted for nothing, including opportunity, after his father succeeded the Columbia founder Harry Cohn in 1958.[29]

Both Rafelson and Schneider fancied themselves heirs of the Beat Generation and wanted to use movies to reach their peers, not their elders. "Bert straightened me out," said Rafelson. "We started a company of our own, and he protected me from all the ugly phantoms of Hollywood." Empowered by the petulance and fervor of the times, their Raybert Productions looked for film projects that would reflect and appeal to boomers.[30]

"Our ambitions were to make movies," recalled Schneider. "We began with a TV series because that was a foot in the door. It was easier to get a pilot of a TV series made than it was to get a movie made." And while Rafelson had had some success with series TV, both he and Schneider credited the Beatles' phenomenal one-two punch, *A Hard Day's Night* (1964) and *Help!* (1965), with convincing Columbia to green-light the pilot for *The Monkees*.[31]

With a $225,000 startup budget from Screen Gems, Raybert set up offices on the Columbia lot in April 1965, and by fall the trades announced auditions for "four insane boys, age 17 to 21," who possessed the "courage to work." Of the 437 who answered the ad, Schneider and Rafelson chose four: a former child actor (Mickey Dolenz), a folksinger (Michael Nesmith), a British stage performer (Davy Jones), and a college dropout/starving musician (Peter Tork). In short order, Raybert dressed them, rehearsed them, and made the boys the Monkees. Larry Tucker (*Bob & Carol & Ted & Alice*) and Paul Mazursky (*Down and Out in Beverly Hills, Scenes from a Mall*) wrote the pilot, and from the moment *The Monkees* premiered on NBC in 1966, the group was an instant hit.

Over the course of two TV seasons, the Monkees sold more than 23 million record albums and captured a huge audience. Manufactured or not, their celebrity inspired a frenzy approaching that of the Beatles. Groupies groped, dealers dealt, and hangers-on hung on in droves. Dubbed "the Prefab Four," the Monkees were no match for the originals either musically or as a cultural phenomenon, but for a time their commercial appeal among American teens ballooned with their Nielsen ratings.

By 1968, Monkees mania did a fast fade. In a fatal moment of honesty, Michael Nesmith told *Look* magazine that the group was synthetic. "This flap started about the fact that the Monkees were not a real rock 'n' roll band, which of course in retrospect seems positively absurd," recalled Nesmith. "[It was] like there being a flap about the fact that the Starship *Enterprise* is not going to outer space." Media outrage over the obvious festered, putting the Monkees in the peculiar position of being both "white hot and miserable," according to Nesmith.

Just at the point when Raybert had convinced Columbia to underwrite a Monkees movie, the scripted TV antics of four insane boys fell from grace. At the same time, the Summer of Love had given way to a winter of discontent, and soon the disastrous Tet offensive in Vietnam would be followed by the assassinations of the Reverend Martin Luther King Jr. and Senator Robert F. Kennedy. The country was in no mood for Monkees. "In the midst of all this incredible success, here was this almost uncompromising hatred from peers and the press," Nesmith continued. "When Jack came on, the ship was sinking."

During the last week of November 1967, Rafelson and Schneider ordered their Monkees to a weekend retreat in Ojai, where they introduced them to Jack, who would write and coproduce *Changes*, the Monkees' answer to *Help!* (1965). With a tape recorder rolling and notepads at the ready, the brainstorming session got lost in giggles and clouds of cannabis. In an aside to Rafelson, Jack muttered, "These guys are mad—they think they're Marlon Brando."

"At this point, they had pretty swelled heads as the major pop stars of their time," recalled Rafelson. "They said, 'Fuck it, we don't need a director. We'll write our own movie.'"

The Monkees did not write their own movie, but, demonstrating the hubris that comes with stardom, they believed that they did. After distilling the free association from the Ojai sessions, Jack and Rafelson crafted a satire that crystallized Monkees malaise. The first day of shooting was scheduled on February 19, but only Peter Tork showed up. The other three Monkees held out for screen credit and an advance against the gross. "Davy and Mike and I had gone on strike the first day of the filming of the movie to get a better deal," said Dolenz. "We had discovered finally after so many years that we were getting ripped off pretty bad."

Indeed, after two successful seasons, each Monkee earned a mere $750 a week. Schneider upped the salary offer to $1,000 to do the movie, and it was left to Jack to act as the go-between, soothing the stars while coaxing them before the cameras. "He's a lovable guy," said Davy Jones. "Happy, smiling, big teeth all over the place."

If contemptuous of the Monkees' ersatz celebrity, Jack sublimated his feelings and convinced each of them that they, too, were in on the joke. Their movie would be a scattergun attack on all things odious in televised America circa 1968, from Madison Avenue's seductive advertising to the wholesale slaughter in Vietnam. More a series of skits flowing into one another than a narrative, Jack's screenplay owed as much to TV's *Laugh-In* as it did to Fellini's *8½* (1963), although Jack, Rafelson, and the few critics who did not savage the finished film preferred comparison to the latter.[32]

Echoing Peter Fonda's grandiosity during the filming of *The Trip*, a beaming Michael Nesmith told one interviewer, "Our film is going to astound the world. I think it is fair to say that not even the Beatles would be able to duplicate what we are doing in this film."

Once cameras rolled in late February, it was clear that anyone looking for a plotline would be disappointed. The first scene shot featured I. J. Jefferson, aka Mimi Machu, in a meaningless kissing contest with each Monkee. Cast as Lady Pleasure, Jack's girlfriend was only one of his pals to pop up in the film. Dennis Hopper wandered through one scene, while Helena Kallianiotes performed her belly dance routine in another. Frank Zappa showed up with a cow, and Victor Mature impersonated the Jolly Green Giant. For no apparent reason, Annette Funicello did a couple minutes of mooning for the camera somewhere in the middle. Wearing a white golf cap, Jack himself did a cameo, as did Rafelson, giving the entire production the feel of a slickly produced home movie.

"What we're doing is not a comedy, but it's funny," Rafelson told the *New Music Express*. "It sounds campy, but it's the enemy of camp. It opens with one of the Monkees committing suicide. It's kind of a trip."

The Trip, in fact, was one of the reasons Raybert hired Jack. Acid dream sequences and wiseass one-liners reminiscent of quips from *Flight to Fury* pop up as non sequiturs throughout the film:

Peter Tork: Nobody ever lends money to a man with a sense of humor.

Davy Jones: Wait! Don't move! I wanna forget you just as you are!

Jack also took the opportunity to satirize the Beatles' guru phase, as well as his soon-to-be ex-wife Sandra's Krishnamurti conversion. A white-robed Eastern swami sitting in a steam room with the heavyweight champ Sonny Liston spouts the same nonsensical speech about "conceptual reality" that Jack's script later plants in the mouth of Peter Tork: "The human mind is incapable of differentiating between reality and the vividly imagined experience. Where there is clarity, there is no choice; where there is no choice there is misery. And why should anyone listen to me? Why should I speak, since I know nothing?"

Once under way, the shooting of the Monkees' movie took on the feel of an ongoing, all-expenses-paid free-for-all. For a birthday party scene staged on a set from *Rosemary's Baby*, Rafelson hired 100 extras; then he put together a crew of 110 to travel to Palm Springs for a week to film desert sequences. One sketch he was forced to leave out was a face-off between the Monkees and Godzilla because he insisted that it be shot on location in Japan—one expense too many. With Columbia as the film's sugar daddy, Raybert went first class, and for the first time, the AIP-trained Jack felt that he was part of a truly big-budget operation, not just as a small acting or writing cog in a much grander wheel, but as one of those who called the shots.

In keeping with the in-your-face sensibility fostered by Raybert, Columbia Studios announced in April that the film had a new title. "Bob Rafelson didn't think any of the titles suggested fit," said Columbia's spokesman. "Someone suggested *Untitled* and we all agreed pronto.[33] Why not?"

Principal photography wrapped by the first week of May. A rough cut was ready for screening in July, and the reaction was "mixed," according to the Monkees' fan magazine: "Some of [the hundred people in the preview audience] said that they didn't understand parts of the film—others thought it was great."

Rafelson, on the other hand, came away satisfied. The ambivalent audience reaction was just what he'd expected.

Later in the summer, the Monkees convened for their final recording session, and Jack was there. Now a self-proclaimed music impresario, as well as a screenwriter and a coproducer, Jack ordered the foursome to sing a self-demeaning version of their TV theme song that he had penned.

He insisted that they perform "like Gilbert and Sullivan," but after

fifteen takes, none met with his satisfaction. At take sixteen, the Monkees tore up their lyric sheets and left. Jack's mean-spirited parody
never made it to the soundtrack, but two months later he was back in
the recording studio—this time by himself, overseeing the soundtrack
album that would be sold in conjunction with the movie, now known
as *Head*.

"Nicholson coordinated that record, made it up from the soundtrack," said Peter Tork. "He made it different from the movie. There's
a line in the movie where [Frank] Zappa says, 'That's pretty white.'
Then there's another line . . . that was not juxtaposed in the movie, but
Nicholson put them together in the [soundtrack album] when Mike
says: 'And the same goes for Christmas.' I mean, that's funny, and
that's very different from the movie. It was a different trip from the
movie. I thought that was very important and wonderful that he
assembled the record differently from the movie. It wasn't just a pale
ghost of a copy. It was a different artistic experience."

As *Head*'s release date approached, Raybert sidestepped Columbia's
well-oiled publicity machine. Based on a passage in *Understanding
Media*, Rafelson and Schneider came up with the incomprehensible
Head ad campaign, still studied in the nation's business schools today
as a worst-case marketing scenario. What worked well in Marshall
McLuhan theory crashed and burned in the real world.

The ad campaign made no reference to the Monkees. Film posters
featured only a head shot of *Head*'s New York publicist, accompanied
by the word *Head*, plus brief information on the upcoming world
premiere at Manhattan's Greenwich and Cinema Studio Theaters. So
convinced were Jack and Rafelson that the campaign would spark
grassroots curiosity, they hit the Midtown streets on their own, plas-
tering posters at subway entrances, on walls, and near bus benches.
An hour before the doors were to open for *Head*'s premiere, police
stopped them.

"Jack is standing behind the cop trying to slap a *Head* sticker on
the helmet, and like a Laurel and Hardy comedy, man, this cop turns
around just at the right moment and Jack nails him on the side of his
face. Bam!" recalled Rafelson. "We're handcuffed and up against the
walls. A squad car takes us away. We've got a flick opening in an hour.
I just wanted to call everybody and tell them we're in jail. And to get
on the radio and sell tickets—because Jack and I had this feeling that
no one was going to see *Head*."

They were right. The movie opened one day after Richard Nixon defeated Hubert Humphrey for the presidency. *Head* closed three days later, never to appear in general release again.[34]

The *New York Times*'s Renata Adler drubbed *Head* as "a film to see if you have been smoking grass or if you like to scream at the Monkees" and compared it with *You Are What You Eat* (1968), a hodgepodge of hippie nonsense featuring David Crosby, Barry McGuire, and Tiny Tim that was making the theater rounds. Critics agreed with Adler, punishing *Head* as a poor parody of *Help!* "*Head* looks like it was made for $1.98 and went needlessly over budget," sniped *Newsweek*.

But at least one *Times* reader refuted Adler and stood by *Head's* satire: "It owes more to *Finnegan's Wake* than to *You Are What You Eat*," wrote Richard D. Horwich in a letter to the editor. "It struck me at least as more mythic than psychedelic."

"In a darkly perverse way," wrote the Monkees historian Eric Lefcowitz, "*Head* had reflected the malignant cynicism of 1968. The brief snippets of war, including the summary execution of a Vietcong soldier, were misinterpreted by critics, who perceived them as smug and flippant commentary on the burning issues of the times."

"Nobody ever saw it, man, but I saw it 158 million times," Jack lamented to Rex Reed two years later. "I loved it. Filmically, it's the best rock 'n' roll movie ever made. I mean, it's anti rock 'n' roll. Has no form. Unique in structure, which is hard to do in movies."

Twenty years hence, *Head* would catch up with its audience (or vice versa), if *L.A. Weekly's* belated appreciation is to be believed:

> Then, nobody knew how to take the Monkees seriously. Now, by grace of this strange artifact, one may at least see them fairly: as four charming guys surfing on a berserk tide of celebrity and cultural upheaval over which they cheerfully admit they have no control. *Yellow Submarine* has long outlived it, but *Head* has preserved the light and air of '68 in a droplet of synthetic amber.

At the time, though, *Head* was just one more setback Jack had to endure on his fruitless Hollywood odyssey. "I hope nobody ever likes it," he said bitterly. "I'm going to remake it with the Beatles and then everybody will love it."

BOOK II

EASY RIDING
1969–1975

6

N THE EARLY MONTHS OF 1968, JACK LOOKED LIKE JUST ANOTHER Hollywood bozo (albeit a *talented* bozo) who'd blown every chance he'd ever had to move up the food chain. He'd gambled his first decade in showbiz and lost his wife, his home, and his child,[1] and he would soon begin losing his hair.

And yet his networking now extended far beyond the alumni of Jeff Corey and Martin Landau, Roger Corman and Monte Hellman and Richard Rush. His axis ran from Laurel Canyon to Topanga, Malibu, and Bel Air, and all points of power in between. In the weeks before, during, and after *Head*, Jack haunted the Raybert offices the way he'd once hung around AIP and Lippert, still hungry and still looking for his main chance. "I'd come into the office each morning and there'd be this guy sitting there, waiting, with the big smile," recalled Steve Blauner, Rafelson and Schneider's Raybert partner.

Jack made himself such a fixture that he became the unofficial fourth partner in the Monkees-spawned enterprise. When Raybert became BBS (for Bert, Bob, and Steve) Productions and moved off the Columbia lot into new quarters on La Brea Avenue, Jack moved with it, taking an office on the third floor. When Jack spoke, Schneider and Rafelson listened. One of Jack's first suggestions was that they meet with Peter Fonda and Dennis Hopper.

Jack had established a bond with his two acting contemporaries during *The Trip*, when they, too, were at critical junctures in their own careers. *The Wild Angels* and *The Trip* had turned Fonda, at twenty-eight, into a youth icon, but fueled in part by LSD-heightened egocentricity, the actor was already trying to move beyond his notoriety as an AIP poster child. Like Jack, he wanted to make movies, not just be in them.

The passive-aggressive Fonda and the hot-headed Hopper made an odd couple. They'd been writing together for a couple of years, turning out an absurdist comedy they called *The Yin(g) and the Yang*, which they tried in vain to sell for $450,000. Another of their pitches—a satire featuring Lyndon Johnson and his top advisers dressed in drag as they discuss the assassination of President John

Kennedy—was for sale for a mere $50,000 and a four-day shooting schedule.[2] There were no takers. Guffaws were impolite. Fonda's counterculture cachet and Hollywood birthright might have secured him meetings in production offices all over town, but his naïveté seemed breathtaking and his film ideas landed with a thud.

Kansas born and California bred, Hopper hadn't the same pedigree as Fonda, but his drug-inspired pitches were equally loony. He'd begun his own acting career back in high school, where classmates dubbed him "most likely to succeed." A 1954 graduate of white-bread Helix High in suburban La Mesa near San Diego, Hopper set out for Hollywood to do what Manasquan High's Jack Nicholson tried for that same year. While Jack floundered, Hopper thrived, first in series TV and then in minor but memorable film roles in classics like *Johnny Guitar* (1954), *Rebel without a Cause* (1955), and *Giant* (1956). James Dean befriended him, and Hopper wept at news of his idol's death. Then Hopper spent the next ten years trying to carry on Dean's legacy.

By the 1960s, Hopper's early triumphs had dissipated. He'd married into Hollywood royalty,[3] but the rebel-without-a-cause cachet wore thin in casting offices, where he tended toward artistic tantrums. When Harry Cohn told his producers they'd have to "take that Shakespeare out of him," Hopper told the mogul to go fuck himself. In a move that would turn out to have been considerably ironic, Cohn barred Hopper from ever setting foot on the Columbia lot again.

Once Hopper had developed a taste for weed and a reputation as "difficult," the roles stopped rolling in. By the time he teamed with his fellow Hollywood malcontent Peter Fonda, Hopper's career was running on hope and hemp. As Roger Corman liked to point out, Hopper's strung-out conversation devolved down to a single word. During an early scene in *The Trip*, Corman's soundman proclaimed a new all-time record.

"He used the word *man* thirty-six times in one speech," he hollered.

"Great," said Corman. "Print it."

But Hopper showed real technical skill behind the camera, and Corman let him direct his second unit for *The Trip*. On the pretense that they were shooting footage for *The Trip* (Fonda in robes, wandering the desert à la *Lawrence of Arabia*), Hopper and Fonda borrowed AIP's camera on weekends to shoot their own footage. They thrilled

at the rushes. A small taste of camera control stoked Hopper's directorial lust, but despair seemed to be his lot. Even more than with Jack,
ten years of sustained defeat took its toll. "I was going off to teach
school in San Jose," Hopper recalled. "I'd given up hope of ever
directing. I'd written three films, but nothing had ever happened."

According to legend, one September morning in 1967, right
around the time Jack was landing his *Head* gig, Hopper's phone rang
at three in the morning. It was Fonda calling from the Lake Shore
Motel in Toronto, babbling over an incredibly hip and very, very *cool*
epiphany he'd had during a promotional tour for *The Trip*. Why not
take the two Corman staples—biker flicks and psychedelic sagas—
and combine them into one heavy-headed acid road trip: a stoned
John Wayne and his trusty sidekick in *The Searchers* out there on the
open plains, hunting for the nation's soul instead of for a kidnapped
Natalie Wood?

"And after a long journey to the East across John Ford's America,
what would become of us?" Fonda blurted. "We would be blasted to
bits by narrow-minded, redneck poachers at dawn, just outside of
Heaven, Florida.[4] And the bed of their pickup would be full of
ducks. *I mean, really full of ducks!*"

Hopper answered in the only way he knew how: "That's great,
man! Fucking great!"

Their first stop was American International Pictures. "When Peter
Fonda and Dennis Hopper asked me to back them for a movie that
combined bikers *and* drugs in a journey across America, I was listening," said Corman. Unfortunately, Sam Arkoff and Jim Nicholson
were not. Despite the success of *The Trip* and *Psych-Out*, they'd had
enough of drug films.[5] Besides, Hopper wanted to direct *and* act, and
there was no way the two AIP partners were going to turn over a
feature film to a doped-out ditz working both sides of the camera—
especially one with as hostile an attitude as Hopper's.

Fonda remained undaunted. Through his sister, Jane, and his
brother-in-law, Roger Vadim, he lucked on to one of the hottest writers of the day, Terry Southern, to help him and Hopper translate his
very cool epiphany into a shooting script. Originally titled *The Loners*, the satirist and screenwriter Southern's first draft was written
during the first weeks of 1968.[6] It centered on the cross-country
adventures of two dope-smoking, drug-dealing hippie bikers who
score big in Mexico and use the money for a joy ride from L.A. to

early retirement in Key West. At one point, the script briefly took on the name *Mardi Gras* because somewhere near the end of the second act the film's two heroes were to stop off in New Orleans for the annual winter saturnalia.

It was Jack who advised Fonda to take their eight-page outline to BBS after AIP turned them down. Bert Schneider loved it. To convince his father and the rest of the aging members of Columbia's board of directors to let BBS bankroll *The Loners*, Schneider screened *The Trip* and several of Rush's biker movies. The message he was trying to convey was that youth films are bankable. Underwhelmed, Columbia chairman Abe Schneider and his brother-in-law, Columbia president Leo Jaffe, still gave Abe's boy a green light and the promise of distribution. In turn, BBS gave Fonda and Hopper a budget of $365,000 for their cross-country epic—a pittance by studio standards, but $365,000 more than they would have received if Harry Cohn had still been alive. Under the terms of their deal, Fonda and Hopper would get a third of the film's profits; the rest would go to BBS.

At the end of February, as Jack and Bob Rafelson were gearing up for *Head*, Fonda and Hopper headed for Mardi Gras to shoot the first 16-millimeter reels even before Terry Southern had put the finishing touches on his script. In Hopper's first five days with a camera in his hand, he shot nearly thirty thousand feet of film. "Dennis was smoking a lot of dope and barely keeping it together," said Donn Cambern, the film's credited editor and one of the few union members who worked on the film.

At the time, Jack could not have cared less about Hopper's movie. He had no interest in being typecast as a biker hippie and had all but abandoned acting anyway. He now thought of himself as a writer-producer who would one day perhaps graduate to auteur. For the rest of the year, he'd have Monkees on his mind, except for a few weeks in the spring when Schneider asked him to head down to New Mexico for a couple of weeks to give Fonda and Hopper a hand.

They didn't need another writer-producer. They needed an actor. "We assigned Jack as our representative to be present during the shooting," said Schneider, "but when Dennis told us that Rip Torn had backed out, we suggested that Jack do the part."

Originally, Hopper had cast Elmore "Rip" Torn as the disillusioned American Civil Liberties Union attorney George Hanson, who meets

Hopper and Fonda in jail, gets stoned, and takes to the road with them—a part that Terry Southern had written with his fellow Texan Torn in mind.[7] "But I was broke," recalled Torn. "There was a tax lien against my bank account for $3,500."

The pitiful nonunion wage Fonda offered did not stand against a stage obligation in New York that paid considerably more. Torn bowed out[8]—but not before he and Hopper crossed swords. Torn didn't like Hopper or his changes to Southern's script, according to Fonda, and the two men got so crazy one night over dinner, they attacked each other with butter knives.[9]

Hopper wasn't wild about casting Jack and told Schneider as much. Power had become as intoxicating as hashish, and fear that someone might take control away began to haunt him. Frequently and without provocation, Hopper snarled at no one in particular, "This is *my* movie! Nobody is going to take away my fucking movie! You got it? This is *my* fucking movie."

At first, Hopper's paranoid objection to Jersey Jack was that he wasn't a real Texan. "I saw him as a Hollywood flasher, not as a country bumpkin," Hopper recalled.

But at last, Hopper accepted Schneider's suggestion and offered Jack $392 a week to replace Rip Torn. "You can wait around forever until a part comes like it did for Jack Nicholson in *Easy Rider*," observed Henry Jaglom. "And that part may never come. Jack didn't know that that film would change his whole life. He didn't want to do that part because it meant he had to get a haircut."

Jack had tackled far more challenging characters for a lot less, but chiefly he accepted the role so he could keep an eye on production for his new benefactors. Rafelson and Schneider weren't as skittish as AIP, but Hopper did have a reckless rep and Jack had demonstrated a knack for diplomacy in manipulating the Monkees. It helped that he was a devoted pothead and lit up a doobie as soon as he checked in with Hopper and Fonda. Conceded Hopper, "Rip Torn and I would have had a lot of fights, and Jack and I never hassled at all."

If anyone could watch the budget and keep the film on schedule without tripping Hopper's switch, it'd be Jack. As for George Hanson, it sounded like just another gig—interesting but still a short supporting role that called for a light touch and a Texas drawl Jack borrowed with ease from Lyndon Baines Johnson. When Jack got his hands on the script, he recognized much more. "He knew when he saw the

script to *Easy Rider* that it was a supporting actor nomination,"
maintained Jack's pal John Hackett. "He knew that."

Before Terry Southern declined a producer role and bowed out of the
Fonda-Hopper project, he gave the finished ninety-page shooting
script its final name. *The Loners* became *Easy Rider*, a euphemism
for "a whore's old man," according to Fonda: "Not a pimp, but the
dude who lives with a chick because he's got the easy ride."

The film Fonda and Hopper envisioned had two such riders easing across the American landscape in pursuit of life, liberty, and hip-
piness. The characters Billy and Wyatt (aka Captain America) weren't
selling sex so much as buying it, but they did so with proceeds from
a big drug transaction in the opening frames of the movie that featured the toothy, frizzy-haired rock producer Phil Spector in the apro-
pos role of coke consumer.[10] In the Corman spirit of keeping costs
minimal, Spector allowed Hopper and Fonda to use his Rolls Royce
and chauffeur during the wordless sequence. Set beneath a busy Los
Angeles Airport runway, the only sound beyond the scream of low-
flying 727s is that of the rock group Steppenwolf prophetically
howling Hoyt Axton's "The Pusher."

Caching their nest egg in Fonda's gas tank, the pair set out on their
odyssey. *Easy Rider*'s baffling period plotline—two L.A. dope dealers
crossing America to get laid during Mardi Gras, only to get shotgunned off their bikes on the last leg of their trip to Florida—would
get yawned out of every agent's office in Beverly Hills today. It was as
if Southern truncated his script with the climactic advice of his fellow
satirist Michael O'Donoghue in his classic 1971 *National Lampoon*
essay "How to Write Good":

All too often, the budding author finds that his tale has run its
course and yet he sees no way to satisfactorily end it, or, in literary parlance, "wrap it up." Observe how easily I resolve this
problem:

Suddenly, everyone was run over by a truck.

—The End—

As one dissenting critic described *Easy Rider* at the time of its
release, "The film preaches a hazy pot-acid philosophy of peace and

freedom, of 'doing your own thing in your own time'—Ayn Rand for the new breed of affluent, half-educated American youth. Like the Watts Tower[s], this film is a primitive, incoherent work of art constructed out of junk."

But in 1968, the culture was in chaos, and Vietnam made clear that death could be instant, inexplicable, and without meaning. From March through June, Fonda and Hopper trekked with their gypsy[11] crew and ragtag cast across California, Arizona, New Mexico, Texas, and Louisiana, gathering hours and hours of stoned footage that would take months more to edit. As zoned as the cast and the crew might have been, all were well aware that Martin Luther King's murder marked the beginning of principal photography; Bobby Kennedy's assassination would punctuate its end. For all of its flaws, *Easy Rider* was destined to become that rarity among films, striking a defiant, resonant chord with an entire disillusioned generation.

After stopovers in a series of desert hamlets, Taos became *Easy Rider's* quasi headquarters, where Jack joined the caravan.[12] One of his first orders of business was to drop acid with Hopper and drive to the nearby grave of D. H. Lawrence.[13] "We laid down in front of his tomb and got into a conversation," Hopper recalled. "I noticed that the insects were circling right over us in relationship to the sun, and Jack said, 'That's really what we are. Just insects.'"

Later on, the pair found a hot spring and an Indian girl, to whom Hopper proposed. Jack acted as the impromptu priest and married them on the spot, just as a drunken Chicano approached. "I want to watch you hippies," he slurred.

Hopper pulled a knife "and got into a whole trip with the guy," he recalled. The next thing Hopper remembered, the sun had gone down and he and Jack were running down a darkened road in front of a set of truck headlights. "We're geniuses!" hollered Jack. "We're both geniuses, Hoppy!"

The following day, Jack told the film critic Rex Reed, he woke up in the top of a tree. The geniuses next set out for Las Vegas, New Mexico, where they shot the scene in which Jack's character first meets Hopper and Fonda in a Texas jail. According to *Easy Rider's* location scout Tony Vorno, no one in the cast or the crew wanted to shoot in the Lone Star state. "Texas, then and now, has such ridiculous laws about drugs that a little pot would have sent them to jail forever," he said.[14] "Dennis, Peter, and Jack wouldn't spend the night in

Texas. They would drive to Taos instead—at least a thousand miles round trip—and return the next day, spaced out."

Hopper directed the same way he acted: frenetically or bombed into moronic levels of "man" babble. Fonda's centered good looks and cool manner at least gave him a Gary Cooper presence, even if Southern's script gave him almost nothing to say. Fonda smoked as much weed as Jack and Hopper did, and he wore spurs throughout the production in order to stay in character.

The film predated the effects of the incipient women's movement, as the only roles for women were silent communal wives, breast-feeding mothers, or the pair of French Quarter whores played by Karen Black and Toni Basil.[15] Outside of the impressive psychedelic soundtrack and László Kovács's dazzling cinematography,[16] the only other clear reason to sit through *Easy Rider*, then or now, was to watch the performance that made Jack Nicholson a star. More than a generation later, George Hanson remains *Easy Rider*'s pivotal role. Jack's delivery of the boozy young Texas lawyer's central thematic line is the one that still rings loudest in the collective memory: "This used to be a helluva good country. I can't understand what's gone wrong with it."

Jack's apparently infinite capacity to ingest drugs never interfered with his self-discipline as an actor. He cut his hair and dressed the part, coming off as more Texas than Rip Torn wearing a ten-gallon hat. Even during the famous campfire scene, when George Hanson wanders off into a stoned soliloquy on Venusians and UFOs, Jack knew his lines and never broke character, despite Hopper's best efforts to rattle him.

"The Pro," Fonda recalled, as he watched Jack carefully work through the scene despite smoking enough cannabis to kill a cow. Among the three of them, they allegedly lit up 105 joints before and during the scene. "My take on that whole thing was that Den-Den *wanted* Jack to be stoned for real; that Jack's 'going up' was part of being stoned, forgetting what you were talking about, losing the thread, as it were," said Fonda.

Jack brought years of craft to the role, despite a respectful and rigorous attention to the words written for him on the page. George Hanson is steeped in Jack's past. The football jersey Hanson wears while he's mounted on the back of Fonda's chopper bears an "M," and his gold helmet resembles the kind Jack's former classmates recalled the Manasquan High football squad using. Like John J. Nicholson Sr., the man who passed himself off as Jack's father, Hanson is good-natured but weak—a philosophical, ineffectual, yet amiable drunk. The glasses Jack wears in the movie are the same sort his grandfather once wore. "It's not necessarily meant for a result, but for what it does for you," Jack explained years later.

Method, not marijuana, controlled Jack's performance. His endearing "nik-nik-nik" shtick, which appeared to have been taken from Shemp in the Three Stooges, was borrowed from one of the bikers hired to work on the *Easy Rider* road crew. When he was getting loaded, the biker flapped one arm like a busted chicken wing and hollered, "Nik-nik-nik!" Jack had the wit to borrow the moment and incorporate it into his character. Nonetheless, Jack is never so buried in the role that a part of himself doesn't shine through.

Fonda invited Jack and Hopper to his sister's Fourth of July bash the summer of 1968, and it became a sort of wrap party for *Easy Rider*. After drafting Roger McGuinn to perform the title song for the movie,[17] Peter arranged for the Byrds[18] to play at the Vadims' Malibu beach house, and the evening evolved into one of the decade's great psychedelic bacchanals. During a break, the band adjourned to Robert Walker Jr.'s place, with Fonda, Hopper, and Jack in tow. Once loaded, they waxed eloquent over the future. "We were free!" recalled Fonda decades later. "God bless grass! God bless us all, each and every one. We were so innocent. Even David Crosby was innocent. We were so angry, so full of hope."

Talk turned to filmmaking. Jack was still supervising the *Head* soundtrack and helping Rafelson to edit his film, but he listened to the *Easy Rider* euphoria and offered his own schizoid observations about working within and outside of the Hollywood system. "I'm not much involved in what the credits are," said Jack. "When I'm *involved* in a film, I'll do whatever I can. I mean, acting is where I started, so I feel most comfortable in that role."

But, as the old punch line goes, what he *really* wanted to do was direct. While he juggled his on-again, off-again acting career, Jack was now hard at work on his adaptation of *Drive, He Said*, which he hoped would make him a full-fledged auteur just like Hopper. At the same time, he massaged the knots in his personal life.

The month Jack's divorce became final, the Democratic National Convention erupted in riots in Chicago. In August 1968, while the generations Jack straddled seemed on the brink of civil war, Sandra took the ten-year-old Mercedes and Jack got the brand-new yellow Volkswagon convertible. They had $8,000 in the bank to divvy up between them. Jack agreed to child support and alimony, and Sandra agreed to weekly visitation. Later on, when Sandra moved to Hawaii, Jennifer went with her. Jack did not object.

"Having the experience myself, I always felt that I did fairly well coming from a so-called broken home, emotionally and every other way," said Jack. "And now I feel that Jennifer is equally as able to survive emotionally and have her own very sure universe and essential living position that she maintains. I don't worry as much about other people in that situation as I would have had I not had the experience."

He was too busy to spend much time with family, anyway. The doors opened by *Head* and BBS would not remain that way forever, and at thirty-one, Jack was getting a little long in the tooth. The anti-war activist Jerry Rubin had just coined the phrase "Don't trust anyone over thirty," and that hostile sentiment was beginning to catch on in Hollywood just as it had in politics.[19] There was no profit in getting caught on the wrong side of the generation gap.

Since June's death, Mud's own health had deteriorated to a degree that she could no longer live on her own, but Jack was now bunking with friends or Mimi. Moving Mud in with him was out of the question.

The spirited Nicholson matriarch stayed on in the Valley, living in June's old apartment for as long as she could and driving her late daughter's car to get around, but diabetes, osteoporosis, and a hernia got the best of her. During the summer of 1968, she collapsed and had to be rushed to a hospital in downtown L.A. Doctors fixed her abdomen but diagnosed a far more insidious and chronic muscular deterioration. Already overweight from a lifetime of Jersey cooking, Mud could neither squat nor sit nor lie on the floor any longer without getting someone to help her. Once she fell in the yard and had to wait hours until her yells were heard. Still, she refused to return to Neptune. "She worshipped the ground Jack walked on," recalled Cheryl Cron, June's daughter-in-law.

Cheryl's husband, Murray, had joined the navy and was stationed at a nuclear plant in upstate New York, while his sister Pamela had married her high school sweetheart eleven days before Jack's twenty-eighth birthday. Pamela was nineteen, a graduate of Laurel Beauty

Academy, and three months pregnant. She followed in her grand-mother's footsteps and became a licensed hairdresser but found as lit-tle time for Mud as Jack did. By default, Mud's care fell to Cheryl, who moved her out of the Valley and into Cheryl's place farther north of L.A. in Canyon Country. "Jack would stop by for fifteen minutes now and then, but then he'd say, 'I have to go,'" Cheryl recalled. "Mud never complained, but you could see the hurt in her face."

Jack was not unfeeling. He helped Mud to buy a pink-and-white mobile home that she had taken a fancy to. Once he thrilled her with dinner at the actress Jennifer Jones's house. Robert Walker Jr.'s mother remarked on Mud's unique nickname, which delighted Mud and sent her into peals of giggles for weeks thereafter.

Mud wore muumuus to cover her girth and had to rely on Cheryl to drive her to the doctor or the store. She talked incessantly of Jack—his successes, the glamorous people he was meeting, and his movies. She remained near to him as long as she could before the inevitable deterioration sent her back to Lorraine and Shorty in Neptune.

With the coming of autumn, Jack geared up for the release of *Head*, but an early screening of *Easy Rider* convinced him that his role in finishing Hopper's movie was not yet over. There were fixes to be made. "Jack invited me to a first cut, which was like ten, twelve fucking hours long," recalled John Herman Shaner. "I didn't think that movie was going to do much for him. I really didn't."

Over twenty-two weeks in the editing bay, Hopper wrestled a rough cut down to four hours and seventeen minutes: 23,130 feet of film, or twenty-three reels of visuals and matching soundtrack. It would require several more months of cutting and recutting before *Easy Rider* was anywhere near releasable. The Mardi Gras footage alone came to more than fifteen hours, and all the grass in Hollywood couldn't seem to aid Hopper in getting the sequence under fifteen minutes.

Along the way, Jack joined the marathon trimming. He took a swipe at the reels that contained his performance, polishing up the best takes to ensure that the scenes he stole as George Hanson would not wind up as butchered as Wickham's in *Flight to Fury* or Bunny's in *Rebel Rousers*.

"Jack was ex-officio producer," said the editor Donn Cambern, who remembered Jack's George Hanson charisma as being "off the screen." "The character as played by Jack is without question much larger than the character that was written," he said. "It was Jack's incredible acting technique that he has and was already in the midst of developing. From an editor's point of view, you'd cut for Jack. You'd go for Jack as often as you could."

As the year wound to a close, the combined pressure of Schneider, Rafelson, Jack, Cambern, and Henry Jaglom (whom Jack brought in to help edit) pared Hopper's opus down to ninety-four minutes. "We all worked very hard to make *Easy Rider* a visible and viable motion picture," said Fonda. "Dennis's reaction? We'd ruined *his* movie."

Columbia, as the movie's backer and distributor, had a "first look" deal. With the approach of the New Year, the studio chieftains grew impatient. BBS had a lot on the line, with no more Monkees left to mollify the money men. Abe's son or not, Bert Schneider had to produce something approaching a hit.

On a Friday afternoon that winter, after *Head* had crashed and burned and vanished from American theaters, Schneider hit the lights and held his breath. The courtly Leo Jaffe sat in the darkened projection room, along with Fonda; Hopper; Cambern; Bert's older brother Stanley, whom Abe had recently named as Columbia's president; Bob Ferguson, who was Columbia's head of marketing; and several other aging studio executives who listened to the whirr of the projector and a raucous soundtrack that featured Bob Dylan, the Band, the Byrds, and Jimi Hendrix.

When the film ended and the lights snapped on, the sixty-year-old Jaffe stood and faced the others, a perplexed look on his face. He cleared his throat, ran his fingers through his thinning white hair, and said, "I don't know what the fuck this picture means, but I know we're going to make a fuck of a lot of money."

7

WHEN *ON A CLEAR DAY YOU CAN SEE FOREVER* HIT Broadway in the spring of 1965, Paramount paid the playwright Alan J. Lerner $750,000 just to secure the film rights: more than double the budget of *Easy Rider*.[1] And why not? Lerner was a winner, tried and true, and he agreed to adapt *On a Clear Day* for the screen. Never mind that his play closed the following year. Paramount still saw silk in a sow's ear.

The best that could be said of Lerner's kitchen-sink screenplay was that it aspired to be timely. In addition to Freud and flower power, the creaky pseudo-psychoanalytic plot insinuated acid rock where there was none and tried to take a light, airy approach to campus rebellion. Paramount insisted on updating the original plot with some student unrest to match the times, but in Lerner's jaded hands the protests came out silly.

To give *On a Clear Day* a touch of hip, Lerner and the director Vincente Minnelli invented a ludicrous beatnik stepbrother for the star Barbra Streisand—a mustachioed Ivy League doofus in a white turtleneck and jeans who could sit in the lotus position and feign playing the sitar and the six-string acoustic with equal ease. After screening *Psych-Out* for its psychedelic lighting effects, Minnelli told the producer Robert Evans that he wanted to test the guy with the ponytail for the part of Tad Pringle, Streisand's stepbrother.

Head had bombed and *Easy Rider* had not yet happened. During the early months of 1969, Jack was back to square one in his so-called career. He'd have to cut his hair again to play Alan Lerner's version of a hippie, but the use of actual weed on or off the screen was out of the question. And yet, faced with insolvency, Jack swallowed his pride and struck the pose of "false confidence" for Minnelli that he'd honed over a dozen years of mediocrity. "You can use me or not," was how he'd begin his spiel. "I can tell you my credits. I can charm you. But really, I'm the *best* actor there is in my age group."

Jack's rival Bruce Dern, who considered himself the best actor in their age group, remembered Jack confiding that "Minnelli intimidated the *shit* out of me."

"They didn't know if I could even carry a tune, so I auditioned," Jack recalled. "Just me and him in the room: me singing 'Don't Blame Me' a cappella to Minnelli . . . it blew my mind!"

Jack got the part, but next came salary. Jack later boasted that he "turned [the role] down five times, but they kept offering me more money."

Evans recalled the negotiations differently. In his version of their first meeting, Evans summoned Jack to his posh suite at New York's snooty Sherry Netherland Hotel. Jack showed up with his agent. "You know, kid, I love your smile," Evans recalled telling him. "I'm going to star you with Barbra Streisand and Yves Montand in *On a Clear Day* and I'm going to pay you $10,000 for six weeks' work."

If Jack was astonished, he hid it well. "That's great," he said, "but I just finished a picture called *Easy Rider*."

"I don't want to hear about that shit," scoffed Evans. "Another motorcycle picture. This is *Barbra Streisand*. You'll be singing a song with her."

Jack stood. "Can I talk to you alone, Mr. Evans?" he asked.

They left Jack's agent in the sitting room and walked to a window. Outside, it was snowing in Central Park. Jack looked at Evans and said, "You know, pal, I just got divorced. I got a kid. I've got no money to pay alimony or child support. Can you make it $15,000?"

"How about $12,500?"

"Do you mean it?" Jack asked.

According to Evans, they hugged and kissed and remained friends from that day forward. It was the most money Jack had ever been paid to act,[2] but it was a pittance compared to what Minnelli and Streisand wasted each day on the set. "The fees are too high," said Jack. "Not just Streisand. She only sets the standard for everybody."

To an AIP veteran like Jack, steeped in the use of borrowed cameras and the kindness of strangers, the standard was way, way over the top. "They spent a fortune on a set," he recalled, "and it doesn't work: the scrim is bad. They could've shot better—and for nothing—on a rooftop in New York."

His Corman frugality insulted, he learned to grin and bear the humiliation of being Tad for the paycheck. "All I am in the movie is bad," Jack said. "It was the clearest-cut job of acting for the money I've ever done. I was supposedly playing a rich hippie. . . . Ways of dressing and stuff like that, they didn't really understand."

Jack found a pair of flashy brown-and-white "spectator" wingtips in wardrobe that reminded him of his father's showy spats, and he thought they might draw attention to his character, but Minnelli nixed the idea. He didn't even want Jack walking around much in front of the camera. "Minnelli always had me leaning against something," Jack recalled.

Jack tried other gimmicks to make Tad more hip, more believable, more au courant, but nobody listened. "I'm glad I did it, though," Jack said. "It didn't hurt me much. It was a good experience."

As Tad, Jack got to sing on camera for the first time. Barbra hummed counterpoint to Jack's solo, "Who Is There among Us Who Knows?" and though he expected the high hat from Hollywood's original Jewish American Princess, he found a pro instead. "Streisand treated me great, man. I don't think she saw *Easy Rider* either, so it wasn't because of that [but] she tried to help me in my scenes, you know?"

Later that year, after Minnelli turned in a director's cut of 143 minutes, Jack's vocal debut vanished from the film. The final edit contained 129 minutes and "Who Is There among Us Who Knows?" was not among them. In fact, most of Jack's performance disappeared— a blessing in disguise.

When *On a Clear Day* premiered on June 17, 1970,[3] critics dubbed its creators the latest and worst example of all that was wretched from Hollywood's old guard. *Newsweek*'s Joe Morgenstern called the sixty-six-year-old Minnelli and his sixty-nine-year-old cinematographer Harry Strandling "custodians of a defunct tradition," while Rex Reed summed up in a single sentence the creaky embarrassment from a playwright and a director whose time had passed: "It gave me the hives."

On a Clear Day cost $12 million, earned $5 million at the box office,[4] and produced a soundtrack (sans Jack) that became the worst-selling LP of Streisand's career. "I don't know a movie that needs to cost $12 million," said Jack. "Offhand, I'd say *Clear Day* is a $2 million musical."

During the winter of 1969, Jack and his pal William Tynan moseyed on down to Guayamas, Mexico, to observe Mike Nichols at work filming *Catch-22*.

Nichols later groused at the screenwriter Buck Henry, who had long been a part of Jack's Sunset Strip coffeehouse crowd, because Henry hadn't told him earlier about Jack. Had he known, the young director said, he would have cast Jack in the film version of Joseph Heller's classic antiwar satire.

But Nichols wasn't about to slip up and lose Jack again. Hollywood's latest whiz kid put Jack on the string for an even darker comedy than *Catch-22*, which he was already cooking up with the cartoonist and playwright Jules Feiffer. *Carnal Knowledge*, originally titled *True Confessions*, centered on the sexual exploits of two adolescent males who never grow up, even as they approach middle age. Jack seemed a perfect fit.

At thirty-two, Jack was maturing, but slowly. Among his pals, he was known as "the Weaver," because either on the page or in bull sessions, he had a windy yet enticing way with words. He often joined friends like Henry Jaglom, Carole Eastman, and Candice Bergen at the Black Rabbit Inn, a West Hollywood pop music business hangout that had table service and a fireplace, and they held forth on liberal icons like Henry Wallace or George McGovern or made fun of the mysticism of Theosophy's founding mother, Madame Helena Blavatsky. Jack had "cobra eyes," observed Bergen. "With all these friends there was an easy exuberance, a sense of camaraderie," she recalled. "This was what I wanted life to be."

But life was about to change for all of them. Along with Jack's master plan for attaining stardom, the law of unintended consequences would come into play soon enough, and the casual klatches at the bistros and hangouts along the Sunset Strip would be history. A souring of the flower-power zeitgeist was in the air, as well as a volcanic shift in modern motion picture making that was about to erupt in the south of France. "I had been to Cannes a couple of times before, and I knew the place like a guttersnipe," Jack recalled. "I was a back-street movie hustler, and I could smell it when something really big was going on."

The previous year, rioting students had threatened to shut down the venerable festival as part of a nationwide general strike aimed at symbols of bourgeois greed and decadence. They jeered at tuxedoed film executives who emerged from the lavish Carlton Hotel, the unofficial headquarters for the three-week film emporium, and presented demands that were meant to democratize the festival's film-selection process.

But the protests didn't alter the way things got done. In 1969, the snob quotient among filmmakers remained status quo. The producer Sam Spiegel, one of Cannes's venerable jurors, rode in like a corpulent Phoenician prince aboard his yacht *Malahne* and anchored a quarter mile offshore.[5] An invitation to martinis at sunset served by Spiegel's Barbadian manservant on *Malahne*'s teak decks meant that a director like Hopper or an actor like Jack had passed through the looking glass and arrived in Hollywood's version of Wonderland. An admirer of both Spiegel's films and his lavish lifestyle, Jack soon became one of Spiegel's "darling boys" aboard the *Malahne* and a regular guest at his St. Tropez villa Mas d'Horison.

A-list parties dominated the nights, and topless starlets posed for paparazzi during the day. The men dressed like James Bond and their women adorned their décolletage with diamonds. Stuffy exclusivity still permeated Cannes in the spring of 1969, and *Variety* trumpeted with relief, "22nd Annual Opens without Incident."

The first film exhibited at the world's best-known film conclave was Bob Fosse's *Sweet Charity* (1969), a politely received big-budget musical from Universal. Feature competition was stiff: *Easy Rider* was up against Constantin Costa-Gavras's political thriller *Z* (1969), which would win the jury prize, and *If . . .* (1968), another drama of youthful revolution from the British director Lindsay Anderson, would take the Palme d'Or.

Jaded journalists yawned at *Easy Rider*. *The Hollywood Reporter's* Odette Ferry scoffed that the film "supposedly describes today's America, its inhibitions and lack of freedom." She was scandalized when "Peter Fonda and Dennis Hopper came to the evening performance costumed as soldiers of the American Civil War," but made no mention of their Confederate companion who strutted up the red-carpeted steps with a leggy brunette draped over one arm. Taking Mimi with him to Cannes was "like taking fine caviar to a good party," Jack later told the director Richard Rush.

The lights went down, the film began, and by the end credits, Jack's days of anonymity were over. "I had been around long enough to know while I was sitting in that audience, I had become a movie star," he said. "Nobody's ever had that experience, I don't think."

The jury honored Hopper as the year's debut director. Later in the week, outside the Cinema Olympia, where he had to pay $3 to get in to see *Easy Rider* just like everyone else, Hopper ran into the *Boston Globe* correspondent Deac Russell. Hopper told Russell he wanted to see what the paying public thought of his film, not just the cummerbund-and-diamonds crowd. What he found was loud, raucous, and way beyond either his highest hopes or his obsessive control. "I suddenly realized that the film was no longer mine," said Hopper. "Now it belongs to the public and there is nothing more I can do to it."

The *Easy Rider* standouts turned out to be Jack and Láslo Kovács, whose lavish travelogue cinematography turned the spectacular scenery of the American Southwest into *Easy Rider*'s unbilled costar. The producer Pierre Cottrell, who'd entered his own movie in the Cannes sweepstakes that year,[6] remarked of Hopper's movie, "I didn't think it was such a great film. I got to like it later, but at the beginning, I thought Jack's sequence really stood out because a lot of the rest was just weak."

Despite disdain from traditionalists like Cottrell,[7] *Easy Rider* premiered in the United States two months later, during the second week of July 1969, breaking records everywhere it opened. "They were lined up around the block at the Beekman Theater in New York, but it wasn't your typical East Side audience," said Steve Blauner. "The management had to take the doors off the stalls in the bathrooms because everyone was ducking in before and after the movie to smoke pot."

Easy Rider became New Hollywood's seminal moment. "Right about the time of *Easy Rider* I had gotten myself locked right into the sociological curl—like a surf rider—and found I could stay right in there, ride this, and cut back against it," said Jack.

With a single outraged and outrageous low-budget road picture, traditional studio notions about content, style, and how movies got made crumbled like nitrate stock exposed too long to sunlight. Every film student in America aspired to become a Dennis Hopper auteur, channeling the twin influences of French New Wave and acid rock onto the big screen. *Easy Rider*'s jump cuts, hand-held cameras, flashbacks, and radical narrative came into vogue. Gypsy film crews took to the streets with their Arriflex shoulder units and Nagra sound recorders, following the windfall example of antiestablishment BBS Productions, which seemed to prove that upstart fortunes could be made by rebels overnight.

When Bert Schneider first hired Jack's pal Henry Jaglom the previous summer to help edit Hopper's marathon director's cut of *Easy Rider*, Jaglom could have accepted a salary of several thousand dollars or he could have taken no money and received half a point of the film's box office gross. Jaglom thought *Easy Rider* too dense for the hoi polloi to grasp, so he took the cash—the most he'd ever earned in his life. Had he taken the half point, he'd have earned nearly $1 million over the next decade.[8]

As star, producer, and writer, Fonda owned 22 percent of the picture and never had to work again. What was more, he'd won his stern star father's unconditional praise. "I am in awe of this boy," said Henry Fonda. "He is more knowledgeable in a technical area of this business than I will ever be. He is a hyphenate actor-director-producer. Can you imagine Peter and Jack Nicholson and Hopper smoking joints and saying, 'Man! Man!' and capturing not only the mint but the reviews, too? *Easy Rider* cost pennies, made a fortune, and Peter didn't even have to get on a horse."

Jack sensed the buzz before he ever left for Cannes. With the prospect of his newfound prosperity, he went house hunting. "I've been trying to buy a house for ten years now," he said. "I've made more attempts to buy houses than any human in history. But when I get the money together, there are no houses available. Then I have to fight to hold the capital together."

At Bert Schneider's urging, Jack bid on a modest two-story frame house with a rectangular swimming pool. The house itself wasn't much, but it straddled a Mulholland promontory along the spine of the Hollywood Hills, and its view of the L.A. basin was spectacular.

Next door on higher ground, Marlon Brando lived in a far grander place once owned by Howard Hughes. Jack's house did not rise so high as Brando's, but his driveway would soon widen and extend so that he'd be sharing it with his idol. Jack's place stood on the precipice above the chaparral and scrub oak of Franklin Canyon, overlooking a reservoir and a park, the sliding glass doors of his living room facing the panorama of his adopted urban dreamscape. "The movement of this house is great," he effused. "You can't get trapped in it."

From the boxy balcony outside his second-floor bedroom he could take in the length and breadth of L.A. and then leap over the wooden guardrail into his pool below. "I built a whole window and balcony on my house because my bedroom is at the end of a very long hall and I have no other way out," said Jack. "I wanted the balcony and I wanted the window, but I definitely know that that's an escape route, because I never want to wake up in my life and find someone I don't know standing over my bed."

Brando's former neighbors signed the house over while Jack was still in France, and the U.S. vice consul in Paris had to notarize the transaction. On July 2, for a sum of about $20,000 (Schneider helped with the down payment), Jack erased forever the notion that he might someday return to New Jersey. Within a short hike from his front porch, he could peek over and see the entire breadth of the San

Fernando Valley spread out on the north side, while the view from his rear deck took in everything to the south. He was finally home. "There's the open quality of it, where you see the sky all the time," he said. "It's a very important and constant phenomenon. That's why it's been the city of the future for so long."

In addition to easing, if not ending, his money worries (like Jaglom, Jack took salary in lieu of points), *Easy Rider* gave Jack what he called "public access." "You've got to break through to that before you can do what you want to do," Jack observed. What he wanted to do was to become a star.

The *Easy Rider* tsunami washed over Hollywood during the summer of 1969, and Jack rode the wave like a windsurfer. The Corman nobody was suddenly in demand. Every studio executive wanted to cash in on the *Easy Rider* phenomenon, and a flood of self-indulgent, antiestablishment films with scant plot, cardboard characters, and overused technical trickery went up on the boards to exploit baby boomers. "*Easy Rider* cost Hollywood hundreds of millions of dollars," said the screenwriter William Goldman (*Butch Cassidy and the Sundance Kid*). "Oh, not the movie itself. *That* was a tremendous success. I am talking about all the idiots who decided to rip it off and capture the suddenly exposed 'youth market.'"

With the same certainty with which he predicted his rise to movie-star status, Jack understood *Easy Rider*'s downside. "Eventually, the industry is going to make all the wrong moves," he said. "They are going to try to make ten more *Easy Riders* and they'll sponsor a bunch of people just because they are young and they are not anything else."

Jack might have been an "overnight success" in the enthused estimation of thimble-deep entertainment writers, but his fifteen-year apprenticeship in the vineyards of Hollywood had not been wasted. He not only understood the vagaries of celebrity before he ever became a star himself; he also understood the economic underpinnings that propelled the Hollywood roller coaster from film to film. "You can't get smart money to finance for $20 million what it can pull back through an investment of 1 or 2 million," he said.

Jack's next film was a case in point. At a cost of $876,000 in tax-sheltered capital, Bob Rafelson was scheduled to begin shooting a Carole Eastman script in the oil fields outside of Bakersfield in November.[9] No studio or sets were involved. The budget was so tight that Jack and Rafelson would bunk together in the same motel room.

"All the dough goes where it can be seen, on the screen," said Rafelson's coproducer Richard Wechsler. "We haven't got studio overhead, no top heavy stuff. Shooting is done with a minimum of top personnel, all live-location."

Jack wasn't sure of the title or all of the plot details but told the *Los Angeles Times*'s Kevin Thomas during the summer of 1969 that Rafelson had Jack in mind as a guy on a train, "returning to his home town, escorting a coffin back."

At the time, Jack was less concerned with his next film than he was with promoting *Easy Rider*. In New York, Philadelphia, and Boston, he wore to his interviews a U.S. Air Force bush jacket, navy bell bottoms, and a thrift store T-shirt that read "Property of the USC Athletic Department," knowing full well the revolutionary effect his appearance would have on the press.

The Broadway Neanderthal Earl Wilson[10] wrote, "This lad Nicholson's pro-pot and has used LSD," but in the entertainment journal *After Dark*, the journalist Neal Weaver detailed some of Jack's pending projects and concluded, "Anybody with that many varied irons in the fire would have to be interesting."[11]

The short Tad Pringle haircut had grown out so that Jack's bushy mane now hung to his shoulders and a beard stubbled much of his face. The sole reminder of *On a Clear Day* was the pair of brown-and-white "spectator shoes" that Minnelli had forbidden him to wear on the set. Jack had not only liberated the footwear from Paramount's wardrobe department, he now made a point of proudly wearing them for reporters. "They are just like the ones my father used to wear in the 1930s in the Easter parade," he told the *Boston Globe*.

Jack was still in Manhattan the second week of August promoting *Easy Rider* when his sister Lorraine called about Ethel Mae. "Mud's in the hospital," said Lorraine. "She's not going to make it this time."

Panicking, Jack made the grim hour's drive to Allenwood, New Jersey, but when he arrived at the nursing home, he found Mud sitting up in bed leafing through a movie magazine. "My son's in this movie," she said, beaming. "He's a *hit!*"

Mud's false alarm only fueled Jack's off-screen anxiety. At the exhilarating height of his new stardom, he juggled trouble on both coasts. In upstate New York, the mass musical gathering at Woodstock might be getting the nation's youth back to the Garden, but in L.A. during those first heady days in August, a more sinister symphony hit its crescendo. Before Jack had even returned to California to move into his new digs in the Hollywood Hills, his place was burglarized. And just one canyon over, the same week that Jack visited Mud in New Jersey, the most sensational massacre in Southern California history was about to hit the papers. Shaken to the soles of his spectator shoes, Jack knew each victim's name as he read it.

On August 9, 1969, the actress Sharon Tate, the daughter of the U.S. Army Intelligence officer Colonel Paul Tate and the pregnant wife of the director Roman Polanski, had been savagely murdered. The other victims—the coffee heiress Abigail Folger, her boyfriend Voytek Frykowski, and the hairstylist Jay Sebring—were all Jack acquaintances.[12] The evening before the four friends died, they'd gone out to eat at El Coyote, a Tex-Mex restaurant where Jack sometimes ate.[13]

Jack was well acquainted with Rudy Altobelli and Stuart Cohen, the pair who rented to the Polanskis the estate up on Cielo Drive. Jack had been invited to the star-studded parties where James Baldwin, Warren Beatty, Ruth Gordon, Barbra Streisand, and fifty or so other celebrities jammed into the living room, the loft, and the bedroom, getting stoned simply by breathing. Had Jack been in L.A., there might even have been a remote chance that he could have hooked up with one of Polanski's houseguests and gone back to smoke a little pot.

Like Jack, all of Los Angeles was traumatized. Doors were dead bolted and double locked. Guard dogs became big business.[14] Gun sales skyrocketed. Over the next three months, rumors ran rampant about sex, drugs, and weird satanic worship in the hills surrounding the city, à la Polanski's *Rosemary's Baby*. Left to speculating, the media tried to link the director's bizarre onscreen fantasies to his very real offscreen tragedy. Polanski, though in Europe working on the screenplay for *The Day of the Dolphin* at the time, was falsely and frequently accused of somehow bringing the horror upon himself.

Besides knowing Polanski, Jack was also acquainted with the previous occupants of the hilltop home at 10050 Cielo Drive.[15] A year before it became a slaughterhouse, Doris Day's music producer son Terry Melcher had lived there with his girlfriend—and Jack's pal—Candice Bergen.[16]

Before the couple had broken up the previous February, Melcher briefly considered recording a guitar-picking ex-con named Charles Manson, who'd come recommended to him by the Beach Boy Dennis Wilson. Manson brought his demo tapes up to the house, but Melcher was not impressed enough to offer a deal. Long after Bergen moved out,[17] it finally occurred to her and to Melcher (who had moved on to his mother's place in Malibu) that Melcher might have triggered Manson's twisted revenge by passing on the wild-eyed little gnome's ho-hum music.

Until Manson and his "Family" were arrested and indicted in November, fear continued to haunt L.A.'s affluent crescent, from the hills above Pacific Palisades to the Cahuenga Pass.[18] In his own new aerie up on Mulholland, Jack took to sleeping each night with a hammer under his pillow.

On November 14, 1969, the *Hollywood Reporter* broadcast that "Jack Nicholson's 'overnight' success in *Easy Rider* has landed him in Mike Nichols' *Carnal Knowledge* but before he starts Mike's first indie film, Bob Rafelson has grabbed him for *Five Easy Pieces*."

The word *easy* is about the only thing *Easy Rider* had in common with *Five Easy Pieces*. *Rider's* soundtrack rocked with Dylan and the Byrds, while *Pieces* rolled alternately between whiny Tammy Wynette and the elastic piano stylings of Fred Chopin. Jack's laconic, alcoholic George Hanson came and went somewhere near the middle of *Easy Rider*, but his Robert Eroica Dupea grinned or grimaced in every scene of *Five Easy Pieces*. And while George Hanson offered comic relief, the dour, introspective Bobby Dupea was about as hilarious as a coronary. "I wanted to do a smashing follow-up to *Easy Rider* and hammer that nail in," Jack explained. "I wanted to get even more distance from being somebody who had some kind of demand for their services versus somebody who is running crazy to try and keep up."

According to the film critic Colin Gardner, the high-concept Bobby Dupea concocted by Carole Eastman for Rafelson boiled down to "musical prodigy turned prodigal son." The title, taken from a child's "fake book" piano primer, carries with it an implied promiscuous subtext, challenging the audience to tick off Bobby's female conquests on the fingers of one hand over the course of the film. "It's about five of the easiest pieces of ass that I ever got," Jack told inquisitive friends. There are only three seductees—the characters played by Karen Black, Sally Struthers, and Susan Anspach—but by the movie's climax, Jack's randy Dupea seems condemned to a lifetime of easy, though emotionally unsatisfying, one- or, at the most, two-night stands.

On the page, "Speed" Eastman's screenplay crackled with original characters, catchphrases, and dialogue so electric that it demanded instant replay. Thirty years before the invention of TiVo, audiences had to line up for a repeat showing of the film to confirm that the characters said what the audience *thought* they said, which may have accounted in part for the long initial release (over a year) of *Five Easy Pieces*. "Line for line, it contains the best dialog—accurate, revealing funny—that I have listened to in a very long time," wrote the *L.A. Times*'s Charles Champlin. "It is the screen equivalent of the John O'Hara ear at its most precise."

Once they roughed out the story, Rafelson left Eastman to her work. His one demand was that she make Bobby Dupea a failed concert pianist. "And give me a moment where he's playing the piano with his hair blowing in the breeze, like Cornel Wilde in *A Song to Remember*," Rafelson added.

Eastman obliged but held off introducing Bobby's musical side until twenty minutes into the movie, during an impromptu ride on the back of a moving truck. Rafelson gets his Cornel Wilde moment, but it's a comic Jack banging out Chopin on an upright piano like Victor Borge as the truck weaves off a freeway ramp during a traffic honkfest.

The most memorable set piece from *Five Easy Pieces*—the coffee-shop scene where Jack fences with a waitress over a toast order—was inspired by Jack's own tantrum ten years earlier when he punctuated a long-forgotten argument at B. J. Merholz's corner table on the patio at Pupi's by sweeping cups, saucers, and silverware to the floor.[19] Like the film's audience, the character Palm Apodaca (Helena Kallianiotes) marvels at Bobby's persistent ability to get past the coffee shop's "no substitutions" rule. But it's Bobby (that is, the older, wiser Jack) who recognizes that neither being clever nor being violent ever got him his toast.

Ending Bobby's odyssey presented Eastman with her biggest storytelling problem. In her original script, Dupea and his dimwit girlfriend Rayette (played by Karen Black) drive off a bridge into a river, and Bobby drowns—Eastman's allusion to the recent real-life tragedy at Chappaquiddick.[20] Rayette swims ashore, berating Bobby for looking like a dead rat washed up on the river bank, only to scream as the credits roll when she finds that he really is dead.

Rafelson was not satisfied with killing off his hero and juggled several other possible endings: Bobby selling ties in a dead-end department-store job, like Bud Eastman, or walking down a country road, his back to the camera, until he vanishes into the horizon. He settled on Bobby hitching a ride at a truck stop, abandoning everything—Rayette, his car, even his clothes.

Beginning in the oil fields of Bakersfield and following Eastman's screenplay to the streets of Eugene, Oregon, and finally, to a small island off the northwest coast of Vancouver, Rafelson kept his crew and repertory company under budget and on the move, completing production in less than six weeks, which included the Thanksgiving, Christmas, and New Year's holidays. The atmosphere on the road was collegial but disciplined. "We all took a vow to stay off pot," Jack later quipped to *Time* magazine. "I'm the only person who stuck to it."

Like a fussy drill sergeant, Rafelson refused to fall behind schedule, while remaining a fanatic perfectionist throughout the shoot. During a scene in which Bobby picks up a pair of hitchhikers, the director recorded the rattle of fifty different car ashtrays before he was ready to call "Action!" "I thought the sound of the car should have its own distinct personality," Rafelson recalled decades later. "So now, when you listen, you can hear the tinkle of the ashtray. Can you imagine how many hours that took? I'd have been better off editing the sequence."

His most famous attack of perfectionism came the day he asked Jack to weep for the camera. "I'm playing a part now, Curly," Jack cautioned, addressing Rafelson by the nickname Jack had given him. "I am *not* being Jack."

"Yes, I know that," said Rafelson, "but I think it would be interesting if this character showed a quality to a mute father that he shows to nobody else during the course of the film."

They debated for a day and a half over Bobby breaking down in front of his paralyzed father. From his earliest days in Corey's classes, Jack learned to loathe cheap sentiment, and he saw crying on cue as the cheapest. "I don't like feelings," he used to tell Charles Eastman.

Jack never forgot his humiliation when the tears of *The Cry Baby Killer* met with jeers and belly laughs among the disbelieving audience. "No one in the world tries to cry except bad actors," said Jack. "Good actors try not to cry. No one tries to laugh except bad actors; people try not to laugh. No one tries to be drunk; drunks try to be sober. You ever see a drunk who wants another drink pick up a drink?"

Nevertheless, while Eastman's sister Carole didn't write tears into her dialogue, Rafelson held out for them.

"This character would never indulge in self-pity," Jack growled.

"Jack, if I don't see the desperation of this character, then I'm not interested in making this movie," Rafelson shot back. "Then this is just a study of alienation, and I won't be touched by his nomadic emotional life."

"What're you saying?" asked Jack. "You want me to cry?"

"Yeah, that'd be good enough."

"No fuckin' way!" Jack shouted. "You know how many directors have asked me to cry before, on screen? It's all a bunch of bullshit."

The debate raged on for hours while the crew stayed on the clock. Rafelson finally dismissed them, canceled the shoot, and came up with a strategy to break Jack's will. He kept him up for forty hours straight, then had him wheel William Challee out to the middle of an open field. No crew. No cast. No spectators. Just the two actors and Rafelson. Rafelson set up the camera for a fixed shot, so that no sideline spectators would watch the private moment he hoped to capture between Bobby and his father, and he handled the microphone himself. "Don't blink. Do nothing," Rafelson whispered to Challee. "Stay in character."

Jack spent a few moments reading through his lines again and groused, "Well, if I'm going to do it, I sure can't do it with this dialogue."

"Look, I don't care if you read me the phone book," said Rafelson. "I want the emotion."

Jack crossed out much of Eastman's dialogue and wrote "Something else?" in the margin. Then he scribbled a new line of his own. Rafelson called for action, and in a single take Bobby delivered his speech. "I guess you're wondering what happened to me after my auspicious beginnings." Jack covered his face and choked back real sobs.

Rafelson made him do a second take but never used it. As with all of his films, Rafelson never saw the finished movie in the theater—a superstitious idiosyncrasy he has stuck to throughout his directing career. The scene became a classic, and the reason, Jack told the *New York Times's* Ron Rosenbaum more than twenty years later, was that he tapped into personal pain in his own memories. "Well, the fact that I was playing it as an allegory of my own career is the secret there," Jack said. "Auspicious beginnings."

Over time, Jack dismissed Bobby Dupea as just another character in the Nicholson canon, but not all those close to him agreed. In many respects, the character came as near as any in his long career to duplicating the offscreen Jack. "I think it's that attractive, tough facade that says, 'I'm tough, I'm cocky, I'm smiling through the difficulties,'" said the director Richard Rush. "But at the same time you can see slightly past the facade to someone who isn't quite as sure, who is looking for the answers and is experiencing the discomfort."

Five Easy Pieces would strike a chord with America's growing disillusion with the Vietnam war. What remained of the nineteenth-century notion of "Manifest Destiny" and the darker shadings of male chauvinism were also targets of the Rafelson-Eastman collaboration.[21] For its time, the movie proved to be both provocative and daring.

In the first third of the film, Bobby and his trailer-trash compadre Elton are openly promiscuous. Bobby impregnates, then dumps, Rayette, while he sneaks a spiteful roll in the hay with his obnoxious brother's icy fiancée, played by Susan Anspach. Helena Kallianiotes and Toni Basil give a homophobic nation a glimpse of a goofy lesbian couple hitchhiking to Alaska, and a generation before Janet Jackson scandalized the Super Bowl, Sally Struthers offered her bared nipple for the world to see.[22]

Ironically, Sally's tempestuous romp with Jack on screen was no reflection of their offscreen relationship.[23] She threw herself at Jack, but he never even offered her a date. "I was so attracted to Jack I couldn't stand it," she said. "I'd find myself one night at about midnight, knocking on his door, going, 'Jack, what are you doing?' I mean, I was crazy for him."

The knock at the door that Jack *did* answer was that of Susan, who was as moved offscreen by Jack's fake book rendering of Mozart's "Fantasy in D Minor" as she was in the movie.

Four days before *Five Easy Pieces* opened in L.A. on September 30, 1970, Susan bore Jack's son and named him Caleb, after James Dean's character in *East of Eden*. In 1974, Susan married the soap star Mark Goddard,[24] who adopted the boy as his own and gave Caleb his last name and the security of family life.

For years, rumors wove through Hollywood hair salons and cocktail parties, but Anspach kept the true identity of the boy's sire a secret for another decade.[25] In a pattern that became both notorious and routine, Jack never acknowledged his paternity but always ascertained that his child was financially secure—an arrangement that some people criticized as "hush money."

As for Jack, he continued to make hay while the sun shined, just as Mud had taught him. Soon enough, he'd be directing his own movie. Nothing lasts forever, and he had no illusions about stardom. Looks fade, fans are fickle, but a director can work forever.

"I'll be out of it by the time I'm forty," he predicted to a reporter in Vancouver, British Columbia, during the final days of filming *Five Easy Pieces*. "I never want to be a household name because those guys' careers end quickly," Jack told another. The important thing was to strike while the iron was hot, yet remain humble. "My mother said two things to me over and over again—'Jack, don't blow your own horn,' and 'Self-praise stinks.'"

Rafelson completed the shooting of *Five Easy Pieces* on January 3, 1970, and took another six months to edit it to ninety-eight minutes. The same week that the film wrapped, word leaked from the Academy that Jack would be nominated for his supporting role in *Easy Rider*. But before the announcement was made official, another call came in from Lorraine. This time, Mud's condition was no false alarm.

Rafelson spotted Jack the money and put him on a plane to New Jersey, but on January 6, 1970, Ethel Mae Nicholson, age seventy-one, died in the Geraldine L. Thompson Nursing Home three miles from the home beauty parlor she had operated when Jack was in high school. "When my mother died, she was a charity patient, and I didn't have any money," Jack remembered. "I've seen every awful thing that can happen when a person needs medical help and isn't well placed. There was a lot of pain in that. So I sometimes have an inappropriate reaction to losing people."

Mud did live to see *Time* magazine declare *Easy Rider* one of the decade's ten most important cinema landmarks, but not to hear that her boy had been nominated for an Academy Award.[26] "If only Mud had lived four months longer," Lorraine lamented.

Once *Easy Rider* broke, Jack never stopped working. He interspersed obsessive writing, rehearsing, newspaper interviews, and preproduction for his next movie with bouts of black depression. Given Mud's deteriorating condition, all that career effort seemed somehow inappropriate in retrospect. "It's how we get reputations for being monstrous people, but this is reality," Jack reflected years later in a conversation with the film critic Joe Morgenstern. "When your friend's mother dies, you almost don't stop eating lunch, 'cause you can't. If your mother dies, you get the day off. At the most. If you have a divorce, you get no time off. Quite frankly, it's the only adolescent resentment I've ever developed toward work in the movies."

8

MUD HAD BARELY BEEN EULOGIZED BEFORE JACK WAS back at his desk at BBS, a portrait of Bob Dylan staring at him from his office wall. Operating more as a film co-op than a corporation, BBS recognized its core capital as the rarefied talent who could make low-budget movies that people actually wanted to see. The partnership not only nurtured proven filmmakers like Jack but held on to them with perks, loans, opportunities, and sage counsel—if not princely salaries. Jack's consolation prize after *Easy Rider* was every actor's dream: Bert Schneider let him direct his own movie. But when it was over, he'd go right back on the treadmill. As Jack himself put it, "[A]cting is no longer a vacation."

On March 5, 1970, *Variety* reported that "Oscar nominee Jack Nicholson completed Columbia's *Five Easy Pieces* and now makes his directorial debut with *Drive, He Said*, a college basketball yarn lensing in Eugene."

Jack described Jeremy Larner's novel as "a narrative dream" told with multiple themes: adultery, drugs, and wacky ways of avoiding the draft—all of them at least as important to the story line as free throws and personal fouls. *Drive, He Said* became an adaptation nightmare—no dramedy but certainly not played for laughs.[1] "The book had a satirical style that worked as a novel," Jack observed, "but would have come out on the screen like *Dobie Gillis*."[2]

Jack brought his Corman-inspired sensibility to the writing, boiling away all but the essence and inventing new scenes to fill in the gaps. Laden with heavy-handed symbols, from apples to flags to reptiles, Larner's original story became self-consciously hip, yet oddly Old Testament. What came together on screen was an unconvincing tragedy as disengaging as it was disjointed: a sophomoric morality tale.

Jack and Larner tangled over cuts, although the novelist wasn't totally dissatisfied with the result. "*Drive, He Said* is not a great movie, but there are touches of genius," conceded Larner, who learned the basics of screenwriting from working with Jack.[3] "He'd slap you on the shoulder and say, 'Jer, we *are* movies!' and you'd believe him. Jack can do this better than your *real* best friend. He's a master of bullshit—totally convincing."

Credited to Jack and Larner, the *Drive, He Said* script was doctored by Terrence Malick,[4] a recent alumnus of the newly created American Film Institute,[5] and by Jack's old friend and former roommate Robert Towne, who also played Karen Black's wooden cuckold of a husband in the finished film. Jack larded the entire cast and crew with onscreen and offscreen talent he'd come to trust as friends during his long Hollywood apprenticeship. He hired his Manasquan High chum Ken Kenney as assistant editor and paid Bruce Dern $1,000 a week for the pivotal role of *Drive, He Said*'s basketball coach. Besides Towne, the cast's Sunset Strip alumni included B. J. Merholz and Henry Jaglom.

Bert Schneider dispatched his brother Harold[6] to Oregon to act as BBS's on-site production manager, while Harry Gittes joined Fred Roos, the BBS partner Steve Blauner, and Jack as the credited producers.

Drive, He Said was supposed to begin in January but got repeatedly postponed, first by Mud's death and later by looming union problems. "When I direct *Drive, He Said*, I know I'll have to use IA and it will make the film that much worse," Jack predicted before leaving for Oregon.[7] "Ultimately, they'll take it out of my ass for talking this way. But I'm only telling the truth."

Like *Five Easy Pieces*, *Drive, He Said* was supposed to be a frugal thirty-day shoot. The contractual deadline would be enforced to keep crew costs minimal. Anything past thirty days turned it into an exorbitant overtime nightmare.

But making a movie was not all headaches and labor troubles. All his life Jack had heard stories of the casting couch; now, he had one of his own. In a lascivious publicity stunt, he invited *Life* magazine to watch him cast an exhibitionist cheerleader.

The first thing an auditioning actress saw when she entered the *Drive, He Said* casting office on the Columbia lot was a poster of a bare, buxom hooker pinned to the wall behind Jack. Jack greeted each young woman with his patented smile, teeth gleaming like an Amana refrigerator: too big to be ignored and too cool to resist. Then he leaned across his desk, his voice low and intimate. "Hi."

The smile held for a minute or more until his prey began to fidget. "Whaddya been doing?" he finally asked.

Each actress responded differently. Usually, she handed across an eight by ten glossy, along with a résumé. Then she relaxed into a monologue about her most recent stage or film gig. Jack let each woman ramble a while before springing the key question: "How do you feel about nude scenes?" On his tongue, the word *nude* elongated into a low verbal leer.

Jack knew it was a show stopper. Sometimes the actress giggled and sometimes she didn't. More often than not, she reddened and stammered that he was just being silly. But on occasion she stood and stripped. For those who hesitated, Jack offered a stage direction and a little directorial coaxing.[8] "This cheerleader looks like Shirley Temple on the outside, but on the inside she feels like that." He pointed past his shoulder at the hooker poster. "There are two scenes that aren't love scenes, where she has to walk around the room naked, because she's the kind of girl who feels *good* naked. So she has to be completely relaxed about it."

"Oh," the actress said

"Now, I'll have to *see* the girl before I hire her. So, would you be able to do that?"

He ogled all of those who were "able to do that" from more than a hundred who auditioned and settled on a young belly dancer named June Fairchild, with whom he had worked in *Head*.[9]

Despite the buildup as to the importance of her nonchalant nudity, Fairchild's scenes in the finished product paled beside the nudity of Mike Margotta, the frizzy-haired actor who played the draft-dodging character (and Dean Stockwell look-alike) Gabriel, whose crucifixion in *Drive, He Said* paralleled that of the Jack cynosure Wilhelm Reich. "His action through the film is the life of Reich," said Jack. "He was right; what he was saying was right; no one believes him, it drove him crazy, and he was institutionalized."

Margotta's extended sequence in the final reel, streaking across campus after a full frontal frolic in a college laboratory, remained in the finished picture, even though Oregon police attempted to confiscate the film.[10]

After the film was finished, Jack admitted to violating an agreement with the University of Oregon that allowed him to shoot on campus with the proviso that there'd be no naked actors. "I knew we weren't supposed to do it," Jack said, "but one very early Sunday morning I went out with the cameraman, a friend, the actor, did the bit and then split. Someone ratted, but we had already gotten the film out of the state across the border."

Drive, He Said's coproducer Steve Blauner secreted the contraband film in the front of his Porsche and made a beeline for L.A. When officials showed up at the Eugene hotel where the film company had set up its headquarters, they allegedly found Jack buck naked and empty-handed. "I quickly took off all my clothes and had them interview me in the nude," he claimed. "It was just one of my whims."

Nudity had obsessed him the previous summer. He'd lived for three months in his new place on Mulholland as a nudist, refusing clothes no matter who dropped by. "Roger Corman came by and didn't like it much," Jack recalled. "I wasn't throwing my wang around or anything, but it startled him nonetheless. My daughter understandably didn't like it." But Harry Dean Stanton did. "He couldn't wait to come over and be nude," said Jack.

Like the nude casting call, Jack made the most of his nude interrogation for maximum publicity, but it was not enough to separate *Drive, He Said* from the glut of campus coming-of-age stories that had emerged in the wake of *The Graduate*. In Eugene, Jack's old compatriot Richard Rush had wrapped his own antiestablishment college saga, *Getting Straight*, which costarred another chum, Candice Bergen. Once studios discovered baby boomers, campus revolt became so au courant that it developed into a separate genre, but *Drive, He Said* differed in that it reflected Jack's own personal ambivalence toward radical politics. "Politically, I'm a humanist. I believe in universal goals," he told *Ramparts* magazine. "I know people are trying to do good things, but I don't see a lot of success in all the attempts. The revolutionaries have created a voice, but I don't see anyone listening to the voice."

In Jack's eyes, campus rebels were more interested in partying than in party politics. When police haul the draft-dodging character Gabriel away in an ambulance at the close of *Drive, He Said*, "you see all the rest of the people on the campus just kind of looking on and it's just another event that day in that society," Jack said. "Everyone's left standing there. That's the way I see it. Things just go on."

At three years past his thirtieth birthday, Jack should have been deemed untrustworthy by the yippie standards of the day, but in fact "Happy Jack" appeared in the pages of *Life* hyping *Drive, He Said* with a doobie between his thumb and forefinger. He radiated more cool than Miles Davis. "He made it okay to smoke pot," said one of his friends. "Toking a joint, right there in the most popular magazine in America."

While disillusioned by politics, Jack became an early and outspoken member of the National Organization for the Reform of Marijuana Laws (NORML), putting a defiant stamp of approval on weed and giving himself an adolescent rebel cachet that matched that of the Chicago 7. At no time was he unaware that his antiestablishment image might also help at the box office.

Still, to Jack, his first stab at directing was less about thumbing his nose at "the Man" than it was about "relationship crisis." "A certain phase of it," he specified. "The most difficult phase that you would pick, you know, the breaking-up point"—not unlike his own unraveling relationship.

Mimi Machu had been his constant companion for three years and was not the least bit naive about either Jack's infidelities or his quasi-scientific rationalizations. Long before Marvin Gaye discovered "Sexual Healing," Jack had learned to self-medicate. "[Wilhelm] Reich said a long time ago that the flat-bellied male martinet is the main problem with our entire culture," Jack preached, vowing never to become such an uptight, abstemious asshole himself.

And yet, while he talked the talk of sexual freedom and Reichian release, there remained enough macho Jersey swagger in his step to keep Jack from walking the walk. At some level, he knew Mimi was as voracious a libertine as he was, but much of the time he lived in denial about her sexual appetites. "Jack liked very thin girls who were twenty," observed Karen Black. "He used to cry after breaking up with his girlfriend. She was blonde and wore overalls a lot."

Mimi, an inveterate flirt, and more, made Jack jealous on purpose and used her promiscuity to punish him, and she knew when she'd hit a nerve. "When that Irish moodiness hit, Jack would grab the back of his neck, throbbing with pain, and look as if he was boiling in oil," she said. When Rex Reed remarked during one of Jack's *Easy Rider* promotion interviews that Mimi's last name sounded like the name of a boat, Mimi flashed him a seductive grin, batted her lashes, and added, "Or a mountain."

Mimi joined Jack in Eugene, bringing along her six-year-old son, Sean, who kicked Jack often in front of the crew, making a difficult situation worse. Mimi had already made no secret of her infidelities. Rumors swept the set about her trysts at Jack's new place in L.A. while he'd been away—once she'd allegedly entertained both of Jack's houseguests, Roger Vadim and Christian Marquand, at the same time. Jack and Mimi's dangerous game of one-upmanship exploded on the set of *Drive, He Said*. With only a tiny role in the movie, Mimi had come to Oregon to make out, while Jack had come to make art. "I work from 8 a.m. to 11 p.m. After 11, I chase around. Laughs," Jack told a reporter. "But don't be a dumdum. The fun *is* the work."

As the thirty-day deadline for completing Jack's film came and went, the union crew's threats to shut the picture down ratcheted up. "The burden of the movie became enormous for Jack," recalled the assistant production manager Lynn Bernay, who also acted in the role of the film's ballet teacher. "He didn't want to get up in the morning. I had to go up to his room, he'd be fast asleep, and we'd all be ready to go on location. I'd say, 'Jack, get up.' He'd say, 'I don't want to do this.'"

Bored and restless, Mimi began to carry on with Michael Margotta, the actor who portrayed Gabriel. At one point, she staged a massage party for members of the cast. When Jack learned what Mimi had been up to while he was filming his opening sequences, he lay down on his back in the middle of the University of Oregon gymnasium, his arms outstretched as if he'd been crucified. He busted loose. Those present watched a rare moment of Jack sobbing, raw and real. "He loved her very much and she left him," said Bernay. "She hurt him a lot. He suffered greatly with that one."

The cast and crew remember Mimi showing up at the set once with a black eye. By late spring, as production ended, so did her relationship with Jack. Mimi, the tall trophy he'd once displayed while she nibbled his fingers and blew in his ear, was now a memory.

At a personal level, Jack identified with Robert Towne's character in *Drive, He Said*: an intellectual who knows his mate is cheating with a younger man, but carries on in the belief that the affair will end and she will come first to her senses and then home.[11] "I was with her for three years, in love, and when she dumped me, I couldn't even hear her name mentioned without breaking into a cold sweat," Jack later admitted.

Mimi saw their passion differently. "We were two maniacs who couldn't live together or apart," she said.

A short time later, after *Drive, He Said* wrapped, Jack ran into John Phillips of the Mamas and the Papas at one of Larry Hagman's beach parties. "Jack was breaking up with a girlfriend and was brokenhearted," Phillips wrote in his memoir. By all rights, Phillips should have been shattered because his ex-wife, Mama Michelle, had recently taken up with Dennis Hopper. But unlike Jack, Phillips had fully embraced the tortured ethics of "free love." Shortly after Jack cried on his shoulder, Phillips met Mimi wandering on the beach and claimed to have bedded her that very night. He said he didn't know she was Jack's heartbreaker until the morning after.

As with *Head*, the pop theories of the Canadian media philosopher Marshall McLuhan crept into the preaching heart of *Drive, He Said*, reflecting Jack's growing contempt for TV. In one scene, after swallowing half a pharmacy to beat the draft, Margotta's addled campus radical whips a sword off a wall while watching a televised parade honoring the Apollo moon astronauts. *"This* is the *instrument* of the *death* of our *times!"* he screams, hoisting the sword above the screen. After destroying the television, Margotta heaves it out a window. "TV is a bad influence, the cancer of film," observed Jack. "What people think they know from watching TV is just a Tower of Babel."

McLuhan warned of television's subtle impact, with its ability to bring together or rend whole cultures, as well as make or break celebrities and politicians by magnifying their mistakes or minimizing their accomplishments. Jack took McLuhan's theories to heart. At the close of the seventies, he told the *New York Arts Journal*, "I did a very smart thing about ten years ago. I decided never to see a single episode of a single television series from beginning to end, not one. So I can't get angry about it."

Jack flat out refused to appear on television. Because of his visceral distrust, he made it a career policy not to grant televised interviews, especially on talk shows.[12] "One of the reasons I never, ever do television interviews is, if you don't resist, they'll make you into their favorite Jack," he said. "They think they know you. You've got to fight that, or the orifice through which you can express yourself becomes narrower and narrower. I'm a person who is very aware of this, maybe because I worked for a long while before I had any say in what I did exactly."

But television remained inevitable over the next decade. Already MCA-Universal had invested in a digital technology that would lead first to the creation of the laser disc, followed by the development of CDs and DVDs. Sony engineers were on the verge of introducing a new machine in Japan that they called the Betamax videotape recorder, which could actually copy television programs as well as play prerecorded movies. While prohibitively expensive (the first model was offered in the United States in 1975 for $2,295), the price would drop precipitously after RCA introduced its American knockoff, the VHS recorder, later in the decade.

But TV's impending transformation didn't end with the VCR. While the cable industry was in its infancy and most homes still pulled in their TV signals from roof antennae, by the end of the century cable would rule. By 1970, a matrix of telecommunications satellites[13] already girdled the globe, offering HBO, Showtime, and a whole host of pay-TV services in the decade that followed.[14]

The resulting video revolution would take TV audiences into uncharted territory, and the colossal impact on the film industry Jack had grown up with would be immediate and irreversible. The medium for which Jack held such unqualified scorn would grow more diverse, pervasive, and persuasive. Most people would see Jack's movies for the first time on the tube, not in the theater. Even Jack was forced to rely on TV for his precious Lakers games, especially when he was away from L.A.

One Hollywood institution that hadn't changed was the Academy

Awards. Because Jack, Best Supporting Actor nominee, was still on location with *Drive, He Said*, he didn't show up for the fortieth annual Oscars ceremony, but his *Easy Rider* director did. Though honored for his directing at Cannes and nominated for the Directors Guild of America's top award, Dennis Hopper had been shut out at the Oscars. That did not keep him from showing up in a double-breasted tux and a white ten-gallon Stetson with Papa John's ex, Mama Michelle Phillips, draped over his arm. He tried to make it clear to those present that Hollywood had a new sheriff and that Jack Nicholson (whom he'd asked to appear in *The Last Movie* [1971], his follow-up to *Easy Rider*) was part of his posse.[15] Speaking for the old guard, a disgusted Henry Fonda told the press, "Any man who insists on wearing his cowboy hat to the Academy Awards and keeps it on at the dinner table afterward ought to be spanked."

Jack was a different sort of rebel. Since he'd been a kid back in Neptune, Jack had a thing for hats—still collected them, in fact[16]— but he'd never have made a sombrero or a fez a fashion statement at the Oscars. Respectful to a fault, he kept his antiestablishment attire down to an ever-present pair of *Breathless* Ray-Bans.

But 1970 wasn't to be Jack's year. He'd already won the first-ever Supporting Actor's award given by the New York Film Critics Association[17] but lost the Oscar to the sentimental favorite Gig Young.[18] Old Hollywood didn't mind taking the boomers' money at the box office, but it would be a while before this generation had enough steam to storm the Academy.

Despite his rising star, Jack agreed to do *A Safe Place* (1971) for Henry Jaglom during the summer of 1970. He and Jaglom continued to share office space at BBS, and, like Jack, Jaglom aspired to auteur status on Bert Schneider's dime. His contempt for the demon television aside, Jack agreed to appear in Jaglom's directorial debut in exchange for a new color TV set. By casting chums like Jack and Tuesday Weld for minimal salary, Jaglom meant to cut costs while translating his play—written in the mid-sixties for the Actors Studio—into his first feature film. "It deals with trying to hold on to the past," said Jaglom.

A Safe Place dealt with a lot more than that. Among other themes, Jaglom jammed fear, lust, darkness, light, id, ego, humor, murder, reality, suicide, and the unfathomable contradictions of the feminine mystique into his screenplay. The most oblique and obscure of any of

Jack's post-*Easy Rider* films, *A Safe Place* sprawled across the screen as experimental and as arty as Monte Hellman's inscrutable existential Westerns—but without the benefit of a coherent plot.

On the first day of shooting, Jack and Tuesday tried to perform according to Jaglom's screenplay, yet nothing rang true. Frustrated, the director told them to fake it. "I threw away the script and made the rest of the movie from my head with the actors," Jaglom said.

And it showed. Jaglom shot a scene, improvised, and then shot some more. Like a sculptor who sees Zeus in a block of granite before ever picking up a chisel, Jaglom saw art in miles of exposed footage before consigning himself to an editing bay for weeks at a time. In all, he printed fifty hours of film and plucked out the bits and pieces to craft into his ninety-four-minute masterwork, "almost like a jigsaw puzzle." His pioneering laissez-faire process launched a long maverick career as an independent—and frequently inaccessible—filmmaker. Thirty years and fourteen films later, he still called his first movie his best. That most audiences did not agree was their own damn problem.

The blame for *A Safe Place*'s short, inconsequential life didn't lie with its cast.[19] In addition to Jack, a bright, luminous young Weld repeated the role she'd performed at the Actors Studio when Jaglom had staged it as a play.[20] For the film version, Jaglom added an inept magician whom Weld meets in Central Park. He wooed the legendary Orson Welles to play the vaguely *alter cocker* role.[21]

Jack's character is a stoned, mustachioed stud who may or may not be Weld's brother and may or may not have murdered his ex-girlfriend before dropping in on the heroine at four in the morning. "I wanted to use him prototypically for what he had become in the American film where he would be the 'hero'," said Jaglom. "He would fuck the girl, fuck the audience, fuck the movie, save the girl, save the audience, save the movie."

But in the end, Jack would save nothing at all. Jaglom described his fantasy as a love triangle, with Weld torn between the decent daytime guy (*Firesign Theater*'s Phil Proctor) she should be with and the dangerous, sexy guy (Jack) who visits her late at night. "She was a woman trapped between growing up and remaining a child," said Jaglom. Upon seeing a first cut, Charles Eastman had a less charitable assessment: "It's a porn movie without sex."

Months later, upon seeing the finished product, Columbia's president

Leo Jaffe thought less about Jaglom's impenetrable story line and lofty themes than he did about his bladder. "Jesus Christ," he said in amazement as the final credits rolled. "I didn't even piss once."

"I don't understand," said Jaglom. "What does that mean?"

"Well, usually I piss—what? Twelve, thirteen times?" He panned his junior executives in the screening room and got a host of serious sycophantic nods. "Yeah, usually I go to the john and piss twelve, thirteen times. And this time I didn't piss once. I haven't not pissed once since—what was it?"

An aide piped up, "*Anastasia*."

Jaffe held up one finger. "That's right," he said. "*Anastasia*. That's the last time I didn't piss during a movie."

"Oh, does that mean you like the movie?" Jaglom ventured.

"No, no, no, it has nothing to do with that. It just means that this movie was so weird that I couldn't take my eyes off of it."

He paused to visit the restroom and returned with a smile. "But I'll tell you one thing," Jaffe continued. "After the movie, did I have a good piss."

Following *A Safe Place*, Jack flew to British Columbia and segued from Jaglom's free-form ad libs to Mike Nichols's tightly scripted *Carnal Knowledge* (1971). Instead of winging it through dozens of reshoots, Jack switched to the kind of acting that calls for memorized lines, complete rehearsals, and single takes. Mike Nichols was low-key and congenial, and his trademark as an actor's director was gentle but confident persuasion. Like the attorney who already knows the answers to his questions, the director of *The Graduate* and *Who's Afraid of Virginia Woolf?* knew his scenes before the cameras ever rolled, yet remained open to his actors' extemporaneous inspirations. A lifelong influence on Jack's own directorial ambition, Nichols gave Jack the mantra "Profit in the doing."

Before launching into *Carnal Knowledge*, which follows the sexual exploits of two 1940s Amherst undergrads from college through middle age, Nicholson and Nichols—"Nick and Nick," as the cast came to know them—screened *Psych-Out* together. Stoney, *Psych-Out*'s amoral hippie protagonist, shared some of the promiscuity of the perpetual adolescent lawyer Jonathan Fuerst in Jules Feiffer's screenplay, but Stoney rallied to waifish Susan Strasberg's side by movie's end. A flinty unredeemed narcissist, Jonathan finished *Carnal Knowledge* with a paid ritualistic blowjob from Rita Moreno. He had Stoney's rag-ing libido but none of his heart.

For its time, *Carnal Knowledge* came as a total shock to audi-ences—so much so that Jack would be tarred by feminists for years thereafter as personifying the American horn dog who cares more about his orgasm than he does about human frailty. Others hailed Jack for risking his newfound star status by debunking a swaggering male stereotype. "It is . . . difficult to envision a star of the past in Jonathan's role" wrote the film historian David Grossvogel. "Stars commanded the screen and it shone with their radiance. They could be as self-centered and as destructive as Jonathan, but never as petty."

Far from being put off by the odious Jonathan, Jack attacked the role with gusto. None of his contemporaries could inhabit Jonathan's sleazy hypocrisy quite so convincingly or deliver a line like "Answer me, you ball-busting, castrating son of a cunt bitch!" with quite the same malicious rage. When it came to cinematic male-female rela-tionships, Jack said he liked to "press on the nerves," and by the end of *Carnal Knowledge*, he'd steamrolled most of America's romantic notions of courtship. In the space of ninety-eight minutes, his unre-deemed misogynist went from arrogant undergrad jonesing to get laid to middle-aged impotence, cursing women throughout as "cunts,"[22] "castrators," or "ball busters."

Off camera, Jack was his usual clowning and confident self. He struck up a lifelong friendship with costar Art Garfunkel, even nam-ing the converted maid's quarters off the kitchen of his Mulholland aerie after Paul Simon's other half. The guest room where Jack invited the crooner to stay whenever he came to L.A. became "the Arthur Garfunkel Suite."[23]

Jack also encouraged the budding romance between Bert Schnei-der and Candice Bergen, whose character both Jonathan and Sandy (Garfunkel) sleep with during the first half of *Carnal Knowledge*. "Jack and Artie and I shared a large house in Vancouver that came to resemble the set of the Amherst dorm," Bergen recalled. "We traipsed home at the end of a day still in our '40s college wardrobe of crew cuts and crew necks, pigtails and pleated skirts, white bucks, saddle shoes and bow ties, bounding in to greet the housekeeper, who cooked and cared for us like a mother as we badgered her for snacks after school."

As in the movie, the trio did everything together. They found time to attend a Greenpeace concert (featuring Joni Mitchell, Phil Ochs, and James Taylor) and watched the Muhammad Ali–Jerry Quarry fight via satellite. When the cast of the director Robert Altman's *McCabe and Mrs. Miller* (1971) threw a party, the cast of *Carnal Knowledge* was invited.[24] According to Jules Feiffer, he first introduced Jack to Warren Beatty there. "Now *that's* what a movie star is supposed to look like!" Jack told Feiffer after Beatty moved off through the crowd. With his penchant for nicknames, Jack dubbed Beatty "the Pro," in deference to Beatty's uncanny ability to succeed at everything—writing, producing, directing, acting, and manipulating the money men.

The fourth marquee name of the *Carnal Knowledge* cast found her career redemption in Mike Nichols's movie. After Jane Fonda nixed the role of Jonathan's willing barmaid Bobbie Templeton, Ann-Margret jumped at the chance to play opposite Jack. They got to be so close that Jack recommended his niece, Pamela, who was then just starting out, as her hairdresser, and Pamela was able to boast that she'd landed Ann-Margret as a client.[25]

Shucking her post-Elvis image, which the *New Yorker's* Pauline Kael had characterized up to that point in the actress's career as little more than "a lewd mechanical doll," Ann-Margret turned her bimbo-with-a-heart performance into a Best Supporting Actress nomination. Jack said she radiated "the same glow of tragedy as Monroe."

Ann-Margret's torrid outtakes with Jack between the sheets were reportedly so pornographic that they made the rounds at Hollywood stag parties. The scene in which she gives her whiny ultimatum, pushing Jonathan into marriage, achieved its own dubious immortality decades later as a perennial set piece on Howard Stern's morning radio show:

Bobbie (lying in bed): I need a life.

Jonathan (angry, getting ready for work): Get a job.

Bobbie: I don't want a job. I want you.

Jonathan: I'm taken. *By me!* Get out of the house! Do something useful, goddam it!

Bobbie: You wouldn't let me work when I wanted to.

Jonathan: That was a year ago.

Bobbie: You throw a tantrum every time you call and I'm not home.

Jonathan: Look, sister, I'm out there in the jungle eight hours a day!

Bobbie: You wouldn't even let me canvass for Kennedy.

Jonathan (ranting): You want a job? I got a job for you! *Fix up this pig sty!* You get a pretty goddam good salary for testing out this bed all day. You want an extra $50 a week? *Try vacuuming!* You want an extra $100? *Try making this goddam bed! Try opening some goddam windows! That's* why you can't stand up in here! The goddam place smells like a coffin!

On weekends, whenever he could get away, Jack shuttled back to L.A. to tackle the final excruciating editing of *Drive, He Said.* "Jack hated to cut, and that's where a movie is made—in the editing," observed Jeremy Larner.

While in L.A., Jack also dropped in on the Charles Manson murder trial from time to time, lingering at the rear of the courtroom, where he took notes. "I just wanted to see it for myself," he said.

For years thereafter, Jack maintained that Manson had been railroaded by overzealous prosecutors who convicted him on the strength of a single fingerprint and the testimony of a murderess who'd been given total immunity: a clear-cut case of the end justifying the means. While some of his friends accused him of typical Jack behavior—taking the contrary position just to provoke a debate—Jack remained adamant about the convicted mastermind of the Tate-LaBianca slaughter. Deny Manson due process, Jack argued, and nobody would be safe from the wrath of the mob.

"Nothing changes in the movie business except prices go up," observed Steve Blauner. "There are two big blockbuster release seasons: summer and Christmas. *Five Easy Pieces* was a nice little picture, but we released it in a time when there was nothing else to write about. In September and October, the summer releases are playing out and a nice little serious film gets more than its share of attention.

We opened in one theater in Westwood in the middle of September and for the next couple months the press was all over it. Free advertising: the best kind."

Within a month of its low-key premiere, *Five Easy Pieces* was on its way to blockbuster status. *Easy Rider* made Jack a star, but *Five Easy Pieces* made him a leading man. The first film could have been written off as a fluke; the second cemented him in the collective imagination as the new American antihero. Critics who already speculated that he might be the logical successor to Brando and Dean now stretched the possibility further: Jack might be the new Bogart.

The same day that *Five Easy Pieces* premiered, the agent Sandy Bresler launched Sandy Bresler & Associates with an ad in the *Hollywood Reporter* in which he announced "the exclusive representation of Jack Nicholson." "I was much sought after," said Jack. "Your name becomes a brand image like a product. You become Campbell's soup, with thirty-one different varieties of roles you can play."

With ascension to the level of Campbell's soup, Jack had more choices than a courtesan to the Russian army, and he needed a sentinel to sort through the offers. Bresler became a gatekeeper more than an agent.

Jack told Bresler to be on the lookout for roles that he dubbed "cusp characters." "I like to play people that haven't existed yet, a future something, a cusp character," said Jack. "I have that creative yearning. Much in the way Chagall flies figures into the air: once it becomes part of the conventional wisdom, it doesn't seem particularly adventurous or weird or wild."

And there was the additional element of money: the kind a star can command simply by attaching his name to a project. With *Five Easy Pieces*, Jack graduated to the level of gross profit participant.[26] Salary, though obscene by mortal standards, now became secondary to owning a piece of the action. Equity became inextricably entwined with the scripts Jack was offered and the roles he wanted to play. "When you get into any kind of position when you're an aid to facilitating the financing of a film, they'll submit anything to you—from George Washington to, you know, Mickey Rooney's biography," Jack observed.

Bresler's job was to find the middle way between art and windfall—to enable Jack to retain the common touch, while frolicking like Scrooge McDuck through his own private Disneyland. And there was yet another variable in the making of a deal: ego.

When John Boorman approached Jack about taking a role in *Deliverance* (1972), Jack said yes, as long as his hero Marlon Brando played opposite him. Encouraged, the director paid Brando a visit. "He said he despised acting," Boorman recalled. "He had learned to be a mimic as a child to get attention. Acting was nothing more than mimicry.[27] A bunch of tricks." Still, Brando agreed to the role.

"How much do you want?" Boorman asked.

"I'll take whatever you pay Jack," Brando answered.

But when Boorman called on Bresler to seal the deal, he got a rude surprise. Jack's agent demanded $500,000—far beyond what Boorman was prepared to offer. When Boorman protested, Bresler said, "I happen to know that Warners is paying Redford half a million to do *Jeremiah Johnson*."

At the time, $1 million for the two male leads was a deal breaker, and the game of one-upmanship ended there. *Deliverance* filmed in the summer of 1971, with Jon Voight in the role earmarked for Jack. Burt Reynolds was cast as the weekend woodsman whom Boorman had wanted Brando to portray.

After *Newsweek* put Jack's face on the cover of its December 7, 1970, issue, there seemed little question that he was on his way to matching, if not superseding, Brando. It took Bob Rafelson to remind Jack just how fickle fame could be. Hailed as America's newest auteur, Rafelson remembered the cruelty surrounding *Head*. "I can't depend on critical support," he said. "From a guy who was considered a complete ass—that's the word people used—with *Head*, I was suddenly brilliant with *Five Easy Pieces*. But I was the same man. You go through that once in a lifetime, never again. Since Jack and I wrote and produced *Head* together, along with my partner Bert Schneider, we're now telling people we made *Five Easy Pieces* so people would go back to see *Head*."

Several critics accepted Rafelson's invitation, and even the withering words of the *New York Times*'s Renata Adler had to be chewed and swallowed: "[I]t was a better movie than most critics allowed," she wrote. "*Head* was a movie that had nowhere to go except down, but in retrospect doesn't seem all that bad."

The same could not be said of Jack's other previous films, which suddenly began popping up on screens across America. After languishing for nearly three years, the ill-fated *Rebel Rousers* found a distributor that ran ads to cash in on Jack's name: "That *Easy Rider* man is here . . . Jack Nicholson. They terrorized the flesh and blood of America. Their creed: 'If it feels good, do it!' *Rebel Rousers*, a four star Excelsior release."

In similar fashion, *The Shooting* and *Ride in the Whirlwind* were suddenly rediscovered and targeted at the art house circuit. "Now they are about to be released in the U.S.," sniffed Jack. "I wonder why."

9

AROUND THE TIME JACK AND MIMI BROKE IT OFF, HELENA Kallianiotes had a blowout of her own. After two bad marriages, she showed up at Jack's door with a shiner she claimed her ex had given her. She was living in her car. Jack told the feisty belly dancer she could move into his guest house—a small building on Jack's promontory that contained a rec room, some weight-training equipment, and simple, semifurnished living quarters.

"I brought a couple of couches from my house," Helena reported years later, long after she never left. Over the next two decades, she lived there gratis, sharing the cottage with Jack's Spanish-speaking housekeeper, mothering her benefactor through his romances, running his errands, and eventually getting him to invest in her business ventures: a skating rink, dance studios, nightclubs, a Sierra resort, and so on.

Helena witnessed Jack's transformation during the first couple of years following *Five Easy Pieces*—a period of adjustment during which the new star switched haunts from Sunset Boulevard's disappearing coffeehouses to more upscale places along Santa Monica Boulevard: hip, but with a cover charge. He still drank Michelob beer and chain-smoked Camels or Marlboros, but he was now becoming a regular at Dan Tana's upscale Italian restaurant, the Daisy in Beverly Hills, and Doug Weston's Troubadour, the trendy West Hollywood club where the Eagles first played and Cat Stevens or Elton John stopped in when they detoured through L.A.

"He has the feet of an aristocrat and the body of a peasant,"

Helena declared of Jack. "He has traveled with kings and knaves and sees no difference between them."

Jack loved the dense pop poetry of Bob Dylan and the raw rock and blues of the Stones, and he made it a point to meet all his musical idols in the wake of his newfound fame. Without behaving like a fawning groupie, he added Mick Jagger,[1] John Lennon[2] and Dylan to his growing network. Warren Beatty introduced Jack to the pop über agent David Geffen and the Canadian chanteuse Joni Mitchell, with whom Jack had a brief romance.[3] According to Jon Epaminondas, Jack was "never an autograph person," but "he knew how to play the game very early by observation. He never imposed on people."

"There were always lots of friends around," said Helena. "Not hangers-on or bloodsuckers, just genuine people. If he liked something, he'd bring it home, whether it was a lampshade or a person. Two or three house guests were around in any single month."

Among her other duties, Helena became a short-order cook, whipping up steak and salad dinners for as many as a half-dozen people at the last possible moment. "He eats out too much," she said. "That's why he always talks about dieting. He's always guilty about what he's eaten the day before."

While Jack didn't play the piano himself, he had a baby grand imported into his living room and kept a guitar or two around the den to pluck—"pacifiers," he called them. Next to the piano, he kept a framed poem by William Butler Yeats: "To a Friend Whose Work Has Come to Nothing." He gave a copy to Dennis Hopper at a low point in Hopper's career.

Jack's art collection began to expand, with a Picasso here, a Modigliani there. Chagalls were now apt to decorate the same walls where he'd displayed his earlier, more modest acquisitions. A voracious pop nerd, Jack set up a Sony speaker system around the pool and stocked long rows of shelves with record albums. He prowled Tower Records or used vinyl stores in the Valley for the newest, the oldest, or the oddest. "I *have* to visit the record store," Jack told an interviewer. "They've got some 'obscuros' there: *The Best of Sam the Sham and the Pharaohs*. Even MGM Records doesn't have a copy! I've always got a list. I asked so many people in so many places in the world if they had a copy of the Beach Boys' *Wild Honey* album that they actually re-released the thing after I'd looked for it for five years. Even Brian Wilson didn't have a copy! Somebody dropped mine—

it's hard to break a 33⅓ album, but it hit on the edge and cracked."

And yet, for all his au courant musicality, Jack was just as likely to serenade himself with Sinatra or Bing Crosby. He extolled "all those songs from those great old pictures" and shamelessly danced across his red-tile floor while crooning along with Bing: "Dinah! Is there anyone finah? In the state of Carolina . . . "

While Jack might have been gaining international recognition, he was not yet so familiar on the streets of L.A. that he risked being mobbed each time he wandered below Mulholland. In his Ray-Bans and buffed-out yellow Volkswagen convertible, he was still able to patrol the boulevards of West Hollywood like a banty rooster, frequently accompanied by a German shepherd named Rue. As added protection against overzealous fans, he dazzled all into submission with what the ex-Vogue editor Diana Vreeland was the first to dub his "killer smile."[4] "He'd pull up at a red light, smile at a bunch of girls and with one smile, he had 'em," recalled Harry Gittes. "It not only worked; it never *not* worked."

Sally Struthers saw him once and honked. He stopped in the middle of traffic, hopped out, ran over and gave her a kiss, then climbed back into his VW and drove off like Valentino in a bumper car. In the infancy of stardom, he remained unguarded. Whenever he saw a familiar face, he'd slow down and holler a smartass remark.

Lesley Ann Warren, who once shared an acting class with Jack,[5] tooled along Santa Monica Boulevard one afternoon with her hairdresser-fiancé, Jon Peters, when Jack rolled up beside them. "*Cinderella* sucks!" Jack yelled.

Notorious for his hair-trigger temper, Peters wheeled round and bore down on the VW like an avenging troll until Lesley Ann shrieked, "No!" She not only cooled her boyfriend but managed to get shaggy Jack added to Peters's growing client list. For $100 a session, the future producer visited Hollywood's high and mighty at their homes, trimming their hair, as well as their pocketbooks, while he learned to play the power game himself.

When Jack first came on to Michelle Phillips, the ex-Mama had already mastered her version of the Hollywood power game, matching wits against some of the finest bullies and basket cases of her generation. For eight years, she'd been indentured to Papa John, until adultery and drugs ended both the marriage and the Mamas and the Papas. In 1970, the same year that she fell for and acted with Dennis

Hopper in *The Last Movie*,[6] she finalized her divorce and retained custody of the Phillips's two-year-old daughter, Chynna. At twenty-six and now going by her real first name of Holly,[7] Michelle next wed Hopper on Halloween, but eight days later—following an ordeal in which a drugged-out Hopper called her a witch, handcuffed her, and fired off guns in the house—she fled and called him from Nashville to tell him the marriage was kaput.[8]

By 1971, just as the Mamas and the Papas reluctantly began to work on a "reunion" album,[9] Michelle gravitated toward Jack, whom she'd come to know through both of her celebrity husbands. Still courtly about dating a bona fide pop star, Jack went so far as to call Hopper in Taos to seek his approval. "Sure," said Hopper.

After *Five Easy Pieces* earned Jack his second nomination in February 1971, he asked Michelle to accompany him to the Oscars, but unlike her crazed ten-gallon date from the previous year, a semirespectful Jack came to her door wearing a dark suit, a shirt, and a tie.[10] "He was very charming arm candy for me that night," she recalled.

Jack chatted up reporters on the red carpet, revealing that he had voted for himself, "though I don't expect to win it. [George C.] Scott already has it sewn up [for *Patton*], whether he likes it or not."[11] At the Governor's Ball and all of the after parties, Michelle called Jack a "fun date," but when the night was over, "Jack dropped me off at my house."

The relationship did not remain platonic, though. She eventually became pregnant; the pregnancy ended in a miscarriage.

Whether it was due to the trauma of being dumped by Mimi or simply Michelle's innate graciousness, Jack began to shift his attitude toward women. "Definition is not good for relationships at any level," Jack pontificated, sounding more like a pop psychologist than a guy looking for the right girl. "It denies very obvious real things—namely, that everyone changes constantly through life and those changes should be in harmony with anyone you're spending most of your time with. So don't define the relationship. Don't even say, 'You're my girlfriend.'"

In the beginning Jack remained attentive enough to Michelle to learn from Hopper's mistakes: now that he'd gotten to first base with a genuine California trophy blonde, he would not overplay his hand.

In August 1971 and at Helena's urging, Jack had paid nearly $40,000 for the modest single-story rental next door. Helena suspected that the previous tenants had broken into Jack's place and made off with part of his early art collection. Owning the house eliminated the threat of transients. Jack coaxed Michelle and her daughter, Chynna, to move in, and Michelle spent thousands more on redecorating. "It was okay, except that Jack was always peering in the windows to see what I was up to," Michelle kvetched. When Chynna was old enough to attend preschool, Jack volunteered to drive her.

As he sat in on Michelle's recording sessions, Jack also got to know the other Mama, Cass Elliott, and the group's ex-manager, Lou Adler. In addition to pop music, all three shared a fanatical interest in sports—basketball, in particular.

Short and stout, Cass resembled Mud, and Jack felt more comfortable watching sports with her than with Michelle. They talked over the phone during games. "We knew that there was a kind of bond between them, based on a mutual love of basketball, but I think Jack also liked Cass because she was smart and he could speak to her on subjects other than just 'You were so good in *Five Easy Pieces*,'" recalled Cass's friend Leon Bing.

Adler had even more in common with Jack, sharing his abiding appreciation for "skunks," as Jack called fascinating but unattainable women.[12] The man who discovered the Mamas and the Papas and would go on to produce the all-time midnight cult favorite *The Rocky Horror Picture Show* (1975) had already sampled Shelley Fabares, Tina Sinatra, Peggy Lipton, Ann-Margret, and Britt Eklund among others. In 1973, when Eklund bore Adler's son, Adler named him Nicholai and asked Jack to be his godfather.

During the 1971–1972 basketball season, the Los Angeles Lakers had a thirty-three-game winning streak, which as of this writing has not been surpassed in NBA history, sealing forever Jack's bond with both Adler and the hometown team. Both men bought courtside seats and seldom missed a game thereafter.[13] Together, wrote the novelist Jim Harrison, who befriended them, Lou and Jack "handled L.A. as if it were their own personal birthday cake."

Through thirty-five years, dozens of "skunks," and legions of one-night stands, they always had the Lakers in common. Speaking in vintage metaphor that other appreciative males might save for the delicious complexity of the opposite sex, Jack observed, as did Adler, "Every basketball season is like a wine. Every wine is different."

· · ·

Jack had lost the Oscar, but he felt far more confident about Cannes. Along with Milos Forman's *Taking Off* (1971) and Jerry Schatzberg's *The Panic in Needle Park* (1971), *Drive, He Said* had been named an official U.S. entry. But while the other two entrants were politely applauded and won awards, the French went bonkers over Jack's directorial debut. "It was a mildly controversial film, but I mean, shit, this was three years after *Easy Rider*," said Jack. "I didn't think it was *that* controversial."

Apparently, it was. First came the screaming and yelling. "I thought I was Stravinsky for a moment," Jack said. Then came the booing. Fistfights broke out in the back of the auditorium. Like a howling omen, Mick Jagger's six-month-old daughter, Karis, began to cry at the opening credits and wailed all the way through.

"They've changed my whole stance toward a work of art that I devoted a year and a half of very hard work to," Jack fumed later on. "Now I'm swimming upstream . . . and I'm depressed by it."

At the press conference luncheon following the screening, angry fans and hostile critics alike demanded to know what the hell he'd been thinking. "Why should we be interested in all these schizophrenic people?" hollered one critic.

"There's this war in Vietnam," Jack answered. Pointing to the lobster, mayonnaise, and cucumber salad then being served, he made his point that dining in the lap of luxury while soldiers and civilians died half a world away was equally schizoid. "And in order to bring these two elements together, we need to refine our facility for schizophrenia to go on functioning."

The French were unappeased. What seemed most to tax the Gallic temperament about *Drive, He Said*, was the sex, not the film's antiwar antics. "They asked me at the press conference at Cannes why I thought the film was being censored, and I said that I felt it was because they didn't have orgasms in American films up until now," Jack deadpanned.

Indeed, the new MPAA ratings board had dealt Jack another blow, giving *Drive, He Said* one of its final "X" ratings before dumping the designation.[14] The locker-room nudity, Margotta's naked romp, and a scene in which Karen Black panted that she was coming[15] during a tryst in the backseat of a VW with the actor William Tepper made *Drive, He Said* officially obscene. Jack, represented by former U.S. attorney general Ramsey Clark, appeared before the appeals board that summer and got the X knocked down to an R, but around the same time, the National Catholic Office for Motion Pictures added its own condemnation. The British film board banned the movie in England.

Milos Forman assured Jack that he liked *Drive, He Said*. So did Tony Richardson, another director Jack respected and with whom he would eventually work. But Roman Polanski agreed with the audience: the film might be cinematically sound, but it wasn't very interesting. "A little bit too naturalistic for his tastes and so on," muttered Jack.

Of all the directors at Cannes, Dennis Hopper empathized the most. Six months before sustaining his own drubbing at the hands of critics upon the September release of *The Last Movie*, Hopper still hurt for Jack. "I identify with him," he said. "I'm very sympathetic to Jack. Jack's a really talented guy. He's a talented director."

Despite the setbacks, BBS still believed it had another boomer hit on its hands. "Bert Schneider expressed to me that he thought it would do business somewhere between the business that *Five Easy Pieces* and *Easy Rider* did," recalled Tepper, who felt like Jack following the release of *The Cry Baby Killer*. "They were quite surprised." Jack wasn't. "It was a commercial disaster," he said. "I knew it was going to set me back."

In June, *Carnal Knowledge* opened in L.A., and although it, too, appeared to suffer at the hands of the MPAA and Catholic censors, the Mike Nichols film finished the year as the sixth-highest-grossing film. A Georgia theater owner's refusal to screen *Carnal Knowledge* was followed by a condemnation of the film at the state's high court. But instead of hurting the film at the box office, this only seemed to drum up publicity.[16] The *Harvard Lampoon* weighed in with its own backhanded compliment by naming Jack "Worst Actor of 1971," even before the October premiere of *A Safe Place*.[17]

To jeers reminiscent of the Cannes reception for *Drive, He Said*, Henry Jaglom's debut film opened the New York Film Festival with brawls and consternation, but thirty years later, Jaglom still judged *A Safe Place* to be among the best of his fifteen films. "It's as good a film as I am ever going to make," he said, following a 2004 retrospective, "but it touches a specific audience very immediately and it does a lot of arm pushing away to a large majority of the audience. . . . I am sort of happy I didn't know more about audiences when I made it. It made my life hard. It was another five years before I could get financing for my second film.[18] Nonetheless, I feel more proud of that film than any film I am ever going to make because it's as pure as I can possibly be."

Jack was not quite so philosophical about *Drive, He Said*. As the year ended, his movie still wasn't on any theater chain's schedule. Following the film's poor reception at Cannes and its ratings troubles, Columbia had already written off Jack's baby. By the first week of January 1972, *Drive, He Said* briefly played a double bill with *Bob and Carol and Ted and Alice* (1969). Then it disappeared from theaters and wasn't screened again for a generation, and it still remains unavailable on DVD, although it can be seen occasionally on cable.

Director Jack's debacle had no visible effect on Movie-Star Jack, who flitted from project to project like an intoxicated butterfly, turning down such roles as the assassin in *The Day of the Jackal* (1973), Robert Redford's grifter in *The Sting* (1973), and *The Godfather*'s Michael Corleone. "I could have played it in spades," Jack boasted to Roger Ebert years later, when he portrayed a very different kind of mafioso in *Prizzi's Honor* (1985).

Jack campaigned for (and lost) the role of the young priest in *The Exorcist* (1973), while at the same time Carole Eastman asked him to star opposite Jeanne Moreau as a guard-dog trainer in a romantic comedy she called *The Second Interval*. Don Devlin would produce and Eastman hoped to make her directorial debut, but Jack declined and the project got shelved for twenty years.

"The only really good role I've rejected—and I could kill myself—was Jay Gatsby in *The Great Gatsby* [1974]," said Jack, who reportedly demanded too much money.[19] "I'm sure Redford will be great, but since I was eighteen, people said I should do Gatsby. I didn't really go after the part, for well, personal reasons I don't want printed."

He was anxious to collaborate with Michelangelo Antonioni on a film the Italian director called *Technically Sweet*, but Antonioni couldn't get the money together. He kept postponing it and made a four-hour documentary called *Chung Kuo-Cina* (1972) about Red China instead, so Jack went with the tried and true: he signed with Bob Rafelson to become *The Philosopher King* (renamed *The King of*

Marvin Gardens). Shooting began on location in Philadelphia and Atlantic City in December 1971.[20]

As with *Five Easy Pieces*, Jack again asked for the SAG minimum for his three months' work, taking his larger share as a profit participant on the back end. "I get paid from the first dollar that comes into the studio," he told the *New York Times*'s Aljean Harmetz. "That's the only way anyone involved in a film *should* make a lot of money: by taking a certain risk."

Knowing that Jack's salary demands had risen well beyond those accommodated by the standard $1 million BBS budget,[21] Rafelson proposed casting a pre-*Godfather* Al Pacino as Jason, the older of the film's two Staebler brothers. Bruce Dern was to play David, the younger, more introverted brother—a character Jack called a "one-roomer" because he lives by himself in a one-bedroom flat. "That's a very specific image, and one that relates to more people than we would care to think about," Jack said.

But whether by happenstance or design, Jack borrowed the script during a visit to Rafelson's, took it home, and got hooked. He spotted his role immediately. "Why can't I play the older brother?" he demanded.

"Well, 'cause that'd be too easy for you to do," said Rafelson, appealing to Jack's contrary sensibility. "If anything, I'd like you to play the younger brother. But I don't think that you'd be interested in doing it because I want a very, very constipated, reticent sense of the personality."

Playing against type at a time when audiences expected Bobby Dupea or Jonathan Fuerst had built-in Jack appeal. He became insistent. "You've *got* to let me do this," he pleaded.

Rafelson relented, and shortly thereafter, the BBS troupe arrived in Atlantic City, the trek taking on the trappings of Jack's homecoming. Neptune was just an hour's drive north on Highway 9, and Jack made a point of taking Michelle with him to a Friday night football game at Manasquan High, showing her off to friends and former classmates. Soon enough, triumph faded and the hometown conquering hero ran afoul of the wrath of his homecoming queen.

While Jack was happy to bunk with Bob and the boys at the Howard Johnson's closest to the next day's location, Michelle demanded upscale quarters more befitting a movie star and his pop diva. She hired a real estate firm to find a beachfront manse, but the

Jersey lad from blue-collar Neptune preferred Ping-Pong marathons, playing the "dozens," and watching sports on TV with his buds back at the motel. When Jack objected to the seaside digs, Michelle berated him as a stupid Irish Mick, packed up, and returned to L.A. Almost immediately, groupies began to materialize, even though the character Jack portrayed was no chick magnet.

The opening shot in *The Philosopher King* is a drab, bespectacled Jack delivering a deadpan elegy in the tradition of the radio monologists Jean Shepherd or Garrison Keillor, who tap deep into subterranean homesick memory. Such performers hit their narrative stride somewhere in the mid-1940s, when Chubs Nicholson was still imagining himself as Jack Armstrong. As the storytelling host of Philadelphia's fictional *Etcetera* radio hour, David Staebler strikes a similar dream-weaving chord. David laments in one of the screenwriter Jacob Brackman's somber soliloquies:

> No one reads anymore. I've been deprived my literary right and I crave an audience. The form of the tragic autobiography is dead or will be soon, along with most of its authors. Goodbye, written word. So I have chosen this form—radio—to author my life. Not because my life is particularly worthy but because it is hopefully, comically unworthy.

When David gets a frantic call from his high-flying brother to bail him out of jail, the fraternal contrast becomes obvious and immediate. Anal and anxiety-ridden, Jack's character catches the next train to Atlantic City. For the first and last time in their four screen appearances together, Bruce Dern gets to play the wisecracking, wild-eyed older brother, and still Jack upstages him.

"Jack can play the bad guy, but you still like him," observed Martin Cohen, who wrote their previous matchup in *Rebel Rousers*. "Bruce tries to do the same thing and the audience doesn't like him."

Dern said that Jack's only weakness as an actor was that he often faked it until after eleven in the morning. He showed up bleary-eyed on the set, his hair exploding across his skull like stiff meringue. He took catnaps during the day to make up for tomcatting at night.[22] "I beg for the late call," Jack said.

The film critic David Thomson compared the bond between the fictional Staebler brothers to "the perfect embodiment of the American manic depressive in pursuit of happiness." Happiness in *The Philosopher King* is represented by a pie-in-the-sky casino resort. Dern seduces his brother into believing they can build their dream on their own Hawaiian islet just off the coast of Oahu. The deal is always just around the corner, "97 percent" complete; all they have to do is convince jaded Japanese investors and a crusty mob boss (Scatman Crothers) to pony up the capital.

As added inducement for Jack's character to hang in on the deal with Dern's character, Dern pimps Jack his mistress (Ellen Burstyn) and her tap-dancing slut-in-training stepdaughter (Julia Robinson).[23] While David Staebler never takes his brother up on his carnal offer, Jack radiates a constricted, sex-starved melancholy that he exposed in none of his other screen appearances before or since. "In my opinion, everything he is credited for in *About Schmidt* [2002] he did earlier and better in *The King of Marvin Gardens*," said Burstyn.

Burstyn was a Hollywood rarity: a nearly middle-aged actress who could still find work. She was up for a Best Supporting Actress Oscar as Cybill Shepherd's loosey-goosey MILF in *The Last Picture Show* (1971) and had already read for Rafelson in auditioning for Rayette in *Five Easy Pieces*.[24] When Burstyn celebrated her thirty-ninth birthday just a week into production of *The Philosopher King*, Rafelson ordered her up to his hotel room where he, Jack, and Dern—all several years her junior—serenaded her in the buff with "Happy Birthday."

As Sally, Dern's aging beauty queen, Burstyn demonstrated what can happen when a used-up woman stretches her plastic smile beyond its limits. At the time, she was in the final throes of an abusive marriage to the drug-addicted actor Neil Burstyn, which added to her onscreen volatility.[25] With one scene in particular, when she menaces her stepdaughter with a pair of scissors, "she went completely bananas," Rafelson recalled, and Jack had to help talk her down. At the end of the day's shoot, Rafelson led the applause, announcing, "This woman has just put in the most remarkable day's work I've ever seen."

"What really happened to those actors during the course of those scenes: they all went nuts," Rafelson continued. "They got so involved in playing these parts that there was murder and mayhem lingering at every moment of every day on that movie. I mean it: I'm not even approximating how horrifying it was. One reason why I don't like to see the movies that I make is that I don't want to review the anguish. It's there for other people to see. I don't want to see it."

Unlike *Five Easy Pieces*, where Jack urged everyone to give up grass for the duration, most of the cast and the crew stayed loaded much of the time. Echoing Burstyn's onscreen butchering of her own hair, Julia Robinson came to the set bald one day except for a single long strand at the back of her head, and she had to be written out of the rest of the film. Dern, the one cast member who never took drugs, lost his mother to cancer during the shoot, which triggered Rafelson's cruel streak as the actor complained about redoing scenes. "We've got all day," he taunted, playing an older, meaner version of the "dozens." "You've got nothing else to do. Your mom's dead."

"Yeah, that's clever," said Dern. "What do you got for Jack?"

"Well, he don't have a mom," said Rafelson.

"Oh, yeah, that's cute," said Jack.

Marking a new high in altered states, quaaludes became the featured drug during the wrap party that followed the end of principal photography.

When *The Philosopher King* opened ten months later in L.A. as *The King of Marvin Gardens*, audience reception was tepid. The producer Julia Phillips (*The Sting*, *Close Encounters of the Third Kind*), who had been invited to an early screening, told Bert Schneider, "Ooooh, I didn't like it."

"I don't care," said Schneider. "I love this movie."

Schneider was in the minority. Jack concluded that boomer audiences simply found *The King of Marvin Gardens* too challenging. It flopped at the box office, but over time, critics who had judged it harshly had second thoughts—Julia Phillips among them. Jack's performance in particular is still singled out as one of his best. "I didn't appreciate *The King of Marvin Gardens* 'til much later," Phillips said. "Like Mark Twain and my mother."

As its partners lost interest in the biz of showbiz and BBS did its fast fade, stars and directors followed the maverick company's lead by taking filmmaking into their own hands. With encouragement from Robert Evans's Paramount, Peter Bogdanovich, William Friedkin, and Francis Ford Coppola formed Directors Company during the summer of 1972. That same summer, Dustin Hoffman joined Sidney Poitier, Barbra Streisand, Steve McQueen, and Paul Newman in First

Artists, which had been modeled on United Artists as an independent venture for financing and releasing films outside the rusting studio apparatus.[26]

Indeed, panicky studio chieftains had met with President Richard Nixon the previous year to warn that Hollywood was "close to collapse." Box office attendance continued to slide, while filmmaking costs crept higher.[27] Nixon offered no tax relief until the former SAG president Ronald Reagan, then the California governor, intervened. By 1972, Nixon signed into law a generous investment tax credit designed to encourage filmmakers to shoot inside the United States rather than go abroad. Movies once again became attractive to Wall Street.

Still blinded by sixties idealism, Jack and friends never saw the symbiotic link between Hollywood and Washington, even if their agents, studios, and business managers did. Thus, when Warren Beatty spearheaded "Four for McGovern," most people didn't understand the irony of picking Tax Day, April 15, 1972, to stage the $100-a-seat fund-raiser to aid Nixon's chief Democratic opponent. Beatty was joined onstage by Carole King, James Taylor, Quincy Jones, and Barbra Streisand, and his gala sold out in eighteen hours. Hollywood's young and affluent filled the sixteen thousand seats of the Lakers' Forum, spilling out into the parking lot and raising more than $300,000 for the senator from South Dakota. To add to the evening's cachet, the celebrity ushers included Carly Simon, Gene Hackman, Julie Christie, Sally Kellerman, and, of course, Jack. "Most of our political involvement is very superficial, including my own," he said. "It is no crime to support the best man."

Just five days earlier, during the 1972 Oscar telecast, Jack wore a McGovern button on his shirt as he presented the Best Picture award to the producers of *The French Connection*.[28] Remaining apolitical at the podium, he joked that Gene Hackman's famous Popeye Doyle chase scene "sounded like I was on my way home."

But McGovern's humiliating defeat in November ended Jack's activism. Bitterly reflecting on the Nixon landslide, he revealed a creeping cynicism about government: Kennedy first betrayed him with the Bay of Pigs, the Cuban missile crisis, and a stepped-up cold war; LBJ perpetuated the tragic fiasco in Vietnam; the year of the Kennedy and King assassinations led to the Chicago police riots and climaxed with Nixon's election; and all of it was followed four years later by McGovern's catastrophic "Children's Crusade."

Jack stopped just short of rejecting Democratic politics altogether. In a stoic understatement proclaiming his resignation from partisan politics, he announced, "I don't look for a superman—a sort of Che Guevara/Ralph Nader to appear on the horizon."

In the summer of 1972, Jack committed to *Three-Cornered Circle*, the director Hal Ashby's remake of *The Postman Always Rings Twice*. Recognizing the couple's often fiery real-life relationship as both an added dimension and a box-office draw, Ashby cast Michelle Phillips as Lana Turner to Jack's John Garfield. But two weeks before cameras rolled, the MGM production chief James Aubrey pulled the plug. He nixed Michelle as just another ex–rock star, and both Jack and Ashby refused to do the film without her.[29]

Michelle reacted to her firing by loading Chynna and her nanny, Rosa, into the car and driving to Mexico, "like a madwoman, all by myself, driving and crying." After a few weeks she returned to L.A., composed and determined to overcome the pop music stigma. She joined the cast of *Dillinger* (1973), relying on the kindness of Jack's friends to assuage Aubrey's injury.[30]

Meanwhile, Ashby quit MGM and moved over to Columbia, where Jack signed on for his next project. Based on Daryl Ponicsan's profane novel, *The Last Detail* (1973) told the story of two shore patrolmen escorting an unjustly convicted sailor from Norfolk, Virginia, to the naval prison in Portsmouth, New Hampshire. "Not exactly a recruiting film," said Jack. Indeed, the script was so scabrous that the U.S. Navy, which routinely opened its arms to Hollywood, disavowed the entire production. The naval vessels and shipyard exteriors had to be shot in Canada, but a Pentagon rebuff made *The Last Detail* appeal all the more to Jack.

He'd read the novel hot off the presses while on location for *Five Easy Pieces*. A girlfriend had slipped him the galleys, and even Jack had to marvel at Ponicsan's frequent and ingenious variations on the word *fuck*. As Jack sang *The Last Detail*'s praises, Columbia was already securing film rights. For $100,000 and a profit percentage, the studio's vice president for creative affairs, Gerald Ayres, bought it from Ponicsan in February 1970. Six months later, Ayres hired Robert Towne to adapt it for the screen.

In the years since Corey's classes, Towne's career path had diverged from Jack's. He still acted, but he gravitated toward writing.

Like Carole Eastman, he opted for his own IBM Selectric over memorizing other writers' lines.

In addition to his first credited AIP film, *Last Woman on Earth* (1960),[31] Towne wrote for early sixties TV (*The Outer Limits*, *Breaking Point*, *The Man from U.N.C.L.E.*), adapted *The Tomb of Ligeia* (1965) for Corman, and tried his hand at a Western, *The Long Ride Home*. Rewritten and produced as *A Time for Killing* (1967), the finished film bore little resemblance to Towne's screenplay, but his version fell into the hands of the actor Warren Beatty, then producing and starring in an Arthur Penn gangster flick, and Towne got a screenwriter's equivalent of Jack's *Easy Rider* break.

It was Towne's uncredited work on *Bonnie and Clyde* (1967) that won over Beatty and cemented Towne's reputation as Hollywood's best-known script doctor.[32] Salting the dialogue with taut one-liners and double entendres, Towne fueled the famous tag line ("They're young . . . they're in love . . . and they kill people") and transformed David Newman and Robert Benton's typical gangster screenplay, originally written for François Truffaut, into a quirky, classic character study. Towne performed similar surgery on Sam Peckinpah's script for *Villa Rides* (1968), Kris Kristofferson's debut in *Cisco Pike* (1972), and the first adaptation of a Joseph Wambaugh best seller, *The New Centurions* (1972).

Before his last acting job, in *Drive, He Said*, Towne had massaged his reputation as a fix-it wizard into a tidy living. By advertising his script-tweaking on *The Godfather* (1972), he raised his profile to a new high in a business that is notorious for denigrating screenwriters.[33]

Towne even found the temerity to tell Paramount's Robert Evans that he was not interested in *The Great Gatsby* (1974).[34] He turned down $175,000 to tailor the role of Daisy Buchanan to Evans's wife, Ali McGraw,[35] because he wanted to concentrate on a spec script he'd been writing for Jack—a sort of Sam Spade detective yarn that he and Jack had first talked about one night while on location during *Drive, He Said*. It was about water, murder, civic corruption, and incestuous noir intrigue in Depression-era Los Angeles, and Jack was keen to get Mike Nichols to direct. Evans was intrigued enough to offer $25,000 for a first-look deal to subsidize Towne's first draft.[36]

But, meanwhile, *The Last Detail* came along, and the raw material of the novel had been too rich and too lurid for Towne to resist. He postponed his spec script and began to juggle expletives for Ayres and Ashby.

It would take more than two years for the fast-moving shifts in film standards to catch up with the taboos Towne scattered throughout his screenplay. One critic grossly exaggerated his estimate of 342 "fuck"s in the first seven minutes alone.[37] Columbia held up the film's release for six months, trying to figure a way to tone down the dialogue and avoid an X rating,[38] but during that time the MPAA itself relaxed its rules, and most of Towne's original vulgarity remained intact.

Ashby, the quirky, mild-mannered director of the sleeper cult film *Harold and Maude* (1971), dismissed the Columbia executives' hand-wringing and used his newly earned clout as an Oscar winner to put *The Last Detail* into production. He saw it as his main chance to climb the final rung to Hollywood's A-list.

Starting out at the showbiz bottom in the mid-fifties, Ashby had been toiling in the vineyards just as long as Jack. He was an assistant film editor at MGM while Jack was still delivering mail for the cartoon division. Ashby's first film as a full-fledged editor didn't happen until Tony Richardson's deadly L.A. satire *The Loved One* (1965). That got Ashby noticed by the director Norman Jewison, who used him on *The Cincinnati Kid* (1965) and *The Russians Are Coming, the Russians Are Coming* (1966). Jewison next asked Ashby to edit *In the Heat of the Night* (1967), which won him an Oscar and his first shot at directing.

But neither *The Landlord* (1970) nor *Harold and Maude* were instant box-office hits. Still, critics praised both films and raised Ashby up a notch in the eyes of studio suits. Unlike the low-budget rebels at BBS, Ashby was moving into the moneyed mainstream, and Jack aimed to go with him. "I figured I'd ride him and take all the credit," Jack said, tongue planted in cheek.

As big a doobie booster as Jack, Ashby was also a vegetarian, a recluse, and an ex-Utah "Jack Mormon" with a try-anything-once attitude. Both men shared an up-by-the-bootstraps backstory, tarnished by a missing father. At fourteen, Ashby lost his father to suicide.[39] He never finished high school and married and divorced before he turned nineteen. Once he'd immigrated to Hollywood, he began to collect art, books, and record albums in order to steep himself in the literature and culture he'd missed growing up, just as Jack had done.[40] "He was deeply frightened, deeply agoraphobic, and deeply panic-ridden most of the time," recalled Ayres, who'd quit his job at Columbia to produce *The Last Detail*.

Ashby's paranoia was not unfounded. Canadian authorities busted him for marijuana possession during *The Last Detail*'s preproduction in Toronto. But once he was back on weed and in the director's chair, Ashby's laid-back style contrasted noticeably with Mike Nichols's stagy orchestration, Henry Jaglom's erratic improvisation, and Bob Rafelson's obsessive-compulsive drive. In lieu of using his power to call "Cut!" or play one actor against another, Ashby called for a wide shot and let his well-rehearsed cast wander in and out of the frame. Before stepping in front of the camera, Jack often borrowed Ashby's viewfinder to choreograph his own performances. "I like the fact that he shot the script," said Ayres. "There are very few moments of improvisation in there. How many directors do that?"

In *The Last Detail*, the two shore patrolmen[41] (Otis Young and Jack) take pity on their naive young prisoner (Randy Quaid), and during the weeklong trek to Portsmouth, Jack's Billy "Badass" Buddusky gives Quaid's timid convict a taste of the world he's going to miss behind bars: brawling, whoring, drinking, and generally whooping it up all the way along the Eastern seaboard. Principal photography began in November 1972 and lasted through the end of January, taking Ashby's cast and crew from Toronto and Norfolk to Washington, D.C., and Boston.

At five-foot-ten and 164 pounds, Jack looked like a leprechaun next to his NBA-size costars. Quaid stood six-foot-four and Young six-foot-two,[42] but like the pipsqueak manager of the Manasquan High basketball team, Jack used mouth and manner to overcome his shortcomings. Towne's outrageous dialogue helped. "I felt that was a breakthrough for me in terms of how much immediate behavior I could get into a character, how free it could be, how wild it was being," said Jack. "And yet it was coming from the text, not improvising."

This was not entirely true. "It was his idea to put the two little bird tattoos on his chest," said Ayres.

It was also Jack's idea to model his behavior after his nephew. Murray Hawley Jr. had spent six years in the navy, raising hell, playing the guitar, and literally spending money like a drunken sailor until he mustered out over disciplinary problems in 1970. Assigned to submarine duty out of New York in the navy's nuclear-powered fleet, Murray bore a strong resemblance to Jack, down to a shyer version of the killer grin and the pensive wrinkles across the brow of his high forehead.

"He [Murray] stole from Jack," said John Herman Shaner, and Jack was loath to forgive. More than once, Jack had to bail Murray out of a jam—a fact of life to which Jack had also grown accustomed with Murray's hell-raising sister, Pamela.

But Murray wasn't Jack's only muse. He had friends and other relatives who had been in the service. When prepping for a role, Jack became a sponge, grabbing motivation and mannerisms from every possible source. "I got an idea for playing *The Last Detail* when I met a guy on a flight home from Vietnam," he recalled. "He was a Chicano paratrooper. So I naturally asked him a few things about what he was doing, and he really summed it all up when he said, 'Listen, I'm a member of the warrior caste.'"

A sailor who performed his professional duty regardless of personal feelings embodied the oxymoron that was, and still is, "military justice." "That's what Buddusky is in the film," said Jack.

Off camera, Jack relaxed with Ashby by passing a joint, although much of *The Last Detail* was shot under a more liquid influence. In one scene that called for beer cans strewn around a room, the actors obliged by emptying the six-packs of Schlitz themselves. In another scene, Ashby wanted his trio blotto on the steps of the Supreme Court building. Chief Justice Warren Burger himself vetoed that plan, so they took their inebriation elsewhere. In still another scene, Jack got a buzz on, dropped his drawers, and mooned a passing commuter train.

"You know what I really like about this uniform?" he told the actress Nancy Allen, who had a brief cameo as a hippie. "I like the way it makes your dick look." And apparently so did the women who gathered around him.

Michelle left Jack the same month that he finished *The Last Detail*. "He was trying hard to keep her, but I could see it wasn't going to work," Towne recalled.

"Men don't leave," Jack philosophized. "Women leave, and when they end the relationship the other guy is already there. They always know where they are going."

The ex-Mama remained mum about the straw that broke their union's back. According to Jack, she was "a real stand-up lady, incapable of anything dishonorable." But with Mimi and now Michelle, his closest friends saw a trend. "These [relationships] were very strong and filled with huge emotional ups and downs, every one of them falling into an identical pattern," said Don Devlin. "Jack is such an overwhelming character that girls were always madly in love with him. Then he starts to behave fairly badly, then he starts to lose the girl, then he goes chasing after her again, then the relationship changes—the girl usually gets the upper hand in the relationship. Then he becomes like a little boy."

To one acquaintance, Jack summed up his regret at Michelle's exit in one sorry sentence: "She's the only one who makes my wee-wee hard."

Jack equated the eternal war between the sexes to a game in which women, unlike men, do not play fair. Women—at least the primo variety he preferred—struck him as far more duplicitous than any of his male friends were. His uncle Shorty Smith put things more succinctly: "I think Jack hates women."

Michelle moved on. She appeared on *The Dating Game* and won a trip to the Orient with a guy named Darryl. She also wound up briefly with Christian Marquand. According to Britt Eklund, Michelle took up with Lou Adler, which broke up Eklund's own long-standing live-in arrangement with the father of Jack's godson. Two years and a couple of TV-movie roles later, Michelle was living with Warren Beatty, who complained that newspaper gossips tried to browbeat the couple into marrying.[43] After she'd run through Hopper, Jack, and Beatty, reporters began referring to her as a femme fatale. "I rather like that," Michelle said. "It's an extremely romantic image. I'm not a gadfly, though. I just found myself involved with a couple of notorious men and assumptions are made."

Jack invested his grief in night life. When he did grow into his nickname, "the Great Seducer," it was at an age far older than most fans realized, and he lived up to it with a vengeance. The mid-seventies ushered in disco: Haight-Ashbury was again a slum, Timothy Leary had gone to prison, and psychedelics were passé. The only pill extant among the young and trendy was the Pill. Cocaine replaced cannabis as the drug of choice, and *Deep Throat* (1972) banished whatever social taboo remained over fellatio.[44] Both blow and blowjobs had gone mainstream. The Me Decade was in full swing, and so was Jack.

Lou Adler made Jack a regular at the VIP room On the Rox above Adler's trendy Roxy nightclub on Sunset Boulevard.[45] Following a revealing Q&A he gave *Playboy* magazine in 1972, Jack began to accept invitations to the publisher's new Holmby Hills headquarters to graze on Hef's Playmates. Echoing Willie Sutton's famous syllogism concerning banks and money, Hugh Hefner concluded, "They all came by because the chicks were here."

During his frequent visits to New York, Jack cashed in on his celebrity to score at au courant East Side clubs like Regine's[46] or, later in the decade, at the West Side's legendary Studio 54. He cultivated friendships among the artsy effete, including the ex–*Vogue* editor Diana Vreeland, the hairstylist turned fashion photographer Ara Gallant,[47] and the pop-art twit Andy Warhol, who had devolved into the Samson DeBrier of Manhattan.

With parodies of tedious home movies like *Haircut* (1963),[48] *Blowjob* (1963),[49] and *Empire* (1964),[50] Warhol had already made a dubious reputation on the college circuit and was well known during the sixties among art-house regulars, including Jack. In addition to the radical chic and the terminally hip, Warhol gathered about him an East Coast entourage of junkies, transvestites, and Gotham "puries," as a younger Jack might have called them: freaks like Warhol himself, who dabbled in film, porn, drugs, and music, as well as in Warhol's unique brand of assembly-line art.

But for Jack, the studio at 33 Union Square West, which Warhol called The Factory, was also a great place to meet "skunks," especially aspiring cover girls.[51] "Moe-dells," Jack liked to call them, arching the famous brows. These tall, willowy, and delectable creatures were never women; they were always girls, as in: "Those girls must be moe-dells."

"They've become a glorified version of what ladies imagine themselves to look like in their fantasy," said Jack's pal Ara Gallant. "And they set a kind of standard. Without models, women in general would have no guideline with which to identify. So they've become icons, the modern icons."

One such fashion model had dual allure to Jack. Not only was the green-eyed beauty young and gorgeous, but Anjelica Huston also carried a strong Hollywood pedigree. Besides marching the runway for Halston and gracing the pages of *Vogue* and *Harper's Bazaar* before she was old enough to buy a cocktail, Anjelica was also the impressionable, coltish granddaughter of the actor Walter Huston and the daughter of the celebrated director John Huston. Jack preferred to introduce her as the "great, great, great-granddaughter of Sam Houston."

"When I was working in New York, it was very difficult to meet real men," Anjelica recalled for Warhol's *Interview* magazine after she'd hooked up with Jack. "It's so easy to become a fag hag if you're a successful model." Jack, on the other hand, was "very definitely a real man, one who gets your blood going," she said.

What would grow into a seventeen-year on-again, off-again relationship began after Jack's breakup with Michelle. Three inches taller than Jack and fourteen years his junior, Anjelica joined her stepmother (John Huston's fifth and final wife, Celeste "Cici" Shane) in an invitation to one of Jack's Mulholland soirees and immediately developed a case of the hots. She confided her lust to her stepmother, who passed the word. Jack was there instantly, impaling her with his smile. "I was mortified, but obviously Jack didn't get put off," Angelica said.

A short time later, she flew back to New York to break it off with her photographer boyfriend Bob Richardson, then lit out West for Jack's place. "It was hard at first," she recalled. "Jack has a lot of friends. I didn't really know anyone. Even though my father is associated with Hollywood, I spent most of my early life in Ireland and England in schools. And then I lived in New York. But Jack sensed it and helped me through this period."

Jack also eased the transition for Angelica by giving her a Mercedes for her twenty-third birthday.

In June 1973, Jack flew to London to start Antonioni's *The Passenger* (1975). Anjelica, whom he'd nicknamed "the Moan" because of her steady stream of Eeyore-style self-criticism, took a modeling job so she could accompany him as far as Europe. He flew on to the Sahara without her.

Originally titled *Final Exit*,[52] and then *Occupation: Reporter*, the bleak tale of a journalist who switches identities with a dead arms trafficker was shot on location in Munich, London, Barcelona, and Almeria on the Spanish coast, but it began in Northern Africa. "I've never been that far from civilization, before or since," Jack told the *L.A. Times*'s Patrick Goldstein more than thirty years later. "We lived in thatched huts out in an oasis in the middle of the Sahara desert. It wasn't unusual to have these huge sandstorms where everything would be covered with this fine pink sand. I can still see Michelangelo walking in the sand, with the wind blowing, picking out shots that he wanted to get."

One was an actual execution that remained in the finished film: an African prisoner dispatched by a three-man firing squad.[53] While easily *The Passenger's* most dramatic fuzzing of fantasy and reality, the killing of the prisoner represented just one of many trips through Antonioni's looking-glass imagination into a "tapestry of ambiguity," according to Jack.

"The Italian crew was serious about eating, so we'd have good food every night, get high, and look up at the sky," Jack recalled. "The first night felt very eerie, because it was so quiet. I didn't know it at the time, but it was the most vivid filmmaking adventure I've ever had."

A maverick who was often misidentified as part of the early sixties nouvelle vague sweep over Europe, Antonioni made his first documentary short during World War II while Mussolini was still in power. He'd been producing films for twenty years before *L'Avventura* (1961) introduced him to U.S. art-house audiences. In 1966, MGM expanded Antonioni's American reach by distributing *Blow-Up* (1966), his first English language feature and a cause célèbre in the United States for its subliminal glimpse of a pair of naked groupies— the first instance of full-frontal female nudity shown in general release. "It now seems that the reason for the success of *Blow-Up* was that it included the first beaver shot in a conventional theater," said Jack. "It's a success such as Antonioni had never had before and hasn't had since."

In the tradition of *Detour* (1945) and other film noir classics of mistaken identity, *The Passenger* became "Antonioni's *North by Northwest*," according to the Nicholson biographer Derek Sylvester, although without Hitchcock's touch of whimsy. "I used to be someone else, but I traded him in," says the journalist David Locke, after swapping passports with the dead arms dealer.

Antoni-"ennui," as his detractors called him, had a great eye but often downplayed or ignored the niceties of story altogether. He tended to linger on landscapes, larding his extended travelogues with all the belly laughs of a vivisection. The somber Italian director treated actors as if they were furniture.[54] "Acting is not the most important thing to me, so don't get upset if you're not the center of attention," he forewarned Jack. "Actors are like cows.[55] You have to lead them through a fence."

If Jack took offense at being compared to an ungulate, he didn't show it. He was delighted to be eating like Tony Soprano and learning film direction at the knee of a master. His understated performance is still numbered among his best. Yet while the role of David Locke was "pure pleasure," Jack admitted that "working with Antonioni has its ups and downs. He never said much in terms of giving direction. He had his images picked out and he really didn't want his actors interfering with his visual tone poems."

Famous for her ample bosom and anal sex with Marlon Brando in *Last Tango in Paris* (1972), the diminutive, dewy-eyed Maria Schneider seemed listless to Jack, like a weathergirl on Valium reading her lines from a teleprompter. Cast simply as "the Girl" who pairs up with Jack through the second half of the movie, she feared being typecast "as the sexy broad with butter up her ass," he said. Jack maintained that Schneider stayed anesthetized through much of the production.

"There she was, having a discussion one night with this very ascetic director, and she was loaded and half nude, with her bathrobe open," Jack recalled. "I thought Michelangelo was going to die. I remember in one scene we did, she was so unconscious that I had to hold the back of her head up when I delivered my lines."

If *The Passenger* tries to make a point, it's summed up in an exchange between Jack's David Locke and the Girl after their last tryst at the Hotel de la Gloria overlooking Spain's stark, whitewashed Mediterranean coast. While assassins catch up with Locke, he sips port and surrenders to circumstances he believes he can't control. He babbles about a blind man he once met whose sight was restored when he was forty. At first, the man is dazzled by the sheer beauty of his vision, but he grows disenchanted, then bored, then desperate. "After three years, he killed himself," says Locke.

Jack wrapped *The Passenger* by September and flew directly to L.A. the same day, arriving at six in the morning. Two hours later, he reported to wardrobe at Western Costume near Paramount Studios to be fitted for another noir film he'd promised to make with his two favorite Roberts: Evans and Towne. With another European director at the helm, the movie was to be an epic exposé of the seedy origins of L.A. itself—the film Evans had commissioned Towne to write nearly two years earlier and for which Jack had loaned him an additional $10,000 to finish.

He called it *Chinatown*.

10

C HINATOWN'S JAKE GITTES PROCLAIMS, "IT LOOKS LIKE half the city is trying to cover it all up, which is fine with me. But Mrs. Mulwray—I goddamn near lost my nose. And I like it. I like breathing through it. And I still think you're hiding something."

Before the evil imp Roman Polanski snapped open a switchblade[1] to slit Jack's nose; before the gumshoe J. J. Gittes or the mysterious widow Evelyn Mulwray or her vile land baron father Noah Cross entered the pantheon of American film archetypes; before Robert Towne ever touched a typewriter key, he lifted the backstory for *Chinatown* from the author Carey McWilliams.

The historian who developed a love-hate relationship with Southern California early in the twentieth century was not the first to write about the creation of modern Los Angeles, but McWilliams was the best and the best known. In 1946, before moving to New York to edit the *Nation* magazine, McWilliams published *Southern California Country: An Island on the Land*, which spilled the sordid details of the infamous fin de siècle Owens Valley water grab in which wealthy L.A. real estate speculators stole a river from ranches in the Sierra foothills to irrigate future subdivisions in the arid San Fernando Valley.

Backed by the chamber of commerce and the publishers of the *Los Angeles Times*, the chief city engineer William Mulholland[2] built a 233-mile-long aqueduct that carried mountain water to the L.A. city limits—the first of several artificial rivers that would transform the western edge of the vast Mojave Desert into the nation's second-largest metropolis. During the waterway's dedication in 1913, Mulholland famously proclaimed, "There it is. Take it." Meanwhile, the lush Owens Valley shriveled to sand.

Towne updated his version of the manmade disaster to 1937,[3] the year of Jack's birth, yet the ruthless history upon which both Los Angeles and *Chinatown* were built remained indistinguishable. He envisioned a script rich in multiple "plot densities" built into deceptively simple detective fiction.

"I figure I do a detective movie and do it about a real crime, which is fucking up land and water rather than stealing a jewel-encrusted falcon," said Towne. "*The Maltese Falcon* is one of my favorite stories. It's about greed and something else, and so's *Chinatown*. But *Chinatown* is about greed and its consequences, not just in the present, but to the future. The land is raped as surely as the daughter, and these things have far-reaching consequences."

In addition to studying acknowledged masters of the hardboiled mystery genre like Dashiell Hammett and Raymond Chandler,[4] Towne was advised by fellow screenwriter Elaine May[5] to prep for his undertaking by dissecting the plots of Agatha Christie, whose murder mysteries were carefully orchestrated riddles. Towne hired a former Pomona College classmate and English major, Edward Taylor, to help him structure his jigsaw plot. With its clues hidden amid newspaper obituaries, obscure land records, and a sinister retirement home, Towne's storytelling paralleled the national mistrust of government during the Watergate era. If the long, rebellious real-life drama of the sixties needed a period at the end of its sentence, *Chinatown* could not have provided a better punctuation mark. In his own fit of Nixonian paranoia, Towne numbered each copy of each draft so that it could be traced if plagiarized or stolen.

Whether by chance or design, *Chinatown* struck note after eerie note that rang with the uneasy truths of Jack's own birth. The movie's central crime might be incest, but illegitimacy and a corrupt father figure lingered as shameful and central facets. And then there were the sexual politics that loomed, both offscreen and on. "One of the secrets of *Chinatown* is that there was a kind of triangular offstage situation," said Jack. "I had just started going with John Huston's daughter, which the world might not have been aware of, but it could actually feed the moment-to-moment reality of my scene with him— 'Are you sleeping with her?'"[6]

"There's an element of my father in Jack," Anjelica observed at the time, comparing her new lover to Huston. "I've never been attracted to weak men. They [Jack and Huston] are both generous, they're both honorable. The most attractive thing about Jack is his humor. And the fact that he's never boring. My father has never been boring either."

One of Hollywood's true renaissance men, with sweeping hedonistic appetites to match Jack's, John Huston relished the role of monster patriarch. The character's initials were the same as those of the all-powerful but low-key former *Los Angeles Times* publisher Norman Chandler,[7] but Towne insisted that he came up with the name for Huston's repellent Noah Cross after meeting Noah Dietrich, who had also been Peter Fonda's father-in-law. Like Huston's character, Howard Hughes's top lieutenant was a genial-looking septuagenarian whose reach had been as long and as pitiless as that of his Machiavellian boss. Noah Dietrich cared less about money than he did about power. Like Noah Cross, Hughes wanted to own the future, and Dietrich was his willing factotum.

In *Chinatown*, John Huston oozed similar decadence. But though he'd been a four-time nominee for Best Director and an Oscar winner for *The Treasure of the Sierra Madre* (1949), Huston would not direct Towne's epic. Neither would Jack's first choice, Mike Nichols. Looking for another hit as commercial as *Rosemary's Baby* (1968), Robert Evans hired Roman Polanski, and despite Polanski's cantankerous reputation as a sharp-tongued Napoleon,[8] Jack, too, was fine with him, "because the little bastard's a genius."

Despite (or perhaps because of) a tragic personal history dating back to growing up in the Krakow concentration camp of World War II and climaxing with the Manson Family murders of his wife and her friends, Polanski's obsession with violence, voyeurism, and humiliation always seemed to translate a unique, hypnotic nightmare quality to the screen. Restless and blunt, the diminutive director clashed with the pensive, procrastinating Towne, whose screenplay "suffered from an excessively convoluted plot that veered off in all directions," according to Polanski. They quarreled over details as small as Polanski's request to misspell a "No Trespassing" sign to read "No Trepassing"—an inside Polish joke. He insisted that Towne slash, prune, and revise, but after two months the script was still overpopulated with superfluous characters and excess verbiage. On Polanski's stopwatch, it timed out longer than *Lawrence of Arabia*.

As with *The Great Gatsby*, Robert Evans saw his wife, Ali McGraw, as *Chinatown*'s Evelyn Mulwray, but even before Towne's first draft came in at a staggering 180 pages,[9] Hollywood's latest golden couple had already split.

Towne had envisioned Jane Fonda as Mulwray, but her recent Oscar win for *Klute* (1971) boosted her ego, along with her demands. By the time Polanski got her to read *Chinatown*, Fonda had become a humorless new mother who found Jack's role too dominant; Mrs. Mulwray was not a large enough part for her to give up breastfeeding her baby.[10]

Evans remembered the high-octane talent agent Sue Mengers being the first to push for Faye Dunaway, demanding $250,000 and raising the stakes by insisting on an answer by the end of the business day "because Faye is considering a picture with Arthur Penn." Knowing full well that Dunaway's career had been slipping since *The Thomas Crown Affair* (1968), Evans countered "I'll give Faye $75,000." When Mengers balked, he said, "Okay, I'm going with Jane Fonda."

Mengers called back an hour later to accept, reportedly at a fee that Evans had lowered to $50,000.[11] Later, she admitted that there'd never been any Arthur Penn picture, and Evans confessed that Fonda had already passed on the part. "All this game playing," sighed Evans, the consummate Hollywood gamesman, "and Sue was my best friend."

There were no such games when Jack signed on to the $3.5 million picture at $500,000 and a net percentage. He'd been Jake Gittes[12] since Towne had conceived the jaded dandy. Bounced from the D.A.'s office, Gittes reinvents himself as a pricey private dick specializing in exposing adulterers in flagrante. Something had happened to ex-investigator J. J. Gittes while he was on the job in Chinatown, but all that is ever revealed to the audience is that his dark secret involved a woman, a wound, and a double cross—a frequent-enough occurrence in Jack's own personal life.

Jack had been every sort of antihero in his twenty years in Hollywood, but he'd never before played the smooth romantic lead. Given this opportunity, he attended to every detail of his character, demanding that the prop department print up official contracts for the J. J. Gittes Detective Agency, even though no one would ever see them on camera, and seeing to it that his shirts were monogrammed "JJG," above the pocket, even though he never removed his jacket. He patterned Gittes's snappy Depression-era wardrobe after the cock-o'-the-walk pinstriped costumes that John Nicholson Sr. once wore on the boardwalk during Bradley Beach's annual Easter Parade. It was not enough for Jack to know his lines; he *became* Jake Gittes. As the film opened and through the first quarter hour, Polanski kept the camera close over Jack's shoulder, making *Chinatown* Jake's story, "an idea Jack was not at first thrilled with," according to Richard Sylbert, "but it works."

After the first camera rolled, Polanski's need for speed ran up against Jack's deliberate speaking style. "Jack, can you do this faster?" Polanski asked.

"Roman, why?" said Jack. "Why are you telling me to do this faster? Give me a chance here."

"I'll tell you why. We've got a hundred-something-page screenplay here. It's a detective picture and we have to get all the facts in. If you talk at this pace, the movie will be three hours long."

But Polanski warred most with Jack's leading lady. Jack had a reputation for turning divisive camps on a set into a team effort, but mediating pitched battles between the abrupt, abrasive Polanski and the temperamental, histrionic Dunaway was a challenge. "She demonstrated certifiable proof of insanity," said Jack.

His favorite illustration of this was the parable of the hair. Evans had flown in Ara Gallant from New York to streak Dunaway's coiffure for the movie, and in the course of one of Polanski's more complicated lighting setups, an errant hair escaped. During a scene set inside the Brown Derby restaurant, Polanski tried to shoot past the loose strand in what would otherwise have been a perfect 1930s marcel: tight, blonde, and lacquered against her skull à la Jean Harlow. But the vagrant hair glowed like a stalk of wild wheat in the klieg lights and Polanski sidled up and plucked it from Dunaway's scalp. She shrieked like a rape victim. "Don't you dare *ever* do that sort of thing to me again!" Dunaway remembered howling before she raced back to her trailer in tears. Polanski remembered it as: "I just don't believe it! That motherfucker pulled my hair out!"

It took a summit meeting in Evans's Paramount office before Dunaway returned to work. Polanski fanned the incident in the press as a perfect example of American star hysterics, while Dunaway insisted the hair wasn't the point. "It was not the hair," she said. "It was the incessant cruelty that I felt, the constant sarcasm, the never-ending need to humiliate me."

According to the author Peter Biskind, Dunaway later exacted her revenge by tossing a cup of urine in Polanski's face. Whatever bile she felt for Polanski did not transfer to her leading man. Following his penchant for nicknames, Jack took to calling her "Dread," as in dreadlocks, but Dunaway chose to see boyish charm, not sarcasm.[13]

Jack had his own famous run-in with Polanski, but with a different outcome. Being Jake Gittes did not preclude being a Lakers fan, and Jack made a fast break to his trailer whenever there was down time on the set. If it had been Bob Rafelson directing, Jack would have left himself wide open to blackmail. "You want to see this basketball game tonight?" Rafelson used to tell him during *Five Easy Pieces* and *The King of Marvin Gardens*. "We're going to fuckin' stay here and shoot this thing, I don't care. I'll change the whole scene to nighttime, Jack, so you better do it."

But Polanski hadn't the patience or the guile, and he freaked over Jack's divided loyalties. He invaded the star's trailer during a Lakers-Knicks game that had gone into overtime and smashed Jack's TV to the floor.[14] "We were yelling, and we both stormed off the set," said Jack. "We weren't three blocks from the studio when I had to stop my car at a light. And I looked over and here's this fucking pixie looking over at me . . . smiling like a monkey."

Unlike Dunaway, who would loathe Polanski for the rest of her life, Jack leapt from his car, embraced his fellow maniac, and laughed it off. He would remain Polanski's long and loyal pal well into the next century, defending him at the nadir of his roller-coaster career, even while Polanski lived in exile.

In the end, Polanski's distaste for Dunaway found its violent way to the screen. Over Robert Towne's loud and angry objections, Polanski killed off Evelyn Mulwray at the conclusion of *Chinatown*. Towne wanted Noah Cross to die while Evelyn escaped to Mexico, but Robert Evans and the production designer Richard Sylbert sided with the director.[15]

"There would be, for Roman, no real justice," said Sylbert. Recalling the Tate-LaBianca murders, still fresh in Polanski's psyche, the director brought the curtain down with brutal existentialism. To save the damsel in distress and waste the bad guy was as predictably old school as TV melodrama or a Saturday afternoon matinee. "The girl died," said Sylbert. "He had lived it." Nevertheless, Towne held a grudge against what he termed "enduring disappointment over the literal and ghoulishly bleak climax."

Fifteen years later, after critics, educators, and film historians hailed *Chinatown* as one of the best detective yarns Hollywood ever produced, Towne still said, "I hated that movie—which is not something I've generally said—when I first saw it. But over a period of time I've come to see it's really an excellent movie, and Roman did a masterful job of directing it.

Ten years old and living with her mother, Sandra Knight, in Hawaii, Jennifer had come to recognize the true value of her bragging rights. As the daughter of Jack Nicholson, she'd already built up a sizable trust fund. Like many fathers of his generation, Jack vowed that she would have the opportunities denied him. When he could arrange it, Sundays were dad days. Jack defined personal terror as fear of losing her: "Once, when my daughter was an infant, I had her in the ocean and on my back, and a wave hit us," he said. "As I turned to grab her, I didn't have physical contact with her for less than two seconds, and that was the most petrifying two seconds in my life."

And yet, Jack remained "very tentative about infringing on Jenny's life. I want to be invited to enter her world, to be admitted gracefully."

The original sixties antihero experienced the generation gap first-hand when he asked if she'd ever heard "I Found a Million Dollar Baby in a Five-and-Ten-Cent Store." "What's a five-and-ten-cent store?" asked Jennifer.

Jack did not dote. His parenting skills fell somewhere between tough love and planned permissiveness. Once, after Quincy Jones's dog nipped Jennifer during a visit, Jack took his hysterical child into the bathroom and lectured past her sobs: "Well, Jennifer, these are the kinds of things in life we have to learn to get through."

For her part, Jennifer had to get used to her father being the center of attention—a position that she'd held back in Hawaii. She inherited "my sense of humor and my nose" from Jack, she said. Recalling her visit to the *Chinatown* set, she "remembered being so amazed as a child how beautiful [Faye Dunaway] looked," especially in her Depression-era Joan Crawford fashions. But the day Polanski filmed Gittes in bed with Mrs. Mulwray, Jennifer was barred from the set. "My dad said it was a kissing scene and I wasn't allowed to watch."

Jack waxed eloquent on the paradox of film and fatherhood. "One of the difficulties of being an artist is that you don't want to exclude your family from your life," he said, "but you don't want your family and your circumstances to intervene with your art."

At times, Jack's line separating reality from his celluloid life fuzzed or disappeared altogether. Like the party meister Samson DeBrier, who furnished his house with stolen movie props, Jack lifted straw chairs from the Mulwray mansion for his own house and installed Jake Gittes's liquor cabinet in his interior patio. His digital wristwatch was an artifact from *The Passenger*, and while it's doubtful that Jack had been tobacco-free for a decade, as he claimed, he did regress to a serious cigarette habit courtesy of David Locke.

Jake Gittes, too, was a smoker. Jack made a real effort to quit following *Chinatown*, getting down to two smokes a day before relapsing. By the following year, he was back up to two packs a day. Still the blue-collar kid from Jersey, he preferred Camels or Marlboros most of the time, but his tastes had also progressed to Cuban cigars now that he could afford them.

The reporter Aljean Harmetz visited Jack at his aerie following the filming of *Chinatown* and chronicled his evolving lifestyle for the *New York Times*.

He flicks his cigarette into a chrome ashtray, rising like a tulip on its thin chrome stem. All the things in the living room of his hilltop house—from the ashtray to the aluminum-and-smoked-glass Museum of Modern Art coffee table to the massive armchairs of rust and dark blue leather to the hot yellow and bright red Strombotne paintings on the walls—were chosen by Nicholson. Even the two pounds of candy in the heart-shaped box were carefully selected by Nicholson. Offering the box, he names each piece.

He had a $3,500 wall-sized TV installed in the den but professed not to watch it much. "I'm still holding out for a world in which people talk," he told *People* magazine.

"Jack has private lines and a private, private line for a few close friends," one of his old crowd told the writer Leo Janos. "The number of the private, private line is constantly being changed because everyone uses it to get through to Jack."

He had three telephone lines, dozens of phones, and a full-time assistant—the veteran character actor Herbert Marshall's daughter

Annie, whom Jack nicknamed "Staff." Her primary duty was to be nearby and bear witness to everything that transpired in Jack's life. "I hired someone whose job it is to watch me while I'm working and that being her job, she is, of course, paid very well," he said.

Despite a brief affair with John Phillips during the late sixties, Annie also remained one of Michelle's closest confidantes. The ex-girlfriend of the pop star Scott McKenzie, Annie pegged her new boss as an absent-minded pack rat. When the first Jack paperback biography was published, she had to call it to his attention. He stuffed every review of every film into a drawer, although she doubted that he read them all. "Jack has a penchant for misplacing items," Annie said. "He can lose seven wallets in the space of a year, and it drives him out of his mind when he can't locate something."

And Jack collected things. As a kid, it had been comics, baseball cards, and 45s. As an adult, his fancy turned to shoes, art, and pigs. "I adopted pigs when they become the symbol of evil," said Jack.

His contrarian interior design theme began with a stuffed melon-colored sow and her six suckling piglets lying on the leather living room couch. A needlepoint pillow depicting a pair of copulating hogs lay nearby. Acquaintances caught on and showered him with oink mementoes, from wood carvings to porcine porcelain.

In the realm of pig flesh, he still loved *carnitas*, but, as it turned out, Antonioni's gourmand film crew infected him with more than a renewed hankering for tobacco. He discovered that he liked fine food, as well as cigars and chocolate. The Italians traveled nowhere without a ready supply of extra-virgin olive oil, garlic, balsamic vinegar, and fresh semolina pasta. They temporarily converted Jersey Jack from tostadas to Tuscan cuisine. "I gain extra weight and I wonder if maybe this time I won't lose it again," he groused. "He can go only so many days without enchiladas," said the Beverly Hills dietitian Judy Mazel, who charged Jack and other celebs $500 an hour for her weight-control advice.

His frequent parties were still of the late-night weed and "make-your-own-taco" affairs, but cosmopolitan pals like Diana Vreeland and Bob Evans were educating him on how to entertain.[16] Evans gave Anjelica a lot of the credit. "He was a glittering vagrant, and she gave him the solid core he needed," Evans said. "Her breeding and culture have refined his life. The man is a diamond, and she's given him a beautiful setting."

Over time, the rough edges began to smooth. Jack's only rules were no crashers and no gossip-column items; violators weren't invited back.

He still parked his yellow VW in the carport, beneath the basketball hoop, but right next to it there now stood a new cocoa-brown Mercedes 600. "I couldn't keep putting people in the back of the Volkswagen," he reasoned.

When Jack ventured out in his new sedan, his Newfoundland retriever, Mr. Fabulous, rode in the backseat. When gawkers saw Jack in traffic, he'd roll down the window, grin his toothiest, and drawl, "Yes, it's Mr. Fabulous."

Jack made a practice of staying up late and getting up later—often after eleven in the morning. He referred to his five o'clock meal as "lunch." To stay fit, he worked out on Nautilus machines and swam each morning. "He swims like Esther Williams," observed Anjelica. In the evenings, he occasionally jogged three miles around the reservoir below his house. Jack warned his girlfriends that "jogging wrecks your tits," but for him the runner's high came as close to God as he cared to be. "I don't have any beliefs, and whatever instincts I've got I actively invest in not believing," he said. "The only praying that ever came naturally to me was during the few periods when I've run. I don't know why."[17]

Then he usually settled into the outdoor hot tub that he would soon replace with a huge fifteen-by-eight-foot black hot tub: "my original symbol of achievement, status, and luxury," which he built beside the swimming pool, between the house and the hillside.[18]

Late at night, when his usual coterie of friends had left, he often tangoed alone in the living room to Beethoven or Bach. Increasingly, he kept his own counsel. "Jack doesn't tip his hand very much," said Anjelica. "He's the kind of guy who walks out into the garden and throws rocks at low-flying planes."

Cats licked his face; dogs lay at his feet. In his distinctive velvet baritone, he could sometimes be heard warbling a mock lament by Randy Newman about having it all.

Just in time for Oscar consideration, *The Last Detail* opened the first week of December 1973—the same week the screen version of Daryl Ponicsan's third novel, *Cinderella Liberty* (1973), went into release.[19] If dueling sailor sagas from different studios and the same novelist were not problem enough, during the first preview of *The Last Detail* the projector failed and half the audience walked out.

Despite marketing gaffes, Columbia had a hit on its hands. As had become his practice, Jack was in for a percentage of the profits. Thus, following a brief vacation in Switzerland to spend New Year's with Polanski ("I've been working every day since last May, and I'm a little tired so I'm taking off and going skiing for a while"), he planned to hit the road with Anjelica to hype *The Last Detail*.

Polanski was now a good-enough friend that Jack let him stay in the Garfunkel Suite whenever he ventured to L.A. The director returned the favor by teaching Jack how to *wedel* on the slopes at Gstaad—a bullet technique that Jack translated to the ski runs he'd discovered the previous year in Aspen, Colorado. "He loves zooming downhill," said Polanski. "His style is like a guy who scratches his left ear with his right hand."

Jack and Anjelica returned to L.A., then stopped over in Vegas to see Frank Sinatra emerge from retirement before they flew on to New York, where they were an instant item in the gossip columns. Despite her own modeling notoriety, Anjelica remained shy and socially awkward and thus an easy foil for Jack. Like a pair of hormonal adolescents, he called her "Toots," a dame with "cla-a-a-sss," while she dubbed him "the Hot Pole." They were both Dylan fanatics, and Angelica became Jack's Joan Baez, down to her penchant for warbling plaintive French and Irish elegies while accompanying herself on a guitar.

Jack showed off his trophy girl during his press interviews for *The Last Detail* and then paraded her to ringside at the second Frazier-Ali heavyweight title bout, the front row of a Joni Mitchell concert, and the Madison Square Garden stop on Dylan's 1974 comeback tour. "There was a song at the Dylan concert—I think it was called 'Forever Young'—that started me wondering just how much anxiety I do feel about growing old," the thirty-seven-year-old actor told one interviewer. "I try to feel that it's just the actual meat that's getting older."

Jack began to obsess on the "dark circles under my eyes that may not go away. My hair is going away. Of course, if I weren't a maniac, I wouldn't be noticing these things. . . . Anyone who reaches a certain age senses a loss of his powers. I just did two movies back to back, and some days I was so tired that I knew I couldn't do what I was supposed to do. That never happened to me before. Oh, I went ahead and did the work, but not really. I guess we all have an anxiety about growing old, about being excluded. Thinking, 'Am I the wrong age now for this kind of behavior?'"

With Anjelica on his arm, Jack wore a red shirt beneath his tuxedo to the 1974 Oscars, where a tipsy John Huston served as one of the hosts.

Once again, Jack was nominated and once again, he lost—this time to Jack Lemmon for his portrayal of a mobbed-up garment manufacturer in *Save the Tiger* (1973). Lemmon made a point of searching for Jack backstage to shake his hand. Crossing palms with the original Ensign Pulver seemed a sign that Outlaw Jack was at last gaining acceptance among the Academy's old guard. A bit more of the chip fell from his shoulder. Afterward, he and Angelica attended the Governor's Ball, where he berated her father for appearing on the telecast "drunk in front of the whole nation."

Jack continued to promote *The Last Detail* at Cannes the following month by "introducing himself and making himself unforgettable, one person at a time," as Harry Gittes put it. Anjelica remembered getting straight-armed. "Young, nubile blondes would be introduced sort of offeringly to him," she said.

Jack tied the seventy-five-year-old Charles Boyer as the festival's Best Actor.[20] He stopped over in London on the return trip, where the director Ken Russell asked him to do a quick cameo as a singing psychiatrist in *Tommy* (1975). Christopher Lee had been cast in the film version of the Who's rock opera but was held up in Bangkok on *The Man with the Golden Gun* (1974). Russell next considered Peter Sellers, but when he heard Jack was in town, he offered Jack $75,000 for a couple days' work.

Jack later admitted that it was the first time he'd sold his services strictly for a paycheck since his pre–*Easy Rider* days, and it showed. He squandered his first opportunity to sing on camera since *On a Clear Day*, looking stiff and sounding hung over. *Tommy* was way overproduced at a cost of $13 million, and its sole cameo worth the price of admission was the electric Tina Turner as "the Acid Queen," certainly not codfish Jack as "the Specialist." Introducing the short-lived "quadraphonic sound" experience to its audience, *Tommy* premiered in New York the following March, grossing more than $96 million worldwide, although the film was considered a flash in the pan in the United States.

But Jack's career seemed to flourish, even while Hollywood floundered. Only 14 million Americans a week went to the movies in 1974, a new all-time low. Meanwhile, the IRS began to patch loopholes that had made cinema such a popular tax haven, drying up whatever capital there was left.

Hard times in showbiz mirrored malaise in middle America. OPEC spawned the first U.S. gas lines, inflation was out of control, and a diehard outfit left over from the sixties calling itself the Symbionese Liberation Army kidnapped the newspaper heiress Patty Hearst, laying claim to the headlines during much of the year.

In Washington, impeachment hearings got under way. By late summer, Richard Nixon would resign. Democrats appeared to be on the comeback, among them the former McGovern campaign manager Gary Hart, who had struck up friendships with Jack and Warren Beatty during the 1972 campaign. Hart called upon them to help him secure a Senate seat in Colorado and they obliged, although Jack had soured on politics. His pretensions became his soapbox. "I believe the real function of the artist is to undermine the institutions of the middle class," Jack preached. "Making movies is the thing I love above all else. I'm where I want to be."

No less a pundit than Orson Welles had Beatty pegged as ravenous for populist power. One day, Welles predicted, the actor might even preen his way to the presidency and drag Jack along with him. Because Jack's politics still smacked of a stealth revolution, Welles saw him in the role of a shadowy Harry Hopkins to Beatty's ebullient Franklin Roosevelt. What once seemed like another Hollywood pipe dream took on increased credibility, given the ex-actor and then California governor Ronald Reagan's recent success, not to mention rumblings of Reagan's own presidential ambitions.

Jack's politics opposed those of the Republican former actor, and yet, unwittingly and ironically, his next movie may have influenced Governor Reagan's successful shutdown of much of California's mental health system. "Michael Douglas talked to me early on about *One Flew over the Cuckoo's Nest* [1975]," said Anjelica. "I don't know if I was the instrumental factor in that, but I mentioned to Jack that Michael wanted to see him about it."

"Marlon Brando and Gene Hackman . . . both turned [the role] down," Douglas recalled. "We were also fascinated with Burt Reynolds.[21] Before Milos Forman got involved, I was talking to Hal Ashby about directing the film, and Hal was pushing Jack, the star of his film *The Last Detail*, which hadn't come out yet. At that point Jack had done passive characters in *Easy Rider* and *Five Easy Pieces*, but when I saw him as the flamboyant yet sensitive shore patrolman in *The Last Detail*, I knew he could play the part."

Jack was in such demand that Douglas had to stand in line. Hal Ashby wanted to reteam on *Bound for Glory* (1976). When Jack passed on portraying the folk legend Woody Guthrie, Ashby solicited Bob Dylan. The role went to David Carradine.

Bernardo Bertolucci had already tried to persuade Jack to star as Dashiell Hammett's Continental Op in Bertolucci's version of *Red Harvest*, while Tony Richardson wanted Jack for *The Bodyguard*, a jet-set murder mystery he cowrote with Sam Shepherd. One of Jack's oldest friends in the business, Richardson preached a mantra that Jack lived by: "Remember, in life it's the things that you don't do that you regret, not the things you do."[22]

Jack gave Richardson's project the nod but postponed after Douglas gave him Bo Goldman's adaptation of Ken Kesey's 1963 bestseller. Richardson drifted off to direct *Mahogany* (1975) for Berry Gordy,[23] and Bertolucci got caught up in his epic *1900* (1976). Thanks to *One Flew over the Cuckoo's Nest*, neither *Red Harvest*[24] nor *The Bodyguard* ever got beyond the script.

"Sometimes I get flooded and think, 'Jesus! If I do all this, I'll be working until I'm sixty-five,'" Jack said. "And at that age I'm pretty sure people won't be that interested in me. I don't know if *I'd* be interested."

In the tradition of Samuel Fuller's *Shock Corridor* (1963), *Cuckoo's Nest* featured a sane protagonist committed to a loony bin—a character Jack had wanted to take on since Kesey first published the novel.[25] "I tried to option *Cuckoo's Nest* as a twenty-six-year-old producer when it first came out in 1963," Jack told the film critic Gene Siskel.

But Kirk Douglas bought the rights for $47,000 while the book was still in galleys and staged it as a Broadway play featuring himself as McMurphy. Following a short run, Douglas could get no studio to turn it into a film.[26] For two years in the early seventies, Richard Rush made the rounds, trying to drum up interest in *Cuckoo's Nest* and Jack as a package, but nothing happened until Douglas turned over the film rights to his son Michael.

Michael Douglas took a leave as costar of ABC's cop drama *The Streets of San Francisco* to produce *Cuckoo's Nest*, settling on the Czech expatriate Milos Forman to direct.[27] But like his father, Douglas got the same thumbs-down from every studio he approached. Following the BBS guerrilla model of moviemaking, he opted to go outside the studio and shoot it on the cheap, Corman-style.

Douglas used the fast-fading tax advantages as a lure to investors, hooking up with a San Francisco jazz record producer who had made millions off the band Creedence Clearwater Revival. The combative Saul Zaentz had already used his capital once to underwrite *Payday* (1973), starring Rip Torn as a country-western scoundrel.[28] A taste of Hollywood readied Zaentz to join Douglas as co-producer if they could convince a star of Jack's caliber to join the package.

For $1 million and a piece of the gross, Jack was in. Once that deal was clinched, Douglas and Zaentz doubled the budget from $1.5 million to $3 million. As the package grew stronger, they got United Artists to commit to distribute, even though the studio had passed on producing.

As the *Cuckoo's Nest* process lumbered forward, *Chinatown* premiered at Hollywood's Chinese Theater on June 20, 1974. Jack was on hand to become the one-hundred-fifty-ninth star to put his foot and hand prints in wet cement in the theater's forecourt.[29] He came via limousine, his VW days now behind him.

But Jack couldn't go to movie openings or sit idle for another six months while Douglas and Zaentz pulled *Cuckoo's Nest* together, so three weeks after the *Chinatown* premiere, Jack began shooting *The Fortune* (1975).

Based on a real crime from the 1930s, *The Fortune* had taken Carole Eastman a year to write. She tailored her odd caper comedy to Beatty and Jack, and it would have clocked in at more than four hours of screen time if Mike Nichols hadn't pared it down.

"Jack and I shared a plane ride to Paris, and I was going on to Warsaw—don't ask me why," recalled Nichols. "I read the first half of the script sitting next to Jack and the second half sitting on my suitcase in the Warsaw airport, waiting to get through customs. Carole wrote it with the boys in mind and the boys brought it to me."

Fresh from shooting *Shampoo* (1975), Beatty joined Jack as the second half of a pair of dimwitted rogues out to fleece the innocent heiress of a sanitary-napkin fortune. Wearing a mustache, a Borsalino hat, and period suits, Beatty was the spitting image of Howard Hughes in his prime, while Jack, with frizzed hair and sweaty brow, approximated Larry Fine of the Three Stooges. Their plan was to play off each other like Oliver Hardy and Stan Laurel.

"The mousebed [the film's colloquial term for sanitary napkins] is a symbol of what men don't know about women, and it parallels the situation in the movie," said Stockard Channing, who played the heiress Contessa Fredrika "Freddie" Biggars-Sullivan.

At Jack's behest, Don Devlin, who'd been producing at Columbia, joined Nichols in co-producing *The Fortune*.[30] Jack also got Randy Quaid and Helena Kallianiotes added to the cast, although both dropped out before cameras rolled. Nichols asked Anjelica to test for the picture, too. "Absolutely not," she said. "I don't want gifts from friends. I don't want handouts."

The thirty-year-old stage actress Channing recalled reading for the part of the heiress while, from the back of the room, Jack and Beatty studied her as if she were an insect. "I couldn't believe how terrible it was," she said. "Jack was in dark glasses and a mink-lined Levi jacket. I'd never seen anybody in a mink-lined Levi jacket." She was offered $20,000, while Jack and Beatty each received 10 percent of the gross from the first dollar earned—an even better deal than Beatty's 40 percent of the gross after *Shampoo* broke even— provided *The Fortune* made a fortune. It didn't.

"One of the lessons of *The Fortune*, in my view, and God knows who else's view, is that it's not enough just to put together good people," said Mike Nichols. "You have to have an idea. You can't just wait for the idea. I don't believe in picking fruit before it's ripe. Eventually, you have to either find an idea or forge one."

Star packaging was on the rise in the mid-seventies, and Hollywood was ripe for boondoggle. Led by the newly formed Creative Artists Agency and International Creative Management, high-stakes agencies filled the power vacuum left by the flailing studios. An array of proven box-office stars coupled with an A-list director meant a green light and a premium price tag, regardless of the quality of the screenplay. The worst of that season was *Lucky Lady* (1975), starring Gene Hackman,[31] Liza Minnelli,[32] and Burt Reynolds,[33] each of whom earned more than $1 million, which jacked up the production price to more than $14 million. While not quite as profligate, *The For-tune* was similarly doomed. Slapstick and murder did not equal hilar-ious, regardless of star power. "Though Jack and Warren—the Bull of Mulholland and the Lion of the Loin—with their dimpled smiles and perfect rows of fighting canines, were very entertaining to watch, they weren't really meant to be Ollie and Stan," observed Carole Eastman.

But once again, if anyone stood out onscreen, it was Jack. The critic Frank Rich got himself invited onto the set of *The Fortune* for *New Times* magazine, and while he found the finished product as wretched as most of his peers did, Jack was a stitch. "Only one scene I saw being shot—one in which Nicholson's Oscar, a bundle of hyste-ria and sweat, unnecessarily confesses a murder plot to cops who are visiting him on another matter—was laughing-out-loud funny, and coincidentally enough, the scene is also the funniest in the finished film," he said.

Off camera, the summer of *The Fortune* turned out to be one of the most traumatic of Jack's life. Two weeks into filming, Mama Cass Elliott died of a heart attack[34] in Harry Nilsson's London apart-ment.[35] "After lunch I found him in the makeup chair weeping," recalled Mike Nichols. "I said, 'Nick, do you want to go home? Would you feel better?' And Jack said, 'I don't want to feel better.'"

By 1974, Jimi Hendrix, Janis Joplin, and Jim Morrison were all dead. The drug-addled Brian Wilson had become a recluse. The Bea-tles, Cream, Jefferson Airplane, the Byrds, Velvet Underground, and Simon and Garfunkel had broken up. What remained of the fecund flower power from which Jack had emerged in 1969 was laid to rest at Mount Sinai Memorial Park on August 3. Along with three hun-dred others, Jack mourned Cass Elliott's passing. But a far larger shockwave hit him around the same time as Mama Cass's death.

Time magazine put Jack on the cover of its August 12 issue, along with six pages of photos and text—the rare sort of *This Is Your Life* tribute the magazine accorded to the most noteworthy standard-bearers of the national zeitgeist. Before running the piece, a researcher gave Jack a final call to double-check the facts and left Jack reeling. Mud was not his mother, he was told, and June was not his sister. Ethel May Nicholson was his grandmother, while the woman he'd known as his sibling had been his mother all along.

When Jack protested, the fact-checker agreed to excise the reve-lation from the magazine article, but after he hung up—according to the popular account that has become Jack legend[36]—Jack called home to Jersey. Shorty, who usually had a blunt comeback to anything Jack had to say, answered the phone.

"I better get Lorraine," he said, turning the receiver over to his wife.

"What's this crap this guy's telling me?" Jack demanded.

"Yes, June is your mother," said Lorraine. His father was another matter—"an X factor," as Jack took to calling him. When the local businessman Don Furcillo-Rose later mailed a fifteen-page letter to the *Asbury Park Press* claiming paternity, Lorraine remained non-committal.[37] "As far as this man is concerned, I don't know," she told Jack. "June dated him, but she dated a lot of people."

Jack claimed to have never brought it up again with Lorraine or anyone else. In 1984, he told *Parade* magazine's Ovid Demaris, "I made a personal decision when I got this information some ten years ago. Since I can't figure out how many of my friends know about it, I decided not to talk about it."

And yet, if ever he wrote his autobiography, Jack declared, the mystery of his father would be at its heart.

11

SHORTLY AFTER JACK LEARNED THE TRUTH ABOUT HIS childhood, Anjelica revisited hers. "I took Jack to Ireland to show him the house where I'd grown up," she recalled. "We walked around the grounds, and I cried a little and felt very nostalgic and told him how much I'd like to get the house back. 'Really?' he asked me. 'You mean you'd be prepared to come and live here?' And after I'd dried my eyes I had to admit that no, I wouldn't."

She'd grown up with her older brother Tony in St. Clerans, a sprawling 110-acre estate dominated by a Georgian mansion and a smaller nearby guest cottage in Galway, along Ireland's rugged west coast.[1] St. Clerans's woods extended for miles, flush with rhododendron and thickets of gorse that afforded the Huston children sheltered adventures through the 1950s and early 1960s. They explored the streams for eel, imagined fairies in the shrubbery at sunset, and practiced a kid's version of death-defying gymnastics on a trampoline their father had built in the barn. He kept fifty thoroughbreds in the stables. Anjelica and her brother learned about sex from studying the coupling of horses.

A swashbuckling tax refugee who abandoned his U.S. citizenship in 1964 after years as an Irish country squire, John Huston staffed his three-story mansion with a dozen servants. He brought home "a parade of beautiful young women that one wanted to emulate, and try on their stockings, and put on their makeup," recalled Anjelica.

She later characterized her father as a "prolific, serious womanizer," but as a child she puzzled over her mother's deadened reaction when Anjelica told her what a great time she'd had with Huston's girlfriends.

Enrica "Ricki" Huston, a former Balanchine ballerina whom the director married when she was just nineteen, lived in the cottage ("the Little House") with her children, separate from the manor ("the Big House"), where John held forth. Too young to appreciate the corrosive effects of Huston's skirt chasing, Angelica and her brother grew up believing that fathers philandered while mothers learned to grin and bear it.

When Jack and Anjelica knocked at St. Clerans's front door in the fall of 1974, the new tenants denied them entrance. They had to be content to wander the grounds, where they met a gardener from the Hustons' era. He recognized the great man's daughter, all grown up. "He had Irish tears brimming in his eyes," Jack recalled.

During much of Anjelica's childhood, her famous father was off in the world making his films, but on his frequent visits home John held court like a feudal lord, entertaining the likes of R. Buckminster Fuller, John Steinbeck, and a host of film folk who accompanied Huston on foxhunts and marathon forays to the local pubs. Anjelica remembered the Huston houseguests as both literary and legion, quaffing tankards of stout; eating from a larder spilling roasted meats, fruit, and cheeses; and speaking of art, culture, and the sad condition of Western civilization.

She recalled for Jack one formal dinner when, as a cheeky youngster, she learned firsthand how little her father suffered fools. She said that she didn't much care for the paintings of Vincent van Gogh.

"You don't like van Gogh?" said John. "Then name six of his paintings and tell me why you don't like them."

Anjelica sat mute and reddened.

"Leave the room!" he roared. "And until you know what you're talking about, don't come back with your opinions to the dinner table."

St. Clerans sold at auction around the time that Anjelica and Jack first met, but the estate had fallen into disrepair since her father and mother had split ten years earlier. Ricki Huston abandoned Ireland during the sixties to raise her teens in London, while John relocated to Puerto Vallarta after filming *The Night of the Iguana* (1964).

Since childhood, Anjelica had dreamed of acting, but her father didn't want a spoiled child star for a daughter. When he thought her ripe enough, he plucked his headstrong sixteen-year-old from her London finishing school to costar opposite the Israeli defense minister Moshe Dayan's son Assi Dayan in *A Walk with Love and Death* (1969).

"She's good," said John. "She's damn good. I think she's going to be a fine actress. I've known that for a long time. Even when she was a little girl, she had that quality that makes good acting."

But the movie, about a fourteenth-century love affair, failed, and although she earned $10,000 for her efforts,[2] a stiff, green Anjelica suffered critical gibes around the globe. Her father moved on to the next directing gig, while Anjelica's confidence had been shattered. "Most of the reviews said I was wooden and not very pretty," said Anjelica. "I was at a particularly unattractive stage of adolescence, and since the role called for a very pretty girl, that made it very hard for me. I came out of the experience feeling quite bruised."

She recalled apologizing on the air for her performance to the TV host David Frost. As if the critical drubbing were not enough, her mother died in an auto accident in the south of France just before the film opened. At the time, Anjelica was understudying Marianne Faithful as Ophelia in Tony Richardson's Broadway production of *Hamlet*. Ricki Huston died at age thirty-nine,[3] having been abandoned by then sixty-three-year-old John years earlier.[4] Anjelica quit *Hamlet* to attend her mother's funeral. It was her last acting job until she hooked up with Jack.

"In a way [Jack] reminds me of my mother a great deal," said Anjelica, who also saw her father in Jack. "He's a Taurus. She was a Taurus. They stand very firmly. And I guess I'm waftier—I'm apt to blow in the breeze a little. It's nice to have someone who's as stable as Jack is. Although I don't think a lot of people think he's stable, in fact, he is so. And he's good blood, Jack; he's true blue."

. . .

Jack and Anjelica toured the rest of Europe that fall, promoting *Chinatown* in public appearances in Stockholm, Hamburg, Munich, Paris, Madrid, and Rome, and stopped over in Manhattan to consult with Dr. Norman Orentreich, "the father of the hair transplant." Jack reportedly underwent the new and painful but quite effective scalp procedure that had already been undertaken by the follicle-challenged Elton John, the thinning Smothers Brothers, and the receding country-western star Roy Clark.

In January, Jack flew to Oregon State Hospital for the Insane in Salem to begin filming *One Flew over the Cuckoo's Nest*. Anjelica went with him and did a brief cameo during a dockside crowd scene near the end of the movie—her first film appearance since *A Walk with Love and Death*.

"Dr. Dean Brooks, who ran the facility and also played the doctor in the movie, gave us tremendous cooperation and let our actors, like Danny DeVito[5] and Christopher Lloyd,[6] sit in on some of the patients' therapy sessions," recalled Michael Douglas, who had arrived with the rest of the cast, well ahead of Jack. "Suddenly, our actors get serious and don't want to break character by going back to their hotel. So Jack arrives not knowing any of this or who these actors were. I'm having lunch with Jack on his first shooting day in the cafeteria with the rest of the actors and inmates, when suddenly Jack pushes his tray aside and storms out of the building. I'm thinking: My first day as a producer and my star is already pissed off at something before we've even finished lunch.

"I follow Jack outside where he's pacing in the courtyard having a smoke.[7] Jack shouts at me, 'Who *are* these guys? Don't they even stop being in character for lunch? Can't they at least let me eat in peace?' Then I told Jack that some of the actors were real inmates. He thought about what I said, then laughed and said something about all actors are crazy, but it will be fun to work with some who don't have to fake it."

The film company took over an entire wing of the eighty-year-old yellow brick hospital, and Jack spent two weeks boning up, getting to know many of the 582 inmates by name. Cast and crew intermingled, and several inmates worked as prop men, electricians, and construction workers. A few in the cast half-joked that they hoped the orderlies would remember they were actors and let them out of the asylum once filming ended. Fiction and reality crisscrossed, and Jack often straddled the line himself. "One of the guys that talked to me was extremely pleasant," said Jack. "He was blond, handsome, and looked about fifty, though he was only thirty. Later on, I found out he killed a guard in prison three weeks earlier. He didn't know the man. He just walked up to him and stabbed him twenty-eight times."

There was the arsonist who set his wife on fire and the serial rapist who played center for the hospital's basketball team. Jack's personal favorite was the drug-addled bank robber whom the court committed after he hit the same bank twice in ten minutes.

But Jack came to appreciate most mental illness as "something different from what people think of as 'crazy.'" Irrational fear, compulsion, searing headaches, isolation, depression, impotence, obsession—these were the mundane symptoms of slippage, as opposed to swinging from trees like an ape or declaring oneself Napoleon or Jesus. "None of these conditions is very charming or romantic," said Jack. "People who suffer them are separate from the rest of the world. I have been in therapy for a particular problem. Did it for a year."

Jack tapped deep into his own broad range of experiences among psychos and pseudo-psychos in preparation for the part of the con- victed brawler and statutory rapist Randle "Red" McMurphy. Before taking McMurphy through the same torturous treatment, he watched two murderers at the Oregon hospital undergo electroshock therapy. At one point Jack dipped so deeply into McMurphy's pathology that Anjelica feared she was sleeping with a sociopath, and she flew back to L.A. early.

Though rich in allegory and subtext, *Cuckoo's Nest's* central conflict—priapic McMurphy versus emasculating Nurse Ratched— bore a striking resemblance to Jack's own struggles with the opposite sex. "Somehow, in the sexual experience, I was making the woman into a sort of mom—an authoritarian female figure," said Jack, recall- ing the results of his own psychotherapy. "That made me feel inadequate to the situation, small and childish. I indulged myself in a lot of masturbatory behavior. I solved none of these problems in therapy; I worked them out for myself."

Dating as far back as Manasquan High's production of *The Curi- ous Savage* and his LSD trips, Jack's memory of life among the loony included several visits he'd paid to the mental ward of L.A.'s Veterans

Administration hospital during the sixties where he assisted Jeff Corey in teaching schizophrenics the fundamentals of acting.

"Jack is a great actor: he can be true and unpredictable at the same time," said pensive, pipe-sucking Milos Forman, whom Jack first met in Cannes during the sixties. "Normally, truth is very boring. . . . Any lie is more interesting than the truth. To be as exciting and unpredictable as Jack Nicholson, that's something."

Although the laid-back Czech director, whom Jack dubbed "Meatloaf," seemed given to improvisation, Jack insisted otherwise. "Milos says that 75 percent is the script, 20 percent is the casting, and the rest is automatic," he said.

Forman himself evoked the philosophy of John Huston: "Half of directing is casting the right actors." Jack was that actor. "You don't direct Jack, any more than you tell Wayne Gretzky where to hit the puck," said Forman. "You just make sure the two of you understand what it's about and you let him go."

On the set, Jack turned scripted lines like "Oh, is that so?" into "Well, I'll be damned and packed in shit." He insisted on the same wardrobe for McMurphy day after day: gray socks, jeans, a dark knit watch cap, and a pack of cigarettes rolled into his sleeve. Where the script called for McMurphy to deliver a whoop upon first meeting the mute Chief Bromden, Jack added a war dance. He wasn't insane; he was insouciant.

"The secret of *Cuckoo's Nest*—and it's not in the book—my secret design for it was that this guy's a scamp who knows he's irresistible to women and in reality he expects Nurse Ratched to be seduced by him," Jack told the *New York Times*'s Ron Rosenbaum a decade after *Cuckoo's Nest*'s release. "This is his tragic flaw. This is why he ultimately fails."

Coldly portrayed by the actress Louise Fletcher in a role turned down by every major actress in Hollywood,[8] "Big Nurse" Ratched controlled the mental ward with a germ-free Stalinist stranglehold, as icy, asexual, and lethal as Moby Dick. "I discussed this with Louise," said Jack. "I discussed this only with her. That's what I felt was actually happening with that character—it was one long, unsuccessful seduction, which the guy was so pathologically sure of."

While Kesey's novel gave "Big Nurse" no first name, Jack asked Fletcher to name her and she came up with "Mildred." At a key point near the end of the film when McMurphy is one-upping Nurse

Ratched, he addresses her as Mildred and Fletcher blushes before redoubling her iron-fisted methods. In her plastic hairdo and starched uniform, the actress so convinced her fellow actors of her smothering frigidity that at one point she stripped to her panties and gave everyone a good look at her naked chest to assure them that she was, in fact, a warm-blooded female.

As with every film Jack had made, from *Drive, He Said* to *Chinatown*, he remained obsessed with basketball throughout production, both on and off camera. "I think one of the things I like about basketball is that the 'game face' has so much to do with acting," he said, comparing players to an acting ensemble who must pretend not to seethe over bad calls or take delight in their opponents' mistakes.

In *Cuckoo's Nest*, McMurphy chides the mute giant played by the six-foot-four ex–forest ranger Will Sampson: "You ever play this game, Chief? Come on, I'll show you. An old Indian game—it's called 'Put the ball in the hole.'"

Forman called for take after retake of *Cuckoo's Nest's* memorable basketball scene to hide the basketball's Voit trademark from the camera. Foreshadowing a long and dubious tradition in Hollywood filmmaking, Voit would not be allowed in the picture without producers paying a product-placement fee à la Reese's Pieces (*E.T. the Extra-Terrestrial* [1982]), Wilson volleyballs (*Cast Away* [2000]), and more tobacco products over the years than the FCC was ever able to ban from television or radio.

Jack told *Women's Wear Daily* that he and Anjelica rented an apartment near the hospital so he could spend evenings and weekends rushing to the nearby universities at Corvallis or Eugene or trekking north to Portland's Trailblazer Stadium to catch as much basketball as possible. At the same time, he lamented to *Newsday* in what sounded like a rehearsed plea for sympathy that life during *Cuckoo's Nest* was virtually monastic. "For more than four months, I spent the days there and would come out only at night, walking down this little path in which my footprints were indelibly marked by the almost constant rain, to the place where I was living. I'd have dinner in bed and go to sleep and then get up the next morning—still in the dark—and go back to the maximum security ward. It was basically being an inmate, with dinner privileges out."

Whichever story was true, Jack's relations with the press had deteriorated to a new level of manipulation and cool star control. Gone

were the frank and free exchanges with reporters. Along with his protective agent, Sandy Bresler, and his loyal personal assistant Annie
Marshall, he'd added a new layer of protection in the rock publicist
Paul "Wasso" Wasserman. Jack's media gatekeeper since *Easy Rider*,
Wasserman used access to Jack as both a carrot and a whip, inviting
malleable media in for a brief audience when it suited Jack's promotional interests, while barring the hostile or overly inquisitive. Wasserman's job, as it had been with Bob Dylan, Mick Jagger, and his other
famous clients, became as much keeping Jack gossip-free as getting
favorable mentions in the papers.

During *Cuckoo's Nest*, muckraking New Journalists such as *Rolling
Stone*'s Tim Cahill and *Playboy*'s Grover Lewis visited the set only to
find themselves herded and contained, fed only the morsels that Jack's
protective entourage wanted them to have. Whether it was due to the
unwelcome revelation visited upon Jack by *Time*'s investigative
research the previous summer or some other influence, reporters who
sought access beyond the actor's comfort zone got shunned or shown
the door. Once so wide-open that he cooperated with a pair of young
film journalists on an entire book of uncensored, self-effacing, and
intimate interviews with himself and many of his closest Hollywood
pals,[9] Jack had become much more the cipher, even among friends
and fellow actors.

"I go to a Jack Nicholson movie hoping that he'll let me in on his
secrets—how to get girls or how to get ahead in the world," said Gene
Hackman. "He always seems to know something that I'd like to know
myself. But he never tells me what it is. And yet I go, film after film,
hoping that this will be the one where I find out the secret."

"We haven't had a heart-to-heart talk in a long time," lamented
Sally Kellerman. During their salad days on the Sunset Strip when she
used to sit in his lap and pour out her heart, she and Jack developed
a "private signal that we still love each other": the catchword *boobs*.
"But I haven't said 'boobs' to Jack in a couple of years," she said.

"I'll see him and he'll hold you at arm's length, and that's the
biggest hug he's ever given anybody," said Bruce Dern. "Even puss.
When he hugs a girl, it's like that, too, and God forbid he kisses anyone until he gives them five breath mints. He's just not going to let
you physically get close to him. I can't imagine what sex with the guy
could be like. Pull out an erector set and Lincoln logs."

"[He] is so wild-eyed and fierce these days that one feels strangely assaulted by his good nature," said Charles Eastman. "A mere hello can knock you off your feet."

"The bottom line with Jack," said Candice Bergen, "is that he's basically unknowable."

Jack kept his demons to himself and only loosed them in private or during those rare bursts on the screen for all the world to see—but where he retained absolute control. No one saw any deeper than he wanted them to see.

At the close of *Cuckoo's Nest*, Jack had a few weeks' respite before leaving for Montana to rustle horses in *The Missouri Breaks* (1976).

The novelist Tom McGuane's offbeat Western was a package waiting to happen when the producer Elliott Kastner, a former talent agent, juggled egos and money to get the green light from United Artists. Unlike most film projects, which can gestate for decades and still die at the moment of birth, *The Missouri Breaks* came together in just six weeks—a half-baked product of the new and frequently faulty studio trend toward pairing stars with auteur directors, while worrying about such niceties as a coherent script after the fact.

"A picture doesn't cost much to make," observed *The Missouri Breaks* director Arthur Penn in a 1997 interview. "What costs more is when there are either one, two, or three stars and all the perks that go with that. The accretions of staff, people, time, and nonsense have an inhibiting effect on production."

The Missouri Breaks cost $8 million to produce at a time when similar films cost half as much, but the most scandalous part of the budget was above the line. Its stars, Jack and Marlon Brando, earned $1.25 million and $1 million, respectively, before they ever set foot on the set. In addition, Brando claimed 11.3 percent of the gross beyond $8.85 million, while Jack's payday—10 percent of the gross—kicked in once the film took in $12.5 million.[10]

The gross, of course, was just that: every penny, peso, centime, shilling, shekel, bhat, or sou collected around the world from box offices, TV stations, in-flight showings, merchandising, music publishing, and soundtrack album sales. For every dollar spent beyond the two stars' respective contractual ceilings, 21.3 cents went straight into their wallets.[11]

Such "gross" deals, coupled with inflated salaries, were squeezing what life remained from the floundering studios. Steve McQueen got

$2 million for *Papillon* (1973), but when Joseph Levine, the producer of *A Bridge Too Far* (1977), asked him to do a cameo turn, he'd upped the ante to $3 million. McQueen turned down *Apocalypse Now* (1979) for the same reason: Francis Ford Coppola couldn't wring another $3 million out of his budget.

"On the other hand, that's very much a part of American filmmaking," Penn conceded. "American stars are the international stars. It's what makes American film an industry rather than an individual labor of love. It's part of what has brought about the packaging of films and making them that way, but studios have come around to an awareness that stars don't necessarily guarantee a highly successful movie."

Not so in the spring of 1975. Such wisdom was in short supply among the young and ambitious studio executives who were desperate to make their mark in a Darwinian industry. Critics later blasted *The Missouri Breaks* for having five directors: Penn, its two stars, the writer Tom McGuane, and the United Artists production accountant.[12] But it was the producer who created the impossible situation of four-too-many bosses.

For Elliot Kastner, Brando was easy. He needed millions to develop his Tahitian paradise, the atoll of Tetiaroa, and he wasn't picky about how he got the money.[13] Kastner waved a big paycheck in front of Brando, sweetening the pot by implying that *The Missouri Breaks* might give him an opportunity to upstage his next-door neighbor. "From my point of view, *The Missouri Breaks* is simply Bucks and Company," Brando told one interviewer.

Jack, on the other hand, saw *The Missouri Breaks* as his chance to team with—maybe even upstage—his idol on the big screen. "It's a pleasure to be in the same sentence with him, no less in the same movie," said Jack.

Kastner gave each actor a different script, in which his character dies in Act III—the idea being that the audience would sympathize with the dead man. Kastner didn't let on that there were two different endings until after Jack and Brando had both signed on.

It also helped Kastner's cause that Jack compared the Western to "the closest thing to classical theater, for America, that exists." During the making of *The Last Detail*, Jack had become particularly enamored of a "spiritual, mystical Western" written by the Oregon novelist Don Berry. Published to critical acclaim in 1971, *Moontrap* tracked the familiar themes of encroaching civilization and frontier injustice. In September 1973, Jack's pal Harry Gittes announced to *Variety* that Jack would direct and the screenwriter Robert Trask would adapt Berry's novel. Jack wanted Brando to star but confessed to Army Archerd that he didn't have the chutzpah to ask until after *The Godfather*. "I had this story and wanted to direct Marlon in it before he got 'hot' again," said Jack.

Set along the Pacific coast in the mid-1800s, *Moontrap* is a moody character study of mountain men trying to come to terms with the trampling of Indian culture—a topic near and dear to Brando's heart. As for Jack, the familiar themes of fatherhood and illegitimate birth run through the story, with the protagonist's Indian mistress bearing a bastard child who is not accepted by the white settlers, which drives her to suicide. "I have my own favorite downtrodden minority, and it's not women," Jack told the *New York Times Magazine*. "It's the bastard, the illegitimately born."

Before *The Missouri Breaks* and for a long time thereafter, Jack optioned *Moontrap* over and over, well into the next decade. "I've been developing and have spent a lot of money on [*Moontrap*]," he said at the end of the 1970s. "In fact, I understand that I've been the sole support of this particular young author for the past four years or so."[14]

While *Moontrap* would forever be the bridesmaid, *The Missouri Breaks* got rushed to the altar without an ending. Everyone, including Jack and Brando, tried to give it one, but even Robert Towne, every director's favorite script doctor, failed to find a satisfying denouement.

Yet Jack anticipated none of these problems in the spring of 1975. He was preoccupied with his annual pilgrimage to the Academy Awards, this time all but certain the Oscar was his.

It was raining the evening of April 8, 1975, but Jack showed up outside the Dorothy Chandler Pavilion with Anjelica clinging to his arm. He'd already been named best actor by the New York Film Critics, the National Society of Film Critics, the British Film Academy, and the Golden Globes. This time, he dressed like a man who expected to win: the requisite tux, Ray-Bans, and a stagy black beret.[15] "Not since Ray Milland guzzled his way to an Oscar in *The Lost Weekend* (1945) has an actor been such a sure bet as Jack Nicholson," crowed the *New York Daily News*.

One showbiz scribe predicted a shoo-in if only half the actresses Jack had slept with cast their ballots for *Chinatown*. Going into the 47th annual ceremony, only *Godfather II* (1974) had as many nominations: ten, including Best Picture, Director, and Actor.

But Francis Ford Coppola's continuation of the Corleone saga swept six of the Oscars that night, including Best Picture, and for the fourth time Jack lost—this time to Art Carney, for his picaresque widower in *Harry and Tonto* (1974).[16]

Hefting the statuette, a surprised but giddy Carney said he was going to double his per-picture price. Out in the audience, those around Jack chuckled, but Jack remained stony behind his shades. He didn't break a smile and muted his disappointment further backstage, cracking wise for reporters: "Maybe in 1976, I'll be the sentimental favorite." He and Carney did not speak, at least not in public.

Despite Jack's loss to yet another Academy *alter cocker*, his old colleague Bert Schneider used the occasion to bury what was left of Old Hollywood. Accepting the Oscar for coproducing the scathing Vietnam documentary *Hearts and Minds*, Schneider read a telegram from the People's Republic of Vietnam, thanking those who opposed the war and wishing "greetings of friendship to all American people." In hypersensitive Hollywood, the stink of controversy already hung over the heartbreaking carnage depicted in *Hearts and Minds* long before the documentary won the Academy Award.

Schneider made no secret of his revolutionary leanings, helping to spirit the Black Panther Huey Newton out of Oakland and into hiding in Steve Blauner's Beverly Hills home when the black leader was on the lam from police.[17] Bert loathed the so-called Establishment far more than Jack did and used what remained of his BBS clout to strike a blow against it. A National Security adviser from the LBJ administration tried to put a temporary restraining order on the distribution of *Hearts and Minds*, but the courts ruled for Schneider. His own father's studio refused to distribute the film, so he had to take it to Warner Bros.

Hearts and Minds "shouldn't be considered a documentary," Schneider declared. "It should be considered a disaster epic, for that's what it surely is."

Fuming over yet another use of the Oscar telecast to promote a liberal political cause, the emcee Bob Hope scribbled a rebuttal.[18] Just before introducing the screenwriting awards, Frank Sinatra read from the podium, "The Academy is saying, 'We are not responsible for any political references made on the program and we are sorry they had to take place this evening.'"

Mixed applause and boos rippled through the audience, marking the divide between boomers and their elders. Meanwhile, civil war erupted backstage, with John Wayne, Sinatra, and Hope representing the old guard and a screaming Shirley MacLaine siding with Francis Ford Coppola and Schneider in speaking for the new. The shouting match centered on patriotism and Vietnam, but control of the Academy of Motion Picture Arts and Sciences was what was really at stake.[19] "Frank Sinatra and Bob Hope are equally entitled to their point of view and I've no argument about their making a statement on their own, but it's wrong to drag the Academy into it," said Schneider, himself one of the younger Academy governors.

Back onstage, the generation gap showed itself once again when the sixty-eight-year-old novelist James Michener named Robert Towne, forty-one, *Chinatown*'s sole Oscar winner that night for his original screenplay.[20] Still harboring his grudge over *Chinatown*'s ending, Towne told the audience, "If you've ever been on a film that didn't quite work out, you know how much you owe to people if it did." He didn't acknowledge Polanski but ended by thanking "Jack, who was really magic."

Several months earlier, Towne had gotten a taste of what he and the *Chinatown* cast would be up against at the Oscars. Soon after shooting wrapped, Coppola invited Towne to his San Francisco–based Zoetrope Studio to see a rough cut of *The Godfather: Part II*—a brilliant if ponderous five and a half hours that made Towne's lengthy unedited screenplay for *Chinatown* look like a Cliffs Notes version of *The Big Sleep*.

But when *The Godfather: Part II* lumbered into theaters the second week of December, Coppola and his team of three editors had wrestled it down to three hours and twenty minutes: still a marathon that rivaled *Gone with the Wind* (1939), but manageable—even stirring—as a blockbuster "event" movie.[21]

The original film *The Godfather* (1972) set a standard for the remainder of the decade and several years thereafter by ushering in the blockbuster era. Budgeted at $6 million and running 175 minutes long, the Mafia melodrama represented the Paramount production chief Robert Evans's biggest gamble to date: that audiences could be persuaded to pay a premium price of $4 (more than double the cost of a standard movie ticket) to watch Brando, Al Pacino, and James Caan emote for three hours. The gamble paid off: the movie grossed $43 million in its first year alone before foreign receipts began to roll in. By the end of the century, *The Godfather's* worldwide box office would total nearly $250 million.

But in raising the bar, *The Godfather* generated unforeseen trouble. Along with Paramount's *The Godfather: Part II* and *The Great Gatsby* (1974), event movies cascaded through the remainder of the decade, delivering such remarkable successes as *Jaws* (1975), *Close Encounters of the Third Kind* (1977), and *Star Wars* (1977), but producing an equal number of expensive duds: *Sorcerer* (1977), *Nickelodeon* (1976), and *1941* (1979), among others.

Meanwhile, production costs spiked and studio output dipped to its lowest ebb since the advent of sound. The average per-picture price of $1 million in 1970 skyrocketed to more than $10 million ten years later, and stars took the biggest budget bites.

With four Oscar nominations under his belt, Jack's salary had crept up from $750,000 (*Chinatown*) to $1 million (*Cuckoo's Nest*) to his $1.25 million coup for *The Missouri Breaks*, but none of that mattered. "You still can't save anything," he complained. "You're never going to be one of the landed gentry. You just have to remember that John Wayne was broke in 1960 to get some idea of how ephemeral movie money can be."

His monthly nut during *Chinatown*—travel, hotels, alimony—topped $12,000 and kept creeping higher. At one point the government sent him a bill for $123,000 in back taxes. More than most people, Jack understood how little Hollywood valued its heroes and why it was necessary to squeeze as much as possible from the studios while the ticket-buying public still loved you. "The fear stories of life to me," he said, "are the Preston Sturgeses[22] and the D. W. Griffiths[23] who wound up in pissy hotel rooms because no one would see them."

Jack skirted the fact that both men were directors, not actors. Nonetheless, Jack resisted the growing blockbuster mentality engendered by *The Godfather*. He played the Hollywood game but still professed to believe in art over commerce. "I've always understood money; it's not a big mystical thing to me," he told *Film Comment's*

Beverly Walker. "I say this by way of underlining that it was then and still is the art of acting that is the wellspring for me."

The day following the 1975 Oscars, *The Passenger* opened in the United States to lukewarm reception. MGM, meaning to cash in on Jack's predetermined win for *Chinatown*, had to jettison newspaper ads at the last minute that named Jack "America's Best Actor." The studio barely covered distribution costs before pulling *The Passenger* from theaters and consigning it to a shelf for a generation. In 2005, Jack re-introduced *The Passenger*, as well as a wheelchair-bound Michelangelo Antonioni, to American audiences.[24] Thirty years had passed, but Jack's nouvelle vague convictions remained unchanged. "My friends and I would go to the art houses expecting to see a masterpiece every week—and we did," he told the *Los Angeles Times*'s Patrick Goldstein. "Whether it was Antonioni, Kurosawa, Godard, Fellini, Satyajit Ray, Truffaut, or Bergman, we knew we were in good hands."

Asked why those films spoke to his generation, Jack said, "Because they took risks—it was the breaking of the form that excited us. Today we have cheap, smart indie movies, but it's not the same thing. Antonioni didn't feel that he needed to get every single point across right away. Today we're just slaves to melodrama."

The Fortune opened in June, and though only eighty-eight minutes long, it seemed far longer to critics and audiences alike. Jack's first real bomb in his post–*Easy Rider* career, *The Fortune* was Mike Nichols's second stinker in a row. Following the dismal *The Day of the Dolphin* (1973), *The Fortune* tanked so badly that it temporarily derailed the director's Hollywood career.[25] Except for a movie version of Gilda Radner's Broadway show, *Gilda Live* (1980), Nichols withdrew into exile in New York and wasn't invited back to direct another feature until *Silkwood* (1983). The film's grim reception devastated Carole Eastman, who went into virtual seclusion, writing nothing for a decade.

But Jack had immunity—at least in the short term. One, two, or even three bad movies in a row couldn't bring down an authentic movie star. He spent a week in New York promoting *The Fortune* and held forth in a corner suite at the Sherry Netherland, twenty-four stories above Central Park, just the way Bob Evans once had done.[26] Jack no longer courted the press; the press came to him, scrambling for their fifteen minutes of predictable questions and pat answers. *Newsday's* Jerry Parker noted that reporters "shuttle in and out as regularly as room service."

Maintaining that he'd shorn his skull for the lobotomy scene in *Cuckoo's Nest*, Jack told an admiring media that he would soon be growing his hair to the proper comb-over shag for his upcoming role as a horse thief in *The Missouri Breaks*. The columnist Earl Wilson trumpeted otherwise: Jack's retreating hairline revealed hair plugs and called for a toupee. Jack, notoriously touchy about his appearance, couldn't speak comfortably about the rising height of his forehead for the next decade. "If you're going to be lit for a photograph," he explained in a 1984 interview, "you put dark powder here [along the hairline] because it keeps the light from making the hair you do have disappear."

His *Missouri Breaks* costar and next-door neighbor wasn't so vain. Whatever movie star conceit Marlon Brando had resurrected during his twin comebacks as *The Godfather* and the randy widower of *Last Tango in Paris* (1972) had been spent in the ensuing three years on sex, sloth, fanciful causes, and food. By the time cameras rolled for *The Missouri Breaks*, the five-foot-ten-inch actor weighed in at 250 pounds, and while he halfheartedly tried various fad diets, his appearance no longer seemed a big concern to him. He was far more interested in bedroom sports, counterculture, and the future of the American Indian Movement (AIM).[27]

The morning after Jack sat through *The Fortune* premiere in New York, a firefight had broken out between AIM and the FBI on the Oglala Sioux reservation in South Dakota. By mid-afternoon, one Indian and two federal agents were dead, launching the biggest pre–September 11 manhunt in the Bureau's history. By summer's end, the AIM fugitives Dennis Banks and Leonard Peltier would slip into L.A. to hide out at Brando's place, right next door to Jack's.

But Marlon wasn't on hand to greet them. That meeting would take place later, after Arthur Penn had put *The Missouri Breaks* in the can. On Independence Day, Brando and his teenage son, Christian, arrived at *The Missouri Breaks* encampment fifteen miles southeast of Billings, Montana, where Penn was retouching the Virginia City sets he'd used five years earlier in *Little Big Man* (1970).

"How do you do? I'm Marlon Brando," the corpulent actor greeted each person he met as he lumbered toward Penn's trailer. "I got the feeling that people really liked Brando and Jack was a politician: a devious type," observed Tom McGuane.

Yet it was Brando who used his schmooze advantage to massage Penn, manipulate McGuane's script, and enlarge his role as Robert E. Lee Clayton, the bounty hunter who was hired to track down Jack and his gang of rustlers. By the time Jack realized what was up and began to protest, Brando had already given Clayton an Irish brogue and was trying to transform Jack's character Tom Logan from a noble horse thief to a noble red man.

While Brando remained bright if quirky on the set, news of the manhunt following the Pine Ridge reservation shootout weighed on him. He was frequently on the phone to his AIM friends, and once a pair of FBI agents showed up at Marlon's big blue trailer to question the actor. Satisfied, they left, and Brando grew weirder, beating his bongos during down time and traipsing through the underbrush, collecting grasshoppers. In a smaller trailer nearby, Jack kept his distance.

Soon enough, the production was past schedule, over budget, and out of control. Jack blamed Penn for caving in to Brando's indolence and careless caprice, but McGuane blamed them all. "Instead of being the ensemble thing that I had imagined, it now had to be a vehicle for two superstars," he said.

Most days, Brando didn't even bother to learn his lines. "Marlon's still the greatest actor in the world, so why does he need those goddamned cue cards?" Jack complained.

Jack's ambivalence about his idol had been building since he first moved in next door to Brando five years earlier. Despite their shuttle diplomacy, the old pro and the young comer still knew each other as little more than nodding acquaintances.

Once, during one of Jack's Halloween bashes, Brando even called the cops on him. "What does Marlon want from me?" Jack asked Adam Roarke. "Does he want me to move back to Neptune?"

But over time, the neighbors became more collegial. Helena Kallianiotes became their most enduring go-between. As with their *Missouri Breaks* trailers,[28] Brando owned the larger home (three bedrooms, four baths, a pool, a guest house, and a pool house), held the higher ground, and exercised the law of primogeniture, taking great pleasure in getting Jack's goat, as well as his girls. "Once Jack moved in next door, Marlon was going after his women and it became another Hollywood game," the actress Pat Quinn told Brando's biographer Peter Manso.[29]

Publicly, Jack heaped nothing but reverential blather on his hero. "Brando is deep," Jack said upon the release of *Last Tango in Paris* (1972). "Brando is deeply into the erotic consciousness of a good percentage of the human beings alive on the planet today. Deeply in it."

And during his *Missouri Breaks* antics, when Brando played coy with the media who were flown into Billings to see the superstar showdown, Jack said, "Marlon is not aloof at all. He's tremendously elusive. It's just his way of communicating. There's a basic stillness about him. You always have the feeling that nothing is being missed when you talk to him."

But at less guarded times, Jack muttered that Brando "is telling us that what we [actors] are doing is shit. He said the other day, 'This is kind of a silly way to make a living, but nothing pays as good.'"

Indeed, Brando cared most about making a killing for the least effort in as short a time span as possible. In a curiously paradoxical Method mantra that Jack would adopt as his own, Brando often recited, "I can't really care. It shows up in the work."

Thus, when Bruce Dern joked to Jack months after the picture wrapped that he thought Brando stole *The Missouri Breaks* out from under him, Jack freaked: "I don't know who the fucking guy is! Lives up the hill from me. What do you want from me?"

Dern accused Jack of jousting with Brando, trying to demonstrate that he had superseded the Master. For his part, Brando did not conceal his contempt. "I actually don't think Jack Nicholson's that bright," he told reporters. "Not as good as Robert DeNiro, for example."

Of course, Brando also suggested that he and Jack might be having an affair, and as preposterous as that sounded, Brando told his fictions with as straight a face as his convictions, leaving the more gullible in the media to sort out the truth.

"Marlon had not much respect for Jack's acting," said McGuane. Penn let both his stars improvise ("You gotta watch these actors," he rationalized), but Jack was the one who came off looking stiff and scripted. "Poor Nicholson was stuck in the center of it all, cranking the damned thing out while I whipped in and out of scenes like greased lightning," Brando boasted.

McGuane wrote the bounty-hunter character as eccentric, but by the end of the movie, Brando had fanned eccentricity into full-blown

Cuckoo's Nest madness, merrily murdering each rustler while humming a tune or making a joke.

The crew watched in genuine horror when Brando plucked a live frog from the river during one scene, took a big bite, then tossed the injured animal back in the water.[30] Wearing a bonnet and a Mother Hubbard dress, he waltzed an uncomfortable Jack in front of the camera, and when it came time for their penultimate showdown, Brando gave Jack a full-moon target by heaving his naked bulk into a bathtub and daring Jack to shoot, like a whale welcoming a harpoon.

Cowed, Jack's character holsters his gun but later stalks the bounty hunter to his camp, where he awakens a silent, bug-eyed Brando with the droll query: "You know what woke you up? Lee, you just had your throat cut."

If *The Missouri Breaks* ended there, it might have been the next big-event movie that Penn, Elliott Kastner, and United Artists hoped it would be, but too many elements remained to be tied together and McGuane had already packed up and left for London to edit his own movie.[31] Even after Jack called in the celebrated Robert Towne, his tacked-on shoot-'em-up ending couldn't save the movie.[32] While destined for respectable business, *The Missouri Breaks* was no blockbuster.

Though critics sided with Jack ("He gave a fine, unusually understated performance—his brashness still present but reined in, his intensity constant but becalmed," one reported), Brando went way over the top to win the publicity sweepstakes. In all his earnestness, Jack had become Brando's foil.

Despite the sniping, Jack had grown close enough to his costar by the end of *The Missouri Breaks* to develop a genuine affection for "Bud" Brando, who stuck around past his contractual five weeks and even paid for the wrap party. Brando persuaded Jack to invest in several of his offbeat business ventures in the years ahead, and they bought adjoining condominiums on the island of Bora Bora.[33]

Jack's hero worship never entirely faded. He couldn't blame Brando for upstaging him during *The Missouri Breaks*, so he took out his pique on Arthur Penn. "I was very hurt," said Jack. "The picture was terribly out of balance, and I said so. Well, an actor isn't supposed to care, I suppose. I mean, Arthur Penn doesn't talk to me anymore because I told him I didn't like his picture. The movie could've been saved in the cutting room, but nobody listened."

The difference between Jack and Marlon seemed to be that Marlon didn't care whether the movie was "saved." As a result, while not his best work, *The Missouri Breaks* became Brando's libidinous triumph, not Jack's.

Along with Jack's precocious twelve-year-old daughter, Jennifer, who played poker with the crew against her father's advice, Anjelica and her ten-year-old sister, Allegra, joined Jack on location in Billings. Polanski stopped by, along with other members of the growing Jack entourage. Mostly, Jack bestowed at least a little of his time upon them. He'd learned to dole out his presence, withdrawing without fanfare when even those he counted closest displeased him.

While Jack soured on McGuane for leaving *The Missouri Breaks* without an ending, he and the screenwriter's friend, neighbor, and fellow novelist Jim Harrison hit it off instantly. A rounder and a hellion with his own ambivalence toward strong, unconventional mothers[34] and feckless fathers, Harrison found instant and enduring common ground with Jack. His glass eye and burly bearing often got him mistaken as Jack's bodyguard.[35] For a time, his 1979 novellas *Revenge*[36] and *Legends of the Fall*[37] looked as if they might be the next big Nicholson projects after *Goin' South* (1978) went south and *Moontrap* failed to materialize.

After other studios passed on *Moontrap*, Jack tried to interest United Artists, with himself directing and the legendary Sam Speigel producing, but the studio would agree only if Jack was also in the movie. His star salary broke the deal. "They [stars] are conglomerates whether they want to be or not," observed Arthur Penn. "In the case of Warren Beatty and Jack Nicholson, they don't want to be, but it goes with them."

The modest $2 million to $3 million *Moontrap* budget that UA offered could accommodate Jack's $500,000 fee as a B-list director but not the marquee money he'd require to maintain his membership in the new "Million Dollar Club": male matinee idols such as Robert Redford, Steve McQueen, James Caan, and Dustin Hoffman, who wouldn't even read a script unless the producers put up a $1 million guarantee. Celebrity gave them the edge. With multiplexes exploding across America, studio executives believed they needed a star just to "open" a picture against competing blockbusters.

Entrepreneurs like Mann Theaters' Ted Mann and National

Amusements' Sumner Redstone had recognized early a subtle migration from the nation's urban centers during the sixties. They followed the Boomers to the suburbs with smaller, multiple-screen versions of the previous generation's movie palaces, and in the decade that followed, the number of screens rose from 13,000 to 18,000 across America, mostly in shopping malls. At the same time, drive-ins and the old single-screen cinemas built during the Depression by Paramount, Fox, Warner Bros., and RKO did a fast fade.[38]

Screen density became the new industry buzzword, and movies no longer had the luxury of building an audience in a handful of movie houses over weeks or even months. BBS gems like *Five Easy Pieces* and *The Last Picture Show* wouldn't stand a chance five years later against a juggernaut like *Jaws* (1975). Smaller ensemble films once caught on through word of mouth following exclusive bookings in two or three theaters in Westwood or Manhattan. No more.

Student filmmakers of the early 1960s, steeped in Jean-Luc Godard, Barbet Shroeder, and Nestor Almendros, produced "interesting pictures which didn't make any money so they abandoned them for blockbuster city," said Jack. "Then a few years passed and Steven Spielberg arrived like the final evolution."

Opening simultaneously on 460 screens coast to coast during the same week that production began on *The Missouri Breaks*, *Jaws* broke new ground with Universal's unprecedented three-day TV advertising blitz. The studio's wide-release gamble yielded a $458 million gross and set the pattern for the rest of the century, upping the ante on special effects, event movies, and star hype. "What's dangerous now is that the financial person doesn't really even want to take a shot anymore if it doesn't have *Towering Inferno's* thing, if it isn't *Jaws*," said Jack.

Again acting against the prevailing wisdom, Jack chose as his next project Sam Speigel's production of F. Scott Fitzgerald's unfinished Hollywood classic *The Last Tycoon* (1976)—and not as its star. Once considered for the title role of the fictitious studio chief Monroe Stahr[39] (which went instead to Robert DeNiro), Jack accepted a salary of just $150,000 and a piece of the back end[40] to play a firebrand East Coast labor leader bent on organizing 1930s Hollywood. It was the first of his roles Jack termed "short parts" or, as the rest of the industry called them, supporting performances. "Certain things you can do in a short part that you wouldn't want to do for a whole picture," Jack said. "A blind man with a Scottish accent who limps and is a yo-yo champion you wouldn't want to do for 311 scenes, but for three scenes it might be interesting."

An array of Hollywood's venerable also did *Tycoon* short parts, including Tony Curtis, Robert Mitchum, Donald Pleasance, Ray Milland, Dana Andrews, and John Carradine. Anjelica tested for the female lead but settled for a smaller role. Even Jeff Corey got hired to portray a long-faced doctor.

The playwright Harold Pinter wrote the plodding screenplay, a mistake that cost *The Last Tycoon* dramatic tension. Despite scenes that had the ring of Fitzgerald's original truth, Pinter organized it like a stage play, and *Tycoon* came across flat. Elia Kazan wrote in his diary of the rough cut: "The picture hangs together . . . the film has subtlety, and even emotional power."

But, in fact, Kazan's final film was doomed at the box office. He agreed to reprise his Oscar-winning collaboration with Sam Spiegel (*On the Waterfront*) after Mike Nichols quit as director, even though Kazan later admitted that he had reteamed with the obstreperous producer "for no good reason except my mother was very sick and I wanted to get money."

It was Spiegel's special genius that brought all these high-profile names to critical mass, even in a fast-changing Hollywood where money didn't talk so much as drown out all dissent. Spiegel baited Jack, for example, by taking out a full-page ad in the Sunday *New York Times* while Jack was making *Cuckoo's Nest* just to offer Jack his "best wishes." "Very seldom can you find an American actor who doesn't care whether he is in the lead or the second or third or fourth most important part," Spiegel spewed to the trades upon signing Jack. "Who just wants to fulfill his professional skill and pride. That's Jack."

The owner of more Oscars than any feature producer in Hollywood, Spiegel was a well-regarded flimflam man, as well as a feudal lord whose celebrated serfs dared not refuse him. During the 1970s, Mike Nichols likened him to "the head of the family" that included Jack, Anjelica, Warren Beatty, David Geffen, Julie Christie, Linda Ronstadt, and Diane Keaton, among others. Like Jack, Sam obsessed over women but not so much over monogamy. He bought art but didn't have Jack's eye. After checking out Spiegel's Cézannes, Manets, and Soutines, the director Joseph Mankiewicz once observed, "Isn't it interesting that Sam has the worst picture by each of those famous painters?"

Spiegel could be as explosive as a wife beater, lavishing praise and gifts following an outburst, somehow continuing to endear himself even to those he'd lashed out at the most. He was an A-list invitee for every power broker from the *Washington Post* publisher Katherine Graham to MCA's Lew and Edie Wasserman. A hedonist and a Zionist, he knew the power of mystery and kept people waiting—a Godot, according to the screenwriter Peter Shaffer, "he was always arriving." To his loyal followers, Spiegel was a force of nature; to his enemies, a control freak, a pervert, and an egomaniac. He claimed to have a third eye with which he could divine the future: he knew what films would succeed and where all his friends were at all times.

But to Jack, Spiegel was Kipling's definition of a modern man: walking with kings while keeping the common touch. They were the same height (five feet, nine inches), had the same disposition, and suffered the same huge appetites for sex, adventure, and adulation. Ultimately, Spiegel's overriding lust was for film. "It was all about the picture, not who you fucked at lunchtime or whether the president came to the set," said Jack.

One of Spiegel's biggest triumphs, *Lawrence of Arabia* (1962), remained one of Jack's lifelong influences. In 2002, he could still quote Alec Guinness at the drop of Spiegel's name: "'Look, Lawrence, you do things according to your real and honest passions of the moment; I do things according to the way in which they should be done traditionally. I ask you to judge which is more trustworthy over the long run.' I love that scene," said Jack.

Anjelica was still wrapping her role in *The Last Tycoon* when Jack headed east for the first leg of a thirty-five-day around-the-world promotion tour for *Cuckoo's Nest*. He still had a hard time processing his good fortune. In Japan, he was given his own geisha. "Instead of massaging me with her hands, she used her body," Jack said.

By now a welcome fixture on the New York party scene, Jack spent his time between interviews migrating from home base at the Carlyle to Andy Warhol's Factory, to Regine's, to Ara Gallant's all-black-and-leather apartment, sampling whatever was offered to him, including at least one old runway crony from Anjelica's modeling days. Anjelica herself had introduced them. Jack's dalliance would come back to haunt him. Boarding a plane to Chicago on his way back home, Jack remarked to a friend, "I think I may have started a few brush fires in New York that could burn all the way to the Coast."

While Anjelica was not so naive as to expect fidelity any more than John Huston's five wives expected it of her father, she did expect discretion—not a revelation in *Ladies Home Journal* that his East Coast junket amounted to "one of his womanizing sprees." The *Journal*'s rival, *Cosmopolitan*, called Jack's brief encounters his "playtime"—not to be confused with his more serious relationship with Ms. Huston.

Far from appeasing, that distinction humiliated Anjelica. Nailing one of her friends after a Gotham all-nighter laced with blue smoke and blow was not her idea of discretion. There'd been flare-ups before, prompting Anjelica to move out for brief periods, but nothing compared to what would soon rattle Jack to the bottom of his randy ways.

He did not visit the Jersey Shore as he had during previous New York sojourns, nor would he again anytime soon. The shattering revelation he maintained that he'd extracted from Lorraine about June, Mud, and his mystery father continued to haunt him. Not yet in a forgiving mood over his humiliation, Jack continued to hold Lorraine, the last of his several mothers, responsible.

On November 19, 1975, *Cuckoo's Nest* premiered, and *People* magazine predicted that the movie "should bring Nicholson his long-overdue Oscar and public acceptance as the first American actor since Marlon Brando and James Dean with the elemental energy to wildcat new wells of awareness in the national unconscious." In one of the few hypercritical reviews, Vincent Canby called *One Flew over the Cuckoo's Nest* "a comedy that can't quite support its tragic conclusion." The *New Yorker*'s imperious Pauline Kael, arguably the country's most influential film critic, named it "not a great movie but one that will probably stir audiences' emotions and join the ranks of such pop-mythology films as *The Wild One*, *Rebel without a Cause* and *Easy Rider*." Of Jack, she wrote:

Nicholson is an actor who knows how to play to an audience; he knows how to get us to share in a character. In *The Last Detail*, his sweet-sadistic alternating current kept us watching him, and we followed his lowlifer's spoor through *Chinatown*. Nicholson is no flower-child nice guy; he's got that half smile—the calculated insult that alerts audiences to how close to the surface his hostility is. He's the people's freak of the new stars. His specialty is divided characters—vulgarians such as J. J. Gittes, with his *Racing Form*, his dumb jokes, and his flashy clothes—who are vulnerable. Nicholson shows the romanticism inside street shrewdness.

The same week that *Cuckoo's Nest* opened, Marlon Brando helped to spirit his felonious houseguests out of the state. AIM's Banks and Peltier got as far as the Idaho border in Brando's Winnebago (he wasn't with them) before Oregon state police pulled them over. Ever the mensch, Jack intervened on Brando's behalf, calling in whatever goodwill he'd earned with Oregon's governor Robert Straub during the filming of *Cuckoo's Nest* in order to lighten the book that was about to be thrown at Brando, Banks,[41] and Peltier.[42]

During the ensuing investigation, Brando was questioned about the dynamite, the cash, the credit cards, and the firearms (including a .357 Magnum that belonged to one of the dead FBI agents) found in the fugitives' possession. Brando admitted to giving Banks and Peltier his RV and later helping to spirit Banks out of the country to Tahiti, but Brando himself was never arrested. He remained defiant and aloof, as only an aging celebrity can, and melded his privileged version of militant activism with a little more personal dissipation each passing year.

The sun had set on Brando's serious acting career. Outside of his sneering swagger through the closing reels of *Apocalypse Now* (1979),[43] the actor's actor so revered by Jack's generation would never again electrify the screen as he'd done in the fifties, sixties, and seventies. Like it or not, the mantle fell to the new kid in town.

Now pushing forty, Jack was hailed as the new Brando. He'd been anointed the new prince of Hollywood, but his crown would weigh heavy in the decade ahead.

BOOK III

WANTED MAN

1976–1984

12

ONE FLEW OVER THE CUCKOO'S NEST DETONATED LIKE A nuclear revelation, touching a universal nerve and elevating Jack to superstardom in the process. While Jack was ringing in the New Year at his new place in the West End of Aspen, audiences around the globe were lining up to buy *Cuckoo's Nest* tickets.[1] Many theaters defied the usual one-week-in, next-week-out trend and extended the film for months. The movie opened in Stockholm on February 26, 1976, and didn't close until eleven years later.[2]

Kirk Douglas, in praising his son Michael for pulling off a phenomenon, said during the movie's premiere, "I kept away from it as far as possible. And I must now say it is a classic film, and Jack Nicholson gives the best performance I've ever seen him do." But in his memoir, Kirk wrote, "*One Flew over the Cuckoo's Nest* is one of the biggest disappointments of my life. I made more money from that film than any I acted in. And I would gladly give back every cent if I could have played the role."

The author Ken Kesey agreed. Kirk Douglas *should* have played Randle Patrick McMurphy while he was still young enough to do so; Jack was too busy playing Jack. "One of the things I really believed," said Jack, "was what Bette Davis, my favorite film actor or actress, said: 'You play the same part over and over again, otherwise they will not know who you are,' and that's how you get to be a movie star."

Kesey was so incensed over what he believed to be the desecration of his magnum opus that he took the producers to court. In February, he sued for breach of contract, claiming 5 percent of the gross and $869,000 in damages.[3] Settling out of court, Kesey vowed never to see the movie, his bitterness lingering until his death in 2001.[4]

But Kesey's was a cry in the wilderness; the *Cuckoo's Nest* juggernaut rolled on. The *New York Times Magazine* dubbed Jack "the Conquering Anti-Hero." Jack was no longer the consummate outsider. Indeed, he wasn't even swimming in the mainstream but now surfed out ahead of the pack. Naturally, the Academy nominated him for his fifth Oscar. He'd grown droll, if not complacent, about always being a bridesmaid. "I'd much rather win an Oscar than a pretty girl," he quipped. "One is permanent and the other is not."

On March 29, 1976, Jack showed up in a tuxedo, a hairpiece, and Ray-Bans, with Anjelica on one arm and his thirteen-year-old daughter, Jennifer, on the other. As the evening progressed, the *Cuckoo's Nest* optimism looked like *Chinatown* redux. Jack Nitzsche's score, Haskell Wexler's cinematography, and the *Cuckoo's Nest* editing were all passed over for Oscars, as was Brad Dourif's impressive film debut as the stuttering Billy Bibbit. In what looked like a repeat of the previous year's nostalgia vote, Dourif lost Best Supporting Actor to George Burns in Neil Simon's *The Sunshine Boys* (1975).

Onstage at the Dorothy Chandler Pavilion, Bo Goldman and Lawrence Hauben won for their *Cuckoo's Nest* adaptation just before the last of the honorary Oscars were handed out. In the buildup to the Big Four—Best Actress, Actor, Director, and Picture—Hollywood's very first Best Actress was honored in a filmed tribute that climaxed with a staged interview. A feeble munchkin, Mary Pickford herself sat propped up in a chair in a blond wig, a satin dress, a white fur collar, and pearls. At eighty-three, she smiled sweetly for the camera as the Academy president Walter Mirisch[5] handed her her second Oscar.[6] "That's wonderful," said the actress and co-founder of United Artists. On cue, a single tear rolled down her cheek. "You've made me very, very happy."

Charles Bronson and Jill Ireland followed with the announcement of 1975's Best Actress: Jack's *Cuckoo's Nest* costar Louise Fletcher, who thanked her deaf parents in sign language. "I want to thank you for teaching me to have a dream," she said, breaking into tears. "You are seeing my dream come true."

Next up, Art Carney opened the envelope and read, "Jack Nicholson." Out in the audience, Walter Matthau, who had also been nominated, leaned to his wife and whispered above the ovation, "It's about time."

Jack removed his shades during his victory walk. Carney hugged him, and Nicholson, cradling his prize, announced, "I guess this proves there are as many nuts in the Academy as anywhere else." He thanked Mary Pickford for being "the first actor to get a percentage of her pictures[7]—and speaking of percentages, last but not least, my agent, who, about ten years ago, advised me that I had no business being an actor."[8]

The final two Oscars went to Milos Forman for Best Direction and Michael Douglas and Saul Zaentz for producing, making *Cuckoo's Nest* the first film to win the top five Oscars since *It Happened One Night* (1934).

Backstage, Nicholson effervesced. "God, isn't it fantastic?" He likened winning to losing his virginity: "Once you've done it, you don't have to worry about it ever again."

"When you were doing *Little Shop of Horrors*, did you ever think it would lead to this?" asked a reporter.

"Yes, I did," said Jack from behind his shades. "I have one more ambition. That is to don gray chauffeur's livery and drive Milos Forman into Prague in a Rolls Royce."[9]

Among the avalanche of congratulatory calls the following day, Bruce Dern told Jack, "Well, you know, you're one for four. One for four doesn't get you in the Hall. That's .250."

"No Hall of Fame," Jack shot back, "but I got gross now."

Fielding as many calls as he could, Jack made a few as well. In all his glory, he remembered what it was like to lose. "The day after the [1976] awards, when I didn't win, my first and only call was from Jack Nicholson—who did win," said Carol Kane, nominated for Best Actress in *Hester Street* (1975).[10] "He and Anjelica took me to lunch because he knew what that day is like. I mean, you think you'll go insane from how many times the phone rings the day before. But the day after, you have to call the switchboard and ask if the phone is broken."

Chinatown made Jack comfortable, but *Cuckoo's Nest* made him rich. His slice of the *Chinatown* box office had come to around $1 million, but *Cuckoo's Nest* would rake in ten times as much. The evening after the Oscars, he took Anjelica and his new pal Jim Harrison to the movies, where they got in free and were offered popcorn gratis. That, as much as all the money and adulation, drove home the fact that Jack had arrived. He was unapologetic about reaching the top of the food chain. "The film industry doesn't run on social principles," he said. "It's Darwinian. No structure. Maybe I get two thousand times as much as another actor, but the studio won't take my money and give it to him." Jack said he'd sooner pay his windfall out in taxes than leave it in a studio's coffer: "I *like* the federal government. I like what they do with my money!"

By 1978, Jack's share of the *Cuckoo's Nest* windfall grew to $15 million, becoming the kind of annuity that just kept on giving. Completed on a $4.4 million budget, *One Flew over the Cuckoo's Nest* became the seventh-highest-grossing movie ever and went on to gross more than $320 million worldwide by the occasion of its twenty-fifth anniversary.

Jack's usual asking price rose to well over $1 million. The question now was what to do next.

He'd come to define the typical protagonist of his time: a laid-back, wiseass Hamlet who makes emotional commitment either reluctantly or not at all. "I'm very grateful for the rhythm of my career," he told the *New York Daily News*. "It's true that some of my early pictures were really horrible, and I'm happy that most people haven't seen them. But I wouldn't have wanted to be successful as a young actor because then you're placed in the position where you have to mature off stage."

The *Village Voice* compared his average-Joe persona to that of Jimmy Stewart. "He is Mr. Smith who has done drugs, Mr. Deeds who has learned to accept corruption in official places," wrote Tag Gallagher, who boasted of sharing a joint with Jack. In interviews, Jack appeared to stay stoned much of the time. During a sit-down with *People*, he lit up a ninth doobie, the remaining eight roaches still lying in the ashtray. "Drugs are a social thing with me, a pleasant evening now and then," he said. "Nobody's ever seen me slack-mouthed. I'm not an advocate of decadence. I've seen friends extremely negatively affected by coke and heroin. But with marijuana, on the other hand, you're making outlaws of an enormous percentage of the population for no good reason."

The previous year, Bert Schneider had been nailed for possession of grass shortly after the release of *Hearts and Minds*. In January, the LAPD raided the home of Jack's pal Ryan O'Neal and arrested him. That same month, pranksters tampered with the Hollywood sign so that it read "Hollyweed." For Jack, who lived in a fortified compound just up Mulholland, a few twisting miles from the sign, the concern was more about price than paranoia. "I'm paying a tremendous amount of money for my dope these days. Seriously, the price has gone up 1,000 percent."

Along with perpetuating the Vietnam War, Jack blamed Richard Nixon for the high cost of weed and the rise in cocaine and heroin use. "Everything that Nixon was successfully involved in, in terms of legislation, always had a result opposite to the reason he espoused the legislation in the first place," Jack said. "I knew that his dope legislation would do just two things: it would increase the use of hard drugs, which it has done, and it would raise the price because the supply would become more difficult."

At the top of his game, Jack radiated confidence. He was in the dharma, riding the zeitgeist with one hand tied behind him. But, as Bob Dylan once preached, the times were a-changing, and for all his cannabis cool, Jack had to work much harder to keep up.

"Part of the myth that people don't understand is that in order to succeed—in order to become a Brando or a Bob Dylan or whatever—you can't just punch a time card, take a nap, and pick up your reviews and your money," he said. "I mean your work is all-consuming. Whether you want to or not, you *do* take your job home with you. . . . In any other job I've done, I could take off when I wanted to and work when I wanted to. I didn't have to show up on Wednesday, whether I was sick or not. But none of this is true for an actor. I can't *not* show up, because otherwise 150 people don't work that day."

By succeeding, Jack seemed to have painted himself into a corner. He was no longer just an actor looking for the next role; he was a corporation supporting a payroll.[11] Flower power was a distant memory, Vietnam had ended, and Richard Nixon was in political exile. During Jack's sprint to the top, the film business had changed as completely as the culture, and so had his fans. "That great movie era subsided in the mid-1970s, when the audience that had seen Nicholson as a symbol of the countercultural raised fist was superseded by a younger, more passive one," wrote the film historian Steve Vineberg. "And for awhile Nicholson seemed stranded."

"Someone like me always worries about the cataclysmic experience that might jerk away the facade and expose you as the complete imbecile that, deep in your heart, you know you are," said Jack. As an actor, he guarded that facade: "An actor's supposed to create an illusion he's somebody else. I don't think it's good for him to let the public know what he's really like."

More than ever, Jack kept his public and private lives separate. A month after the Academy Awards, David Geffen invited him to an entertainment industry seminar he taught at UCLA. Jack had grown wary of the media but still made himself available to undergrads. Since he first leaped to fame, he'd been meeting with aspiring filmmakers and discussed his craft as frankly this time as in the past.

When *The Missouri Breaks* came up, he confided to Geffen's students, "I don't think it's very good—but don't tell anybody."

One of the students turned out to be writing for UCLA's *Daily Bruin*. The following week, Jack's candid quotes appeared, were picked up by wire services, and were propelled across the country just as *The Missouri Breaks* opened. Affirming Jack's distrust of journalists, the incident prompted Warren Beatty to cancel his own scheduled appearance at Geffen's class.

Like Jack, Beatty developed an approach-avoidance media relationship, manipulating the public's endless appetite for gossip with a constant aloofness. Any reporter who was ambitious enough could reach Beatty by phone, and "the Pro" might even speak at length, but he rarely revealed anything. Asked by *Vanity Fair*'s Nancy Collins about the accident of celebrity, Beatty said, "The world is filled with accidental celebrities. What you mean is that no one remains the focus of media attention . . . accidentally."

Unlike celebrities who "find themselves a pretty thing to be moved around by others," Mike Nichols observed that Jack and Warren were a rarity in showbiz: actors who control their image and business "without visible technique or method."

Following the huge success of *Shampoo*, Beatty moved from his long-standing residence in the "El Escondido" penthouse atop the Beverly Wilshire Hotel to a large white Mulholland dump that his new neighbor Jack dubbed the "Hospital Ship."[12] Around the same time, Michelle Phillips quit Beatty. Her reasons sounded familiar: "The closer he gets, the more afraid he gets," she said. "And so he goes off and has another meaningless affair."

Like Jack, Beatty refused to take responsibility and evaded the issue when Phillips confronted him—a pattern he repeated often enough that she accepted his philandering as a chronic personality disorder. She could play the game herself, getting even by getting laid, or she could move on and find a man who didn't hide out in another woman's bedroom. "I finally faced up to it and got out," Michelle said.

Anjelica did not. Oscar-night appearances to the contrary, she and Jack had entered choppy waters. As passive-aggressive as her boyfriend was, she played right into his imperious sleep-around game. "I never adjusted my life for her presence," sniffed Jack. "If she comes here in the middle of a party, the party goes on." He fatuously described their relationship as like that of Jean-Paul Sartre and Simone de Beauvoir.

Anjelica's description was neither so lofty nor so cavalier. In classic Freudian lockstep, she'd found a man very like her own father and then set out to reform him. Short of that, she sought revenge. She'd heard about Jack's Manhattan spree the previous autumn and, humiliated, moved out of Mulholland into a Beverly Hills apartment. During her retreat, she found solace with the actor Ryan O'Neal.[13] Thus, when she met Jack in London during a promotion for *The Missouri Breaks*, Anjelica checked into O'Neal's hotel, not into the posh Connaught with Jack—a deliciously lurid fact that didn't get past Fleet Street. "All I know is that Anjelica is in London and she's not with me," Jack groused. "I don't want to be mentioned in the same sentence with O'Neal. We are no longer friends, but I don't want to talk about why."

As late as July, Jack and Anjelica were still together, celebrating her birthday at Beverly Hills's venerable Chasen's restaurant with such Jack stalwarts as Beatty, Robert Evans, David Geffen, and Dustin Hoffman. But by August, Anjelica had left him again—a come-and-go pattern that would endure through another decade. "I was upset about it at the time, but I'm not now," Jack told the *London Daily Express*. "When you have a problem like that you can only deal with it and move on."

By summer's end, Jack had had quite enough questions about his love life. He spent the rest of his vacation aboard Sam Spiegel's yacht in St. Tropez, where he embossed his aging adolescent image by dropping his drawers and giving the media an eyeful of his bare ass.

"I wouldn't describe Jack as a jealous man," said Anjelica, who became engaged in the game, lunching with Jack one day and ricocheting back to O'Neal's place in Malibu the next. "Possessive more than jealous. Jealousy involves insecurity. My father is mad about him."

John Huston, whom Jack considered his father-in-law, counseled a strong hand with his daughter. Jack tried, but by fall, she'd decided to torture him by accompanying O'Neal to the Netherlands, where he was on location for *A Bridge Too Far*. At various points, Jack professed to want to marry, but Anjelica refused. "Every time someone got divorced, Anjelica would say, 'Look, there's no reason to get married,'" recalled Helena Kallianiotes. "But Jack wanted to."

When friends split, Jack admitted that he was often more shaken than they were: "Because when you're struggling to get some harmony in your life and you see a twenty-year marriage break up, it's a blow," he said. "Man-woman relationships just seem to get harder and harder all the time."

The entire Anjelica-O'Neal episode had an indelible effect on Jack, but it was no deterrent. When he wanted a woman, he still ordered out on occasion, dispatching a limo for pickup and delivery. Orgasmic Reichian release didn't solve his more immediate emotional dilemma. Like a contrite philanderer fresh off the analyst's couch, he described in one interview how his need for strong females went back to childhood: "It's all tied in with the fact that, as an infant, I knew my survival depended on a woman—my mother," he said. "I still treat the women in my life with that same feeling, attaching my survival to our relationship."

Then he'd whipsaw right back to obeying his gonads. Decades later, he reflected, "If you told me twenty years ago that some woman could go off and fuck one of my best friends and I'd end up reading about it in the newspapers, and then four years later I wouldn't even give a shit, I'd say, 'You're talking to the wrong guy here. That's not the way I am. I might want to be that guy, but I'm not.'" He then clapped his hands and raised his inevitable eyebrows. "Now, I am."

Like his libertine mentor Sam Spiegel, Jack had taken to collecting paintings the way he'd once collected baseball cards. "Jack lives in a $500,000 house with a $100 million art collection," observed one friend.

Many works were on display, but just as many weren't, resting in their frames in neat stacks until Jack could find a place for them on his walls, in his life. "My pictures," as he called them, included Tamayo, Modigliani, Botero, Soutine, and Matisse, all illuminated with specially designed lighting. In deference to Anjelica's taste, he bought paintings by Tamara de Lempicka, a force in the art deco movement of the 1920s and 1930s.[14] Even his furnishings had an art deco quality. Floor lamps with coiled-snake bases and Gallé glass shades lit the living room. He owned a Rodin marble and indulged his penchant for nineteenth-century Western art. "I hate to call them an investment; its banking rather than investment," he said, adding, "I'm not a trader or a collector, but I'm aware that I don't throw $10,000 out the window."

An early Picasso of an angular, cubic woman hung in the hall that led to his living room. An Alma Tadema hung on one wall, while a green-and-blue Chagall shone from inside the bathroom.[15] A Pierre Bonnard rendering of the harbor at St. Tropez served as a constant reminder of Spiegel vacations along the Côte D'Azur. He delighted in being his own docent, expounding on Picasso's clean, confident lines and palette-knife work or the magic-hour primary colors of American Luminists. Along the upstairs hallway, he displayed a small gallery of Mud's paintings and drawings. "She was quite talented," said Jack.

Following his Oscar triumph, Jack didn't take the year off, but neither was he as fevered about moving from movie to movie. Cocooned with his paintings and his insecurities, he pondered his options.

When Stanley Kubrick called upon him to consider collaborating on Stephen King's new novel *The Shining*, Jack told Sandy Bresler to make the deal before he'd even read the book. It wouldn't be his next project because Jack remained determined to spend some of his *Cuckoo's Nest* clout on another crack at directing, but Kubrick was still high on the list of auteurs with whom Jack intended to work.[16] The meticulous, secretive, but sought-after director had been courting Jack since *Easy Rider*, when he offered Jack the role of Napoleon.

"I can't imagine Stanley Kubrick making an uninteresting film, and if that's the subject that he wants to tackle, I mean, I would love to let Napoleon move in on me for six months or so," Jack said at the time. Then he watched the director's enthusiasm fade as quickly as it had arisen. "I raised the money for the project—it took me a day—and then he changed his mind and did *Clockwork Orange* (1971)," said Jack. "He used a lot of the Napoleonic material in *Barry Lyndon* [1975]."[17]

While Kubrick's Napoleon never got beyond talk, it did launch Jack's lifelong obsession. He became so intrigued with the self-proclaimed French emperor that he created his own shrine: Napoleonic lithographs, and maps, and books.[18] At one point, he asked Towne to write a screenplay that Jack would direct. As early as his first Oscar nomination, Jack reminded one columnist of the fleeting value of awards, using the pint-sized Corsican's insight as an example: Napoleon said he could subdue the whole world if he had enough ribbons to award his soldiers. Jack seemed well aware that the studios had similarly hoodwinked actors with shiny trophies called Academy Awards.

Besides Napoleon, Jack lured Towne into another long-standing fancy: a *Chinatown* sequel. Following the film's success, Robert Evans began jonesing to produce *Chinatown Deux*, envisioning the same sort of franchise he'd created with *The Godfather* saga. Towne came up with a Jake Gittes trilogy, documenting the despoiling of Southern California that began with *Chinatown*'s 1937 backstory of water theft and land grab. *The Iron Jew*, later retitled *The Two Jakes*, would be set eleven years later, in 1948, documenting the rise of the automobile, oil, and postwar subdivisions. The third and concluding segment, titled *Cloverleaf*, would chronicle an aging Gittes in 1959, witnessing the unholy marriage of freeway and urban sprawl.[19]

Now independent of Paramount, Evans would produce, while Towne, who was already noodling with a script, hoped to direct.[20] Evans advised Jack to abandon his own directing ambitions and grab the million-dollar acting jobs while he could. Stars that shone brightly, he counseled, inevitably faded. "Wait 'til you're an old man to direct," said Evans.

Jack had grown accustomed to getting hit up from old friends but now found himself deluged with scripts: everyone had one with a part perfect for Jack. Pals long-standing and newly acquainted implored Jack to read theirs first. "I have this dream that my poor deceased mother is going to come up out of her grave to me someday and beckon me over," said Jack. "'Psst! Come here, son, I want you to have a look at this script I've got for you.'"

When the producer-writer Polly Platt sent him a copy of *Pretty Baby* (1978), her director, Louis Malle, chafed. He knew that so direct an appeal would rub Jack the wrong way. When Jack passed, the role of the Storyville photographer Bellocq went instead to David Carradine.

Similarly, the brash and predatory Andy Warhol cast Jack and Anjelica as Jackson Pollock and the artist's girlfriend Ruth Kligman before Warhol even bothered to ask whether they were interested.[21] *The Last Detail* producer Gerry Ayres had a Pollock script, too. *The Painter* was tailored for Jack. Jack was not interested.

Hal Ashby was also looking to reprise *The Last Detail* partnership, asking Jack to be the impotent, wheelchair-bound veteran in *Coming Home* (1978). He'd play opposite his old rival Bruce Dern. Jane Fonda urged Jack to sign, but again, no deal. The role went instead to Jon Voight, who earned an Oscar for the effort.

Polanski wanted Jack for *Pirates*, a fanciful costume adventure set in the eighteenth century along the Spanish Main, but Jack wouldn't cut his deal-busting $1.25 million asking price even for an old friend. *Pirates* had to wait until 1986, when Walter Matthau took on the role of the crafty buccaneer written for Jack.[22]

Orson Welles's fast friend Henry Jaglom also approached Jack to help moviedom's elder statesman make *The Big Brass Ring*, a Welles screenplay about the unmasking of a gay U.S. senator. Jack named Welles along with Akira Kurosawa and John Ford as his three all-time favorite directors, and while *The Big Brass Ring* would have been the director's triumphant final film, Jack nixed the project when the subject of his salary arose.[23] "I'd charge my mother my fee—and she's deceased," he told *Variety*'s Army Archerd.

Steven Spielberg could afford Jack and wanted him to play the lead in *Close Encounters of the Third Kind* (1977), but Jack begged off. Sandy Bresler told the producer Julia Phillips that Jack wouldn't play second fiddle to an eye-popping spaceship.

"I can't believe he's turning it down," said Phillips. "He's big enough for the effects."

"You know this 'no' is final," said Bresler.

"Nothing is final in Hollywood," scoffed Phillips.[24]

Spielberg's matinee rival George Lucas had his own space movie in the works, and while Jack was no part of it, *Star Wars* (1977) would affect him and every other Hollywood actor for years to come. "There is not a frame in *Star Wars* that I would have let through my editing machine," Jack observed. "George Lucas made a good science fiction film for him, but it just wasn't good enough for me. That shows how wrong I can be."

At $461 million, *Star Wars* was destined to dwarf Spielberg's $260 million *Jaws* box office and make special-effects spectaculars as routine a summer tradition as the Fourth of July. Sealing the blockbuster formula and ensuring sequels well into the next century, *Star Wars* and *Jaws* gave rise to the *Indiana Jones* and *Back to the Future* series but also brought on the soulless machine-made cinema of the mid-eighties—"little herpes, monsters, and Jell-O movies," as Jack liked to call them.

Jack wanted no part of Spielberg or Lucas. In his post-*Cuckoo* incarnation he wanted a place behind the camera, not in front. Beyond *Moontrap*, he had developed his own growing roster of directing projects. "I was very attracted to *Dune* for a long time," said Jack, "but it'd be a huge job for me to approach."[25] He also vowed to "come out with the real Howard Hughes," backing off only after Warren Beatty began to obsess over the billionaire as Jack had over Napoleon.

For years, Jack had wanted to turn *Lie Down in Darkness*— William Styron's grim but lyrical story of intergenerational alcoholism and suicide—into a grim but lyrical movie. In *Henderson the Rain King*, he saw great comic potential. For the rest of the century, Jack kept optioning Saul Bellow's rollicking tale of an unhappy Manhattan millionaire who finds satisfaction as an African shaman. "Well, I could pull that movie off if I could figure out Pygmies," said Jack. "It's hard to fake Pygmies in any way."

While Bellow welcomed the option money,[26] the peevish Nobel Prize winner recalled his initial meeting with Jack as something of a bust. Jack's world and the middle-class New England neighborhood where Bellow lived couldn't have been more different:

> His white stretch limousine could not make the narrow turn between my gateposts. Silent neighbors watched from a distance at the long car with its Muslim crescent antenna on the trunk. Then Nicholson came out, observed by many.
>
> "Gee, behind the tinted glass I couldn't tell it was so green out here," Jack observed.
>
> He lit a mysterious-looking cigarette and brought out a small pocket ashtray, a golden object resembling a pillbox. Perhaps his butt ends had become relics or collectibles. I should have asked him to explain this, for everything he did was noted and I had to answer the questions of my neighborhood friends, for whom Nicholson's appearance here was something like the consecration of a whole stretch of road.

The Bellow episode belied Jack's claim to have developed "a facility for hiding out in public." For years he'd depended on his everyman looks to limit double takes. Occasionally, he'd don the chauffeur's cap and drive himself.

But it grew harder to blend in. Not long after moving to Mulholland, Jack bought a beach retreat and drove there in his VW,[27] but the simple task of getting to Malibu unrecognized was no longer a snap.[28] Venturing out anywhere evolved into an ordeal.

Colorado was different. "Aspen people, like Parisians, tend to leave their noteworthy citizens alone," observed Jim Harrison.

By the late 1970s, Jack was the unofficial "King of Aspen," joining Don Henley, Glen Frey, Jimmy Buffet, Jill St. John, Bob Rafelson, John Denver, Lou Adler, Hunter Thompson, and other affluent sixties survivors in an upscale mountain resort that Thompson called Fat City and Andy Warhol referred to as Toy Town. Jack wintered for the Zen of the slopes but liked to range through the wilderness on his Harley during the spring and the summer.

In January 1977, Jack took a few days off from skiing to sit in the front row at the French chanteuse Claudine Longet's Aspen murder trial. Unlike the Manson trial seven years earlier, where Jack came and went unnoticed, his presence generated media delirium and helped to cinch the mountain resort's reputation as "Hollywood in the Rockies." Longet, charged with shooting her live-in lover, the Olympic skier Vladimir "Spider" Sabich,[29] got a twenty-one-day sentence for criminal negligence and married her defense attorney: an early version of the oxymoronic "celebrity justice" that O. J. Simpson and Robert Blake would enjoy two decades hence.[30]

Jack flew from Aspen to Washington, D.C., to join Warren Beatty in celebrating an end to the Nixon era at President Jimmy Carter's inauguration. Afterward, they partied first at the Lion D'or, where they met up with John Lennon, Yoko Ono, and Muhammad Ali, and later at Pamela Harriman's party, where "Master B" talked politics while Jack tried to sell *Moontrap*. United Artists had given the film a thumbs-down, so Jack cornered Lester Persky, one of the moneymen behind *The Last Detail* and *The Missouri Breaks*. After Persky passed, Jack found a couple of Israelis with film money. For the lead, he advised them to think Lee Marvin, not Jack Nicholson, who, he again stressed, would direct, not star. Without Jack in the cast, the Israelis weren't interested. "There's always a different group of people, a different philosophy at a given studio of what makes them make funds available to a filmmaker to make a film," Jack complained.

At month's end, Jack was back in New York, "looking a little older and heavier," by Andy Warhol's estimation. Nonetheless, Jack partied hard. He made the Regine's rounds, the glam parties upstairs at Zoli Rendessy's modeling agency, the nonstop action at Ara Gallant's place, or anywhere else the thin young Amazons now dubbed "supermodels" might gather. Well past the loss of Michelle Phillips, Beatty tagged along on Jack's "skunk" expeditions with the sleek Somalian cover girl Iman in tow.

Disco gripped Manhattan. Nose candy was the drug du jour. No less an ironic student of the era than Roman Polanski observed, "The relatively innocent use of psychedelics and grass was on the wane. Cocaine and quaaludes were now the rage."

Dissipated into a complete junkie, Papa John Phillips hit up Jack and his fellow party animal Mick Jagger for $5,000 loans, ostensibly to help him past a rough financial patch but, in fact, to sustain a $500-a-week coke habit. Everyone from Tony Franciosa to Linda Blair got busted for cocaine. Tommy Rettig, who played the adorable young owner of Lassie in 1950s television, got five years for smuggling. Before the decade's end, it seemed as if every celebrity had his own personal dealer or knew someone who did.

In the clubs, willing supermodels replaced the Holly Golightlys of the Jet Set. Linked with Lauren Hutton,[31] Apollonia von Ravenstein, and Zou Zou, among others, Jack wallowed in sensory overload. Studio 54 opened that spring and grossed $7 million during its first year of operation, even though two years later its founders would go to prison for drug trafficking. Closing briefly, the legendary nightclub reopened and remained a New York fixture and a favored Jack haunt until 1986, when it was shuttered permanently as a club; it reopened years later as a venue for Broadway musicals. Jack trolled, entreated, and usually got his way with women. Recalling her late friend the fashion princess Gia Carangi,[32] the party girl Toni O'Connor recounted one instance when he did not: "Jack Nicholson tried to put the make on her at Studio, and I flipped out. He was in love with Gia; he worshipped the ground she walked on. She got off on it. She was like, 'I can't stand him; he's an *old* man.'"

Jack had his secret doubts. He was losing his hair and developing a belly. He'd lost Anjelica to hunky Ryan O'Neal. And perhaps the biggest slap of all, he couldn't even get *Moontrap* off the ground. As his fortieth birthday approached and *Moontrap* looked more and more iffy, Jack retreated to Aspen. Meanwhile, back in L.A., events unfolded that would land him and Anjelica in a scandal that made Claudine Longet's gunplay look like jaywalking.

On March 11, 1977, the LAPD arrested Roman Polanski for drugging and raping thirteen-year-old Samantha Geimer. Talking about her ordeal twenty years later, the chain-smoking young mother of three recalled for a *People* staff writer how Polanski had seduced her in Jack's outdoor hot tub, first with the prospect of shooting her for a *Vogue* fashion layout and later with whispered promises of stardom.[33] Courtesy of her high school boyfriend, the precocious Samantha had already lost her virginity, but the sex she described with the forty-two-year-old director during a quaalude-and-Cristal sodomy session was bewildering at best and psychically searing at worst. When she told him that she used no birth control, Polanski turned her around to penetrate her anus and fell to his knees for Samantha's first dazed experience with cunnilingus—a numbed sensation she described as Polanski lapping at her like a terrier.

It was Anjelica's misfortune to stumble upon this tryst. She was still in the drawn-out process of breaking up with Jack and had dropped by to pick up more of her belongings when she found Polanski and the girl in flagrante in Jack's TV room. After Anjelica satisfied herself that no one seemed to be hurt and she bought Polanski's story that Geimer was old enough for consensual coupling, the girl and the director left.[34] Only later, after he'd taken Geimer home to Woodland Hills and she revealed to her sister and her mother what had happened, did Polanski's pedophilia mushroom into an international incident.

The next day, police confronted the director in the lobby of the Beverly Hills Hotel. Polanski cooperated to the degree that he volunteered to take detectives to the scene of the alleged crime. Anjelica let them in. During the ensuing search, the cops turned up half a gram of cocaine in her purse and a small container of hashish upstairs in a chest of drawers. After Anjelica's arrest, it dawned on her what the cops were up to.

Jack returned to L.A. for the Oscars, presenting Best Picture to the producers of *Rocky* (1976) on March 29, 1977, but revealing nothing about the obvious turmoil surrounding his private life. Two weeks later, police got a court order to take his fingerprints so they could compare them to those found on the confiscated hashish container. They could make no match, but Jack saw the pattern: first Bert Schneider, next Ryan O'Neal, then Anjelica.

Fortunately for Jack, no one knew about the shaving cream or the coffee containers with the false bottoms or the sliding wall at the rear of his bedroom closet, which hid a cedar-lined stash that even trained dope-sniffing police dogs could not penetrate.

half-brother, Murray Hawley, at [t]een, a decade before he became [insp]iration for Jack's portrayal of [the "]Badass" Buddusky in *The Last* [*Detail*] (1973).

Murray, June, and Jack's half-sister, Pamela, at the beach in California in the late fifties.

[Jack's] mother, June Nicholson [Hawle]y, at twenty-three.

Jack's first home, on Sixth Street in Neptune City, New Jersey.

Ethel May "Mud" Nicholson (second from right) surrounded by Murray's in-la
circa 1963.

Murray and Cheryl (Cron) Hawley, circa 1963.

Jack's half-sister, Pamela,
eighteen, upon graduatic
beauty college.

ck's home during his high school years in Spring Lake, New Jersey.

ack, far right, playing
for the MGM basket-
all squad, circa 1957.

Jack's first movie role
as *The Cry Baby
Killer* (1958), with
Carolyn Mitchell.

Jack swaps dialogue with Barbra Streisand in the overproduced musical *On a Clear Day You Can See Forever* (1970).

As Texas ACLU lawyer George Hanson, Jack finally broke through to stardom in *Easy Rider* (1969).

Jack during a break while directing *Drive, He Said* (1971).

...d Ann-Margret in *Carnal Knowledge* (1971).

In *The King of Marvin Gardens* (1972), Jack shifted gears, playing against type as an introverted late-night radio host opposite cocky con man Bruce Dern.

Billy "Badass" Buddusky, one of Jack's most enduring characters.

Gittes in *Chinatown* (1974), pictured here with costar Faye Dunaway,
t only landed his fourth Oscar nomination, he also graduated from
er roles to leading man.

Polanski (left), John Huston (center), and Jack during a *Chinatown* break.

Jack in his first Oscar-winning role, as Randle Patrick McMurphy in *One Flew over the Cuckoo's Nest* (1975).

Milos Forman, Louise Fletcher, and Jack, Oscar night 1976.

Marlon Brando in *Missouri Breaks* (1976).

(standing, second from left, behind costar Mary Steenbergen) in *Goin' South* (1978),
...ed by his real-life uncle George "Shorty" Smith (left) and B. J. Merholz (right), with
...Begley Jr. (far right).

Jack and Anjelica
Huston at the Oscars
the night he won
Best Actor for *One
Flew over the
Cuckoo's Nest*.

Jack and daughter Jennifer (left) with actress Joan Hackett (right).

In Stanley Kubrick's *The Shining* (1980), Jack left the critics cold but created a high-water mark for onscreen insanity and cleaned up at the box office.

Jack's sixth Oscar nomination, for his portrayal of playwright Eugene O'Neill, came courtesy of pal Warren Beatty's *Reds* (1981). Twenty years hence, Jack and Diane Keaton would reteam in *Something's Gotta Give* (2003).

Jack and Jessica Lange with Bob Rafelson (left) on the set of *The Postman Always Rings Twice* (1981)

Big winners at the 56th Annual Academy Awards included James L. Brooks for directing, writing, and producing *Terms of Endearment* (1983), costarring Shirley MacLaine and Jack.

pping for the over-the-top monsters he would portray in *Batman* (1989), *Wolf* 94), and *The Departed* (2006), Jack romped through *The Witches of Eastwick* 37) with costars (from left) Cher, Susan Sarandon, and Michelle Pfeiffer.

ronweed (1987), Jack patterned the alcoholic ex–baseball player Francis •lan after his grandfather. The film earned both him and costar Meryl Streep •ar nominations.

"Joker" Jack in *Batman* (1989).

As marine colonel Nathan Jessep
A Few Good Men (1992), Jack sp
best-known catchphrase: "You ca
handle the truth!"

For *Hoffa* (1992), costarring and directed by Danny DeVito, Jack earned both a b
(Golden Globes) and a worst acting (Razzies) nomination. He won neither.

Jack wooed Michelle Pfeiffer in *Wolf* (1994), his fourth pairing with director Mike Nichols.

In one of the three roles he played in Tim Burton's sci-fi farce, *Mars Attacks!* (1996), Jack went over the top and kept going.

ood as It Gets (1997)
ed a first-time
emy Award for
n Hunt and a third
g Oscar for Jack.

Jack's fiftieth high school reunion, his aunt Lorraine sitting at his right.

Jack and his former classmate Miller "Punky" Preston, five decades after they were both cut from the Manasquan High basketball squad.

Following arraignment on six felony counts, Polanski posted $2,500 bail. Prosecutors offered to drop charges against Anjelica if she'd cooperate. Two months later, the district attorney announced that the actress would testify—a prospect she later denied. "She reacted strongly to being mislabeled, and the D.A.'s office wrote her a letter of apology," said Jack.

Throughout his persecution, Polanski protested that Samantha was a conniving Lolita. At no time did he compare himself to Professor Humbert Humbert. Even after all but one of the charges were dropped, he continued to maintain that he was the victim: Samantha and her mother had misrepresented her age and conspired to blackmail him.

Jack defended Polanski, perhaps forgetting that his own daughter was Samantha's age. As the scandal grew and the future of both his pal and his ex-girlfriend remained in jeopardy, Jack made an abrupt decision.

In April, he signed with Paramount to direct himself in a Western—not his pet project *Moontrap* but *Goin' South*, a raucous comedy about a renegade forced into a frontier marriage. The screenplay, written by his old pal John Herman Shaner and Al Ramrus, had been sitting on the shelf for years. Bob Rafelson's ex, Toby, hired on as production designer. Two more old pals, Harold Schneider and Harry Gittes, would produce. *Goin' South* was shot in Durango, Mexico, far from subpoenas, lawyers, police, and media, which began to gather in L.A. in anticipation of a titillating summertime trial.

With a $6 million budget and a free hand to cast and control as he saw fit, Jack accepted *Goin' South* as his directing consolation prize. It was also a very good time to get the hell out of Dodge.

Jack had wanted to make *Goin' South* with Jane Fonda as early as 1970, but the studio originally intended it for Elliott Gould and Candice Bergen, with Mike Nichols directing. *Goin' South* told the tale of the con man Henry Lloyd Moon, who was rescued from the gallows by a homesteading woman who takes advantage of a fanciful Texas custom: sparing condemned men if they marry and obey their wives.

Jack's early Westerns, beginning with the long-forgotten *The Broken Land* and continuing through the stark, dark *Ride in the Whirlwind* and *The Shooting*, informed and resonated through *Goin' South*

(1978)—at least, in his imagination. Instead of seeing the movie as a clumsy comic rewrite of the Shaner-Ramrus script, he viewed it as what the two screenwriters had intended: a sober drama about the outlaw legacy of the Civil War.[35]

"No one extracts the serious plot from *Goin' South*," Jack complained. Like the ragtag crew pursued by the evil marshal in *The Broken Land* or the posse in *Ride in the Whirlwind*, *Goin' South*'s Henry Lloyd Moon and his pals "were once all members of Quantrill's Raiders, the original guerrilla warfare unit in America," said Jack. "And what do you do with these people once they're now home? The fact that this wasn't even touched on critically was disappointing to me."[36]

Most of *Goin' South*'s conflict centered on Henry Moon's love interest, played by tall, dark-haired Mary Steenburgen. The twenty-four-year-old Arkansas native resembled Anjelica, fueling speculation that Jack had meant the role for Huston until she renewed her fling with Ryan O'Neal. Anjelica, saddled with her cocaine bust and her conflicted feelings about Jack, was notably absent throughout the filming of *Goin' South*.

But the neophyte Steenburgen was a publicist's dream. She'd been a sometime actress and a full-time waitress at the Magic Pan Creperie on Fifty-seventh Street in New York until Jack plucked her out of obscurity. In a field that included such pros as Jessica Lange and Meryl Streep, Steenburgen walked in for a cold reading and got the part. In June, she quit the New York comedy ensemble Cracked Tokens, where she'd been honing her improv skills, and gave notice at the Magic Pan, where her boss wrote in the "Termination" heading of her personnel file, "left to star in a movie with Jack Nicholson." Not since the legendary MGM flak Howard Strickland imprinted the "discovery" of the "Sweater Girl" Lana Turner on fans' fevered imaginations had an untried actress been given the full studio hype Paramount accorded Steenburgen.[37]

Jack also got credit for casting John Belushi[38] in his first motion picture: the cameo of a Mexican sheriff, which earned the *Saturday Night Live* star $5,000 and the directorial attention of his acting idol.[39] Belushi said the experience made him "a shark in front of the camera," adding, "Nicholson taught me that."

Production began in late July on a Western set outside of Durango that John Wayne had dubbed "La Tierra del Cine" when he and John Ford made *Rio Grande* (1950). Although Mexico forbade foreign ownership, the Duke somehow wrangled possession of the property with the blessing of the Portillo government and shot or sponsored seventy Westerns there during the next quarter century. For $400 a day, the *Goin' South* company rented the same adobe town that Wayne had ridden through in *Chisum* (1969). The only new element was a gallows, where Henry Moon faced perdition before Steenburgen's character claimed him as a husband.

Jack reveled in the Durango desert, which he called "strikingly breathtaking." "Some scenes will even be resembling the landscapes of Maynard Dixon, who did those beautiful paintings of Western sunsets where mountains and plains stand out in light and shadow," he said.[40]

Before *Goin' South*, Clint Eastwood cautioned Jack to "get twice as much sleep as everyone else on the movie." There's no evidence he followed Eastwood's advice, but Jack did surround himself with friends tolerant of his late-night habits and unpredictable mood swings. He took the ranch house nearest to the set for himself, alternately brooding or exulting over the film's progress. On a down day, he'd growl, "There's absolutely nothing I care about anymore. Does it show on the screen?"

The next evening he might throw open the doors and invite everyone in for lasagna and booze, chortling and canoodling until dawn. With Ruth Etting belting blues from the stereo, Jack could mesmerize with eloquence and erudition, rambling through the night about death and cancer, sex without enthusiasm, Nietzsche, drugs, and an ever-evolving philosophy about the dark side of human nature.

Cuckoo's Nest cronies Danny DeVito and Christopher Lloyd joined the cast, as did Ed Begley Jr., B. J. Merholz, and Jeff Morris, one of Jack's early acting coaches. Veronica Cartwright was among the actresses who admitted sleeping with Jack during the four-month shoot. Inevitably, there were others.

Annie Marshall, who also made her brief screen debut as a "painted lady," was Jack's gatekeeper, as well as his permanent social secretary. No one got to Jack except through her. Relatives came to watch. Jennifer flew in from Hawaii to visit, and Jack gave his "Uncle" Shorty Smith the role of Luana Anders's husband in the film's opening sequence.

Though Shorty's legs were bad and he was slowly dying of emphysema, he took his film debut as seriously as Belushi or Steenburgen did theirs. A former dancer from his Eddie King days, he once cut a mean rug with Lorraine at the Elks Club dances back home in Neptune, but even a short shuffle and a jig during *Goin' South* left him breathless. Jim Harrison, who also visited at Jack's invitation, affectionately called the indomitable Jersey roughneck with the defiant lust for living "preposterous."

Harrison, who began his novella *Revenge* during his stay, said that Jack insisted upon becoming his patron: "After about a week in Durango I was getting mildly nervous about what I was doing there, but then Nicholson drew me aside to address the problem. I was staying at his rental, and every evening we had spoken about literature and movies until late, but now we were talking about money, which for me had always been a ghastly issue. I was put at ease when he merely asked about my debts and what I needed to come up with for a year of writing. When I got home two days later, the check was already there."

If one had neither the time nor the inclination to spend it, Jack called such excess cash "dead money." He preferred putting his to work and did so in Harrison's case by underwriting *Revenge*. John Huston would direct, with Jack to star. But even after the deal to make *Revenge* fell through years later, Jack never demanded Harrison's film rights as a premium on his $50,000 subsidy. When Harrison got far enough ahead, Jack asked only that he repay the loan. "Many people can afford to behave this way but very few actually do," Harrison observed.

Despite a casual working atmosphere that the cast and the crew raved about, Jack again found himself at odds with the International Alliance of Theatrical Stage Employees (IATSE)—the same union that gave him fits during *Drive, He Said*. If it were up to its members, IATSE might have coexisted with the Mexican nationals whom the government demanded that Jack put on the payroll. But the union's business agent back in Hollywood would not be placated. Because Jack used Mexican labor as well as American, IATSE demanded that its trademark be removed from the finished *Goin' South*.

But Jack's movie would not be finished for some time, even though he took advantage of the latest advances in technology. Using the newest video playback machine before and after a scene immediately allowed him to see how he looked on camera and made the job of directing himself all the easier. Yet even with that aid, he ordered retake after retake. Using two separate cameras and shooting on a ratio that would make Dennis Hopper blanch, Jack came away with more than 400,000 feet of film. It would take three editors and the better part of a year to boil it down to 101 minutes of screen time.

For the first time on an extended location shoot, Jack also had to contend with his health. In October, his horse tripped and Jack flew from the saddle, splitting his lip, bruising ribs, and breaking his wrist. Borrowing a page from the Duke, he taped himself up and got back on the horse, but there would be back trouble in his future.

Jack also developed a constant nasal drip, and for almost three and a half years after *Goin' South*, rumors dogged him that he had both a drug problem and a coke temper. Although he denied both, it did not help his case that his next screen role would be that of an explosive psychopath.

"I'm tired. I've never been tired before," Jack droned as *Goin' South* wound to a close. "If this film doesn't work, I can never direct again."

On August 8, 1977, Roman Polanski circumvented an L.A. show trial by pleading guilty to unlawful intercourse with a child. The following day, he busted a paparazzo's camera as the photographer snapped a shot of him visiting Sharon Tate's grave on the eighth anniversary of her murder.

Jack's support never wavered. In December, the night before the director entered a forty-two-day psychiatric evaluation at the California state prison in Chino, Jack joined Tony Richardson and the *New Yorker* critic Kenneth Tynan in a Polanski send-off dinner.

That same month, Jack's family secret hit the papers, and not in a small way. The venerable Sunday supplement *Parade* magazine printed the staff gossip Walter Scott's tantalizing revelation in a Q&A that named Ethel May as Jack's grandmother, June as his mother, and the New Jersey businessman Donald F. Rose as his real father. Jack had been born, Scott reported, at St. Vincent's in Manhattan, not at home on the Jersey Shore.

By now a successful semiretired owner of several beauty salons, Don Furcillo-Rose got a late-night call from Jack a short time after the item ran. It was during this pleasant exchange that the man who once had a summer fling down at the Jersey Shore with June Nicholson assured June's boy Jack that they were, in fact, father and son.

Jack wanted to know whether Furcillo-Rose needed anything, and he answered no. He'd done well for himself and his family, to a degree that he was able to purchase horses, season box seats at Monmouth Racetrack, and a vacation home in the Poconos. Furcillo-Rose's overriding concern was reconnecting with the son whom he'd been forced to watch grow and develop from afar—a result, he said, of Mud's abiding fury over his impregnating her daughter and ruining June's showbiz career. The one essential bit of information the aging Furcillo-Ross withheld was that Mud had lusted after him as much as June had, and this mother-daughter jealousy guaranteed that the Nicholson matriarch would never allow Jack to know his real father.

Jack never tipped his hand as to what he did or did not believe about his origins, but neither did he acknowledge Furcillo-Rose's paternity. Thereafter, Furcillo-Rose heard from Jack only through his attorneys, Abe Somer and Ken Kleinberg. The tone grew icier over time, culminating in Kleinberg's final threat on November 14, 1980: "Our client refutes and repudiates as without foundation the statements made by you alleging that you are Mr. Nicholson's father. Such statements are false and defamatory."

And then, silence.

13

JACK RETURNED FROM ASPEN TO BEGIN THE MARATHON editing of *Goin' South* just as the New Year began. Polanski finished his psychiatric evaluation about the same time and was once more out on bail, awaiting sentencing. Still unshaven and brimming with jailhouse chitchat about his prison celebrity, he dined with Jack on the last Monday in January. Tuesday morning, the director fled to London, then Paris, never to return to the United States. "He was in the best of spirits when I saw him Monday night," said Jack. "I just can't believe it."

Through the Paramount producer Howard Koch, who'd run into the sentencing judge at the Hillcrest Country Club, Polanski had learned that he might have to undergo another psych evaluation.

Probation might be recommended, but it seemed equally likely the judge could make Polanski an example and send him to prison for the next twenty years—a prospect Jack found hard to fathom. "I think he would have gotten off because the girl's father had entered the case and taken her out of state," he said. "She would not have testified."

But the media pressed Jack further. He rationalized Polanski's behavior on grounds that Polanski's actions were neither rape nor wrong in the European culture Polanski had come from. While Jack conceded nothing, the Polanski episode left a sobering imprint on his own propensity for young women. "I believe Roman is under the classification of 'fleeing felon,'" Jack said. "I think that it's a completely unjust decision. I, of course, wasn't there, so I know less about the actual events than anybody else."

On March 29, Jack presented the award for Best Picture to *Annie Hall* (1977),[1] but the spotlight belonged to the Best Supporting Actress Vanessa Redgrave, for *Julia* (1977). Redgrave, in her acceptance speech, upheld her favored minority—the Palestinian refugee— and condemned the Jewish Defense League as "a small bunch of Zionist hoodlums whose behavior is an insult to the stature of Jews all over the world." Signaling an end to the type of seventies political grandstanding that made the Oscars a bully pulpit for Vietnam, Native Americans, and now Palestinians, the playwright Paddy Chayefsky rebuked Redgrave later in the telecast. "A simple 'thank you' would have sufficed," he said, and got a standing ovation.

Asked his opinion, Jack feigned ignorance. "I guess it's fine," he deadpanned. "But I'm not a well-read person, you can see that. What are these Zionists? Are they Reds? There've been threats? I've been skiing."

Jack had to look no further than his next-door neighbor to see the sorry result of airing one's convictions on TV. He kept his opinions off the tube, where he ran the risk of rubbing his fan base the wrong way. While acknowledging the medium as inevitable as Marshal McLuhan had predicted, Jack resisted with all his might. "Everyone's afraid of television," he preached. "Television is the strongest single element in every area of American society, including government. All you have to do is look at the polls; every time the president makes a speech on television the polls in the country change drastically, no matter what he says and no matter what the issue is. Charles de Gaulle said you cannot run a government without controlling television. Television is a mighty, mighty monster."

Once as politically active as Beatty, Brando, or Bert Schneider, Jack kept his own counsel and parried pointed questions with quips. Nobody heard him quote Nietzsche or speak like a wonk while cameras were rolling. Playing the clown always seemed the safer course.

Jack's time began to look as though it had passed, yet he remained philosophical. "Movies change like the fashion of skirts, up and down, up and down," he said.

As Jack supervised the wrangling of seventy-five miles of negative into a screen-worthy *Goin' South*, he also prepared to take up residence in London. *The Shining* (1980) would begin with exteriors of the Timberline Lodge on the southern slope of Oregon's Mt. Hood, but the expatriate Stanley Kubrick—a British resident since *Spartacus* (1960)—refused to shoot on American soil unless he had to.[2] Except for the Sno-Cat chase scene, shot on an access road leading to the grand old mountain inn, *The Shining* was filmed on interior sets built at London's EMI-Elstree Studios. Production got under way the last week of May 1978.

Although Kubrick announced a twenty-five-week shoot, he had a long history of going way over schedule. Jack checked in at the five-star Dorchester, but as Kubrick asked for more and more time, Warner Bros. saw the wisdom of moving Jack to a cheaper four-bedroom manse on the Thames at a mere $1,700 a week: a so-called rag-head rental because wealthy Arabs moved in and out of the neighborhood with some frequency.

Jack's pals and hangers-on followed him to his London lair. Anjelica and her sister Allegra stayed for a while and then left, the Ryan O'Neal episode not quite over. Harry Dean Stanton, in England to film *Alien*, dropped by.[3] John Huston visited, as did Jim Harrison, who discussed their progress on *Revenge*. Mick Jagger, George Harrison, and John Lennon paid their respects. When Bob Dylan came to Covent Garden, Jack and Bianca Jagger basked in his presence, according to the journalist Michael Gray. Musicians, models, and Manhattanites were always welcome at Jack's place.

Diana Vreeland recalled a late-night dinner at San Lorenzo's when Jack's *Goin' South* back injury pained him so that he could not sit. He paced, fidgeted, tore cigarettes to bits, and complained that the injury threatened to hold up production of *The Shining*. Vreeland took him to task like an avenging grandmother. "I'm fed up with your back!" she said. "You take every pill on the market, but you don't do as I say. Tonight I'm fixing you up."

She borrowed Jack's Daimler and his driver, George, who took her to an all-night pharmacy in Piccadilly. Purchasing a couple of back plasters, she returned to the restaurant and ordered Jack to drop his trousers. A small audience gathered to gawk as she complimented the star's bum: "Wonderful condition! I must say your chemistry is really good! Plump and pink."

She ordered Jack to wriggle so the plaster wouldn't stick too tight. "Otherwise, you'll never move again," she warned. The plaster did the trick; he was able to continue with *The Shining*, while Vreeland took full credit for literally saving his ass.

When Jack wasn't dining out, the studio hired its star a live-in cook. Otherwise, George ferried him from hot spot to hot spot, as Jack changed women as frequently as he did cuisine.

Margaret Trudeau, the estranged wife of the Canadian prime minister Pierre Trudeau, recalled joining Jack one evening.[4] In her 1982 memoir *Consequences*, she boasted, "I discovered just how much room there is in the back seat of a Daimler," but in typical Jack fashion, he returned to Anjelica and left Trudeau feeling "crushed and like a fool" after their brief affair graduated to the gossip columns. Likewise, Christina Onassis had her fling with Jack— power attracted to power—but it was over as quickly as it began. Fleet Street linked Jack to Melanie Griffith, Jill St. John—a veritable smorgasbord of the starlets of the day. How much was true and how much fanzine fiction was left to the imagination—just the way Jack liked it. "I'd say if you cut half of his pussy in half, you'd have it about right," said Bruce Dern. "And still he probably gets more than anyone around."

Invariably, Jack returned to the stylish Anjelica, a friend and a lover who'd also mastered the graces of a great hostess. She spoke French and Italian, saw to the caterers, and held her own in a debate, while rolling a joint better than Jack could ever hope to. But still she wanted to act.

Jack had grown ambivalent toward marriage, especially to another actor, as illustrated by his reaction to his old pal Henry Jaglom's announcement that he would star his wife, Patrice Townsend, in

Sitting Ducks (1980), his first film since *Tracks* (1976). "You're crazy," said Jack. "This is one of the few really good marriages I've seen in my life. Don't endanger it by making her into an actress. You're nuts."

The Jagloms were divorced three years later.

Stanley Kubrick's eyebrows matched Jack's in flexibility and sheer arch power.[5] Beyond that, all comparisons failed. "Define Kubrick?" said Jack. "Umm . . . gives a new meaning to the word *meticulous.*"

Kubrick's epic approach to storytelling dwarfed Francis Coppola's grandiosity, and his perfectionist camerawork made the detail-obsessed Bob Rafelson look like an amateur with a Kodak camera. Following the resounding global success of *2001: A Space Odyssey* (1968), the Bronx-born ex-*Look* magazine photographer became the most sought-after director in the world, and he used his auteur power to wring what he wanted out of Hollywood. For a time, Kubrick held the *Guinness Book of World Records* title for most retakes (156) of a single scene.

He pioneered the most extensive and effective use to date of the Steadicam during *The Shining*. Propelled by a wheelchair rig, the camera was virtually another cast member, its Cyclops eye moving from room to room, around corners, and through the artificial maze at the end of the film.[6] In a sequence often aped, Kubrick used the Steadicam to stand in for the little boy Danny, who scooted through the spooky hotel hallways on his Big Wheel.

And yet, the roly-poly Anglophile with a passion for chess and a penchant for secrecy was so technology adverse that he created his shooting scripts using hunt-and-peck on a manual typewriter. He rewrote constantly, prompting Jack to borrow Boris Karloff's old trick of underlining his character's lines each day just to keep up. For the first time, Jack played a father, but one not like any other father—alleged, pseudo, or real—he'd ever known. Jack Torrance was a paternal nightmare.

"Grand Guignol was [*The Shining*]'s classification for me," said Jack, referring to the French theater of the grotesque that thrived in Paris during the first half of the twentieth century.[7] Terming *The Shining* "the first horror movie about writer's block," Jack portrayed an over-the-top author who retreats for the winter with his simpering wife and psychic son to a haunted mountain inn. There to write the

Great American Novel, Jack instead descends over two and a half hours of screen time into murderous madness.

Recalling the endlessly typed line "All work and no play makes Jack a dull boy," he said, "That's the one scene in the movie I wrote myself. That scene at the typewriter—that's what I was like when I got my divorce."

Jack parodied Ed McMahon's widely known intro to *The Tonight Show with Johnny Carson*, turning "Heeeeere's Johnny!" into a send-up that became the movie's enduring catch line and Jack's first major foray into self-parody.[8] Because Kubrick lived in England, he didn't understand its significance, but Jack was one of the few actors he allowed to improvise. Only Jack could find the funny side of Charles Manson. Both actor and director understood the delicate interplay between horror and comedy. "There's something inherently wrong with the human personality," observed the sardonic director of *Lolita* (1962), *Dr. Strangelove* (1964), and *A Clockwork Orange* (1971). "There's an evil side to it. One of the things that horror stories can do is to show us the archetypes of the unconscious: we can see the dark side without having to confront it directly."

Evil was what he wanted from Jack, and, during a grueling schedule that stretched to thirteen months, evil was what he got: a cross between Richard III and the Big Bad Wolf, concluded Pauline Kael. "[Kubrick] was trying to get performances that came out of extremity, exhaustion," theorized Kubrick's fellow director John Boorman.

In a scene in which Jack takes an ax to the seventy-year-old Scatman Crothers, Kubrick ordered more than forty retakes. Jack, who usually went along with his director, begged off on Crothers's behalf. Kubrick soldiered on until he got what he wanted. At Kubrick's behest, his cast overacted to the point of parody, pulling back just before *The Shining* spilled over into an absurdist retread of *The Terror*. "As the takes stacked up, Jack Nicholson and Shelley Duvall began to move through a range of emotions from catatonia to hysteria," wrote the Kubrick biographer Vincent Lobrutto.

The pressures alone were enough to drive a man to drink.

On July 9, 1978, Jack's half-brother, Murray Hawley Jr., died of heart failure and cirrhosis at the Veteran's Administration hospital in West Los Angeles. He was thirty-three, twice married, ex-navy, and a former bartender at Clare & Coby's Inn in Old Bridge, New Jersey. He bore a striking resemblance to Jack, down to the high forehead that wrinkled with Murray's own version of the killer smile. His ex-wife, Cheryl Cron, remembered him as the inspiration for Billy Badass in *The Last Detail*. "I don't know why he had to die in a VA hospital," she said. "And I don't know why they dumped him in the ocean instead of burying him beside his mother. Jack could have done better for his brother."

Murray's ashes were scattered at sea. Like his grandfather, he'd succumbed to alcohol: the same family curse that contributed to the early deaths of his mother and father. "They both drank," recalled Murray Sr.'s sister Nancy Dilsea. When the Hawleys were still married in the late 1940s and June used to visit, Dilsea recalled her sister-in-law always making a beeline for the bar. "She poured herself a big stiff one right away," Dilsea said.

When it came to anesthetizing the pain of living, Murray Sr. turned as often to spirits as his ex-wife had. If cancer hadn't prematurely claimed them, alcohol would have—as it did their only son. For Jack, Murray Jr.'s legacy was an appeal for vigilance about his own drinking. Pot eased his blackest moods but left him his liver.

Pamela liked her cocktails as much as her late brother had, but she tended hair, not bar. Now a professional hairdresser, as well as a wife and a mother, she moved with her husband, Doug Mangino, from the San Fernando Valley to the California Gold Rush hamlet of Georgetown. There, with a loan from "Uncle" Jack, she opened the Hilltop Beauty Shoppe, and for the next twenty years, she followed in both her grandmother's and her grandfather's footsteps. Like Mud, Pam operated her salon out of the family home; like her grandfather, she greeted many days with a hangover.

Jack had bailed out both Pam and Murray throughout the 1970s. When Murray welshed on a Beneficial Finance loan that threatened to ruin his credit, Jack came to the rescue. Burned by Pam's profligacy, he made her sign a promissory note secured by the Manginos' homestead before lending her any more money. He learned to exercise equal caution with friends. When the *Drive He, Said* star Bill Tepper fell on hard times and borrowed from him, he repaid Jack in full some time later.

Jack raised the famous eyebrows and said, "Tep, I've got money out to two dozen people. You're the only one who's ever paid me back."

Harold Schneider, who borrowed $280,000, which Jack secured with a lien on Schneider's Mulholland home, summed up the actor's circumspect generosity in a single advisory: "Don't ask him to put out $100 for dinner, but if you need $100,000 there's no problem."

Jack kept shredded currency heaped in a bowl on his living room coffee table, which, in addition to being his favorite conversation piece, put his riches in perspective. Once used as an ashtray, the bowl became home to dead dollar bills after a visit from the novelist Richard Brautigan, who demonstrated his own contempt for cash by pulling a pair of fifties from his wallet, tearing them up, and tossing them into Jack's fireplace.[9]

"Well, the next morning, I find some of the torn $50s on the floor and I just mindlessly put them into this thing here," said Jack. "It's some sort of a candy dish, but everybody always used it as an ashtray." Thenceforward, no one dropped their ashes in the bowl. "Instead, people would always ask me about it—what's with the torn money in the dish?" Jack continued. "And I started to realize that I was creating a work of art. It was sculpture, as much as that Salvador Dalí piece over there. In fact, of all the things that are in this room— the Picassos, the Francis Bacon, the Magritte—this bowl of money is the one piece of art that always draws the most comments and attention."

Squeaky frugal, Jack wasn't skilled at making money in traditional ways. He dabbled in the stock market but picked loser after loser. When he got to thirteen, Jack admitted, "There's another field I used to think I was a genius in."

Thanks to Brando, Jack became an early investor in solar-powered vehicles. "There's nothing wrong with that car," he insisted. "The conversion of water to hydrogen using photovoltaic cells is inevitable.[10] Petroleum's days are numbered. It's an antiquated power source and it's finite. And, okay, maybe it won't be a hundred years, but in a thousand years, it must be because it simply must be."

At one time generous to a fault, Jack no longer shared his riches without getting some assurances in return. While Polanski loved him like a brother, he labeled Jack "stingy." To a permanent professional entourage that included Sandy Bresler, Paul Wasserman, and Annie Marshall, he had added the rotund business manager Robert "Mr. C" Colbert, who encouraged him to temper his charity.

It was this Jack who was forced to confront his own past

indulgences in a flurry of publicity that came and went in the late seventies without the mainstream press catching on. "We had guarded the secret for years, but everyone knew except the public," Susan Anspach told the *Village Voice*. "Recently, an article appeared in print. Jack and I got together, decided how to proceed. We basically agreed not to talk about it."

Divorced and in need of a permanent home, Anspach bought a place in Santa Monica in 1979 for herself and her two children, including Jack's now eight-year-old son, Caleb. Jack would later help her with the mortgage. Like so many of Jack's secrets, the truth about his love child remained submerged in plain sight, at least for a time.

Jack took September off from *The Shining* to return to New York for a sneak preview of *Goin' South*. He invited Ara Gallant, along with the rest of the Warhol crowd. "I'm not sure—I think it was a light comedy," Warhol wrote in his *Diaries*. "It didn't say anything, though. It's good in the beginning and you think something's going to happen, but it doesn't."

The following month, Paramount released *Goin' South* with a resounding thud. Mary Steenburgen received praise; Jack got poison. "His impression of a scalawag is scenery chewing of the broadest kind," wrote the *London Guardian's* Steve Vineberg, in one of the kinder assessments.

Pauline Kael's take was as merciless as her review of *Cuckoo's Nest* had been fawning. The *New Yorker's* grand dame found particularly galling a loose and lurid mannerism Jack first played up onscreen as Red McMurphy. "[W]orking his mouth with tongue darting out and dangling lewdly, he's like an advertisement for a porno film. Wasn't there anybody on the set who'd tell Nicholson to give it a rest?" she lamented. "An actor-director who prances about the screen maniacally can easily fool himself into thinking that his film is jumping. Nicholson jumps, all right, but *Goin' South* is inert."

Kael also detected an annoying nasal drip. She heralded half a hundred other critics over the next few years who concluded that sniveling Henry Lloyd Moon suffered from a septum deviated by dope—an assessment that Jack angrily refuted during what was left of the seventies. Nevertheless, *Goin' South* would join *Under the Rainbow* (1981), *Sorcerer* (1977), *Personal Best* (1982), *One from the Heart*, (1982), and *Popeye* (1980) as spectacular duds delivered by the best and the brightest of the current crop of brilliant young film-makers. Capping an otherwise remarkable decade with dreck, these films all had a coke buzz and the unmistakable odor of plots on pot.

Goin' South's chilly reception plunged Jack back into a pigeonhole. The failure of his second directorial effort left him in a foul mood for months thereafter, as his daughter, Jennifer, noted during her annual holiday visit. "My dad was really weird then," she recalled. "It was like Christmas with an ax murderer."

"Jack and I have similar but different backgrounds," said his old pal Harry Gittes. "He's well-read, a deep guy, while I skate over everything. After *Goin' South*, I'm depressed he didn't cultivate directing, but he chose to be a movie star. Not a movie actor, but a movie star. If he'd been a movie actor, it might have been different."

Jack Warner, the last of the Warner brothers, as well as the last of the first generation of Hollywood's moguls, died that autumn along with *Goin' South*. Jack lamented Warner's passing, as he did that of Mary Pickford, who died the following spring. Both of them hailed from an era when "every guy who was the head of a studio was also a gambler." For actors as successful as Jack, the prospect of a Louis Mayer or a Harry Cohn or one of the Warner brothers blackmailing him into a single successful characterization over and over again, à la Clark Gable or Bette Davis, was no longer a threat. Like Pickford, he'd assumed control of his own destiny.

But in the emerging era of the deal maker, when studio heads "are making themselves the stars," Jack saw a different kind of trouble. "They're on the covers of magazines," he said. "Their salaries are now quotable. Why? Because it isn't about movies anymore."

As his bitterness grew, Jack became as pecuniary as a producer. He gobbled an ever larger chunk of the gross and cut his fee for no one. "I work for a guaranteed sum against a percentage of the profits—and every film I make exceeds that guarantee," he said. "If I don't take the money, it only disappears into one of those studio-owning conglomerates."

In January 1979, fire gutted one of *The Shining* sets.[11] Reconstruction cost $2.5 million and delayed Kubrick's already much-delayed Grand Guignol by two more months. Warner Bros. grew impatient, then worried. In all, Kubrick had kept his cast in front of the cameras off and on for thirteen months. *The Shining*, scheduled for a 1979

Christmas release, was pushed back yet again to Easter of the following year. It began to look as if it would rival *Apocalypse Now* (1979) in sheer number of postponements.[12] Coinciding with *Goin' South's* failure, *The Shining's* many delays reflected the New Hollywood's growing pains.

Another oft-delayed opus, United Artists' *Heaven's Gate* (1980), would end the decade with a whopping price tag of $44 million and an anemic return at the box office of just $3.5 million. Commemorated in the former United Artists executive Steven Bach's bestselling *Final Cut*, the Michael Cimino blockbuster did what neither *Cleopatra* (1963) nor *Mutiny on the Bounty* (1962) had been able to do: bring down an entire studio. Before *Heaven's Gate* virtually bankrupted United Artists,[13] the studio resurrected Hal Ashby's proposed remake of *The Postman Always Rings Twice*, again with Jack in mind.

Through all of these debacles, Jack's star remained aloft. Ashby attempted to cast him opposite Clint Eastwood in a screen adaptation of the novelist Richard Brautigan's "gothic Western" *The Hawkline Monster*, and Michael Douglas offered him the Jack Lemmon role in *The China Syndrome* (1979). But as Kubrick's *The Shining* marathon ground to a close, Jack remained noncommittal about his next project, much to the annoyance of those who clamored after him.

"I abhor the lack of manners that too often characterizes show business power," said David Brown, the coproducer of *Jaws, The Sting*, and a long string of hits. Counting Jack among "the worst offenders," he wrote in his 1990 memoir, "We are still waiting to hear from Jack Nicholson to whom Richard Zanuck and I submitted a script more than eleven years ago."

It would take Warren Beatty to pull Jack out of his funk. "The Pro" wasn't offering a starring role. That belonged to Beatty, who'd planned since the early seventies to direct himself in a revisionist retelling of the birth of bolshevism. *Reds* (1981) was the story of the communist writer John Reed, whose good friend, the Nobel Prize–winning playwright Eugene O'Neill,[14] played the same sort of sidekick in pre–World War I Greenwich Village that Jack seemed to play to Warren in post-Vietnam Hollywood.

"I hadn't done much biographical acting, and I really felt I got good brain contact there with Eugene O'Neill," said Jack, who claimed to have read six thousand pages by or about the playwright in preparation for another "short part," much like that of the labor leader Brimmer in *The Last Tycoon*.

But even more than Brimmer, Jack found special resonance with O'Neill. The famed playwright's parents and older brother all died within three years of one another, alcohol and drugs playing central roles in forming the dark basis upon which O'Neill created *Long Day's Journey into Night*.[15]

"I'm not saying I'm as dark as he was . . . but I am a writer, I am Irish, I have had problems with my family," said Jack. At one point during the making of *Reds*, he joked with Army Archerd, "It makes me want to retire and become a writer—and be a drunk."

Jack celebrated his own birthday in 1979 without much fanfare, although it carried considerable personal significance to him. "When I was a little kid I remember the first time I thought somebody was old," said Jack. "It turned out that they were forty-two, and that number stayed with me, all my life. So I had a thing about forty-two. Once forty-two went by and I still felt like a child, I was okay."

At Cannes, Polanski resurfaced and spoke about returning to Hollywood to face a sentence he expected to be "anything from probation to three years." "I do not think of myself as an international fugitive," he said. Jack concurred. "The elements of hysteria will no longer be predominant," he predicted after visiting Polanski in Paris. "Already I feel people are looking at the case in a more rational light."

Beatty's long, sprawling saga of the Russian Revolution began filming in August, courtesy of Paramount's Barry Diller, who'd supplanted the now independent Robert Evans as studio chief. Like the Warner Bros. production head John Calley, who ran interference for Kubrick on *The Shining*, Diller waived his usual draconian mania over missed deadlines and red ink. Even so, in that cautionary *Heaven's Gate* era, Beatty strained friendship to the breaking point.

Reds was filmed over fifteen months in England, Finland, and Spain, busting its $20 million budget twice over. It would take another year and a half to edit the 130 hours of footage to its essence. The finished product would come in fifteen minutes short of *Gone with the Wind*, with a final price tag somewhere between $33 and $55 million, depending upon who did the estimating. By the time Beatty borrowed the last of the cash to finish *Reds*, Barclay's Bank held the mortgage. Through the entire ordeal, Beatty called in chits from all his pals to finish his masterwork.

"Warren worked me to death, repeating some scenes as many as twenty times," said Jack. "I ate more than humble pie because I believed in him and in the film. Conclusion: there is nothing like hard work to bring an actor's ego down a few notches."

Nearly as secretive as Kubrick, Beatty doled out script pages to featured players only and not until the hours before they were to appear before the cameras. "I don't know who I play because I never read the script," complained Gene Hackman.

Only Jack and Diane Keaton got complete scripts. Beatty began *Reds* with his leading lady linked to him offscreen, but by the end, he and Keaton were kaput. "Just look at how many movies 'The Pro' has made with girlfriends," said Jack. "Of course, there are classic pitfalls. Making a movie is psychologically brutal."

As with Julie Christie in *McCabe and Mrs. Miller* (1971), *Shampoo* (1975), and *Heaven Can Wait* (1978), Beatty planted Keaton on a pedestal soon after they began dating in 1978, using her as a sort of muse to jump-start *Reds*. "I love her work, and she makes me laugh, she makes me cry," he said, adding somewhat cryptically, "and in that sense, the old thing, you know: character is plot. Diane is plot."

Gossip columnists turned the *Reds* breakup into a triangle, with Jack featured as the third leg. While he admitted developing a "real crush" on Keaton, Jack maintained that "absolutely nothing happened between Diane and me."

Like Beatty and his muse, Jack was not above using his crush as part of the Method on screen. "If you were mine, I wouldn't share you with anybody or anything," Eugene O'Neill confesses to Louise Bryant, Keaton's character. "It'd be just you and me. We'd be the center of it all."

In the movie, before Bryant dumps O'Neill to run off to Russia with the revolutionary John Reed, O'Neill hands her an envelope containing a poem, but it wasn't just a prop. It was a genuine artifact poured from Jack's heart. "That poem I gave to Miss Keaton: I wrote a real poem that was extremely revealing," he said. "It's the kind of thing no one else sees, but you know it's there."

Years before *Reds*, Beatty and Jack had turned their long-standing friendship into a well-publicized "skunk" rivalry, often competing for the same women as if they were bowling trophies. Their competition wove itself deep into the fabric of Hollywood fable. "He and Beatty have contests about it," said Bruce Dern.

With their fellow satyr Polanski tagging along on occasion, they cruised the Sunset Strip during the seventies, "twin chauvinists—picking up broads," as Faye Dunaway told the *Los Angeles Herald-Examiner* on the night she won her Oscar for *Network* (1977). As *Shampoo*'s randy George Roundy,[16] Beatty spoke for every aging adolescent male who ever lusted after his best friend's prom date: "Let's face it: I fucked 'em all. . . . It makes me feel like I'm gonna live forever."

"Look, he levels that wonderful you-are-the-only-person-in-the-room expression on you and you fall in love with yourself," said Beatty's sister, Shirley MacLaine. "It's not about him. It's about what he makes them feel about *themselves*."

The Mulholland males club kept on sampling like sultans, and whenever they were called on their bad behavior, Jack invoked the ghost of Wilhelm Reich, while Beatty just shrugged and grinned like a kid caught with his hand in the cookie jar.

MacLaine shrugged, too. In response to Barbara Walters's *20/20* word-association gimmick, the actress answered Walters's utterance of her brother's name with "Unrequited love." "That popped out of my mouth," said MacLaine. "I was as surprised as anybody."

The Great Seducer and the Sexiest Man Alive earned their nicknames at a price. In the rare moment when Jack wasn't basking in the glow of his latest conquest, he stopped crowing long enough to speak about the cost of coitus. "Sometimes a married woman, who's a friend of mine, will seek me out as a confidant when she starts to feel the old wings going," he said. "And the first thing I say to her is, 'Don't think you're going to go out and find some glorious sexual freedom. Don't think that's what's moving you. Because I know a lot of adepts in this area, and people lie. It's not a vibrant bed of sexuality out there; it's not a free and easy and marvelous exchange. The times it comes together really elegant are scarce as hen's teeth. Yes, there are people out there and yes, it can be exciting and blah, blah, blah. But it's way overrated. Way overrated.'"

Still, the ties that bind seemed like shackles to Jack. He'd been married once and purportedly had asked Anjelica to make it legal, but his freedom always came first. When she was in the mood, he wasn't, and vice versa, so they evolved into friends who slept together as infrequently as an old married couple. At the time, Warren hadn't advanced to even that level of commitment. "Warren does respect women," said Jack. "He has a real respect for . . . well, basically he has respect for his sister and mother. I think he has . . . uh . . . a real curiosity about who women are because his mother wasn't sure about who she was. That's what's really going on."

As the 1970s lurched to a close, Jack continued to search for a new balance. Slipping into Eugene O'Neill's skin for a time helped. Critics who decried his broad comic lunacy in *Goin' South* and *The Shining* saw his restraint as the brooding Irish playwright as a "return to form." *Reds* marked the opening of his second act, both onscreen and as a middle-aged movie star who no longer had the rebel-without-a-cause license of a young actor—or even a thirtysomething leading man.

At decade's end, he was asked by a London tabloid reporter, "What makes you a superstar?"

Without missing a beat, Jack shot back, "I am not a superstar. I am a mega-superstar."

14

THE POSTMAN ALWAYS RINGS TWICE (1981) STRUCK A dissonant chord at the outset of the eighties—a grim counterpoint to the tattoo of Ronald Reagan's "Morning in America." "I don't particularly want a guy who murders a man and then fucks his wife on top of her husband's body to be all that charming," said Jack, commenting on his role as *Postman*'s doomed narrator Frank Chambers.

Jack's fee alone ate nearly a third of the $9 million *Postman* budget; still, he maintained that he did it for art and to help out an old friend. "When Jack decided to do *Postman* in '81, I had, prior to that, produced and/or directed maybe four or five movies," groused Bob Rafelson. "And Jack's fee, as I recall, was more than the cost of all those movies put together."

While the director might kvetch over the star salary, the value of Jack's support was inestimable. Just months earlier, Fox had dismissed

Rafelson from *Brubaker* (1980). At a low point in the former BBS partner's career,[1] Jack steered *Postman* Rafelson's way, demonstrating typical loyalty by vowing that he would make the movie with no one else despite the *Brubaker* brouhaha. Originally meant to star Jack, the $10 million Robert Redford prison drama had screeched to a halt ten days into a fourteen-week production schedule. Hectored for free spending and falling behind schedule, Rafelson blew up and allegedly punched out a Fox vice president who'd been sent to the set in Columbus, Ohio, to prevent another runaway production à la *Reds*. The day following the donnybrook, the Fox chief Alan Ladd Jr. himself flew to Ohio to fire Rafelson. Rafelson retaliated with a suit for slander and breach of contract, upping the ante on his reputation as a hothead at a time when freewheeling or coked-out directors, from Dennis Hopper and Francis Coppola to Robert Altman and Michael Cimino, were being reined in, replaced, and blackballed by the studios.

But beyond saving Rafelson after he was canned from *Brubaker*,[2] Jack shared a common bond with him over James M. Cain's existential storytelling. *Postman*, banned when first published in 1934, wrestled with the blurred border between love and lust and literally drew blood, equating nipped lips, orgasmic screams, and feral coupling with the inevitability of Puritanical perdition. The narrator's tragedy made Frank an existential insect that both Jack and Rafelson meant to study. "Did you know that Camus named *Postman* an inspirational source for *The Stranger*?" Jack asked one interviewer.

While he revered the original 1948 version of *Postman* with John Garfield in the drifter's role, Jack maintained that MGM's censorship during the 1940s had muted Cain's raw sexuality. He and Rafelson preferred *Ossessione*, the grittier Italian version produced in 1943 by Luchino Visconti.[3] Before careening into noir irony, Cain's novel opened with one of the most loaded understatements in American literature: "They threw me off the hay truck about noon." Together, Jack and Rafelson meant to throw *Postman* on the screen with as much blind fornicating and blunt-force trauma as they claimed the author intended.

Like his noir contemporaries Raymond Chandler and Dashiell Hammett, who both tried their hand at screenwriting, Cain dabbled in film but concentrated on his novels. Though embittered by the sanitized MGM version, he left no script behind that was based on his highly visual novella. At Jack's urging, Rafelson first asked Jim

Harrison to adapt it. The author had bounced back as a screenwriter since his *Goin' South* low point but now had a three-picture contract stemming from *Revenge* and had no time for *Postman*.

Jack and Rafelson turned next to the Chicago playwright David Mamet, who translated Cain's gloomy sin fest nearly word for word to the screen. Rehearsed since January, the remake of the MGM classic began in May. The key role would be that of Cora. Meant for Raquel Welch, the role attracted a string of actresses. Among those considered was Meryl Streep; she offered to work in the nude if Jack would.

The part that sultry Lana Turner first made mandatory for millions of masturbatory males in the 1940s went to Jessica Lange. "She's got that terrific farm-girl-goes-to-the-city aura about her," said Jack.

Recognized at that time as little more than the ape's screaming consort in the 1976 remake of *King Kong*, Lange was anxious to show range beyond Fay Wray. As it turned out, Jack did get naked at one point, but Jessica never had to.[4] Knowing that pornography plays best in the imagination, Cain wrote *Postman*'s sex either fully clothed or suggested but never shown. Ever the purist, Jack allegedly tried for forty-five minutes to whip up an erection for a tumescent trouser silhouette,[5] but gave up after Jack Jr. refused to stand at attention for a live audience, even one that consisted of a mostly male union crew on a closed set.

Nevertheless, Jack will be forever remembered for provoking Jessica onto a butcher block in the kitchen of the Twin Oaks roadhouse café. "Jack did it, he provoked her, and boy, she stayed provoked," Rafelson recalled.

During junkets promoting the film, Jack did little to discourage speculation that real, raw coitus had gone on. The actors' snarling huffs and puffs remain among the hottest couplings ever filmed, even though not a pube, poke, or penetration is ever onscreen. Given Jack's grubby portrayal—including an omnipresent five o'clock shadow and a thickening waistline that would soon grow to paunch proportions—his animal allure baffled *Postman*'s critics, who saw few sparks between Jack and Jessica. They might be raw and rambunctious but were oddly inauthentic in their passion. "Jack will always go for the ugliest, least likable choice, and he'll say, 'What's the matter with that?'" said Rafelson.

Despite Jack and Jessica's attempt at onscreen chemistry, it was the other woman in the cast with whom Jack had his continuing offscreen soap opera. He urged Anjelica to take the part of Madge, a lion-taming German temptress with whom Frank has a brief fling. It wasn't much, but it gave Anjelica more screen time than either of her previous cameos in *Cuckoo's Nest* and *The Last Tycoon* had. During her Ryan O'Neal interlude, she'd taken a nonspeaking role in *Swashbuckler* (1976), but the screen intimidation her father had instilled during *A Walk with Love and Death* remained slow to resolve.

"When I first met Jack, I decided I did not want to work for a year, and then it became two," Anjelica said. "Before I knew it, I hadn't worked for five years, and when I was living with him, it was to all intents and purposes as a housewife without my own center. Not that I didn't have a good time. I traveled a lot on his films, but at a certain point I became thoroughly disillusioned with myself for not having an aim, and this was merely aggravated by the fact that we were surrounded by very motivated people all day long."

If ever Anjelica needed an epiphany, it came head-on one night after filming a last scene in *The Postman Always Rings Twice*. A sixteen-year-old drunk driving his BMW on the wrong side of Coldwater Canyon plowed into her as she was traveling toward the Valley. Like her thirty-nine-year-old mother who'd died in a car crash ten years earlier, the twenty-nine-year-old Anjelica wasn't wearing a seatbelt. "I went through the windshield and broke my nose in four places and had an appalling headache for a week," she recalled.

Following six hours of plastic surgery, she convalesced at Jack's place as he finished *Postman*. She awakened one night in convulsions. It was then that she decided to get serious about acting. At Jack's insistence, she began to study first under the acting coach Peggy Feury[6] and later with the actress Lee Grant, David Craig, and Jack's old coach Martin Landau—a process of discarding bad habits and learning new techniques that Anjelica called "kindergarten."

While Anjelica recuperated, Jack took a *Postman* break to head east to New York for the opening of *The Shining* and a little healing of his own. By the time he returned, Anjelica had begun to look for her own place. Later that year, she bought a pink adobe bungalow[7] up Beverly Glen, where she lived with her dog, Minnie, and five goldfish.[8] "I used to have four cats, but one got run over and the coyotes ate the others," Anjelica said.

She remained welcome on Mulholland, but henceforth, no one could accuse her of cramping Jack's style. "Am I living in the Little

House and Jack in the Big House?" she asked. "I guess it's unavoidable that one's lifestyle should be shaped by one's parents."

At a party at Mick Jagger's[9] place following *The Shining* premiere, Jack met the rock groupie Bebe Buell.[10] At five foot ten, she resembled Michelle Phillips and later wrote in her memoir that she would have slept with Jack that very night except he slipped off into Mick's bedroom with the Australian actress Rachel Ward.

The following day and for days thereafter, Jack came on like gangbusters, sending Buell flowers every hour, phoning relentlessly, and even going so far as to call her mother. His method of seduction was full-court press: make it impossible for the girl to say no. "The other important thing with women is to pay attention to what the girl you are with is saying—and this many people find difficult to do," Jack said.

As the supermodel Janice Dickinson described his technique in her own memoir during an interlude two years hence: "[H]e was irresistibly funny, and he really, really wanted me. He was surrounded by some of the most gorgeous models in the business, but he behaved as if I were the only woman in the room."

But there was a morning after. As Dickinson sped off from Jack's suite at the Carlyle Hotel the next day to keep a modeling appointment, Jack called out from the bed: "I want you to do me a favor. Don't tell anyone you've got star cum inside you." "He wasn't kidding, either," Dickinson wrote. "He was lying there naked, propped up on the pillows, grinning that famous grin. I couldn't believe he could be so full of himself."

While Jack partied, Warner Bros. was looking for a fast return on its $18 million investment. The strategy was to open *The Shining* in New York and L.A. on Memorial Day weekend, supplementing word-of-mouth during the next four weeks with an ad blitz over ABC, the network most favored by eighteen- to thirty-two-year-olds. By July, the studio hoped that *The Shining* would be ready to compete in wide release with *The Empire Strikes Back*, *The Blues Brothers*, and *Brubaker*, despite the drubbing Jack and Kubrick were taking at the hands of the critics.

Many Manhattan reviews were derisive. Pauline Kael, in her first article since returning to the *New Yorker* following an abortive year as a Paramount production adviser, called Jack's diabolic performance "cramped, slightly robotized"; *New York*'s David Denby said the movie was "stiff and pompous, an anthology of horror-film flourishes";

and the *Wall Street Journal* declared that *The Shining* "not only fails as horror, but on almost every other level as well."

There were just as many slams in Jack's adopted hometown. The *Los Angeles Herald-Examiner* condemned it as "completely fake and banal," while *Variety* predicted that it would be Warner Bros.'s "biggest box office disappointment since *Exorcist II*."

"After viewing Stanley Kubrick's *The Shining*, I find myself wishing that Kubrick, like Graham Greene, would let us know when he's being serious and when he's merely providing us with 'an entertainment,'" Arthur Knight wrote in the *Hollywood Reporter*.

None among the cognoscenti seemed to appreciate the fine line between humor and horror that brought young film audiences back to theaters again and again. *The Shining* was a box-office smash, second only to *Cuckoo's Nest* as Jack's most profitable film up to that time.[11] And reappraisals in the years since have put it near the top of Kubrick's finest achievements. In 2004, the American Film Institute named *The Shining* number 29 on its list of the 100 all-time best thrillers.

"In some eerie fashion, it gets better every year," Vincent Canby wrote in the *New York Times* several years after its release. In 1997, ABC-TV remade *The Shining* as a six-hour miniseries more closely adapted to Stephen King's novel, but it had little of the impact of Kubrick's version. "There's a lot to like about it," King told *American Film* in 1986, regarding Kubrick's version.[12] "But it's a great big beautiful Cadillac with no motor inside. You can sit in it and you can enjoy the smell of the leather upholstery—the only thing you can't do is drive it anywhere."

But *The Shining* did drive TV addicts back to theaters, and in many ways, that was enough for Jack. With *The Shining*, British theaters used video projection for the first time, prompting an outcry from film projectionists whose jobs were being phased out. Similarly, the combined threat of technology and TV would send the Screen Actors Guild to the picket lines for the first time in twenty years over the issue of higher residuals from videocassettes, cable, and pay-TV. "Television is the worst thing that ever happened to the movies," observed Jack. "Everything that comes out pops up on cable TV three months later. We're gonna run out of product before long."

By the late seventies, TV's endless appetite had already nibbled at Jack's earliest films. When ABC aired a sanitized version of *The Last Detail*, the very idea made Jack apoplectic. "I hate it when my movies are on television," he said. "Too small. And the commercials befoul and overwhelm. The overall concept of a film is the story, the pace at which it's told, the progressions, the aesthetic viewpoint. The object is to make all of that a part of an audience's life, for that period of time. But on television, you are turned on and off. They can make you different colors. They can relate you to potato chips."

Jack continued to demonize TV as the monster responsible for the industry's ills, but he rarely addressed blockbuster budgets bloated by celebrity greed. "Jack Nicholson could easily get $3 million for a film," his old pal Roman Polanski told the French film journal *Cinématographie*. "And for the last five or six years I've had the impression that actors aren't at all interested in their roles or their films, only their salaries. It's obvious that people like Marlon Brando aren't interested in cinema anymore."

And yet, despite TV and overpaid stars, movie ticket prices crept past $2.50 and total admissions in the United States again topped the 1 billion mark for the first time since 1948. The average film budget now hovered at $10 million, an unprecedented seventeen thousand screens had popped up across the nation, and annual box office receipts totaled nearly $2.8 billion. Unlike Brando, Jack still cared about acting, but with the Hollywood gravy train now bulking into the billions, he wasn't about to cut his fee for anyone.

Begun on location in El Paso two weeks before the start of the SAG strike in the sweltering summer of 1980, *The Border* (1982) had been written for Robert Blake with a proposed budget of $4.5 million. But Blake, Jack's early rival for Sandra's affections and the star of TV's *Baretta*, rubbed the suits at Universal the wrong way. Demonstrating a lifelong propensity for snatching defeat from the jaws of victory, the pocket-sized actor lambasted the studio on *The Tonight Show with Johnny Carson* and once again made himself anathema.

When Tony Richardson next asked Jack to take the role of the incorruptible INS patrolman Charlie Smith, *The Border*'s budget shot past $14 million to cover Jack's star salary, as well as the added production values of a genuine star vehicle. Jack meant to play Charlie as a middle-aged Bobby Dupea, with limited brain power and an omnipresent set of reflector sunglasses that hid his I.Q. "Charlie is simply 'a man who don't like his job,'" said Jack. "That's the closest he can come to saying what's wrong."

Speaking with an ironic urgency that continued to fall on deaf ears a quarter century later, Richardson said he knew what was wrong. Illegal immigrants were everywhere, even among the extras in his movie. The border, he said, was a sieve, and *The Border* would be a real message picture. "I think the subject of the tide of illegal aliens streaming into America has terrific significance," Richardson preached to the press at the outset of production. "The aliens create a conflict between two societies living side by side—one country unbelievably poor with high unemployment and a minimum standard of living and the other the richest and most powerful country in the world. It is a fascinating canvas to work on."

Symbolically, Jack's character would be saving an entire downtrodden nation by saving the pregnant Mexican girl and her newborn at the end. But from the outset, Jack didn't seem up to the film's demands. Early reports on location in Texas had him "out of it," arriving hours late, and failing to learn his lines. The back trouble he developed following *Goin' South* and further aggravated during *The Shining* slowed production.[13] Jack worked out with free weights, but precious time was lost.

When the SAG strike halted shooting after just two weeks, water still flowed in the Rio Grande. But following the nine-week work stoppage, the river was bone dry. That was only one of Richardson's many production headaches. An entire year would pass before he realized he'd have to recall the cast and shoot another ending at an additional cost of $1.5 million. The first ending—Jack blowing up INS headquarters and going off to prison—didn't work with either preview audiences or nervous Universal executives, who didn't want the responsibility for giving border anarchists any ideas. *The Border* seemed plagued at every step, all the way to the box office.

During the SAG work stoppage, Richardson complained, "I don't have any place to go. I rented my home in Los Angeles. I have a home in the south of France, but I don't want to travel that distance only to be called back as soon as I get there."

The distance between El Paso and St. Tropez didn't intimidate Jack. He spent the rest of the summer with Sam Spiegel. Learning to speak halting, hilarious French over dinner, he regaled Sam's guests by retelling an entire novel, complete with redundant nouns and badly conjugated verbs. For the first time in months, Jack relaxed. He even gave some thought to moving to France, "mainly because of the aesthetic climate. I'd like to have the distance from the whole insane corporate level of moviemaking."

Age was catching up. Jack got his first pair of reading glasses in 1980. The good life—Spiegel's life—sat well with him. He began to favor Cohibas and Monte Cristo cigars as much as he did Marlboros. His belly hung a bit over his swim trunks, and he didn't bother hiding the beginnings of a double chin. "No point in trying to pretend it isn't there," he reasoned.

He tried something called "the Pineapple Diet"—what he termed "the latest Hollywood way to starve." But once he relaxed his discipline, backsliding became an avalanche. "When I'm filming, I build up excess energy that has to be repressed so I reward myself by eating—sweets, spaghetti, milk, cheese," Jack explained. "Food is a fabulous passion with me."

In St. Tropez, where sauce was king, he ate like an emperor. By the time *The Border* resumed in September, his waistline had expanded to kingly proportions.

Neither did he limit or disguise his drug use. In a *People* interview, he spoke of doing everything from marijuana to mescaline in front of his seventeen-year-old daughter. He'd once tripped out on "peach mescaline" during a rafting trip.

Until the *People* magazine interview, there'd been speculation that John Huston might hire Jack as Daddy Warbucks opposite the Jeff Corey alum Carol Burnett in Ray Stark's production of *Annie* (1982). Burnett's terse response to Jack's interview put an end to that possibility. In *People*'s letters to the editor, the mother of three wrote:

Dear Jack,

Drugs "ain't no big thing"? Maybe not in your home.

With love and hope,

Carol Burnett

Shortly thereafter, Albert Finney got the Daddy Warbucks role and Jack dropped the curtain on his drug use, at least in interviews. "I don't feel obligated to go on with the cause [of championing drug use]," he told *GQ* magazine. "I'm not feeling philanthropic enough to expose myself any longer." And later, to *Cosmopolitan*, "I'm sorry I ever said I smoked pot."

The gulf between Jack and the media, already gaping, became a chasm, and it wasn't just reporters he dissed. He'd come to hate still photos that caught him unawares. Unless Ara Gallant, Herb Ritts, or some other trusted pal was behind the lens, Jack tended to say no to photos. Jim Harrison remembered Jack hiding behind an Evian bottle when approached by paparazzi because he knew most editors would not publish a snapshot that contained a brand name.

"You're always exposed when you do interviews," Jack complained. "First of all, I don't like to be photographed while I'm talking, so it's like, I don't have cameras around my house."

He grew surly and evasive, canceling interviews or leaving journalists waiting. "Sly, slippery, smart, he accepts questions with contempt, answers with condescension and, one suspects, is playing Jack Nicholson," wrote the *New York Daily News* arts editor Susan Toepfer, who fenced with Jack during a 1980 interview. She tried to make sense of Jack's oddball gibberish while her tape recorder ran but suspected he was doing more than relieving himself during his frequent visits to the restroom.

"Collectivism is king," Jack babbled. "In other words, I belong to the only living minority: the all-white, affluent father. I don't like collectivism. It's the main thing going wrong on a mass sociological basis here. My response is that I have hired my own lobbyist."

"Your response is . . . ," Toepfer began.

"My response is that *I have hired my own lobbyist*," said Jack.

"I don't understand that."

"I don't know how to say it any clearer." Jack transubstantiated into high dudgeon, exploding into Billy Badass fury. "*I have my own lobbyist!*"

"Okay," said Toepfer, as Jack stood and stomped from the room. During his absence, she leaned toward Jack's publicist, who sat in on the session, and asked, "Do you understand what he meant?"

"No," said the publicist. "But why don't you try asking directly, like, does he mean he pays a guy in Washington?"

After Jack returned, Toepfer tried again.

"Okay, Jack, let's just go back. Now, you got very irritated with me when you said you had hired your own lobbyist and I didn't understand that. Are you saying that you actually pay a person to represent you or are you speaking symbolically?"

"I was represented symbolically for a period of time," he answered. "Everything went exactly as I planned it and beautifully. But no. I actually hired my own lobbyist. Currently, just to represent my point of view. He sends me reports."

Afraid of sending him spinning off again, Toepfer let the matter drop, never learning anything further about the mystery lobbyist or his reports.

Stoned or sober, Jack couldn't be entirely faulted for media paranoia. He never left messages on answering machines for fear of his voice being misused. He avoided signing autographs or commenting for roving TV crews, even at Lakers games. When Art Garfunkel criticized Jack's cold behavior during a Lakers-Knicks matchup, Jack demonstrated what warmth got him. He signed one autograph and fans began lining up. He never got to see the rest of the game.

If he stood still, strangers kissed him in airports. When he walked anywhere, he'd advise companions, "Whatever you do, don't stop." If he kept moving, fans stared but rarely approached. "I feel like I'm the mayor of the world," he groused.

Upon accepting her Oscar for Best Supporting Actress in *Melvin and Howard* (1980) on March 31, 1981, Mary Steenburgen said, "If anybody had a patron saint, it was me. In 1977, when he insisted on casting me as his leading lady in a film called *Goin' South*, everybody told him he was crazy, but thank goodness for me he was and is, Jack Nicholson."

Jack was in New York for the premiere of *The Postman Always Rings Twice* but dashed her a note. He'd nicknamed her, like every other one of his friends:

Dearest Chair[14]—

Congratulations on Oscarhood, motherhood[15] and, for me, sainthood.

Jack

Jack felt good. He'd lost eighteen pounds since *The Border*, and *New York* magazine's David Denby proclaimed *Postman* the end of

Jack's "Devil-eyed, rump-shaking, high-Kabuki period," although Denby's praise was in the minority.

"*Postman* was the picture that was really punished at the box office—and by the critics, I think—in America," observed Bob Rafelson. "But you can't go anywhere in the rest of the world without people thinking it was some kind of weird, gigantic hit—which it was—and a masterpiece of some sort."

Jack remained oblivious. It was once again party time in Manhattan, and Jack's old pal Ara Gallant threw a humdinger. "It was wall-to-wall models," said Andy Warhol. "I told Jack how great he was in *Postman* and everybody thinks Jessica Lange is great."

During his New York *Postman* celebration, Jack met Winnie Hollman, a former Miss Denmark who'd been married briefly to the late Tom Sullivan, a high-rolling rock 'n' roll drug dealer and the title character in Andy Warhol's *Cocaine Cowboy* (1979). Sullivan had overdosed, and Jack invited his tall, gorgeous widow to mourn with him in Cannes, maybe stay awhile at Jack's place in California. She accepted with visible results. On July 27, 1981, Warhol wrote in his diary:

> Ran into Winnie Sullivan on the street. I thought she looked a little fat. I asked her how she was doing, did she miss Tom a lot and she said, "He died but I'm pregnant." I asked her if it was Tom's baby, and she said "I've been seeing a lot of Jack Nicholson." She's very calculating, Winnie. But who knows, maybe it is Jack's and he'll marry her.[16] She's very pretty.

Three months earlier, with Winnie on his arm and *Postman* praise still ringing in his ears, Jack held forth during *Postman*'s European premiere. Even as U.S. audiences were staying away in droves, Jack told the French press he might soon portray the Roman despot Caligula, complete with cross-dressing. Or he might do a Fred Astaire biopic with the eighty-two-year-old dance meister himself directing. The world was Jack's oyster. "I'm the only one between me and what I want," he announced.

Peter Fonda had come to him with a script for *Biker Heaven*, an *Easy Rider* sequel that would reunite Hopper, Fonda, and Nicholson, kicking off with Jack riding out of heaven on a Golden Harley to the Louisiana road where the good ol' boys had shotgunned Captain America and Billy back in 1969.

The actor-filmmaker and Fonda co-conspirator Zack Norman once went so far as to arrange to have Jack driven from the set of *The Border* to a sports arena, where a helicopter lowered a chopper with a copy of the script attached to the seat.[17] In the film fantasy, a reanimated George Hansen would bring his pals back to life, and off they'd go once more, in search of the real America while doing battle with The Man. It did not occur to Fonda or Norman that Jack might have *become* The Man.

Bruce Dern also tried to resurrect the biker genre, with a script called *The Last Ride*, based on four aging Harley heroes. "Of course, it was going to be Jack, Dennis and me," said Dern. "We were going to pick a fourth guy and a twelve-year-old kid. . . . We're there for a last ride because we know the outlaw biker era is over."

Jack loved it, according to Dern, but like so many projects Jack professed to love, it never got made. Bob Rafelson had written an original musical, for example: *Acts*, in which Jack would play a writer-composer in a father-son story. Jack loved it, too.

He loved Jim Harrison's *Warlock*,[18] still toyed with doing *Moontrap*, and there would always be Napoleon. He'd also fallen for the fat, flatulent medieval scholar Ignatius J. Reilly in the 1980 Pulitzer winner *A Confederacy of Dunces*.[19] He considered an American big-screen remake of Dennis Potter's eight-part BBC miniseries *Pennies from Heaven*. He leaned toward a "biographical approach" in his upcoming projects, he said, regarding narrative vehicles in his star future the way a medieval lord might regard the succulent platters of meat on his creaking banquet table. "I'd also like to direct something which will put across the ideas of Wilhelm Reich," said Jack.[20]

Everywhere he looked, he saw another potential movie. His frequent visits to Hawaii[21] to visit Jennifer and Sandra would introduce him to *My Old Sweetheart*, Susannah Moore's[22] intergenerational novel about the island struggles between a mother and a daughter— yet another novel he'd option with the intent of directing it into a film.

He did none of these films.

In June, Jack attended Jennifer's graduation from the Punahou School in Honolulu. A self-described "surfer chick," she'd been raised with the knowledge that her father smoked tobacco and "tea" and ingested pharmaceuticals, but Jennifer spurned drugs. She joined Kappa

Kappa Gamma at USC and declared herself both a fine arts major and a vegetarian. She worked on the fringes of her father's filmmaking but asserted that growing up as Jack's daughter never fazed her.

"I remember when Jennifer was going to school in Hawaii," said Sandra. "She was in tenth grade and *The Shining* was out. She came home one day and said, 'Mother, you cannot believe what a girl said to me today. She came up to me, put her arm around me and said, "Oh my gosh Jen, what a horrible childhood you must have had."'

"And Jennifer said, 'Why?' [The girl] said, 'Because of your father.' And Jennifer said, 'What do you mean?' And she said, 'Well, I just saw *The Shining*.'"

Friends wanted to know if her father was really nuts. "And I'm so bored with the question that I say, 'Well, a little,'" said Jennifer. Actually, she saw Jack as no different from her classmates' fathers, save for his uncanny ability to get the best table at the best restaurant or last-minute front-row tickets to sold-out concerts.

"He is a sweet and good man, and he knows how to treat a woman, and that includes me," she said years later. "He has always treated me in a very feminine way."

Come September, Jack responded to Manhattan's clarion call. When the super moe-dells returned to Midtown, Jack was there to greet them. He hung with the toxic Warhol crowd for the gala reopening of Studio 54. Everyone wanted to know what Jack was up to next. He had no answer.

He flew to Aspen for Thanksgiving, then returned to L.A. for previews of *The Border*. The film had been withdrawn and recut after Richardson's initial print disappointed the suits. Like most products that were homogenized by committee, *The Border* wound up pleasing no one. During its opening weekend, it brought in a tepid $500,000 at the box office and went downhill from there. For the first time since *The Fortune*, Jack headlined a real stinker.

He returned to Aspen for a month before making another trek to New York—this time for the opening of *Reds*. While a resounding critical success, three months into its theatrical run Warren Beatty's magnum opus had earned just $31 million—well below its estimated $40 million production cost. This, added to *The Border*'s tepid reception and Jack's general malaise, made 1982 look to be another troubling year.

Despite poor box office, Jack protested, "This is traditional literature for America. It's traditional that an American literary personage be in conflict with the authority of some kind or another and that that conflict is noble. This is what's indigenously interesting about American work."

But while he wasn't looking, the era of the antihero had given way to a national lust for superheroes, the more swashbuckling the better. Following *Jaws* and *Star Wars*, Hollywood obsessed first over the $50 million and, later in the decade, the $100 million summertime blockbuster. The same summer that *Postman* sank, Hollywood's two newest power players joined forces to elevate the old-time movie matinee serial to *Raiders of the Lost Ark* (1981): the multimillion-dollar Indiana Jones franchise was born. With *E.T.: The Extraterrestrial* (1982) the following summer, Steven Spielberg would score $435 million, rising even higher in the dollar pantheon than Luke Skywalker.

Jack tried to put on the best face. "Steven Spielberg arrived like the final evolution," he said. "He is the top of the mountain of that particular thing, and that's good for me."

Jack held the film business to be cyclical. Whiz-bang comic-book villains and heroes might reign for a time, but Hollywood had to return to human stories. "I figure that anybody who's not a puppet and who's left standing in three or four years is going to be in a very good position," said Jack. "A few years from now, if you can still portray a human being, you'll be quite a valuable commodity."

While the Spielberg-Lucas juggernaut steamrolled the corporate landscape, more than half of Hollywood's twenty-two thousand union members were out of work. All the cash seemed to flow uphill to Skywalker Ranch or Amblin Entertainment, and another round of mergers to match those of the late sixties began to hit Hollywood.

"Our country is becoming corrupted little by little by conglomeration and conglomerative thinking," said Jack. "Look at Columbia. Coca-Cola owns them. Coca-Cola also owns part of TriStar.[23] Coca-Cola runs its business based on market share. Period. That's the way they run it. . . . . It has nothing to do with any one movie. And that's where the business is being corrupted."

On March 5, 1982, John Belushi became Hollywood's latest overdose victim. Just two and a half weeks earlier, he'd been up to Jack's place, sprawling out on the horseshoe-shaped couch in the TV room at five in the morning, awaiting Jack's counsel. Like every other aspiring actor in America, Belushi both admired and envied Jack. "John had always behaved toward me as if I were an uncle," said Jack.

After hits like *Animal House* (1978) and *The Blues Brothers* (1980), Belushi's girth, drug habit, and ego had expanded accordingly, but he still tried to weave his way through the Hollywood labyrinth. His agent, Mike Ovitz, had managed to swing him a sweet deal to cowrite and star in *Noble Rat*, a caper comedy for which he'd earn $1.85 million, but now Belushi was late on the rewrite and pissed over his deal. "They're busting my balls," he complained. Jack advised him to suck it up and finish the rewrite. Belushi had a different plan. "They can wait," he said.

He was stoned, but Jack, Ed Begley Jr., and Harry Dean Stanton, who had also dropped by, gave Belushi room to bluster. His next role, he announced, would be that of God in a Ken Russell musical. After dipping his vast body in Jack's hot tub, Belushi toweled off, dressed, and left.

Jack later told Bob Woodward, the *Washington Post* editor who documented the tragedy in *Wired: The Short Life and Fast Times of John Belushi*, that it was the last time he saw the comedian alive. After Belushi learned that Jack might be earning as much as 10 percent of the gross on the back end, Belushi went ballistic. The *Saturday Night Live* star ordered Ovitz and his manager, Bernie Brillstein, to get the same deal for him. Jack was off to Aspen when the comic turned up dead.

Belushi had just turned thirty-three. Once the coroner established that his drug dealer had shot him up with a "speedball" combo of coke and heroin, the bastions of the film industry went into damage control. The former Academy president Howard W. Koch, who produced the Oscar telecast that year, forbade Dan Aykroyd to mention his Blues Brother's name on the air. Jack didn't need to be told to keep silent. "I wouldn't be part of a tribute to Belushi," said Jack. "I couldn't face myself if I were."

Up for Best Supporting Actor in *Reds*, he told Army Archerd that he looked forward to "a nice, relaxed evening." He expected Sir John Gielgud to take home the Oscar.[24] "I'm hoping for a win for Warren," said Jack.

Reds lost Best Picture to *Chariots of Fire* (1981), but Best Director did go to Beatty. From the stage, Warren focused on Jack. "Mr.

Nicholson," he said, "I know that you're enjoying my being up here almost as much as I am in being here." Jack grinned, but his sunglasses remained impenetrable.[25]

One morning Jack woke up feeling burned out. "I'd worked every day for three years," he said. "I did *Goin' South*, *The Shining*, *Reds*, *The Border*, and *The Postman Always Rings Twice*—one right after another."

He paid a visit to John Huston, the closest person he had to a father at the time. "For the first time I started thinking: Jeez, do I want to do this every day 'til I'm eighty or something? I mean, this is an awful lot of life, and I'm not a brain surgeon."

Huston answered him with a story about the most successful horse trainer he'd ever met. After the trainer had enjoyed a long and distinguished career, someone demanded to know the trainer's secret. "And the guy just told him that he never allowed himself to get horse sick," said Jack. In the spinning of Huston's yarn, Jack recognized his own dilemma: "I had gotten movie sick. The doing of the deals took its toll."

For the next two years, Jack gave up on film. "Everyone said, 'Oh God, you won't be able *not* to work for six months. You'll be a dead man,'" Jack recalled. "Well, I never missed it."

But at more candid intervals, when he saw his image sag in the mirror, he confessed a different sentiment. "You don't really know there are splinters in the ladder until you start going down."

15

W ITH THE MAIDEN BROADCAST OF *ENTERTAINMENT Tonight* in September 1981, the floodgates opened on so-called entertainment news—a thinly disguised sobriquet for gossip, celebrity hype, and the eternal envy of being a Hollywood insider. Otherwise intelligent, sophisticated adults returned to a high school frame of mind each time an "entertainment reporter" breathlessly revealed how the rich and famous squandered time, money, and talent. Paramount's then production chief Ned Tanen summed it up best: "Everyone's in two businesses: their own and the movie business."

From prewar *Photoplay* through *Confidential* in the 1950s, the fanzines of the 1960s, the *National Enquirer* in the 1970s and beyond, studios exploited their stars like the prize cattle most of them were. The subtext was always the same: with a little luck and the right connections, anyone might become the newest heifer and win a ticket in the Hollywood lottery.

But *Entertainment Tonight* offered a new televised twist on an old con. Supplemented by a brace of newly invented celebrity magazines such as *People*, *Entertainment Weekly*, and *Premiere*, as well as a daily dose of "entertainment news" published in every American newspaper, the faux promise of celebrity at the L.A. end of the U.S. rainbow ballooned. With a helping hand later in the decade from the tabloid TV of *Access Hollywood*, *Inside Edition*, *Extra*, *A Current Affair*, and E! Entertainment, the appetite for industry news grew insatiable. It began to seep into late-night and morning programming and eventually into the venerable networks' evening news. The average American who once had scant interest in the mechanics of moviemaking now spoke with authority about casting choices, above-the-line talent, and the contractual difference between gross and net points. Each Monday morning, everyone knew the weekend grosses. Studios, agents, and publicists fed this new appetite by serving up clients for self-aggrandizing interviews. Celebrities got in line for a "grilling" at the hands of Barbara Walters and her clones. Except for Jack.

"Every time he has a movie, he steadfastly refuses to do an interview—he is the biggest holdout in Hollywood," the *Entertainment Tonight* producer Pete Hammond complained to *TV Guide*. Jack handled ambush interviews at public events by ducking or doing "his Jack thing," according to Hammond. "He just walks on by."

"It is the ever-onward, ever-upward hype which gets to people," said Jack. "And if it doesn't go onward to upward, what are you supposed to do? Think your life is over? That's rubbish."

That didn't mean he shut the media out. During fifteen years of star schmoozing, Jack had perfected the art of the interview. He took the most savvy print reporters into his confidence, doing one-on-ones in which he managed to convey unspoken confidence, giving the impression that what he said in his hypnotic baritone was strictly for their ears alone. "Sitting at the other end of a sofa, he concentrates so fully on the interviewer that when the interviewer leans toward the coffee table to pick up a glass, Nicholson leans, too," wrote the *Chicago Sun-Times* film critic Roger Ebert. "And then [he] leans back in unison when the movement is completed."

Jack's seductive conversation ranged from the sublime to the ludicrous and all points in between. "I used to think that one of the great signs of security was the ability to just walk away," he confided to Ebert. "I'd think that I could be in the middle of Africa, and I could always say, 'Excuse me.' And walk away. The thing is though," he said, sighing a long sigh, "the line of work I'm in now I can't walk away. Because there is no 'away.' Wherever I walk to, I'll be known. There's *alone*, but there's no *away*. Maybe I could retreat into a kind of exterior."

"If you can't get 'away,'" asked Ebert, "where do you go? Where do you spend your secret time?"

"Last winter I was up in Colorado with Dr. Hunter S. Thompson, continuing our study of American history," said Jack.

"You are referring to the author of the *Fear and Loathing* books?"[1]

"Yes. At the time, Hunter was cranking up to cover the Pulitzer trial for *Rolling Stone*," said Jack.[2] "To set the stage for his reportage, he and I were reading the life of Lord Dangerfield, who founded the Hellfire Club in England. You are familiar with Dangerfield?"

"The Rodney, yes, but not the Lord," said Ebert.

"Lord Dangerfield was one of the great supporters of the American Revolution in the Britain of his day. As a young man, he and his tutor went off to Italy for one of those lordly sabbaticals which was allegedly devoted to studying art and was actually devoted to getting drunk as hell. They came upon this religious shrine where all the devotees were flagellants who beat themselves with tiny whips. The next day, Dangerfield returned with a big black cape and he bull-whipped some three hundred people into submission, shouting, 'You want penitence? I'll give you penitence!'

"Well, wouldn't you know, he then had a religious conversion where a four-eyed monster appeared to him in his room. But when his tutor later convinced him that he had overindulged and that the four-eyed monster was actually only two copulating cats, that was when he founded the Hellfire Club."

To have Jack Nicholson put you on was very nearly as big a hoot to a jaded film critic like Roger Ebert as having the original Gonzo journalist do so. A far more indulgent and well-advertised consumer of pharmaceuticals than Jack, Hunter Thompson lived in Woody Creek, a few miles down valley of Jack's Aspen home, where he'd developed an undomesticated reputation as the mountain community's most eccentric, dope-smoking, gun-toting local color. As with Bob Dylan, his other counterculture literary hero, Jack had been aware of Thompson since the sixties, when *Hell's Angels* became the underlying text for most of Roger Corman's bike fantasies. After exploding across the American consciousness in the seventies, "Uncle Duke"[3] Thompson gravitated toward his famous neighbor. The match seemed preordained. "We hardly ever tell the truth to one another," said Jack. "He attacks me endlessly. Insists on calling me Adolf Hitler or something that suits his fancy at the moment and I, of course, always accuse him of being raving out of his mind."

Jack spent much of the early eighties skiing, eating, biking, and sleeping alone. When a storm passed through Aspen, he'd buck his usual late-riser routine and wake before dawn, bundle up like the Hulk in a Hefty bag, and catch the powder on Ajax Mountain before the hordes arrived.

The screenwriter Ned Wynn, grandson of Ed and son of Keenan, once challenged Jack and Bob Rafelson to a downhill race, but Rafelson declined. "He never turns," Rafelson warned. Jack remembered slipping over the edge and zipping straight down Aspen Mountain, right beside Jack, who tucked and picked up speed. "The greatest skiers in the world turn," Wynn recalled later. "Jack goes straight."

Wynn waited for the inevitable pull to the right or left, but it never came. As Jack grew smaller and smaller rocketing ahead, Wynn gave up the chase, turning too late and slamming into a snowbank. As he dug out, Rafelson caught up to him.

"Lose Jack?"

"Uh, yeah," said the younger, sleeker Wynn, spitting snow.

"Guy never turns," said Rafelson.

When Jack wasn't on the slopes, he claimed that his Victorian digs were so laid back, he'd "take along some cassettes of the National Dog Show to watch in the evening." "I go there for a kind of middle

America insular living," he said. "I live a little out of town. I tap in when I want, and other than that I ski all day, and I'm in so goddam bad condition that I'm exhausted all night and I sleep."

Celebrity meant little to the locals. Gawking idolatry was rare inside the city limits, all of which appealed to "the mayor of the world." He could share a drink with Reggie Jackson at the Jerome Hotel or eat alone at the Abetone restaurant without fear of being mobbed or even noticed.

Anjelica showed up at Jack's place from time to time. She came for Christmas, during which she and Jack ran into Andy Warhol, who could not resist noting that Margaret Trudeau had just published her tell-all memoir *Consequences*. In it, the former Canadian first lady detailed her affairs with Jack, Ryan O'Neal, and the late Tom Sullivan. Jack listened politely but did not reveal that during that same holiday season, Sullivan's widow had secretly given birth to Jack's daughter.

A quarter century later, Honey Hollman broke her silence about her father's identity. Winnie Hollman had carried on a five-year affair with Jack right under Anjelica's nose. For a time during the summer of 1981, the Danish beauty even lived in Jack's Mulholland compound, but she returned to Copenhagen to raise their daughter.

"My dad's never been a stranger," said Honey. "When I was a kid, my mom took me to see him, and when I got older I went on my own. . . . I think we have a regular father-daughter relationship. We have similar facial features and my mom says I have the same temper as him. . . . I scream and shout a lot."

Jack and Anjelica brought in the New Year in 1982 at a party thrown by Jimmy Buffett. Warhol was there. So were Barry Diller and Diana Ross. The atmosphere was Hollywood on holiday. There was no mention of Jack's latest child.

Losing himself in the mountains had never meant that Jack had become a total hermit. Bert Schneider and Harry Dean Stanton visited often, Bob Rafelson and Annie Marshall each owned their own Aspen retreats nearby, and Jack's fellow Laker fanatic Lou Adler joined Jack in front of the TV set during basketball season. Once they even chartered a plane to San Antonio to watch the Lakers take on the Spurs.

But most of 1982 was a self-imposed Hollywood hiatus, during which Jack's assessment of film and culture took a dark turn. "I feel it's a violent country we're living in today, that people thirst for violence," he said.

Still an occasional guest at the Playboy Mansion, Jack revised his take on free love, declaring an end to Hugh Hefner's sexual revolution after *Time* carried a herpes cover story in August 1982. Jack saw the rise in STDs as just one of the dividends of the orgiastic seventies.

"The results of the sexual revolution are streets littered with dead emotions," he said. "I'm interested in sex. I'm preoccupied with sex. I love it. But, you see, most sex is about non-feeling. People are afraid of their feeling in this area. Not just in the Western world but in all cultures. The world fears the sexual animal. The only therapy I've ever been in is Reichian, and Reich says we form our personalities, our families, our governments around this neurotic armor. We're all victims, victims of the furies."

During the earliest signs of AIDS hysteria, Jack saw people as "living with the fear of the death fuck," although he believed the threat was exaggerated.[4] "One of my friends, during the original onslaught of the AIDS epidemic, said, 'God! Who'd've thought three years ago that getting fucked in the ass seven times a day would be bad for ya?'" Jack wisecracked.

He maintained that he did not use condoms, which he compared to making love wearing "a warm garbage bag." Such precautions eliminated spontaneity and intimacy. He was far more concerned about the damage that the growing fear of sex and sexuality did to popular culture. "There is just less personal freedom," he said. And years later, "Once you deny that normal, simple organic sexual flow, the country is going to move right."

As Jack saw it, the timing could not have been better for a seminal anachronism with the unlikely name of Garrett Breedlove.

At the close of 1982, Jack planned to end his self-imposed retirement by re-teaming with Mary Steenburgen[5] in MGM's *Roadshow*, based on Robert Day's novel *The Last Cattle Drive*, a story about a modern-day Kansas cattle drive, costarring Timothy Hutton.[6] But the director Martin Ritt (*The Long, Hot Summer* [1958], *Norma Rae* [1979]) went to war with the studio and lost his film to Richard Brooks (*In Cold Blood* [1967], *Looking for Mr. Goodbar* [1977]), who read the script but never would commit. After interminable delays and a change in MGM management, *Roadshow* died. In settling his pay-or-play arrangement with the studio, Jack won cash as well as distribution rights to *The Passenger*.

As it turned out, Jack would return to film under the aegis of another Brooks: the TV producer-director (*Taxi*, *Mary Tyler Moore*) and fellow New Jersey refugee James L. Brooks. Originally a come-back vehicle for Jennifer Jones,[7] *Terms of Endearment* (1983) was a bittersweet saga of a Texas mother and daughter based on a best-seller by *The Last Picture Show* novelist Larry McMurtry. When the actress lost interest, Brooks urged Paramount to purchase Jones's rights. Then he began to shape a screenplay using *The Best Years of Our Lives* (1946) as a model.

Terms of Endearment would star Debra Winger and Shirley MacLaine, Warren Beatty's sister, as the battling daughter and mother at the center of the story. Coming off the successful *Urban Cowboy* (1980) and *An Officer and a Gentleman* (1982), the twenty-eight-year-old Winger was Paramount's top female star, although *Terms* would be her last big hit, demonstrating the short shelf life of most actresses. MacLaine was the Hollywood exception who still had marquee value even while she was pushing fifty. In taking the role of the prim, middle-aged Aurora Greenway, she turned down a biopic based on the life of the French chanteuse Mistinguette.[8] "She's been lots of places on her psychological map," Jack said in retrospect. "She was fun to work with."

Brooks offered Burt Reynolds first crack at the gone-to-seed astro-naut Garrett Breedlove, but Reynolds refused to doff his hairpiece or expose his middle-aged spread. It was Winger[9] who lured Jack to the role after Reynolds passed. In typical Jack fashion, he nicknamed her Buck, as in "buck and wing[er]."

Introduced to film audiences as the righteous heroes of *The Right Stuff* (1983), America's much celebrated rocket jockeys would soon enough have to count the black sheep Breedlove among their number. Chasing skirts with a comical humanizing hedonism, Breedlove was an age-inappropriate "cusp character" who matched Jack's own sexual preoccupation. Like the apocryphal aging horn dog who stands on a busy street corner propositioning every woman who passes by and getting slapped for his trouble, Breedlove might explain himself thus: "Every once in a while, one of them says yes."

In one of his first tipsy appearances, Garrett demands to know why he can't coax a Houston coed into his lair after she dumps him in his driveway.[10]

Doris: Because you're much older than the boys I date. Because you're drunk. And because when I went there tonight to see a United States astronaut give a lecture, I didn't expect him to prowl after us all night long. I didn't expect some silly flirt who had to keep his jacket open because his belly's getting too big. I expected a hero.

Garrett (swaying, indignant): Well, okay, Doris, don't come in.

[Then, a moment later, to the other girl in the car]

Garrett (hopefully): Lee Anne, would you like to come in?

"I'm in my forties and if I'm going to continue to grow as a person and an artist, I can't keep playing thirty-five-year-old ideas of romance," reasoned Jack.

Bringing ruthless sitcom efficiency to movie production, Brooks had grown up in TV as a successful writer-producer and showrunner who differed from Kubrick, Tony Richardson, or even Warren Beatty the way a sprinter differs from a marathon man. With an $8.5 million budget that had no room in it for Jack's $3 million asking price, the director put on his producer's hat to persuade Jack to swallow his braggadocio about never cutting his fee. "And remember, at that time, anybody from television was really a leper," said Brooks.

Jack rationalized, "I thought [Terms] would definitely hit the bull's eye because it wasn't about mechanized robots or puppets or monsters or special effects."

No longer so hot at the box office, Jack agreed to second billing after the two female stars and deferred most of his gross-point compensation to the back end. Brooks began filming in mid-March, with minimal time allotted to rehearse, block, light, and shoot. Jack had to be on location for only two weeks. The movie wrapped three months later, and Brooks had it edited, tested, and packaged for distribution before the end of the year.

In part, Jack built Garrett Breedlove, "an astronaut and a swimmer," around Murray Hawley Sr., whom he recalled as a swashbuckling World War II pilot. "At that point in aviation there just weren't any other people who could show up in Long Island and say they'd just arrived from Cairo," said Jack.

Jack also studied the career of the Apollo astronaut Russell Schweikart, in part because Schweikart had graduated from

Manasquan High two years ahead of Jack.[11] Jack wore the same kind of expensive watch that astronauts wore. MacLaine marveled at Jack's style of withholding emotion, which he said would move an audience "because they identify with their own inability to express their feelings." He'd talk about acting after the fact, but when getting into character, he went mute "because of the gypsy fear of losing the magic.

"Primarily, we're superstitious," Jack said. "We [actors] have to feel that everything's a struggle while we're making it."

Jack wanted a hero who'd stayed a mite too long on the pedestal, a rooster on the brink of losing barnyard control. During production, he stayed at a Houston spa, where "I could keep in shape without getting trim, so to speak." He found a bathrobe in wardrobe that he thought his character would wear when he wasn't attempting to swim himself back to Adonis condition. He lived in the robe, according to Brooks, rehearsing his celebrated gut. "For that bedroom scene I just swelled it out to make it look as huge as possible," said Jack. "My baby elephant look, I call it."

An experienced quipster, Brooks larded Breedlove's fifteen-year courtship of the widow Aurora Greenway with as many double entendres and cutthroat punchlines as he'd given his best TV comedies:

> Aurora: I just didn't want you to think I was like one of your other girls.
>
> Garrett: Not much chance of that unless you curtsy on my face real soon.
>
> [and]
>
> Garrett: You need LOTS of drinks.
>
> Aurora: Why?
>
> Garrett: To kill that bug up your ass.
>
> [and, upon finally agreeing to have lunch together]
>
> Aurora: Imagine you having a date when it wasn't necessarily a felony.

The comic portrayal of middle-aged intimacy came as a counterprogramming revelation to youth-obsessed Hollywood. When Aurora finally broke her tea-cozy character and told her daughter that sex with the astronaut was "fanfuckingtastic," she signaled hope to menopausal women everywhere. Jack saw Breedlove as a similar beacon for men.

"One of the things that motivated me with that character is that everyone was starting to make a total cliché out of middle age," said Jack. "Everybody was supposed to have a middle-age crisis, they were dissatisfied, they hated their job. I just went against the grain of the cliché. I just wanted to say, 'Wait a minute, I happen to be this age and I'm not an object of scorn and pity by anybody ten years younger than me. There's got to be other people like me, so I'd like to represent that in this movie.'"

Terms of Endearment opened over Thanksgiving weekend and took in $4.5 million. Normally opposed to studio dog-and-pony shows, Jack saw wisdom in flying the Paramount jet to Las Vegas for ShoWest, the annual convention of the National Association of Theater Owners. He shook hands. He schmoozed. With a little hype, his comeback vehicle would soon join the list of the highest-grossing films of 1983.

Jack retreated to Aspen for the holidays, where Warhol saw him and recorded in his diary, "[H]e's fat now."

Anjelica remained in L.A. to finish MGM's *The Ice Pirates*. Following her auto accident, she'd moved from performing in tiny L.A. theaters[12] and playing a mentally disturbed extra in *Frances* (1982) to making appearances on her pal Penny Marshall's show on ABC-TV, *Laverne and Shirley*, and more serious TV productions, including HBO's *A Rose for Emily*. She credited Jack with helping her out of her professional stall. At one point, he considered directing her in a biopic chronicling the troubled life and career of Maria Callas. "I've seen a lot of [opera]," Jack said. "It's very exotic."

The newer, stronger Anjelica also learned to turn a blind eye to Jack's serial sexuality. Once cowed in the shadow of the older men in her life, Anjelica had matured. Comfortable in her own skin, she even turned a little cruel toward Jack. "It was always the same with Jack and his women," said Charles Eastman. "They'd start out as sweet as Myrna Loy, get their second wind, become Barbara Stanwyck and then go after him with their tiny little manicure scissors."

By now, Jack and Anjelica were as intimate and old hat as any long-married couple, yet they were still as capable of exploiting each other's vulnerabilities as teens feeding off the cycle of negative excitement: break up, make up, and break up again. "Aspen was his escape, but he could never get away from Anjelica," observed the screenwriter Eric Hughes, who'd come to know them both through Helena Kallianiotes.

Jack remained both promiscuous and oblivious. Like Warren Beatty, he wanted license to play, while he remained reluctant to grant his main squeeze similar freedom. "Of course, being overly possessive is obviously going to irritate the person you're having a relationship with," Jack said. "But I don't like to share my lady, really. And I assume she feels the same. Everyone gets the impression that because you are a film star, you can pick and choose any girl you want. Damn it, I expect my women to be loyal and faithful. If they look over my shoulder—I kick them in that direction. Sharing a woman is not my idea of enlightenment. I try not to be possessive, but when it comes to the crunch—I am."

He traveled to Europe in 1984 with the supermodel Veruschka, hung out in Monaco with Princess Caroline, dated the actress Kelly Le Brock, and went out on the town in London with Petula Clark's daughter Cathy Wolff. He even had his old flame Susan Anspach up to the house on Mulholland for occasional trysts. "Jack didn't live with women, but he did live with his drugs," Anspach later told Jack's British biographer, Peter Thompson. "That was a commitment he seemed to have no problem making."

But no longer in public.

When Rupert Murdoch's *London Sun* reported in February that Jack had "a string of drug busts," Jack sued. The *Sun* story came at a particularly irritating time for Jack, as he had been off the recreational merry-go-round for nearly a year, trying to lose weight and stabilize a digestive problem. Not only did the *Sun* concede its lie and settle out of court, the paper apologized. "The truth is that he has never been arrested for drugs or any other offenses either in America or elsewhere," said Jack's lawyer, disingenuously adding, "The article also quoted Mr. Nicholson as saying that he loved to get high four days a week."

More than a mere legal victory, the *Sun* suit represented Jack's final word on public discourse over his recreational drug use. With the national embrace of Nancy Reagan's "Just Say No" campaign, scofflaw toking, snorting, and swallowing had passed out of fashion.

"People are so convinced of the present drug policies that they don't even consider the alternatives," complained Jack. "One alternative is to legalize them and see what happens. What about the crime that illegal drugs encourages? A couple of my friends who don't like what I have to say about legalizing drugs both have lost children to drugs. They think I'm extreme."

Jack might still indulge but never within range of a microphone or paparazzi. He kept his hypocrisy well hidden.

Following publication of *Wired: The Short Life and Fast Times of John Belushi*, Jack slammed the author, Bob Woodward, for revealing one of Jack's chintzier drug secrets: his penchant for distinguishing between his "upstairs" quality (that is, he kept it in his bedroom) cocaine, which was reserved for VIPs, and the "downstairs" variety, available to common folk. Unlike with the *Sun*, Jack found no grounds for suit, but he did lash out at Woodward as "a ghoul and an exploiter of emotionally disturbed widows."

Jack had warned Woodward when he granted an interview not to write a "coke Hollywood sensation book," based on the unique star access that Belushi's widow provided him. "You don't understand what the karma will be on you," fumed Jack. "This guy is actually finished. I believe that."

But Jack's prediction was way off the mark. Not only did *Wired* ride the top of the *New York Times* best-seller list for several months, the Watergate journalist went on to write nearly a dozen more nonfiction best-sellers during the next quarter century while retaining his position as assistant managing editor of the *Washington Post*.[13]

Jack had planned to sit out the Academy Awards in Aspen, but like the dutiful burgher he'd become, he returned to Hollywood on April 9, 1984. He spoke not a word to fans as he and Anjelica entered the Dorothy Chandler Pavilion. The first Oscar of the evening, for Best Supporting Actor, went to Jack. He doffed his shades, strolled to the podium, and kissed the hand of the presenter Mary Tyler Moore. Garrett Breedlove was a far more courtly character than the triumphant antihero Randle Patrick McMurphy who'd mounted that same stage a mere eight years earlier.

"I was going to talk a lot about how Shirley and Debra inspired me," he quipped, "but I understand they're planning an interpretive dance later right after the Best Actress Award to explain everything about life."[14]

What defiance Jack had left in him he saved for an exit line he aimed at his oldest friends and newest party pals: "All you rock people down at the Roxy and up in the Rockies, rock on."

Later in the evening, after she accepted the Best Actress Oscar,[15] Shirley MacLaine announced that bedding Jack had been "such middle-aged joy." Backstage, Jack underscored his crack about interpretive dance by doing a flying leap behind MacLaine as she addressed reporters.

For his part, Jack told the press, "I feel happy with this. I'm going to go for a lot more, you know; I'm after three or four more, and it feels great."[16] Echoing his parting shot from the stage, he told a reporter for USA Today, "I'm going down to the Roxy, get loaded, tell a lot of fake jokes."[17]

Jack's fellow nominee Rip Torn, whose supporting performance in Cross Creek (1983) lost to Jack's, assessed the Oscar outcome as evidence that Jack had evolved into everything Easy Rider's George Hanson had deplored: "Come on. He wasn't a supporting player. His name was up there above the title. Anyway, I didn't care. Actors say it's an honor to be nominated because it's our peers who nominate us. But the fix was in. Nicholson was going to win."

The day after Jack accepted his second Oscar, the Manasquan High School Drama Club awarded its first annual Jack Nicholson Drama Achievement plaques to the school's two best drama students. The Class of '54 was about to celebrate its thirty-year reunion, but Jack wouldn't be there. When he got back home to Mulholland, he put his new Oscar on a "top shelf along with my bowling trophy and my original pair of [bronzed] cowboy boots."

In its first two months of release, Terms had earned $25 million. The final box office for the year would total $174 million. By June, Paramount was already offering cassettes at $39.95 each. The studio's home video chief, Tim Clott, effused, "This is the first time we're going to get this kind of quick availability of an Academy Award winner. This is a chance for the public to own a cassette of the Best Picture of the Year."

In October, the gossip maven Liz Smith put Jack's take of the Terms pie at $9 million.[18]

After burglars tried to break into Marlon Brando's place, the actor responded with a security gate at the foot of the road that wound up to "Casanova Corner," as the compound he shared with Jack had come to be known in the tabloids. Weighing as much as a locomotive, the intimidating eight-foot-high structure was secured by two separate code systems and topped with spikes wrapped in razor wire. Helena Kallianiotes had planted a small grove of trees around the entrance to hide the hideous contraption.

Inside, all that separated Jack's place from Brando's was a long hedgerow of bamboo. Like every other Southern California suburbanite, they were nodding neighbors but hardly close. A sign above Jack's address on Marlon's security gate read, "If you arrive before 10 a.m., please ring the next address over."

"I stopped by Jack's house not long ago, just goofing around," recalled Nick Nolte. "The whole street's locked up. I punched the button on the big iron gate. Lights came on, cameras started to roll, a voice came out 'Who are you? What do you want?' I said, 'Is Jack there?' The voice said, 'It's four o'clock in the morning, pal.' I said, 'Oh, oh, okay.' The cameras were still going when I left."

While no one was paying attention, Jack had become a Hollywood grandee. He now owned a blue Mercedes 450 SEL, in addition to his larger red Mercedes 600. He loaned a white Cadillac El Dorado convertible to friends visiting from out of town. He housed all of his rolling stock in a huge garage through which visitors entered the house. A tennis ball hung from the rafters as a guide so that he wouldn't drive one of his cars into a wall. Tucked in one corner of the garage was the ubiquitous yellow VW convertible—the constant souvenir of his youth.

West Hollywood's exclusive Maxfield Bleu men's shop tailored Jack's sports coats.[19] His clothes reflected his grandfather's grandiosity before he began hitting the bottle, all the way down to a pair of size 9½ D double-buckled black suede spectator shoes with gray linen insets and black-and-white-flecked stitching. He bought Missoni tops, Armani shirts (15½-inch neck), and trendy painter's pants to top out an already bulging wardrobe.

Jack now retained dealers on both coasts to track artists who intrigued him. He added Frederic Remington to his growing collection of Western paintings. At a Sotheby's auction of impressionist art, he paid $430,000 for *Woman in a Fur* by Henri Matisse and began buying works of the late nineteenth-century French academic master (and Matisse teacher) William Bouguereau, who was also a favorite of Sylvester Stallone.

"There is always that Calvinist thing about not wanting to admit something is good for fear that it will be taken away from us," said Jack. "But the reality is that I prefer good times to bad."

His epicurean's delight extended to his favorite spectator sport. He didn't make it to half the Lakers games but still held two season floor tickets, each worth $160 a night. "The difference between sitting on the court for a game and sitting in row 99 is the difference between living in the Hollywood Hills and renting on the outskirts of Nashville," observed Jack's Aspen neighbor Hunter S. Thompson.

When Anjelica joined Jack on the Lakers bench, the couple carried on at times like a pair straight out of a James L. Brooks sitcom.

"Jack, why is Larry Bird so pale?" asked Anjelica. "I wish he'd get a tan."

"Whaddya mean, why is Larry Bird so pale? Where does he live? Boston, right? What time of year is basketball season? Winter, right? What time of day does he do his job? At night, right? Now how the hell is he gonna get a tan? I like him just like he is, anyway."

When Jack attended the night ballet by himself, he could be counted on to rant like Randle Patrick McMurphy and swear like Badass Buddusky.

Through the eighties, Larry Bird's Celtics were the Lakers' chief rivals. Led by Kareem Abdul Jabbar and Earvin "Magic" Johnson, the Lakers took five NBA championships, and Jack watched them all.

The Celtics president Red Auerbach swore that Jack gave the Lakers a two-point advantage every time they came to Boston Garden, because officials were star-struck. When L.A. faced off against Boston during playoffs, Celtic fans wore T-shirts that read "Hit the road, Jack" and waved placards suggesting "Jack, choke on coke." Security wouldn't guarantee his safety. During one memorable playoff game, Jack distinguished himself by dropping his pants in his skybox seat and mooning the stadium. While Celtic fans chanted, "Fuck you, Jack!" Nicholson grabbed his crotch. "I find it quite flattering in a certain way," he said. "But to hear an entire basketball stadium chanting 'Fuck you, Jack!' I felt entitled to shake my dick at them."

Basketball ranked right beside Wilhelm Reich as Jack's favorite form of therapy. "It was the only thing he liked and lived for— basketball," said Kareem, who'd known Jack since Kareem joined the Lakers in 1975. "He probably got all his aggressions out when he could on the court. He loves the game."

. . .

During the 1984 summer Olympics, Jack escaped to John Huston's Caletas hideaway south of Puerto Vallarta, where the two settled in to watch the Olympic boxing trials via satellite, far from L.A.'s clogged freeways. Inaccessible by auto and approachable only by boat, Huston's place rivaled Aspen as a sheer sybaritic sanctuary.

Even after Jack's ardor for Huston's daughter had cooled, Huston regarded him as Anjelica's protector, a son-in-law, and one of the best actors of his generation. Besides, Jack had "a fine eye for painting, a good ear for fine music, and [is] a lovely man to drink with," observed the director.

But there had been another motive to Huston's invitation this time. While recuperating from directing *Under the Volcano* (1984), the aging filmmaker had found a property he knew he could craft into a screenplay that would bring his daughter and his prospective son-in-law together on screen, if not in real life.

Huston had come across a set of galleys of *Prizzi's Honor* and decided that the novelist Richard Condon's comic send-up of *The Godfather* would be his next film. He advised the producer John Foreman to snap up the rights, only to learn that the book had been published three years earlier. The galleys had been collecting dust in Huston's villa since 1980. But the film rights were still available. Huston had only to ask and Jack was in.

After Jack returned to L.A., he exercised his renewed box office clout to throw in with another "family" project. He sat down with his two favorite Bobs and swore an oath to make Bob Towne's *Chinatown* sequel. Bob Evans recalled the three old cronies sitting around the inlaid mahogany table in Evans's storied projection room next to the tennis court of his Coldwater Canyon bachelor flytrap.

"None of us were going to take any money and we'd own a good percent of it ourselves," Evans said. "We all put our hands together and swore no agents or lawyers were going to screw us up."

Both Bobs suffered setbacks in the 1980s. Towne's directorial debut, *Personal Best* (1982),[20] tanked, while Evans's career spiraled downward with a highly publicized cocaine bust, followed by the disastrous *The Cotton Club* (1984),[21] during which his coproducer Roy Radin was murdered. For a time, Evans himself was implicated.

Jack alone had weathered Ronald Reagan's first term as president with his star status untarnished, yet he waived his going rate of $4.5 million a picture and was the first to put up $1,000 of his own money to incorporate TEN Productions (an acronym for Towne, Evans, and Nicholson) in December 1984. Towne, Evans, and Jack met over a weekend at Jack's place in Aspen to seal their agreement, naming *The Two Jakes* the "Venture" and themselves the "Venturers": a filmmaking collective and a new model for melding high-priced talent without attorneys or studios taking their slice and ruining the project before it ever got off the ground.

"The way American movies are made," said Towne, "a producer packages a bunch of strangers and says, 'Be intimate with each other.' It's amazing that any sort of unity or clarity comes through at all. Generally speaking, when the people are friends, when they know each other, the results are better."

Jack and Evans deferred their salaries. Only Towne got any upfront money—$125,000 for his screenplay sequel fee. Paramount agreed to a $6 million distribution cap on a film budgeted at $12 million, which meant that the studio waived its normal 30 percent bite on *The Two Jakes* earnings above $18 million. Any income beyond $18 million would be evenly divided between the studio and the three TEN partners—a stunning deal during the voracious Reaganomics era, when greenmail and greed seemed to underwrite every transaction. Paramount would pay for production, but the finished movie would belong to the three principals.

At a Hollywood power party late that same year, as Jack and James L. Brooks—now simply "Brooksy," in Jack shorthand—surveyed a room full of producers, studio executives, and other high-octane Industry players, the director leaned in and whispered, "You got the feeling that somehow these people *own* you?"

"Absolutely not," snapped Jack. "I'm one of the few people *alive* that that question isn't hypothetical for. I'm the pawn in no one's game."

BOOK IV

IDIOT WIND
1985–1992

16

AFTER TOMASINO "TOMMY" BARATTA HAD JACK OVER FOR dinner one Aspen winter evening, Jack tasted the essence and inspiration for *Prizzi's Honor* (1985). Despite Jack's chronic digestive problems, his deadpan hit man, Charley Partanna, put on thirty additional pounds from Baratta's cooking. "I fixed some gnocchi, a salad, a pot of strong coffee—espresso," recalled the Greenwich Village restaurateur to whom Art Garfunkel first introduced Jack.

"Why can't I eat like this all the time?" raved Jack. "Simple food, tasty food, not all covered up with fancy sauces, but not boring."

As John Huston launched the New York segment of *Prizzi's Honor*, Jack urged him to hire Baratta to teach the cast linguine linguistics. "He and I went over to Brooklyn to get some of that Brooklyn-Italian background flavor," said Baratta, who also had a bit part as an opera tenor in *Prizzi's Honor*. Off camera, he was making dinner for the entire crew, including the Hustons, Jack, and his costar, Kathleen Turner. Thanks to Baratta, Charley Partanna's specialty among the Prizzi mob would be pasta, garlic, and tomatoes, in addition to contract murder.

Like Shorty Smith, Baratta had a comforting appeal: a personality as robust and lacking in pretense as any of his recipes. Each year from *Prizzi's Honor* forward, Baratta left his three East Coast restaurants to underlings so he could cook for Jack while he was on location or just to spend a few weeks at home with him in Aspen or on Mulholland, training his personal chefs in the fine art of satisfying their boss.[1] A *paisan* like the ones Jack had grown up with in New Jersey, Baratta became a regular among the growing entourage now known as the Jack Pack.

Prizzi's Honor was the first time Jack played son to an on-camera father (John Randolph as Angelo "Pop" Partanna) since *Five Easy Pieces*, but Charley Partanna was as different from Bobby Dupea as a Nerf ball is from a diamond. The story of two assassins who fall in love, marry, and discover the truth of the cliché about living by the sword could be played as tragedy or the blackest of comedy. Huston chose comedy. "It seems to me, Jack, everything you've done is informed by intelligence," said the director. "And you can't have that with this film. It's got to be dumb, very dumb."

Charley Partanna is dense but dogged—and deadly. He crosses and rolls his eyes but sets them as blank as a line of lemons on a slot machine when he goes in for the kill. At an emotional level, Kathleen Turner's character is as different from Charley as a streetwise con is from a stone-cold sociopath. As she hustles to cover her lies, Charley evaluates her in his slow, stolid way as if she's under a magnifying glass, and he is torn between Prizzi loyalty and his unfortunate passion for a fellow killer. "I always decide what this guy's IQ is and hit it to the decimal point," said Jack.

Prepping for the role, Jack practiced his Sicilian mobster walk and imitated Brando's cotton-stuffed cheeks in *The Godfather*, using cotton to stiffen his upper lip. "I'm not the first actor to notice Italians don't move their upper lips when they talk," Jack said. "Charley's eyes I took from the eyes of my dog when he killed another dog." Behind those eyes is "the mind of a killer: that slightly deeper level of reality . . . there's no angels in there to save you."

Huston, then seventy-eight and suffering from the emphysema that would kill him, worked fast and with the certitude of a pro, wrapping the movie in record time. He did "more one takes" than any director whom Jack recalled working with since Roger Corman. "It reminded me of what Truffaut always told his editor: 'Remember, better is the enemy of good,'" said Jack. "When John thought he had it good enough, that was it."

"We can make movies good and we can make 'em bad," said Huston. "Bad is just more expensive."

As the third side of a loopy love triangle, Anjelica blossomed in *Prizzi's Honor*. The talent that John Huston had sensed before miscasting her fifteen years earlier in *A Walk with Love and Death* had ripened, and he proclaimed her "the eternal matriarch" of the Huston dynasty.

Her long-suffering Maerose Prizzi even upstaged Jack at times:

Maerose: So let's do it.

Charley: With all the lights on?

Maerose: Yeah. Right here. On the Oriental. With all the lights on.

Off camera, Jack and Anjelica stayed in separate rooms on the thirty-first floor of the Carlyle Hotel. Anjelica made the excuse that "at the end of a long day of work, you need space to recover your own identity." Jack recovered his identity on the party circuit. He always did when he visited New York. Right there. On the Oriental. With all the lights on.

Following *Prizzi's Honor*, Jack dieted and toned up, getting back into leading-man shape for his Jake Gittes reprise in *The Two Jakes*. In a meeting at his place in Aspen the third week of January, he sealed the deal with the two Bobs, and the partners trumpeted in *Variety* that they'd found "a new model for studio sponsorship of movies with high-priced talent."

The Two Jakes was to be a "negative pick-up" for Paramount: the studio would treat the film like an independent production. Without underwriting the budget, the studio charged no overhead, which tacked as much as 15 percent onto a movie's cost. The previous spring, Evans had partnered with the brothers Fred and Ed Doumani, who'd made their fortune in Vegas casinos and bankrolled Evans's ill-fated *The Cotton Club*, reportedly looking to *The Two Jakes* as their next venture.

For *The Two Jakes*, TEN Productions hired Kelly McGillis and Cathy Moriarty as the female leads, rounding out the cast with Dennis Hopper, Joe Pesci, Perry Lopez, and Scott Wilson. In his second time directing,[2] Bob Towne envisioned Dustin Hoffman as Jake Berman but rewrote the ruthless real estate developer for Bob Evans, down to the former Paramount chief's annoying real-life penchant for humming on the golf course.

The obsequious archetype of the modern producer, Evans hadn't been in front of a camera since *The Best of Everything* (1959), a pre–women's lib soap opera in which he portrayed one of the office studs who prey on the girls in the steno pool. His brief acting career, which began as a young soldier in the historical potboiler *Lydia Bailey* (1952) and kicked into second gear as Ava Gardner's matador boy toy in *The Sun Also Rises* (1957), coasted to a halt before his thirtieth birthday. "I was sure of one thing," Evans wrote in his 1994 memoir, *The Kid Stays in the Picture*. "I was a half-assed actor."

With *The Two Jakes*, Evans planned to return to the screen following the cocaine bust and his precipitous decline as a producer.[3] At fifty-five, he unfurled a star vanity that took even Jack by surprise, getting a face lift, followed by a "slim-down" Tahiti vacation. Once Evans trimmed and tanned his torso, he primped like Faye Dunaway during *Chinatown*, spending hours with hairdressers and hours more in makeup.

Just four days before shooting began, Towne got cold feet. Several screen tests confirmed Evans's own later assessment: he couldn't act. "I'm really scared this guy could cause a lot of delays," Towne confided to friends. When he mustered the *huevos* to tell Evans he was out, Towne incited civil war. "I'm so humiliated," said Evans. "He has made such a fool of me."

At first, Jack remained neutral, fleeing to his trailer, but when the screaming matches reached such high decibel levels that cast and crew began to buzz, Jack stepped in on Evans's behalf. Echoing the future title of Evans's memoir, Jack ordered Towne to keep him in the picture. "Don't fuck with me, Robert," Jack said. "I'm the movie star here."

But, as director, Towne pulled rank. On the eve of production, agents, lawyers, and studio executives bivouacked with the three principals at Evans's Woodland estate in Coldwater Canyon, where Jack again sided with Evans. The following day, April 30, 1985, Evans showed up at the Bel-Air Bay Club for rehearsals. While cast and crew cooled their heels through the day, noshing on lobster Newberg and chateaubriand, no cameras rolled. The following day they convened farther up the coast at the Ventura Holiday Inn, and again, there was no shooting. The film's publicist blamed the fog.

With expenses mounting, Paramount had had enough. The studio pulled the plug, sending the film into turnaround and postponing production indefinitely. Jack pulled out all the stops trying to salvage his movie. He called on "the Pro" Warren Beatty to replace Evans as producer and, perhaps, to play Jake Berman. When Beatty passed, Jack pleaded his case to John Huston. "I've looked it over," said the grand old man. "There's no way . . . it's out of control."

Evans remained stubborn about his comeback as Jake Berman, while Towne holed up in his office in Culver City, awaiting final word from Jack. It came in a phone call from New York. "The picture is dead," said Jack.

The cost to Paramount of canceling the pay-or-play contracts, striking sets, trashing $100,000 worth of lumber, and paying off subcontractors came to nearly $4 million, according to the *Hollywood Reporter*. The studio needed to clear the soundstages where *The Two Jakes* sets had been constructed to make way for *SpaceCamp* (1986).[4] Six Directors Guild of America members joined more than 120 IATSE members who filed grievances, claiming they hadn't been paid for two weeks' work.

The Two Jakes script was supposed to end with a real-life event: snow falling on L.A., which had happened just once in living memory, in January 1949. Instead, the movie ended without a snowflake or a whimper. Although the three partners made several feeble attempts to resurrect *The Two Jakes*, the lawsuits and losses triumphed.[5]

Towne observed during a 1980 interview, "Movies are like wars. The guy who becomes an expert is the guy who doesn't get killed."

Literally weeping over the death of Jake Gittes,[6] Jack had become a movie expert—a highly paid professional, but no match for the face-less studio bureaucracy or the irrational tantrums of his two best friends.

The houseguest who never left, Helena Kallianiotes felt a deep and abiding compassion for the plight of celebrities. Jack listened when she empathized. "Of all the public people I know, I'm the least comfortable in public," he said.

Neither Jack nor any of his famous friends had anywhere to go at night without fear of being mobbed. "Mother Teresa feeds the poor," Kallianotes reasoned. "The rich need it more."

After her memorable dyke hitchhiker in *Five Easy Pieces*, Kallianiotes had dabbled in acting throughout the seventies, tagging along with Bob Dylan during his 1975 Rolling Thunder Review[7] and appearing opposite Raquel Welch as a tough-as-nails roller-derby queen in *Kansas City Bombers* (1972).[8] That role inspired her first attempt at babysitting the stars: a regular Monday evening lease of a Reseda roller rink that she dubbed "Skateway" night. Underscoring the exclusivity of Skateway's clientele, she got the pop artist Ed Ruscha to paint "No Press or Photographers" on the front door and brought in Cher to act as her cohostess. "If I saw a flash go off, I'd skate over and smash the camera," said the short but raw-boned Kallianiotes.

Skateway became an eighties L.A. version of the Studio 54–Warhol mindset that had given rise to A-list exclusivity in Manhattan during the seventies: only pretty people who passed muster with Helena got through the front door. Her prevailing rule was that no one hit on anyone else once they were inside.

"People are art," she said. As her personal *objets*, the Richard Geres and Lily Tomlins, Brandos and Nicholsons would be allowed to skate or schmooze in peace, far from gawking autograph hunters.[9]

While Helena's critics likened Skateway to 1950s roller derby mania—dead-end nostalgia like the marathon dancing of *They Shoot Horses, Don't They?*—she turned her exclusive Mondays into an idiosyncratic success.

But Helena's real passion remained dancing. Without fanfare, she ventured into a seedy neighborhood west of downtown Los Angeles to apply her talents, but not among the rich and famous. "I taught folk and belly dancing to divorced women, the poor, the basket cases," she said. "It was like therapy for me."

Helena instructed the underprivileged of Silverlake, a then largely poor Hispanic neighborhood, in a large gray building across Temple Street from the Rampart Division of the LAPD. No sign out front indicated that it was a dance studio. At the beginning of 1985, after years of scraping by, the studio's owner told Helena that he would have to shut down. She offered to operate it as a successor to her Skateway star sanctuary and went to Jack for backing. By April, L.A.'s most exclusive nightclub was born.

"I called up a few people and they didn't know where the fuck Temple Street was," said Kallianiotes. "And they were afraid to come down there. A year later, they were standing in line, trying to get in, and I said, 'See you later.'"

Jack showed up on opening night carrying a cake decorated like a set of D-cup boobs. Nobody was there.

"Helena, where is everybody?" he asked. "It's your opening night."

"I didn't invite anybody," she said. "I didn't have an opening. I wanted to do it slowly."

Three months later, on the occasion of Anjelica's thirty-fifth birthday, Helena's slow opening strategy had proved even more effective than Skateway. Jack gave Anjelica the baby elephant she'd once said she wanted. She fed it carrots, and the animal took a dump on the dance floor. When the cake came out, Anjelica asked all the women to remove their rings, place them over the candles, and join her in making a wish. The lore of Helena's began to build, flashing through

Hollywood faster than any Gotham myth surrounding Regine's,[10] Warhol's Factory parties, or Ara Gallant's legendary orgies.

"It became *the* spot, but in a way that doesn't exist today," recalled the screenwriter Eric Hughes, one of Helena's charter members. "She had a doorman, but *she* had to meet and approve everyone who came through the door."

The scrutiny was so exclusive that the two busiest nights—Friday and Saturday—had A and B lists. People she allowed in on Saturdays seldom got in on Fridays. Inside were a bar and a small dining room with about twenty tables and a fireplace. Table nine, between the dining room and the dance floor, was always reserved for Jack and his guests. "The Ivy had its VIP list and its V-VIP list, and at the time, Chasen's and the Bistro were in their last days, but there really was no other place in L.A. for Pacino or DeNiro to sit down and have a nice dinner with Jack," said Hughes.

At first, fare was humble, consisting of soup and salad. Drinks were limited to cappuccino, espresso, and wine—none of the notorious "Drop Your Pants and Forget Your Name" punch served in snifters at Regine's. Later, the wait and cook staffs expanded along with Helena's notoriety, and the quirky proprietor made it exclusive on all fronts. While she paid lip service to forbidding drugs and hookers, alcohol was okay, and the bar began to offer vodka, Scotch, and tequila. Some members, like Michelle Phillips, brought their own.

Jack drank Cristal and was the only guest who was allowed to pour from his own bottle or ask for an extra glass. He seldom table-hopped, but sat and studied the shifting clientele, letting others come to him. "Everybody did cartwheels as soon as the Joker walked in," recalled one of Helena's waiters.

Helena's was a paparazzi wet dream, but none ever got past the owner. Likewise, those who dared to speak to the media about what went on inside risked losing their membership. With her cracked leather voice and severe dominatrix appearance, Helena protected her clientele's privacy like a she-wolf.

"Kallianotes is a formidable person when you first meet her," said Carol Kane. "Turns out she's more like a child than anything else."

Taylor Hackford and Helen Mirren might have been dishing at one table, while Don Henley and David Geffen schmoozed at the next. The biggest night in memory was when Jack brought Mick Jagger as his guest. Short of the fawning worship that Helena frowned upon, everyone from waiter to guest paid obeisance or averted their eyes.

When Jack wasn't in Aspen or on location for a movie, he could be expected to roll up each Friday night in his limo and stay until way past closing. Carol Kane, Ronee Blakely, Michael Douglas, and Bud Cort were all among Helena's regulars. "The town suddenly came alive," recalled Cort. "It was enchantment, a dream, and the nightly mixture was unbelievable: painters, poets, architects, tango dancers."

For a time, Robert Duvall staged Tango Night each Tuesday. Following Anjelica's bash, everyone wanted to celebrate his or her birthday at Helena's. Melanie Griffith turned twenty-eight there. When Goldie Hawn celebrated forty, her boyfriend, Kurt Russell, led a surprise party with everyone wearing Goldie masks. Jade Barrymore threw her daughter Drew's twelfth birthday at Helena's. The future rehab candidate reportedly got her first taste of beer there.

Requiring prepaid memberships, coupled with a careful screening at the door, Helena's attracted the crème de la crème of 1980s Hollywood: Mel Gibson, Roy Scheider, Barbra Streisand, Meryl Streep, Ed Begley Jr., Bill Murray, Elton John, Meg Ryan, Wayne Gretzky, Warren Beatty, Jane Fonda, Sly Stallone, Marcus Allen, Dennis Quaid, Eddie Murphy, and on, and on. "It was a rare space where people felt really safe," said Marcia Avnet, Helena's original cocktail waitress. "They had none of the bridge and tunnel folk around pestering them."

Sean Penn wooed, wed, and broke up with Madonna there. For two months in the summer of 1985, the pop diva deejayed for Helena midweek, when dinner traffic was slow. Invoking a "just plain folks" trump, Helena justified her caprice as to who got in and who did not on the flimsiest grounds. Anyone who accompanied Jack was allowed. Anyone else was open to whim. When Prince tried to get in without a card, Helena barred the door. "I detest royalty," she said. "Fuck the prince. I never heard of him. He can apply for a membership like everybody else does."

She snubbed the billionaire Adnan Kashoggi when he showed up with the *Entertainment Tonight* hostess Mary Hart. Lynne Wasserman, the only child of Universal's Lew Wasserman, the reigning king of Hollywood, was told she couldn't buy a membership no matter how much she offered.

Brando showed up on such rare occasions that each time was an event. The reclusive godfather to all of Helena's patrons preferred eating out alone at an Indian restaurant on Lankershim or an all-night coffee shop on Ventura, where he drove himself on the rare occasions that he ventured out of the Bad Boy compound.

But Helena's other benefactor was ever present and always "on." "He had a smile that was a cross between a Cheshire cat and a gargoyle," said Avnet.

"You'd get your bill on a silver tray," said Hughes, "but Jack never paid. At the end of the night, though, he'd ask one of the waiters to bring him one of the trays and then he'd disappear with it into the back seat of his limo."

When he emerged, he was good 'til dawn.

The 1980s had evolved into the epoch of the young urban professional: a consumptive time dedicated to designer jeans, Nike shoes, platinum Michael Jackson albums, and junk bonds. *The Cosby Show* dominated television, and movies were as much about power ties and Wall Street as they were about storytelling. In the decade-defining role of Gordon Gecko, Jack's old bud Michael Douglas not only won an acting Oscar but gave the era its dubious motto: "Greed is good."

The Wall Street feeding frenzy unleashed by the profiteer Michael Milkin and Drexel Burnham Lambert Inc. touched network TV, all eight movie studios, and dozens of independent production companies during the 1980s. At $4 million a picture, Jack's latest asking price kept him in tune with the times.

Prizzi's Honor opened on June 13, 1985, the same day that Jack's beloved Lakers won the NBA World Championship. Critics likened the film to Huston's 1953 black comedy *Beat the Devil*, which had also inspired Jack's ill-fated *Flight to Fury*. Making $4.2 million its first week in release, *Prizzi* grossed $26 million.

As *The Two Jakes* debacle faded, Jack prepped for a substitute film to meet his Paramount obligation. Mike Nichols's $19 million *Heartburn* (1986) was "the perfect antidote for sitting around on your ass talking to lawyers," said Jack. He replaced Mandy Patinkin[11] as Meryl Streep's faithless husband in the author Nora Ephron's thinly disguised *roman à clef* about her failed marriage to the philandering Watergate reporter Carl Bernstein.

Before the September start date for *Heartburn*, and one month after *Prizzi's* premiere, Jack flew to Philadelphia for Live Aid.

Network television had discovered that people were dying of hunger in the Horn of Africa in 1985, just as they had been for centuries. But the video wake-up call inspired knee-jerk alarm and a tsunami of celebrity-driven compassion. The clarion call went up all over Hollywood: save Ethiopia and burnish your public image at the same time.

Fanned by all-star hits like "Do They Know It's Christmas?" and "We Are the World," a series of pop charity events culminated in a rockfest to rival Woodstock and the largest satellite link-up in broadcast history. Jack, the sworn enemy of TV,[12] put in an appearance to introduce his main musical idol to the 90,000 fans at Philadelphia's RFK Stadium, as well as to an estimated audience of 1.5 billion watching around the globe. "Some artists' work speaks for itself; some artists' work speaks for his generation," Jack thundered from the stage. "It's my deep personal pleasure to present to you one of America's great voices of freedom. It can only be one man: the transcendent Bob Dylan!"

Like Jack before he regained his footing with *Terms of Endearment*, Dylan had fallen from fashion during the early eighties. His divorce cost him $15 million, his epic *Renaldo and Clara* (1978)[13] crashed at the box office, and his earliest albums outsold his latest ten to one. Dylan floundered in middle age, at risk of becoming as much a sixties anachronism as Jack was before Garrett Breedlove. Without the benefit of Jack's Reichian panacea, Dylan immersed himself in born-again theology, first as a Christian and later as an Orthodox Jew, in search of the transcendence Jack still believed that Dylan had already achieved.

In fact, Dylan hadn't been "transcendent" since his 1976 album *Blood on the Tracks*. His newest album, *Knocked Out Loaded*, was one of the worst and worst-selling of his career. Even as he floundered, his friend Jack's name appeared among the 120 people whom Dylan thanked in the liner notes.[14]

As the final Live Aid act, Dylan punctuated his three-song set[15] with a plea for America to help its own farmers instead of shipping cash overseas. The result was Farm Aid, Hands Across America, and a resurgence in domestic charity. Dylan cared more about the homeless at home than about the stubborn ignorance that infected Africa.

The lesson was not lost on Jack: with just a few words, a minstrel, a poet—perhaps, even an actor—had more potential impact on the shrinking global community than any politician had.

Whatever discipline Jack had as a writer during his salad days in Hollywood dissipated with stardom. Even his interviews had devolved into what *Vanity Fair*'s Stephen Schiff described as "no known tense": "The past runs into the present, wishes sprout into *faits accomplis*, old wounds bleed again. Yet as fuzzy and undisciplined as his conversation becomes, one recognizes a profuse, buzzing intelligence in it."

Lucy Kaylin, who wrote about the actor in *GQ*, described a Jack monologue as "the pretzel logic of hipster-speak: sentences that rove around, abandon their subjects and spiral off in unexpected directions."

Jack attempted to dazzle like Dylan but didn't achieve the same effect. He admired Dylan, quoted and praised him, but he'd never rise to his level of poetry without the help of a camera and a script.

"It was like meeting Mick Jagger or Bob Dylan," Meryl Streep recalled of the day when Jack first showed up outside her trailer door.

Mike Nichols tried to keep his two Oscar-winning *Heartburn*[16] superstars apart, on the theory that there would be more spontaneity if they met for the first time on the set. Jack foiled that plan by asking Streep if he could use her toilet. She put aside her awe, her makeup, and her hair curlers and let him take a whiz. "He was a big deal," she recalled. "But he's not a big deal in his own mind. He sort of plants himself in front of you and he's already in your life."

In 1978, Streep had married the sculptor Don Gummer. She moved to Connecticut, had four children, and never sacrificed monogamy to Jack's venerable appetites, regardless of the inevitable gossip mongering. One report had the stars coupling between takes inside Streep's trailer; another paired them as Rhett and Scarlett in an upcoming remake of *Gone with the Wind*. Neither actor discouraged speculation, perhaps aware that curiosity could only help *Heartburn* at the box office. The sad comedy about the hard harvest that grows from the seeds of infidelity brought out philandering Jack's windy philosopher.

"This culture fears freedom," he said. "These two characters, are they better off divorced? That's their inevitable progression. We have very, very specific, rigid moral principles relating to sexual fidelity. But are these people better off because they're gonna go through the form? Or is there some adjustment they might have made that was better off for them?"

Fucking was a fact of life. Why not lie back and enjoy the ride? Fidelity, Jack concluded, was overrated. Like his two-timing character in *Heartburn*, he preferred spontaneity. "I'm back to that point where it's on the moment, and everything that you are is included within it, and that's the way to be," said Jack.

Like *Prizzi's Honor*, *Heartburn* opened with a wedding. Both were staged in the same Brooklyn Heights church: St. Ann and the Holy Trinity. Beyond that, the Mafia and yuppie love stories had few similarities, save one: in the end, Jack's character comes through unscathed, while the women he professed to love are either dead or devastated.

George W. "Shorty" Smith died at age sixty-six on June 27, 1985. Jack had been juggling publicity for *Prizzi's Honor* with final bedside visits to New Jersey, but when he returned for the funeral, he was accompanied by Anne Steinmann, a New York psychologist who specialized in men's identity crises. In addition to coauthoring *The Male Dilemma*, a 1974 study of men coping with women's lib,[17] Steinmann was connected to Hollywood through her husband, Herman Steinmann, who produced the much-praised Holocaust survivor saga *The Pawnbroker* (1964), and her daughter, Shelley List, who created the Emmy Award–winning *Cagney and Lacey* TV series.

Jack's friends had to figure out for themselves who Steinmann was, because he never introduced the seventy-eight-year-old therapist. He broke into sobs during the service and clutched at her arm.

At year's end, he said, "I lost three of the really great men in my life this year. Sam Spiegel, Orson Welles, and Shorty Smith. They just happened to be three older dudes who I got along great with for a long, long period of time." Welles passed on just before Halloween. Spiegel died on the last day of the year.

In a benediction that could just as easily have been applied to Jack, the producer Max Youngstein said, "You accepted Sam in total; you didn't accept him piece by piece. You knew he was a mixture of good and bad, but he had style, a kind of courage, an innate ability to handle things that other people could not handle without showing their nervousness."

Another significant death that year was that of Eddie King, who succumbed to lung cancer on December 20, 1985. He was a retired musician; his biggest claim to fame was a 1957 appearance on NBC's

Today show. He'd led the Asbury Park Boys' Club orchestra and once ran the most successful dance studio along the Jersey Shore. King had long been a Nicholson family friend. He'd come to Shorty's funeral, but Jack didn't attend his.

Born Edgar A. Kirschfeld in Liepaja, Latvia, in 1910, King came to New York in 1925 aboard the German liner SS *Esthonia*. He played the piano in the ship's band, but once in port, he went AWOL and made his way to Neptune City, where he changed his name and opened the Eddie King Studios. He became a big entertainment fish in a small suburban pond, and by the mid-1930s he'd branched out to vaudeville. He staged a Saturday morning program over WCAP-AM: *Eddie King and His Radio Kiddies*.

One of those kiddies was June Nicholson, Eddie's chief protégée and regular partner during many a dance exhibition up and down the state. Ten years her senior, Eddie even listed her as co-owner of his dance studio when she was just fourteen years old.

June was seventeen and six months pregnant when U.S. immigration authorities caught up with Eddie. He was shipped to Ellis Island, where he spent 1937 fighting extradition. Meanwhile, June had her baby, passed him off to the world as Ethel May's son, and hit the road to stardom once more, but without Eddie as a partner. After Eddie beat extradition, he returned to Neptune, allegedly ignorant that he might be a father.

Eddie King married and had two children, Eddie Jr. and Pamela. When he died in the Jersey Shore Medical Center, King was an Episcopalian, an army veteran, and a pillar of his community, outside of which he remained as anonymous as his old dancing protégée, who was, by then, already more than twenty-two years in the grave.

Long after Jack had confirmed that his sister June was his mother, he continued to tap dance around the issue of his birth. "I made a personal decision when I got this information," he said. "Since I can't figure out how many of my friends know about it, I decided not to talk about it."

As Don Furcillo-Rose found more news outlets who'd listen to his story about siring Jack, the silence on Mulholland became deafening. Jack grew slightly more comfortable answering questions about his mother but changed the subject whenever the interview segued into paternity.

"I must see my son," Furcillo-Rose insisted. "I must have the chance to tell my side of the story. I want to explain to Jack the reason why I left his mother fifty years ago. Then if he still doesn't want to see me, fine."

Retired and legally blind, Furcillo-Rose maintained that he and June had eloped to Elkton, Maryland, in the autumn of 1936, where he paid a justice of the peace $10 to marry them, but because she was underage—and he was still married to someone else—the marriage was annulled. She had their child without him, but he held a torch for June another twenty years before marrying a third time in 1955. Jack knew the story by heart but refused to acknowledge Furcillo-Rose.

Speaking for the first time to *Rolling Stone* about his birth, Jack said, "Illegitimacy is still the heaviest prejudice in the world. . . . Everything I do in the movies is autobiographical, no matter what the surface says. I think it's a great asset by now to be of dubious parentage."

17

EAGER TO CAST JACK AS BETTE MIDLER'S HUSBAND IN *DOWN and Out in Beverly Hills* (1986), Paul Mazursky joined him at his Mulholland compound on New Year's Day, but the director found that he and his script had to compete with cannabis and the Rose Bowl. "Merely sniffing the stuff got me a little high, and I became a bit concerned—I didn't want to meet a stoned Nicholson," said Mazursky. "Rumor had it that Jack was almost always high, but that he functioned well and was totally professional."

Jack passed on the *Down and Out* role, which went to Richard Dreyfuss,[1] but he was never so stoned that he didn't consider the flood of offers that kept coming his way. Brian DePalma wanted him as Elliott Ness in Paramount's version of *The Untouchables* (1987),[2] while Barry Levinson saw Jack as Dustin Hoffman's brother in *Rain Man* (1988), a role that would raise Tom Cruise's profile from matinee idol to serious actor.

"The actor is the *littérateur* of his era," Jack pontificated to the *New York Times*, while scoffing that most efforts of Hollywood's "Brat Pack" generation left him cold.[3] Movies like *Ferris Bueller's Day Off* (1986) made him feel "119 years old."[4] "I literally walked out of there thinking my days are numbered [in Hollywood]," he said.

Since *The Shining*, horror films enjoyed a renaissance, but the melodramatic "slasher" genre typified by *Friday the 13th* (1980), *A Nightmare on Elm Street* (1984), and *Halloween* (1978) smacked of Roger Corman on a higher budget. Jack also hated the bumper crop of eighties cop comedies, from *Police Academy* (1984) to *Robocop* (1987). "You know, it's like a great sickness," he said. "I thought *Beverly Hills Cop II* (1987) really flat-out stunk, for the lack of a more tempered phrase, but it wasn't as bad as the movie before, *Flower Brain Child* or whatever that was."[5]

He found little to admire in 1980s TV-infected cinema. To Jack, the best of the recent harvest were David Lynch's offbeat *Blue Velvet* (1986)[6] and the charming coming-of-age Swedish import *My Life as a Dog* (1985).

Thus, when Warner Bros. offered him $6 million and a share of the distributor's gross to spend the summer of 1986 playing Satan in New England, Jack saw a devil of an opportunity, and a helluva payday for just twelve weeks' work. By contrast, Jack's old friend Don Devlin spent more than three years developing *The Witches of Eastwick* (1987) from the John Updike best-seller, although his salary as one of the film's two executive producers came to only $300,000. Before he and his partner Rob Cohen could option the novel, the producers Peter Guber and Jon Peters swooped in with $200,000 to purchase the film rights.[7] They then forced the original producers to work for them at reduced fees. Not only did Jack fail to interfere, he went on to work with Guber[8] and Peters again a couple years later in *Batman* (1989).

As Devlin's fortunes faded, Jack's had exploded.[9] And, as the actor had grown fond of telling everyone, Jack Nicholson cut his fee for no one, not even his oldest friends. "He was the anti-Establishment guy, which is why young people always loved him so much," said Devlin. "Well, the irony now is, because of the length of his career and how successful he's become, Jack *is* the Establishment."

An icy mantra had crept into Jack's lexicon: "Business is business." He'd been burned often, lending money that he never saw again, and not just to deadbeat relatives. Over a five-year period, he'd sub-sidized Charles Eastman for a total of $110,000 while the once "hot" screenwriter-director struggled to get back on his feet. "I was never able to pay him back," Eastman said with regret.

He wasn't the only one. While generous in his way, Jack laced char-ity with contempt. Members of his early entourage who came to him hat in hand were labeled "lame-o's" for failing to sustain what Jack saw as the fiscal rigor that he and his fellow success story Warren Beatty had achieved. "They were always talking about the common man, but they cheated their contractors and paid production assistants nothing to work in their films," said the architect Bob Silvestri, who had done extensive work for both actors.

Jack could be dismissive even among his oldest and closest friends. As a star, he rarely had to show his parsimony. Robert Colbert and the best lawyers money could buy were his bulldogs.

Sam Spiegel hadn't been dead six months before Jack sued Spiegel's Academy Pictures over his share of the profits from *The Last Tycoon*. Even those close to Jack were made to know not to cross him; there was legal muscle behind his pique. Suing the electronics giant NEC became a personal vendetta when the TV manufacturer dared to use a still from *Prizzi's Honor* to advertise its VCRs. The magazine layout carried the caption "The Best Brains in Television"—a state-ment that Jack deemed a cancer on his movie-star reputation. He demanded $15 million in damages for soiling his face and name with video.[10]

Colbert complained that doing Jack's dirty work became all the more difficult when Jack was in character. For weeks, sometimes months after a production wrapped, the business manager didn't know whether he was collecting money on behalf of a Mafia hit man, Meryl Streep's philandering husband, Mephistopheles, or Jack. It grew harder and harder to tell where the screen persona ended and the real Jack began. Dunning for the Devil was challenging.

Riding the crest of his *Ghostbusters* (1984) popularity, Bill Murray had been the Australian director George Miller's first choice to play devilish Daryl Van Horne in *The Witches of Eastwick*.[11] Don Devlin convinced the successful director of the *Mad Max* thrillers that Jack was evil incarnate.[12] A full decade earlier, Jack had told the *Chicago Tribune*, "I'd really like to play the Devil. Lucifer. The Fallen Angel. The character has been in a lot of things, but unfortunately I've never played him. Playing the Devil would be easy. It's juicy; you can work with it."

Arthur Miller had once asked Jack to be Satan on Broadway, but Jack declined. As a movie star used to moving from camera setup to camera setup, he was not interested in the hard work of sustaining a character two hours each night onstage, week after week. He waited for the right movie and found it in Michael Cristofer's screen adaptation of the Updike novel.

Before transforming himself into Old Nick, Jack had to recover from a winter skiing accident that resulted in a broken elbow and several pulled ligaments. He ended a Sun Valley vacation the first weekend in March to cinch the *Witches* deal.

The following month, while still a little stiff from surgery, Jack was able to join Anjelica at the Oscars. Nominated for *Prizzi's Honor*, he lost to William Hurt,[13] but as Maerose Prizzi, Anjelica won the 1986 Best Supporting Actress award. Her father, who'd been nominated Best Director for the tenth time,[14] also lost, but he broke into tears, as did Jack, while the strobes caught his daughter's star moment. "I feel like the world's oldest debutante," Anjelica deadpanned.[15]

After making the rounds of the post-Oscar celebrations, she and Jack adjourned to Helena's, where they kicked back, ordered in burgers from a fast-food chain, and celebrated until dawn. For a brief time, in Helena's admiring words, they were once again "just plain folks."

In reviewing *The Witches of Eastwick* for the *London Observer*, the critic Joan Goodman pegged Jack's "bravura performance" as coming "dangerously close to self-parody."

Indeed, Jack's Satan, in Updike's whimsical fantasy about three Rhode Island women who conjure up the devil, converted the supernatural comedy into uncomfortable autobiography at times. Daryl Van Horne seduces and sates but loses the upper hand after hopping from bed to bed, woman to woman. His three witches banish him from their lives once he has impregnated each of them, and Daryl is left where Jack began—shrieking in tantrums like the brat from Neptune City who didn't always get his way with the trio of females who raised him.

Nevertheless, George Miller praised Jack's acting as "a revelation." "I'd imagined he'd be a frivolous, spoiled movie star, but he was just the opposite," said the director. "He is absolutely fearless. How many actors would dare play a modern-day devil, dressed in pink and covered in feathers and cherry pits, ranting on about God and women in a church and throwing up at the same time? Yet he makes it work. He's masterful."

Jack nicknamed the production "Floating Anxiety," ostensibly for his costars' hormonal angst, but the term could just as easily have been applied to him. When it came to gender equality Jack talked a good game, but his much-hyped love of women always belied a deep-seated misogyny. He remained convinced that men were prisoners of their own penises, while most women lived emotional lives of quiet desperation. "So, yes, I understand the resentment rage of women," he told the critic David Thomson. "But nature's a balancing element. Women still control men. Not necessarily in the sense of gross national product or income, but if you look at relationships, the everyday walking-around nature of life, I think you'd see that the female controls the home. And in a relationship the woman has the power that comes from man's inability to think about anything but women."

Anjelica auditioned to be one of the three Eastwick witches, but Miller chose Cher, Susan Sarandon, and Michelle Pfeiffer instead. Their combined salaries didn't approach Jack's and still, the actresses professed to adore him. "When we wanted something, we went to Jack," said Cher. "He stuck up for us."

As with the battles between Shirley MacLaine and Debra Winger during *Terms of Endearment*, Jack adopted a paternal role as arbiter and referee. At one point, Cher used her clout to force Sarandon to switch roles and let her be the sculptress witch.[16] Pissed, Sarandon settled for the part of a sexually repressed cellist, while Pfeiffer took the character of a fertile (six children) small-town newspaper reporter. Jack saw himself onscreen and off as a soother of feminine egos, maestro of the catfight.

The screenwriter Cristofer liberally salted his adaptation with dialogue drenched in Jack truths.[17] The audience first catches a glimpse of Daryl Van Horne being chauffeured into town in a brown Mercedes 600, not unlike Jack's. He cheats at doubles almost as if he had the hometown advantage on Bob Evans's tennis court. He sweats a lot. He's as crude as a kindergartner who's discovered the magic of the word *fuck*, smiling wickedly while telling Cher's character, Alexandra Medford, "I always like a little pussy after lunch."

And he's proudly porky, briefly displaying a torso the size of Orson Welles's before his manservant mercifully covers him with a silk dressing robe. Then Daryl stretches like a Goodyear advertisement across his king-sized bed, only slightly appalled when Alexandra tells him how repulsive he really is. A creature of appetites, Daryl overcomes all objections.

In one of the more telling exchanges, Cher describes to Michelle Pfeiffer a physical peculiarity found in ferrets, similarly described by some of Jack's former lovers as being a characteristic of the real-life Jack:

> Alexandra: He has this most amazing penis. It bends the wrong way.
>
> Sukie: What do you mean it kind of bends the wrong way? Wait a minute. What?
>
> Alexandra (hooking the end of her index finger): I mean it kind of bends like that.

While screen shtupping was strictly simulated, off camera Jack continued an on-again, off-again romance with Veronica Cartwright that dated back to *Goin' South*. The actress, who plays a supporting role as Eastwick's uptight town matron, hollers perhaps the movie's most ironic line of dialogue, just before she collapses, vomits, and dies: "I have nothing against a good fuck, but there is danger here. *Somebody* has to do something about it!"

On or off the set, Jack persisted in invoking the dubious wisdom of Wilhelm Reich to anyone who cared to listen. Between rationalizations, Jack attended to character details well beyond the terms of his contract. Even though his violin playing is dubbed in the movie, he hired an instructor to teach him the instrument. He read up on Satan, showing Mick Jagger's sympathy for the devil while studying the twisted engravings of Gustave Doré in an illustrated version of Dante's *Inferno*.

"I came across a century-long debate about the definition of God," Jack said. "And the only thing they could come up with is that anything definite you can say about God must be supported by its paradoxical opposite. And that's what life is all about, this paradoxical situation."

On a $20 million budget, shooting began south of Boston in mid-July before moving on to Little Compton, Rhode Island, later in the summer. There, Miller and his cast met local protest in the form of the Board of Deacons of the United Congregational Church, which labeled the movie "satanical slime."

From within his film company, Miller also ran into problems. Jon Peters wanted to clip Miller's budget, while larding the ensemble farce with special effects. At one point, the producer planned to dump Miller and replace him with a more malleable director, until Jack interceded. When Peters tried to bully Jack, there was no contest. The dynamic had changed considerably since Lesley Ann Warren kept her then husband from busting an unknown B-movie actor in the chops one charged afternoon twenty years earlier.

"You know you *can* talk to me this way," Jack told Peters. "But if you keep doing this, I'll turn off. And if I turn off, you'll be in a lot of trouble."

No producer, director, or studio head now had the power Jack did. As one anonymous agent put it, "If Jack wanted Canada, some studio boss would buy it, paint it red, and park it in his driveway."

Even with Jack's backing, Miller compromised with Peters and his penchant for special effects. He commissioned a pair of puppets, one-sixth life size, that would illustrate Jack's grotesque metamorphosis into Mephistopheles near the end of the movie. The second of the two puppets—a demonic baby—bore an uncanny resemblance to Eddie King.

Jack savored his final line in the film. His face resurrected into a bank of TV sets, the now-disembodied Daryl Van Horne tells the three toddlers whom he conceived with their witchy moms: "I reassured them." Then the witches pull the plug, the TV sets go dark, and the end credits roll.

While *Heartburn* opened to a tepid box office in July and set no records in the summer of 1986, a year later Blockbuster couldn't keep it on the shelves. Something was happening to audiences conditioned only to see "hit" movies. Like Hal Ashby's *Harold and Maude*, which didn't find its audience until years after its short theatrical release, "failed" movies like *Heartburn* were getting a second chance.

"In another era, that might have been the end of *Heartburn*, at least until it showed, briefly, on pay TV or on free television, sliced up like last week's newspaper," wrote the *New York Times*'s Vincent Canby. "This would have been the film's only hope. That, however, was in the old, pre-videocassette days. Today movies that haven't been smash hits in their theatrical engagements turn up less than a year later in video rental shops."

Jack still preferred "the big silver" to TV and continued to watch most films in Evans's or Beatty's screening rooms. He reserved his own big-screen television for sports. As loathsome as he found TV to be, Jack embraced the idea of satirizing the enemy.

When James Brooks came to him with a comic sendup cameo of a TV anchor in *Broadcast News* (1987), Jack didn't hesitate. He even agreed to play the pompous ass Bill Rorich without star billing and for minimal compensation.

"Spiffed up and slicked back, Nicholson nails network superstars to the wall with his straight-on portrayal," wrote Duane Byrge in the *Hollywood Reporter*. "Dashes of Brinkley, Cronkite and Rather[18] glimmer in his mannerisms; all the while his own great and goofy aura naturally sabotages the all-knowing, deity-like status of network anchors."

During the fall of 1986, Jack also opted to flex his litterateur muscles. He'd been doing a lot of reading: Herman Hesse, C. P. Snow, David Halberstam. His next movie was going to be William Kennedy's Pulitzer Prize–winning *Ironweed*, a novel he could not read without his glasses. "I first noticed I needed them when I couldn't tell the faces at the far end of the court," Jack said following a Lakers game. Henceforth, even his shades were prescription.

As Jack's eyes worsened, he began to carry a small magnifying glass with him to read restaurant bills. Presbyopia caught up with him during *Ironweed*. "I don't mind reading it down the middle," he said, finding Kennedy's prose less enticing than its hype. "I don't feel as if I'm missing anything."

Jack preferred the larger type and the leaner drama of Kennedy's screenplay, which the author had written and sold to the Brazilian director Hector Babenco a year earlier. On the strength of the script, Jack concluded that the sad Depression-era story of a schizophrenic alcoholic's homecoming would contrast well with the high camp of Daryl Van Horne. He played the faded baseball star Francis Phelan from his own memory of the drunk who was his grandfather. "He was a great baseball player in the late '20s and early '30s," said Jack. "I don't know this firsthand, of course, but Ma always said he never took a drink until Prohibition was over. Then one day, after the firehouse baseball game, he got drunk on apricot brandy and never stopped drinking. Never, never stopped. He started drinking in his mid-thirties and died in his mid-fifties. . . . Yeah, *Ironweed* was close to the bone."

But not so close that Jack was ready to address the question of his real father. Paternity loss loomed large through *Ironweed*, which Babenco saw as an Irish Catholic parable of poverty and the expiation of sin. Francis Phelan is haunted by the memory of dropping and killing his infant son, as well as by the deaths of friends he could have saved but did not. "The Irish have a big hole between the memory of the past and now," said Babenco. "It is as if nothing else happened in between."

Filmed at a cost of $27 million over seventeen weeks in the New York state capital of Albany, *Ironweed* kicked the city's usual political headlines off the front page. The two most celebrated movie actors in the world had come to town, and everyone wanted their autographs. The movie reunited Jack and Meryl Streep, who submerged herself so deep into character that fans mistook her for a real bag lady. "You'd have police lines three blocks away to keep the crowds away," remarked Kennedy, who lived, taught, and wrote in Albany.

Streep lived in Connecticut and drove the forty miles home to her family at the end of each day, but Jack stayed in town. Anjelica flew in to visit once, but mostly he lived alone in a rented house with an indoor pool, where he tried to swim off some of Daryl Van Horne's 210 pounds. Francis Phelan looked like "the best fed, plumpest hobo in history," according to the *Times of London*.

But as a proud, broken derelict, Jack hid his weight as well as he hid all the other Jacks. Cocaine and cannabis, pussy and pomp had no place in the terminal story of a character as alcohol-soaked and ruined as John Joseph Nicholson Sr. At *Ironweed*'s bitter end, Jack's hollow-eyed Phelan huddles in a freight car that clip-clops out of town, light and dark strobing over him with tortured hypnotic precision, defeating in its harsh truth that there is no home left to go to anymore.

Except for a $1,000 contribution to the failed senatorial bid of then Governor Edmund G. Brown Jr. in December of 1982, Jack stayed out of politics through most of the 1980s.[19] "I don't campaign too

openly because my image as a rebel is perhaps a little counter produc-
tive," he said.

Indeed, during a Barry Diller fund-raiser for Michael Dukakis in
1987, Jack and Warren Beatty got a lukewarm reception when they
cozied up to the bar with the Massachusetts governor. Stars and politics still mixed, but at a distance. Beatty's candidate—and Jack's—was
the same for 1988 as he'd been in 1984: the Colorado senator Gary
Hart. But when the fifty-year-old senator got into hot water over his
affair with the twenty-nine-year-old model Donna Rice, only Beatty
went to his aid. Jack faced his own problems with twentysomething
women. "I hate being one of the older people in films," said Jack.
"God, fifty brought me crashing to my knees." Unlike previous birth-
days, the half-century mark "landed on me like a ton of bricks. That's
when I really realized my mortality. . . . I couldn't do nothing for a
year except think I was dying."

Still, he remained the gracious host to his middle-aged entourage.
"His house has become for me and a lot of his friends, a locality, a
vicinity, a watering hole," said John Herman Shaner. "We don't have
the corner candy store here anymore. It's a place where people talk
about everything. He's hospitable: lets you help yourself to drinks,
make your own sandwiches. It draws people to be intimate about
themselves."

During one of Jack's last celebrations as a forty-nine-year-old, he
had members of his old posse up to the house on the evening of April
6, 1987, to watch Sugar Ray Leonard face off against Marvelous Marvin Hagler. During the twelve rounds, Jack matched HBO's on-air
announcers comment for comment, offering his own expert advice.
When he got testy, Jack punched the air and curled his lips over his
teeth, punctuating each sentence with "pal."

The fight ended with a split decision that favored Leonard. One by
one, Harry Gittes, Don Devlin, and the others thanked Jack for his
usual hospitality and left. There would be no partying until dawn.
They had wives and children to go home to.

"I was alone with Jack and we talked for a couple more hours,"
recalled the final visitor that night. "He brought out this special golf
club that had a 45-degree angle to it and talked about how someday
all clubs and baseball bats would be made with that kind of angle to
drive the ball better. Of course, that never happened, but Jack speaks

with such authority, especially when he's coked out, that you think maybe he's right, even when he's not.

"At some point, I started talking about the [Black] Panthers and how they killed the sixties—these murdering, ass-raping thugs like Huey Newton who we all believed in.[20] And Jack says, swinging that golf club: 'Yeah, but think about what it *means* to be a murderer.' And the way he said it sent a chill through me. It was like he didn't have any sense of people; like he had no feeling for them whatsoever. It's shocking to suddenly think of someone you *know* behaving like that. I got up and left.

"Now, that could just as easily have been him acting. Jack always enjoyed putting me on. But I have never been able to shake that memory and the way he looked and the way he said it: 'Think about what it *means* to be a murderer.'"

Jack said the same thing, only slightly more diplomatically, in an unnerving interview with the *Sunday Express*: "[T]here's a surprisingly nondramatic quality to murder in real life. I've read a lot of books about murderers, as it happens. It was one of my favorite reading areas even before I was an actor."

In speaking of his life growing up in Neptune, he had alluded once to being a witness to a murder. He never elaborated, but now, at fifty, those boyish criminal fantasies kept surfacing and submerging, like a joker in a deck of cards.

The Witches of Eastwick opened in June 1987 and raked in $30 million at the box office.[21] It finished out the year in the top ten, earning more than $125 million—well ahead of either *Heartburn* or *Prizzi's Honor*.

Toward the end of the summer, John Huston collapsed on location during filming of the TV movie *Mr. Corbett's Ghost* (1987), which his son Danny directed. Working clear to the end, Huston had recently wrapped *The Dead* (1987), his final film as a director. Based on a James Joyce short story about Irish love and loss in the early twentieth century, the film was shot in a warehouse near L.A., but the set was the interior of an Irish country home much like St. Clerans. Fittingly, the screenplay had been written by Tony Huston and starred his kid sister Anjelica as a thirtysomething wife who tearfully outlines to her husband the innocent passion of her first love: a teenage boy long dead of consumption. "I could just look at my father and think of Ireland," Anjelica recalled. "It was all there."

In performance, direction, and execution, *The Dead* made a fitting epitaph to Huston's own lusty life, brimming as it had for nearly sixty years with appetite but connected to others by a few precious epiphanies.

While Huston was hospitalized in Newport, Rhode Island, Jack flew to see him and purportedly made a deathbed promise to look after Anjelica. On August 28, Huston died. A somber Jack accompanied Anjelica to the funeral.

And yet, exercising a reckless perversity that would return to haunt him again and again, Jack spent the night before the memorial chasing another woman around his bedroom with a ping-pong paddle—a twenty-three-year-old British actress and model with whom he'd been sleeping since they'd met eighteen months earlier in Aspen. "I had to wonder why he wasn't consoling Anjelica instead of making love to me," said Karen Mayo-Chandler in a *Playboy* interview two years later.

For all of his zeal to remain authentic in front of the cameras, Jack had become a study in contradiction and deceit. He pictured himself the sworn enemy of mendacity, while his own life was riddled with it. "Shorty's death was a catalyst," said his old friend Jon Epaminondas, suggesting a trigger for Jack's emotional Russian roulette. Huston's passing only accelerated the self-destruction. With a heedless grandiosity and impunity that only Jack's ionospheric level of money and celebrity could afford, he upped the ante on wine, women, and bong.

For public consumption, he waxed vainglorious about his "eternal" relationship with Anjelica and persisted in comparing their long-term affair to that of Jean-Paul Sartre and Simone de Beauvoir. The founder and the first lady of French existentialism had lived under separate roofs but maintained their mutual affection throughout their lives, and so it was with Jack and his lady.

For her part, Anjelica seemed a little weary of "her glittering vagrant," as Bob Evans had once called Jack, but she still wanted to have his child. For years, she'd been timing and testing her fertility, trying for pregnancy. "I love children," the thirty-five-year-old actress told *Cosmopolitan* not long after she won her Oscar. "It's part of a long-range plan that I would get to a satisfactory point in my career and then take time off to have a child."

She kept a room down the hall from Jack's, but she'd abandoned any hope of monogamy. Most of the time she stayed at her place in Beverly Glen. "We both believe in keeping our freedom," she said.

Jack parried questions of marriage by playing reporters, telling them that Anjelica wouldn't be in the mood whenever he proposed and vice versa. "She never called me—I always call her," complained Jack. "It's just her nature. You can ask any other friend of hers. Anjelica doesn't call people."

All Anjelica asked was that Jack not rub her nose in his faithlessness. If anything, she confided to friends, being so readily identified as Jack's old lady might be impeding her acting career.

Sandwiched between his occasional tryst with Anjelica and the inevitable one- or two-night stands with a budding actress or a Lakers cheerleader, Jack juggled several other long-term lovers, from Mayo-Chandler and his old flame Veronica Cartwright to a cunning cocktail waitress who not only could satisfy and keep secrets but could also play the stud poker of showbiz like a pro.

Born the same year as his daughter Jennifer, the wide-eyed, pouty-lipped, golden-haired Rebecca Broussard resembled an outsize version of Mimi Machu. She quit the University of Louisville after one year and went to New York to study hairdressing and become a model. From there, Broussard returned to her native Colorado, where locals remember her waiting tables at Aspen's Ute City Banque. As Jack's pal Jim Harrison once observed, "If you've known a lot of actresses and models, you return to waitresses because at least they smell like food."

After they met, Jack reportedly cast her as Jake Gittes's secretary in the 1985 go-round of *The Two Jakes*. The following year, Helena hired her as a cocktail waitress. A year after that, Broussard, then twenty-four, married one of Helena's regulars: the Pointer Sisters' forty-five-year-old record producer, Richard Perry.

Their wedding was in July, but by Christmas, the relationship teetered on dissolution. During an Aspen ski vacation, the Perrys attended the same round of parties as Jack and Anjelica, including a New Year's bash hosted by Don Johnson and Barbra Streisand. But in Jack, Broussard saw an opportunity to trade up, while Jack began to imagine relief from his own midlife crisis in the vivacious company of another man's youthful wife. At first stunned by the relationship, Jack's daughter, Jennifer, became good friends with Broussard. "It's

Ten North Frederick," said Jack, casting himself in the role of an aging Gary Cooper, who sees a last chance at love in a woman half his age.[22]

"I was feeling fat and old and generally miserable," he recalled. "I wasn't happy with any of the projects that were coming my way and it seemed pretty bleak out there to me. I didn't feel like I was able to have fun the way I used to. But when I met Rebecca, she kind of shook me up. She has a strong character and she would bully me to get into shape and stop feeling sorry for myself."

The public response to his two latest films hadn't helped his gloomy disposition. *Broadcast News* opened in December, as did *Ironweed*,[23] and while the former scored $24 million at the box office in its first twenty days of release, the bleak story of Francis Phelan hadn't even earned enough to cover Jack's $5-million acting fee.

He didn't begrudge James L. Brooks's success. In fact, Jack recognized the director's focus and energy as "an army against anything that can go wrong with the movie." "I admire the fact that the man won three Oscars in his first directing job and nobody pays that much attention to him," said Jack.

On the last day of February 1988, Jack turned up at a Hollywood reception for the Duke and Duchess of York with Karen Mayo-Chandler on his arm. The British tabloids jumped all over "Jack the Lad" and his latest "sexcapade," while the jaded U.S. media got as excited as Claude Rains discovering gambling at Rick's.

Jack couldn't keep it in his pants. Everybody knew it, including Anjelica. While they were still a couple in the public imagination, she had already begun to move on. The actress put up for sale the Beverly Glen cottage that Jack had helped her to buy, and she moved into larger ranch-style quarters on Hutton Drive in Benedict Canyon. She further flexed her independence by going in thirds on a Sierra retreat near Sequoia National Park.[24]

Careerwise, she committed the then unpardonable sin of signing on for a TV miniseries. Anjelica took the role of Clara Allen, Tommy Lee Jones's old flame in Larry McMurtry's epic Western *Lonesome Dove*. After watching the much-honored CBS miniseries, even the film snob Jack had to rethink his video attitude. His long-gestating *The Murder of Napoleon* might be perfect miniseries fodder in the right hands.[25] "Maybe I made a mistake not doing television," he admitted. "Now it might tempt me."

But not as much as Rebecca Ann Broussard did. Even as he squired Karen Mayo-Chandler around Hollywood right under Anjelica's nose, Jack laid plans to lay Rebecca. She'd left Richard Perry in January, claimed "irreconcilable differences" in May, and moved into 9959 Westwanda Drive in June, just a five-minute drive from Jack's Mulholland compound. Jack paid her rent. Given the deal he was about to sign with Warner Bros., he could afford to pay a thousand rents.

He now commanded $6 million a picture. Only Robert Redford, Sylvester Stallone, Dustin Hoffman, Clint Eastwood, and his old pal Warren Beatty had as high an opening bid.

But Brando still held the record for the biggest paycheck on a single motion picture. The Godfather traded nine minutes of screen time in the original *Superman* (1978) for an $18.5 million salary plus a percentage of the gross. Jack's reclusive neighbor might be a bilious shell of the actor he'd once been, but when it came to cash, Brando still represented star power's high-water mark. With the prospect of taking on the Joker in the $40 million summer blockbuster *Batman* (1989), Jack stood to supersede him in the *Guinness Book of World Records*.

As early as *The Witches of Eastwick*, Jon Peters had offered Jack the role of Batman's nemesis. "You've got to be crazy," said Jack.

Guber and Peters had been courting Jack ever since, but a third voice now joined the chorus. Tim Burton was a Goth wunderkind from the burbs of Burbank who backed into showbiz via the California Institute of the Arts, where he learned animation and obsessed over the acting of Vincent Price. Like Jack, Burton turned a love of movies and a talent for caricature into a career. He sketched and painted his way into a Disney apprenticeship, just as Jack had gotten his foot in the door through the MGM animation division.

Unlike Jack, Burton's path remained behind the camera, although his direction turned out to be far too dark for Disney. *Frankenweenie* (1984), his directorial debut about a resurrected family pooch, got him invited to leave. He moved on to Warner Bros., where he directed the surprise hit *Pee-Wee's Big Adventure* (1985). The studio showed its continued faith in his zombie vision by giving him the off-beat horror comedy *Beetlejuice* (1988) as his next project.

But the big one was *Batman*. Following the recurrent success of its campy 1960s TV series starring Adam West as the Caped Crusader,

Warner Bros. spent years and millions of dollars trying to figure a way to bring Gotham City to a theater near you. By the mid-eighties, the studio had settled on a face-off between Batman and the Joker, the worst of Bruce Wayne's foes, but the movie would not be played for laughs. Owing as much to the novelist Frank Miller's graphic novel *The Dark Knight Returns* as to the original DC Comics, Burton's *Batman* loomed and brooded like a high-concept bad dream.[26]

The director's *Beetlejuice* box office triumph in the spring captured Jack's attention. He accepted the studio's invitation to fly him via corporate jet to London, where Warner was investing $6 million in set construction across ninety-five acres on eighteen soundstages at Pinewood Studios.

Following his London expedition, Jack called on *Batman*'s comic book creator Bob Kane to get a read on the Joker's origins and discovered that the cartoonist had based him on the title character of a 1927 Universal silent film called *The Man Who Laughs*. As a boy, the title character's cheek muscles are slit so that he always grins. Jack found a print and studied the film. Meanwhile, to entice Jack to join the cast, Kane doctored the famous "Here's Johnny!" still from *The Shining* for him, giving Jack white skin, green hair, and ruby-red lips.

By summer, Jack stopped playing hard to get. He accepted a $6 million salary, while he had Sandy Bresler hammer out a gross participation on the back end that would become the most lucrative acting contract in Hollywood history. "The thing Jack learned from the Monkees, as the story goes on, is the power and value of merchandise," said Davy Jones. "When he did *Batman*, he got 10 percent of merchandising."

When Jack sat down with the director and the screenwriter, he opted to put the Joker so far over the top that, as one critic put it, "you can't see the top."

"He was like an encyclopedia of culture and history and art," said the screenwriter Warren Skaaren, whom Jack summoned to discuss *Batman* before the first cameras rolled. "I threw out a line from Nietzsche and Jack jumped on it and *he* threw out a line from Nietzsche."[27]

After his initial reluctance, Jack now embraced the Joker as an exaggeration of his own glowering id: the apex of self-parody that began with *The Shining*, in which "Jack" overpowered his own acting. The Joker became a burlesque of the Jack persona, including his mania for total control.[28] At one point, the Joker excuses his murder and mayhem on grounds that he is an artist, not a killer. In Jack and Burton's first tête-à-tête after Jack took the part, he told Burton, "Remember it's dark. Just like basketball, it's night comedy."

"He can come up with different approaches to a scene time after time, and I'd find myself wanting to do extra takes just to see what he would do," said Burton.

It was Jack who came up with the Joker's evil non sequitur "Ever dance with the devil in the pale moonlight?" and Jack who counseled his costars Michael Keaton[29] and Kim Basinger[30] to become one with their costumes: "Let the wardrobe do the acting, kids."

Jack was so taken with his own duds that he paid $70,000 to keep them once the twelve-week production was over: twenty-five shirts, six suits, and a dozen hats, all in various shades of orange, purple, and turquoise. Price was no object. At the end of a week's shooting, Jack reportedly turned to another cast member and said, "Ah well, that's another Matisse."

Batman got under way in October and wrapped after the holidays. The Joker moved Jack past the horror of turning fifty. After spending two hours in makeup each day—one to transform him into the Joker and another to return to just plain Jack—it was clear that dour Frances Phelan had been vanquished by Daryl Van Horne on steroids. With hyper Jack dancing like the devil in the pale moonlight, *Batman* seemed destined to become "the Trump Tower of movies," in the words of the producer Julia Phillips: more corrupt, shiny, and *big* than any blockbuster that had preceded it.

18

HAL ASHBY DIED OF PANCREATIC CANCER ON DECEMBER 27, 1988, two doors down from Bruce Dern's place on the beach at Malibu. Despite Ashby's remarkable track record, his career collapsed after *Being There* (1979). The final indignity came when Columbia locked Ashby out of his editing room for *The Slugger's Wife* (1985) because not enough scenes contained Neil Simon's dialogue. Ashby's death became symbolic of the drug-propelled flameout and the bloodless impersonality of the New Hollywood. "It's had a singular effect, this drug," Anjelica said of cocaine. "I think it's made people numb, and I think it's made them angry under the numbness."

Unlike the standing-room-only memorial for John Huston the previous year, Ashby's postmortem at the Directors Guild Theater filled less than half of the five hundred seats. Jane Fonda, who owed Ashby her second Oscar, wasn't there. Jon Voight, who also won for *Coming Home* (1978), failed to show. Jack was on location for *Batman* and sent a telegram. To their credit, all had stopped in to say good-bye in Ashby's final days, but they made no public display of their grief.

A martyr to coke and cash, the fifty-nine-year-old director was only the latest victim of sixties excess. Andy Warhol had died ten months earlier at fifty-eight, and Abbie Hoffman, fifty-two, would soon commit suicide. Another Nicholson touchstone, the eighty-three-year-old Diana Vreeland, would be gone within the year. Time compressed and accelerated all at once, giving Jack and his entire generation a kind of dervish urgency codified in Billy Joel's 1989 anthem "We Didn't Start the Fire."

Jack's rebel spirit remained strong. He still trusted art over the media. "As time goes on, it's more and more risky to confront the public through the press—unadorned by trappings of the story," he said. "It's just . . . it's a slightly more vicious thing."

While no one was looking, the stakes of movie making had risen, and the party-on-down celebrities that the New Hollywood bred either got with the program or perished. Jack might be as plagued by self-doubt as the next guy, but he never let on. He watched helplessly as *conglomeration*, now one of his favorite words, continued unabated. "I've been screaming against conglomeration on behalf of America, not just the movie business," he railed. "It's one of those things that's too sophisticated for the mass media. Conglomeration was illegal in 1928! They sent people to jail!"

An earlier generation's effort to keep monopoly out of the movie business fell by the wayside during the 1980s. Free-market Reaganomics opened up studio cross-ownership of TV, radio, satellite, and cable and allowed Hollywood to auction itself off to the highest bidder, even if the new owners spoke no English.

By decade's end, Sony[1] paid Coca-Cola $3.4 billion for Columbia

Pictures, and the Sony rival Matsushita Electric angled to purchase MCA-Universal for a whopping $6.6 billion. In the biggest U.S. merger to date, Time-Life and Warner Bros. became Time-Warner under the funeral-parlor heir Steve Ross.

Paramount and the sad artifact that had once been MGM-UA would both be on the auction block soon. Rupert Murdoch's Fox juggernaut stalled and threatened to plunge toward bankruptcy, but the Aussie press baron answered his critics with audacity, launching BSkyB, Europe's first international satellite TV operation: a cash cow and the next logical step in the evolution of motion-picture delivery.[2]

The movies that got delivered were slipping. The Ashby generation of directors had given way to a newer, slicker breed. The best continued to court Nicholson, once *Batman* had lifted him to a whole new level of superstardom. Robin Williams, whom Tim Burton considered for the role of the Riddler in his *Batman Returns* (1992) sequel, summed up Jack's post-Joker place in the Hollywood pecking order during a televised interview with ABC's Barbara Walters: "There's Jack, and then there's the rest of us."

Jonathan Demme tried casting Jack as Hannibal Lecter and reteaming him with Michelle Pfeiffer in *The Silence of the Lambs* (1991)—roles that went instead to Anthony Hopkins and Jodie Foster. John Badham wanted him to be an NYPD detective in *The Hard Way* (1991), a part that went to James Woods. Jack dismissed Oliver Stone as "too full of himself." Tony Scott asked Jack to consider *The Last Boy Scout* (1991) for Warner Bros., but Bruce Willis took the title role of the cynical detective Joe Hallenbeck.

At the end of the yuppie decade, Jack preferred his own cynical detective. After *Batman*, he resurrected *The Two Jakes*. Determined not to let lawyers and the Paramount suits bury Bob Towne's greatest creation, this time he had both the money and the juice to revive J. J. Gittes. Jack had fallen into the Paul Newman model: make a film for money, then make a movie he loved—but always make sure there's a paycheck. For every big-budget *Exodus* (1960), Newman would push for *The Hustler* (1961); for every super-hyped *Torn Curtain* (1966), there was a *Cool Hand Luke* (1967); for each potboiling *When Time Ran Out . . .* (1980), there was an *Absence of Malice* (1981).

Thus, for Jack, Batman meant a return to Chinatown.

. . .

For four years Jack had been trying to bring *The Two Jakes* back to life, but every time he did, another lawyer's letter arrived. "I was the only person who had any money, so the lawsuits went after me," he complained. "It bored me to death. When I work, I don't just step in and learn my lines. I have to play a year in advance. And I had to work my schedule around the lawsuits."

He demanded a complete rewrite before he'd commit. Towne maintained that Jack and Jake were interchangeable. "Jake Gittes handles people the way Jack does, alternately intimidating and coaxing," said Towne. "He has Jack's ability to manipulate people in a funny and reflective manner. Gittes's love of clothes comes from Jack and his blue-collar arrogance. There's a sense in which Jack has always put a stamp on what I write."

While Towne was the wordsmith, Jack believed himself to be the one who'd "worked twelve-hour days since two years ago," to shepherd the *Chinatown* sequel to the screen. Over Christmas, Towne delivered a shooting script while Jack was in London wrapping *Batman*.

"I pigheadedly said I wouldn't let this die, because I didn't want big-time personal things in my life affected by making a movie," said Jack. "We all know—from being in this business—hundreds of people who don't speak to one another for years over some fucking dress in a movie, or something. I had worked this long without that, and I wasn't about to let it happen now. Between these two guys, one camp or another, they know 80 percent of my friends in life."

Jack told Bob Evans he'd still get to produce but would not appear as the second Jake. Towne's role was reduced to that of screenwriter. Jack would have preferred to let Roman Polanski direct, but, as with the first *Jakes* go-round, Polanski was out of the picture.

Towne had flown to Paris in 1987 to help the director tweak *Frantic* (1988) and witnessed first-hand Polanski's abject fear of prison. Showing a persistent preference for *jeunes filles*, Polanski had married the twenty-two-year-old Emmanuelle Seigner, Harrison Ford's *Frantic* leading lady. Thirty-three years Polanski's junior, she'd also made him rethink his hot-tub tryst at Jack's house ten years earlier. "He decided he did in fact do something wrong," said Jack. "As an honest man, he admitted that, though he didn't have to."

But contrition didn't mean a willingness to risk jail. There was no way Polanski would return to the United States for *The Two Jakes*, and there was no way Jack would give Towne another crack at directing.³ He tried to interest either Mike Nichols or Bernardo Bertolucci. Both passed. If Jack had any hope of resurrecting Jake Gittes, it appeared that he'd have to direct himself. "I know perfectly well that people would rather invest in my acting than my directing," he told Roger Ebert in a prophetic interview. "I'm at risk here. If it's not well received, I think I'll be humbled by the experience, and say, 'Well, maybe it's not what I should do.' I won't really believe it, but maybe I'll go that way."

At the beginning of February, Jack signed to star, produce, and direct. A fifth of the relatively modest $25 million budget went to him.⁴ The movie he set out to make was about the inevitability of karma in the shifting Los Angeles he'd come to call his own, but "you can't make a movie called *Fucking Karma* and not be pretentious, so I called it *The Two Jakes*." What he had in mind was an L.A. elegy.

"The reason why I originally liked it here still exists," said Jack. "It's just the easiest place to live. It's nothing original, but you can't beat the climate—the desert by the sea. You know, my ears pop when I drive up here on top of the Santa Monica hills. It's high enough for a boy who comes from New Jersey."

He recalled his first trek to Hollywood across the rolling Baldwin Hills, past a vast dried grass panorama interrupted only by the occasional oil well derrick. Street lights had yet to be installed along two-lane La Brea Avenue, so he made the long hike back to June's place in inky darkness. Thirty-five years later, he lived on top of the void. "If you laid L.A. out the way Manhattan is laid out, this is Fifty-fifth and Fifth Avenue," said Jack. "This is dead center."

The L.A. of his earliest memory had become a neon monument to light pollution and incessant traffic but was still "a town to get lost in," Jack insisted. "It has that line between dream and illusion. When I moved here, there was only one freeway. You could see through the air then."

He and Towne were still retooling the script when principal photography began on April 18, 1989. Early in production, life imitated art.

"We went out to shoot a doctor's house in an orange grove that I'd been to twice," said Jack. "I'd scouted the area twice. The day we get out there the orange grove's been cut down, there's nothing but a dirt field. And not only that, they forgot to cast the actor I had in the part. Every day there was something. Every day."

Nicholson's L.A. had entered the final stages of shedding its agrarian roots. From Disneyland to Riverside and beyond, dairy farms and orange groves had given way, one by one, to concrete and mortar. *Chinatown's* arid San Fernando Valley had become wall-to-wall subdivisions. As Jack's old flame Joni Mitchell once put it, they paved paradise and put up a parking lot.

Los Angeles now belonged to a very different breed of immigrant: it was no longer New Jersey refugees hiking to Hollywood. Freeway offramp signs announced such neighborhoods as Thai Town, Little Tokyo, Koreatown, and Little Saigon. Salvadorans owned MacArthur Park; Rampart, where Helena had opened her club, was known as Filipinotown; and displaced Ethiopians began to dominate the old Jewish neighborhood along Fairfax Avenue. British expatriates and Russkis overran Santa Monica. The largest Cambodian population outside of Phnom Penh occupied central Long Beach.

Los Angeles was second only to Mexico City as the largest Spanish-speaking urban center in North America. Spanish radio stations now outnumbered Anglo stations by half, and the Telemundo and Univision networks rivaled CBS, ABC, NBC, and Fox for Nielsen ratings. Salsa superseded disco along the Sunset Strip. Hollywood, as Jack first knew it, had gone into fast fade. "People used to talk about going to the Bahamas or some other exotic place to get away from it all," Jack told the *Los Angeles Times*. "There is no away anymore. No matter where you go in the shrinking global community, you run into your past. Somebody will say, 'Hey, I never expected to see you here.' You've got to deal with it without running away."

Everyone ignored the sign on Jack's trailer door that read "Do not disturb unless urgent." The interior was appropriately strewn with sunglasses. Jack gained thirty pounds to become the middle-aged Jake Gittes. Throughout the shoot, he battled his waistline by living on Marlboros, Evian, and "frothy, purplish" shakes he dubbed "the elixir of life." "I'll never be able to eat what I want," he grumbled. "I'll never get around to preferring salads. I will never crave butter lettuce. I crave butter, cream, steak."

The Two Jakes gave him ample opportunity to review his own life, as well as the changing landscape of his adopted home. *Chinatown's* Jake differed as much from the J. J. Gittes of *The Two Jakes* as young Jack's *The Cry Baby Killer* differed from Garrett Breedlove.[5] The times were no longer a-changin'; they'd flat-out changed.

In one *Two Jakes* scene, Jack stood on a hillside in the northwest reaches of the Santa Clarita Valley, where arid meadows and blue skies still approximated the unspoiled feel of the San Fernando Valley circa 1948 or the Baldwin Hills circa 1954. "Ah, the rape of the land," he muttered.

He filtered his high-brow artistic temperament into his film direction, ordering the cinematographer Vilmos Zsigmond to contrast the angular cityscapes and the claustrophobic interiors of the early-twentieth-century artist Charles Sheeler with the open range and desert vistas of Maynard Dixon. He told the artist Julian Schnabel,[6] "The story of Jake Gittes is about reflecting back to his youth, to his childhood, and another woman besides Faye Dunaway. The lesson of the whole is, 'Hey, stay out of Chinatown.'"

Eleven years might have elapsed between *Chinatown* and *The Two Jakes*, but the theme was the same—and the similarities to Jack's own comfortable life revealing. "It is not a story of what happened in between," said Jack. "Where Jake is now tells that story. He is engaged. He does belong to a country club. He is fat and sassy. He does own his own building. . . . All this indicates the whole fabric of this guy's life. He's everywhere. He's Perino's, he's tuxedo, he's golf club, he's managing the idealized postwar life. He's gotten away from Chinatown."

But what Jake Gittes comes to appreciate is that you never get away from Chinatown. Like a lover betrayed, a tarnished childhood, or a long-lost father, Chinatown persists as a lewd reminder of what once was, what might have been, and what, in the end, never fades from memory.

"One of the main elements in it is the family, the chaos that results from mankind not being in a family way," said Harvey Keitel, who played opposite Jack as the second Jake (Berman).[7] "These people are in despair, hopelessness, agony. And they're all in search of a family—the Nicholson character, the Meg Tilly character, my character. We're all people without family, without children."

"The power of memory is his central motivation," said Jack. "When this specter of the past rises, when it comes into his life, all of the life he's developed since falls away from him. Gittes is pretending this is just another job, but you can see by the way others around him react—his secretary, his assistants—this is an obsession. He tried to do something good once—of that he's sure—and he doesn't want to lose that. He can try to subvert the past. He can try to bury it in old files. But time is continuous and circular."

Throughout production, Jack surrounded himself with his own extended family. Jennifer, now twenty-six and struggling to gain a foothold in Hollywood, signed on as an assistant to the film's two production designers. Like her old man, she'd studied with Jeff Corey after she left USC, but she preferred art direction over acting.[8] She'd been offered a job working on the TV series *Miami Vice* and joined her father on the set of *The Witches of Eastwick* as a production assistant before *The Two Jakes*.

In her debut performance as Jake's secretary, Rebecca Broussard received personal coaching from the master. Jack gave her her very own backstory: her fiancé, a member of Jake's army unit, had died during the war. Like everyone else in *The Two Jakes*, Rebecca's character tried to forget the past—not that the audience could tell from her few moments of screen time.

"I've got a friend in this movie now named Jeff Morris," said Jack.[9] "Jeff was in *Goin' South*. I then put him in *The Border*, and in *Ironweed*, and now this. I've known Jeff twenty fucking years"

"He doesn't forget the guys he knew before he became famous," said Tracey Walter, a veteran character actor who played a *Two Jakes* geologist following his role as Bob the Goon, the Joker's right-hand stooge in *Batman*.

Jack Pack cronies peppered the cast. As an inside joke, Jack cast Will "Red Dog" Tynan as a judge. Michael Daves, whom Jack met during *Ensign Pulver*, was his first assistant director. Luana Anders played a florist, and Jack brought John Hackett out of retirement as his stand-in. He also gave bit roles to John Herman Shaner and Annie Marshall and made Ara Gallant a "special consultant."[10] Van Dyke Parks, who'd scored *Goin' South*, reprised that role for *The Two Jakes*. As with *Drive, He Said* and *Goin' South*, Jack again called upon Harold Schneider as his line producer, although he tortured Schneider this time around with his new best friend and future business partner Alan Finkelstein, whom he brought on as Schneider's associate producer.[11] His nickname, courtesy of Jack, was "The Shadow," in deference to his dogging Jack's every step.

As production proceeded, Jack kept discovering script problems, particularly with the ending. He returned to Towne for rewrites, but as Polanski had observed fifteen years earlier during *Chinatown*,

Towne was "a very slow writer, delighting in any form of procrastination, turning up late, filling his pipe, checking his answering service, ministering to his dog."[12]

There was also Towne's simmering resentment over Jack directing his screenplay. As production rolled toward its climax, Towne took a vacation in Bora Bora, making himself unreachable by phone or fax through most of June and leaving Jack to fend for himself: an unforgivable breach of loyalty. Jack was forced to narrate part of the story himself, banking on his familiar voice to bridge expository lapses that a good script doctor might have been able to resolve.

Jack's penny-pinching worsened. Even though Roger Corman wasn't there, his make-do spirit pervaded production.[13] In lieu of paying exorbitant studio soundstage fees, Jack used the same Valencia warehouse where John Huston had shot *The Dead*. When a scene aboard a yacht called for actresses to wear expensive 1940s bathing suits and hairstyles, Jack told Schneider, "We'll wrap them naked in towels and put hats on 'em." To save time, he cut meal breaks and told cast and crew to eat when they could, either from craft services or take-out. One wag called the hurry-up atmosphere on the set "*Gone with the Wind* in the morning and *Dukes of Hazzard* in the afternoon."

But Jack spared no expense on himself. His parking place at Paramount Studios bore the sign "Reserved for Jake Gittes only" and he drove a shiny, detailed, classic two-door convertible to the lot each day, just like the one Jake drove in *Chinatown*. When *Batman* premiered in June, Jack hired a helicopter to ferry himself from *The Two Jakes* set near Santa Barbara to the red-carpeted theater in Santa Monica. He invited Harold and Amy Schneider along for the ride. Jack sat behind the pilot, facing the Schneiders, but as Amy recalled, "The whole way, he didn't speak a word. He just sat there getting loaded."[14]

As expected, *Batman* obliterated all competition at the summertime box office, earning back its entire production budget during its first weekend and eventually grossing more than $250 million. While clearly its star, Jack turned down $7.5 million for the sequel. The Joker, he grew fond of saying, was dead.

But that grinning image remained a part of Jack's public persona. He learned to sketch the Joker's trademark smile and made it a part of his autograph, like Mick Jagger's lewd comic lips and lolling tongue, which had become a permanent part of the Rolling Stones. In the mad blink of the Joker's eye, Jack's morbid fear of turning fifty had vanished as a whole new generation embraced his stardom. When *The Two Jakes* production shifted to a warehouse section in downtown L.A., the throngs who showed up along the sidewalk to catch a glimpse of Jack were teens who couldn't care less about L.A. nostalgia. The chant beyond the line of rent-a-cops was "Joker! Joker!"

Once, as Jeremy Railton passed through the halls of the Ventura County Courthouse following a *Two Jakes* scene, the production designer marveled at Jack's continuing ability to delight. "All the ladies are popping their heads out and he's talking to everybody, and as we left, I looked up at the courthouse and every single window in the courthouse had a smiling face," Railton recalled. "And I thought to myself: what a gift to be able to walk into a place, not really talk to people, not make any scenes, and walk out and leave this huge build-ing of people all grinning."

Jack's bad-boy image had evolved; he was now a bad man, but not so bad that fans recoiled. They labeled him *eccentric* or *naughty*— words that come with an automatic excuse and gave him license to behave badly again and again.

"He's nobody's father, but he is everybody's mad uncle," con-cluded the *London Guardian*'s Adrian Turner. "The guy who disap-peared round the world to run a whorehouse in Manila or a fishing sloop in Puerto Vallarta and now regales nephews with tales of high adventure and gives nieces sitting in his lap their first whiff of carnal knowledge. Were he not so charming he would be locked away."

In July, Anjelica told the *Sunday Express*, "I don't like the word *com-mitment*. It has a gloomy sound. *Understanding* is a better word. Jack and I have an understanding."

The following month, Jack told the *London Daily Mail*, "One area in my life where I am not as happy as I might be is not having a sec-ond child. I'd like one; more than one. But at my age the possibility becomes less likely. Not because I can't have children but because the age gap between them and me would be so huge."

Then two months later, the *Los Angeles Herald Examiner*'s Mitchell Fink dropped the bombshell.

Nicholson is going to be a father. And the mother is neither (Karen) Mayo-Chandler nor Nicholson's longtime girlfriend, Anjelica Huston. The mother, according to some of our best sources, is record producer Richard Perry's ex-wife Rebecca Broussard.

The 26-year-old Broussard plays Nicholson's secretary in *The Two Jakes* and our sources say she's 2½ months pregnant with his baby.

Anjelica had just returned from shooting Paul Mazursky's *Enemies: A Love Story* (1989) in New York. Based on an Isaac Bashevis Singer story about a Holocaust survivor who juggles three women—his mistress, his wife, and the wife he thought had perished in a concentration camp—the movie bore uncomfortable parallels to Anjelica's own life. She played the concentration camp wife, returning to her husband only to find he is having a child by another woman.[15] "That very much reflected what was going on in my life directly after I came back to Los Angeles after the movie," she told *Vanity Fair*. "That was pretty close to the bone, I would say."

One afternoon after the news leaked, Anjelica showed up at the *Two Jakes* office and began pummeling Jack. Following their two-hour confrontation, she allegedly told him, "This is the last indignity I will ever suffer."

"It never feels good to have been left and to have been left for a younger woman," she reflected a decade later. "I was very devastated by our having to separate, but there was no choice. There was no way I could go on being with Jack, who was fathering a child by another woman. I'm not that kind of woman."

Jack again blamed the gossip columns for eliminating "the privacy and the intimacy" and reluctantly took responsibility before retreating into fortune cookie wisdom. "Where there's clarity, there is no choice," he said. "Where there's choice, there's misery. The fragility of an infant's skull reduces all this talk to gibberish. There was nothing else I could do but what I did."

Anjelica staunched her grief by going back before the cameras in *The Grifters* (1990) during the fall of 1989. She played the con artist mother of a con artist (John Cusack) and was invited to sit on the jury at the next Cannes Film Festival.

Whatever feelings Jack had about so very publicly ending his seventeen-year relationship with Anjelica were superseded by yet another sex scandal, which he now rode out like a seasoned rodeo clown, oblivious to the buck and bellow of the media.

Rachel Ryan, a porn star who used the screen name Serina Robinson and had most recently appeared as a corpse in *Batman*, said she had had a three-month fling with Jack, which the tabloids the *Globe* and *News of the World* misrepresented as a three-way fling with Rebecca.[16] Ryan sued for $10 million, maintaining that "we had only normal sex . . . we never did it with another girl and I've never even met Rebecca."

Meanwhile, *Playboy* paid Karen Mayo-Chandler $150,000 to detail her life with Jack in the months prior to the filming of *Batman* and published the results in its December issue. For $5.50 at the newsstand, Jack's fans got to see what he and Mayo-Chandler's gynecologist got to see. Though it was as lurid a spread as any that the nation's premier skin magazine[17] prided itself on publishing, the far greater revelations were folded into the "interview" she gave her publicist, the ex-Fleet Streeter Kenelm Jenour. With predictable sleaze and come-hither artifice, Jenour wrote down Mayo-Chandler's purported first-person impressions of Jack, which accompanied her pictorial: "He really is a horny little devil. He has this image of being a bit like Bogart, a lovable rogue, a naughty little boy, if you like, and that's just how he is."

The lovable rogue's S&M episodes left marks that "took the make-up girl all of two hours to cover up" when Mayo-Chandler reported for her latest film. But beyond the *Playboy* pubes and pouty lips, and beneath Mayo-Chandler's account of the "mad, wild and wonderful" sex, Mayo-Chandler's own pitiable voice resonated from her supposed direct quotes. While the seasoned jade Jenour pimped up Jack's penchant for Polaroids, paddling, and peanut butter sandwiches ("to keep his strength up"), the doctored *Playboy* copy carried an unmistakable subtext of a woman not so much scorned as desperate.

> Jack was like a drug to me. He was very addictive. Life was one big high when he was around. He had me completely hooked for a long time. Of course, all good things must end.
>
> Sometimes when men throw themselves at you, the only way to treat them is badly. You lose respect for them and you

move on. So Jack went to London to make *Batman* and I got on with my career. I guess the age difference told in the end. Actually, Jack is about the same age as my mother. Perhaps I should have introduced them—that's a joke. Ha, ha! My mum will kill me for that.

In a subsequent interview, Mayo-Chandler said she did not go ahead with the *Playboy* deal without first checking with Jack. She said that he told her the publicity would be good for both of them and, indeed, Jack came off to the average aging voyeur as a standard-bearer for lust unencumbered by intimacy.

But confronted by those same journalists who sought his take on Mayo-Chandler's *Playboy* tell-all, Jack played the injured party and planted the dagger deep. "It was a violation," he said. "It's like when your apartment is robbed. You imagine you're not going to be able to deal with it, but in fact your sympathies are with the criminal, because karma is instant. Ultimately, she is going to suffer more than I. The person who was driven to this is in a much more difficult slot in life and doesn't understand it."

Like voodoo, Jack's cruel prediction came to pass. Mayo-Chandler's formal training at the Italia-Conti and Guildhall drama schools in London and a subsequent decade of paying her Hollywood dues counted for nothing. What screen work she was able to get subsequent to the *Playboy* article was as a third- or fourth-billed bimbo in straight-to-video sci-fi horror flicks. From 1998 until her death from breast cancer in July 2006, she didn't work in film at all.

In the days prior to her memorial, held in a Sherman Oaks chapel at the base of the mountain where Jack still lived, her mother celebrated Mayo-Chandler's life as misunderstood and her end tragic. She was just forty-seven and left behind a nine-year-old. Of her daughter's short-lived relationship with the Joker, Karen's mother, Mrs. Norma Mayo-Chandler, had a clipped, bitter assessment. "It was an unfortunate incident," she said.

In August 1989, Jack took off from editing *The Two Jakes* to fly to Monte Carlo to meet with the man who bought Robert Evans's house.

Evans, the onetime czar of Paramount, had fallen even further from grace after his 1985 implication in the so-called *Cotton Club* murder. He took the Fifth Amendment when Assistant District Attorney David Conn put him on the witness stand, which might have saved him from an indictment in the April 1983 murder of his coproducer Roy Radin,[18] but the court of public opinion had already convicted Evans.[19] For a time he became a Hollywood pariah. Except for Jack, who kept Evans's name in the credits on *The Two Jakes*, the producer didn't work for a decade. "Loyalty," said Evans. "That he's given to me like no one else."

Evans became so despondent and desperate for cash that he mortgaged everything he owned for $1.1 million and sold his much-storied French Regency bachelor pad at the foot of Coldwater Canyon, only to immediately regret the decision.[20] Friends like Jack and Warren Beatty scolded him for unloading a landmark in which more sex, drugs, and film deals had been consummated than in half the studios in Hollywood.

Jack's Monte Carlo visit was a mission of mercy, in which he used his substantial clout to undo a two-week emergency escrow on Evans's $5 million real estate deal and give the producer back his house. Jack claimed that his action wasn't selfless: he needed Evans's legendary screening room in order to watch *The Two Jakes* dailies. "He [Evans] and John McEnroe are my only two Republican friends," said Jack.

In order to qualify for Oscars, Paramount had already booked the film at theaters in New York and L.A. for release during the last two weeks of December, going wide to twelve hundred theaters in February, three days after the announcement of Academy Award nominations. Jack felt the pressure but refused to hurry. "Cinema is a visual poetic form," he said. "I have a lousy narrative sense and feel like I'm more of a poetic director." There would not be "a lot of popcorn stops in *The Two Jakes*," he promised. "This is a real movie."

Indeed, Jack seemed to toil over the tiniest nuance. Watching himself getting it on with Madeleine Stowe in one scene, he echoed what he believed would be the audience's voyeurism as he discussed visual poetry with the film's editor.

"I love when she does [that with] her little mouth," Jack said.

His editor nodded. As Gittes girdled Stowe's ass with his hands, Jack leaned forward. "I love this, too."

"Yes," said the editor, grinning. "I put it back in for you."

And as Gittes engulfed the girl, Jack added, "I love seeing the little garters through the opening in the furniture there"

Jack's erotic attention to detail did not propel the story—a criticism that the film critic David Denby would echo when he recalled that Jack's two previous directorial efforts had not been "particularly coherent as narrative."

December came and went without delivery of *The Two Jakes*. Jack pleaded for more time. Paramount cancelled the theater bookings and moved the release date up five months to April, a dead zone for film and rarely a time when Oscar contenders open, but—as it turned out—a very good month in which to have a child.

At year's end, one British journal quoted Anjelica as saying that the news of the baby was "the worst Yuletide present I ever had." But her feelings didn't dampen Jack's Christmas. Rebecca rode out the initial media firestorm in retreat with her family in Montana, but by the holidays she was visibly pregnant, and Jack proudly jockeyed her from party to party all over Aspen in his Land Rover.

"He broke up with Anjelica Huston, if indeed that was ever serious to the point of getting married and having children," said Jack's old friend Jon Epaminondas. "Then he comes up with this new woman. He's in a more familial mode, more forging and gentler. Someone's decision to become a real father has to be tied up with their idea of their own father."

Lorraine Broussard Nicholson was born at dawn on April 16, 1990, six days shy of her father's fifty-third birthday. Of course, Jack wasn't about to change his routine over impending fatherhood. The night before her birth, he saw the Lakers play, then stopped off at Evans's house to screen a movie before getting to Cedars-Sinai in time to help Rebecca through her four hours of labor. The professed atheist Jack Nicholson named Don Devlin as the infant's godfather and doted on Lorraine, whom he called "a boon from divine nature."

He bought Rebecca her own Beverly Hills 5,500-square-foot, five-bedroom home for $2 million and established a $200,000 bank account for her and the baby, but he continued to live alone in Xanadu with his personal chef, Paul, his art, and his usual Jack Pack entourage of cronies and hangers-on. Meanwhile, he continued to tinker with *The Two Jakes*. Paramount postponed it again. The movie wouldn't open until the fall.

19

O N THE EVENING OF MAY 16, 1990, MARLON BRANDO'S slacker son Christian got loaded with his sister Cheyenne over dinner at Musso & Frank's Grill. She confided that her live-in boyfriend had been slapping her around, so they drove back home to Mulholland Drive, where Christian found a gun and shot his sister's boyfriend in the face.

When police arrived, Dag Drollet still dangled a cigarette lighter from one hand and the TV remote in the other, but the .45 slug that passed through his skull prevented him from ever using either again. At the time, Cheyenne was an emotional basket case and eight months pregnant with Drollet's son. Immediate speculation pointed to a brother-boyfriend tiff, fueled by booze and Cheyenne's alleged lies about Drollet's abuse. Police concluded that the argument had escalated to homicide.

With just a tenth-grade education and a history of dull-witted but spoiled violence, Christian was a thirty-two-year-old unemployed tree surgeon who still lived at home with his dad. Later, it developed that Christian allegedly had an incestuous crush on his sister and that Brando himself might also have put the moves on his own daughter, a former fashion model until cocaine and prescription drugs rendered her unemployable. Like everyone else within Brando's orbit, Cheyenne was chattel and as subject to Brando's whim as a child of Don Corleone, or perhaps Noah Cross. In one of the great Hollywood understatements, Brando told reporters, "I think perhaps I failed as a father."

Indeed, incest and drugs and alcohol underscored his family's entire sordid history. Eleven years Christian's junior, Cheyenne had been using drugs or staying drunk since she was sixteen. The night her brother killed Drollet, Christian's blood alcohol level was twice the legal driving limit. And while both Christian and Marlon later insisted that Christian shot Drollet by accident, there had been no sign of a struggle—just a dead 270-pound Tahitian sitting in Brando's living room.

The once-revered actor had grown equally hefty in the fifteen years since he costarred with his next-door neighbor in *The Missouri*

Breaks. Brando tipped the scales at somewhere between 300 and 400 pounds and was so obese the studios shunned him.[1] He'd lapsed into a paranoid bunker existence. Members of his codependent family seldom strayed from their routine lethargy, all but guaranteeing some sort of eventual tragedy. Behind the barbed wire, the electrified fence, and the bamboo curtain that separated Brando's place from Jack's, a pair of mastiffs stood guard. Most of the time Jack and his houseguests kept their distance.

Brando still had manic bursts of enthusiasm over organic foods, environmental gadgets, or New Age claptrap, but mostly he sated himself with sex and food like a latter-day King Henry VIII. He acknowledged having nine children, most of them illegitimate, including three by his housemaid, and had a reputation of many years' standing of refusing to admit women into his mountaintop lair unless they had sex with him. He feared anything or anyone he couldn't bribe or seduce. All that remained of his once-hallowed American Indian Movement was an arsenal he'd stockpiled in the unlikely event that an imaginary enemy staged a Wounded Knee assault on his compound. At the rear of the house, he kept an M-14 assault rifle, a MAC-10 machine pistol, a shotgun, and a .44 caliber carbine with a silencer.

The arsenal alone convinced the L. A. district attorney to charge Christian with premeditated murder: Brando's son knew where to find a gun, according to the prosecution's theory, and coolly plugged Drollet with it. There was even talk that he and his father might have plotted the killing together.

While both Jack and Helena Kallianiotes filed sworn statements attesting to Christian's good character, Jack's relationship with Brando's son had been strained since Christian was a teen. Jack had shared his weed with the boy until he caught Christian stealing his stash. Afterward, Christian got giggle mileage with fellow slackers by mimicking Jack's scolding: "You do that again and I'll *break* your fucking *fingers*, man!" Marlon blamed Jack for his boy's drug problems.

Though Jack kept his distance, Helena helped the stricken clan next door. She ferried Christian's younger brother Miko in and out of the compound, while raising hell with the tabloid press, which had gathered outside the Mulholland gates. TV crews set up satellite feeds and reporters picked through trash as Marlon descended the mountain to plead for bail lower than the $10 million demanded by the prosecution. Playing the wounded father, Brando won over the courts and the media. On his son's behalf, he wept on the stand, manipulated public sympathy, and got Christian out on a $2 million bond.

But his sense of filial responsibility did not extend to his daughter. A week after the killing, Helena dropped by the Brando kitchen and found a whacked-out Cheyenne licking Comet cleanser from her fingers. Before the prosecution could issue the troubled young woman a subpoena, Marlon spirited her back to Tahiti for the duration of the trial. In subsequent depositions, Cheyenne hinted at drugs and incest beneath her father's roof.

The attorney Robert Shapiro, who'd represented Robert Evans in the *Cotton Club* murder case, copped a manslaughter plea for Christian. Shapiro got him ten years, five of which he served, with time off for good behavior.

In the meantime, the anorexic Cheyenne was diagnosed a schizophrenic. She ballooned in size to her father's proportions, lost custody of Drollet's son, and spiraled into despair. On Lorraine Broussard Nicholson's fifth birthday, Cheyenne Brando committed suicide on the other side of the world, just as California prepared to parole Christian.

While Brando endured heartbreak, Jack wrestled with his own personal paradoxes: paternal responsibility versus party animal; monogamy versus masturbatory one-night stands.

In the best-selling tell-all *You'll Never Make Love in This Town Again*, one of madame Heidi Fleiss's girls claimed to have had a fling with Jack, but never for money. According to Alexandra Datig, aka "Tiffany," Jack prided himself on helping himself but never paying for it like a common John. "I'm too Calvinist, and besides, I'm big Jack," he once boasted in the pages of *Vanity Fair*. "I don't have to pay for it."

Datig reported that Jack "hauled off and hit me hard" once after a roll in the hay. Similar stories circulated throughout Hollywood about Jack testing the limits of hedonism.

While the affairs could last all of one night or linger for months, they followed the same three-act pattern: seduction, passion, adios. The first act featured bashful yet masterful Jack and brimmed with lavish gifts, flowers, limos, and attentive late-night dining; Act Two was strong yet gentle Jack demonstrating his stallion prowess and bedroom endurance; Act Three was the old heave-ho, usually signaled by never returning a phone call or a more spectacular climax, like a wild-eyed tantrum over his absolute need to defend and preserve his independence.

One constant was younger and younger women: the low twenties seemed about right. The Beverly Hills gumshoe Frank Monte, whom Jack once hired to investigate a fraud, claimed that Jack slept with a sixteen-year-old but never faced the statutory wrath Polanski did because neither the girl nor her parents reported the alleged misdeed. Jack's affairs reportedly ranged from porn stars such as the one-time *Playboy* photographer Suze Randol to Hollywood royalty like Katharine "Kat" Kramer, the producer Stanley Kramer's daughter. In any case, women who matched Jack's own advancing years rarely met his qualifications.

Yet all the while Jack continued to play proud papa to Lorraine and husband of sorts to Rebecca, even though they lived outside his compound in the home Jack bought for them.

The crease above Jack's eyes had permanently etched his brow. He smoked with a tar-reducing filter, using cigarettes as props to draw out conversation and talk around a subject, tapping each stalk thoughtfully on the edge of a coffee table before lighting up.

Hedonist or sage? Should he act the Joker or behave like a grown up? Why choose if he didn't have to?

If Jack felt any kinship to Brando, it wasn't as a father or a husband. He saw no ironic parallels in the illegitimacy of his own children or the potential for pain in indiscriminate rutting. His life wasn't Brando's. Whatever dysfunctionality Jack's own situational ethics showered down, his personal demons couldn't hold a pitchfork next to those that roosted in the house next door.

In a larger context, down on the Hollywood flatlands, the new decade was shaping up as a cultural civil war, with Jack hovering above on his mountaintop. Having replaced the Godfather as the most celebrated actor of his era, Jack was now also its richest. "Remember, in the 1980s, Hollywood was all about the Benjamins," wrote the *New York Times*'s David Carr. "In the '90s, it was more about the stars, who received a lot of Benjamins."

Jack welcomed the windfall but claimed to still be bothered by the defeat of yesteryear's hard-won lessons during the cash-driven yuppie decade just past. "Life can only be understood in retrospect," he rhapsodized. "You can only get a picture of it when you look back." When he wasn't filling his personal void with sex, drugs, or rock 'n' roll, Jack looked back often.

"A couple of years ago I needed new chairs," recalled Robert Evans, whose screening room Jack visited each Thursday night. "The old chairs were there for twenty-two years, cotton was coming out of them," Evans continued. "It looked like the Salvation Army. I designed a chair and got six of them made and put them in. "Nicholson comes over and asks, 'Where are the old chairs?' I said I was looking to give them away to the Motion Picture and TV Fund convalescent home so I could get a write-off on them. He said he wanted them.

"So he sent down a truck and had them picked up. Two weeks later he comes back and says to me, 'You gave me the greatest gift I ever got. Those chairs. They're the most valuable chairs in all of Hollywood history. Do you know what happened in those chairs over the last twenty-five years? Mike Nichols wants one, Meryl, Warren, Bernardo. . . . Everyone wants a chair.'

"I didn't know what I owned," concluded Evans. "He said, 'I may give one to Meryl and to Bernardo. I'm not giving one to Warren.' Suddenly, I didn't like my new chairs anymore. And Jack won't give me back the old ones."

The past haunted Jack as it did Jake Gittes, but like his fictitious alter ego, he chose to live in a city without memory, and the geography was catching up with him. Just as Marshall McLuhan had predicted, media triumphed, especially in L.A., and the results were a growing superficiality and a childlike addiction to televised fad or fashion: Joker, *si*, Jake Gittes, no. Sound bites and spot news eclipsed the past. In the 1990s, anything older than a dozen years was primeval and convenient misinformation took the place of history. "Every day something graceful is ground out by mendacity," lamented Jack.

Sober sanctuary—especially for the world's best-known actor— became a pipe dream. John Henry Shaner maintained that his old friend practiced a kind of amnesia. The last line from *The Two Jakes*—"Does it go away?"—became Jack's newest mantra.

"My living motto for the eighties as a person has been: There is no *away*," said Jack. "You can't run. There's no away anymore. Certainly not for anyone like me."

Whatever Jack had yet to achieve as an artist, he had already achieved a thousand times over in fame and accounts receivable. He could no longer pretend to be Everyman. While he strove to remain what Peter Fonda called the "Tom Joad of our era," he was rivaled only by Arnold Schwarzenegger as the wealthiest man in showbiz.

"I don't make bad money decisions," Jack boasted—a fiscal point of honor since his Corman days. "The happiest thing that's happened to me is, about a month ago, I got my first overage check on *Goin' South*, which took my record from 47 and 3 to 48 and 2. No one else has that record. With a couple of exceptions, all the movies I've made since *Easy Rider* have gone into [net profit]. The only two movies I haven't received bonus premiums on are *The Border* and *The Fortune*. I call that account the 48-and-2: my superstructural Jack Nicholson account. I don't draw on it unless I have to, and I don't fool myself into thinking that it's based on anything but the returns."

On the other hand, he maintained that he still balanced commerce with art. "I consider my profession to be extremely respectable and very little of it is by chance," Jack told the *New York Times's* Aljean Harmetz. "How do you manage an esthetic body of work? Not without design."

He put some of his money into real estate, expanding the tract he'd purchased thirteen years earlier in the Santa Monica Mountains by forty-one acres, and bringing the size of his seaside spread at the northwestern end of the Mulholland Highway to nearly seventy acres. He also expanded his art collection, turning his enviable domestic displays into a veritable museum with a different masterwork on every wall. "Impressionist masterpieces coupled with Modernist giants," marveled Michael Volpe, an East Coast buyer who catered to Hollywood. Unlike his client Barbra Streisand, whose walls bore mostly images of herself, "Nicholson doesn't show off who he is or what he's become," said Volpe. With a docent's sense of wonder, he recalled his first visit to Jack's place: Chagalls, Cézannes, Magrittes, Picassos.

But blue-collar Jack never gave in to faux sophistication. As corny as it might seem, one of his favorite pickup lines was, "Wanna come up and see my artwork?" And yet, he had only the vaguest sense of his collection's worth. "I don't care to sell any paintings, so I don't care how much they appreciate," he said. "Their value will be a tragic problem for those who come after me."

As a Hollywood grandee, Jack took up golf after *The Two Jakes*. He preferred a noon start and called the game "Zen archery." He left how-to golf manuals and magazines all over the house and kept a stack of golf instruction tapes next to the TV. Along with Clint Eastwood, he invested in Lynx Golf, a start-up club manufacturer, and added a putting green to his house. He drove balls off his deck overlooking Franklin Canyon, sending Helena down to fetch them. "I've only played a couple of rounds of golf in my life," Jack told the *Los Angeles Times* in August 1990. "It's going to become one of my main activities. It's a divinely infuriating activity that teaches you patience and inner poise."

Michael Douglas said that he and Jack both decided they were golfers around the same time because "we can play it for the rest of our life whereas a lot of other sports you can't." Said Jack, "I always planned to take up the rich-boys sports—tennis, skiing, golf—at the ages just after I could fantasize total competition in them because I wanted to just enjoy the leisure of it."

But not *too* much leisure. Once he joined Bel-Air, Sherwood, and Lakeside Country Clubs, Jack's competitive streak rose to the fore. He earned a prickly reputation on the back nine, inner poise devolving shamelessly into shaving strokes. "I bet, but not with him," said Douglas. "I don't necessarily like the way he keeps score." Observed *Golf Digest*'s Tom Cunneff, "Nicholson has been known to take six shots on a par three and say after holing out, 'These bogeys are killing me.'" He fumed at slowpokes who blocked him from playing through: "Would you mind getting the fuck out of the way? I paid my money!"

Like the belligerent child to which he often reverted, Jack breached no criticism. He cheated with impunity and gave himself ten points on his handicap. As with bedroom and boardroom, he was Big Jack, and no one dared to challenge him. Offered tips, even by PGA pros, Jack returned the advice with: "Go fuck yourself."

Negotiations to land Jack for *Man Trouble* (1992) began the same month Paramount finally released *The Two Jakes*. Panned by critics, the glacially paced *Chinatown* sequel took in just $3.7 million its first weekend. *The Two Jakes's* final tally—$10 million—barely covered Jack's fees before the ghost of Jake Gittes faded from the public imagination.

Harry Gittes, on the other hand, was still going strong, at least in Jack's imagination. Unlike other sixties "lame-os" whom Jack had left in the dust, Gittes never let go of Jack's coattails. He was the first to boast in *Variety* of trying for a third pairing of Jack and Meryl Streep.

But having pushed himself to exhaustion on *The Two Jakes*, Jack held off on costarring with Streep in *Man Trouble* until the following year. By then, the actress was pregnant with her fourth child and had to be replaced by Ellen Barkin. Jack used his clout to salt the rest of the *Man Trouble* cast with his usual pals: Harry Dean Stanton played an ancient gangster and Veronica Cartwright had a speaking role. Even Rebecca Broussard took time off from motherhood to do a walk-on as a hospital administrator.

Outmaneuvering Gittes, Carole Eastman got herself named coproducer of *Man Trouble*. An updated version of *The Second Interval*, her antic and romantic Manson-era comedy, *Man Trouble* featured a frightened diva (Barkin) who hires a guard-dog trainer (Nicholson) and falls for him. For the fourth time, Jack's other old friend Bob Rafelson hired on as director, but Jack's salary nearly derailed the project before it began. Old friends or no, he demanded 10 percent of the gross and a $7 million slice of the $30 million production budget.

At the same time that Eastman wooed him for *Man Trouble*, Danny DeVito wanted Jack as the working-class hero in *Hoffa* (1992).[2] As early as 1982, a biopic had been in the works, but it wasn't until 1989, when the producer Edward Pressman got Fox to underwrite a $1 million David Mamet revision of the original script, that the project took on steam. Barry Levinson signed on to direct until "creative differences" drove him away.

Pressman saw the vanished Teamsters leader as King Lear—"a complex individual with a capacity for great violence and love of his men." Likewise, Pressman believed the heavyweight who would portray him needed "this chameleon quality as an actor and also the star magnitude to carry a movie." He asked both DeNiro and Pacino to star before considering Jack. By 1990, *Hoffa* had become an orphan. Pressman lost his name director, no stars were attached, and no one rushed to rescue the Mamet script from limbo, until Danny DeVito stepped in.

Hot off two comedy hits, Jack's fellow New Jersey transplant wanted to show that he could direct drama.[3] DeVito latched on and would not let go, even as the production budget swelled beyond what Fox was willing to pay, even for a star of Jack's magnitude.

"He knew I had the script in '89, and I really bothered him about it," recalled DeVito. "I kept calling him up. He was flying to New York and I would offer to come up with him on the plane so he could read it with me, and then I offered to fly back with him."

Even from close friends, Jack handled pitches with lip service. He did the same with DeVito. He promised to read the script and consider the role. But, as DeVito told it, the breakthrough didn't come until the bantam actor-director sneaked past the Brando security gate and waited outside Jack's bedroom window. "He opened the curtains of his house in Los Angeles one morning with this incredibly panoramic view, as befits a man of his stature," DeVito recalled, "and he looks down, does a double take, and I'm standing there asking and begging. . . . This little guy!"

Jack relented. He committed to the movie just before taking off for a fall vacation in Aspen with Jennifer and baby Lorraine. "I'm not a negotiator—I'm a movie maker," Jack told Army Archerd, when asked about his *Hoffa* salary. He left the money details to Sandy Bresler, who got him $9 million.

At the Grammy Awards on February 20, 1991, Jack made a rare TV appearance to present Bob Dylan his Lifetime Achievement Award. As Dylan took the stage with a back-up band that looked like refugees from *The Blues Brothers*, Jack introduced the strung-out troubadour as a "riot." Dylan was not.

Just in time to tweak George H. W. Bush and the onset of the first Gulf War, Dylan performed an indecipherable rendition of "Masters of War." Jack stood by and beamed. As he handed Dylan his award, Dylan accepted in deadpan character, without a hint of emotion. From the podium, he squinted at the audience like Rip Van Winkle.

"Well, my daddy, he didn't leave me too much, you know," Dylan began. "He was a very simple man. What he did tell me was this. He did say, 'Son,' he said, um . . .'"

Jack joined the audience in nervous laughter, straining in anticipation during the long pause.

Dylan continued, "He said so many things, you know. . . . He said, 'It's possible to be so defiled in this world that even your mother and father won't know you. But God will always believe in your ability to mend your ways.'"

With that, Dylan left the stage without thanking his agent, his manager, Jack, the audience, or any of the family, friends, and rabbis who populate most award winners' acceptance speeches.[4] Far from being abashed, Jack redoubled his applause. He marveled at Dylan's refusal to be sucked in by the trappings of celebrity.

"The biggest star in the music business, until he dies, is Bob Dylan," said Jack in a *Rolling Stone* interview. "Even though Bobby may not be the biggest commercial artist at the moment, you can never deny the quality of his work, which is always fabulous. Let's put it this way: stack his albums and they're that high." Jack held his hand two feet off a table. "That's a lot of albums. You say, 'How's the album, Bob?' And he says, 'Its all original songs and all good musicians.'"

Dylan never pretended to be anything more than what he was: a singer-songwriter who hoped he had something worth saying to his audience. His absolute silence in any other context kept fans guessing, including Jack. "No matter what people think, they don't know *anything* about Bob Dylan," the singer declared during a rare TV interview in the mid-eighties.

In reviewing a critical Dylan biography a few years earlier, the *New York Times*'s Stephen Holden focused on Dylan's genius at overcoming private contradiction while maintaining the popular myth. "Treated like a king for the last twenty-five years by an adoring entourage, Mr. Dylan is shown playing games of mental cruelty on his family and followers," wrote Holden, who decried a celebrity's constant plague of yes men who will not speak truth for fear of losing favor.

"Surrounded by people who are paid to speed them along and shield them from life's unpleasantness, how do they maintain an independent self-critical perspective?" Holden asked. "Contradictory feelings of being cursed by stardom and being obsessively addicted to it are shared by almost every pop star I have met. And all things considered, Mr. Dylan is a relatively hardy survivor." Holden could have substituted Jack's name for Dylan's and still have been accurate.

After watching Jack introduce Dylan at the Grammys, the director Rob Reiner asked Jack for a few good scenes in *A Few Good Men* (1992): four, to be exact, and at a premium price. Reiner saw him as the hard-assed marine colonel Nathan Jessup in an upcoming film version of the writer Aaron Sorkin's hit play about murder, court martial, and military cover-up. After seeing *A Few Good Men* when

Sorkin first mounted it on Broadway in 1989, both Robert DeNiro and James Woods were among the actors who sought the brief but riveting role.

But after hiring Tom Cruise for the lead, Reiner went to Jack. Reiner's five-year-old Castle Rock Entertainment had already agreed to pay Cruise $12.5 million to star as Lieutenant Daniel Kaffee, Jessup's adversary in *A Few Good Men*.[5] As a contractual ego bonus, Cruise also got the biggest on-location dressing trailer. Cruise was hitting his star stride the way Jack had in the years following *Chinatown*.

Jack earned a mere $5 million and got a smaller trailer but worked only ten days of the sixty-eight-day shoot. After Jack and Cruise each negotiated their piece of the back end to help defray Castle Rock's upfront costs, Jack swallowed his vanity over earning less than Cruise, who was twenty-five years Jack's junior. Cruise got the best of Jack's patriarchal villain at the explosive climax of the film, but the Joker in Jack didn't care as long as *A Few Good Men* afforded him a few good lines and a fat paycheck. Even with the Cruise-Nicholson back-end concessions, the budget bulged from $33 million to $41 million and could climb higher if cameras did not roll on schedule.[6]

But Jack had other matters on his mind. He still had to finish what he'd begun, which included *Man Trouble*. With the sting of *The Two Jakes* still fresh, Jack told interviewers that he planned to shut up, hit his marks, and just stick to acting for a while. "I went out of my way not to put my two cents in," Jack said, deferring to Eastman and Rafelson during the two-month summertime shoot.

"He and I work in a very odd way," said Rafelson. "It's usually by finger snaps. We know each other pretty well and only in case there's a major disagreement about how to play a scene—and there are enough of those, too—it's all done like this." Rafelson snapped his fingers and pantomimed switching poses for the camera. "Look one, look two, look three, look four, look five—give me another one."

While Jack responded to Rafelson's finger snaps the way dogs were supposed to respond to *Man Trouble*'s Harry Bliss, Jack was still being a producer. He'd committed to underwriting another noirish revenge melodrama, more dark and downbeat than *The Two Jakes*. The first film he'd ever made on his own, *Blue Champagne* was yet another labor of love—or, more accurately, *for* love.

In Rebecca Broussard's first role as something other than background scenery, she starred opposite the TV sitcom actor Jonathan

Silverman in the $10 million production. If Jack had doubts, Rebecca vanquished them. A month before production, she sealed the deal by conceiving their second child.

Blue Champagne was also to be the first showcase for Jennifer, who'd heretofore worked on her father's movies but never in front of the cameras. Jack agreed to bankroll most of the film himself, indulging his two favorite women, even going so far as to turn over his Mulholland home for many of the location shoots while he was off in another part of the Hollywood Hills with *Man Trouble*.[7]

As a story, *Blue Champagne* smacked of stillborn impotence: a castrating wife schemes against her vengeful, murderous husband, and vice versa. Its ambitious writer-director Blaine Novak thought he'd found the elusive formula for Hollywood success with Jack. Like others who'd languished in the Hollywood vineyards, Novak had struggled to make a name for himself since Jack's generation first burst through the studio barriers. In the early seventies, Novak had apprenticed himself to independent success stories such as John Cassavettes and Peter Bogdanovitch.

By 1983, Novak had moved on to a third sponsor in Jack, who commissioned him to write *Children's Heaven*—a confusing fantasy about a philandering basketball team owner who can't remember which of his girlfriends was the mother of his twelve-year-old son. Susan Anspach maintained that Novak's eighty-nine-page screenplay was a thinly veiled burlesque based on Anspach, Jack, and their illegitimate son, Caleb Goddard. According to the actress, it was no coincidence that the God in *Children's Heaven* resembled a middle-aged wreck who rarely made personal appearances, groused offstage in voiceover, and left most dirty work to a teenaged sexpot simply named "Girlfriend." "If this is not a paean to sexism, I don't know what is," Anspach told Jack's British biographer, Peter Thompson.

Children's Heaven never got beyond a script, but *Blue Champagne* did. Rebecca saw Novak's thin plotline as her breakout role, and Jack went along. She wanted her name above the title in her own movie. Like Charles Foster Kane, Jack paid the price. "It was an income tax nightmare," Bob Colbert told his wife, Samantha.

Meanwhile, *Man Trouble* wrapped, and Jack hired a personal trainer to help him shed fifty pounds for his upcoming role as Colonel Jessup. In late August, he flew with Jennifer, Rebecca, and baby Lorraine to Antibes. Despite a minor gossip item that had Rebecca briefly consorting with her *Blue Champagne* costar, all seemed smooth as Jack headed into *A Few Good Men*. Rebecca's pregnancy began to show, and Jack blew off questions about his or her fidelity.

The third week of October, Colonel Jessup marched onto the set of *A Few Good Men*, and an all-star cast, which included Cruise, Demi Moore, Kiefer Sutherland, and Kevin Bacon, came to attention. Wearing a flattop reminiscent of his Manasquan adolescence, Jack personified spit-polished arrogance. "I felt like the Lincoln Memorial walking into that first reading," said Jack. "There were a lot of wonderful young actors in that picture. I'm usually very uncomfortable with the Jack part of it all. I'm too in admiration of so many people who do what I do. But because of what this picture is, I walked into that reading differently. I went in there to get them. I went in there ready to read this damn part and you better all be ready."

During Jack's key scene, when Cruise brings him down as the mastermind behind a deadly military hazing, Jack bellowed what was to become his best-known movie line ever:[8] "You want the truth? You can't *handle* the truth!"[9] It resonated with another well-known Jackism from twenty years earlier, when *The Last Detail*'s Billy Buddusky screams, "I *am* the motherfucking shore patrol!"

As with *The Last Detail*, the Pentagon refused to cooperate.[10] With arrogation worthy of Colonel Jessup, the Defense Department condemned Sorkin's screenplay for reinforcing the conclusion that "criminal harassment is a commonplace and accepted practice within the Marine Corps." Whereas Tom Cruise made the military seem glamorous in *Top Gun* (1986) (indeed, the navy used the movie for recruiting), *A Few Good Men* did the opposite and got the U.S. Marine Corps's cold shoulder.[11]

With *People*, *Star*, and the *Enquirer* breaking the news of Rebecca's pregnancy, Jack's other old flame let the tabloids know she'd moved on. "He is a soulmate," said Anjelica. "There is not one aspect of my life that has not been touched by him, and I hate to think of a world without him. It would be dismal."

As Jack wrapped *A Few Good Men*, Anjelica moved in with the celebrated L.A. sculptor Robert Graham Jr., and though still keen on having a child, even if it meant adoption, the forty-year-old actress was no longer sure she could do so as part of a couple.[12] "I haven't heard the biological clock ticking," Anjelica said.

A year later, she and Graham married and remained the quintessential childless L.A. professional couple. He created a windowless concrete cocoon for her in the artsy seaside barrio of Venice and surrounded it with a forty-foot fence. There they withdrew from an oppressive megalopolis. "For a town that the rest of the world looks upon as exuding such sexuality with its lifestyle, Los Angeles has always struck me as a remarkably unsexy place," Anjelica observed.

Indeed, Magic Johnson made his dramatic announcement that he was HIV positive as Jack finished *A Few Good Men*, and Jack called his favorite Laker to offer support. "I was stunned, brokenhearted. Still am," said Jack, who once spurned the use of condoms by announcing, "I asked my doctor, who said, 'Look, if you're not shooting up and you're not an active homosexual, you're as likely to get AIDS as have a safe land on you.'"

Delivering a sobered benediction on AIDS, Jack now added, "The times have changed dramatically. Life was getting freer and freer for so long. But now it's not."[13]

He took solace in fatherhood. In the garden outside his bachelor's manse he installed a child's swing. Babies put him in a mood to quote Bertrand Russell: "Love is everything. All the rest is standing on the edge and staring into the abyss."

He claimed to have started a daily diary once Lorraine was born and promised to give it to her when she grew up. By 1992, Jack also claimed to spend up to three hours a day, three days a week at her preschool when he wasn't working, and once he finished *Hoffa*, he vowed to take two years off to watch his children grow.

Rebecca delivered him a son on February 20, 1992. For public consumption, Jack maintained that he'd wanted to name him Landslide, but he and Rebecca agreed on Raymond.[14] "The baby looks like Rebecca—thank goodness—but he's got my dick," Jack said.

All about him, his oldest friends were in a marrying mood, and with far younger women. In March, Warren Beatty, fifty-five, married his *Bugsy* (1991) costar Annette Bening, thirty-four, two months after Bening gave birth to their first daughter. In April, Lou Adler, fifty-eight, married Daryl Hannah's sister Page, twenty-eight, who was six months pregnant with their first child. Even Roman Polanski and the confirmed bachelor Harry Gittes had recently married, each of them fathering two children.

Among Jack's inner circle, only Harry Dean Stanton, sixty-five, and the much-married (five times as of 1992)[15] Robert Evans, sixty-two, remained unattached. But at some level, Jack remained deaf to the ticking clock. The 1990s might mark the triumph of political correctness—family values, moderation, monogamy—but he wasn't fooled. "Behind every holier-than-thou sanctimonious Dan Quayle type I'll show you a man who pays two transvestites to piss on his face," said Jack.

During a Paris visit to see Polanski, Jack tried to shock a young female reporter during an interview with: "You know, in the old days, after twenty minutes of this I would have tried to fuck you."

"Oh that's funny," she retorted. "Twenty years ago you tried to fuck my mother."

Jack celebrated his own fifty-fifth birthday by crouching on the April 1992 cover of *Vanity Fair* dangling a pair of babies while a third peeped up at the camera from between his legs. Readers had to go to the fine print inside to discover that all three infants were models and not his own. Between his career update and various views on the state of the world in the accompanying interview, Jack detailed his living arrangements with Rebecca: she and the children lived in the Valley, while he remained perched on the Hill.

And yet, the original Hollywood lech still got a "pass" from middle America. In the letters to the editor published the following month, a Kansas woman related the story of her nephew who got a call from Jack as the boy lay dying in a hospital from brain cancer. Jack sent photos of the Joker and checked in several times before the boy passed away. "It is so easy to assume that we as the viewing public know 'the truth' about celebrities," wrote the dead boy's aunt. "My family is thrilled to know the caring Jack Nicholson."

But on the same page, a New York reader wrote:

Congratulations to Jack Nicholson for his brilliant transition from the socially conscious 60s to the Me Decade. His wealth affords him a family in one house and his bachelorhood in a second. Mr. Rebel is the epitome of Mr. Hollywood. What next? Gold chains and a Ferrari?

A classic study in the shifting quicksand of 1990s movie making, *Hoffa* teetered on bankruptcy before the first camera rolled. For nearly a year, DeVito and the producers Pressman and Joe Isgro warred with Fox over the budget, which the studio capped at $35 million. As expenses crept past $40 million, then $45 million, the producers bought a completion bond and paid overages themselves. DeVito so wanted to see *Hoffa* through that he agreed to direct and act for scale. His sacrifice carved nearly $7 million off the budget, while Pressman picked up another $5 million by preselling European pay-TV rights to the French studio Canal Plus. And still, the movie's price tag climbed, topping out at nearly $50 million. All the while, Jack never budged a dime on his salary.

The four-month *Hoffa* odyssey began on location in Pittsburgh the same month Ray was born. Jack shared none of his producers' budgetary angst. He and DeVito split the top floor of a luxury hotel, where rooms ran to $1,450 a night. When he wasn't on the set, Jack was on the golf course or taking in a Lakers game in his penthouse. Even David Mamet failed to see the irony in Jack's delivery of a key bit of proletarian dialogue when Hoffa states, "We have taken the Teamsters, and the Teamsters have taken the American Working Man into the middle class, and *buddy* . . . we intend to stay."

"When he said that line, it was one of the finest moments I have ever seen on film," the screenwriter declared.[16]

Jack got into character by pacing the set the way he'd seen Hoffa do in dozens of newsreels, chanting, "That's right . . . that's right" in Hoffa's flinty Midwestern twang.[17] Jack called in Tommy Baratta to help him bulk up as the beefy Teamsters' boss. With a prosthetic nose and Hoffa's white-sidewall haircut, Jack so closely approximated the mobbed-up labor leader that Hoffa's own son, James P. Hoffa, did a double take on the set. "He really had the character down," said the younger Hoffa.

DeVito hired a videographer to tape everything he and the crew did for behind-the-scenes use in the videotape release, foreshadowing the attention to back matter that would become an essential part of selling DVDs in the twenty-first century. The film wrapped seven days over schedule with what Jack and DeVito believed was Jack's finest performance to date.

Meanwhile, *Blue Champagne* seemed on track. While still editing, the director Novak announced that there'd be a sequel. Production would begin in June on *Love Me if You Dare*, another Rebecca showcase about "a man's affair with an abused woman and a turbulent sister-brother relationship" that would again costar Jonathan Silverman.

Indeed, 1992 looked to be another good year for the self-described "existential romantic" of Mulholland Drive until *Man Trouble* crashed in July. The bewildering comedy took in a scant $4 million, and Jack took a nasty drubbing at the hands of critics.

By fall, *Hoffa* hemorrhaged more red ink and, from where Jack sat, so did *Blue Champagne*. His extravagant gift to Rebecca looked awful in early prints, and her spell over him was not so strong that he'd willingly toss good money after bad. Before filming on *Love Me if You Dare* began, Jack pulled the plug on it.

Worst of all, Rebecca began dating a younger man—twenty-five years younger than Jack, to be precise. A brief spring fling Jack had with the French actress Julie Delpy found its way into the gossip columns and looked to be the final straw. Jack's separate-but-equal lifestyle, in which he alternately partied and brooded while the mother of his children stayed in a separate home with the kiddies, appeared to have failed.

Jack and Rebecca made up in September, attended the Barcelona Olympics, spent a few weeks in Cap-Ferrat, then returned home to watch the World Series and the presidential debates together, but the reconciliation didn't last. Things began to fall apart. The center of Jack's well-crafted universe wasn't holding. Single at fifty-five and on his own once more, the Master of Mulholland found that all his petulance, all his star wattage, and all his yes men would have a tough time putting the Joker together again.

BOOK V

THINGS HAVE CHANGED

1993–2005

20

F ROM EARLY AUTUMN IN 1992, FOX AND COLUMBIA DUELED over the first-ever head-to-head Jack match: a winner-take-all experiment in megastar marketing. Hollywood focused on December 11, when both *Hoffa* and *A Few Good Men* hit the nation's multiplexes. While the Motion Picture Association of America didn't forbid it, member studios never opened a film with the same big-name actor on the marquee within the same week—and certainly not on the same day.

But the face-off turned out to be no contest. By mid-January, the winner of "the Jack Nicholson Wars"—with a payday headed toward the $200 million stratosphere—was *A Few Good Men*. At $24 million, *Hoffa* barely dented the box office. "One company handled one movie perfectly and the other one did the opposite," summarized Jack.

Columbia preordained *A Few Good Men* a grand slam "because of the star power involved," reported the *Los Angeles Times*. "Even if you screwed up the marketing it could still make $100 million."

The movie carried an R rating, but MTV promoted it early and often, zeroing in on the prime moviegoing demographic: testosterone-driven males, twelve to twenty-eight. Castle Rock's casting formula offered something for everyone: Cruise for hunk worshippers, Demi Moore for the guys, and Jack for the older crowd. In what Columbia called "the first time a world premiere will truly be a world premiere," *A Few Good Men* opened in fifty-three countries around the globe, all within the same week. "As all the countries of the world continue to move closer together, it was only a matter of time before the global village concept was translated into a global premiere," said Columbia's international distribution chief.

Jack went to the *A Few Good Men* premiere at Westwood's Village Theater but didn't sit all the way through. He slipped out to a waiting limo after the lights dimmed so he could make that night's Lakers game and still return in time for Castle Rock's postpremiere party at the nearby Century Plaza Hotel.

At an Academy benefit days later, Fox rolled out *Hoffa*, followed by a similar gala in the studio's back lot. Each lucky attendee received a gift bag containing a *Hoffa* baseball cap and a toy Teamsters truck. The Lakers weren't playing that night, so Jack stayed for the entire evening. Glad-handers praised him for literally *becoming* Jimmy Hoffa, but even among the friendly crowd, which included the Fox overlord Rupert Murdoch, the plodding biopic got more lumps than kudos. "Why do all these directors have to prove to us how brilliant they are and make us sit there?" one producer complained during the after party. "What happened to the word *pacing*?"

Hoffa opened in selected theaters, going wide later in the month, but its strategy of banking on a single superstar backfired. Jack played the Teamsters chieftain as "a cross at times between Bogart and Bugs Bunny," sniffed one critic. *Time* magazine's two critical Richards—Schickel and Corliss—further denigrated *Hoffa*, slamming Jack's portrayal as

> an utterly externalized view of the corrupt, crusading boss of the Teamsters, James R. Hoffa. . . . Who is he? The movie gives not a clue. Jack Nicholson looks eerily like his subject, (but) . . . instead of a hard-edged portrait, we get painting on velvet. It's epic-style vamping around the void of epic character.

"I didn't like it," said James P. Hoffa, who saw little of his father behind Jack's near-perfect makeup. "The ending was too graphic, and they didn't depict the way he was."

Movie audiences agreed. Along with Jack's retarded Harry Bliss in *Man Trouble*, his *Hoffa* got him a nomination but not for an Oscar. Had Sylvester Stallone not stunk up theaters with *Stop! Or My Mom Will Shoot* (1992), Jack might have taken home the Golden Raspberry for worst actor.[1] Danny DeVito, also Razzie-nominated, wasn't even considered for the Oscar. "I guess I just have to put up with the fact that I'm the eternal outsider," he whined. "The Bob Dylan of film directing."

Jack redeemed himself in *A Few Good Men*, although he hardly seemed to care. Played against the starry support of *A Few Good Men*'s ensemble cast, Rob Reiner's exacting direction, and Aaron Sorkin's carefully crafted screenplay, Jack's portrayal of Colonel Jessup earned him his tenth Oscar nomination. Nonetheless, Jack got no boost from the nomination and spoke of calling it quits for a while. "For the first time in my work, there are lots of parts I simply couldn't play because I'm too old," he said. "I've always had a big conflict about how much acting I am going to do. I like it, but it's all-consuming, more than most jobs. I work more than anybody. But now I'm thinking: Work less—or don't work at all."

At the beginning of 1993, he had too much in the pipeline to simply walk away. He'd already struck the deal to star in *Wolf* (1994) for $13 million, and the director, Mike Nichols, wanted a late spring start.[2] In his fourth turn directing Jack, Nichols described the world's best-known movie star as "a kind of walking id. It's not that he's a wild man. It's that his nature is absolutely free."

For Jack, *Wolf*'s theme could not have been more appropriate: the protagonist is betrayed by his wife, his best friend, and a culture that decided he was dispensable. "It has been the toughest lesson of my middle life to accept that everyone is betrayed by everyone," Jack said. "To some extent, betrayal is the theme of us all."

After Geena Davis passed as Jack's she-wolf, Nichols settled on the *Witches of Eastwick* alumna Michelle Pfeiffer. James Spader completed the triangle as the ambitious understudy who wants Jack's character's career, wife, and mistress. Still, Jack was in no hurry to get into hairy-faced makeup and rip Spader's throat out.

"Nicholson more than any other major star I've met knew how to protect himself, how to live a private life with his books and paintings away from the public eye," said Jim Harrison, who'd begun crafting the *Wolf* screenplay a dozen years earlier.[3] "It was a matter of controlling all incursions whether in Beverly Hills, New York, Paris or London. This requires a good deal of precision and energy, of knowing what you want."

One thing Jack wanted was a private place to party. Lou Adler's On the Rox had lost its heat, while Helena's recently became a victim of L.A.'s fire laws. Instead of complying, Helena shut her bistro down. Jack tended bar during the wake for his favorite downtown haunt and began to look for another watering hole.

He found it in the Monkey Bar. As with Helena's, Jack was a founding partner, as well as its most celebrated customer. This time, his front man was Alan Finkelstein, whom Jack met in New York during the 1980s. A hirsute professional party boy with roots in Studio 54 and an anachronistic appearance that included an East Village shuffle and a Fu Manchu mustache, Finkelstein operated a Madison Avenue boutique called Insport when he first latched on to Jack. A consummate hetero hound dog in the largely gay world of New York fashion, he was also simpatico with Jack over controlled substances: Finkelstein knew where the best were to be found, and Jack knew how to use them.

Finkelstein insinuated himself into Jack's insular life, building on their powdery friendship to eventually help himself to producer credits in *The Two Jakes* and the ill-fated *Blue Champagne*. Simultaneously, he quit New York for new digs near Aspen and another home just down the Mulholland Highway from Jack's place.[4] When Jack traveled to London, Alan traveled to London. When Jack played a round of golf, Alan played a round of golf. Similarly, Jack's new best friend did not stand idle when Jack fretted over the passing of Helena's.

Finkelstein located the Carriage Trade, a former West Hollywood restaurant that catered to a gay clientele, and transformed it into the Monkey Bar in 1993. The building resembled a pink stucco speakeasy on the north side of Beverly Boulevard. A single barred window marked its guarded and canopied entrance, and its rooftop terrace was perfect for A-listers who wanted to rise above the hoi polloi by stepping outdoors to tweak a little fresh air. The new owners imported the celebrated Chef Gordon Naccaroto, an Aspen fixture of long standing, and upgraded his menu. Presto! The newest L.A. hot spot was born, complete with rap artist–size security to keep out the Friday night riffraff.

Inside, the same celebrity mix that once populated Helena's now packed the Monkey Bar: John Travolta, Don Henley, Bob Evans, Nick Nolte, Mick Jagger. But without the screening presence of Helena, eventually the Monkey Bar opened its doors to lampreys from all walks of life, including well-connected coke distributors and high-class hookers from the notorious Heidi Fleiss stable. Over time, star traffic tapered off.

But during the first year or two, Jack and Finkelstein did manage to reinvent a more rambunctious version of Helena's. Jack had a place to celebrate holidays and Saturday nights, while Chef Naccaroto wowed Jack's out-of-town guests with his signature lobster tacos. Jack could bring Rebecca or Jennifer, appear in blackface for Halloween, and get plastered on New Year's Eve: so gloweringly loaded that he didn't mind stepping outside to piss on the lawn when the men's room traffic got too close.

The waitresses Finkelstein hired weren't bad-looking either. Perhaps another Rebecca lurked somewhere in their midst.

Mike Nichols called for an April start on *Wolf*. In preparation, Jack flew to New York to visit Random House and get a feel for the kind of publishing firm he'd be running as the tweedy fiction editor Will Randall. With Tommy Baratta's help, Jack lost nearly fifty pounds from his *Hoffa* high and patterned his slimmed-down character's post-preppy wardrobe after the Random House editorial director Jason Epstein.

Jack poured himself into his subject, studying medieval animism and werewolf mythology, as well as the precious politics of publishing. He visited the zoo, studied nature films, and consulted movement coaches to get the gait right. The more Will Randall gave in to his inner wolf, Jack believed, the more he embraced a Native American mysticism that approximated the atmosphere Jack once hoped to capture with *Moontrap*: "The truth is in the blood and the stories are in the stones."

On the days he went from Will to Wolf, Jack spent hours in makeup. His aging joints and old back injuries might not be up to a werewolf's leaping athleticism, but that's what stuntmen (eight) and animatronic wolf effects specialists (nineteen) were for. Jack had to remain in front of the camera up to seventeen hours a day during the three-month shoot, but he never gave up his golf or Lakers breaks. When there wasn't a game on, he hit his marks and delivered his lines low and breathless. *Wolf* had something profound to say about the taming of the modern American male, but in a routine Jack had followed since *Man Trouble*, he deferred to his director on just what that "something" might be.

Wolf's author saw that as a mistake. According to Jim Harrison, Nichols dumbed down his story. "[Nichols] took my wolf and made it into a Chihuahua," Harrison complained. "I cracked up for ten minutes and then went out into the country and stood in front of a wolf den and apologized while my dog hid under the truck."

Wolf ended Harrison's twenty-year affair with Hollywood and sent him packing back to his native northern Michigan in disgust. He vowed to finish out his career writing books, not scripts. While his immediate quarrel might be with Nichols, Harrison found fault in a system as old as Hollywood itself: writers were courted like royalty but eventually viewed with suspicion, envy, or contempt—sometimes all three. "Studios are corporations, like publishers," he said. "Sometimes they treat you quite wonderfully. And sometimes they're like a rich uncle with severe Alzheimer's, and you don't know in any given week which it's going to be."

Giving Will Randall "wild man" license in Nichols's rewritten script allowed Jack one more opportunity to overact and spread the gospel of Wilhelm Reich. In making *Wolf*'s protagonist a furry-faced retread of *Eastwick*'s Darryl Van Horne, Jack demanded a Gene Simmons tongue to thrust down Michelle Pfeiffer's throat as he imagined amorous wolves might do. He also suggested an image straight out of Roman mythology, instructing Pfeiffer to suckle his nipples like Romulus and Remus. Nichols nixed both ideas, but in a scene resonant of Karen Mayo-Chandler's description of Jack's belief in the staying power of peanut butter, Pfeiffer did feed him PB&J sandwiches prior to their first onscreen tryst.

"Oh, I think it's nice if one guy does all the fucking," said Jack. "This is something that a wolf has. The Alpha wolf in the pack and the Alpha female do all the fucking because the pack can't get any larger than the land that supports it. There's something in that that human beings could learn about."[5]

Shot mostly on the Sony lot, *Wolf* wrapped in July, but an early screening proved dismal so its Christmas release was postponed. Nichols returned to the editing bay, tightening and overhauling the score. Until the retooling, the final price tag for the film had been put at $49.3 million, but that would rise.

Jack's plan following *Wolf* was to direct a Nick Nolte road picture called *A Strange New World*, but the fast-growing independent film movement caught up with him first. Sean Penn, his young friend from Helena's, wanted to make a movie about the tragic consequences of drunk driving, and for the first time since *Broadcast News*, Jack allowed friendship and an artful script to prevail over the almighty dollar.

Based on Penn's original screenplay, *The Crossing Guard* (1995) typified a new breed of low-budget filmmaking, spawned in the late eighties, when the bigger, starrier, blockbusting plotboilers created in the Spielberg-Lucas tradition virtually obliterated character-driven "little" movies.

While film schools cranked out more graduates with derivative spec scripts and higher hopes each year, the chances any of their work would ever get made—let alone be seen—diminished at the same pace as the B-movie, now all but banished from American life. Studios no longer made them, and TV, including cable, opted for happy endings and formula melodrama over the gamble of original vision. Even the venerable artiste Roger Corman moved on to soft-porn bloodlust (*Bloodfist*, I through V; and *Sorority House Massacre* I, II, and III) and showed scant interest in mentoring another generation of Coppolas, Scorseses, or Nicholsons.

In 1985, Robert Redford used his own star cachet as a down payment on an independent film experiment.[6] He loaned his formidable name to the Sundance Institute, located in Utah's ski country in the southern Rockies. Designed to showcase student films, the institute's annual Sundance Film Festival evolved into a midwinter Hollywood holiday, its scope soon expanding well beyond the average 16-millimeter short subject required for graduation from film school. Some of the best movies anywhere were premiering in Park City, not Hollywood.

By the time the twenty-five-year-old wunderkind Steven Soderbergh's *Sex, Lies, and Videotape* (1989) exploded as the first real Sundance success story, both the festival and the indie movement it spawned were a significant counterweight to the star-driven, special-effects-laden blockbusters that obsessed Hollywood.[7] Between 1986 and 1991, the number of American features made and distributed without major studio backing doubled. Riding the crest of this new wave was the next generation of directors: Soderbergh, Quentin Tarantino, and Robert Rodriguez, among others.

Sean Penn was the same age as these emerging outsiders, but he had an insider's pedigree. His mother was the veteran actress Eileen Ryan and his father the blacklisted TV director Leo Penn. When Sean Penn was still in his teens, he was already doing television. By twenty-one, he emerged as a Brat Pack standout in films like *Taps* (1981) and *Fast Times at Ridgemont High* (1982).

Throughout the eighties, Penn was better known as Madonna's hot-headed husband, but the marriage ended in 1989 following Penn's arrest for domestic assault. Professionally, he carved out an enviable acting career (*The Falcon and the Snowman* [1985], *Colors* [1988]), while he worshipped maverick directors like John Cassavetes and Hal Ashby. With Penn's first effort, *The Indian Runner* (1991), he picked up the maverick mantle himself.

The low-budget character study of two radically different brothers (stoic David Morse and angry Viggo Mortensen) failed in the United States, taking in less than $200,000 at the box office, but it got a warmer reception at Cannes. In much the same way that Monte Hellman's existential Westerns *The Shooting* and *Ride in the Whirlwind* became cult classics in the 1960s, *The Indian Runner* developed its own European following. Back in the United States, cable TV picked it up, giving the movie a second chance.

With *The Crossing Guard*, Penn produced, directed, and wrote. His $11 million budget came courtesy of Miramax, the biggest indy distributor of the 1990s. While Sundance opened the door to young filmmakers, Miramax closed the deal. At the time Penn sought backing for *The Crossing Guard*, the independent company's founding brothers, Harvey and Bob Weinstein, had become so successful that Disney paid them an $80 million merger fee and left them to control their company. Ultimately, the Disney merger proved a Faustian bargain (the Weinsteins bowed out ungracefully, though even richer, in 2005), but for the remainder of the nineties, Miramax dominated Hollywood's independent filmmaking and underwrote young directors like Penn, making it possible for him to afford Jack. "He only wanted what was fair, and what was fair with Jack is a *lot*," said Penn.

To Jack, *The Crossing Guard*'s real appeal was "first-person acting." "No makeup, no wardrobe, no haircut, no limp, no accent, no voice, no nothing," said Jack. "Just the emotion."

A vengeful father whose child died at the hands of a drunk driver would be his first real immersion *acting* since Frances Phelan in *Ironweed*, and there was the bonus of lending his twenty-four-karat name to a good cause. "Having maybe dropped the ball myself on my own directing aspirations," said Jack, "I always felt as an actor that I could be helpful to directors—because pretty much anything off-center needs support to get it going."

Like *The Indian Runner*, *The Crossing Guard* was way off-center. Penn took his inspiration from the recent tragedy of the rock legend Eric Clapton's son: while not the victim of a drunk driver, the boy died equally senselessly.[8] *The Crossing Guard*'s stormy storyline had grief, gunplay, and sex, typical of Hollywood fare, but none of the climactic resolution that American audiences had come to expect. A revenge plot that ends with tragic empathy instead of wholesale slaughter, *The Crossing Guard* might reflect life's ambiguity but not the melodramatic expectations of *Batman* fans.

Penn's spare screenplay further encouraged Jack. Penn labored through the summer at his new $4 million estate overlooking the jagged Malibu coastline, and yet his final draft came in at only ninety pages. Mostly dialogue, *The Crossing Guard* gave its repertory cast broad leeway to interpret their roles—a rarity in a medium that had largely been conceded to special effects, studio oversight, and anxiety-ridden auteurs.

While concentrating on writing, Penn combined self-discipline with domesticity. In August of 1993 he and his fiancée Robin Wright had their second child, a son whom they named Hopper Jack Penn in honor of Dennis Hopper and Jack.[9] As casting for *The Crossing Guard* began a month later, nature and circumstance slowed Penn's momentum.

On November 3, the Santa Anas blew in from the east, fanning L.A.'s worst fire in a generation. While the flames lapped near the edges of Jack's Malibu ranch, 268 nearby homes were incinerated, including that of the Penns. Robin moved into a hotel with the babies, but Sean stubbornly set up a trailer in the ashes. He learned to barbecue on the stoop outside his door (Jack was a frequent guest) and worked by lantern light, fine-tuning his screenplay. He also angled for a casting coup: the reunion of Jack and Anjelica, who both agreed to a February start date for *The Crossing Guard*. "Jack's a great actor," said Anjelica. "Who wouldn't want to work with Jack? Anyway, it was more about Sean's script than about Jack."

While Anjelica and Jack had long since buried the hatchet, their screen angst as a couple divorced over the death of a daughter finally put a public resolution to their very bad breakup. Ironically, Jack and Rebecca's on-again, off-again relationship began to look like it might explode in much the same way Jack and Anjelica's had ended.

Pitched battles over Jack's insistence on his "freedom" worsened over time, and even separate houses didn't resolve differences. Jack's perpetual next-door neighbor Helena recalled a typical quarrel: "Rebecca was running out of the house in tears, and he was running down the steps saying, 'I've worked too hard for my lifestyle. No female is going to turn it around. No woman is going to change me . . . take me away from my recreation.' And then he went to play golf."

Adding to the domestic upheaval, golf wasn't Jack's only recreation. He didn't know it yet, but he was going to be a father again—not with Rebecca, though. Following nearly a year of surreptitious dating, he'd impregnated the Monkey Bar waitress Jennine Gourin. "My friends were asking who this older man was and how I could buy a new car on my salary," the young woman later told the *London Daily Mail*. "At first I told them he was someone in real estate."

Following habit and with characteristic hauteur, Jack handled his latest female troubles through denial. In an oft-repeated quote that he gave the journalist Nancy Collins, he summed himself up in a sound bite: "You only lie to two people in your life: your girlfriend and the police. Everybody else you tell the truth to."

Hollywood's "King of the Deal" Irving Paul "Swifty" Lazar succumbed to cancer on December 30, 1993.[10] In the weeks leading to his death, the legendary eighty-six-year-old agent anointed Jack his successor as host of his annual Oscar bash: *the* preeminent A-list event in the envy-infected cesspool that is showbiz. Jack eulogized the fallen Hollywood icon for "going ahead with his party" but politely declined Swifty's honor.

"If you are lucky enough to have a career as an actor, it becomes vital to save your own life inside that," Jack said. Somewhat disingenuously, he added, "One of my new vows is not to talk about my personal life in public."

He didn't have to. Potheads, paparazzi, strumpets, and suck-ups did it for him. The *Sunday Times of London* observed that Jack's life had become a Fitzgerald fantasy: "He gives extended parties at his house and is furiously on the telephone, leading people to Los Angeles Lakers' games and then on to fashionable nightspots. Like Jay Gatsby, he remains smilingly gregarious, but the smile is there to protect those secrets known only to him."

Jack's ongoing domestic troubles, further exacerbated by fallout from the Malibu fire, capped a testy year. At the beginning of the new year, Jack attempted to circumvent future catastrophe by donating sixty acres of overgrown hillside to the Santa Monica Mountains Conservancy. While giving himself a nice tax write-off, he also shifted responsibility to the state for keeping the canyon adjacent to his house fire safe. But for public consumption, Jack sounded like a concerned and generous environmentalist.

"When I first bought my house, I suggested to my neighbors that we buy up the empty parcel that goes straight down the hill, so we'd always have the land the way we like it," he said. "They all agreed to it, but when we had a meeting they all ended up nitpicking over stupid little things. So I bought it myself—and in those days [1973] it was a financial stretch. You know, sometimes you just get fed up with the nonsense, and you've got to do it yourself." It helped Jack's self-sacrificing image that he was following the lead of Barbra Streisand and Warren Beatty, who had previously donated property to the conservancy.[11]

But Mother Nature, it seemed, could not be bought off so easily. Just before dawn on January 17, 1994, the ground shook and fifty-seven people lost their lives in the Northridge earthquake. Out-ranked up to that time only by Hurricane Andrew as America's costliest natural disaster, the quake caused $15 billion in damage. Up on his ridge, Jack escaped injury. The only damage he sustained was that some rare Tang vases were broken.[12] When the inevitable rains came later that winter, Jack dodged another bullet: his house held firm while others slid off their foundations.[13]

Cursed by a geography that the urban anthropologist Mike Davis dubbed "the ecology of disaster," L.A. suffered fires, floods, and temblors that season. Unnatural disasters also swirled around Jersey Jack: foul air, fallout from a riot,[14] road rage, freeway gridlock. Drivers confronted one another in the fast lane, threatening to turn their cars into battering rams. Snipers picked off motorists on the Harbor Freeway for no apparent reason. The cancer of unchecked urban sprawl had spread from Palm Springs to Malibu and all points in between. The City of Angels began to resemble the City of Dis.

Yet when it came to real disaster, Jack remained exempt. Forces might conspire to accelerate the ruin of his promised land (predicted with unnerving accuracy by Lawrence Kasdan's *Grand Canyon* [1991]), but from where he stood on the isolated precipice of the Hollywood Hills, Jack's adopted city still looked like a sparkling neon quilt, especially after midnight. "I have an abiding fear of the dark," said Jack, "which is strange because that's supposed to be a fear of your own subconscious, which is something I constantly try to rupture the membrane of to get it working into my own job."

Despite Jack's vague sense of doom, life on Bad Boy Hill remained both stable and sweet. The American Film Institute had just announced plans to honor Jack as its youngest-ever recipient of the AFI Lifetime Achievement Award. Jack continued to live the Gatsby dream. There seemed little chance that he'd wake up anytime soon.

On February 4, 1994, Harold Schneider dropped dead of a heart attack at his Ojai Valley home. Unlike Bert,[15] with whom Jack had a falling out over *The Two Jakes* years earlier, Harold remained Jack's faithful friend for a quarter of a century. Loud, abrasive, and smart, Schneider held a movie together by force of will—a throwback to another era when the producer outranked the director on a set and made square pegs fit in whatever holes were necessary to bring a film in on time and under budget. A year younger than Jack, Harold was held in such esteem that Jack asked him to produce every movie he ever directed. It wasn't until *Hoffa* that they parted ways.

When Danny DeVito's cost overruns got to be too much, Schneider objected, but the diminutive director kept spending. Schneider asked Jack to intervene, but Jack sided with DeVito to keep the peace. Instead, Jack offered Schneider a personal loan of $150,000 until he collected his producer's fee, then counseled him to quit. Harold used part of the loan to open a restaurant with his wife, Amy.

Meanwhile, DeVito replaced Schneider with his own line producer and blamed a "personality conflict" for Schneider's departure. When the film wrapped and Schneider still hadn't been paid, he again sought Jack's counsel. Jack told him to sue. At the time of Schneider's death, the suit had reached the stage of settlement talks.

At the funeral, Jack offered Amy his condolences, but in the days leading up to and following Schneider's death, he was also steeping himself in his *Crossing Guard* character.

When the cameras rolled, Jack was ready. He'd virtually become *The Crossing Guard*'s Freddy Gale. The raging father who bursts into anger through much of Penn's movie menaces everyone in the cast from Anjelica to David Morse, the drunk driver who killed Gale's little girl. Penn praised Jack early and often for his bitter and deranged acting, until the morning of February 8, when Jack and Freddy Gale became the same guy.[16]

Three miles east of Mulholland, thirty-eight-year-old Robert Scott Blank pulled his 1969 Mercedes out in front of Jack in "a crazy piece of driving that almost ran me off the road," Jack recalled. He chased Blank to a stoplight, removed a two-iron from the rear of his own late-model Mercedes, and whacked the startled driver's roof several times before smashing the front windshield and showering Blank with glass.[17] "It was a graphite golf club," Jack later explained in his own defense. "I thought it would shatter. And after all, he was trying to run me over."

Nine years earlier, during a rambling interview with the *Washington Post*'s Paul Attanasio, Jack gave a far better and more honest explication of his tendency to tantrum: "I behave well in some situations, and I feel kind of good about it, and sometimes I'm liable to take all of the repressed anger of something that's very important to me, and take it out on the ice cream man. And then I feel like a schnook. And I am a schnook at those moments. I don't think I'm better or worse than anybody else."

In blaming Blank, schnook Jack forgot his conditional contrition. Gleeful Fleet Street regulars accused him of doing "a Basil Fawlty on Blank's car." The irony rose another notch when news photographers discovered that Jack's face decorated posters all over town promoting the 23rd Police Celebrity Golf Tournament. Even while street cops charged him with misdemeanor assault and vandalism, the LAPD brass were boasting that none other than "Joker" Jack Nicholson would be hosting their annual police charity fund-raiser.[18]

In court, Jack's lawyer, Charles English, cited "some extraordinary circumstances going on in his life," including the tough demands of *The Crossing Guard* and the shock of Harold Schneider's death. But Deputy District Attorney Jeff Harkavy didn't buy either excuse. He argued for full prosecution, pointing out that Jack had aimed for Blank's face when he whacked the windshield. English complained that Harkavy was just singling out his client because of his celebrity. Harkavy warned that going easy on Nicholson would only invite outcries of preferential star treatment.

Pending trial on criminal charges, English entered into settlement talks with Blank's attorney. But in the meantime Jack continued to face the emotional challenge of bringing his "A" game each day to *The Crossing Guard*. A harsher setback to his acting or his personal life was hard to imagine.

An hour after closing time on February 28, 1994, someone put three .22 caliber rifle slugs in Pamela Hawley Liddicoat's head.

For nearly twenty years and through two marriages, Jack's dreamy kid sister had lived anonymously in the Gold Rush hamlet of George-town in the Sierra foothills near Sacramento. Except for the occasional tourist, life there was as rural as Mayberry. Hunting, fishing, and drinking—not necessarily in that order—were the chief pastimes. More than once, Jack had to lend Pam money. Like her grandmother and her mother and aunt before her, Pam was a beautician, though nowhere near as successful as they had been. She proudly hung her California state license on the wall of the Hilltop Beauty Shoppe, which she ran out of her home just off Main Street. But mostly Pam lived on past glory, drank too much, and was perpetually in debt.

She divorced her high school sweetheart, Doug Mangino, in 1982, and for eleven years she was married to Mannie Liddicoat, George-town's best-known down-on-his-luck day laborer. She had recently filed for divorce a second time. Four months before she died, Jack loaned her $10,000. Pam was hitting the bottle again. He urged her to get professional help. She didn't. The El Dorado County Sheriff's blotter read:

> The victim is the half sister to actor Jack Nicholson. She was a long-time resident of the Georgetown area and owned a beauty shop in that area. While fairly well known in the Georgetown area, Pamela Liddicoat was not held in particularly high esteem by members of that community and had been refused admittance to nearly all of the establishments which serve alcoholic beverages.

During the full moon of February 27, Jack's forty-eight-year-old half sister picked up her gal pal Michelle "Shelly" Burns, twenty-five, and they drove to Chiquita's cocktail lounge. They were a couple of ladies just blowing off steam. Pam drank diet Dr Pepper and rum, while Shelly drank whatever any guy was willing to buy her.

"Pam was recently divorced," said Detective Scott Stewart. "Michelle thought she was looking for a sexual relationship."

"When Pam got drunk, she got kind of amorous," recalled her friend Andrea Weaver. "She got kind of just, not sleazy, but you know, just kind of nice, touchy-feely kind of nice to everybody."

After getting a buzz on, the women returned to Pam's place, where Shelly recalled that they "bullshitted and tried on clothes." They decided to go out for a nightcap, but the local bar had already closed, so they headed up Highway 192 to the Coloma Club. Long past midnight, Pam pulled her Mustang into the parking lot. The girls waltzed inside and found three male prospects sitting at the bar. "As we walked in the door, it was last call," Shelly later told police.

But Pam kept on drinking and the more she drank, the more she tended to flip her hair, call herself "the Princess," and do a little dance out on the barroom floor. "She loved to dance," recalled her former sister-in-law Cheryl Cron. "Pam would dance in front of everyone else, all by herself."

A night of drinking did not make for princess behavior. When Shelly got snippy with Pam about losing her figure and her good looks, Pam countered by boasting that she could sleep with Shelly's boyfriend "any time I want." As the Coloma Club closed, they quit their catty one-upmanship and settled for a threesome with a total stranger. The women left with a one-eyed gun enthusiast, rottweiler owner, and unemployed thirty-three-year-old white-water river-rafting guide by the name of Michael David Fellows.

What happened next remains an open question. The one certainty was that a 911 call came in to the El Dorado County Sheriff's office at 7:09 the next morning. Shelly phoned from a neighbor's house a quarter mile away from Fellows's isolated mountain shack.

When deputies showed up, they found Pam's naked body sprawled in a back bedroom, covered with Hefty trash sacks and a sleeping bag. Fellows later admitted having dragged her from the bathroom, where investigators found a pool of blood. Pam also had a bruised forehead, scratches on her face and neck, defensive wounds on her hands, and scrapes on both knees and elbows.

"I could be real graphic with you," Detective Stewart warned reporters. "I've got some very good photos out there that probably would make you sick. But it's all to me and to [his partner] Steve and to everybody else around here . . . it's evidence. It's Pam Liddicoat. She's dead. Her spirit went on. The body's the house she used to live in. And that body contains evidence. And that's all it is to us. And it's black and white. This is 1994. This is the age of science, okay?"

Perhaps the motive was jealousy. Maybe it was alcohol-fueled rage. Some people in Georgetown speculated that Pam had just received another loan from her rich and famous brother and that she had been out boasting, winding up the victim of rape and robbery.

Police arrested Shelly Burns and Michael Fellows, charging them both with murder. Fellows accused Burns of shooting her friend in a jealous rage, while Burns pointed the finger at Fellows, claiming that she had to sleep with him after he'd killed Pam, just to calm him down. Eventually, they both pled guilty to voluntary manslaughter and got six years each.

The coroner released Pam's body to her family. They buried her in the Georgetown Pioneer Cemetery.

"She was a pretty mixed-up little gal," said Carol Olsen, a coworker at Hilltop Beauty Shoppe.

"I knew Pam," said her friend Elaine Charkins. "She was a good woman."

According to the locals, Jack didn't make it to the funeral. As in the final reels of *Ironweed* and *The Two Jakes*, a terrible melancholy settled over Georgetown. For weeks thereafter, residents expected to see a limousine idling outside the graveyard one day, but none ever came.

One week after the murder, twelve hundred of Hollywood's rich and famous donned Ray-Ban "Clubmasters" and stood at attention in the Beverly Hilton Hotel. Dustin Hoffman fell to one knee as the band played "Born to Be Wild" when Jack entered the ballroom. Lights blazed and TV crews trained their cameras on the man of the hour as he made his way toward the dais to receive the 1994 AFI Lifetime Achievement Award.

All ten women who joined him at his table had once been his leading ladies: Shelley Duvall, Mary Steenbergen, Louise Fletcher, Ellen Barkin, Kathleen Turner, Candice Bergen, Faye Dunaway, Madeline Stowe, Cher, and Rebecca Broussard.

Much more intriguing were the no-shows. Anjelica Huston wasn't there. Neither were Susan Anspach, Mimi Machu, Michelle Phillips, or Winnie Hollman. Sandra Knight Stephenson's name was not on the eight-page seating chart. Bob Rafelson was there, but not Bert Schneider or Steve Blauner. Roger Corman came; Robert Towne was absent. Alan Finkelstein showed; Bill Tynan didn't. Carole Eastman was invited, but Charles wasn't. Old flames and expendable colleagues had no place on the guest list. Yet, inexplicably, the hierarchy of Occidental Petroleum, headed by Chairman Dr. Ray Irani, had an entire table to itself.

Once dinner was finished, praise, toasts, and folderol began. Soon enough, adulation gave way to one-liners, and the lovefest quickly took on the trappings of a roast. It was television, after all.

"Jack made being in a mental institution like being in a mental institution," quipped his *Cuckoo's Nest* costar Louise Fletcher.

"He will go to great lengths to be in a good mood. Farther than I will," said Warren Beatty. "Jack takes an oblique approach to conversation."

Beatty complimented Jack on his homemade rice pudding but pointed out that Jack didn't much care to eat fruits or vegetables. "And," Beatty added, "he's every bit as vain as I am."[19]

Shirley MacLaine contradicted her brother, claiming that she'd seen no such vanity in Jack during their nude scene together in *Terms of Endearment*. "I adore the fact you don't care how you look," she told Jack. She did kibitz over his scene stealing and salary demands. "First you steal the money, then you steal the movie."

Slyly implying that Jack still dealt drugs, Dennis Hopper confessed, "I'm the schmuck who didn't want Jack Nicholson to get the role in *Easy Rider*."[20]

"He has proved that self-indulgence was uncommitted inspiration," said Sean Penn, who brandished a putter with a mace attached.[21] "It's my no-witness club," he confided to the appreciative crowd.

A diehard folkie who once headlined his own country band on weekends, Harry Dean Stanton joined Art Garfunkel in an impromptu serenade. They sang the Everly Brothers' "Dream" for Jack, while Bob Dylan sat silent nearby at Stanton's table, never once cracking a smile or speaking a word.

"I was touched by Jack's feeling of undeservability," recalled Shirley MacLaine some years later. "He never liked to speak in public. Like many actors, he needed the camouflage of a character. When we went around the country accepting our awards for *Terms*, he was never comfortable, and on this AFI night nothing had changed."

Calling himself a "hick actor," Jack finally took the podium near the climax of the three-and-a-half-hour testimonial. His voice was thick with emotion and laryngitis from days of shouting during *The Crossing Guard*. His hands shook. His mouth trembled. The adoring women who surrounded him at his table maintained that there were tears in his eyes. "I've been yelling a lot this week. I'm drunk and lucky to be at large," Jack said. "So this speech is bound to come out muddled and confusing, sputtering like my life, but I'm gonna do it that way. I hate making a speech and talking about acting and showbiz."

He acknowledged Lorraine, who had come all the way from New Jersey to fete her younger brother. He introduced Jennifer and pointed to Rebecca, "the mother of some of my children." His eyes lingered a while. "She changed her mind a lot of the time," said Jack. "She's coming, not coming, coming, not coming. Let's take the babies. Well, you know maybe she's right. I thought that they were too young to drink."

Later, Jack told Shirley MacLaine how "deeply embarrassed and unworthy" he felt, but on the evening of his greatest public triumph, Shirley recalled, "He stopped for a long moment, looked around the room and actually said, 'From now on I might fall in love with myself.'"

Jack concluded with praise for his profession. "I love this work," he said. "It's dangerous. I'm proud of all my collaborations. My work motto is 'Everything counts.' My life motto is 'Have a good time.'"

Then he borrowed his exit line from Jackie Gleason: "You ain't seen nothin' yet."

Jack partied through the night with Rebecca. They finished at the Monkey Bar at six in the morning and went home together. For a moment, it looked as if they were a couple again.

But April came and with it more reality. Just after Sean Penn called a wrap to *The Crossing Guard*, Jack and Rebecca were about to board a plane for Maui when Jennine Gourin called. She told Jack she was carrying his baby. She didn't want to but felt as if she had no choice but to go to the tabloids. "Do what you have to do," he said.

While he and Rebecca vacationed, Jack's lawyers negotiated a settlement with Robert Blank's attorney. Rumored to be in the mid–six figures, the payoff was submitted under seal to Judge Martin Suits. As Deputy District Attorney Harkavy predicted, the case against Jack was summarily dismissed.[22]

Harold Schneider's widow did not get off so easily. Following weeks of turmoil, Amy Schneider placed a call to Jack. When Harold died, he'd left her and their seven-year-old daughter enough debt to shut down their restaurant and force the sale of their home. Furthermore, without Harold there to testify, his wrongful termination lawsuit against *Hoffa*'s producers deflated. A settlement offer dropped to

$25,000, but Amy was still on the hook to Jack for $150,000. She swallowed her pride and asked him to forgive the loan. "I'll never forget what he told me," Amy recalled. "He shouted into the receiver, at the grieving widow of his supposed dear friend, 'What kind of a fucking hack lawyer did Harold hire anyway?'"

Jack accused her and her late husband of trying to screw him. After asking for a review of her assets, he demanded whatever cash settlement might come from the *Hoffa* suit, plus a rare wine collection that he'd acquired with Harold. Amy signed over what remained of the $25,000 *Hoffa* settlement after paying her lawyer but sold the wine for $22,500 to help pay her bills. When Jack sent her a dun notice, she called his business manager.

"Business is business, Amy," said Robert Colbert.

"Well, Bob, that's where I think you're wrong," she answered. "As far as I'm concerned, this isn't about business. Is Jack going to sue me for the money?"

"I don't know," said Colbert. "Jack's in a bad place. I don't know how far he'll go."

Amy wrote Jack a letter and poured out her heart, her rage, her disappointment:

As I told you soon after Harold died, he wasn't ready and unfortunately things were left undone. Harold had grand visions but at 55, not one of them had come to fruition. The inventory assets list that was just sent to the probate referee reads like a bad joke. He loaned a lot of money too, Jack, and no one ever paid it back. The list of bad debts is long and gruesome. Without boring you with the details suffice it to say I am still cleaning up the mess. . . .

I don't understand why you said what you said in the US magazine interview when asked about your erratic, uncontrolled behavior with the golf club incident. You blamed it on the death of your dear friend and producer Harold Schneider. Was that true? Or was that an "Oh, don't I sound compassionate" line? If it was true, why would you be asking Harold's widow and daughter for $22,500 when you know my situation? When you know my needs? How could $22,500 be so important to you? Is that money really more important than your 25-year relationship with Harold?

Harold died, and he didn't die because he owed you money, although that was one of his mounting stresses. Harold had this undying loyalty to you, Jack. I never understood it. I always questioned it. He said he couldn't explain. He'd just laugh his throaty laugh. I want to believe he was right. I want to believe in his judgments, but right now I can only be disappointed.

Amy never sent the letter, but neither did she pay any more on the debt.

In similar fashion, Jack went after the meager assets of his late sister. For more than two years following Pamela's murder, Colbert tried to exact cash from Mannie Liddicoat on the supposition that he'd inherited what little remained of the $100,000 that Jack had loaned Pam during the previous twenty-five years. With interest, Colbert figured the debt down to the penny. Mannie Liddicoat owed his former brother-in-law $206,822.83.

Liddicoat paid none of it.

21

I N 1994, DISNEY BECAME THE FIRST STUDIO TO GROSS $1 BILLION at the box office, most of which came from Europe, Australia, South America, and Asia.[1] The MPAA estimated that gross receipts for all six major studios totaled a whopping $5.7 billion, but for the first time in Hollywood's history it earned more distributing movies abroad than it did showing them at home.

While ticket sales were up 20 percent in the United States over the previous decade, movie demand hadn't kept pace with the glut of movie houses. A total of 37,396 screens were now scattered across the country, with drive-ins accounting for less than 1,000 of them.[2] Yet even as multiplexes multiplied, VCRs and satellite and cable TV kept audiences at home. Fans simply didn't flock to the movies the way they did when Jack was a kid.

It was movies themselves that were the problem. They cost more to make, admission to see them now topped $4, and there were fewer to choose from. Studios that once released nearly a thousand films a year now barely produced a hundred. As the stakes rose, the problem facing Hollywood remained as old as P. T. Barnum: finding events so compelling, so delicious, so spectacular that popcorn buyers couldn't resist lining up like lemmings to get inside. Box-office champs like *Batman Returns* (1992), *Jurassic Park* (1993), and *The Mask* (1994) upheld the tent-pole theory that bigger and bolder were better, but just as many "spectaculars" proved to be jaw-dropping bombs. By mid-decade, the studios had dumped hundreds of millions into lemons like *Hudson Hawk* (1991), *Last Action Hero* (1993), *Stargate* (1994), *Waterworld* (1995), and *Judge Dread* (1995).

"In all my experience—and it goes back rather a long way—I've never known a time when there was so much crap around," Jack complained. "It makes me very angry because those responsible are mostly idiots and charlatans. They know nothing about the cinema and they care very little, too. They just think in terms of 'fast' and 'slow' and 'where's the rooting interest?'"

"I thought that the swing to melodrama, frankly, would be over four or five years ago already. But it seems like the movies are becoming more formally the circus. It's the bigger explosion and the wilder escape from the more pyrotechnical situation, and it's not very rewarding for the actor when everything is either soap opera or pure melodrama or special effects. And by now it's been going on for so long that the audience is unused to anything else."

Not without sin, Jack should have cast fewer stones. Before *Wolf* ever got near a theater, both he and Mike Nichols sensed trouble. The film, larded with special effects and a plot left howling at the moon, resulted in a final cost hovering near $70 million. After a year in and out of editing rooms, Nichols's retooled *Wolf* still had problems. *Wolf* was set to open opposite *Forrest Gump* (1994), but thanks largely to breathless handicapping among entertainment reporters, it took on the trappings of a storm-watch event. Would *Wolf* take a bite out of the box office or sink like *Howard the Duck* (1986)?[3]

Publicity began early with a Nancy Collins cover story in *Vanity Fair*. An attractive blond journalist hired specifically to play cat and mouse with elusive celebrities like John Travolta, Michael Douglas, and Jack, Collins coaxed details about Jack's now broadly known maternal mix-up, his paternal mystery, and the usual provocative rationales he gave for indiscriminate sex. Jack appeared on the cover in wolfish muttonchop makeup just in time for the 1994 Academy Awards and also made the July cover of *Rolling Stone*, but he never once broke his taboo about giving TV interviews.

It didn't help that *Wolf* had been upstaged by a real-life bloodfest just before the movie opened. On June 12, Nicole Simpson and Ron Goldman were savagely butchered on the steps of Nicole's Brentwood condo. The bloodlust that dominated the final reels of *Wolf* suddenly ran counter to a newly awakened public revulsion. Following O. J. Simpson's arrest and subsequent trial, Jack remained cautiously sympathetic when questioned about his fellow golfer, whom he'd befriended on the links at Bel Air. "I've always liked Juicy," he said. "He's a sweet man when you're around him. I'm not a close friend of his, but he's always been very nice with me. I mean, if the world's worried about this, if they're worried that a guilty man has gotten away with something, they should stop and think what it's like to have to lie to your children for the rest of your life."

In late June, Jack made a surprise appearance at Southern California's annual Weekend of Horrors. Drawing the largest crowd of fantasy and horror movie fans in that event's ten-year history, the convention, sponsored by *Fangoria*, "America's Horror Magazine," was a perfect place to pump up the buzz.

Jack and Nichols also agreed to a junket with the Hollywood foreign press. While Nichols lasered in on *Wolf's* thrills and entertainment value, Jack veered off on renewed attacks against TV and movie studio conglomerates. "You have only to have had an International House of Pancakes breakfast *before* it was conglomerated and *after* to know the difference," said Jack.

Like home cooking that descends into cafeteria food, movies once carefully crafted by a BBS or Jack's late producing partner Harold Schneider had become assembly-line products of faceless monopolies headquartered thousands of miles away from Hollywood. "TV changed everything," Jack declared, recalling his childhood when he couldn't wait to get out and play. Just a few years later he witnessed his kid brother and sister, Murray and Pamela, huddled indoors, glued to *The Howdy Doody Show*. They weren't much younger than he was but were already held hostage. "I'm a World War II baby and my whole life, no matter what the paper said or what Mom said or what the school said, every day I felt I moved a little closer to the truth," said Jack.

He witnessed America evolve into the "What It Is" generation, as he called it: people believed only what they saw on TV. "Truth is literally altered by this phenomenon," said Jack.

Jack had been offered $10 million to do a voice-over commercial but turned the easy money down. "Something has been lost," he persisted. "As we go on, we want less conflict in our lives. We become more conservative. My job is to provoke people to deny this. Just because you are sixty or seventy doesn't mean you are less vital."

After a mediocre opening weekend, *Wolf* was dismissed by *Entertainment Tonight* and its clones, and yet, while perceived a loser and utterly forgotten by Oscar time, *Wolf* had legs. By summer's end, it had grossed more than $65 million and eventually took in $150 million. "It's perfectly possible for people, during a single summer, to be bored with how much a movie did its first weekend," said Jack. "They just suddenly say, 'Who gives a fuck? So what if it's been a preoccupation of the media?'"

Jack had had enough of Hollywood and headed east to make good on his vow to take a year off. He started with Barbra Streisand's comeback concert at Madison Square Garden. "We're walking, walking, walking to our seats—dead front-row center!" recalled Jennifer, who accompanied her father and Rebecca on the first of their several vacations. "I'd been invited. I never get to do stuff like that on my own. Only with him does that happen.

"Barbra didn't notice him until the second half of the concert, but when she did, she said, 'Hi, Jack,' and it was the only person she said anything to during the whole concert. Afterward, we went backstage, and they invited us to go out for dinner. I was picturing a big dinner party, but we go and it's a whole restaurant that's been closed down, with one table in it. And it was Barbra Streisand, the people that she worked with, me and my dad, and two of our friends. It was really fun."

At thirty, Jack's oldest child sounded as giddy as a teenager, but such was the effect her famous dad still had on women—even the ones whom he'd fathered. "We went to a play and I walked in and they were all screaming 'Rebecca!'" said Jennifer. "My dad turned around and said, 'Her name is *Jennifer*.' It kind of bugged me, but I'm used to odd things, I guess."

When they flew to London to attend Wimbledon, Jack borrowed a bobby's helmet and clowned for the paparazzi. He brought along

Jennifer and a thirteen-year-old blond girl named Honey whom he introduced as his daughter. The media didn't bother to pursue the obvious question as to who the girl's mother might be. Their cameras, microphones, and questions were always trained on "Jack the Lad," as he was known on Fleet Street.

At the trendy Tramp nightclub on Jermyn Street, the usual coterie of adoring actresses and models surrounded him: Naomi Campbell, Kate Moss, *L.A. Law*'s Amanda Donahoe, and Jennifer's latest friend, the aspiring actress Amanda de Cadenet.[4] Whenever a young woman asked to dance, Jack would lewdly growl, "Wrong verb, honey, wrong verb."

In a rare televised interview with the BBC, Jack elaborated on his long-standing libertine notions. He made sex sound like Method acting and spoke of coitus with the detachment of a Masters and Johnson volunteer: "I felt in my heart every time I was in the sublime sexual embrace that in order to feel it fully you had to allow for its full reality!"

Whether in London or Hollywood, he still invoked Wilhelm Reich as his raison d'être whenever young pussy passed his way.

"They tell you in Reichian therapy that the totally hard penis is not the best instrument for feeling sexuality," Jack instructed a disbelieving writer for the *Sunday Daily Telegraph*.

"Are you making this up?"

"No, this is science," insisted Jack. "I'm not a prurient person. If I wanna talk dirty, honey, believe me, I got a different approach to this."

"There's a very good reason why a man goes to someone of breeding age for a sexual situation," said clinical Jack. "It's the way we're set up. By nature. Nature doesn't care what you think about marriage; it cares about reproduction." But sensitive Jack made this observation: "I'm still in love with all the women I ever loved. I'm very shy. I'm not that easy to fuck, you know."

In August, Jennine Gourin gave birth to Jack's latest daughter. He sent her flowers. "Jack was my first love," Gourin recalled for *Star* magazine. She and her daughter lived in a New York brownstone that Jack subsidized along with the girl's education. "I thought he loved me," Gourin said. "I had the best time of my life with him."

But if Jack was still capable of loving anyone, it was Rebecca. She went with him to the Venice Film Festival in September to continue the global *Wolf* hype. They traveled again to the south of France, and he renewed talk of settling there, at least until the next picture. In December, in Aspen, he gave her a diamond "sort of an engagement" ring. He hadn't counted on a "No, thank you."

At the time, the tabloids had Rebecca dating Adam Storke, a young actor best remembered as Julia Roberts's preppie boyfriend in *Mystic Pizza* (1988). It turned out that Rebecca wasn't interested in marriage. After two children and nearly six years of living under separate roofs, she'd gotten Jack's point. Ring or no ring, he wouldn't change.

In January 1995, Jack told Susan Anspach he was foreclosing on a loan that would force her from her home. As with Amy Schneider and Mannie Liddicoat, it was just business and no reflection on Jack's feelings toward Caleb. "I don't feel obligated to save Caleb's mom," Jack told Anspach.

It wasn't until 1980 that Jack acknowledged the actress's child as his, but the master of the nickname still couldn't bring himself to call Caleb "son." Susan demanded a medical history at the time because ten-year-old Caleb was briefly hospitalized and his doctors needed to know what role DNA might have played in his condition.

One morning four years later a fed-up Susan appeared unannounced outside the Brando gates and demanded an audience. Jack buzzed Susan and Caleb inside. Caleb was now almost fourteen and needed to meet his father, the testy actress said. Jack got past his morning grump and focused on his son. "You've got my eyes," Jack told Caleb.[5]

For the next ten years, theirs was as typical a father-son relationship as showbiz dysfunctionality and Jack's special brand of narcissism would allow. Caleb continued to live with his twice-divorced mom and his half-sister Catherine in Susan's two-story, four-bedroom home in Santa Monica, but like his still-smitten mother, Caleb made the infrequent pilgrimage to Mulholland. Slowly, a bond developed.

A basketball fan himself, Caleb preferred the Celtics over the Lakers. Jack enjoyed this competitive camaraderie and on occasion shared his courtside seats with the boy. From afar, Jack followed Caleb's progress. Their estrangement may not have healed exactly, but it developed scar tissue, and when Caleb headed east to Georgetown University, Jack footed the bill.

He had only one inviolable command: he was Jack, not dad, and demanded no publicity. For public consumption, he had just three children: Jennifer, Lorraine, and Raymond. That he had sired at least three others out of wedlock was a fact the mendacity-loathing but still quite illegitimate John Joseph Nicholson could not tolerate.

The first time Caleb remembered Jack ever acknowledging him as his son was in a phone conversation on December 27, 1995. He was twenty-five years old, working for CNN, and living in New York at the time. "We discussed the fact that this was the first time in my life that he had called me his son directly," Caleb recalled.

The precision of his memory had the weight of sworn testimony behind it because Caleb wrote it in a declaration in support of his mother's lawsuit. The thing that Jack feared most—the antiseptic glare of publicity—lit up this part of his private life like a soundstage throughout 1995 and didn't dim until more than a year later, after the worst of his mean-spirited intolerance lay ugly and exposed in the press. Like a flat coyote who tried once too often to beat the traffic on the Mulholland Highway, Jack got in trouble believing he was the wolf who answered to no one.

The Anspach episode began with a letter to the editor of *Vanity Fair*. In its June 1994 edition, the magazine published Susan's response to Nancy Collins's *Wolf* interview with Jack. In her letter, Susan pointed out that the article mentioned only three of Jack's children; Caleb had been omitted. "I have asked Jack about this oversight and his response to me is that he doesn't really want to talk about his children in interviews. He feels that it's not his responsibility if the reporter neglects to mention one or two of his children."

Jack went ballistic.[6] Among other things, Caleb's mother was "an idiot," "an unpredictable cunt," and "a miserable, drunken bitch"— epithets he hurled over the phone at her with the velocity of physical blows. "I do not agree with this endless publicity-seeking and so forth about personal affairs," Jack offered in his defense, but his tongue nearly tripped into gibberish when he got to the heart of the matter: "And we had a discussion not unlike it at other times when this particular something that I consider a confidence in private was used in a public way to exploit the situation."

As with many wars, this one began with good intentions and a fundamental misunderstanding. In 1988, when Anspach's second marriage failed, she had trouble finding acting work. Arrears on her refinanced mortgage began to mount, and she went to Jack. During the bullish years when she'd hitched her star to *Blume in Love* (1973), *The Big Fix* (1978), and *The Devil and Max Devlin* (1981), Susan's career paid off handsomely, but the casting calls stalled in the late eighties while her living standard did not. She estimated that she needed $200,000 a year to keep going.

Through the pension fund of his Proteus Films production company, Jack arranged a bail-out.[7] He rescued her from foreclosure when creditors that included two banks and the Small Business Administration claimed she had defaulted on a series of loans totaling $629,286.

According to Susan, Jack promised her that she could keep the house even if she could not repay his loan, so she didn't. But following the *Vanity Fair* incident, all bets were off. He demanded $400,000 in back payments and interest. When Susan failed to respond, foreclosure proceedings began.

For seventeen years, Susan had lived at the corner of Marguerita and 16th Streets with Caleb and Catherine. At the time that Jack tried to evict her, Anjelica's older brother Tony Huston had moved in temporarily and was living in Caleb's old room. Jack's daughter Jennifer was also moving in soon across the street. Among other arguments, Susan pointed out that Jack had cosigned the loan on his daughter's new $2.475 million home. Why treat the home where his son grew up any differently?

Despite a generous public record that seemed to indicate otherwise, Jack was Simon Legree, according to Susan. In November 1995, she struck back with a $1 million suit alleging that Jack's loans were never intended to be repaid. She painted a picture of Jack and his lawyer as sexually harassing, chauvinistic henchmen conspiring to bring her down, not because of profligacy, but because she was a woman.

Admitting only to a "vague antipathy" toward Susan, Jack called her feminist pose just that: another stratagem to win public sympathy while extracting money from him. With Christmas on the way, he had a message for her: "I'm not Santa Claus."

Over the next year, Jack did four back-to-back projects, beginning with *Blood and Wine* (1996). For a fifth and final time, Bob Rafelson reteamed with his old crony, launching their crime caper feature on location in Miami just one week after *The Crossing Guard* crashed and burned at the box office.

Despite a year of editing,[8] an encouraging August preview at the Venice Film Festival,[9] and unprecedented star power for an indie feature,[10] *The Crossing Guard* opened the week before Thanksgiving and took in just $864,972 before getting dumped from theaters. R-rated and somber to the point of resembling "therapy . . . unfolding in a blearily confessional mode at 3 a.m.," *The Crossing Guard* nonetheless achieved a "stirring, spiritual vision of the path to grace," according to the *New York Times's* Janet Maslin. Unfortunately, holiday crowds were in no mood for somber therapy and flocked instead to *Toy Story* (a $191 million box office), *GoldenEye* ($106 million),[11] and *Ace Ventura: Pet Detective* ($72 million).

But Sean Penn's box-office failure did not mean Jack was any less in demand.[12] Clint Eastwood recalled Jack once telling him that *The Crossing Guard* would be his last film. "I said I would do *In the Line of Fire* and *A Perfect World*, and that would be it," said Eastwood. "Well, he went on to act in about ten more movies, and I went on to act in or direct six more. They keep saying yes to you, so you keep going."

Before Jack agreed to *Blood and Wine*, a revitalized MGM[13] asked him for a cameo in *Mulholland Falls* (1996),[14] Warner Bros. wanted him opposite Jodie Foster in Carl Sagan's *Contact* (1997), Morgan Creek[15] wooed him with a remake of *Diabolique* (1996), and Sony's TriStar division envisioned him as an obsessive baseball nut in *The Fan* (1996).

But it was Rafelson who was able to sweet talk Jack into forgetting *Man Trouble* and signing on to one more movie. The director described *Blood and Wine* as the third part of his Jack trilogy, wherein Jack played a son (*Five Easy Pieces*), a brother (*King of Marvin Gardens*), and finally, a father (*Blood and Wine*). The story was "a $15 million Oedipal film noir," according to Rafelson, although the finished product more closely resembled an unfunny black comedy: a philandering wine salesman teams with a Cockney oaf to fence a stolen necklace. Illicit sex and bloody mayhem ensue.[16] Jack persuaded Michael Caine to costar, despite a low ebb in the British actor's long career. "It wasn't fun anymore—and I wasn't getting the roles," Caine complained. "Jack restored my heart in doing roles—and my faith in the business."[17] Jack told Army Archerd, "He's a champion. I love

Michael when he plays a hard man. And he's like me—when we finish a role, we rush to our cars!"

It took a star of Jack's caliber to get *Blood and Wine* off the ground. He'd become a de facto producer, according to Rafelson. Long a brand name, Jack became the reason that the new Fox Searchlight division committed to the movie.[18]

"Approval of the director, approval of the project, approval of the final script, approval of the costar, sometimes a coterie of makeup and wardrobe, the trailer—that comes with the actor," said Rafelson. "You're hiring aboard considerably more than you were twenty years ago when you hired an actor, certainly more than forty years ago when the actor was under contract to the studio. Things have changed; the actor is not starting work the moment he's offered the part. He's now part of the production." Even so, Jack "hasn't altogether lost his sense of irony about himself," said Rafelson. He paused briefly to reconsider. "He's lost it a bit, but not completely."

James L. Brooks had nothing to do with *The Evening Star* (1996), and it showed. The $25 million sequel to *Terms of Endearment* began production while Jack was still in Florida, but he agreed to do a few scenes after Rafelson wrapped *Blood and Wine*. *The Evening Star* gave Shirley MacLaine a chance to reprise her Oscar-winning role as Aurora Greenway, and Jack became Garrett Breedlove one more time as his Valentine—February 14 being one of the three days that he appeared before the cameras.

Unfortunately, *The Evening Star* director-screenwriter Robert Harling had never directed before, and Jack's expensive star presence was wasted. The continuing saga of Aurora raising her late daughter's three unruly children came off as contrived, and Jack added nothing beyond the Brooks original. After doing little more than speak his lines and arch a brow, he moved on to his next project for the *Batman* collaborator Tim Burton.

But before Jack did, Jim Brooks reemerged in his life—not in conjunction with *The Evening Star*, but rather with a romantic comedy appropriately titled *Old Friends*. Since 1994, Brooks had been reworking the Mark Andrus love story set in New York City about an obsessive-compulsive author, his gay neighbor, and a single mom. Kevin Kline, Ralph Fiennes, and Holly Hunter were the original leads, but when Jack agreed to star, Brooks snapped him up. In a deal the trades described as "very hard to make," Jack lowered his salary in exchange for a "significant back end."

At first, cameras were to roll in May, but *Old Friends* got delayed until August while Jack wrapped up a hammy smorgasbord of way-over-the-top clowning in Tim Burton's all-star sci-fi spoof *Mars Attacks!* (1996). "I was location scouting and I phoned Jack from the plane and asked him, 'Which part would you want to do?'" Burton recalled. "He answered, 'How about all of them?'"

Like Peter Sellers in *Dr. Strangelove*, Jack took on three roles—two credited (President James Dale[19] and the Vegas hotelier Art Land) and one that was not. This last part, the vaguely Strangelove-like scientist who messes up a Martian translation and unwittingly provokes the destruction of the planet, was Jack's favorite. "Jack really saved our butt," said the *Mars Attacks!* screenwriter Jonathan Gems, who marked the beginning of casting as the day Jack signed on. "We started getting requests from more stars than there were parts for it. It was like a tidal wave when Jack came on."

With the whiff of *Batman* billions flaring in their agents' feral nostrils, Glen Close, Pierce Brosnan, Sarah Jessica Parker, Annette Bening, Rod Steiger, and a host of other names queued up for the next Nicholson-Burton blowout. Jack even brought Rebecca on board to play a brief scene as a streetwalker. He affirmed Mike Nichols's pre-*Wolf* assessment of his sheer omnipotence on a movie set: "He can pick a whole picture up by its ass and swing it around his head."

Burton built his $80 million tribute to 1950s sci-fi flicks around a rare series of 1962 Topps bubble gum trading cards that featured little green men invading the Earth. Shot on location in Las Vegas; Washington, D.C.; Arizona; and Kansas; as well as on L.A. sound-stages, *Mars Attacks!* was originally budgeted at $120 million. Crammed with animation, special effects, and stunts that Jack normally found odious, Burton's extravagant vision included the actual implosion of the Landmark Hotel on the Vegas Strip.[20]

But the outsize budget was based on the oddball director's long string of big-profit Warner Bros. hits, beginning with *Beetlejuice* (1988) and *Batman* (1989). Following the disappointing *Ed Wood* (1994),[21] Burton's budget dropped to $70 million but crept up another $10 million before *Mars Attacks!* headed to theaters. By then, it was too late. Not even Jack could pick *Mars Attacks!* up by its alien ass, let alone swing it around his head.

. . .

While Jack went from movie to movie, the Anspach war escalated. In March, he told Susan's lawyer, "My spirit was simply to help a friend" when he lent her money. "I'm a humanitarian," said Jack. "I believe in being good and charitable to my fellow man."

But provoked to anger during his deposition, he lashed out at a system that allowed anyone to take advantage of his celebrity and his perceived fortune. "I have three cases like this," Jack complained. "And what happens to me? They sue and I wind up settling and paying *my* lawyers and *their* lawyers."

In his rage, he let slip a glimpse at his complicated finances, which the media believed to be limitless but were in fact as subject to taxes, mismanagement, embezzlement, and moochers as those of his fans—just on a much larger scale. "There are some problems in my Proteus Plan," he told Susan.[22] "There! Another gift! I gave you the gun, but I don't want to give you the bullets. I trust no one. They're incapable of holding a decent relationship with a benefactor. They're all parasitic and dangerous enemies that benefit from my professional life, which is all that matters to me."

Jack's fortune, especially after the oft-repeated *Batman* windfall, carried with it the curse of a lottery win. Everyone near him wanted a taste, transforming friends, children, and lovers into debtors as frequently as the inevitable parade of Hollywood parasites. Long ago, Jack's perceived generosity soured into cynicism, suspicion, and resentment.

A much calmer Jack told *Playboy* magazine in 2004, "I came to realize that ill-gotten gains are never good for the person receiving them. The contrary is true. So when you're paying an extortionist, there's a bit of diabolical delight and contempt in handing over that check. It's like when you get robbed. You would think I'd be furious, but pretty soon I always feel bad for the person who has to lead that kind of life."

With assets that now included homes in Aspen, a Malibu ranch, three houses inside the Brando gates, profit positions in dozens of hit movies, and an investment portfolio[23] that generated more than enough to pay $1,000 a game for courtside seats at the Forum, Jack was indisputably wealthy. What missed public scrutiny were the secured and unsecured loans he'd doled out, frequently off the books, for a generation—many of which went unpaid. "When I make a loan I collateralize it; it just makes good sense," he said, although he didn't always follow his own advice.

After two years, his $10 million *Blue Champagne* gamble came up snake eyes. After the film was twice rejected in competition at Sundance, Jack ordered Rebecca's showcase shelved, not out of pique so much as because of the obvious fact that all the recutting in the world would not make a bad movie better.

He'd also only recently learned that he and Brando had been among those clipped for an estimated $6 million embezzled from a California pleasure spa. The *New York Daily News* reported that the two Mulholland recluses had invested in a "health ranch" that Helena Kallianiotes persuaded them to help her develop near Anjelica's Three Rivers property in the Sierra foothills. In an extension of Helena's nightclub philosophy, an exclusive clientele who passed her strict membership standards would helicopter in for swimming, sweating, and recreation among scantily clad hostesses who'd never allow a drink to go unfreshened—a sort of rustic Playboy Mansion set among the sequoias.

It was Jack's partner in another losing proposition, the Monkey Bar's Alan Finkelstein, who hired the detective Frank Monte to track down the missing money. Cash that Helena's Colombian business partner was supposed to pay to contractors was rerouted to Swiss and South American banks at about the same time the business partner vanished. Monte told his clients that they weren't likely to see the Colombian or their money again.

Meanwhile, Helena's latest scheme ground to a halt and for the first time in a quarter century, Jack banished her from his compound. He believed that the Colombian embezzler might pose a threat to Lorraine and Raymond,[24] made Helena a six-figure loan to get started elsewhere, and ordered her exit. She moved into the Venice compound, where Anjelica and Robert Graham settled, and tried to revive Helena's, first as a nightclub and then a dance studio, but without Jack's help and with far less success.

Yet Susan knew nothing of Jack's various setbacks. She just wanted to save her house. In June, she filed for Chapter 11 bankruptcy protection. "If the house is sold, I will be left with nothing after [Jack] and the mortgage holder, Merrill Lynch, have been paid," she said. In one of her greatest understatements, Anspach told *People* magazine, "there's something psychological going on."

That summer, a copy of Blaine Novak's *Children's Heaven* screenplay landed on her doorstep. The bizarre fantasy arrived in a plain brown envelope that bore an Aspen postmark and no return address. In her reading, Susan saw herself, Caleb, and Jack among the characters. Caleb was the bastard child, trying to get into heaven and Susan was his mother. Jack played two parts: the boy's philandering father and God. "God just can't show affection and tenderness to boys who have imperfections, and this boy's imperfection is that he never had a father," Susan said. "That's what this is saying."

By summer, *Old Friends* was in front of the cameras but not with James L. Brooks's original cast. Holly Hunter took a pass and Jack's girlfriend in the movie became Helen Hunt, the star of NBC's hit sitcom *Mad about You*. The same age as Rebecca, Hunt took the part of the single mom-waitress Carol Connelly[25] on the condition that Brooks stretch production over a year to accommodate her *Mad about You* schedule.[26]

The third lead also came from TV, from the part of that medium Jack loathed the most. A broadcast journalist who had paid his dues as an E! Entertainment red-carpet storm trooper, Greg Kinnear was breaking from being typecast as the host of E!'s *Talk Soup*.[27] He passed Brooks's audition for the plum part of the gay artist Simon Bishop, then found out he also had to read for Jack. "Unfortunately, I was so nervous I ate myself sick on spaghetti," Kinnear recalled. "So I went to Jack Nicholson's house bloated with pasta."

If Jack recognized Kinnear as one of E!'s wide-eyed predators, mandated to corner and coax bon mots from reticent stars, he didn't show it. After the reading, Kinnear was hired.

"Hey, are you hungry?" asked Jack. "Want some spaghetti and meatballs?"

Still bloated on pasta, Kinnear sat and ate. "Jack Nicholson was asking me to eat dinner with him and James L. Brooks," he said. "This was one of those high points in life. All I could think was, 'Gee, I hope this is a long meal.'"

Once production got under way, *Old Friends* became *As Good as It Gets* (1997), "a love story where you do nothing but aggravate somebody," according to Jack.[28] Skillfully played for laughs, his obsessive-compulsive Melvin Udall resonated with sweet and sour notes from Jack's own offscreen existence. A grumpy recluse given to the sneering, blunt remark, Jack's character stopped short of self-parody.

In *As Good as It Gets*, the best-selling novelist Melvin Udall has both means and motive to help those around him in genuine need, but he cannot connect on an emotional level, even with the waitress Carol upon whom he dotes. In one memorable misogynistic exchange, Melvin confronts a fan of his romance novels. She asks, "How do you write women so well?" and Melvin carefully intones, "I think of a man . . . and I take away reason and accountability."[29]

During the opening sequence, when homophobic Melvin tosses Simon's incontinent dog Verdell down a trash disposal chute, the only difference from the way Jack would have reacted in real life was "he would choke it to death right on the spot," according to Bob Rafelson. Despite mean-spirited sarcasm and occasional cruelty, Melvin comes around. In an exchange with Carol halfway through the film, he confesses the redemption she has brought into his life: "You make me want to be a better man."

Similarly, he is the unlikely savior of his gay neighbor. When a beaten, broke, and defeated Simon Bishop runs down his three-by-five card of "Friends to Ask for Money," he gets universal rejection. Even his own parents deny him.

But Melvin takes him in, partly because he's grown attached to Verdell. Like Jack, who helped dozens at low ebbs in their careers over the years, Melvin Udall can be called upon in a pinch but with strings attached. Like Jack, he has his own self-serving interpretation of the Golden Rule.

After Melvin hires a doctor[30] and pays to save Carol's asthmatic son's life, she pours out her soul in a long thank-you letter. But when Melvin asks Carol to accompany him and Simon on a road trip to Baltimore, she balks.

Carol: Melvin, I'd rather not.

Melvin: What's that got to do with it?

Carol: I thought it was a strong point.

Melvin: Write a note, ain't she sweet. I need a hand and where'd she go?

Carol: Are you saying accepting your help obligates me?

Melvin: Is there any other way to see it?

Carol: No.

However hesitant Melvin might have been in putting the moves on Carol, Jack, of course, had no second thoughts. Had Helen Hunt not survived and thrived in the showbiz septic tank since childhood (her first professional acting gig was at age eight), Jack might have had her up to his place to see his artwork.

But there were always "skunks" to be had in London, and that's where he headed in September, just before the *Blood and Wine* premiere at Spain's San Sebastian International Film Festival. He hooked up with the producer Michael White, whose scandalous *Voyeurz* had just opened in London. *Voyeurz*—a 1990s version of *Oh! Calcutta!*—centered on lesbian fetish-club performers, one of whom caught Jack's eye. After "a memorable night," twenty-four-year-old Christine Salata told *People* she received flowers with a note that read "Thanks for everything. Jack."

Jack the Lad's clubbing was an annual London ritual. He was as well-known at the five-star Connaught Hotel as was visiting royalty.[31] The *London Evening Standard* columnist Henry Porter said that Jack's enduring persona "causes in men a wistful remembrance of their own prowess. And in women, a pleasant tingle of revulsion."

After Jack returned to L.A., his prowess got him in trouble again. A self-described "wardrobe designer" named Catherine Sheehan called the LAPD in the early morning hours of October 12, 1996, from just outside the Brando gates. She said that Jack had been "slapping her with both his hands" after refusing to pay her and another woman $1,000 each to wear "little black dresses" for an all-night three-way. Jack grabbed her by her hair, she said, and dragged her several feet, slamming her head to the ground.

Once she broke free and ran, he yelled, "I'm going to kill you!" When she threatened to call police, he came back with, "I'll give you a good reason to call the police," then grabbed her shoulders and threatened to toss her over the wall into Franklin Canyon. She finally locked herself in her friend's car until they could get away. Cocaine may have fanned the flames, but the tantrum had ignited over money. As a long-standing point of pride, Jack *never* paid for sex.

Officers who were dispatched to Mulholland investigated, and the L.A. City Attorney's office took Sheehan's complaint, but when she failed to show for a hearing, the criminal accusation was taken off-calendar. Sheehan later sued for $10 million, accusing Jack of rupturing her breast implants, but settled out of court for $32,500. In 2000, Sheehan returned to court, claiming that her hospital bills had topped $60,000, but after the furor over this later suit settled, it, too, quietly faded from the docket.

Blood and Wine tanked in the fall, earning a paltry $1.1 million at the box office. But TV and video had changed the movies, and Rafelson's movie got a second life as one of the first features to get repeat airplay on STAR, Rupert Murdoch's newly acquired Hong Kong–based satellite operation. From Jakarta to Beijing, *Blood and Wine* became one of Jack's best-known films. At the time of its release, most critics adopted the position of the *San Francisco Chronicle*'s Edward Guthmann: "They should pass out Wash 'n' Drys wherever this movie plays."

Despite a sleaze factor that turned off Americans, *Blood and Wine* earned its money back on cable and satellite and took on cult status with the supplemental *Making of Blood and Wine* documentary marketed ten years later: an example of the revitalizing influence of DVD. It even caught the twenty-seven-year-old Jennifer Lopez on the cusp of her *Selena* (1997) superstardom, playing a Cuban maid with whom Jack has a deadly affair.

Critics also savaged *Mars Attacks!* and *The Evening Star*. For the first time since the face-off of *Hoffa* and *A Few Good Men*, a pair of Jack movies opened against each other, but the media didn't seem to notice. In conjunction with the *Mars Attacks!* premiere, Jack showed up to get his star on Hollywood Boulevard. The publicity did little to save a movie that *Newsweek*'s David Ansen called "a goofball alien-invasion parody that is so defiantly inconsequential it makes *Pee-Wee's Big Adventure* look weighty." Of Tim Burton's space folly, the British journalist Beverley D'Silva posed two key questions: "How has Burton spent so much money making a film that looks that cheap?" and "If it was billed as a comedy, why wasn't it funny?"

In a year when the box office champs *Independence Day* ($306 million) and *Mission Impossible* ($180 million) clearly showed the growing influence of video gaming on movies, the whiz-bang pyrotechnics of *Mars Attacks!* sputtered on the launchpad. Burton's unintentional homage to *Plan 9 from Outer Space* (1959) earned a mere $37.8 million.[32] *The Evening Star* fared even worse at $12.5 million but didn't cost the price of a Boeing 747 to make. While *Mars Attacks!* wasn't nominated for a Razzie, it still rang down the curtain on 1996 as one of the year's biggest losers.[33]

From all outward appearance, Jack's star had appeared to dim. Obviously, his name on the marquee didn't have the same wattage it once had. Yet with his sixtieth birthday looming, Jack's long, enviable career as Hollywood's best-known star looked to be in decline. He'd had a good run, though. No one could say that Jack's career wasn't as good as it gets.

22

WHEN THE DIRECTOR'S GUILD OF AMERICA HONORED Stanley Kubrick in March 1997 with its highest accolade, the director of *The Shining* asked Jack to accept the D. W. Griffith Award on his behalf. Deep into production on *Eyes Wide Shut* (1999), Kubrick sent along a short video with Jack, in which Kubrick observed that despite Griffith's genius, he died in poverty, forgotten by the very industry he helped to create, and thus became a sort of high-flying Hollywood Icarus.[1] "I've compared Griffith's career to the Icarus myth," said Kubrick, "but at the same time I've never been certain whether the moral of the Icarus story should only be, as is generally accepted, 'Don't try to fly too high,' or whether it might also be thought of as, 'Forget the wax and feathers and do a better job on the wings.'"

Jack quipped to the DGA audience, "Stanley's money's on better wings."

Lofty art versus earthbound commerce was a point not lost on Jack. He debated the issue with Sean Penn, whom he regarded as something of a younger version of himself. "I've hung out with Sean," said Jack. "Our esthetic is similar. I like his instincts, his intelligence, his poetry."

But starving poets didn't dine at Indochine or live on a Malibu estate.[2] Speaking from personal experience, Jack called a *succès d'estime* like *The Two Jakes* or *The Crossing Guard* no match for a genuine box-office hit. "Sean, you're so entertaining as an actor," Jack told him. "Now will you try with your next movie to do one where you're not *doomed* before you start to having [sic] a marginal audience?"

Following Jack's advice, Penn picked William Faulkner's tragic farce *As I Lay Dying* as his next project. He subsidized himself with acting fees and nightclub investments[3] while he developed the script for the Polish director Jerzy Kromolowski, lassoing Jack and Leonardo DiCaprio to costar.

Penn kidded Jack as still spunky for "an older guy," but after blitzing through five movies in two and a half years, Jack rested. A month following the Kubrick DGA award, he celebrated sixty at home with an aging entourage that included Brando, Mike Nichols, and Warren Beatty. He flew Tommy Baratta out from Marylou's to make his favorite pasta.[4] "The only thing wrong with turning 60 is there's no guarantee you'll be alive 'til you're 160," Jack observed. "You know what I'm saying?"

L.A., too, was aging. The land of possibility where he'd arrived more than forty years earlier had become a minefield of opportunism. Everyone was on the make. "If it's nine months making a deal and three weeks writing a script, then you don't have to ask what's wrong with the movie business," said Jack.

Movies had evolved into plot-driven assembly-line products, and the emerging Internet promised to accelerate that transformation even further. "You can't really get a good rewrite anymore because of the computer," Jack complained. "The writers go home and dip into their memory bank and there's something lost in that process."

The population of Southern California had doubled since Jack first trekked across the Baldwin Hills. A single L.A. freeway in 1955 had spawned twenty-seven others. More than 10 million commuters now put 100 million miles on their odometers each day. Beaches were often so polluted they had to be quarantined. Citrus orchards were long gone. The American Lung Association rated the very air Jack breathed as the worst in the nation. And still he remained a booster. "Painters and musicians always do their very best work here, and I always thought it was because of the space," Jack insisted. "When you live in a metropolis, it shapes your perceptions. When the throw of your vision is never more than a few yards or it's down an alley, the human being is affected by this. You're effectively thinking in these types of metaphors: shortsighted. I came to Los Angeles as a teenager in the fifties from the East Coast, and there's nothing that's in another city that isn't here. But you have to generate it. You have to get to it."

The suburbs predicted by *The Two Jakes* now extended far beyond Claremont, where "Beaner" Towne once attended college; or Canyon Country, where Mud lived in her pink trailer; or the San Fernando Mission, where Mrs. June Nicholson Hawley lay buried along with the secret of Jack's birth. "I'd like to meet two broads today who know how to keep a secret to that degree," he said. Calling himself an "amateur psychologist," Jack pondered telling the story himself. "June Nicholson was a prototypical woman of the twentieth century. I might write this someday." But when asked point blank by the film critic David Thomson, "Do you know now who your father was?" Jack bristled, "No, and I really hadn't much curiosity about that."

With Don Furcillo-Rose still protesting in the media, Thomson's question lingered. Every year or two, another article appeared, quoting the retired beauty salon operator about the son who refused to speak to him. Beneath the glaring headline "H'wood Bad-Boy Jack Snubs Dying Dad," the *New York Post* reported on June 23, 1997, that the eighty-eight-year-old Furcillo-Rose lay bedridden and forsaken in a Florida nursing home, dying from cancer. The old man revealed that Jack had been conceived in an upstairs bedroom at the Sixth Street bungalow in Neptune City where Jack's birth certificate falsely stated that he'd been born. "He told me he wants nothing to do with me," Furcillo-Rose said. "He told me not to write any more letters—and to, like, go away."

Jack's psychiatrist advised him that some of his early experiences were best left repressed. Among them, apparently, was the identity of his father. "I'm inured to emotional blackmail . . . because of the kind of family I come from," said Jack.

Furcillo-Rose died a month later on July 27 and was shipped home to New Jersey for burial. Jack sent no condolences.

"I would be so happy if I didn't smoke, for a lot of reasons," said Jack. "I can't believe that I can't break the habit. I don't want to be lying around, dying in Cedars-Sinai Hospital and thinking that I was stupid enough, a man who is as petrified of dying as I am, to have done it to myself. I'm a real fraidy-cat about mortality."

He indulged his tobacco habit in spite of changing laws that forbade smoking in virtually any public venue, from Jack's own Monkey Bar to the Forum. "I sneak into the men's room at halftime, like when I was in high school, and take my drags there," he said. If he needed a drug stronger than nicotine, Jack sought the privacy of the photographers' darkroom inside the Forum press room.

At New York City's Madison Square Garden, he found broom closets. Most New York restaurants discouraged smoking, too, but Tommy Baratta actually built a $40,000 air-conditioned and insulated addition at Marylou's in the Village to accommodate Jack and his Pack. "When I finish my pasta, I'm gonna kick back and smoke a big, fat Cohiba for dessert," Jack said.

Invariably, Jack's whims were accommodated. While Jack took in *Swan Lake* at Lincoln Center one fall evening, he ordered an assistant to tape the third game of the World Series so that he could watch it when he got back to his hotel. During the ballet's intermission, when the discussion turned to the score at the bottom of the third, Jack snapped, "I don't want to know," and all talk of baseball hushed.

The following night he headed to a party in Chelsea hosted by Alan Finkelstein.[5] His chums Art Garfunkel, Michael Douglas, and Sean Penn showed, but Jack excused himself to watch Game 4 of the series. For Jack, and only Jack, the owner set up a TV at the back of the restaurant.

"I don't go out much now," Jack said. "It seems like I do because people see me at a basketball game two or three times a week, and my friends in London or Paris think of me as a bon viveur, but I don't go out anywhere but London and Paris, not even in New York. And I'm much more at home than I was, say, ten years ago." Jack grappled with what he termed the "cybernetics" of being "singular."

Gossip columnists discovered that Rebecca had a new boyfriend in the soap opera star Daniel Quinn, but Jack reacted with uncharacteristic calm. He adopted the convention of referring to Rebecca as "the mother of my children."

Following Helena's departure, Jack began to outfit the house next door, to accommodate his growing children. "One of [the houses] is tricked up for the kids for when they're staying here," Jack said.

Whatever mistakes he might have made with the other children Jack now seemed determined to correct with Lorraine and Raymond. He distilled a lifetime of experience into a single Calvinist counsel: "All I'm going to say is, everything they say is bad for you, pretty much it is bad for you."

He hired no less an instructor than Tai Babilonia to teach Lorraine how to ice skate. He sat in the back row to avoid recognition but attended most of her soccer games. He took up watercolors with his children, recalling that he'd had some talent himself as a kid. More than just a Disneyland dad, Jack spent quality time with both youngsters at his Malibu ranch. He hired a full-time nanny. The children were pampered and protected. "Liddy Poo" had her mom's pouty lips and her dad's exclamation eyebrows. Stocky and as sweet-natured as his late uncle Murray, Raymond had dark hair that curled naturally. When he smiled, his cheeks dimpled. He baited Jack, declaring himself both a Bulls and a Michael Jordan fan.

At the same time that Jack indulged his youngest children, he became a grandfather. On February 20, 1996, Jennifer gave birth to Sean Knight Nicholson.[6] A year and a half later, she married Sean's father, her fellow Panahou School graduate Mark Norfleet. The marriage didn't last, but motherhood did. As a divorcée, Jennifer produced a second son, Duke, in 1999.

After *Blue Champagne*, Jennifer's acting career waned. She planned to appear in a one-woman play her mother had written, followed by *King City*, a movie Sandra coauthored with her husband, John Stephenson, but neither project clicked. Jennifer switched her interests to costume design. With Jack's help, she opened the Pearl boutique on Santa Monica's stylish Montana Avenue and began a successful line of designer clothing: "fun, girly, sexy and playful . . . part Andy Warhol, part beach-influenced."

Without Jack's help, Caleb moved on from CNN to Yahoo. In May 1998, Jack put an end to his public feud with Susan Anspach over the home on 16th Street by deeding the property to Caleb. A few years later, the property was sold.

After more than a year in production and at a reported cost of $75 million, *As Good as It Gets* opened in December 1997.[7] Art Garfunkel sang the ironic theme song, "Always Look on the Bright Side of Life," borrowed from the crucifixion finale in Monty Python's

Life of Brian (1979). Reviews were mixed, ranging from "an emotional hodgepodge" (*Dallas Morning News*) and "tiresome" (*Variety*) to "the best and funniest romantic comedy of the year" (*Los Angeles Times*).

Jack answered potshots over the age difference between him and Helen Hunt by returning to Biology 101. "I have a sweet spot for what's attractive to me," he said. "It's not just psychological. It's also glandular and has to do with mindlessly continuing the species."

With Melvin Udall, Jack battled the convention that men lose their sex drive with age and that actors eligible for Medicare got relegated to roles he characterized as "Judge Hardy and Uncle Bim."

To overcome the critics' ambivalence, Helen Hunt hosted *Saturday Night Live* the week *As Good as It Gets* premiered. During a skit featuring the head-banging "Roxbury Guys," the *SNL* regulars[8] Chris Kattan and Will Ferrell broke character in the waiting room outside their therapist's office when a wild man emerged raving, "You want the truth? You can't handle the truth!" It was Jack, of course, ending his self-imposed boycott of series TV for the first time in thirty years. How much the *SNL* stunt casting helped the movie couldn't be measured, but after the first of the year, *As Good as It Gets* had taken in more than $85 million and all three leads received Oscar nominations.[9]

Jack set out on a global public relations push,[10] beginning with Australia and eventually ending in Europe, where he stopped in Paris to visit Roman Polanski.[11] Whenever TV cameras appeared, Jack ordered them turned off. A brief *SNL* spoof was one thing; television Jack could not control was quite another.

By Oscar night, the box office for *As Good as It Gets* had already shot past $100 million. At year's end, the movie tallied $147.6 million—the sixth-highest-grossing film of 1998.

Rebecca accompanied Jack to the 70th Annual Academy Awards telecast, as did Jennifer and her husband, Mark Norfleet. Early on, the host Billy Crystal ventured into the audience and sat in Jack's lap, singing, "Sit back, relax. Forget *Mars Attacks!*"

Jack was one of seventy past recipients of Best Actor or Supporting Actor Oscars who took the stage for a cameo-by-cameo introduction. As names and winning roles were called out, the camera lingered on each of the best male film actors of the twentieth century, gathered together for the one-time-only tableau.[12]

Near the end of the evening, the 1996 Best Actress winner Frances McDormand opened the envelope containing the name of the Best Actor winner, and the largest TV audience in Oscar history heard her say, "Jack Nicholson."[13]

Later backstage, the familiar Jack persona sniggered, "Welcome to the nineties. I like a career that covers three decades."

But ever so briefly as he stood at the podium, the facade slipped. A sexagenarian who still suffered self-doubt had the good grace to publicly recognize each of his fellow nominees, as well as two fallen comrades who never approached Jack's level of celebrity. "Some of the other nominees are very good friends, and I'm very honored to be on the list with you, Bobby;[14] Dusty;[15] you and your father, Mr. Damon;[16] my old bike pal Fonda.[17] We're very proud of the picture, but I've had a sinking feeling all night up 'til now," said Jack, referring to *Titanic*'s winning streak.[18]

He dedicated his Oscar to the late character actor J. T. Walsh,[19] his costar in *A Few Good Men* and *Hoffa*, and fought back tears as he recalled the early Jeff Corey graduate and recent cancer victim Luana Anders.[20] Then hubris took over. Jack had beaten the odds and was still on his game at sixty—the winner of more Oscars than any actor alive.[21]

However trying Jack's recent years, his fortunes suddenly reversed with *As Good as It Gets*. Even the LAPD signaled an end to the golf-rage jokes by taking out a full page in the *Hollywood Reporter*, saluting Jack as a past host of the annual Police Celebrity Golf Tournament.

In May, a triumphant Jack celebrated by taking Rebecca and their children on a European holiday. "I'm on a constant honeymoon with the mother of my children," he told paparazzi.

He and Rebecca flew to Havana in June, stopping in at a cigar factory and spending three hours at Revolution Palace as guests of Fidel Castro. Anticipating criticism, Jack kept comments terse and to the point: he was there to talk about film and found Cuba "very beautiful, very lovely, a paradise."[22]

In July, Jack returned to London for his annual Wimbledon sojourn, bringing a cache of Cuban cigars along with him but suggesting no noticeable shift to the left in his politics. He might fancy himself a lifelong liberal, but he understood his fan base and would never jeopardize his good fortune by flaunting radical opinions.

That autumn, the Hollywood Foreign Press Association named Jack the latest recipient of its Cecil B. DeMille Life Achievement Award. Liberals and conservatives alike loved him. It wasn't until a president of the United States stood to lose his job over a little adultery that Jack jeopardized his perceived neutrality.

In December 1998, Congress impeached President Bill Clinton for lying about having sex in the Oval Office. A White House intern half his age named Monica Lewinsky boasted over getting her presidential kneepads and thus rechristened the center of global power the Oral Office. "Blow job" became an accepted phrase among presidential pundits. Naturally, Jack came to Clinton's defense. "What would be the alternative leadership?" Jack asked. "Should it be somebody who *doesn't* want to have sex?"

The week of the impeachment, Jack joined Barbra Streisand at a rally in front of the Federal Building in Westwood to demonstrate his support. "I wanted to come down today because the presidency of the United States is at stake," Jack told the crowd. "Both parties could stop this tomorrow morning. I'm just here to wish you all a Merry Christmas and say I hope they do."

When Bill Clinton was first elected, Jack sent him a $350 golf driver. They hit the links together, and Jack likened their relationship to that of Falstaff and Prince Hal. "He's a modern president," said Jack. "And I've been asking for this guy for twenty-five years. He's different. And as a result, he's quietly getting more done than any president in my lifetime."

But near the end of Clinton's first term, this logical successor to the 1960s Democrats Jack admired most ran into a chainsaw of criticism from televised talking heads. Jack's advice: hang in there. "I hope that Clinton, after his rough start, will settle down and transcend the power of television," he said. "We now have government by sound bite. No man is bigger than the television, not even the president of the United States. Television determines the schedule, who sits where and what's said. It's monstrous."

In a satirical return to 1960s truth-telling, Warren Beatty tried to show the result of compromising personal integrity. In *Bulworth* (1998), the fictional Senator Jay Bulworth simply speaks his mind without regard to the television minefield. He shocks constituents by taking on the very politically correct timidity of modern politics, when ever-present cameras catch and magnify each slip and doom whole campaigns by looping a faux pas that repeats ad nauseum, news cycle after news cycle.

While often suggested as a candidate—and one whom Jack vowed he'd support—Beatty said during the *Bulworth* marketing blitz that he'd be far more effective and truer to his convictions if he did not run for office. "I have this great luxury of not having a career as a politician," Beatty said, "so I can say what I want to say."

As did Jack, but his Christmas message outside the Federal Building turned out to be his first and last public defense of the blow job heard 'round the world. Comparisons between Jack and Bill were inevitable, and once made, Jack backed away. "Like Clinton, Jack was raised by women without the restraining presence of a man on the premises," observed the *London Daily Telegraph*. "Also like Clinton, he became a famous lover of women, except the kind that try to make you stay home at night."

America's conservative mood implied that Jack's Clinton endorsement might carry more potential damage than balm. The impeached president missed conviction in the Senate by a single vote. The support of Hollywood's most notorious rake could not have been much help. For the remainder of the 1990s, Jack's momentary return to politics faded. He contributed $750 to Al Gore in the months leading up to the California primary but otherwise held his tongue. Once again, he'd had an object lesson in mixing celebrity with politics, and he calculated that speaking out as Beatty did was a losing proposition.

Jack saved his soapbox for filmmaking, which he declared to be a vital part of the learning process. "We learn how to kiss, or to drink, talk to our buddies," he said. "All the things that you can't really teach in social studies or history, we all learn them at the movies."

Lately, matinee matriculation left a bad taste in his mouth. The target audience remained "post-literate" youngsters numbed by explosions, mindless mayhem, knifings, and worse. "I think [U.S. film distribution] is bad for people who want to see movies," Jack said. "It's nerve-racking if you are making a movie. These days, it is all about takeoff and landing. It's a shame."

Nevertheless, he agreed to reprise his very violent Joker in *Batman Triumphant* until Warner Bros. canceled the project. For a senior citizen concerned with making meaningful movies, the news had to come as a mild relief. Studios had taken wide release to absurd new levels in the late 1990s with a simultaneous blast of two or three new video game–influenced films over as many as 2,500 screens each week. "You can't get to *Batman* [revenues] without the children," said Jack. "I have no disrespect for *Batman* audiences. I also don't have any illusions about it. But it's been a long time since we've had an alternate view."

Jack still read for pleasure, preferring the mysteries and thrillers of John D. MacDonald, Tom Clancy, and James Ellroy to the predictability of *Law and Order* and other prime-time procedurals. "I'm very nocturnal, and [reading] keeps me from watching the same movies all night long," he said. "It's a kind of recreational reading. And because I'd directed three movies and hadn't had any commercial success with them, I always thought, 'One day I'll do a thriller.'"

Unfortunately, screenplays—even those adapted from the thrillers that Jack enjoyed—pandered to stunted attention spans and slash-and-burn videocy. Indeed, one of the biggest box office surprises of the 1990s was a plotless black-and-white terrorfest called *The Blair Witch Project* (1999), which cost $35,000 but took in more than $141 million. "The more literary a movie becomes, the less audience it's relating to," said Jack. "The last time I can remember that kind of a movie being really successful was *Cuckoo's Nest*. And that was twenty-something years ago."

Jack's talk seemed cheap to critics who demanded that he use his star power to improve, rather than pander to, Hollywood. In a scathing critique at Oscar time, *Esquire*'s Tom Carson named Jack a leading cause of movie mediocrity:

> By now, after a quarter century of loaning out his swagger to safe projects whose inanity guarantees he'll have pizzazz, Nicholson's gloating roguishness just rots the screen. Yet he may have no choice but to soldier on as "Jack" into senility, since on the rare occasions when he pursues his former hobby, acting—as in 1992's *Hoffa*—he can't hold an audience's interest.

Jack turned to old friends to help him find his next *Cuckoo's Nest*. Mike Nichols asked him to reteam in *Primary Colors* (1998), but Jack's price was too high. He flirted with Jim Harrison over turning the author's novella *Julip* into a movie. Harry Gittes developed a Universal project for him called *American Caesar*. John Henry

Shaner wrote a sequel to *Goin' South*. Fred Roos wanted him to be an Ohio State football coach in a comedy called *Him & Her*. And Clint Eastwood angled for Jack to reprise a Garrett Breedlove character in *Space Cowboys* (2000). "I like working with actors who don't have anything to prove," said Eastwood.

Jack said no to all of them and still had no follow-up to *As Good as It Gets* when he presented the 1998 Best Picture Oscar to Miramax for *Shakespeare in Love* (1998). By summer, he was back in the news but not because he'd finally decided on his next picture. At sixty-two, he'd overdosed on estrogen again. This time, he nearly made a left turn into eternity.

Jack vacationed over the July 4 weekend at Martha's Vineyard but rendezvoused upon his return with the actress Lara Flynn Boyle over *salsa y cerveza* at El Cholo in downtown L.A.

Pale and freckled, with brows perfectly plucked above her indigo eyes and a pout always at the ready, Boyle's given name was Sally, like her mother's, according to court filings. But the diminutive (five-foot-three), anorexic (96 to 105 pounds, depending on her most recent meal) star of ABC-TV's hit series *The Practice*[23] maintained that she'd been named after the hapless Russian beauty portrayed by Julie Christie in *Dr. Zhivago* (1964). Growing up poor, pretty, and shy and the only child of a Chicago stage mother, Lara Flynn got her first taste of film when she was sixteen. One of Jack's least favorite movies, *Ferris Bueller's Day Off* (1986), was shooting on location, and although none of Lara made it into the finished film, she got some screen time and was hooked on Hollywood.

The Boyles moved to L.A. immediately after Lara finished school, and her mother began carting her to auditions. By 1990, when Lara Flynn first tweaked the popular imagination as one of the regulars in David Lynch's surreal ABC-TV series *Twin Peaks*, she was already a veteran of nearly a dozen movies.

Nine years later, when she met Jack in the men's room at a Hollywood party, she was a bona fide star. "He was sitting there having a cigarette," she recalled. "I went in and talked to him. You certainly don't run out of things to talk about with him."

At twenty-nine, the raven-haired actress was thirty-three years Jack's junior but every bit his contrarian match. "Hey, I'm an actress, and I have a Napoleon complex," she said.

When it came to truck-stop language and outrageous behavior, Lara Flynn smoked, drank and dueled Jack to a draw. They began secretly dating. Beneath the tailored, lawyerly exterior of her TV character, she concealed a pair of tattoos: a Celtic cross on her ankle and a shamrock on her pelvis. She still lived with her mother (also her manager) and renounced her father, who'd left them when she was six years old. While not literally true, Lara Flynn liked to say that she and Jack had in common the fact that they were both bastards abandoned early by their fathers. The soundstage served both of them as a substitute for psychotherapy. "Actors live in a world where there are no consequences," she told US magazine. "You don't ever have to grow up. It's a great gig."

At around the same time that Lara Flynn hooked up with Jack, Rebecca reportedly began dating Al Corley, a former regular on the TV show Dynasty. These casual betrayals, which seem to inhabit Hollywood like herpes, might have gone as unnoticed and unremarked as a thousand other trysts that had come before, if only Jack had been paying closer attention to the road on the ride home from El Cholo.

At the dimly lit Mulholland turnoff on Coldwater Canyon, Jack turned his new black $120,000 Mercedes directly into the path of a speeding BMW. The impact totaled both cars and sent the bumper of the Mercedes flying five hundred feet. Miraculously, no one was seriously hurt.

Attila Henry Hegedus, the twenty-three-year-old uninsured driver of the BMW, recalled a panicky woman emerging from the Mercedes shortly after the crash. "I can't stay here. I can't be seen with you," she hollered at the driver as she ran off from the scene.

When the LAPD showed up, Hegedus was questioned and given a sobriety test, which he passed, but he recalled Jack being handled with kid gloves. "He didn't even apologize to us," Hegedus told the London Daily Mirror. "He just sat in his car looking ahead. When the police arrived, they quickly put him in a car. It's outrageous that just because he is a movie star, he gets preferential treatment from cops. I had to talk to officers while he was whisked away." An LAPD spokeswoman, Charlotte Broughton, explained later, "He lives a few blocks away, that's all. That's just a courtesy they offered him."

Police said that neither driver was legally drunk and laid the blame for the accident on both of them: Hegedus for excessive speed and Jack for an unsafe left turn. Jack cut his right hand seriously enough to see a doctor, and Hegedus later claimed medical and wage losses of $38,887, but the lawsuit he filed was dismissed.[24]

While at first ducking her role as the runaway passenger, Lara Flynn fessed up when she saw the publicity possibilities. She threw over the *Just Shoot Me* star David Spade and moved into Jack's Mulholland sanctuary, characterizing the actor as "the most well-read man in the world." Over the next year, she became Jack's arm candy at everything from awards shows and film festivals to tennis tournaments and Lakers games. "He's the chief, right?" she asked. "What else is there to say? It's not bad sleeping with Einstein."

Jack gave Lara Flynn a $50,000 set of designer earrings and put a framed photo of her in the bathroom where he'd once kept Anjelica's. At year's end, he took her with him to the New Millennium party at the Clinton White House, but unlike his other mistresses[25] and even his own children, whom he'd repeatedly warned never to speak to the press, Lara Flynn would not shut up. "I'm not a home wrecker," she said. "I'm not dating married men. I'm not a glutton for punishment. I was raised to believe that if you want something, don't ever bank on a man getting it for you. Do not rely on him to put a roof over your head, a car in your garage, or to give you happiness. Rely on him for intimacy, and that's all I do."

While never claiming to date Jack exclusively, Lara Flynn took full advantage of his limelight. In August 2000, they vacationed together in St. Tropez, where Jack had once spurned paparazzi by dropping his drawers and mooning them. No more. Despite gossip that Lara Flynn had been seeing Bruce Willis on the side, Jack demonstrated a wisdom that comes only with experience by refusing to answer questions or show his ass to reporters.

In September 2000, Lara Flynn moved out of Jack's place, but the Jack-Lara breakup was neither traumatic nor permanent. Much to the dismay of Jack's cronies, who saw her as an interloper in their "guys only" basketball and beer klatches, Jack and Lara Flynn remained on-again, off-again. The Jack Pack might refer to her as "the Witch," but she shrugged them off, just as she did the media. "The whole country has a love affair with Jack," she said. "Why can't I?"

While Lara Flynn made no secret of her boyfriends, Jack took his relationship with her seriously enough to ask her to accompany him on a trip down memory lane. On November 30, the *Asbury Park Press* reported:

Actor Jack Nicholson paid a surprise visit to his alma mater, Manasquan High School, last week, and now the school is hoping for an encore—a guest appearance at a ceremony naming the auditorium after the Hollywood star. Nicholson, Class of 1954, arrived unexpectedly Nov. 21 accompanied by his current girlfriend, actress Lara Flynn Boyle, ostensibly to show her where his show-business career got its start.

Manasquan High did rename its auditorium the Jack Nicholson Theatre and hung his black-and-white portrait above its entrance, but not with Jack present. There was no movie to promote or industry honor to be bestowed, and thus nothing to be gained by submitting to a gaggle of Asbury autograph hounds.

Lara Flynn's publicist might trumpet the visit and wring the last bit of Page Six notoriety out of the hometown hero's triumphant return, but whenever Jack visited on his own, he preferred to go incognito.

After serving Jack for nearly thirty years, the publicist Paul Wasserman understood the fungible line that clients drew between public relations and personal privacy. In addition to Dylan and the Rolling Stones, Jack had protected his image under Wasserman's watchful eye since his BBS days, and "Wasso" remained one of Jack's oldest and most trusted advisers. Those within Jack's tight inner circle seldom left except over ill health, and even then Jack stood by them. When a brain tumor forced his personal assistant Annie Marshall to retire, Jack took care of her. When Sandy Bresler had a sextuple bypass, it didn't end his forty-year tenure as Jack's agent.

Loyalty was everything, and that extended to publicity. Whenever a reporter had a Jack question, he or she had no choice but to call Wasso. Long ago, Wasso had stopped putting out press releases. His job involved killing rumors, downplaying or making a joke of gaffes such as Jack's golf rage incident, or simply issuing a blanket "no comment." Like Bresler, the attorneys Abe Somer and Ken Kleinberg, and the business manager Bob Colbert,[26] Wasso was a permanent cog in the Jack star machinery.

While rising to the very pinnacle of the Hollywood publicity game, however, Wasso had acquired the same addictions that often threatened his clients. To feed them, he began to trade on Jack's name as early as 1990. By the time his frauds caught up with him in the

summer of 1999, Wasso had created the very public relations nightmare he'd been paid so well for so long to spin beyond the public's
imagination.

The disaster was called Neptune Investment Inc.—a quiet insiders' hedge fund created after Jack's huge *Batman* payday, or so
Wasserman told his marks. Here was an opportunity for Wasso's
business acquaintances to discreetly attach themselves to Jack. It was
a classic Ponzi scheme, but the magic of Jack's name allowed Wasserman to string "investors" along for years. When one demanded his
money, Wasso would pay him with another's investment, and if there
wasn't enough to cover it, he'd scold the person for his impatience. As
Wasso wrote to one Neptune investor: "I didn't realize that you had
nothing on paper that your investment for $25,000 in *Hoffa* and *Man
Trouble* rolled over to *A Few Good Men*. As you know, *A Few Good
Men* made money. How much is the issue to be agreed on. But whatever that amount is . . . interest will be tacked on to the amount."

Jack was equally ripe for the plucking in the art world. His collection now numbered more than six hundred paintings and spilled over
to Aspen, where he displayed many of his most treasured Western
pieces. *ARTnews* magazine recognized Jack as a leading U.S. collector. His broker, the Manhattan art dealer Tod Volpe, took much of the
credit.

Their symbiosis went back a decade, when Volpe used Jack to land
other Hollywood clients and Jack relied on Volpe's connections within
the rarefied New York art and auction house circles to find him the
best deals on quality work. When Volpe came across a rare original of
the art deco illustrator Maxwell Parrish's *Chef with Lobsters* for a
mere $75,000, Jack gave him the go-ahead to buy it. Jack issued the
same standing order on any deals Volpe could find on the Scottish
artist Jack Vettriano.

It wasn't until Volpe got twenty-eight months in prison for
swindling celebrity clients that the truth came out. He had never
delivered *Chef with Lobsters* or the Vettrianos. In all, Volpe had
defrauded Jack to the tune of $224,000. But once Volpe did his time,
he wrote a book-length apology detailing his misdeeds and offering a
mea culpa. "Lying to myself, I blindly walked a path of illusion, wor-
shipping the false idols of celebrity, fame, and material possessions,"
he said.

But whatever lessons Volpe learned, his accusers had not. Among the first questions the FBI leveled at him was, "Tell me . . . what is Nicholson *really* like?"

When Wasso was arrested, he learned that friends will desert you. Jack refused to comment on the case or come to his defense. Like Volpe, Wasso served a short sentence and had to pay restitution, but unlike Volpe, he didn't write a book. "What am I going to do?" Wasso asked *Los Angeles Magazine*'s Amy Wallace during a jailhouse interview in 2000. "Tell interesting stories about clients? That doesn't seem right. You see how moral I am?"

During the winter of 1999, Sean Penn finally found enough backing to direct his third film, and his second starring Jack, but it wasn't Faulkner's *As I Lay Dying*.

Based on an existential murder mystery by the Swiss novelist Friedrich Dürrenmatt, *The Pledge* (2001) turned the typical crime drama on its head. What begins as a noble pursuit of evil twists somewhere in the third act into a study of the corrosive effect of ends justifying means.

Shot on location, mostly in British Columbia to take advantage of Canadian tax breaks, *The Pledge* focused on Jerry Black, a retiring Reno cop played by Jack, whose last case involves the murder of a young blond girl at the hands of an elusive predator known as "the Wizard." While the sensational and unsolved 1996 murder of Jon Benét Ramsey resonated throughout *The Pledge*, Jack's personal touchstone was his own beautiful blond child, whom he'd guarded against kidnapping but knew he might not always be able to protect. It is no coincidence in *The Pledge* that Jerry Black's fishing boat is named *Sweet Lorraine* after Jack's daughter.

The Pledge is a promise Jerry Black makes to the murdered child's grieving mother (Patricia Clarkson) at the beginning of the film: the retiring cop will not rest until he's brought the Wizard to justice. Long after fellow officers are convinced they have the killer—a self-confessed mental case (Benicio Del Toro)—the now-retired Jerry Black is convinced that the Wizard still lurks, biding his time, waiting to strike again. As Jerry Black, Jack says as much to another cop, played by Sam Shepherd. "I'm very proud of the last line in that scene where [Jerry Black] says, 'I made a promise, Eric. You're old enough to remember when that meant something,'" said Jack. He added, "That's me speaking out to my times, you know?"

As with *Mars Attacks!* Jack became the magnet for a stellar cast that included Vanessa Redgrave, Helen Mirren, Mickey Rourke, and Jack's old standby Harry Dean Stanton.[27] But Jack cut Sean Penn no breaks on his fee, as he had on *The Crossing Guard*. "Jack got his full price this time, and by the time we paid Jack, we didn't have a lot of money for the other actors," said the casting director Don Phillips. "Plus, they were going to have to fly into Vancouver. But you get to work with Sean Penn and do a scene one-on-one with Jack."

The newcomer Aaron Eckhardt (*Erin Brockovich*, *In the Company of Men*) said his biggest kick up to that point in his career was "waiting to shoot a scene for *The Pledge* and hearing Jack Nicholson go, 'Where's Aaaaa-ron?'" He also got his best career advice from Jack: "Make best friends with the editor."

Jettisoning his "Jack" persona, Jack grew a mustache and got a buzz cut for the role. He became all but invisible to the locals, driving himself to and from locations in the Canadian outback.[28] "It was frightening, those huge lumber trucks that you see throughout the picture—and rain, and night, and curling mountainous roads," he recalled. "I mean, Canada is very much wilder than I thought once you get up north there."

As with *The Indian Runner* and *The Crossing Guard*, Penn had to go outside the studio mainstream to finance *The Pledge*. Though Warner Bros. signed on as distributor, the budget came from Franchise Pictures, the latest in a growing number of independents that bankrolled movies on the strength of star names.

The founder, Elie Samaha, a Lebanese wheeler-dealer who had moved up fast from Studio 54 bouncer to Beverly Hills dry-cleaning mogul to Hollywood producer, launched Franchise in 1999 after four years of successfully making TV and straight-to-video features. Samaha's philosophy was simple: sign the star and the money will follow, usually from Europeans who care more about a Sly Stallone or a Bruce Willis than they do about story or character. In the cases where stars include a good script and their own professional entourage, the Franchise strategy worked well enough. Bruce Willis had a hit with *The Whole Nine Yards* (2000).

But when the star alone was the deal, the failures could be spectacular. *Get Carter* (2000), Stallone's Franchise debut, cost the company $40 million, but the magic of the Stallone name brought in only $14 million at the box office.[29] Strictly on the strength of John

Travolta's name, Franchise Pictures also underwrote *Battlefield Earth* (2000), which cost $73 million, took in $21 million at the box office, and supplanted *Plan 9 from Outer Space* as the worst motion picture ever made.

With *The Pledge*, Franchise Pictures got a bargain. While the subject matter was grim and the ending too ambiguous for most U.S. audiences, the script and its characters were expertly drawn and the director so dedicated that he went into his own pocket to subsidize his budget. "I go broke all the time," said Penn. "I can't do what I've been doing. I keep doing projects and not getting paid for them."

At a cost of $45 million, *The Pledge* premiered in L.A. the second week of January and went on to earn $19.7 million. And while deemed a flop, *The Pledge* became a darling of the critics. "The gloomy things *The Pledge* has to say about manhood are antithetical to the heroic rites of Hollywood action-adventure films and professional sports through which American mass culture channels and idealizes male violence," wrote the *New York Times*'s Stephen Holden.

Roger Ebert gave Jack's performance a thumbs-up as his best in years, and the *London Guardian* called *The Pledge* "brilliantly accomplished." But even as *Variety*'s Todd McCarthy praised the acting, Sean Penn's directing and Jerzy Kromolowski's script, he correctly predicted that most of Jack's Joker fans would pass on Jerry Black. The *Village Voice*'s Michael Atkinson summed up *The Pledge* malaise by calling the film "an alienated fable of justice and luck, personified by Jack in the twilight of his iconicity, babbling to himself at the crossroads of nowhere."

23

THE WORLD CHANGED THE YEAR *THE PLEDGE* PREMIERED, and so did Jack. A month after the nation's September 11, 2001, nightmare, Jack made the pilgrimage to ground zero during a break in the World Series and joined a celebrity phone bank for a telethon that raised $150 million for the survivors. In the years ahead, the tragedy inspired Jack's switch from bleak drama to comedy. Jack needed a chuckle. So did his countrymen.

After years of developing projects that Jack rejected, Harry Gittes hit on a comic winner in *About Schmidt* (2002). For the first time since *Goin' South*, the producer who'd been comfortably closeted on the Sony lot for a decade on the strength of his friendship with Jack finally found an actual Nicholson project by matching the forty-one-year-old director Alexander Payne with the world's best-known movie star.

At sixty-five, Jack "paved the way for how older people should be picking their roles," wrote *Empire* magazine's Colin Kennedy.[1] "Now Harrison Ford and Robert DeNiro are starting to do indie stuff as well. I think Alexander Payne is certainly the kind of director he should be working with. You can add him to a list—Spike Jonze, David O. Russell, Steven Soderbergh—of people who are doing the kind of interesting stuff that was going on in the '70s."[2]

Based on Louis Begley's novel about the transgenerational troubles of a retired New York lawyer, *About Schmidt* owed much of its plot to *The Coward*, Alexander Payne's own unproduced comedy on the same subject. Premised on a man enduring his retirement, Payne's Schmidt is an Omaha[3] insurance adjuster, although, just like Begley's lawyer, he is also a widower and a father to a contrary daughter. Jack, who'd weighed retiring "since before *The Two Jakes* was written," bought into the story instantly.

Payne's *The Coward* found laughs in a single ironic story line. "Wouldn't it be funny," he asked, "if there were a guy, and he were sixty-six and he really fucked up all of his decisions and now he's paying for it?"

Jack declared *About Schmidt* "a dark comedy—and that's what I am. It's like a Hal Ashby road movie."[4]

Newly widowed and retired, Warren Schmidt cruises Middle America in a thirty-five-foot Winnebago, searching for the life he lost while in the insurance business.[5] Schmidt was "the man I might have become if I wasn't lucky enough to wind up in show business," observed Jack.

Distraught over his daughter's impending marriage to a doofus water-bed salesman, Schmidt finds his only emotional satisfaction in a one-sided running correspondence with Ndugu, a six-year-old Tanzanian pen pal he's adopted through a late-night TV pitch for an African children's charity.

"You see that somehow, whether he's deluded or not, there's a center to this man, there's something left," said Jack. "I don't think the film says what will be the result of that, but I think the gradual taking away of the things that have supported him throughout his life gets him down to his basic essence."

To get into character, Jack questioned veteran actuaries on how to become part of the wallpaper. "One [thing] I remember is that they told me an actuary looks down at his own feet when he's talking to you and he's embarrassed," said Jack. "The other is you ask an actuary what time it is, and he tells you how to build a clock."

During production, Jack couldn't bear to look at a mirror. In the finished film, he cringed at the dumpy old man on the screen. The actress June Squibb, who played his wife, was Jack's age, but looked even older. "Who is this old woman who lives in my house?" Schmidt grouses at one point.

And yet, as he discovers in love letters he stumbles upon shortly after her death, it was his wife who'd been carrying on a torrid affair while her cuckold of a husband trudged to the office each day for forty years.

For the first time in his long leading-man career, Jack didn't get the girl. The one time Schmidt makes a pass at a younger woman, he hightails it out of the RV park where he's decamped, just ahead of the outraged woman's husband. In a celebrated hot-tub scene, Jack gets naked with Kathy Bates, the mother of Schmidt's future son-in-law, but the match-up of the substantial actress and the world's oldest "skunk" hunter was played strictly for smirks.[6] Ten years Jack's junior, Bates bravely demonstrated that American women bulk up just as American men do, regardless of the thin fictions advanced by both Hollywood and *Vogue* magazine. "Jack was a real gentleman," said Bates. "He never let his eyes stray from mine as I was getting in and when it was all over, he said, 'Beautiful work, honey.'"

Jack praised Payne for giving him the best single-line direction he'd received from a director since Roger Corman. "Now Jack," said Payne, "you're going to be playing a small man in this movie." The few instances when Payne asked him to play Schmidt bigger, Jack hesitated "because he was so much in the vibe of this small man with very suppressed and repressed emotions," said Payne.

Jack didn't cripple the $32 million budget by taking his usual $15 million fee. Instead, he loaned his name to the production for a piece of the back end, putting his faith in Payne's proven skill at preserving irony without plunging into slapstick.

The comedy that put Payne on the Hollywood map was *Election* (1999), a hilarious case study of high school politics at its Machiavellian worst, starring the twenty-three-year-old Reese Witherspoon as a perky, precocious sociopath. Rising quickly from his Sundance roots, Payne had positioned himself in the Quentin Tarantino mold as one of the new "backlot rebels."[7]

But with apt irony, it was Jack who'd first given the young director a leg up in Hollywood. Although he'd grown up in Omaha, Payne earned degrees at Stanford in the 1980s before moving south to UCLA's School of Theater, Film, and TV. In 1988, he was the first recipient of the newly endowed Jack Nicholson Distinguished Student Director Award. Since then, more than two hundred students have gone on to benefit from Jack's philanthropy. "I didn't dream I'd ever get a job out of it," said Payne.

Four years after Bill Clinton lauded Bob Dylan as a Kennedy Center Honoree, George W. Bush similarly affirmed Jack's legendary status. Along with Julie Andrews, Van Cliburn, Quincy Jones, and Luciano Pavarotti, the president feted Jack in 2001 as "one of the true greats of this or any other generation of actors. America cannot resist the mystery, the hint of menace, and, of course, that killer smile," said President Bush during the 23rd Kennedy Center Honors, an annual exalting of the nation's highest cultural achievers.

Back in 1997, Dylan had received similar treatment. As twin symbols of the sixties, Dylan and Jack had survived sex, drugs, and rock 'n' roll to perform another day. The same year that Jack had bounced back with *As Good as It Gets*, Dylan released *Time Out of Mind*. Like Jack's Oscar-winning fifty-third movie role as Melvin Udall, Dylan's forty-fourth album marked both a creative resurgence for the poet laureate of the sixties and his first hit record in years. "Not Dark Yet," the standout track on the album, sounded a new anthem for his and Jack's generation, defying age this time instead of an intolerant government, an immoral war, or an amorphous Establishment, of which both he and Jack had unwittingly become a part.

The two antiheros also shared enormous wealth and celebrity schizophrenia well beyond middle age. Their admiring public knew precious little about their innermost secrets, their personal insecurities, their health, their family lives, and their day-to-day well-being, and that was just how they liked it.

Dylan still toured a third of each year, while Jack stayed in touch with fans through his movies and an occasional magazine interview, but neither star seemed interested in revealing much, nor were they about to leave the stage. "Retirement is what happens to other, frailer talents," wrote Danny Leigh for the British film journal *Sight and Sound*. Loved by most and criticized by few, Jack had become "Hollywood's Pan, living the very highest of lives in a secluded house up on Mulholland Drive"—an unassailable, if isolated and rather lonely, idol.

"Nature forces you to be a better person," observed Jack, even as nature caught up with him. He didn't need Warren Schmidt's actuarial tables to remind him of his own mortality. Don Devlin, *Eastwick*'s producer and one of Jack's oldest amigos, died from lung cancer in 2000. Stanley Kubrick's heart gave out the previous year. A year earlier, Frank Sinatra—Jack's oldest New Jersey role model—died at eighty-two. A year hence, Jeff Corey—his oldest acting coach—would be gone at eighty-eight.

All four men passed away with wives at their sides, but it looked more and more as if Jack wouldn't. Rebecca Broussard married in 2001, and Lara Flynn Boyle flitted in and out of his life, behaving more like a mordant sidekick than a stand-by-your-man sweetheart. And although Jack had the occasional women up for the evening, none could be termed serious.

"I'm a different guy here in my sixties," Jack told *Newsweek*. "I don't have the same libido. It used to be that I didn't think I could go to sleep if I wasn't involved in some kind of amorous contact or another. Well, I spend a lot of time sleeping alone these days. That's different. And very liberating. It wasn't until the last few years that I became completely comfortable with it."

Friends said that Jack's happiest years were the early ones with Rebecca.[8] While Lara Flynn had a certain grace, she'd never been able to permanently dispel Jack's melancholy.

Though not so comforting as the spouse he never found, Jack's enduring star legacy gave him some satisfaction. His recycled films ricocheted across the digital universe. The same month the tabloids reported that Lara Flynn had left him once more, this time for the soap star Eric Dane, TBS trumpeted the broadcast premiere of *As Good as It Gets*, drawing the largest audience—5.4 million households—in cable history. "There are stars who have made bigger pictures, but there's no one who is as known around the world as he is, who still connects with teenagers," said his old pal Robert Evans. "Every kid knows him. Jack stands alone. He's an original. He's not playing anybody. That's who he is."

Cable had finally matured in the new century, joining the Internet and the satellite dish in obliterating a half-century of network domination before taking on the studios themselves. For the first time in Jack's long cold war against the Demon Tube, even he had to relent. He subscribed to HBO and locked into TiVo for those Lakers games that he couldn't get to in person.[9] Once Jack became addicted, he admitted to becoming so fascinated by such traditional network fare as *C.S.I.*, *Without a Trace*, and *Monk* that he felt compelled to record them, too.

Meanwhile, the industry he so loved lumbered along like a dinosaur. The studios adapted glacially to the lightning shifts in digital technology. Muscle-bound moguls who'd controlled movies for most of Jack's career lost their grip. But in this brave new world Jack remained a fixture, and the profiteering multinationals like News Corporation, Sony, Vivendi, and Viacom that now ran Hollywood still vied for his services. In a fast-changing multimedia environment, stars were still the only constant.

With box office headed in the same direction as the buggy whip, showbiz economics were forced to retrench, then retrench again. None of the studios' efforts kept pace with the dot-com revolution. Amid the seismic shifts in media choices, the only logical hope of bringing audiences back to the theaters seemed to be quality filmmaking and original storytelling, and while independent filmmakers like Sean Penn[10] or the Sundance Kids tried to follow that model, Hollywood still opted for star power.

Jack obliged with *Anger Management* in 2003.

"I've always wanted to do a Martin and Lewis film or a Hope and Crosby picture, and I thought this was as close as I was going to get," said Jack.

A month before production began in February 2002, Jack got cold feet, but the *Anger Management* director Peter Segal so desperately wanted Jack's name above the title that he later said he "basically customized the part for him."

As Dr. Buddy Rydell, Jack got free rein to play "Jack," down to the detail of smashing a car window in a fit of rage. The car was a Lexus and the weapon a bat instead of a golf club, but the reference to Jack's own explosive behavior from eight years earlier was plainly the sendup. From the "Here's Johnny!" menace to the Joker's fey-but-deadly mannerisms, the psychiatrist he portrays in *Anger Management* was so obvious a parody of the Jack persona that he might just as well have been billed as Dr. Nicholson.

With scraggly beard and jaunty beret, his trademark shades glinting along with his bleached teeth, Jack got to make his menacing presence felt among a whole new generation; as *the* Hollywood icon, he could just as easily have graced the cover of *GQ* or the *AARP* magazine. His nails buffed and manicured, clothes always stylish and neatly tailored, he'd been quietly setting the fashion pace for decades, and he demonstrated that he still had panache, from his two-toned shoes to his Pellegrino water (though lately he admitted to having acquired a taste for Earl Grey tea).

Anger Management's thin comic premise—that a nebbish businessman (Adam Sandler) framed in an air-rage incident winds up with a psychotic shrink (Jack) as his court-appointed therapist—was made even thinner by the talent mismatch. Sandler was no Nicholson, and it showed in every frame, even during their "I Feel Pretty" duet from *West Side Story*. While the film is predictably watchable and occasionally amusing, both stars performed by rote, and Jack clearly had the upper hand.

Of his costar Sandler, who reportedly took $25 million of the $75 million production budget, Jack said, "He's real smart and a man of his word." And while the ex–*Saturday Night Live* comedian shared top billing, Jack put himself first, on and off the set. He once stood up production for hours so he could go to a Lakers game. Before shooting began, he took his costar with him courtside a few times to get a taste of Shaquille and Kobe up close, and he spoke graciously about the opportunity that Sandler afforded him by exposing him to *Anger Management*'s younger audience. Later that year, Jack was one of the few celebrities Sandler invited to his super-secret Malibu wedding.

Anger Management wrapped before *About Schmidt* premiered at Cannes. Jack joined Alexander Payne to promote the film well ahead of its planned Christmastime release in the United States, but upon arrival in the French resort, Jack holed up in his hotel instead of meeting the press. He watched local TV news to study how critics dealt with festival participants before venturing out on the Promenade de la Croisette himself to answer questions. "He's smart about being smart," said Harry Gittes. "When Jack's turn came, he was so prepared. He gave a virtuoso performance of an actor giving a press conference."

"The character was miserable to inhabit," Jack confided to the rapt gaggle of reporters. "I thought I would never return to my normal self." Jack characterized Warren Schmidt as "a sedentary American with a bad diet."

But come December, when *About Schmidt* finally rolled out on six screens in New York and L.A. in limited release in order to qualify for the Oscars, Warren Schmidt hit a national nerve. Jack's star, tarnished by the poor box office of *The Pledge*, glittered anew. *About Schmidt* went on to earn $63.7 million, as well as Oscar nominations for both Jack and Kathy Bates.[11]

And proving that synergy and timing are everything in the big leagues, Jack's Oscar heat spilled over onto the April premiere of *Anger Management*. "The concept is inspired. The execution is lame," wrote Roger Ebert. "*Anger Management*, a film that might have been one of Adam Sandler's best, becomes one of Jack Nicholson's worst."

Regardless of the ruthless reviews, *Anger Management*'s marketing was as good as it gets. The saturation onslaught began with a thirty-second spot during the Super Bowl XXII telecast.[12] Before critics could prevail or word-of-mouth leak out, the thin comedy had already been released on more than 3,551 screens and took in $44.5 million during its opening weekend—the largest first-week gross either Jack or Sandler had ever generated. It didn't matter that by the second week, audience numbers began to tumble. By June, *Anger Management* had grossed more than $133 million and was well on its way to earning $178 million worldwide.

By 2003, the Lakers had settled into their new home at the downtown Staples Center. Outfitted with luxury skyboxes that catered gourmet tacos and nonfat decaf lattes while affording panoramic views of the action in the sort of regal privacy to which Jack had become accustomed, the arena was just a basketball court to Jack. He preferred $1,800-a-game floor seats where he could reach out and slap Kobe on the ass if he so chose.[13]

Jack was a loyal Yankees fan, and he kept up with the Rams and the Raiders before they moved out of L.A., but his obsession had always been the Los Angeles Lakers. Since the sixties, when he had to sit up in the cheap seats at the L.A. Sports Arena, Jack had put his faith in the hometown team.

In the sound-bite culture, when little time was given over for reflection, basketball became Jack's ritual of hope. The Lakers won some, they lost some, but there would always be another game, another season, and one more chance to triumph. The downside of his loyalty was that people knew where to find him whenever the Lakers played a home game. Over the years, he'd been assailed by those seeking as minor a favor as an autograph or as outrageous a demand as a roll in the hay.

Everyone wanted a piece of him, and Jack had stopped giving years earlier, regardless of who did the asking. He called himself the Dodger, "because I've learned how to slip away from the party and the photographers." When Bob Costas approached him during a Bulls game and asked for a quick courtside interview, Jack responded to Costas's rolling cameras, "No fucking way."

More than once he sprang cursing from his seat during a TNT broadcast. In lieu of bleeping Jack's language, the cable channel cut to the "Here's Johnny!" clip from *The Shining*. The basketball court remained a safe place for Jack to flip out in public. He told the *London Sunday Times* that he still blew up "for absolutely no reason," despite decades of psychotherapy. "Every once in a while, I just have to let it out," he said. "I always regret it later. . . . Not regret it, because when I let go, there is no way out for me. But I find myself thinking a couple of hours later: 'Could I have solved that without blowing up?' It seems ridiculous that, after all these years, I have no other way."

According to Jack, *Something's Gotta Give* (2003) was once going to be called *Love Me or Leave Me*, which would have been a far better single-line plot summary. In November 2002, he signed with Columbia and the director Nancy Meyers to star with Diane Keaton in the as-yet untitled romantic comedy in which Keaton played a poised, middle-aged playwright torn between a doting younger physician (Keanu Reeves) and an aloof, aging music mogul who, like Jack, lusts after much younger women.

Indeed, the little ditty about Jack and Diane opened with Jack dazzling her thirty-year-old daughter (Amanda Peet) before switching attention in mid-seduction to a more age-appropriate Keaton. Ultimately, Jack must decide whether to commit to Keaton or continue chasing silicone and thong underwear for the remainder of what appears to be a shortened life. Jack makes several comic visits to the E.R., although his coronary alarms turn out to be overblown. Yet they still have the effect of a wakeup call. "He has a heart attack. It changes him. People tend to forget the story," said Jack. "Brushes with mortality straighten a man up."

At the beginning, and for the benefit of those still enamored of the Jack myth, he oozed Hollywood hubris down to his gold chains and hot car. Comparing himself to the leonine Harry Sanborn, his *Something's Gotta Give* character, Jack poked his tongue in his cheek and told a reporter, "We're rich. We're funny. Women are crazy about us. Every age. All over the world. We don't care. We're happy."

But in a far more sober interview with *People* magazine, he reflected on the changes that time had enforced on his real-life appetites. "A younger woman is not necessarily for me," he said. "I'm pretty old, so almost everyone is younger. I won't pretend that I haven't been a rogue most of my life, because I have and would still be if I had the energy. I sat in a restaurant recently, and I could've knocked off two thousand of them—every age, and their mothers, too. Right now, though, I just can't do the dance. And if I bother, they've got to be a good dancer."

Though they'd seldom seen each other since *Reds*, Jack still called Diane "Special K" and rekindled their own dance to the degree that they'd spark some chemistry onscreen. Whether invented to sell tickets or spawned in the f-stops of fanzines, the real-life romance was only imagined, according to Keaton, who'd adopted two children in middle age but never married. "But, I tell you, the best way to get to know someone is to spend a week or two with them in bed," she added.

On the flashes of nudity she and Jack had to deliver, Keaton spoke of her full frontal in the jargon of an actress prepared to bare all for her art. "At this point, does it really matter?" asked the fifty-seven-year-old actress. Jack summed up his own position with: "I'm very proud of my ass."[14]

While they were double billed above the title, Keaton dominated *Something's Gotta Give*. Unlike *Anger Management*, where Jack out-mugged his costar Adam Sandler in every scene, Keaton's return to the mixed emotional messages of her Oscar-winning role as Annie Hall transformed Harry Sanborn into a lovesick sap, especially near the film's climax. Keaton provoked herself to comic tears every time she got near Jack, and her ambivalence very nearly made her decision to dump a vital young hunk like Reeves for an ancient lech like Jack believable. The secret of her sobs, she said, was listening to Macy Gray on the soundtrack album of *8 Mile* (2002). "The music was just so pounding, but sad," she said. "It would get me crying every time."

The closing scenes set in Paris gave Jack a chance to spend some time with Raymond and Lorraine along the Côte d'Azur, where he was still regarded with the same awe he'd inspired decades earlier. During the European premiere of *The Two Jakes* back in 1990, the French culture minister Jack Lang bestowed on him the Commandeur des Artes et Lettres and summed up Jack for the ages: "Your angular eyebrows, your ironic smile, your taste for exaggeration have etched out characters who are memorable, sometimes satanic."

During *Something's Gotta Give*, Diane Keaton may have stolen the show stateside, but Jack's star remained undimmed in Europe. When striking French actors interrupted a scene on a bridge over the river Seine, Commandeur Jack got the cameras rolling again by shouting in broken French to the strikers: "The struggle continues!" In deference to Jack, the picket line dispersed.

But the movie may well have been Jack's Gallic swan song. Over the closing credits, Jack warbled an English translation of the Edith Piaf standard "La Vie en Rose."[15] Somewhere beneath the nicotine gravel of his Pepé le Pew growl, Jack approximated the bittersweet longing of a strung-out romantic.

Defying Hollywood's conventional wisdom, *Something's Gotta Give* took on Tom Cruise in *The Last Samurai* (2003), an all-star cast (Nicole Kidman, Renée Zellweger, and Jude Law) in *Cold Mountain* (2003), and the third part of the blockbusting *Lord of the Rings* trilogy, *The Return of the King* (2003), during the 2003 Christmas season. Not only was the middle-aged love story a hit, it held over in multiplexes for weeks. When *Something's Gotta Give* topped the $100 million mark in mid-January, the director Nancy Meyers threw a celebration where Jack held court with admirers who tried to plumb the secret of his staying power.

Something's Gotta Give's success also made it a prime target of Hollywood's latest scourge. While still in theaters, a pirated DVD turned up on the Internet, setting off a renewed outcry from the MPAA for federal enforcement of copyright laws. Studios lost as much as $3 billion a year to bootleggers.

But what bothered Jack most in the post-9/11 world wasn't the death of Hollywood so much as death itself. "I mean, I get depressed like everybody," he said as he lit another cigarette during a *Rolling Stone* interview. "I have angst. I have anxiety. I worry about the world. Nobody was expecting the kind of fearful times that we live in. It's really out of the blue. It's like, 'My God, what the hell is happening?'"

In a laudatory 2004 *Esquire* cover story published in conjunction with the release of *Something's Gotta Give*, and subtitled "What I've Learned [from] the Master," Jack admitted to beseeching God about the apocalyptic state of world affairs. "I do pray," he said. "I pray to something . . . up there. I have a God sense. It's not religious so much as superstitious. It's part of being human, I guess."

He offered advice on parenting, social graces, golf, and, of course, sex. But politically, Jack exhibited a turn to the right. Describing his brand of liberalism as "the right to question without being called a heretic," he pledged support of George Bush and the occupation of Iraq. He also supported the administration's profiling of Arab Americans and the president's right to privacy.

In response to Jack's musings, Daniel Cochran of Emeryville, California, wrote to the *Esquire* editors the following month:

> I'm always a bit tickled when I see actors dispense advice and provide insight on the common human experience as if they are as fully connected as the rest of us. What they always seem to forget is that they've probably been wealthy for more than half their lives, live in an environment that is almost by definition totally focused on themselves, and spend most of their professional careers pretending to be someone else.

. . .

In February, Jack attended the Berlin Film Festival to promote *Something's Gotta Give*, and a reporter tracked him to dinner with the skating star Katarina Witt. Jack said that his three-hour meal with the thirty-nine-year-old Olympic gold medalist wasn't a date. "Dating just does not happen to be my scene at the moment," he said. "I am not into it. You know, I don't wanna queue up, I don't wanna get in line, I don't wanna hear the racket. I don't wanna say, no, I don't dance. There are just too many things. And I always believed that if you are not going to go out and contribute, don't go out.

"Of course, I miss the real thing. Of course, I get lonely. Not lonely the way I might have been when I was twenty-five and it would have filled me with angst. But I wish I had a partner. The success of this movie does not have the snap on it that it would if I was sharing it firsthand with someone. And so forth. All those things. But you know, I am lucky. I have a relatively rich life and a lotta friends."

Asked if his life had gone quickly, Jack didn't hesitate. "Honey, it's been like smoke through a keyhole."

On February 13, 2004, six days short of her seventieth birthday, Carole Eastman lost a lingering battle with pulmonary edema. During a private memorial luncheon that her niece Claire Cordary staged two months later at the Bel-Air Hotel, a formidable sampling of the surviving rebels who came of age with the fallen writer of *Five Easy Pieces* gathered to pay their respects: Warren Beatty, accompanied by Annette Bening; Ed Begley Jr.; David Geffen; Jerry Schatzberg; Faye Dunaway; Monte Hellman; John Herman Shaner; Joni Mitchell; Helena Kallianiotes; and, of course Jack, just back from Europe.

Resting mid-room on a simple easel, Carole's youthful black-and-white portrait advertised that she had once been a dark-haired beauty who graced the covers of *Vogue* and other glam magazines. Before she took up screenwriting, she'd been a dancer as well as a successful model, and she remained even now a fiercely independent and formidable presence in a room filled with celebrity. "This is the party she couldn't throw for herself," said her brother Charles.

Charles characterized his sister as the arch contrarian among her Hollywood peers, once holding her producer David Geffen hostage to the unfinished screenplay of *Man Trouble* for more than a decade. After dozens of blown deadlines, Geffen asked to see what he'd been subsidizing for so many years, and she told him, "You're not going to pressure me, are you?"

When she reluctantly handed him 247 pages, Geffen gasped that it was longer than *Gone with the Wind*. "Has Jack read it?" he asked.

"He'll read it when it's finished," she snapped.

"He'll be dead!" said Geffen.

When it was his turn to speak, the L.A. litterateur and public radio host Michael Silverblatt, who had come to know Carole in her later years, retraced her path of disillusion, distrust, and inevitable divorce from Hollywood following her *Five Easy Pieces* triumph. "She knew after *The Fortune* the world had changed," he said. "Literary movies were over." A devotee of the iconoclastic poet James Tate, Carole tried for poetry in her screenplays, "where it doesn't live comfortably anymore," Silverblatt lamented.

In Carole's lifetime, she bitterly and helplessly watched so-called auteurs conspire with the studios to subsume, spindle, and mutilate that which she'd put on the written page. After Mike Nichols decided to cut the first forty pages of *The Fortune*, she vowed never to let her work fall from her control again.

But when she bought *Man Trouble* back from Geffen and at Jack's insistence hired Bob Rafelson to direct, even Jack's star presence and Carole's role as a producer couldn't save it. The anxiety of a big budget, meddlesome studio oversight, and no time for retooling had combined with one of the worst marketing ploys in memory to doom *Man Trouble* before the film ever made it into theaters. A lobby poster featuring Ellen Barkin on all fours in a dog collar with Jack holding her leash raised protests from the National Organization for Women and helped to hasten the ruin of what remained of Carole's work. "The world does not know how to live up to the expectations of its outsiders," Silverblatt concluded.

There was irony in *Man Trouble*'s feminist backlash. Carole had led the storming of the chauvinist stronghold that belonged almost exclusively to male actors, writers, directors, and producers during the sixties. *Five Easy Pieces* gave her clout that she gladly wielded, but not as a ball-busting Amazon. "She was the biggest tiny woman I ever met," said Jack when it came his turn to speak. He followed with smartass aplomb: "One of the things you didn't know is she didn't like any of you."

After the laughter died down, Carole's oldest showbiz partner replaced the wisecracking with his earliest L.A. recollections, before *Easy Rider*, before *The Shooting*, even before Roger Corman, when

Jack had few friends beyond Jeff Corey's classes, and the Eastmans took him in. "I had never been invited into the home of any family in California before," he said.

The Eastmans were an oddball clan of upscale bohemians who lived in Palos Verdes, and Jack was an instant fit. While both Carole and Charles had their eye on Hollywood at the time, Jack had his eye on Carole. "The girl had moves," he said, shucking and jiving for his peers with the classic Jack smirk scrawled across his face. They were pals. They took shots at each other. He painted badly, while she wrote poetry. He remembered baiting her once and she came back with, "There's *nothing* too sacred for you to stomp on with your victim's boots."

Then, moments later in his remarks, Jack was fighting back tears. "She was as constant as the speed of light," he said.

Carole was afraid of elevators. She was a recluse and an animal rights activist. She had never married, but she rescued wounded birds and made a home for stray cats and dogs. Her brother intoned, "She'd looked in the elephant's eye and she had seen the cruelties we do each other. Death is a grim accomplishment. She did it majestically."

But it was Carole's writing that she was obsessed with all her life. Her slingshot imagery articulated character in just a few spare words: "cabbages with faces," "amputee meatloaf," "creeping foreskins." As it turned out, Carole was meant to be the writer all along, while Jack, the greatest success of their generation, was meant to be the interpreter of her words. As Geffen recalled during his eulogy for Carole, "It was always for you, Jack, every script."

In the years that followed *Man Trouble*, Carole continued to write, but Hollywood had moved on and her final efforts weren't even pitched to the assembly line that produced superheroes, dumb-guy comedies, inspirational sports stories, bland sequels, and blockbusting spectacles now demanded by Generations X, Y, and Z. She died with only thirty pages of her final screenplay written—a thriller about a woman lawyer who lives with a serial killer. Charles finished it for her, but it was too cerebral. No one in the new "New Hollywood" showed any interest.

Jack had moved on, too. He might recite Carole's poetry in private, but after *Man Trouble* his public face was that of the Joker. He could have made another movie with Carole, but he chose not to. Addressing the easel where her photo stared unblinking at the lunch crowd,

Jack spoke directly to Carole, recalling with regret an unrequited moment that had come and gone years before. "You remember when I went with Georgiana?" he told her. "You had asked me out."

There was genuine innocence in Jack's voice, predating all the dope and dames to come. He addressed Carole as if she were in the room, confessing to a lost opportunity she'd given him half a century earlier. His words cracked with the belated grief of teen romance, and not simply the Learish howls of an old man. "I would have gone out with you," he sobbed, shaking his head while he wiped at his nose and eyes.

And when he recovered, he recited a poem for her: an ode to an accelerated era, when birds die needlessly and heedlessly on the freeways of a mechanized, high-speed culture that has forgotten, somewhere in the midst of an interminable L.A. traffic jam, how to slow down, how to savor, and how to reflect on the roads not taken. "Look around. Perhaps it isn't too late to make a fool of yourself again" said Jack, recovering his stentorian self. "Perhaps it isn't too late to flap your arms and cry out, to give one more cracked rendition of your singular, aspirant song."

EPILOGUE

MARLON BRANDO DIED FOUR MONTHS AFTER CAROLE Eastman did. A couple of years earlier, Jack had told an interviewer, "I don't see him much lately. He plays classical music late at night, and if I'm out walking around in the moonlight, I hear it up there. He's the perfect neighbor." As an afterthought, Jack added, "When he goes, we'll all move up a place."

The greatest actor of his generation descended into dementia at the end, finally succumbing to pulmonary fibrosis at age eighty. Brando hadn't done a movie since *The Score* (2001). Plagued by diabetes, congestive heart failure, and a host of other ills, Don Corleone slipped quietly from the limelight.

During Brando's last years, he'd tucked inside himself like a snail, exhausted by the punishing excesses of the public's right to know. Comparing Brando to his celebrity neighbor, the novelist Daphne Merkin distinguished the two actors: "Unlike Nicholson, who appears always to be smirking in self-satisfaction behind his dark glasses, Brando seemed like a small boy chased by furies."

In his own Brando epitaph, the critic David Thomson saved his applause for Jack who, unlike his late neighbor, "has not given up on us yet. A very rich and rather lonely man, perhaps, Jack Nicholson cannot be fooled on the toughness of the world, and still he conjures up unexpected, worthwhile films—*The Pledge, About Schmidt, Something's Gotta Give*—and still he has that grin that goes all the way back to Gable and says that loving stars isn't crazy."

Jack, too, wrote his Brando appreciation. Sidestepping their long rivalry and Brando's bitterness toward him following the Drollet murder, Jack praised his onetime idol in *Rolling Stone*, as if Brando were an American Caesar. "Marlon Brando is one of the great men of the 20th and 21st centuries, and we lesser mortals are obligated to cut through the shit and proclaim it," he said, waxing on for another eighteen hundred words over Brando's unparalleled contributions to the culture.

But practical Jack now stood alone on the Mulholland mountaintop. He was the sole occupant of the Bad Boys' Xanadu. Another year would pass before the *Los Angeles Times* reported it, but Jack bought Brando's house for $6.1 million. After years of disrepair, it was a falling-down wreck. Jack vowed to plow it under and plant a flowerbed.

Just before Don Furcillo-Rose died, Donna Rose swabbed the inside of her father's mouth and saved it, hoping that Jack might someday submit to a DNA test to determine whether they shared the same father. Jack refused.

"Jack's movie *The Pledge* was amazing in coincidences," said Donna. Certain that magical realism laced Sean Penn's movie, she looked for signs of her father and noticed an eagle during one scene, flashing in the background over a computer screen-saver. "Everyone called dad 'Eagle,'" she said, adding, "Dad always joked he'd come back as a butterfly. This movie features butterflies, including one that lands directly on Jack's shoulder."

A former New Jersey radio broadcaster, Donna Rose set out to tell her father's story after his death. She found a coauthor in the journalist Linda Allen, and together they published *You Don't Know Jack: The Tale of a Father Once Removed* (Oakland, CA: Virtual Publishing Inc., 2001). After selling a handful of copies, the publisher went out of business, and Donna fell ill with cancer. She died in the autumn of 2005. "But when she was in the hospital, Jack finally called," recalled Linda Allen. "They talked for a long time and they cried and he told her that their parents' mistakes weren't their responsibility. They were both just kids. They had no power."

Cancer flushed out further testimony regarding the mystery of Jack's father that season. Pamela Hamernick, the sixty-two-year-old daughter of the late Eddie King, admitted just months before her own death that she and her family had kept their secret for more than half a century.

In the summer of 1936, twenty-five-year-old Eddie King had conceived a child with his underage dance partner just months before his arrest as an illegal alien. Transported to Ellis Island, the former Eddie Kirschfield faced deportation to his native Latvia. He'd already been branded an undesirable for sneaking into the country and eluding authorities for more than a decade. Any chance he might have had to remain in the United States would definitely have vanished if his and June Nicholson's secret became public.

In retrospect, and seen through the prism of the sexual revolution, the sins of a dance teacher and his hot young protégé seem almost quaint next to the shameless exhibitions of the twenty-first century. But at the time of Jack's birth, June and Eddie agreed on the lie and set a course that would survive seventy years of rumor. With the vocal support of hundreds of WCAP-AM's Saturday morning listeners, who signed petitions and called their congressmen to prevent the deportation of the amiable host of *Eddie King and His Radio Kiddies*, Eddie returned triumphant to the Jersey Shore six months after Jack's birth. He married, but not June. She still had stars in her eyes. She left Jack with Mud and hit the vaudeville circuit again. During their lifetimes, none of them spilled the beans. "We knew," said Eddie King Jr., Pamela Hamernick's younger brother, "but no one talked about it while my mother was alive."

In a series of phone interviews in 2006, King confirmed his sister's story. At the time of Jack's American Film Institute tribute twelve years earlier, Eddie Jr. had lived down the hall from Mrs. Lorraine Smith in a high-rise condo building that overlooked Neptune's Shark River. He and Lorraine "did a lot of soul searching," he recalled, and decided to keep the truth between themselves.

The aunt whom Jack had known most of his life as his older sister told Eddie that it was all true: Eddie's father and Jack's mother had once been lovers, and Jack was the result. Eddie King Jr., an Allenhurst, New Jersey, insurance broker, and Jack Nicholson, a god of Hollywood, were indeed half-brothers.

Eddie had seen nothing to be gained in advertising the fact. His mother was still living then and his father was only six years in the grave. Besides, such delicate matters weren't discussed in Neptune City. The world might have eroded to such an indiscreet degree that

Pamela Anderson and Paris Hilton could blow their boyfriends over the Internet with impunity, but Eddie and his neighbors along the Jersey Shore still subscribed to the bumper-sticker philosophy that harkened back to another time "when air was clean and sex was dirty."

Eddie King Jr. thought it best to let his father and June Nicholson Hawley rest in peace.

In the fall of 2004, Jack returned to Manasquan High for the fiftieth reunion of the Class of '54. Security was tight. No one outside of the reunion committee knew the favorite son was coming home. When Jack rolled up in his limo at the Riverview Pavilion just before dinner, he had his aunt Lorraine on his arm. As soon as he'd glad-handed his way through the crowd, the doors were locked from the inside. Inevitable giddy cell phone calls went out to relatives, but no crashers were allowed to turn an otherwise pleasant evening into a media event. "He looked just the same," said the varsity football hero Dave Bramhall. "Same goofy guy."

Jon Epaminondas sidled up and overheard a classmate regaling Jack over a memory that never happened. "'Remember the time we did such-and-such?'" mimicked Epaminondas. "The guy never even *knew* Jack in high school! People remember what they want to remember."

But most of them could be forgiven for basking in Jack's reflected glory. Many who showed up for the reunion had never left the Jersey Shore during their long lives. "After you haven't seen somebody for fifty years, you might recognize them, but you don't know them," said Miller "Punky" Preston. "But I saw Jack and I *knew* Jack! Other people might be strangers, but I *knew* Jack."

Cut from the Manasquan basketball squad the same year as Jack, Miller remained in his hometown and became a schoolteacher. But Manasquan's most famous graduate didn't judge Miller's parochialism. Jack treated him with the same cordiality that he tendered the rest of the class. They talked basketball, and Jack assured Miller that the Lakers were doomed to rebuild during the 2005 season. Only the return of Phil Jackson as head coach would resurrect the glory days of Shaq and Kobe.

As the night rolled on, Jack relaxed into his "Nick" persona. As a gift for everyone, he'd had a seven-CD box set created that featured a year-by-year selection of 1950s music—the end of the Big Bands and the beginning of rock and roll. For the cover, Jack drew a caricature of himself, complete with shades and his long-lost ducktail haircut.

At nine thirty that evening, Jack delivered his exit lines, excused himself, and took his eighty-five-year-old aunt home. His oldest acquaintances stayed on for hours, prattling over the return of the hometown hero.

In February 2005, Hunter S. Thompson put a shotgun to his head and pulled the trigger. In a note he left for his wife, Anita, he wrote, "No More Games. No More Bombs. No More Walking. No More Fun. No More Swimming. 67. That is 17 years past 50: 17 more than I needed or wanted. Boring. I am always bitchy. No Fun—for anybody. 67. You are getting Greedy. Act your old age. Relax—This won't hurt."

Jack, who was also sixty-seven, remembered Thompson as the Aspen neighbor who once made Jack's youngest daughter a gift of a rubber rat, caught in a trap. An attached card read:

Dear Lorraine,

This will be a very valuable reminder to you that men aren't always what they seem to be. Knowing this will save you a lot of time in your life.

You're welcome, Uncle Hunter

In his own requiem for the Father of Gonzo journalism, Jack recalled a gentle nut job whose years of correspondence with "Reasonable Jack" he someday hoped to publish, all proceeds to go to the Aspen School of Music. "His behavior was provocative," Jack wrote in *Rolling Stone*, "but it was less dangerous than we all felt because, after all, Hunter was an expert at provocation. Pretty much, he knew what he was doing."

In the spring of 2005, Jack joined Leonardo DiCaprio, Matt Damon, and Mark Wahlberg in Boston to film Martin Scorsese's *The Departed* (2006). All in their thirties, none of Jack's costars had been born before *Five Easy Pieces* was filmed. "This is a Darwinian business in a Darwinian world," said Jack, "and maybe I think I should keep doing it because I can."

When DiCaprio first asked Jack to talk to Scorsese about the role of the mob boss Frank Costello, Jack wasn't interested. *The Departed* was a "lay down script." "All you do is lay it down," explained Jack. "Any moron could play the part, and the movie would still be great."[1]

What Jack needed was a challenge. As the screenwriter William Monahan had written Costello, he was just another mob boss. "I was looking for a bad guy," Jack told Army Archerd. "I just did three comedies."

The *New York Daily News* reported that "Jack didn't feel there was enough Jack in his character," so he asked Scorsese if he could improvise. The director gave him the nod, and Jack created a party monster to rival the Joker, only more attuned to the gross-out standards of the present day. There would be nudity and drugs, to be sure, but also strap-on dildos, porn theatrics, and lots and lots of blood. "Jack suggested using a [prosthetic appendage]," reported one gossip column. "He also wanted to dust the ass of one of the actresses with cocaine."

The Departed became a Boston bloodbath patterned after the highly successful Hong Kong film *Infernal Affairs* (2002) about two young cops assigned to infiltrate and spy on unlikely rivals: the mob and the organized crime unit of the state police. The screenwriter Monahan substituted Irish-American thugs for a Chinese Triad gang, but otherwise the cat-and-mouse drama remained intact. The Costello protégé Matt Damon becomes a rising star on the state police force, while the undercover cop Leonardo DiCaprio apprentices himself to the worst (and at times, most unintentionally funny) crime boss to hit the screen since Brando's parody of Don Corleone in *The Freshman*. As Frank Costello, Jack pulled out all the stops and went for popcorn, burning whatever serious acting currency he'd regained in *About Schmidt*. "I wanted him to be more corrupt than anything I'd seen on TV," explained Jack. "I needed this to be different."

Costello is patterned after the fugitive Boston mobster James "Whitey" Bulger, a near-legendary serial murderer, sadistic bisexual, and Godfather bully who disappeared in 1994 one step ahead of arrest. Within the nihilistic context of *The Departed*, Jack played Costello off his fellow actors like a pinball, reveling "in perpetrating the unexpected," as Shirley MacLaine once described Jack whenever she went up against him in front of the cameras. "Planned response to Nicholson was not a good move," she said, following *Terms of Endearment*. "Better to leave yourself open. Homework was better left at home. He challenged me to take a chance and not plan my moves or feelings."

Jack did the same with DiCaprio and Damon, catching them off guard and behaving outrageously to elicit authentic surprise. He spilled lighter fluid and lit a table on fire without telling DiCaprio beforehand and unexpectedly whipped out his strap-on in a porn theater scene with Damon.

Jack not only spoke *The Departed*'s most memorable dialogue, he also dominated the action throughout the first three-quarters of the movie, which fell to pieces after Costello was eliminated. By the time credits roll, the body count exceeds the last act of *Hamlet*. Billed as a war between those who uphold the law and those who refuse to abide by it, *The Departed* owed more to its Chinese original than to Shakespeare.

By year's end *The Departed* topped the $120 million mark at the box office—one of the biggest hits of 2006—but unlike *Hamlet*, its bloody denouement defied any serious postmortem and stuck to the ribs like a helping of chow mien. *The Departed*'s point seemed as hopeful as a suicide bomber and was summed up by Jack in the most widely advertised non sequitur from a movie larded with sound and fury. "When I was your age they would say we can become cops, or criminals," Costello tells Matt Damon's character. "Today, what I'm saying to you is this: when you're facing a loaded gun, what's the difference?"

The era of Paris Hilton, Lindsay Lohan, Jessica Simpson, and William Hung had made celebrity a joke. Talent counted for less than chutzpah, adding weight to Andy Warhol's throwaway prophecy that everyone would be famous for fifteen minutes. Jack's old flame Janice "Big Dick" Dickinson seemed to prove the point in 2006, graduating from a judgeship on UPN's *America's Next Top Model* to her very own modeling series on Oxygen: a no-talent hostess featuring no-talent contestants in a no-talent reality program.

Amid the chaos, Jack persisted. "My generation is the new old," he told the *Hollywood Reporter*. "We're living longer. If I can't find real models, my idea would be to inspire that."

He had no plans to go gentle into Dylan Thomas's good night, but rather to defy the odds like that other Dylan. "Just because I'm in *The Departed* doesn't mean I'm ready to go," Jack growled.

He and Bert Schneider mended fences and began to show up at Lakers games together. When Bert nearly died from a coronary aneurism in 2006, Jack moved him to his compound to recuperate. They both remained unrepentant dope smokers. "Baby Boomers are the first generation that is facing a drug and overdose epidemic in their middle age," said John Newmeyer, an epidemiologist and drug researcher at the Haight-Ashbury Free Clinic in San Francisco. "They started using drugs recreationally or regularly over twenty years ago, and they aren't really slowing down."

Tobacco was an equally tough habit for Jack to break. He was able to go for only ten to fifteen minutes between cigarettes—approximately the same for trips to the urinal. He decried "those old boys' bladders" and drank a beige diet liquid to keep his weight down but still refused to eat fruits and vegetables. He added Prilosec, Lipitor, and baby aspirin to his diet but ate pudding for breakfast.

"The Great Seducer" still had an appetite for women, but his fantasies were taking an odd turn. While suggesting to one interviewer that "fucking Britney Spears would be a life-changing experience," he admitted to another that he lusted after Rosalynn Carter, the New Age guru-ette Marianne Williamson, and the ghost of Eleanor Roosevelt. He embarrassed himself at the 2006 Oscars by hitting on Nicole Kidman three months before she married the country music star Keith Urban. Jack later apologized.

In the blogosphere, Jack was derisively described as "bald, paunchy and definitely a B-cup." Jack preferred "seasoned" and "singular," as opposed to the far less hopeful "single." "Recall the old Chinese saying: 'A man does not fall in love if he's dead,'" he said. "I keep that in mind, and now I do yoga every morning."

On the increasingly rare occasion that he got a woman to agree to a little Reichian therapy, Jack kept his demands low key. One ex reported that he liked his women shaven as clean as a Barbie doll. An early Hollywood acquaintance described him as still having "an immense facility to arrange his secret satisfactions." "I can't help but notice that women, especially when they're in any sort of amorous mood, don't say my name that much, so I like when they do," he said. "I like being called 'Jack.' I like being identified by my name. At that moment."

His female friends and ex-lovers rallied to him. With rare exceptions, even those who'd been jilted tended to recall their time with Jack fondly. Upon breaking up with him, Anjelica said, "I don't think relationships come to an end. Period," and sixteen years later, the fifty-four-year-old Mrs. Anjelica Huston Graham added this coda: "He's still a great-looking man. A sense of humor goes a long way. His smile got us through a lot of bad moments. He has a great smile."

Jack sketched and painted. He didn't go out much, preferring to stay home and read, sometimes until the sun came up. When he peered in the bathroom mirror each morning, he saw little more than a blur. "I can't see myself too clearly these days. Sometimes I go ahead and put the glasses on."

Jack told *Playboy* he'd thought about turning his life story into a screenplay but contradicted himself a year later in the *Times of London*: "I swore I would never write a memoir and I'm sticking with that. If you are going to recount your life in that way, you don't live it as well."

A full generation after *The Last Detail*, Jack planned to reteam with Randy Quaid on a sequel in 2007. In *Last Flag Flying*, the aging Billy Badass would run a bar and Morgan Freeman would step into the role of the late Otis Young. Again, Harry Gittes planned to produce, while Richard Linklater, the forty-five-year-old director of *Dazed and Confused* (1993), *School of Rock* (2003), and *Fast Food Nation* (2006), was to direct.

But that deal fell through after Rob Reiner came to Jack with another Morgan Freeman dramedy—this one centered on a pair of cancer patients who team for one last road trip. *The Bucket List* began shooting in the fall and was targeted for a late 2007 release.

Roll up the red carpet, shut down the lights, mute the talking heads, and tinseltown becomes a desert landscape of greed and fear, where the axiom that "power corrupts" shifts ever so slightly to read that Hollywood corrupts absolutely. Most of the time, Jack seemed to have risen above it all, and while it might be argued that his hilltop monastery remains a long way from heaven, it was as good a place to call home as any in the City of Angels.

In a quick inventory of his life that he recently gave a reporter, Jack said, "I haven't seen the Pyramids yet. I never hit .380 in the American League. I'm less likely to direct another movie than I was. I never became a master chef, and I'll probably never take a cooking class. I never became fluent in another language. I never decided I had to write a novel. I used to think I was going to do all those things."

Shortly after the October premiere of *The Departed*, Jack checked into Cedars-Sinai Medical Center, reportedly to have a stone removed from a salivary gland, but the *National Enquirer* quoted "insiders" who called it a cancer scare. A month later, the Hollywood Foreign Press Association picked Lorraine to hand out the 2007 Golden Globes. The annual selection of a star's daughter was as close an approximation as Hollywood had to the sort of "coming out" cotillion thrown on behalf of East Coast debutantes. Though looking a little frail following his hospital stay, Jack sat through the ceremony, beaming each time his daughter shone in the spotlight. Uncharacteristically, he remained in the audience when his old pal Warren Beatty received the Cecil B. DeMille Lifetime Achievement award. Tom Hanks was the presenter, leading to speculation that Jack might be more ill than he let on.

At Oscar time two months later, Jack's bald and bloated presence during the 79th Academy Awards added to the guesswork surrounding his health, but the answer he let seep into his fan base was that he'd shaved his head merely for the part of a cancer patient in the upcoming film *The Bucket List*. By summer, Jack was again healthy enough to be caught on camera floating in a boat on the Mediterranean, surrounded by a bevy of young women in bathing suits who navigated while Jack snacked on a hero sandwich, sipped a Diet Coke, and flagrantly lit up a cigarette. From the *London Daily Mail* to TMZ.com, Jack's critics might carp about his flabby death-defying appearance or his comical pursuit of bikini-clad babes long past the grasp of more mortal men, but Jack gave not a damn.

Jack ran into Sidney Poitier at the golf course not long ago. The Bermuda-born actor, who is ten years Jack's senior, assured him that "you get a huge burst of energy at seventy."

"I'm waiting for that," said Jack, "hanging on by my fingernails."

ACKNOWLEDGMENTS

I always begin by thanking my first line editor, my litmus test, my little red-haired girl, Sharon McDougal, whose instincts never fail. I may be the writer in the family, but she is the reader, and without her, the more dreadful examples of my alliterative pompous purple prose would populate these pages. Thank her. I can't seem to help myself.

Along with my Wiley editors Lisa Burstiner and Eric Nelson and Eric's able assistant, Constance Santisteban, I must add my old bud Patricia McFall, who went through the manuscript in its early stages, tightening and reminding me once again that brevity and a comma after each appositive beats faux Faulknerian excess every time. I could wax on at length, as she well knows, but in keeping with her counsel I will simply say, Thanks. Ditto Deborah Caulfield Rybak, my Minneapolis copy editor, and J. P., the lady with the flaw in her eye.

Here's where I thank family, and there is a lot of it. At eighty, my mother, Lola McDougal, still takes a little time between bingo matches to read, and lately concedes that her son might actually have a future trafficking in words after all. My older brother, Patrick, recently finished reading all of my books and now feels a little better about repeatedly saving my worthless butt from neighborhood beatings when we were growing up in Lynwood, California. My sister, Colleen, worries that my head will swell larger than it already has while my kid brother, Neal, worries that his waistline will swell as large as mine and, thus, devotes his spare time to running 10Ks. Still, all my siblings support this odd hobby of mine.

My children make me proud. Jennifer, Amy, Kate, Fitz, and Andi are, respectively, a social worker, a lawyer, a schoolteacher, an Internet entrepreneur, and a budding accountant, making their way in an increasingly Darwinian world while simultaneously raising talented, energetic dynamos of their own. They are securing for each of my ten grandchildren the best possible educational advantages in a Bush-whacked nation where children shamefully get left behind in droves, every hour of every day. My eleven-year-old granddaughter Megan Dominguez Cole recently summarized my own feelings about books far better than I ever could: "Books are very important to the world. If everyone had a book to read, the world would probably be a better place to live in. . . . Those less fortunate don't have an education usually. Those who can read can teach the ones who can't. Eventually poor people will be so smart that they will be accepted into college, get a good job, and buy a house. . . . If everybody had a job by reading, no one would be homeless."

Unfortunately, Megan goes on to endorse Harry Potter and not her grandfather's efforts, but, hey, I can wait. I'm not sure I want my pre-teen princess reading up on Jack Nicholson, anyway.

Alice Martell has been my agent now for more than twenty years. During that time, I have had students, acquaintances, and friends ask me to define what a good agent does, and I have responded with the following checklist. A good agent:

- Keeps up on the book market and the players who pass through the turnstiles of the quixotic publishing world
- Understands contracts and copyright law
- Reads voraciously, critically, and broadly
- Balances commerce with art
- Fights for clients like a rabid wolverine on steroids

Lastly, I would add that an exceptionally good agent gives you all of her telephone numbers, including her cell, home, fax, and secret land line at the cabin in the Berkshires, and invites you to call any time, night or day. Alice is exceptional in every way.

Since I moved to Tennessee a year ago, my compatriot Bill Knoedelseder has kept me apprised of the goings-on in Jack Nichol-son's L.A. by calling me each morning from an eternal traffic jam on the Ventura Freeway. Likewise, Pat and Jim Broeske fill me in on the latest gossip and give me a place to stay when I make my infrequent return visits to my native Southern California. Danelle Morton serves similar duty as innkeeper, bartender and Jungian analyst whenever I'm near San Francisco.

Early on, the Jack biographer Patrick McGilligan generously opened his archives and his musings to me, giving me a tremendous head start on *Five Easy Decades*. All too often, biographers forget that they are part of a continuum. Theirs is seldom the last word on their subjects and it would behoove them to help those who come after them, not impede, sabotage, or mislead all for the sake of book sales and ego. If the end goal is to more clearly understand the subject of the biography, sharing information seems not only natural but mandatory. As Patrick told me over a very expensive dinner (for which I paid) in a restaurant overlooking Lake Michigan, "It's not as if I'm going to write *another* Jack book."

Similarly, I must thank all those other brave biographers who came before me, especially Peter Thompson and Edward Douglas, who ran the same gauntlet as Patrick and me, dodging flaks, suck-ups, and phoneys at every turn who seem bent on preserving their respective versions of the Nicholson legend, whether Jack wants them to or not.

In no particular order, I also need to thank: Jeff Ross, David Cay Johnston, Peter Biskind, Michael Cieply, Brian Zoccola, David Crook, Bob Zeller, John and Christine Beshears, Richard Kyle, Adeline Otto, David and Sheila Murphy, Karen Koch, Dorothy Korber, Steve Luckman, Katharine Lowrie, Betty Lukas, Linda Marsa, Mary Murphy, Jack Myers, Phil Marshak, Ira Abrams, Pam Pierce, Jim and Tish Coblenz, Frank Dana, Steve Molton, Susan Daniels, Michael Randolph, Sharrone Dearmore, David Vokun, Ray Dominguez, Corey Mitchell, David Vokoun, John and Jessica Trent, Chris and Erin Peck, Marty Plotnick, Mike Riley, Luke Ford, Mark Gladstone, Diane Goldner, Neville Johnson, Peter Jones, Dana Kennedy, Ron Parker, Peter and Linda Knutson, Sean Mitchell, Craig Modderno, Harry Press, Dixie Reid, Sue Russell, Megan Rosenquist, Gus Russo, Ed Sallee, Bob Sipchen, Christopher Silvester, Lionel Chetwynd, Bill and Mimi Silverman, Sarah Spitz, Lyndon Stambler, Lieutenant Richard L. Sullivan (ret.), Joanna Harcourt-Smith, Jill Stewart, Tom Szollosi, Brian Tessier, Audrey Dills, Dietrich Timmerman-Carpio, Edwin P. Wilson, Leslie and Jeremy Welton, Linda Allen, Marcia Avnet, Cynthia Basinet, Steve Blauner, Samantha Colbert, Cheryl Cron, Tom Cunneff, Dave Danforth, Bernard Dick, Sabrina DeGuiseppe,

Charles Eastman, Jerry Eisenberg, Jonathan Epaminondas, Charles Evans, Harry Gittes, Monte Hellman, Preston Miller, Beverly Gray, Chuck Griffith, Helena Kallianiotes, Eddie King, Graham King, Diane Ladd, Jeremy Larner, Peter Manso, Nancy McClelland, Arlene Moss, Monica Rosenquist, Amy Schneider, Fred Roos, Peter Rainer, Brian O'Neal, Tom Piechura, Marina Zenovich, Tony Vorno, Bill Tepper, John Henry Shaner, Bob Silvestri, and Marc Wannamaker. And irascible, irreverent, irreplaceable Irv Letofsky—my editor, my friend, the last of a breed.

If I left anyone out, I apologize. I'm only ten years Jack's junior, and, like the Great Seducer, my memory isn't what it used to be, though I'm not yet at a point where I have to wear earwigs in order to have script girls read me my lines.

Lastly, I thank Jack himself, who did me the great favor of leaving a lifetime of clues while assiduously avoiding meeting me face to face and seducing me into sycophancy as he has film fans, journalists, and *jeunes filles* by the score during an enviable and priceless career of hiding out in plain sight.

Thanks for the movies, Jack. Unlike a good many of your contemporaries, I'm pretty sure that you can handle the truth. Your like shall not pass this way again, I'm afraid, and all of us are the lesser for it.

NOTES

PROLOGUE

1. In his own enviable career, the runner-up, Spencer Tracy, was nominated nine times and won twice, his second Oscar awarded in 1938 for *Boys Town*. Tracy's lifelong love, Katharine Hepburn, remains the top winner, tying Jack's twelve nominations but winning four acting Oscars for *Morning Glory* (1933), *Guess Who's Coming to Dinner* (1967), *The Lion in Winter* (1968), and *On Golden Pond* (1981). In 2003, Jack told *Entertainment Weekly*, "I noticed when I passed Spencer Tracy and Laurence Olivier because that made me laugh, and also because my kids love that I'm in the *Guinness Book of World Records*."

CHAPTER 1

1. At the 1981 Cannes Film Festival, Nicholson told reporters he'd like to portray Fred Astaire in a biopic and have eighty-two-year-old Astaire direct, but in the same press conference, he also said he'd like to play the Roman emperor Caligula as both a man and a transvestite.

2. In 1995, Jack alluded to yet another alternative, adding further obfuscation to the Nicholson myth: his mother had traveled fifty miles north of Neptune to Manhattan's East Side to give birth at Bellevue Hospital. New York was "the city of my birth," he told the *New York Times*'s Chris Chase.

3. The last presidential candidate for whom Jack actively campaigned was George McGovern in 1972, although he has supported most of the same Democrats that his pal Warren Beatty has over the years, from Jimmy Carter and Gary Hart to Michael Dukakis and Bill Clinton.

4. "Abortions" is the first alphabetical listing in the 2005 edition of Asbury Park's *Verizon Yellow Pages*.

5. It was a vain streak that Jack inherited, from his pegged pleats and blue suede shoes to turtleneck sweaters and fancy footwear.

6. One such rival turned out to be Don Furcillo-Rose, the crooning barber's son, who opened a pair of nearby beauty shops after his showbiz career fizzled.

7. The mayor of Asbury Park from 1973 to 1985, Kramer ran restaurants with his brother Lou for more than fifty years and may have been the namesake for Nicholson's son by Rebecca Broussard.

8. Jack led a drive to get his sixth-grade teacher to take the entire class to see the movie, which pits a troubled boy (Roddy McDowell) against his emotionally distant father (Preston Foster).

9. By 1951, 10 million American homes had TV sets.

10. At one point, Jack wanted to be a sports announcer like his hero Bill Stern, the host of NBC's *The Colgate Sports Newsreel*.

11. Until its demise in 1950, the long-running serial that was sponsored by Wheaties had a lucrative sideline of selling "premiums" to millions of kids who sent in a dime and a Wheaties box top. Young listeners could look forward to finding a Torpedo Flashlight, an Explorer Telescope, a Secret Bombsight, a Dragon's Eye Ring, or an Egyptian Whistling Ring in the mail.

12. Jack received first communion in 1944 at St. Elizabeth's in Avon, New Jersey.

13. The skin condition persisted into Jack's thirties and required medical attention. The acne left scars across his back that he always kept hidden.

14. After decades as a Latin lothario in both movies and TV, Romero struck his most indelible note in the late sixties as Batman's archrival, the Joker—a role Jack would reprise in 1989 for the director Tim Burton.

CHAPTER 2

1. In Switzerland, Professor Hans Laube developed a process that reproduced odors in a theater, leading to Smell-O-Vision, which began and ended with *Scent of Mystery* (1960).

2. While still in high school, Jack took to wearing a jaunty black porkpie with the brim flattened: "I'd gotten [the hat] from the freeway in a motor accident that involved a priest, so it had a lot of juju on it."

3. Until he married, Jack suffered from *ejaculatio praecox*. As he explained it to *Playboy*, "You find yourself making it with a chick and, like, you poke her eight times and right away you're coming."

4. Following *The Wild One* (1953) and *On the Waterfront* (1954), Brando disappointed his more angst-ridden fans by singing and dancing his way through *Guys and Dolls* at the same time that *East of Eden* was in theaters.

5. Trying his hand as a photographer in L.A. after graduating from the University of Massachusetts, Gittes shot portraits of Jack, Elliott Gould, and Liza Minnelli, among other aspiring actors. He returned to New York in 1963, where he wrote advertising copy and shot album covers. Gittes met Bill Cosby at the Bitter End in Greenwich Village and talked his way into producing Cosby's pilot for the Saturday morning animated series *Hey, Hey, Hey: It's Fat Albert* (1969). On the strength of that credit, he returned to Hollywood the following year, where he hitched his star to Jack's.

6. Best known for his role as the bumbling Captain Binghamton on TV's *McHale's Navy* (1962–1966), Flynn was a regular in Disney films and on the *Tonight Show* in the early 1970s, but he broke his leg and was found at the bottom of his pool on July 19, 1974, weighed down by the cast. His death was ascribed to a heart attack. Flynn was fifty.

7. The 150-seat theater on Melrose Avenue burned down in 1968.

8. Dennis Hopper was the original lead in *Tea and Sympathy* until he dropped out to take a role opposite James Dean in *Giant* (1956). Landon became "Little Joe" on *Bonanza*; Byrnes became "Kookie" on *77 Sunset Strip*; and Fuller had stints as the wrangler Jess Harper on *Laramie* and the trail master Major Adams on *Wagon Train*.

9. Hosted by John Conte, *Matinee Theatre* produced about 650 half-hour live TV dramas for NBC from 1955 through 1958, employing some seven thousand actors and actresses. One of the earliest programs broadcast in color, *Matinee Theatre* also employed writers such as Frank Price, who eventually became the head of production at both Universal and Columbia Pictures in the 1980s.

10. Taylor went on to his own long career, directing TV movies and episodes of such series as *Star Trek* and *Law & Order: SVU*.

11. Born Michael Gubitosi in Nutley, New Jersey, Blake came to L.A., where his parents put him to work at age four in *The Little Rascals*. He went on to the *Red Ryder* serials and several movies during the 1940s, but by the mid-fifties, when he met Nicholson, Blake was a washed-up child star who had to start over from scratch. He marked his comeback with *In Cold Blood* (1966), followed by the *Baretta* television series (1975–1977), before lapsing back into obscurity in the late 1990s. He again rose to notoriety in 2001 when the LAPD accused him of murdering his wife—a charge of which he was acquitted following a 2005 trial. In a civil trial later that year, a jury found him responsible and ordered him to pay his dead wife's heirs $30 million.

12. Corey charged $50 a head and insisted on punctuality. When a young actor named David Crosby showed up late once too often, he got the boot and never came back, opting instead to become a musician—specifically, a Byrd.

CHAPTER 3

1. The British Film Institute's *Sight and Sound* journal gave *The Cry Baby Killer* one of its few positive notices—a fact Jack never forgot in his general appreciation of foreign journalists over the domestic variety.

2. Carolyn Mitchell, who was cast as Nicholson's teen heartthrob, married the actor Mickey Rooney a few months after the release of The *Cry Baby Killer*. They had four children but separated in 1965 when twenty-nine-year-old Mitchell began an affair with twenty-four-year-old Yugoslav actor Milos Milosevic, who had a small role in *The Russians Are Coming* (1966). The Rooneys attempted to reconcile, but on January 31, 1966, Milosevic murdered Carolyn, then turned the gun on himself.

3. Jack's sophomore year as an actor wasn't much better. He earned $1,900 in 1959.

4. The first of Corman's AIP productions, *The Fast and the Furious* (1954), cost $50,000 to make and earned an immediate profit, just like the nearly four hundred other movies he produced during his fifty-year career in Hollywood.

5. Another of the short-lived watering holes that Jack's crowd frequented along the Strip was the Fred C. Dobbs coffeehouse, named for Bogart's character in *The Treasure of the Sierra Madre*. A favored stopover for itinerant musicians, Fred C. Dobbs's was on Dylan's itinerary whenever he drifted through L.A.

6. A painting that Jack hung in his living room for years featured a pair of cowpokes, one of whom was clearly Jack.

7. Susan Strasberg, who never attended her father's famous Actors Studio, knew Jack had once auditioned and failed to make the cut when the West Coast franchise first opened at the end of 1966, but she shrugged it off. "Sometimes my father said no because he felt the person wasn't going to change so much."

8. Berman, who had been promised 50 percent of the profits in lieu of a salary, eventually had to hire the attorney Melvin Belli and sue Corman in order to get paid.

9. In typical Corman style, the cameras had been borrowed from an AIP production to be shot in the Caribbean. Because *The Wild Ride* was Corman's own production, distributed through his separate Film Group company, he had a two-week window before the cameras had to be returned.

10. Hellman's *Beast of the Haunted Cave* (1959) invited audiences with the poster tagline "Screaming young girls sucked into a labyrinth of horror by a blood-starved ghoul from Hell!"

11. The author of *Beyond Laughter: Humor and the Subconscious* (1957), Grotjahn said that "actors have no proper identity. When someone assigns them an identity, they can do that very well, but when they get off the stage, they collapse. . . . Even actors who seem to be the exception really are not." While maintaining that actors "are almost

impossible to treat successfully," Grotjahn admitted shortly before his death in 1988 that he was attracted to them as clients because most could afford to pay lavish fees.

12. Several actors were called back for reshoots weeks later, but Jack was not among them.

13. The first, *Bucket of Blood*, is another cult classic, featuring a mad sculptor who turns murder victims into statuary, and the third, Monte Hellman's *Creature from the Haunted Sea* (1961), involves a heist from Castro's Cuban treasury, a gun moll, a dimwit gangster, and a sea monster. *Creature* was also the second screen turn for Robert Towne, who played Sparks Moran, Agent XK150.

CHAPTER 4

1. Marlon Brando earned $1.3 million as a very fey Captain Bligh, one of his most lackluster performances, but he caused so many delays in the shooting schedule that the director Lewis Milestone complained publicly that the actor had tacked $6 million onto the production costs.

2. After selling off its back lot for $43 million to make way for what would become Century City, Twentieth Century Fox used part of its capital to pay Elizabeth Taylor $1 million to star in the bloated $40 million Roman epic, which took in just $39.8 million at the box office. Fox sued Taylor's MCL Films, Inc., for $50 million, claiming that her well-publicized extramarital affair with costar Richard Burton kept boycotting audiences away. Taylor countersued, and they settled out of court. She ultimately wound up with a pay-day of more than $7 million. In 2006, *Forbes* magazine named *Cleopatra* the most expensive movie ever made, adjusted for inflation.

3. *The Broken Land* was also released under the title *The Vanishing Frontier*.

4. Jack and Devlin liked to coin their own words and came up with *bufist* to describe overly serious film actors. "They're neither Mahatma Ghandi nor Michelangelo, we decided," said Jack. "They're a 'bufist.'" Similarly, Jack later coined the term *kookamoola* to describe the perfect camera shot.

5. During the mid-seventies, Jack kept a startlingly lifelike JFK ventriloquist's dummy atop the piano in his living room.

6. At one point, Sandra returned briefly to Blake before resuming her relationship with Jack, thus setting up a lifelong rivalry between the two actors.

7. A Greek émigré, Kallianiotes grew up in Boston, where she learned her art at Greek reunion picnics: "I did an impromptu belly dance and people threw pennies. I thought, 'Hey, this is a far-out way to make money.'"

8. According to Los Angeles County records, Jack and Sandra got their wedding license on a Friday but were married two days later on a Sunday.

9. Trained by Moe Disesso, filmdom's premier pet wrangler who gave the world Ben the rat in *Willard*, *The Raven*'s raven, "Jim Jr.," won a Patsy (the Oscar of the animal world) despite its loose bowels.

10. According to Charles Eastman, Jack did in fact borrow rent money from him once but paid the $400 back as soon as he was able.

11. Corman got triple mileage out of Karloff, holding on to twenty minutes of unused footage from *The Terror* and turning it over to his protégé Peter Bogdanovich, who made his directing debut five years later with *Targets* (1968), the story of an aging horror film star who confronts a teen killer. Shot in twenty-five days for $130,000, *Targets* was a minor hit, leading Bogdanovich to *The Last Picture Show* (1971), for which the Academy nominated him for Best Director and Best Adapted Screenplay.

12. Upon screening *The Terror* for the first time, Peter Bogdanovich recalled thinking, Gee, I hope Jack makes it as a director or a writer because he's not much of an actor here.

13. The *Asbury Park Press* ran June's obituary in two different editions with her name misspelled as June Harley.

14. Hawley died a year earlier than June, on August 29, 1962, in Toronto, following an auto accident. He was forty-eight. He left a widow and three sons, in addition to June's children.

15. Mary Martin knew Logan from Broadway, specifically *South Pacific*, in which she was a naval officer—a role that Mitzi Gaynor played in the movie version.

16. First and best known as a suave satyr in Vadim's *And God Created Woman* (1956), which made Vadim's then wife, Brigitte Bardot, an international sex symbol, Marquand also directed Buck Henry's script of Terry Southern's notorious novel *Candy* (1968) and appeared as a French rubber plantation owner in *Apocalypse Now Redux* (2001).

17. Following their initial success in 1967, Phillips and Mama Michelle bought Jeannette MacDonald's Bel Air mansion, where they threw lavish Hagman-like bashes and included Jack among the regularly invited.

18. Fox dumped Lippert Productions in 1966, and Lippert himself quit the business after a series of heart attacks. He produced his last movie, *The Murder Game*, in 1965 and died at age sixty-seven in 1976.

19. Narrated by Marlene Dietrich, *The Black Fox* (1963) documented the rise and fall of Adolf Hitler, pairing actual footage of the dictator with illustrations from the medieval fable of Reynard, a trickster fox that always seemed to put one over on the aristocracy.

20. *Beat the Devil* was adapted by Huston and Truman Capote from a James Helvick novel. The droll adventures of rival crooks and con artists sailing on the same boat to Africa to lay claim to uranium is more comedy than caper.

21. Along with an official stamp of approval from the Department of Defense, *Back Door to Hell* enjoyed army surplus props and uniforms, as well as free naval assault and infantry footage, which Hellman used to add authenticity to his finished film.

22. In 1966, *Alfie* became the first American film that was allowed to use the word *abortion* in its dialogue, under the strictures of the MPAA Production Code.

23. Carole Eastman adopted the pen name Adrian Joyce to differentiate herself from her brother Charles, then an up-and-coming writer-director in his own right.

24. Although Warren Oates was married at the time, he and Millie Perkins made no secret of their affair.

25. Hellman and Jack later asserted that this gimmick was influenced by the televised murder of Lee Harvey Oswald. "With Carol, one of the things she does is incorporate events into her script the way a painter uses paint," Jack explained. "In *The Shooting*, that ending with the jerky movements is like the film of Jack Ruby coming out of the crowd at the Dallas Courthouse."

26. In his seminal *Understanding Media* and *The Medium Is the Massage*, the Canadian media philosopher Marshall McLuhan sounded the cautionary alarm about the impact of TV's "cool," passive hypnosis during the late sixties.

27. By 1965, more than 161 million television sets were in operation around the globe, according to *Daily Variety*. The following year, ABC paid Columbia Pictures a record $2 million for the rights to air *The Bridge on the River Kwai* (1957), and 60 million tuned in.

28. The script was not hokey enough for Colonel Tom Parker, Presley's legendary counsel on bad taste, who begged for a rewrite so Elvis would have a talking camel for comic relief.

29. The director Mike Nichols's hit also introduced Dustin Hoffman, the first teen heartthrob without the pretty-boy glamour of Tab Hunter, Fabian, or Frankie Avalon. An unknown stage actor born the same year as Jack, Hoffman commanded $200,000 a picture after *The Graduate*. "They saw every actor I had lunch with," complained Jack, adding, "I couldn't even get interviewed for *The Graduate*."

30. The prestigious Cinémathèque Française held a retrospective of thirty Corman films in 1964, praising his work as inventive and inspired, despite the general lack of interest among major Hollywood studios.

31. Corman paid Jack and Dern $550 a week, $175 above scale.

CHAPTER 5

1. This was *Harper's* hundredth anniversary issue.

2. During the filming of *The Chase* (1966), the producer Sam Spiegel still feared that speed-loving Brando might kill himself James Dean style and leave a big hole in the middle of his picture. "Marlon didn't bring his motorcycle, did he?" Spiegel frequently asked the director Arthur Penn.

3. *The Wild Angels'* surf rock soundtrack, easily its most memorable element, was produced by Davie Allan and the Arrows, but California's future lieutenant governor Mike Curb took co-credit in his then role of recording mogul.

4. "I think it's the only movie of mine I've never seen," Jack said in a 1986 interview about *Rebel Rousers*.

5. Corman resurrected Cohen (briefly) from obscurity to produce *Humanoids from the Deep* (1980).

6. Following *Hell's Angels on Wheels*, Solomon made *Angels from Hell* (1968); *Run, Angel, Run* (1969); *Wild Wheels* (1969); and *Nam's Angels* (1970), which carried the tagline "Hell's Angels vs. the Viet Cong!"

7. As late as 2005, the Los Angeles County assessor indicated that Jack and Sandra co-owned a $327,000 condominium in Venice, while Hawaiian records showed joint ownership of property in Kailua on the island of Oahu.

8. Commenting in 1987 on the twenty-year decline of television and pop culture, Nicholson told the journalist Nancy Collins, "Let me put it this way. In 1967, you could hear Krishnamurti in the Oak Grove, in Ojai. Now he's on Channel C in New York City between the porno shows."

9. Nestled into the foothills some sixty miles north of L.A., the hamlet that Frank Capra filmed as Shangri-La in *Lost Horizon* (1937) had become the Holy See of Southern California–style mysticism decades before anyone knew there was a New Age.

10. As Stanton interpreted Krishnamurti, the Self consists of memories, many of which are self-defeating, distorted prejudices. He credited the yogi's meditations with helping him wipe his "Self" slate clean for the next half century, making him one of the most successful and recognizable character actors in Hollywood.

11. Sandra and her husband since 1982, the ceramic muralist and screenwriter John Stephenson, follow the precepts of "The Infinite Way"—a Christian-based mysticism pioneered by the "revelator" Joel S. Goldsmith (1892–1964). The Stephensons operate Aloha Mystics (www.alohamystics.com) from their home in Kailua, Hawaii.

12. In 1978, Neil Young paid Jack $200,000 for a stretch of Mulholland Drive property adjacent to Jack's place.

13. *Guns of Will Sonnett's* other producer, the *American Bandstand* impresario Dick Clark, took a shine to Jack and commissioned a screenplay on the same psychedelic subject matter that Nicholson had poured into *Love and Money*.

14. The Whiskey a Go Go was co-owned by Jack's pal Elmer Valentine.

15. The first eight stars on the Hollywood Boulevard Walk of Fame included familiar names like Burt Lancaster, Joanne Woodward, Ronald Colman, Preston Foster, and Louise Fazenda, but also the obscure—Olive Borden, Edward Sedgwick, and Ernst Torrence—whose immortalization ironically seemed to capture the fleeting desperation of Hollywood celebrity.

16. Credited to the screenwriters David Newman and Robert Benton, the producer-star Warren Beatty hired Robert Towne for rewrites, launching his stellar reputation as an uncredited script doctor long before his first major triumph: adapting Daryl Ponicsan's novel *The Last Detail* (1973) for Jack.

17. Striking a symbolic death knell to old Hollywood, Universal brought doddering seventy-seven-year-old Charlie Chaplin out of retirement to direct Brando and Sophia Loren in this lame comedy—one of the biggest box office disappointments of the decade.

18. John Lennon wrote the Beatles' "She Said She Said" based on Fonda's description of one of his first trips: "I know what it's like to be dead."

19. The nation's leading men's magazine was still in its airbrushed heyday. Another year would pass before Hugh Hefner openly acknowledged that his centerfolds did, in fact, have pubic hair.

20. One year later, under pressure from parents all over the United States, the MPAA ushered in a new era with its own rating system, labeling films G (general audiences), M (mature audiences), R (no one under 16 without an adult), and X (not recommended for any audience).

21. *The Trip* was actually banned twice—once in 1967 and again in 1988, when it was released on video and was still deemed too seamy at the time for British audiences.

22. Both the Nazi Party and the Communist Party denounced Reich during the 1930s, leading to his flight to the United States.

23. When Reich refused to appear, he was sent to jail. In the meantime, the Food and Drug Administration joined with the New York attorney general to destroy Reich's legacy, at one point burning six tons of his books and research materials. Despite a lengthy FBI investigation, the government never proved its case. A Reich museum and study center still operates today at Mooselookmeguntic Lake near Rangeley, Maine.

24. No less a sexual philosopher than the journalist Dan Rather once characterized the distinction between making love and having sex as the difference between true lightning and lightning bugs.

25. Thirty years later, Susan Strasberg fell victim to breast cancer and opted to treat it holistically rather than undergo a mastectomy. She died at age sixty in 1999.

26. Jaglom's letter of inquiry to J. D. Salinger was never answered.

27. The Lido and the Sunset, both now defunct, were among the art movie houses that Jack and friends once haunted on L.A.'s west side.

28. Bob's uncle Samson Raphaelson was one of the most venerated writers in screen history, starting with *The Jazz Singer* in 1927. Classic Raphaelson films include *The Shop around the Corner* (1940), *Suspicion* (1941), *Heaven Can Wait* (1943), and *Green Dolphin Street* (1947).

29. "King" Cohn died of a heart attack after turning his "poverty row" studio of the 1930s into a powerhouse rivaling the larger and more formidable Warner Bros., MGM, Paramount, and Twentieth Century Fox. Schneider and his brother-in-law Leo Jaffe carried on Cohn's tradition in the 1960s, delivering such classics as *Lawrence of Arabia* (1962), *A Man for All Seasons* (1966), and *Guess Who's Coming to Dinner?* (1967).

30. Before the Monkees, Raybert announced plans to adapt the novelist Gavin Lyall's *Midnight Plus One* for the screen and commissioned the novelist William Wood to write his first screenplay, *The Crucified*. Neither script ever got to the screen.

31. Rafelson originally wanted to cast the Lovin' Spoonful, but the group's first hit record, "Do You Believe in Magic?," put the group out of Raybert's price range.

32. *Cue* magazine said the film was "as if 8½ had been made by a flower child."

33. Dolenz wanted to call it *The Monkee Movie Starring Victor Mature, Annette Funicello, and Sonny Liston.*

34. The French, however, hailed *Head* as a masterpiece in much the same way that they exalted the work of Jerry Lewis and Roger Corman. The movie screened for weeks in Paris.

CHAPTER 6

1. Jack lost his child only during the work week; he insisted on having Jennifer as often as possible on weekends and vacations and splitting the holidays with Sandra.

2. Fonda and Hopper's satire was based on *The Queen*, a play by the beat poet Michael McClure.

3. From 1960 through 1969, Hopper was married to Brooke Hayward, the daughter of the talent agent–producer Leland Hayward and the actress Margaret Sullavan, who had also been briefly married to Henry Fonda in the early 1930s. Hayward and Sullavan's other daughter, Bridget, was once Peter Fonda's love interest when they were teenagers. Like her own mother, as well as Fonda's, Bridget ended her life with a drug overdose. Peter later named his daughter, the actress Bridget Fonda, for her.

4. Once a brothel and a gambling house, the Blue Heaven restaurant in Key West had a rich bohemian history. Ernest Hemingway once refereed boxing matches in its courtyard, where cockfighting was another entertainment staple. The restaurant became a prime hipster destination during the 1960s.

5. Little more than a year later, Corman quit AIP in a dispute over the release of his end-of-the-world satire *Gas-s-s-s!* (1971).

6. The screenwriter of *Dr. Strangelove* (1964) and *The Loved One* (1966), Southern helped Vadim to adapt the sci-fi comic character Barbarella for a screenplay directed by Vadim and featuring Jane Fonda in the title role. Southern so loved Peter Fonda's biker film idea that he waived his usual $100,000 fee and worked on *The Loners* for $350 a week.

7. Hopper preferred Jack Sturit, an old friend and ex-football player from Texas. Bruce Dern was also briefly considered for the role.

8. Through much of Torn's career, the story persisted that he "walked out" on *Easy Rider*. When the *New York Times Magazine* repeated it in a 1977 article, Torn forced a retraction: "Mr. Torn has informed the magazine that while he was asked to read the script of *Easy Rider*, he never agreed to play any role in the film and was never on the film set, and, therefore, never 'walked off the picture.'"

9. In 1994, Hopper told Jay Leno during the *Tonight Show* that Torn pulled a knife on him. Torn sued, claiming that it was Hopper who pulled the knife, and he won a $475,000 judgment, which Hopper appealed. The appeals court upheld Torn's verdict and doubled the judgment.

10. On February 3, 2003, Phil Spector, the sixty-two-year-old creator of rock's "Wall of Sound," was arrested and charged with murdering the actress Lana Clarkson, forty, in his L.A. mansion, following a night of drink and drugs along the Sunset Strip.

11. At a time when the guilds, the Teamsters, and the International Alliance of Theatrical Stage Employees conspired with the studios to keep Hollywood a closed shop, the few microbudget productions that were mounted outside the studio system used nonunion or "gypsy" personnel, but at the very real risk of having each film shut down by the unions and the cast and crew blackballed from future union productions.

12. Hopper fell so hard for the high desert town that once he was flush with his own *Easy Rider* windfall in the early 1970s, he splurged on Taos's venerable Mabel Dodge Lujan adobe hacienda, opened his own art gallery, and purchased the local El Cortez Theater so that he'd have a place to screen his movies when he was in town. He fell out of love with the place in the summer of 1975, when Taos police busted him for leaving the scene of an accident and carrying a .357 magnum.

13. The British author of *Lady Chatterley's Lover*, *Sons and Lovers*, and other works died in Vence, France, on March 2, 1930, but his widow moved to New Mexico soon thereafter and asked her lover, Angelo Ravagli, to bring Lawrence's ashes to her for reburial near Taos. Years later, after his lover's death, Ravagli revealed in a drunken confession that he had tossed the author's ashes into the Mediterranean in order to save the expense of shipping and substituted other ashes when he arrived in New Mexico. Though the tomb was a literary shrine at the time *Easy Rider* was made, it contained none of the remains of D. H. Lawrence.

14. Fonda had already been busted once for pot in Los Angeles and would have been a high-profile trophy for an ambitious Texas Ranger.

15. A dancer by training, Antonia Basilotta appeared briefly in *Five Easy Pieces* as Helena Kallioniotes' silent girlfriend. She gained further notoriety during the disco era with her 1981 hit single "Mickey" and went on to choreograph everything from music videos to Gap ads.

16. To capture the wipe-out scenes when Billy and Wyatt are shotgunned, Kovács had himself strapped to the bottom of a helicopter, which took three tries before lifting off in the heavy bayou air. "They would never allow you to do that shot in a copter today," said the location manager Vorno.

17. After granting permission to use "It's Alright, Ma" on the film's soundtrack, Bob Dylan wrote the lyrics to the "Ballad of Easy Rider" and gave them to McGuinn to set to music, according to Fonda. Dylan took no credit for the song.

18. According to Hellman, Carole Eastman planned a film created around the Byrds, similar to *Head*, although far more serious.

19. Ironically, Jerry Rubin was a year younger than Jack but just past his thirtieth birthday when he uttered his famous homily.

CHAPTER 7

1. After Jack's star finally rose, he maintained that Lerner had offered to write a musical for him because Lerner knew from *Clear Day* that Jack could carry a tune.

2. By contrast, Robert Evans offered Yves Montand $200,000 for the role of Dr. Marc Chabot, and Montand countered with $400,000. To Montand's surprise, Evans paid it.

3. A month before *On a Clear Day*'s 1970 premiere, National Guardsmen shot four students dead on the campus of Kent State University.

4. Over time, the domestic gross of *On a Clear Day* rose to $14 million.

5. The national student strike of 1968 froze mass transit and shut off gasoline supplies, spurring several festival regulars to swim to Sam's yacht and bum a ride to a port, where they could then find a ride home.

6. *Ma Nuit Chez Maude* (1969), directed by Eric Rohmer, was nominated for the Palme d'Or and in the Best Foreign Film category at the 1970 Oscars.

7. Katherine Hepburn said that she "loathed" *Easy Rider* but "found Nicholson brilliant."

8. Heir to a fortune, Jaglom didn't need the money.

9. Under a federal tax change enacted in 1969, investors were allowed 100 percent tax exemption on cash they put into movies.

10. Earl Wilson dubbed Baby Boomers "the Genitalia Generation" and predicted that weed and "Vitamin C" (cocaine) would ruin Hollywood.

11. In addition to Rafelson and Mike Nichols, the director Larry Peerce asked Jack to star in *The Sporting Club* (1971), Peerce's grim follow-up to his hit dramedy *Goodbye, Columbus* (1968).

12. Jay Sebring was one of the inspirations for Warren Beatty's character George Roundy in *Shampoo* (1975).

13. Jack's favorite, then and now, however, was El Cholo.

14. Carole Eastman wrote a screenplay about this widespread paranoia, which would evolve from drama to comedy and would take another twenty-two years to produce: *Man Trouble* (1992). Bob Rafelson turned it into a light romance, pairing a frightened star (Ellen Barkin) with a guard dog trainer (Jack).

15. The estate where the Tate-LaBianca murders occurred was demolished in 1994.

16. Others who had lived at the estate since it was first built for the French film star Michèle Morgan in the late 1940s included Cary Grant and Henry Fonda.

17. Candice Bergen eventually hooked up with Bert Schneider through her association with Jack.

18. The Manson girl Susan Atkins later boasted that the Family had a star hit list that

included Elizabeth Taylor, Richard Burton, Tom Jones, Steve McQueen, and Frank Sinatra.

19. "That's rubbish," Rafelson maintained decades later. "The diner scene that everyone talks about was based on something I used to do, not on Jack."

20. On the night of July 19, 1969, Senator Ted Kennedy's car went off a bridge connecting the Massachusetts island of Martha's Vineyard to its Chappaquiddick peninsula, and Kennedy's secretary Mary Jo Kopechne drowned. "In *Five Easy Pieces*," said Jack, "because it was a film that involved family, home and brotherhood all concentrated in one area together, the idea of going off the bridge was sort of *bang* . . . Ted Kennedy."

21. In December 2000, the Library of Congress added *Five Easy Pieces* to its National Film Registry, making it a permanent part of the nation's film history. Other Nicholson movies in the collection of 425 films include *Easy Rider* (1969), *Chinatown* (1974), and *One Flew over the Cuckoo's Nest* (1975).

22. A year later, Sally Struthers immortalized herself as the virginal Gloria Stivic for seven years on CBS-TV's groundbreaking sitcom *All in the Family*, with no apparent stigma resulting from her seminudity with Jack. In later years, she became the spokeswoman for Save the Children and, more recently, a regular on CBS's *Still Standing* and the CW series *The Gilmore Girls*.

23. The coupling couple got so rowdy on the second take that Jack put his hand through a plate glass window and ended shooting for the day while the crew bound up his wound.

24. On Thanksgiving 1963, Goddard and his first wife had discovered the body of Karyn Kupcinet in her West Hollywood apartment, long believed by conspiracy theorists to have been strangled to death because she knew who assassinated President John F. Kennedy.

25. Jack didn't even know until a party at Bert Schneider's house in the mid-seventies when Susan sat on his lap and told him the truth. Twenty years later, he described his reaction at the time as "suspicion" and "vague antipathy."

26. The other nine films were Jean Luc Godard's *Breathless* (1961) and Federico Fellini's *La Dolce Vita* (1961), which sparked U.S. interest in European film; *Dr. No* (1963), which launched the James "Bondwagon"; *A Hard Day's Night* (1964), which broadened the Beatles' international appeal; *Dr. Strangelove* (1964), which satirized nuclear war; *The Sound of Music* (1965), which spawned endless musicals; *Bonnie and Clyde* (1967), which instituted a new kind of gangster film; *The Graduate* (1967), which started the youth revolution; and *I Am Curious (Yellow)* (1969), which became a modest hit and made a mockery of the MPAA's "X" rating at the bottom of its new ratings system.

CHAPTER 8

1. Taken from the last stanza of the poet Robert Creeley's "I Know a Man," the title *Drive, He Said* implied a reckless, headlong rush through contemporary life. Misquoted in the film (and infuriating Creeley), the lines actually read:

drive, he sd, for
christ's sake, look
out where yr going.

2. A CBS sitcom that ran for four seasons (1959–1963), *The Many Loves of Dobie Gillis* was an influential and multiple point-of-view teen comedy starring Dwayne Hickman that created such venerable stereotypes as the beatnik slacker Maynard G. Krebs (Bob Denver) and the brainy but aggressive Zelda Gilroy (Sheila James), while boosting the fledgling careers of Tuesday Weld, Michael J. Pollard, and Warren Beatty.

3. Larner won an Oscar for Best Original Screenplay in 1972 for *The Candidate*.

4. A Harvard grad, a Rhodes scholar, and the son of an Austin oil executive, Terrence

Malick carved out his own legend with *Badlands* (1973), a much-heralded directorial debut, and the pastoral *Days of Heaven* (1978), after which he left for Paris to teach for the next two decades. He reemerged with *The Thin Red Line* (1998) and *The New World* (2005) and is once again regularly producing Hollywood films.

5. Patterned after the older and more venerable British Film Institute, AFI was created in 1967 as one of President Lyndon Johnson's executive swan songs. As one of its first students, Malick produced and directed his first student film, *Lanton Mills* (1969), costarring Jack's pals Harry Dean Stanton and Warren Oates.

6. Harold Schneider was known as "The Screamer," a nickname based on his shrieking—usually over getting off schedule or overspending—when a calming word or two might have been sufficient.

7. With a long and colorful history as a Chicago union spawned by the Capone Mob during the Depression, the International Alliance of Theatrical Stage Employees was rivaled only by the Teamsters as the most powerful and, arguably, the most corrupt union in Hollywood—both willing and able to shut down film production.

8. Roman Polanski developed a similar scenario with Jack in mind for *The Magic Finger*, an "inside Hollywood" satire he wrote with his partner Gérard Brach, in which a producer tests prospective actresses by having them suck his pinky with different emotions: love, revulsion, hatred, and abject devotion.

9. Born June Wilson in 1946, Fairchild was the 1964 Mardi Gras Queen at Aviation High School in the L.A. suburb of Redondo Beach before graduating to Hollywood. She fell deep into drugs following *Drive, He Said*, making her final film appearance in Cheech and Chong's *Up in Smoke* (produced by Lou Adler) as the Ajax Lady—so named because the character snorts cleaning powder like cocaine. In real life, Fairchild was similarly out of control, failing through two marriages and winding up on welfare in the 1990s. In 2001, a *Los Angeles Times* reporter found her living in a cardboard box on L.A.'s Skid Row. A year later, Fairchild was taking acting classes and trying to resurrect her career.

10. According to Jack, Margotta's streak across campus was a precursor to Robert Opal's famous 1974 televised streak at the Academy Awards.

11. Towne retooled the dialogue so that his cuckoldry was both oblique and poignant. "The way that Towne helped rewrite that scene, the point came across light rather than heavy-handedly," said coproducer Harry Gittes. "It's a lesson I'll never forget."

12. Early on, Jack did violate his own edict at least once, granting a TV interview in 1971 to England's Granada Television series *Cinema*, but he ever gave equal access to any similar U.S. program.

13. AT&T launched the first Telstar satellite in 1962. The same year, the British pop group the Tornados came out with an instrumental single with the same title that hit the top of the Billboard chart.

14. For a flat monthly fee of $6, subscribers to HBO got the first nontheatrical look at recent releases.

15. Shot in Chile with an eclectic cast that included Kris Kristofferson, Samuel Fuller, Sylvia Miles, and Henry Jaglom (but not Jack, who declined Hopper's invitation to be in the film), *The Last Movie* was originally to have been a BBS production, but MCA-Universal lured Hopper with a promise of cash and autonomy. *The Last Movie* was to be the first of its new low-budget "youth" division films. While the division delivered classics like George Lucas's *American Graffiti* (1973) and Peter Fonda's *The Hired Hand* (1971), Hopper's film opened and closed in a week, a victim of Hopper's war with the MCA chairman Lew Wasserman over his director's cut. When Hopper refused to make changes, Wasserman kept distribution and promotion to a contractual minimum. Few fans of *Easy Rider* ever got a chance to see *The Last Movie*.

16. Jack also collected shoes: seventy-five pairs by the mid-1980s, ranging from

huaraches and sneakers to exorbitantly priced Italian and English footwear. He refused to go before the cameras barefoot and counted among his favorite short stories Philip Roth's "Eli the Fanatic," which ends with the protagonist closeted with his shoes. "Jack is a foot fetishist," said a pal, only half in jest.

17. With Mimi on his arm, Jack accepted the award at the association's annual dinner at Sardi's and personally sent a thank-you note to each member the following week.

18. Gig Young's career peaked with his win for *They Shoot Horses, Don't They?* and slid quickly downhill over the next decade. Three weeks after marrying his fifth wife, the German actress Kim Schmidt, age thirty-one, on September 17, 1978, the sixty-five-year-old Young shot her to death, then turned the gun on himself with his Oscar standing nearby. "For Gig, the Oscar was literally the kiss of death, the end of the line," said his fourth wife, the actress Elaine Williams.

19. The erotic poet and diarist Anaïs Nin gave *A Safe Place* a temporary reprieve two years after its release with a gushing review in the nation's alternative press, urging women to embrace Jaglom as something of a feminist revolutionary.

20. Originally, Karen Black had the lead opposite Jaglom himself in the Actors Studio rendition.

21. For the rest of his life, Welles entered into a symbiotic relationship with Jaglom, who championed his films, struggled with Welles to find financing at a time when Hollywood had turned its back on the great director, and coaxed him into writing a screenplay specifically for Jack—a film that never got made.

22. Jack liked to say the word was an acronym for "Can't Understand Normal Thinking."

23. Carol Kane became a Garfunkel Suite regular following her first Hollywood sortie as Art's teen mistress in *Carnal Knowledge*. She also roomed at Jack's during her performance in *The Last Detail*, during which Jack took note of her blonde hair and preference for white wine and nicknamed her "Whitey."

24. Both movies were shot on location in Vancouver at roughly the same time.

25. Pamela also had a brief falling out with Jack when she sold early photos of him and Sandra to a supermarket tabloid.

26. According to Charles Eastman, the only two major players in *Five Easy Pieces* whom BBS shut out of profit participation were Carole Eastman and Karen Black.

27. Commenting on Jack's whirling dervish parody of the Atlantic Records CEO Ahmet Ertegun, Diana Vreeland compared him to Brando, in that both had "something all great actors have—he's a great mimic." He was also known to do animal impersonations and a dead-on Jackie Gleason.

CHAPTER 9

1. Jack was the godfather to one of Mick Jagger's sons.

2. *Imagine* (1971) was produced at Lennon's Berkshire estate. The recording session visitors included Andy Warhol, Miles Davis, and Jack.

3. In "People's Parties," from her 1973 album *Court & Spark*, Joni Mitchell turned her gimlet eye on the beautiful people who masked a deeply felt inferiority behind cocktail chatter and desperate laughter, including "Jack behind his joker . . . and me in my frightened silence."

4. "Jack must know it's devastating," Vreeland told *Time* magazine, "because he uses it very rarely."

5. Leslie Ann Warren enrolled in Landau's class following her early success as the nineteen-year-old lead in Rodgers and Hammerstein's *Cinderella* (1965).

6. "We were high in the Andes, literally and figuratively, and most of the film was just . . . made up as we went along," said Michelle Phillips. "There was a script, but it wasn't something that we adhered to very closely."

7. Holly Michelle Gilliam was born June 4, 1944, in Long Beach, California.

8. Four months earlier, Hopper had threatened to sue *Life* magazine over a June 19 cover story implying that he used drugs. "The only thing I shot up with is Vitamin B-12 and my only habit-forming vice is cigarettes," he told *Variety* with a straight face.

9. The last and worst of the Mamas and the Papas' four albums, *People Like Us* was forced on the quartet by Lou Adler's Dunhill Records, whose lawyers threatened the singers with a $1 million contractual penalty if they didn't return to the studio one final time before heading off on solo careers.

10. Jack had shown up at the Golden Globes four months earlier in stone-washed Levis and tennis shoes.

11. George C. Scott stayed home to watch a hockey game on TV instead of attending the Oscars. "The ceremonies are a two-hour meat parade, a public display with contrived suspense for economic reasons," he told the press the following day.

12. As opposed to *chippies*, Jack's favored term for groupies.

13. After Jack and Lou Adler took up skiing in Gstaad and each bought a home in Aspen, they found they could not get TV reception and went halves on the old Judge Shaw house, a historical landmark in a section of the mountain town that had better reception—chiefly so they could go there to watch Lakers basketball.

14. The American Civil Liberties Union first publicly slammed the MPAA two years earlier on grounds that its "X" rating flew in the face of First Amendment freedom of expression.

15. "I'm coming," was the only line the British Board of Film Classification ordered cut from *Drive, He Said*.

16. On June 24, 1974, the U.S. Supreme Court reversed the Georgia Supreme Court's ruling that *Carnal Knowledge* was obscene.

17. Candice Bergen was "Worst Actress," according to the *Harvard Lampoon*.

18. Originally written for Jack, Henry Jaglom's *Tracks* (1976) starred a drugged-out Dennis Hopper as a drugged-out Vietnam vet named Jack, who utters the line "When the going gets rough, I think about my childhood."

19. In anticipation of huge crowds, some theaters advertised marked-up ticket prices, adding a $4 premium to the usual $2 price of admission "so you won't have to stand in line." Word of mouth proved more powerful than studio ads. At a cost of $7 million, *Gatsby* earned $14.2 million at the box office—quite respectable, but hardly the big hit Paramount expected.

20. The three BBS partners sold out to Columbia that same month. *The King of Marvin Gardens* became one of the company's final films.

21. Bert Schneider's deal with his father called for a $5 million match from Columbia to spend on prints and advertising for each BBS film that remained under the $1 million budget, provided the finished movie was released in at least a thousand theaters.

22. Taking catnaps was a trick that Jack claimed to have learned from Gene Autry.

23. The seventeen-year-old tap dancer was allegedly "discovered" by Jack. During filming, Julia Robinson carried on an affair with the husband of the Andy Warhol girl Baby Jane Holtzer. According to Papa John Phillips, she had another affair with Phillips's second wife, Genevieve, after he and Michelle divorced. Robinson died in a fire two years after the release of Rafelson's movie, her first and last film appearance.

24. Burstyn lost Best Supporting Actress to Cloris Leachman but was nominated Best Actress two years later for *The Exorcist* (1973) and took home the Oscar the year after that for the title role in *Alice Doesn't Live Here Anymore* (1974).

25. In November 1978, Neil Burstyn killed himself by leaping out of a ninth-story window of a New York building.

26. Charlie Chaplin, Mary Pickford, Douglas Fairbanks, and D. W. Griffith banded together to form the original United Artists in 1920 as a distributor for their films, independent of the major studios.

27. Attendance bottomed in 1973 with ticket sales of only 864 million—one-seventh of the 4 billion sold in 1946, when movie attendance hit its all-time high.

28. Jack's performance in *Carnal Knowledge* was nominated for a Golden Globe but not an Oscar.

29. The prescient former CBS executive James Aubrey wanted Raquel Welch in the role instead.

30. The Roger Corman alumni Warren Oates starred as the notorious bank robber and Harry Dean Stanton as his sidekick. Michelle was Billie Frechette, Dillinger's moll.

31. To save money, Corman also starred Towne in the sci-fi horror quickie shot on location in Puerto Rico.

32. For $25,000, Beatty started Towne working on the script for what would become *Shampoo* (1975), shortly after *Bonnie and Clyde* (1967) wrapped.

33. From the podium at the 1973 Oscars, Francis Ford Coppola thanked Towne by name for rewriting the key scene in which Vito Corleone passes the Godfather's mantle to Michael.

34. Evans next asked Coppola to write it. He agreed and used his adaptation of *Gatsby* as a stepping-stone to directing *The Godfather*.

35. Ali McGraw did *The Getaway* (1972) instead, fell for leading man Steven McQueen, and divorced Evans, prompting the Paramount production chief to agree to the casting of Mia Farrow as Daisy.

36. Against $250,000 plus 5 percent of the gross if Paramount made the movie.

37. Not true. In fact, *The Last Detail*'s "fuck" quotient was minimal by twenty-first-century standards. Not until *The Departed* (2006) did Jack hit his stride with a film that logged in 237 "fuck"s or nearly 1½ "fuck"s per minute. *Hoffa* (1992) came in as the runner-up at 150 "fuck"s.

38. In the summer of 1972, Columbia called in Ponicsan to rewrite the script, but his work and screen credit never showed in the final film.

39. Days before his death in 1988, Ashby told the actor Jon Voight that he still had not forgiven his father.

40. Ashby also had a fling with Mimi Machu after she left Jack. She locked Ashby out of his own beach house following an argument.

41. Columbia originally wanted Jim Brown, David Cassidy, and Burt Reynolds in the roles that eventually went to Young, Quaid, and Nicholson. Ashby considered John Denver and John Travolta for the sad-sack sailor facing eight years for petty theft, before awarding the part to Quaid.

42. Ashby cast Jack's old friend Rupert Crosse (six-foot-five) as "Mule" Mulhall, but Crosse—who'd appeared opposite Jack only once, as a villain in *Ride in the Whirlwind*—died of cancer that same year at age forty-five.

43. Michelle called Jack for his blessing just as Jack had called Hopper before he asked Michelle to move in with him. "I thought it was fabulous, because I like them both very much," said Jack.

44. When the Justice Department indicted the actor Harry Reems for obscenity in 1976, Jack was one of the first Hollywood figures who stood in his defense.

45. The Roxy was once the home of the director Preston Sturges's short-lived nightclub The Players during the fifties.

46. Moved in 1976 to the eleventh floor of the Delmonico Hotel until it shut down in 1991, the disco on East Fifty-fourth Street had a peephole through which members and guests were required to flash their gold membership cards, which they carried in Cartier cases.

47. Ara Gallant was born Ira Gallantz in 1932 in the Bronx.

48. *Haircut* was shot in three stupefyingly monotonous black-and-white versions; the "plot" involves Andy Warhol's boyfriend Billy Name silently cutting hair.

49. In *Blowjob*, forty-one equally silent minutes of the camera focused on the grimacing face of an Andy associate getting a blowjob.

50. Warhol's film *Empire* consists of a 485-minute tripod shot of the Empire State Building during a single day in 1964, without benefit of time lapse photography.

51. The original "Silver Factory" (1963–1968) was located in a building on East Forty-seventh Street.

52. Like Jean-Paul Sartre's bleak existential play *No Exit*, the brooding hopelessness in Antonioni's so-called American trilogy (*Blow-Up* [1966]), *Zabriskie Point* [1970], and *The Passenger* [1975]) was as perplexing and (except for the hugely successful *Blow-Up*) as unpopular at the box office then as today.

53. Antonioni told the film historian Ned Rifkin, "the events . . . did actually transpire as represented," but the director had to swear secrecy as to where and when the execution took place.

54. Antonioni's oddly emotionless stagecraft had been pioneered early in the century by the German playwright Bertolt Brecht, who called his technique *Verfremdungseffekt*, which roughly translates as "alienation effect." Jean-Luc Godard and Ingmar Bergman later translated *Verfremdungseffekt* to the screen.

55. Hitchcock famously referred to actors as children or cattle, "but children grow up and cattle can be legally slaughtered in most states."

CHAPTER 10

1. Specially made with a hinged tip, the blade was designed to give the illusion of cutting Jack's nostril, but it didn't always flip back as it was supposed to. Jack's apprehension at getting cut was real.

2. William Mulholland's name became part of Jack's home address, as well as the inspiration for *Chinatown*'s Hollis Mulwray.

3. The production designer Richard Sylbert remembered choosing 1939 license plates for *Chinatown*'s vehicles because it was both "the year [Raymond] Chandler's *The Big Sleep* was published and the greatest year in movie history."

4. Towne maintained that he was also influenced by a Sunday feature story in the *Los Angeles Times*'s *West* magazine detailing Chandler's influence on L.A. noir culture and vice versa.

5. Elaine May was also Mike Nichols's former stand-up comedy partner before they both went to Hollywood.

6. Anjelica and her new pal Carol "Whitey" Kane, a frequent guest in the Garfunkel Suite since her hooker roles in *Carnal Knowledge* and *The Last Detail*, often visited the set to kidnap Jack for tacos at El Cholo restaurant. He so loved its food that he had the restaurant cater his birthday party each year.

7. Champions of the Owens Valley water theft, the all-powerful Chandler family dominated Southern California politics for most of the twentieth century through its daily newspaper, the *Los Angeles Times*.

8. Polanski stood two centimeters taller than the Corsican dictator.

9. A script usually ranges between 100 to 120 pages. The standard Paramount writer's contract that Evans had Towne sign was more than 60 pages long.

10. Troy Garrity, Fonda's son by her new husband, Tom Hayden, was born on July 7, 1973.

11. *Chinatown* led to Dunaway's second Oscar nomination, and by the time she finally won the Academy Award for *Network* (1976), her salary demands had climbed to $500,000.

12. The character was named for Jack's producer pal Harry.

13. Many psychologists maintain that nicknaming is a means of showing domination over another, as seems to be the case with President George W. Bush, who has a pet

name for everyone from the former FEMA chief Michael "Brownie" Brown to the White House political adviser Karl Rove ("Turd Blossom"). "There is almost always a hint of derision concealed within [nicknames]," according to the Boston psychiatrist and author Dr. Ronald Pies.

14. The set turned out to have been borrowed from the assistant director Howard Koch Jr.

15. Sylbert remembered Towne's climax as a pistol-wielding Dunaway chasing her father into a seaside salt marsh during a torrential rainstorm. At a fishing tackle kiosk on the coastline, Huston hides in a huge, three-dimensional albacore with the word *BAIT* painted across it, and Dunaway plugs it full of holes. "After a few moments," continued Sylbert, "blood starts to leak out of the holes and is washed down the side of the fish by the cleansing rain. THE END."

16. Diana Vreeland came to Hollywood in the spring of 1974 to study the movies' influence on fashion for the Metropolitan Museum's Costume Institute but wound up instead shuttling with Warren Beatty to Jack's all-night parties. She rationalized that hob-nobbing with Cher, Brenda Vaccaro, Marjoe Gortner, and a hundred other celebrity ephemera who were drawn like mayflies to Jack's place after dark constituted a certain kind of research.

17. On a detailed Web site titled "The Religious Affiliations of Jack Nicholson" (www.adherents.com/people/pn/Jack_Nicholson.html), an impressive case is made for Jack's fall from Roman Catholicism and resurrection in the orgasmic mysticism of Wil-helm Reich.

18. Installed in 1976, the frothing playground consisted of a half-dozen interlocking circles, like misshapen Olympic rings, and served as a prelude to hundreds of trysts.

19. On the Fox production of another yarn with a very different hook, *Cinderella Liberty* (sailor James Caan falls for hooker Marsha Mason and becomes a surrogate father for her son), the navy refused to cooperate, just as it had with *The Last Detail*. Ponicsan saw a third effort quashed when the producers of *Countermeasures*, his story about mur-der onboard a nuclear aircraft carrier, did not pass the navy's public relations muster.

20. Boyer won Best Actor for the director Alain Resnais's *Stavisky* (1974), which turned out to be Boyer's penultimate film in a career that spanned more than five decades. He overdosed on barbiturates two days after his wife's death in 1978.

21. Jack told his old pal Bruce Dern that he, too, was under consideration but that Jack was holding out for his first $1 million role and was certain that he would get it.

22. After fathering two daughters with the actress Vanessa Redgrave (Natasha and Joely Richardson), Richardson adopted a gay lifestyle and died of AIDS in 1991.

23. Gordy took the director's credit although he never directed before or since.

24. Bertolucci finished the script shortly after he completed *Last Tango in Paris* (1972), only to have it passed over, unproduced, and consigned forever to Hollywood limbo.

25. "One day I took some peyote and didn't come off it for ten months, and then my book was finished," the author Ken Kesey deadpanned.

26. *Cuckoo's Nest* was viewed by Hollywood's old guard as downbeat tragedy rather than black comedy. The closest Kirk Douglas came to cinching a deal was with Avco Embassy's Joseph Levine, who ultimately passed in 1969.

27. After *Cuckoo's Nest* swept the Oscars, Douglas's character Steve Keller went on a permanent leave from police work to take up teaching.

28. Steve Zaentz's Fantasy Films brought *Payday* in at $746,000—$62,000 under budget.

29. Jack was the first to do so under the theater's new name, Mann's Chinese The-ater. Built by the legendary showman Sid Grauman in 1927, one of Hollywood's few ven-erable landmarks hosted more premieres than any other theater in the world. When the

Minnesota theater chain owner Ted Mann purchased it in 1973, Grauman had been dead twenty-three years. Following a ripple of protest, the city fathers and the fickle public accepted Mann's name, just as he predicted they would.

30. Don Devlin had just finished *Loving* (1970), starring George Segal and Eva Marie Saint. Partnered with Harry Gittes, he chose as his next film *Harry and Walter Go to New York* (1976).

31. Hackman's next role was in the all-star bomb *A Bridge Too Far* (1977), which featured A-list talent like Robert Redford and Michael Caine but failed to break even on its $26 million price tag.

32. Minnelli segued to *A Matter of Time* (1976), her father's swansong for American International Pictures. He went over budget, the film tanked, and Liza moved on to *New York, New York* (1977), one of the director Martin Scorsese's few box office turkeys.

33. Reynolds scored a raspberry in *At Long Last Love* (1975), the director Peter Bogdanovich's abortive $6 million tribute to 1930s musicals.

34. Mama Cass Elliott did not choke on a ham sandwich, which was a popular urban legend in the 1970s.

35. On September 7, 1978, the Who's drummer Keith Moon died in the same apartment.

36. Some of Jack's earliest friends contest his total surprise. Charles Eastman specifically recalls a day at Hermosa Beach in the summer of 1963 when Jack tearfully confessed a version of the June-Mud story shortly before he left for Mexico to film *Ensign Pulver*. "He knew," said his sister-in-law Cheryl Cron. "He knew before June died that she was his mother."

37. Among others, the journalist Eve Berliner has detailed Furcillo-Rose's claim to paternity, including love letters, early photos, and a purported wedding certificate tying Furcillo-Rose to the underage June Nilson (June Nicholson's stage name). Berliner's findings are available at www.evesmag.com/nicholson.htm.

CHAPTER 11

1. The former talk show host, hotelier, and *Jeopardy* creator Merv Griffin owned St. Clerans, having decorated everything from the doors to the pillowcases with his personal crest: a heraldic symbol depicting the mythical creature with the body of a lion and the wings of an eagle.

2. *A Walk with Love and Death* cost $1.5 million to produce.

3. More than a decade after Tony and Anjelica, Ricki Huston bore a third child, Allegra, in 1965, but John was not the father. Nonetheless, following Ricki's death, John raised the girl as his own.

4. In 1962, John fathered the future actor Danny Huston by the actress Zoe Sallis.

5. Another New Jersey native whose sister ran a beauty parlor, the diminutive DeVito was seven inches shorter and seven years Jack's junior and came to *Cuckoo's Nest* via an Off-Broadway production, where he played the role of Martini in a revival of Kirk Douglas's original stage version.

6. While *Cuckoo's Nest* was his impressive film debut, neither Lloyd nor DeVito established their celebrity bona fides until they costarred in NBC's *Taxi* (1978–1983).

7. Jack made one of his halfhearted attempts to kick smoking during *Cuckoo's Nest*, betting Michael Douglas $1,000 that he'd quit first. "We both lost," Douglas told *People* magazine.

8. The role of "Big Nurse" Ratched was turned down by Jane Fonda, Anne Bancroft, Colleen Dewhurst, Faye Dunaway, Angela Lansbury, Ellen Burstyn, Geraldine Page, and Jeanne Moreau.

Jack blamed the emergence of women's lib, but Moreau decried the story's misogyny. "My God, the hatred of women," she said, adding her interpretation that Chief

Bromden and McMurphy behaved like closet lovers. "Remember when the Indian holds Jack Nicholson before he kills him? I was fascinated by that scene."

A plum role, Big Nurse was worth an Oscar, but it typecast Fletcher as a prim misanthropist. The remainder of her long career was generally limited by casting directors to television or secondary film characters.

9. *Jack Nicholson: Face to Face* by Robert David Crane and Christopher Fryer (New York: M. Evans & Co., 1975).

10. Sensing box office trouble a week before the movie opened, Jack hedged his bet by selling back 5 percent of his eventual gross to Elliot Kastner for $1 million in cash. Kastner agreed but didn't pay, prompting Jack to sue later that year.

11. Brando claimed that *The Missouri Breaks* eventually earned him more than $16.5 million, a bigger payday than his legendary cameo in *Superman* as Christopher Reeves's father, Jor-El: $15 million for three days in front of the cameras.

12. Five years later, cost overruns would bring down the entire studio when *Heaven's Gate* (1980) did to UA what *Mutiny on the Bounty* almost did to MGM in 1962 and *Cleopatra* did to Fox in 1963.

13. In addition to expensive experiments with wind and solar power, Brando tried to farm sea tortoises and Maine lobsters in his lagoon.

14. The young writer was six years older than Jack and the author of a celebrated Oregon trilogy built around the frontier character Elbridge Trask. Before Don Berry died at seventy in 2001, he moved from the typewriter to cyberspace, publishing most of his later work on the Internet.

15. Newspapers speculated that the beret covered healing hair plugs Jack had recently had installed. When confronted by a Roman paparazzo who asked him to doff his beret for a snapshot near the Colosseum, Jack said, "Oh no, I never take the hat off. I even sleep with it on."

16. Ironically, Jack's twelfth Oscar nomination for *About Schmidt* (2002) chronicles the odyssey of the retired insurance salesman and widower Warren Schmidt, who crisscrosses the country like Carney's Harry Coombes.

17. When Daniel Ellsberg was on the lam after the 1971 publication of the Pentagon Papers, Jack similarly offered the former Rand Corporation Vietnam expert safe haven for awhile. "Back when he was on the run, Ellsberg played the piano in this house in his underwear," Jack told *Rolling Stone*. "He played beautifully, by the way."

18. Two years earlier, the Oscar winner Marlon Brando sent Sacheen Littlefeather (actually, the actress Maria Cruz made up like Pocahontas) to refuse on his behalf, having her slam both the nation and the Academy for discriminating against Native Americans. When Jack called his next-door neighbor at two-thirty that morning to offer his congratulations, Brando didn't answer the phone.

19. President Gerald Ford would effectively end the argument two weeks later during a speech at Tulane University, where he declared Vietnam "a war that is finished as far as America is concerned." As the last Americans to leave Saigon, the U.S. Embassy's marines turned out the light at the end of General William Westmoreland's tunnel by the first of May 1975.

20. Coppola, thirty-six, and the author Mario Puzo, fifty-five, shared the award for adapting Puzo's novel for the screen.

21. *Gone with the Wind* three hours and forty-two minutes, but neatly bisected by an intermission that graced neither *Godfather*.

22. Jack counted Sturges's *The Lady Eve* (1941) as one of his all-time favorite comedies, but following the celebrated director's string of 1940s successes, Sturges alienated the studios in the 1950s as a profligate perfectionist. He died unemployed and nearly broke in the Algonquin Hotel in 1959.

23. D. W. Griffith was Hollywood's first and most famous innovator. The director of

Birth of a Nation (1915), Griffith was forced into retirement in 1931 after directing more than five hundred films. While living alone at Hollywood's kitschy old Knickerbocker Hotel, he suffered a cerebral hemorrhage in 1948 and died in the lobby.

24. Introducing Antonioni as "one of my favorite dudes," Jack presented an honorary Oscar for career achievement to him during the 1995 Academy Awards. Nearly a year later, the Oscar was stolen from Antonioni's Rome apartment during the Christmas holidays.

25. Mike Nichols's next movie was to have been *The Last Tycoon* (1976), but after repeated clashes with Sam Spiegel, the producer replaced Nichols with Elia Kazan. Nichols similarly warred with Robert DeNiro over *The Man Who Looked Like Bogie*, walked off the set, and did not return to Hollywood until he directed *Silkwood* (1983).

26. Evans quit Paramount three days after the 1975 Oscar telecast to become an independent producer. His first foray was the hit *Marathon Man* (1976), followed by the more modest *Black Sunday* (1977) and the bomb *Players* (1979). After his career hit the skids with the debacle *Popeye* (1980), it took a full decade and a helping hand from Jack for Evans to recover.

27. An early supporter, Brando supplied AIM with money, sanctuary, and the power of his celebrity throughout the turbulent 1970s.

28. Brando had a big silver "Executive" sign posted on the side of his.

29. One of many former Brando paramours, Pat Quinn played the title role in Arthur Penn's *Alice's Restaurant* (1969).

30. *The Missouri Breaks* is one of Hollywood's few products condemned by the American Humane Society for its treatment of animals, although the animals in question were horses, not frogs.

31. Based on McGuane's best seller *92 in the Shade* (1975) was written and directed by the author and costarred Jack's pals Harry Dean Stanton, Peter Fonda, and Warren Oates, as well as McGuane's then wife, Margot Kidder.

32. Robert Towne's next script doctoring assignment was *Orca* (1977) for Dino De Laurentiis.

33. In 1978, Brando persuaded the pop star Jackson Browne and Jack to invest in photovoltrolysis, a process using solar power to break down water, producing hydrogen to power auto engines.

34. *Dalva* (1988), a story of a wayward Nebraska woman searching for her bastard son, resonates with the recurrent Nicholson theme of illegitimacy, and Jim Harrison's roman à clef, *True North* (2004), tells the tale of a reckless alcoholic father's lifelong effect on his sensitive son.

35. Harrison lost his left eye playing doctor with a female playmate when he was seven years old.

36. First published in *Esquire*, *Revenge* was brought to the screen in 1990 by the director Tony Scott. It starred Kevin Costner, Anthony Quinn, and Madeleine Stowe.

37. The lead in *Legends of the Fall* went to Brad Pitt, thirty, and the role of his father to fifty-six-year-old Anthony Hopkins. Although Jack was Hopkins's contemporary, Jack chose to play far younger than his fifty-six years. The same year that *Legends* became a movie, Jack took the lead in *Wolf* (1994), based on another of Harrison's stories. Both Jack and the author believed that *Legends* should have been far grittier but the author did not complain about the money. The film rights sale pushed Harrison's annual earnings from $12,000 to $650,000.

38. Even Mann's venerable Chinese Theater went from one to six screens, although Sid Grauman's original rococo exterior remained untouched.

39. Based on the MGM "boy wonder" Irving Thalberg, who created a legend by producing a string of hits during the earliest days of talking motion pictures; marrying the biggest star of the moment, Norma Shearer; and dying at age thirty-seven before the excesses of Louis Mayer and middle age shone a spotlight on the cracks in his genius.

40. Two percent of the gross up to $15 million and 3 percent thereafter.

41. With Brando's help, AIM's cofounder successfully lobbied California govenor Jerry Brown for amnesty and didn't return to South Dakota to face the Pine Ridge charges until ten years later. Banks served an eighteen-month prison sentence before returning to Hollywood, where he segued into a successful acting and recording career.

42. Shot by Oregon police trying to escape, Peltier fled briefly to Canada and was caught, tried, and sentenced for the killing of the two FBI agents. While the other AIM members implicated in Pine Ridge were either acquitted or served minimal jail time, Peltier has been imprisoned continuously since 1976 and remains a cause célèbre to many.

43. Along with Redford, Pacino, Hackman, and Caan, Jack turned down Martin Sheen's role in *Apocalypse Now*. Playing opposite Brando once was enough.

CHAPTER 12

1. Jack's green, two-bedroom, nineteenth-century Victorian farmhouse, located on the same street as Lou Adler's in the West End, was next door to Elizabeth "Pussy" Paepke, the grand dame who, with her late Denver industrialist husband, Walter, had put Aspen on the map in the late 1940s. Whenever Jack wanted to pull the octogenarian widow's chain, he went to the front door and hollered, "Here, pussy, pussy!"

2. Although it was banned in Eastern Bloc countries because the director, Forman, was a Western defector and the antiauthoritarian theme made every heavy-handed party apparatchik seem like Big Nurse, no less a fan than Vladimar Putin confessed to Jack at the 23rd Moscow International Film Festival in June 2001 that *Cuckoo's Nest* was his favorite movie.

3. Kesey maintained that Saul Zaentz and Michael Douglas had contracted with him to adapt his novel to the screen, but when Kesey insisted on narrating the tale through the eyes and the voice of Chief Bromden, as was done in the novel, Milos Forman and the producers rejected his script.

4. When Universal tackled Kesey's second novel, *Sometimes a Great Notion* (1971), five years earlier on location in Newport, Oregon, Kesey bitterly described the cast and the crew as "the Hollywood dream-makers who made a lot of promises, got three women pregnant, and suddenly, they were gone.

5. Warren Beatty, who accompanied Mirisch to Pickfair for the remote TV feed, later told friends that the actress suffered from acute alcoholism.

6. Born Gladys Marie Smith, Pickford received her first Academy Award in 1930 for *Coquette* (1929). She retired from acting in 1933 after making 247 films but continued to produce until 1949. She was considered among her peers to be the quintessential cold steel actor-businesswoman who could weep for the camera without ever losing sight of the bottom line.

7. Jack's praise hadn't abated eighteen years later when he told an interviewer, "She found that of all the movies shot by Paramount, only hers made money."

8. Neither Jack nor the film's other winners thanked Ken Kesey—an outcome the novelist likened to "pumps trying to say they're more important than the well or the water."

9. The director was promoting one of his early films in the fall of 1968 when the Soviet army infamously crushed Czechoslovakia's embryonic democracy during "Prague Spring." Forman remained in the United States rather than return to his native country.

10. "It was Jack who told me to study Bette Davis on film and watch the way she used her eyes, which are similar to mine," said Carol Kane. "He taught me so much about film."

11. To develop properties like *Moontrap*, Jack incorporated Proteus Films, named for the son of Poseidon (Neptune) in Greek mythology—a soothsaying sea god who

minds his father's harem and changes form every time a mere mortal gets too near, rather than reveal the future.

12. Built for the Danish opera singer Lauritz Melchior in the 1930s, the International Style barn had to be gutted and remodeled from scratch. Among other amenities, Beatty added a self-contained safe room comparable to the sanctuary where Jodie Foster hid out from the bad guys in the movie *Panic Room* (2002).

13. No slouch himself in the roué department, Ryan O'Neal juggled Anjelica with the newly divorced Melanie Griffith over the next year, ultimately settling on neither.

14. A bisexual Polish bohemian with bourgeois roots, de Lempicka and her husband—a well-heeled Austrian baron—fled Europe at the outset of World War II and settled in King Vidor's Beverly Hills manse, where fanzines dubbed her "Favorite Artist to the Stars." Tyrone Power, Greta Garbo, and Delores del Rio, among others, bought her androgynous oils and visited her studio. After her death in 1980, the artist's life became the basis of the hit participatory play *Tamara*, which starred Anjelica Huston in the title role during the 1985 Hollywood edition. Besides Jack, Madonna avidly collected de Lempicka.

15. In later years, the privy's showpiece was a pair of nudes with their tongues in each other's mouths, painted by the German Dadaist George Grosz. A rattlesnake was embedded in the clear plastic toilet seat, and a collage above the loo read, "Does size matter?"

16. Two others with whom Jack tried to work, but never succeeded, were Bernardo Bertolucci and Lina Wertmuller, another Italian and the first woman director ever nominated for an Oscar (*Seven Beauties* [1975]).

17. *Barry Lyndon* starred Ryan O'Neal, Jack's rival for Anjelica.

18. After the book's publication in 1982, Jack reportedly paid $100,000 for the rights to *The Murder of Napoleon* (New York: Congdon & Lattes). The authors Ben Weider and David Hapgood based their book on the theory of a Swedish dentist who spent twenty years dissecting historical evidence and concluded that Napoleon was poisoned while in exile.

19. Towne insisted that the final installment would be titled *Gittes vs. Gittes* and would be about "a detective who's spent his whole life in matrimonial cases, getting sued by his own wife."

20. The three men were so obsessed that at dinner one evening at Scandia's restaurant, Evans's tipsy date threw up as the trio hotly debated *The Two Jakes*. None of the men noticed until after Anjelica had covered the mess with a napkin and she and Towne's wife led the woman off to the restroom.

21. In the December 12, 1976, entry of his scabrous *Diaries*, Warhol wrote, "I read the Ruth Kligman book *Love Affair* about her 'love affair' with Jackson Pollock—and that's in quotes. It's so bad—how could you ever make a movie of it without making a whole new story?" A decade later, the pop artist was still pestering Jack to star in his biopic.

22. *Pirates* bombed, but a similar tale featuring the same story line and a seriocomic Johnny Depp in the lead cornered the box office in the summer of 2003. *Pirates of the Caribbean: The Curse of the Black Pearl* and its 2006 sequel, *Pirates of the Caribbean: Dead Man's Chest*, grossed well in excess of half a billion dollars. *Pirates of the Caribbean: At World's End* (2007) appeared to put the Disney franchise within striking distance of the $1 billion mark.

23. Best remembered during the seventies as a hefty TV shill for Paul Masson wines ("We'll serve no wine before its time"), Orson Welles died in 1985 never having directed another film. His final feature-length release was the masterful *A Touch of Evil* (1958).

24. For $500,000 and 5 gross points, Richard Dreyfuss took the part in *Close Encounters of the Third Kind*.

25. Jack was so taken by the elastic Face Dancers in Herbert's *Dune Messiah* that he declared the characters "my influence."

26. Though Jack was too old to star in it himself, he still held the rights to *Henderson the Rain King* as late as 2001. Like Jack, Bellow was a follower of Wilhelm Reich, once investing in his own Orgone boxes.

27. Police once ticketed Jack for crossing the yellow line as he emerged from a tunnel on treacherous Malibu Canyon Road. He groused, "Christ, these fucking guys, don't they know who I am?"

28. In 1977, Jack bought an additional twenty-eight acres of undeveloped ranch land in the Santa Monica Mountains above Malibu, not far from a similar undeveloped tract that Bob Dylan purchased and later quitclaimed to his ex-wife, Sara.

29. "Spider" Sabich was the model for Robert Redford's *Downhill Racer* (1969).

30. Longet's trial inspired *Saturday Night Live*'s satirical "Claudine Longet Invitational Ski Tournament," in which rifle shots picked off "competitors" as they flew off a ski jump.

31. When Jack and Lauren Hutton first met, he boasted to his posse, "She flew in from the East Coast just to fuck me."

32. Gia died of AIDS in 1986. She was twenty-six years old.

33. Married to a carpenter, Geimer lived in a Maui mobile home with her family, which she subsidized by part-time work as a legal transcriber. She later moved to Kailua, the same Oahu town where Jack's ex-wife, Sandra, and her husband live.

34. Anjelica's younger sister, who stayed with her off and on, was eleven, while Tatum O'Neal, who regarded her father's new girlfriend as a role model, was also thirteen.

35. Paramount called on Charles Shyer and Alan Mandel, the team that created *Smokey and the Bandit* (1977) and *Housecalls* (1977), to rewrite *Goin' South* for laughs.

36. Patty Hearst was arrested in 1975 and imprisoned the following year, effectively putting an end to an era, as well as to the Symbionese Liberation Army. Like returning Vietnam vets or *Goin' South*'s Quantrill's Raiders at the close of the Civil War, the SLA's alleged raison d'être was over.

37. Lana Turner was just another MGM starlet until the studio publicity machine spread the lie that she'd been discovered by a talent scout while sipping a soda at Schwab's drugstore on the Sunset Strip.

38. Belushi first caught Jack's attention when he parodied Nicholson in an SNL version of *Cuckoo's Nest*, featuring Raquel Welch as Nurse Ratched.

39. When Belushi demanded per diem for postproduction dubbing, Jack's producers sent over a woman in a Subaru to pick him up at his hotel and paid him $100 in quarters, dimes, and nickels.

40. An early twentieth-century protégé of Fredric Remington, Maynard Dixon produced highly stylized "snapshots" of the Old West that became prizes among Jack's growing collection of oils.

CHAPTER 13

1. Cast as Woody Allen's friend Tony Lacey in the film, Paul Simon describes a New York party as "mellow. Small. Jack and Anjelica will be there."

2. The Timberline Lodge was transformed into Colorado's fictitious Overlook Hotel. Room 217, where the Torrance family stayed in King's novel, became room 237 in the film so that future Timberline guests would not be afraid to sleep in the real room 217.

3. Kubrick offered Harry Dean Stanton the role of Lloyd the bartender, but *Alien* kept Stanton out of *The Shining*.

4. Because of Jack's penchant for consummating in cars, his first coupling with the rock wannabe and notorious groupie Bebe Buell ("wholesome backseat sex," in her words) led to a lyrical commemoration of that act in Buell's song "Normal Girl."

5. Compared to McDonald's golden arches and "twin Mt. Fujis hovering in his forehead" (Pauline Kael), his brows got singled out for comment because of "Reichian particularism," said Jack. "People are dismembered in order to negate them. With a woman, they pick out one tit, one leg and show each part, one at a time. It's to stimulate the fetishness in the mass mind."

6. Made of hundreds of ersatz hedges and topiary stapled to the floor of a soundstage, the artifice was so intricate and complex that stagehands got lost in it.

7. Until shutting its doors forever in 1962, the Grand Guignol fostered a bizarre, horrifying, sleaze-laden brand of Parisian theater that reveled in murder, prostitution, perversion, and the supernatural. Paula Maxa, the Grand Guignol's best-known star, died on stage for close to two decades in more imaginative ways than had any other actress in history, expiring from gunshot, scalping, strangulation, rape, disembowelment, guillotine, hanging, burning, scorpion bite, arsenic, mountain lion, whipping, quartering, scalpels, stabbing, and mutilation with an invisible Spanish dagger. She also kissed a leper and "simply decomposed on stage in front of an audience," according to one critic, but she never failed to please.

8. Jack first used the gimmick in *Carnal Knowledge*, tossing the line "Heeeeere's Bobbie!" at Ann-Margret during one of their marathon blowouts.

9. Richard Brautigan was a one-time client at Oregon State Hospital for the Insane, where *Cuckoo's Nest* was filmed. The troubled counterculture writer shot himself to death in 1984. He was forty-nine.

10. In the autumn of 2006, BMW announced plans to test 7-Series sedans powered by 12-cylinder internal-combustion engines capable of burning gasoline or liquefied hydrogen.

11. George Lucas had planned to use the set next for *The Empire Strikes Back*.

12. Originally scheduled for a six-week shoot in the Philippines, Francis Coppola's Vietnam paean to Joseph Conrad's *Heart of Darkness* wound up taking sixteen months.

13. For $380 million, MGM bought the troubled studio from the San Francisco insurance company Transamerica, reducing UA to a distribution arm of the larger studio.

14. Beatty originally thought of another playwright, the sometime actor Sam Shepherd, for the role.

15. Both of O'Neill's sons suffered alcohol and/or heroin addiction and committed suicide. He disowned his eighteen-year-old daughter, Oona, after she married fifty-four-year-old Charlie Chaplin in 1943. In his memoir, Don Furcillo-Rose claimed to have had "a brief fling" with Oona while she was just thirteen and growing up on the O'Neill estate in New Jersey, two years after Furcillo-Rose said that he had fathered Jack. Nicholson met with the then fifty-three-year-old Oona in 1979 in preparation for *Reds*.

16. The lead in *Shampoo* was patterned after the Beverly Hills salon operator Gene Schicove, who cut Beatty's hair once a week when he was living at the Beverly Wilshire Hotel.

CHAPTER 14

1. Following a freak accident that cost their young daughter's life, Rafelson divorced his wife, the set designer Toby Carr Rafelson—a move that set the director adrift professionally and personally for several years. Until *Postman*, he hadn't finished a film since *Stay Hungry* (1975), the oddball weightlifting comedy that introduced Arnold Schwarzenegger to American audiences.

2. Directed by Stuart Rosenberg, *Brubaker* earned back its production cost within the first three weeks of release in the summer of 1980, even though it was up against *The Shining* and other blockbusters.

3. One of the founding fathers of neorealism in Italian cinema, Visconti presided over the Cannes Film Festival jury that nominated *Easy Rider* for the Palme d'Or in 1969.

4. Though Anjelica did, briefly exposing her backside in the film.

5. In *This Is Spinal Tap* (1984), which featured Anjelica in a small role, Harry Shearer's character solved the public erection problem by substituting a pickle wrapped in tin foil until airport security unsheathed his deception.

6. A latter-day Jeff Corey, Feury opened the Loft Studio with her husband, Bill Traylor, in 1973 and trained Michelle Pfeiffer, Sean Penn, and Jeff Goldblum, among many others.

7. Jack might ban photographs at his place, but Anjelica opened her doors to *Architectural Digest*.

8. By the time Anjelica moved to larger quarters, there were just four fish: Ruby, Opal, Spot, and Jade. Pearl, alas, had passed on from the fishbowl to the toilet bowl.

9. Anjelica is the godmother to one of Jagger's children.

10. Todd Rundgren, Mick Jagger, and Steven Tyler were among her lovers. She was also the mother of the actress Liv Tyler.

11. Despite being panned by critics, *The Shining* finished out the year second only to *The Empire Strikes Back* at the box office.

12. Kubrick baffled King and audience alike by snipping *The Shining*'s two-minute epilogue after the New York previews. In the lost ending, the hospitalized Wendy (the actress Shelley Duvall) learns that her husband's body was never found, implying that she might have been unbalanced and that her terrifying stay at the Overlook Hotel was all imagined.

13. A possible delayed reaction to Jack's wrestling match six years earlier with the hydrotherapy unit in *Cuckoo's Nest*.

14. Steenburgen's character in *Goin' South*, Julia Tate, avoided emotional confrontation with Henry Lloyd Moon by hanging chairs on the wall.

15. Steenburgen and the actor Malcolm McDowell had had their first child, the actress Lily McDowell, in January.

16. Honey Hollman was born near the year's end and grew up with the knowledge that Jack was her dad, although she did not go public with the information until twenty-four years later, in 2006.

17. In a similar stunt, Zack Norman booked all but one of the first-class seats on a flight from L.A. to San Francisco that he learned Jack would be taking. He then put a copy of the script on every empty seat, including Jack's.

18. Jack reportedly optioned the author's *Legends of the Fall*, a novella that eventually devolved to other producers and launched Brad Pitt into the box office stratosphere in 1994.

19. Ignatius J. Reilly was a part John Belushi wanted to play.

20. The Serbian filmmaker Dusan Makavejev made an absurdist paean to Reich in *Sweet Movie* (1974), one of Jack's favorite films. Complete with displays of bulimia, pedophilia, defecation, golden showers, dildoes, and public sex, the bizarre fantasy of two women wading through nearly every imaginable taboo remains so raw it continues to be banned in Britain.

21. In March 1982, Jack bought a home in Kailua.

22. From 1972 to 1976, Moore was married to Richard Sylbert, the production designer for *Blood and Wine*, *Chinatown*, *The Fortune*, *Reds*, and *Carnal Knowledge*, among others. During Jonathan's "Ball Busters on Parade" slide show cataloguing the castrating women in his life, Moore's snapshot appears, along with that of the *Carnal Knowledge* still photographer Mary Ellen Mark.

23. HBO and CBS each owned a third of TriStar.

24. Sir John Gielgud did win, for his role as the butler in *Arthur* (1981).

25. Now Jack's sunglasses were also prescription; his casual Ray-Ban days had given way to presbyopia, and his shades were no longer of the boutique variety.

CHAPTER 15

1. The opening line of *Fear and Loathing in Las Vegas* ranks with that of *The Postman Always Rings Twice* as one of the best known in twentieth-century American literature: "We were somewhere around Barstow on the edge of the desert when the drugs began to take hold."

2. In a media circus foreshadowing the show trials of O. J. Simpson, Michael Jackson, Robert Blake, and a host of other unfortunate, indiscreet celebrities, the newspaper heir Peter Pulitzer divorced his wife, Roxanne, after running her down in court as an unfit mother and a coke slut who had earned her nickname "strumpet with a trumpet" after sleeping with her favorite musical instrument.

3. "Uncle Duke" was immortalized in Garry Trudeau's "Doonesbury" cartoon strip.

4. One of the plague's earliest victims, the Manhattan modeling agent Zoltan "Zoli" Rendessy was forty-one when he died in 1982. He had supplied Jack and Ara Gallant with "moe-dells" since the early seventies.

5. The role was originally intended for Diane Keaton, followed by Debra Winger.

6. Hutton later sued MGM, accusing the studio of lying about the switch in directors to keep him from committing to other projects and depriving him of months of employment while he rode the crest of his popularity as the Oscar-winning star of *Ordinary People* (1980). In 1989, a jury agreed and awarded Hutton $9.75 million, but by then, his star window had shut and he was just another second-tier actor.

7. Jennifer Jones optioned the novel in 1979 and originally angled for Al Pacino as her costar.

8. The role was first offered to Anne Bancroft and Louise Fletcher, but MacLaine understood prim. She had to take matters into her own hands during one raucous scene when she and Nicholson were in bed and Winger sneaked in under the covers, licking their thighs. As Jack held MacLaine's shoulders and Winger, her legs, it looked as if she were about to experience an involuntary threesome until she grabbed Jack's testicles and refused to let go until they both backed off.

9. Paired with the Nebraska governor Bob Kerry at the time, Winger would marry Timothy Hutton in 1986 and divorce him four years later, shortly after Hutton won his *Roadshow* suit against MGM.

10. Jack's advice on playing a drunk was to walk as if everything might break—the furniture, the walls, even the floor.

11. Janet Schweikart was a cheerleader in Jack's class and had a part in *The Curious Savage*.

12. In one short-lived original staged in a basement in downtown L.A., Anjelica played a predatory sixty-year-old Hong Kong lesbian for a microscopic audience.

13. When a film version of *Wired* was attempted five years later, however, it failed miserably. In his first movie role, the actor Michael Chiklis later said he felt that his career suffered for a time because he'd naively accepted the role of the late comedian when no other actor would do so.

14. MacLaine had just published the first of her New Age manifestos, *Out on a Limb*, which detailed her otherworldly views of spirituality. Winger, a survivor of a near-fatal auto accident ten years earlier, held a similar set of beliefs about the search for life's meaning.

15. Nominated four times but previously never a winner, Shirley MacLaine started her speech with "I really deserve this."

16. Jack told *Rolling Stone*, "I'd like to win more Oscars than Walt Disney [nineteen], and I'd like to win them in every category."

17. By the late 1990s, the Roxy founder-owner Lou Adler had turned over management of the Sunset Strip night spot to the oldest of his seven sons and Jack's namesake, Nic.

18. Six years later in 1990, the *Hollywood Reporter* stated that *Terms of Endearment* had five net profit participants and had paid out $4,989,000 to each of them.

19. For Jack's forty-third birthday, Anjelica bought him a cigarette lighter from the boutique for $67.50 so he could light kindling in his fireplace.

20. Bob Towne had written the part of a UCLA coach who sleeps with a student athlete for Jack, who politely passed.

21. *The Cotton Club*'s production designer, Richard Sylbert, called the pretty, pointless finished film "a coffee table movie."

CHAPTER 16

1. In 1996, Baratta and his sister Mary Lou—for whom their original Greenwich Village restaurant was named—published *Cooking for Jack* (Pocket Books). In addition to Jack's favorite recipes, the Barattas threw in Danny DeVito's Escarole and Bean Soup, Mike Nichols's Penne with Tomatoes, Kathleen Turner's Sicilian Steak Giardiniera, and Joe Pesci's Mother's Sweet Potato Gnocchi.

2. Joining the growing ranks of writer-directors, the immensely successful screenwriter Bob Towne directed *Personal Best* (1982), a flat and poorly received love triangle featuring a college track coach and his two star female athletes, the twist being the lesbian relationship between the two women.

3. After *Marathon Man* (1976) and *Urban Cowboy* (1980), Bob Evans's descent into drugs began to show first in the coked-out production of *Popeye* (1980), followed by the troubled and similarly coke-plagued *The Cotton Club* (1984).

4. *SpaceCamp* was another public relations nightmare. The family action-adventure was scheduled for theaters within weeks of the *Challenger* explosion on January 28, 1986. Claiming seven astronauts' lives, the space shuttle accident involved a solid rocket booster problem similar to the malfunction in the movie. When *SpaceCamp* was finally released later in the year, it grossed less than $10 million.

5. In August, the *Los Angeles Daily News* reported that Harrison Ford would replace Evans as the second Jake while Dino De Laurentiis would step in as producer. For legal reasons, the project was to be renamed. The following year at Cannes, Evans attacked Cannon Pictures over an internal memo saying that he was out of the picture entirely. Evans swore that *The Two Jakes* would never get made without him.

6. "Mind you, Jack is notorious for crying," said an assistant. "He'll cry because it's the best-looking spaghetti he's seen in his life."

7. Kallianiotes appeared as herself in the ill-fated *Renaldo and Clara*.

8. The cult classic *Kansas City Bombers* grossed five times its $1 million production cost and featured ten-year-old Jodie Foster in one of her earliest roles. Helena convincingly played "alcoholic lesbian hostility," according to *Time*; she was "one of the Trojan women on wheels," said *Newsweek*.

9. Anjelica was headed to Skateway the night of her head-on traffic accident in 1980.

10. A taskmistress like Helena, the New York grand dame once expelled the wife of the Indonesia dictator Sukarno, who retaliated with a $4 million lawsuit. The court awarded her one franc.

11. Nichols reportedly paid Patinkin half a million to walk away after less than a week on the set. Nichols also considered Dustin Hoffman, who had played Carl Bernstein in *All the President's Men*, and Kevin Kline.

12. Jack also agreed to narrate the soundtrack to *Elephant's Child* (1986), TV fables based on Rudyard Kipling's stories, including the story of how the elephant got its trunk. He won a Grammy for Best Recording for Children. Jack's readings were part of a twenty-two-minute animated video titled "How the Rhinoceros Got His Skin and How the Camel Got His Hump," incorporating both tales on laser disc, the forerunner of both the CD and the DVD, which would dominate music and video in the next century.

13. Directed and cowritten by Dylan, the four-hour film collage of fantasy sandwiched between concert footage of his Rolling Thunder Revue closed before it opened and remains seldom seen.

14. Others Dylan thanked in the liner notes included the Dodger pitcher Steve Howe, the New York Mets' Sid Fernandez, and the actor Martin Sheen.

15. Dylan's three-song set was "The Ballad of Hollis Brown," "The Hour That the Ship Comes In" and "Blowin' in the Wind."

16. The future Oscar winner Kevin Spacey made his feature film debut in *Heartburn* as a subway mugger, as did TV's *Monk*, Tony Shaloub.

17. Subtitled *How to Survive the Sexual Revolution*, the book (coauthored by David J. Fox) maintained that the American male was drowning in a sea of estrogen, trying to submerge his true identity in order "to become the kind of man he believes women want."

CHAPTER 17

1. Dreyfuss was coming off a highly publicized cocaine addiction and fresh out of rehab, so the 1977 Oscar winner accepted Disney's cut-rate salary of $600,000—a price Jack wouldn't have considered, regardless of the back-end offer.

2. Kevin Costner played Ness to Robert DeNiro's Al Capone in the David Mamet script.

3. Playing off Sinatra's 1960s Rat Pack, the 1980s version included Rob Lowe, Demi Moore, Judd Nelson, Anthony Michael Hall, Molly Ringwald, Emilio Estevez, and Ally Sheedy, among others.

4. And yet the musical set piece, with Matthew Broderick leading a St. Patrick's Day parade in a raucous lip sync of the Beatles' version of "Twist and Shout," has become a cinema classic.

5. Jack was referring to *The Golden Child* (1986), Eddie Murphy's bizarre follow-up to the original *Beverly Hills Cop* (1984).

6. The director David Lynch's masterwork exhumed Dennis Hopper's drug-addled career and made perversion in small-town America obsessively fashionable.

7. They were commemorated for their greed and profligacy in the 1996 best-seller *Hit & Run: How Jon Peters and Peter Guber Took Sony for a Ride in Hollywood*.

8. Guber bought a 648-acre retreat in Aspen in 1987 near Jack's place and called it Mandalay. Each year on the Saturday before New Year's Eve, he threw a star bash, and Jack was always invited.

9. *The Witches of Eastwick* was Devlin's final movie. One of the first people to publicly accuse Universal's Lew Wasserman of keeping two sets of books, Devlin increasingly turned away from Hollywood and focused his attention on the emerging possibilities of the Internet until his death in 2000.

10. Jack sued RTO Rents of Georgia for the same amount because the firm used his picture in its flyers advertising VCRs. Both NEC and RTO settled with him out of court in 1990.

11. Murray reprised Jack as the masochistic dental patient in a musical remake of *Little Shop of Horrors* (1986).

12. The sci-fi series first popularized its star Mel Gibson in the United States.

13. For *Kiss of the Spider Woman* (1985), which was directed by Hector Babenco.

14. John Huston's only directing Oscar was for *The Treasure of the Sierra Madre* (1950).

15. Unlike Jack, she felt no compunction about cashing in on Oscar, taking $250,000 for a magazine layout advertising Cuervo Gold in the months following her win.

16. Cher had just won Best Actress at Cannes for *Mask* (1985) and was on her way to an Oscar for *Moonstruck* (1987).

17. Cristofer's next adaptation on behalf of Guber and Peters was the dreadful megabomb *The Bonfire of the Vanities* (1990).

18. Jack modeled his pompous character on NBC's Chet Huntley.

19. During the Iran-Contra affair, one wag suggested a miniseries starring Treat Williams as Oliver North, Fawn Hall as herself, and Jack as the Devil.

20. The cofounder of the Black Panther Party and a close chum of Bert Schneider and Steve Blauner, Newton was himself murdered by a drug dealer in 1989 after once being accused of killing a police officer and an underage prostitute.

21. In 2000, the Broadway producer Cameron Mackintosh (*Cats, Phantom of the Opera*) turned *Witches* into an award-winning musical starring Ian McShane as Daryl Van Horne. It ran for eighteen months in London's West End before closing shortly after September 11, 2001.

22. In *Ten North Frederick*, the 1958 movie based on a John O'Hara novel, a fifty-ish lawyer hooks up with a twentysomething woman who befriends the lawyer's troubled daughter, also in her twenties.

23. *Ironweed* did earn both of its leads Oscar nominations, but when Streep learned what Jack had been paid, she went public with her anger. She launched an indignant campaign to boost actress's salaries, which continued to lag 40 to 60 percent behind those of their male counterparts.

24. Anjelica's partners in the retreat were the production designer Jeremy Railton and the writer Tim Wilson.

25. In 1991, Jack renewed rights for $250,000 and hired *The Deerhunter* screen-writer Deric Washburn to write the script. He poured himself into all things Bonaparte, reading as many as twenty-three books on the deposed emperor of France.

26. In 2006, Warner Bros. cast Heath Ledger as the Joker in *The Dark Knight* (2008), the studio's latest *Batman* sequel.

27. A favorite of Jack's, particularly as it pertained to male-female relationships: "If the model of your ethical life is defeating you, change the model."

28. Even the Joker's real name is Jack: Jack Napier, the master criminal who murdered Bruce Wayne's parents. By the time the film premiered, Jack and Joker literally became synonymous.

29 Before awarding Batman to Michael Keaton, Warner Brothers considered Mel Gibson, Bill Murray, Charlie Sheen, and Pierce Brosnan.

30. Replacing the actress Sean Young, who broke her leg on the eve of filming, Kim Basinger was famously and frequently quoted as praising "crazy, nasty" Jack as "the most highly sexed human being I ever met."

CHAPTER 18

1. Two years earlier, the Japanese electronics giant paid $2 billion to acquire CBS Records.

2. In 1985, Murdoch gave up Australian citizenship in order to satisfy one of the few remaining FCC ownership requirements: that only U.S. citizens could own U.S. TV and radio stations.

3. In Towne's *Tequila Sunrise* (1988), a minor character's dialogue seemed to echo his own bitter feelings over the bust-up of TEN Productions: "Who says friendship lasts forever? We'd like it to maybe, but maybe it wears out like everything else. Like tires."

4. The *Hollywood Reporter* put his take from the movie at closer to $11 million.

5. The director John Waters spoofed Jack's earliest effort with *Cry Baby* (1990), starring Johnny Depp.

6. Julian Schnabel used Jack's toothbrush to paint the actor's portrait.

7. Harvey Keitel once described hanging with Jack as "like being in the grip of a really good novel."

8. Jennifer eventually dabbled in interior decorating, her father and Courtney Love among her first clients.

9. A Lubbock native who attended high school with Buddy Holly, Morris last appeared with Jack in *Anger Management* (2003) before his death from cancer in July 2004.

10. A permanent L.A. transplant by the early 1980s, Gallant hoped to use Jack's leverage to launch a directing career. Gallant killed himself in a Vegas hotel room in 1990. He was fifty-eight.

11. Jack also lobbied for Bert Schneider as a producer, but Paramount vetoed Harold's older brother on grounds that Bert was not up to the job. When Jack failed to stand up to the studio on Bert's behalf, it sparked a feud between them that lasted for more than a decade.

12. Towne so loathed the bowdlerized version of his screenplay for *Greystoke: The Legend of Tazan, Lord of the Apes* (1984) that he gave the writing credit to his dog. P. H. Vazak presumably became the first Oscar-nominated Hungarian komondor in screen history.

13. While Jack spent most of 1989 making *The Two Jakes*, Corman produced fifteen movies: *Warlock, Ministry of Vengeance, Bloodfist, Under the Boardwalk, Wizards of the Lost Kingdom II, The Terror Within, Time Trackers, Barbarian Queen II: The Empress Strikes Back, Heroes Stand Alone, Hollywood Boulevard II, Lords of the Deep, Masque of the Red Death, Primary Target, Silk 2,* and *Stripped to Kill II: Live Girls,* which starred Karen Mayo-Chandler.

14. Bob Rafelson remembered a similar helicopter ride to a Lakers game with Jack during the filming of *The Postman Always Rings Twice,* when Jack insisted, "'Come with me and we'll talk on the way back.' I would go along with him and, of course, he'd get so wasted we'd get nothing done."

15. The role in *Enemies: A Love Story* brought Anjelica a second Oscar nomination.

16. Rachel Ryan also dated *Batman* himself, Jack's costar Michael Keaton, before wedding the TV sitcom actor Richard Mulligan (*Empty Nest*) in 1992. The star of *Honey Buns* and *Deep Obsession* divorced Mulligan after just ten months of marriage.

17. Once the undisputed leader in loin uncoverage, Hefner's *Playboy* was nearly overtaken in the 1980s first by Bob Guccione's *Penthouse* and later by Larry Flynt's raunchfest *Hustler.* Only "tasteful" celebrity crotch shots and true confessions of the Mayo-Chandler variety kept the magazine competitive.

18. Roy Radin, a one-time Broadway impresario, was executed gangland style in a remote stretch of desert northeast of L.A. Prior to his death, Evans had proposed that Radin coproduce *The Two Jakes,* among a slate of other films.

19. In 1991, a jury convicted Evans's and Radin's cocaine dealer, Lanie Greenberger, along with her bodyguards, and sentenced them to life in prison.

20. Evans mortgaged even his Picassos, Dalís, a Rembrandt, and a Toulouse-Lautrec, all the way down to the silverware, a $9,000 mink-tail bedspread, and a J. C. Penney clock radio.

CHAPTER 19

1. Tim Burton wanted Brando to play the Penguin in *Batman Returns,* but Warner Bros. objected and Jack convinced Danny DeVito to take the role instead. Brando didn't return to the screen until *Don Juan DeMarco* (1995), in which he played Johnny Depp's psychiatrist for $3.25 million and 12.25 percent of the gross.

2. Jack's old Corey classmate and rival Robert Blake also played the labor leader in the 1983 made-for-TV movie *Blood Feud,* for which Blake was nominated for an Emmy.

3. DeVito directed, as well as acted in, *Throw Momma from the Train* (1987) and *The War of the Roses* (1989).

4. In an interview with the journalist Mikal Gilmore ten years later, Dylan said he had been running a temperature of 104 degrees that evening and that his remarks were aimed at four musicians who were to have offered a musical tribute but failed to show—a manifestation of his general bitterness about a business that, like the movies, had become more about money than about art.

5. Castle Rock Entertainment was founded by Reiner and four partners in 1987. The first and among the most successful of several "mini-majors" straddled the distance between the eight major studios and bare-bones independent production houses that emerged during the 1990s. Like New Line, Miramax, and a handful of others, Castle Rock began with a goal of producing premium entertainment from A-list talent but wound up catering to star demands just as the majors did. Castle Rock had to partner with Columbia in order to finance *A Few Good Men*. The mini-majors eventually had to merge or go out of business. Castle Rock sold to Turner Broadcasting in 1994.

6. The first nine Castle Rock productions cost about $20 million each and averaged grosses in the $40 million range. *A Few Good Men*, the company's tenth movie, was by far its most expensive.

7. Jack also used his Mulholland home for scenes set in Jake's house in *The Two Jakes*.

8. It was number 29 on the American Film Institute's 2005 list of the "Top 100 Movie Quotes." Jack's only other entry was "Here's Johnny" from *The Shining* (number 68), although the character actor Joe Mantell's unforgettable "Forget it, Jake. It's Chinatown" came in at number 74.

9. Before his 2001 execution, the convicted Oklahoma City federal building bomber Timothy McVeigh borrowed from a cable TV viewing of *A Few Good Men*, telling interviewers who believed he did not act alone: "You can't handle the truth because the truth is, it was just me."

10. Resonating *The Last Detail*'s vulgarity, David Mamet's *Hoffa* script used "fuck" 157 times.

11. Sorkin based his stage and screenplay on the trial of three young marines charged with the 1986 hazing of another marine at Guantanamo. In April 1994, one of those tried and expelled from the marines was himself murdered near his Massachusetts home, his body clad in a Marine Corps jacket. The crime remains unsolved.

12. A year younger than Jack, Graham catapulted into Southern California culture during the 1984 Olympics with the two headless *Olympic Gateway* bronzes outside the Los Angeles Memorial Coliseum. He created a similar *Torso* bronze on Rodeo Drive in Beverly Hills and capped his career with the twenty-five-ton bronze doors for the new Cathedral of Our Lady of the Angels, unveiled in downtown L.A. in 2003.

13. Thereafter, Jack made a point of weaing a red AIDS ribbon on his lapel at the Oscars and other public events throughout most of the rest of the 1990s.

14. Jack also gave his pet Lhasa apso the name Ray. When German shepherds killed the tiny animal, he eulogized, "If only I was as good a person as my dog. I'll never have the character that Ray had." When Jack's son, Ray, was old enough to own a dog, he got a shih tzu and named it Beanie.

15. At seventy-two, Evans married a sixth time in 2002, only to divorce two years later, remarry, and file for divorce a seventh time in 2006.

16. Using precisely the same deadpan phrasing, Jack described Mercedes McCambridge to Mamet: "When you looked at her early films, you *knew* . . ." and he paused a while for effect, "that she would be one of those women who, in later life, would wear excessive wrist jewelry."

17. The film crew celebrated Jack's fifty-fifth birthday with a cake that read "That's Right, Jack, It's Your Birthday."

CHAPTER 20

1. Since 1980, the "Razzies" have been announced the day before the Oscars to "dishonor" the worst film achievements of the previous year. Stallone is the all-time winner, with thirty nominations and ten wins.

2. Jack's deal was $7 million in salary, plus a $6 million guarantee against 10 percent of the gross. He was now working for what he termed *dead money*: back-end cash that would roll in to his heirs after he died.

3. The screenplay had no relation to Harrison's first novel, *Wolf: A False Memoir* (1971).

4. Jack underwrote Finkelstein's mortgage at 12644 Mulholland in 1992 and put both of their names on the deed.

5. Responding to a *Vanity Fair* cover story hyping *Wolf*, a reader sent a single-sentence letter to the editor: "Someone should tell Jack that wolves are monogamous."

6. "Jack's not like Redford," said Jeremy Larner. "He's not trying to write Boy Scout books about ecology."

7. Not only was Soderbergh's screenplay nominated for an Oscar, its $1.2 million budget transubstantiated into more than $24 million at the box office: cash register music to MPAA ears.

8. On March 20, 1991, Eric Clapton's four-and-a-half-year-old son fell fifty-three stories to his death through an open window in his mother's New York apartment. Clapton poured his own grief into the hit song "Tears in Heaven."

9. Sean Penn and Robin Wright's first child, a daughter, was named for Bob Dylan.

10. Married to the same woman for thirty years, the repulsive Hollywood power figure who resembled the Six Flags song-and-dance gnome was both as flirtatious and as tenacious as Jack, but Lazar did not use his position to consummate the same level of coital conquest that Nicholson took pride in achieving.

11. After years of building without permits in Ramirez Canyon, Barbra Streisand donated twenty-four acres in 1993 when it became clear that she would not be able to sell her property without substantial and costly repairs. Warren Beatty also donated twenty acres in 1986.

12. Jack's neighbors the Beattys did not fare so well. The ceiling fell in on their Mulholland home, and they moved to the Beverly Hills Hotel until Annette could find a Coldwater Canyon rental near the ruined estate.

13. While not the wettest year in L.A. history (2004 with thirty-seven inches), the 1993–1994 season brought down twenty-four inches on the denuded hills of Malibu, triggering massive mudslides.

14. The six days of violence in April 1992 were triggered by the "not guilty" verdicts in the Rodney King beating trial. The riots claimed fifty-two lives and caused $1 billion in damage.

15. A recluse living on Oak Pass Road above Benedict Canyon, Bert Schneider lost his young wife to a drug overdose in 1994. After failing to produce *The Two Jakes*, he returned to a pastime of pot and collecting Charlie Chaplin films, often not getting out of his bathrobe all day.

16. The Toluca Lake intersection of Moorpark and Riverside Drive is commemorated in Hollywood guidebooks and on maps to the homes of the stars as the hallowed spot where Jack lost it.

17. Jack's former golf instructor Ron Del Barrio took perverse pride in Jack's vandalism, boasting to *Maximum Golf* magazine, "You have to have a near perfect grip and a killer shoulder turn . . . and I taught those to Jack Nicholson."

18. The following year the boxer Sugar Ray Leonard succeeded Jack as the tournament's grand marshal.

19. Long rumored to be the subject of Carly Simon's stinging critique "You're So Vain," Beatty had mellowed with age, while Jack continued to keep one eye in the mirror to watch himself gavotte.

20. Rafelson, Schneider, and Blauner planned to release a twenty-fifth anniversary commemorative video of *Easy Rider*, using interviews and unseen footage, only to discover that Columbia had destroyed it all. To appease the BBS partners, the studio turned over rights to all of the Monkees' recordings and films, including *Head*, which in turn were sold to Rhino Records in 1994.

21. When the Oscars host David Letterman staged a similar golf club spoof a year later during the 67th Annual Academy Awards, Jack was not amused. Asked about the pounding that the comedian administered to a New York cab during the opening segment of the telecast, Jack grumbled, "David Letterman should stick to the East Coast."

22. "I never knew what ticked the guy off, but I can tell you this: within the past year I got a letter of apology from [Blank]," Jack said during a January 2004 Q&A with *Playboy*.

CHAPTER 21

1. Thanks chiefly to *The Lion King* (1994), which had grossed over $328 million for Disney as of 2006.

2. At their zenith during the 1950s, 3,775 drive-ins operated in the United States. By 1997, the number had dropped to 815.

3. *Howard the Duck* was considered one of the great bombs of the 1980s. At the box office, the story of a duck from outer space took in less than half its $30 million production cost.

4. An L.A. version of Tramp nightclub operated in the basement of the Beverly Center for a brief time in the early 1990s under the aegis of MGM's short-lived CEO Giancarlo Paretti.

5. Both Jack and his son Caleb wear corrective lenses.

6. Jack maintained that Graydon Carter tried to use Susan's letter to blackmail him: it would not be published if he would come to the 1994 *Vanity Fair* Oscar party.

7. Proteus Films was named for the Greek god of the sea, who could change his appearance at will.

8. To edit *The Crossing Guard*, Penn used the new Avid digital console, which would soon become the industry standard but at the time "was a little bit like electric invading acoustic"—Penn's reference to Bob Dylan's legendary switch from folk to rock at the 1966 Newport Folk Festival. Splicing, taping, and waiting two weeks for a print to come back from the lab would soon be history. Despite grumbles from diehard purists like Jack, computerization was the future of film.

9. Jack attended the preview of the *The Crossing Guard* at the Venice Film Festival, but his preoccupation was golf. "They've got a great course on the Lido built by Herman Goering," he said. He stopped over in Paris to visit with Roman Polanski on the trip back.

10. In addition to Jack and Michael Caine, the cast of *The Crossing Guard* included Jennifer Lopez, Judy Davis, and Stephen Dorff.

11. The international take for the nineteenth entry in the James Bond franchise, featuring the fourth Bond (Pierce Brosnan), underscored the importance of global ticket sales at the end of the twentieth century. *GoldenEye* took in more than $351 million worldwide.

12. Although Penn's directing was snubbed at Oscar time, his acting wasn't. He was nominated for his role as a condemned man in *Dead Man Walking* (1995), while his costar and *Eastwick* witch alumna Susan Sarandon won Best Actress for her portrayal of the anti–death penalty activist Sister Helen Prejean. Backstage, the real Sister Prejean had a pleasant conversation with Jack about the devil.

13. Following an audacious international fraud perpetrated upon MGM's chief underwriter Credit Lyonnais by the Italian flimflam man Giancarlo Paretti in the early 1990s, Kirk Kerkorian bailed out the studio a third time and used its chief asset—James Bond—to restore MGM and United Artists to a semblance of their former glory.

14. Jack joined the Eagles' Don Henley in successfully keeping a nine-mile stretch of the Mulholland Highway near Jack's Malibu ranch permanently unpaved. Known as "Dirt Mulholland," the road was a throwback to Jack's earliest years in Southern California.

15. A very successful independent "mini" studio founded in 1988 and run by the father-son production team of James and David Robinson, Morgan Creek was responsible for *Robin Hood: Prince of Thieves* (1991), *True Romance* (1993), and the *Ace Ventura* series.

16. In one scene reminiscent of the Robert Blank affair, Caine pounds Jack with a golf club, after which Jack smothers Caine with a pillow.

17. Maurice Micklewhite (aka Michael Caine), the Cockney son of a charwoman and a London fishmonger, was the only actor besides Jack to be nominated for an Oscar in every decade since the sixties. In 2003, Caine was nominated for Best Actor for *The Quiet American*.

18. A "specialty film" distributor created in 1994 to cash in on the indie film movement, Fox Searchlight offered smaller budgets for character-driven movies, competing with Warner Independent Pictures, Miramax, Universal's Focus Features, Sony Pictures Classics, and Paramount Classics, later renamed Paramount Vantage.

19. President James Dale was a role for which Burton originally sought Warren Beatty. In *Dr. Strangelove*, Sellers played President Merkin Muffley.

20. Once the tallest structure in Clark County, the thirty-one-story Landmark Hotel was razed in November 1995 to make way for a Las Vegas Convention Center parking lot.

21. While a darling of critics and an Oscar winner for Jack's old acting coach Martin Landau, *Ed Wood* cost the Touchstone division of Disney $18 million but grossed less than $6 million at the box office.

22. Under federal law, the pension fund could not be used for personal loans without triggering heavy penalties. By Robert Colbert's calculations, paying off Susan Anspach's $625,000 mortgage would have cost Jack $1.8 million.

23. Shortly after the 1996 Pfizer patent of Viagra, Jack became one of the erectile dysfunction drug's early investors, according to the *Globe* supermarket tabloid.

24. Such threats were very real to Jack. Despite the Brando gates, there were occasional break-ins at the Mulholland compound, which remained virtually unprotected from the steep canyon side. And several of Jack's closest pals were crime victims. Lou Adler was once kidnapped at gunpoint for ransom and, on January 20, 1996, three men broke into Harry Dean Stanton's place just down the road from Jack. They roughed him up, then stole his stereo, TV, and 1995 Lexus.

25. Helen Hunt's mother is played by the actress Shirley Knight, who is one year older than Jack.

26. Helen Hunt and her co-star Paul Reiser earned $1 million per episode during the final season of *Mad about You*.

27. Kinnear hosted the gossip and talk show roundup for four years in the early 1990s, graduating to NBC's *Late with Greg Kinnear* before leaving broadcasting for movies.

28. Jack campaigned for the title *Warm Rolls and Wet Pants*, which would also be the last lines he and Hunt exchanged in the movie. Standing outside a bakery at four in the morning, Melvin says, "Ummmm. Warm rolls" and Carol responds, "Ummmm. Wet pants." Brooks said no.

29. *The Witches of Eastwick* author John Updike reportedly delivered the same response when asked that question.

30. The role of the doctor was a cameo by the director-writer Lawrence Kasdan.

31. For nearly ten years following Jack's very public set-to over Anjelica's fling with Ryan O'Neal, the stuffy old-school hotel banned Hollywood actors. All was not forgiven until the end of the 1980s.

32. *Plan 9 from Outer Space*, a sci-fi horror movie sprung from the febrile mind of Ed Wood, is frequently cited as the worst motion picture ever made.

33. In a year when Tom Arnold headed a family called *The Stupids* (1996) and Brando looked like a dirigible in *The Island of Dr. Moreau* (1996), competition was stiff, but the Razzie went to *Striptease* (1996), regarded even today as Demi Moore's bump-and-grind nadir.

CHAPTER 22

1. Adding further ridicule, the politically correct DGA dumped Griffith's name from its Lifetime Achievement Award in 1999 because the director's landmark *The Birth of a Nation* (1915) "helped foster intolerable racial stereotypes," according to the DGA president Jack Shea. Though Shea's own contribution to the craft included twenty-one episodes of *The Jeffersons*, ten of *The Ropers*, and fourteen of *Designing Women*, including one titled "There's Some Black People Coming to Dinner," the previous Griffith Award winners Francis Ford Coppola and Robert Altman concurred with Shea's decision to change the trophy's name.

2. Alan Finkelstein opened Indochine, his latest très trendy restaurant, on Beverly Boulevard following the 1996 close of the Monkey Bar by the state Department of Labor for failure to meet payroll taxes.

3. In addition to MacInerney's, Sean Penn would soon own a piece of another Manhattan restaurant called Man Ray's.

4. Located on West Ninth Street in Greenwich Village, the café was named for Baratta's sister. His nephew cooked; his mother counted the cash. His wife and his four sons also operated restaurants in Florida.

5. Still cashing in on Jack's goodwill, Finkelstein spent seven years patenting a credit card with a built-in magnifying lens before he sold the gimmick to Chase Manhattan Bank. Following dinner one evening in 1991 at an Aspen restaurant, he'd watched presbyopic Jack pull out a plastic magnifier to squint at the check, which gave him the idea. Finkelstein founded InCard Technologies, shaved his mustache, and moved back to Manhattan, where he further parlayed his Hollywood connections to launch a chain of New York-style pizza parlors.

6. Named for Sean Penn.

7. A young actor named Owen Wilson was an associate producer of *As Good as It Gets*.

8. The *SNL* alumnus Chris Farley died the following week at the same age and of the same drug overdose that killed his hero John Belushi. A later *SNL* regular, Maya Rudolph, made one of her first screen appearances as a policewoman in *As Good as it Gets*.

9. Only the Best Supporting Actor nominee Greg Kinnear failed to win.

10. In the emerging and increasingly important Chinese market, the title was a literal translation of Melvin Udall, which came out in Mandarin as *Mr. Cat Poop*.

11. Polanski had recently petitioned for—but had not been granted—readmission to the United States.

12. As the only past winners who he refused their Oscars, neither George C. Scott nor Marlon Brando was invited.

13. That year 57.55 million households tuned in to the Annual Academy Awards.

14. Robert Duvall, nominated for *The Apostle* (1997).

15. Dustin Hoffman, nominated for *Wag the Dog* (1997).

16. Matt Damon, nominated for *Good Will Hunting* (1997). His father, Kent Damon, was a Massachusetts investment banker, stockbroker, and realtor.

17. Peter Fonda, nominated for *Ulee's Gold* (1997).

18. The number 1 movie of the year, *Titanic* (1997), not only won Best Picture but also became the highest-grossing film of all time, taking in more than $600 million.

19. An Irish rounder who'd been a social worker, an encyclopedia a salesman, a bartender, a junior high school teacher, and a reporter before taking up acting in his late thirties, J. T. Walsh died of a heart attack three weeks before the Oscar telecast. He was six years younger than Jack.

20. Following a failed regimen of Mexican homeopathic treatment, Luana Anders died of breast cancer on July 21, 1996. Jack paid for her medical care the last year of her life. She was fifty-three, had never married and, like Jack, never knew her father, who was listed as "unknown" on her death certificate. She named Sally Kellerman her executor.

21. At ninety, Katherine Hepburn was still the winningest actress, with four Oscars, and still held the title at her death in 2003.

22. Years later, the Cuban defector Delfin Fernandez, who had been in charge of Castro's wiretaps, said, "The American actor Jack Nicholson was another celebrity who was bugged and taped *thoroughly* during his stay in the hotel Meliá Cohiba."

23. As the cool, hard-edged prosecutor Helen Gamble, Lara Flynn Boyle appeared in 115 episodes over six seasons, beginning in 1997.

24. Hegedus's passenger, Olga Kharitonovich, claimed losses of $3,470.

25. One of them, the singer Cynthia Basinet, maintained that Jack dumped her for Lara Flynn, but Basinet kept her silence until years later when it became clear that he'd shut her out of his life. Bearing an uncanny resemblance to Jack's mother, June, and his sister Pamela, the jilted redhead philosophized, "When you love somebody like that, it's like loving a ghost."

26. Colbert died of cancer in December 2005. Jack did not attend the funeral.

27. The actress Lois Smith, who played Jack's sister in *Five Easy Pieces*, was the mother of the Wizard (Tom Noonan) in *The Pledge*.

28. In one early shot that briefly focuses on a photo of Jerry Black as a young man, the portrait is that of Jack Torrance in *The Shining*.

29. The aging hunk also landed his record-breaking fourteenth Razzie nomination with *Get Carter*.

CHAPTER 23

1. With typical British modesty, the monthly fanzine calls itself "the World's Best Movie Magazine."

2. Among others, these "Indie"-era directors born in the sixties and early seventies and lauded as successors to the seventies rebels led by Francis Ford Coppola, Martin Scorsese, and Robert Altman, included Wes Anderson, Paul Thomas Anderson, and David Fincher.

3. In addition to being Payne's hometown, the Nebraska metropolis produced several actors who influenced Jack, including Brando, Fred Astaire, Henry Fonda, and Montgomery Clift.

4. Hal Ashby was Payne's favorite director.

5. The RV belonged to Payne before and after *About Schmidt*.

6. In an offense to his Midwestern neighbors, a naked Jack puttered through his rented house in his off hours during the shoot, prompting requests that he keep his shades drawn.

7. Payne's first major feature, *Citizen Ruth* (1996), starring Laura Dern as a stoner mom, was a Grand Jury nominee at Sundance.

8. Married or not, Rebecca was not above calling for help when she got into trouble. In June 2002, she drank too much on a Los Angeles-to-London flight, punched a flight attendant who refused to serve her more alcohol, and forced an unscheduled landing in Winnipeg, where she was arrested and jailed. With Jack's help, she was able to post $15,000 bail, surrender her passport, and return to L.A. She pleaded guilty to assault and paid damages that totaled $26,000 a year later.

9. It took the digital recorder five years from its September 1999 debut to turn a profit, but TiVo's impact devastated viewing habits and sent traditional commercial-supported broadcasting into an even steeper tailspin. A documentary on the making of *About Schmidt* became one of TiVo's first independent "on demand" offerings.

10. When nominated for Best Actor for his portrayal of a retarded father in *I Am Sam* (2001), Penn announced that he'd boycott the Oscars on grounds that the Academy had snubbed Jack's performance in *The Pledge* (2001), but Jack cautioned him against Brando-George C. Scott obstinence. "I'm going to get him to go," said Jack. "I know he'd enjoy it. I've never heard him say anything bad about the business. It sure can be a fun evening."

11. The Academy named Roman Polanski Best Director for *The Pianist* (2002), but Harrison Ford had to accept on Polanski's behalf after an attempt to repatriate the sixty-nine-year-old director fell through. In 2002, even his victim Samantha Geimer publicly forgave Polanski, but, the Los Angeles D.A.'s office did not.

12. Intermedia Advertising Group said that the ad boosted viewer's "intent to purchase" admission to the movie by 200 percent.

13. By 2006, the cost of a courtside seat climbed to $2,200—per night.

14. Having been familiar with her father's nudity since she was a child, Jennifer commented, "He's always done things that embarrassed me, so it's not odd. But it's still embarrassing because it's my dad's ass."

15. Literally, "life in pink," though the idiom translates into English as "life through rose-colored glasses."

EPILOGUE

1. According to Jack, among the "lay down scripts" in his own past were *Easy Rider*, *One Flew over the Cuckoo's Nest*, *Terms of Endearment*, and *Something's Gotta Give*.

BIBLIOGRAPHY

BOOKS

Abramowitz, Rachel. *Is That a Gun in Your Pocket? Women's Experience of Power in Hollywood.* New York: Random House, 2000.

Adams, Alex, and William Stadiem. *Madame 90210: My Life as Madam to the Rich and Famous.* New York: Villard Books, 1993.

Amburn, Ellis. *The Sexiest Man Alive: A Biography of Warren Beatty.* New York: Harper Collins, 2002.

Bach, Steven. *Final Cut: Dreams and Disaster in the Making of Heaven's Gate.* New York: William Morrow & Co., 1985.

Base, Ron. *"If the Other Guy Isn't Jack Nicholson, I've Got the Part": Hollywood Tales of Big Breaks, Bad Luck, and Box-Office Magic.* Chicago: Contemporary Books, 1994.

Baxter, John. *Stanley Kubrick: A Biography.* New York: Carroll & Graf, 1997.

Bergen, Candice. *Knock Wood.* New York: Simon & Schuster, 1984.

Bingham, Dennis. *Acting Male: Masculinities in the Films of James Stewart, Jack Nicholson and Clint Eastwood.* New Brunswick, NJ: Rutgers University Press, 1994.

Biskind, Peter. *Down and Dirty Pictures: Miramax, Sundance, and the Rise of Independent Film.* New York: Simon & Schuster, 2004.

———. *Easy Riders, Raging Bulls.* New York: Simon & Schuster, 1998.

Bosworth, Patricia. *Marlon Brando.* New York: Viking Penguin, 2001.

Brown, David. *Let Me Entertain You.* New York: William Morrow, 1990.

Brown, Gene. *Movie Time: A Chronology of Hollywood and the Movie Industry from Its Beginnings to the Present.* New York: MacMillan, 1995.

Buell, Bebe, with Victor Bockris. *Rebel Heart: An American Rock 'n' Roll Journey.* New York: St. Martin's Griffin, 2001.

Burstyn, Ellen. *Lessons in Becoming Myself.* New York: Riverhead Books, 2006.

Cardullo, Bert, Harry Geduld, Ronald Gottesman, and Leigh Woods, eds. *Playing to the Camera: Film Actors Discuss Their Craft.* New Haven, CT: Yale University Press, 1998.

Collier, Peter. *The Fondas: A Hollywood Dynasty.* New York: G. P. Putnam's Sons, 1991.

Collins, Nancy. *Hard to Get: Fast Talk and Rude Questions along the Interview Trail.* New York: Random House, 1990.

Conover, Ted. *White Out: Lost in Aspen.* New York: Random House, 1991.

Corman, Roger, with Jim Jerome. *How I Made a Hundred Movies in Hollywood and Never Lost a Dime*. New York: DaCapo Press, 1990.

Crane, Robert David, and Christopher Fryer. *Jack Nicholson: Face to Face*. New York: M. Evans & Co., 1975.

Cronin, Paul, ed. *Roman Polanski Interviews*. Jackson: University Press of Mississippi, 2005.

Crosby, David, and Carl Gottlieb. *Long Time Gone: The Autobiography of David Crosby*. New York: Doubleday, 1988.

Dern, Bruce. *Things I've Said but Probably Shouldn't Have: An Unrepentant Memoir*. With Christopher Fryer and Robert Crane. Hoboken, NJ: John Wiley & Sons, 2007.

Dick, Bernard, ed. *Columbia Pictures: Portrait of a Studio*. Lexington: University Press of Kentucky, 1992.

Dickinson, Janice. *No Lifeguard on Duty: The Accidental Life of the World's First Supermodel*. New York: HarperCollins, 2002.

Douglas, Edward. *Jack: The Great Seducer*. New York: HarperCollins, 2004.

Douglas, Kirk. *The Ragman's Son*. New York: Simon & Schuster, 1988.

Dowling, David. *Jack Nicholson: A Biography*. Briarcliff Manor, NY: Stein and Day, 1983.

Dunaway, Faye, with Betsy Sharkey. *Looking for Gatsby: My Life*. New York: Simon & Schuster, 1995.

Eastman, Charles. *The All-American Boy Blues: A Memoir*. (Unpublished manuscript.)

Eastman, John. *Retakes: Behind the Scenes of 500 Classic Movies*. New York: Ballantine, 1989.

Ekland, Britt. *True Britt*. New York: Berkley Books, 1980.

Fiegel, Eddi. *Dream a Little Dream of Me: The Life of Cass Elliott*. Chicago: Chicago Review Press, 2005.

Finstad, Suzanne. *Warren Beatty: A Private Man*. New York: Harmony Books, 2005.

Fonda, Peter. *Don't Tell Dad: A Memoir*. New York: Hyperion, 1998.

Fonda, Peter, Dennis Hopper, and Terry Southern. *Easy Rider: Original Screenplay*. New York: Signet Books, 1969.

Forman, Milos, and Jan Novak. *Turnaround: A Memoir*. New York: Villard, 1994.

Fraga, Kristian, ed. *Tim Burton Interviews*. Jackson: University Press of Mississippi, 2005.

Fraser-Cavassoni, Natasha. *Sam Spiegel*. New York: Simon & Schuster, 2003.

Fried, Stephen. *Thing of Beauty: The Tragedy of Supermodel Gia*. New York: Pocket Books, 1993.

Goldman, William. *Which Lie Did I Tell? More Adventures in the Screen Trade*. New York: Vintage, 2000.

Gray, Beverly. *Roger Corman: An Unauthorized Biography of the Godfather of Indie Filmmaking*. Los Angeles: Renaissance Books, 2000.

Griffin, Nancy, and Kim Masters. *Hit and Run: How Jon Peters and Peter Guber Took Sony for a Ride in Hollywood*. New York: Simon & Schuster, 1996.

Grimes, Steven. *Heroes and Villains*. New York: Dutton, 1986.

Grobel, Lawrence. *Conversations with Brando*. New York: Hyperion, 1991.

———. *The Hustons*. New York: Scribners, 1989.

Gross, Michael. *Model: The Ugly Business of Beautiful Women*. New York: Perennial, 2003.

Grossvogel, David. *Vishnu in Hollywood: The Changing Image of the American Male*. Lanham, MD: Scarecrow Press, 2000.

Hagman, Larry, with Todd Gold. *Hello Darlin': Tall (and Absolutely True) Tales about My Life*. New York: Simon & Schuster, 2001.

Harmetz, Aljean. *Rolling Breaks and Other Movie Business*. New York: Alfred Knopf, 1985.

Harrison, Jim. *Off to the Side: A Memoir.* New York: Grove Press, 2002.

Harvey, Stephen. *Directed by Vincente Minnelli.* New York: Harper and Row, 1989.

Hill, Lee. *Easy Rider.* London: British Film Institute Publishing, 1996.

———. *A Grand Guy: The Art and Life of Terry Southern.* London: Bloomsbury, 2001.

Hopper, Dennis. *A System of Moments.* Ostfildern-Ruit, Germany: Hatje Cantz Publishers, 2001.

Kael, Pauline. *When the Lights Go Down.* New York: Holt, Rinehart & Winston, 1980.

Kelly, Richard T. *Sean Penn: His Life and Times.* New York: Canongate U.S., 2004.

King, Geoff. *New Hollywood Cinema: An Introduction.* New York: Columbia University Press, 2002.

Kolker, Robert. *A Cinema of Loneliness: Penn, Stone, Kubrick, Scorsese, Spielberg, Altman.* 3rd ed. New York: Oxford University Press, 2000.

Larner, Jeremy. *Drive, He Said.* New York: Bantam Books, 1964.

Leaming, Barbara. *Polanski: The Filmmaker as Voyeur.* New York: Simon & Schuster, 1981.

Lefcowitz, Eric. *The Monkees Tale.* Berkeley, CA: The Last Gasp of San Francisco, 1985.

Lessig, Lawrence. *Free Culture: How Big Media Uses Technology and the Law to Lock Down Culture and Control Creativity.* New York: Penguin Press, 2004.

Levy, Emanuel. *Cinema of Outsiders: The Rise of American Independent Film.* New York: New York University Press, 1999.

Lindsay, Cynthia. *Dear Boris: The Life of William Henry Pratt a.k.a. Boris Karloff.* New York: Limelight Editions, 1995.

Lobrutto, Vincent. *Stanley Kubrick: A Biography.* New York: Donald J. Fine Books, 1997.

MacLaine, Shirley. *My Lucky Stars: A Hollywood Memoir.* New York: Bantam, 1995.

Mair, George. *The Barry Diller Story: The Life and Times of America's Greatest Entertainment Mogul.* New York: John Wiley & Sons, Inc., 1997.

Manso, Peter. *Brando: The Biography.* New York: Hyperion, 1994.

McGee, Mark Thomas. *Fast and Furious: The Story of American International Pictures.* Jefferson, NC: McFarland & Co., 1984.

McGilligan, Patrick. *Jack's Life: A Biography of Jack Nicholson.* New York: W. W. Norton, 1994.

Mottram, James. *The Sundance Kids: How the Mavericks Took Back Hollywood.* New York: Faber and Faber, 2006.

Neale, Steve, and Murray Smith, eds. *Contemporary Hollywood Cinema.* London & New York: Routledge, 1998.

Nogowski, John. *Bob Dylan: A Descriptive Critical Discography and Filmography, 1961–1993.* Jefferson, NC: McFarland & Co., 1995.

Parker, John. *The Joker's Wild: The Biography of Jack Nicholson.* London: Anaya Publisher, 1991.

———. *Polanski.* London: Villiers House, 1993.

Phillips, John, with Jim Jerome. *Papa John: An Autobiography.* Garden City, NY: Dolphin Books, 1986.

Phillips, Julia. *You'll Never Eat Lunch in This Town Again.* New York: Random House, 1991.

Phillips, Michelle. *California Dreamin': The True Story of the Mamas and Papas.* New York: Warner Books, 1986.

Polanski, Roman. *Polanski.* New York: William Morrow, 1984.

Puttnam, David. *Movies and Money.* New York: Alfred A. Knopf, 1998.

Reed, Rex. *Big Screen, Little Screen.* New York: Macmillan, 1971.

Richardson, Tony. *The Long-Distance Runner: An Autobiography.* New York: William Morrow, 1993.

Rifkin, Ned. *Antonioni's Visual Language*. Ann Arbor: UMI Research Press, 1982.

Robin, Liza, Linda, and Tiffany. *You'll Never Make Love in This Town Again*. Los Angeles: Dove Books, 1995.

Salamon, Julie. *The Devil's Candy: The Bonfire of the Vanities Goes to Hollywood*. New York: Houghton Mifflin, 1991.

Sandoval, Andrew. *The Monkees: The Day-by Day Story of the '60s TV Pop Sensation*. San Diego, CA: Thunder Bay Press, 2005.

Sherman, Eric. *Directing the Film: Film Directors on Their Art*. Los Angeles: Acrobat Books, 1976.

Siegel, Barbara, and Scott Siegel. *Jack Nicholson: The Unauthorized Biography*. New York: Avon, 1990.

Sinclair, Andrew. *Spiegel: The Man behind the Pictures*. Boston: Little Brown & Co., 1987.

Steinmann, Anne, and David J. Fox. *The Male Dilemma: How to Survive the Sexual Revolution*. New York: Jason Aronson, 1974.

Stone, Judy. *Eye on the World: Conversations with International Filmmakers*. Beverly Hills, CA: Silman-James Press, 1997.

Sylbert, Richard, and Sylvia Townsend. *Designing Movies: Portrait of a Hollywood Artist*. Westport, CT: Praeger, 2006.

Sylvester, Derek. *Jack Nicholson*. New York: Proteus Books, 1982.

Thomas, Marlo. *The Right Words at the Right Time*. New York: Atria, 2002.

Thompson, Peter. *Jack Nicholson: The Life and Times of an Actor on the Edge*. Secaucus, NJ: Birch Lane, 1997

Thomson, David. *The New Biographical Dictionary of Film*. New York: Alfred Knopf, 2005.

———. *The Whole Equation: A History of Hollywood*. New York: Alfred Knopf, 2005.

Travers, Peter, ed. *The Rolling Stone Film Reader: The Best Film Writing from Rolling Stone Magazine*. New York: Pocket Books, 1996.

Trudeau, Margaret. *Consequences*. New York: Bantam-Seal, 1982.

Vadim, Roger. *Bardot, Deneuve, Fonda: My Life with the Three Most Beautiful Women in the World*. New York: Simon & Schuster, 1986.

Van Gelder, Peter. *That's Hollywood: A Behind-the-Scenes Look at 60 of the Greatest Films of All Time*. New York: Harper Perennial, 1990.

Volpe, Tod. *Framed: America's Art Dealer to the Stars Tells All*. Toronto, ON: ECW Press, 2003.

Vreeland, Diana. *D.V.* Cambridge, MA: DaCapo Press, 1997.

Williams, Lucy Chase. *The Complete Films of Vincent Price*. New York: Citadel Press, 1995.

Wolf, William, with Lillian Kramer Wolf. *Landmark Films: The Cinema and Our Century*. New York: Paddington Press Ltd., 1979.

Woodward, Bob. *Wired: The Short Life and Fast Times of John Belushi*. New York: Simon & Schuster, 1984.

Wright, William. *All the Pain That Money Can Buy: The Life of Christina Onassis*. Simon & Schuster: New York, 1991.

Wyatt, Justin. *High Concept: Movies and Marketing in Hollywood*. Austin: University of Texas Press, 1994.

Wylie, Mason, and Damien Bona. *Inside Oscar*. New York: Ballantine Books, 1986.

Zucker, Carole. *Figures of Light: Actors and Directors Illuminate the Art of Film Acting*. New York: Plenum Press, 1995.

NEWSPAPERS

Abcarian, Robin. "Never a Borrower or a Lender Be . . ." *Los Angeles Times*, May 29, 1996.

Abramowitz, Rachael. "The Key of Jack." *Los Angeles Times*, November 3, 2002.

———. "He Knows Jack," *New York Post*, November 18, 2002.

Academy Awards Press Release. "Nicholson Named Oscar Presenter." February 11, 1999.

Adams, Cindy. "Jack Nicholson." *New York Post*, July 10, 1992.

———. "Jack's Sis Keeps Her Pledge to Dad." *New York Post*, February 5, 2001.

Akerman, Piers. "This Is the Car That Jack Built," *Times (London)*, 1980.

Alberge, Dalya. "I'm Too Vain to Bare It, Admits Nicholson." *Times (London)*, May 23, 2002.

Albright, Diane, and Ed Susman. "Marriage-Shy Jack Nicholson Is Dumped by Long-time Love." *National Enquirer*, March 22, 1988.

Alvarez, Maria. "Wildlife, Jack and Warren at 60." *Daily Telegraph*, March 1, 1997.

Ammon, Jack. "Five Easy Pieces Rolls in Canada." *Variety,* January 14, 1970.

Archerd, Army. *Variety*, March 9, 1976.

———. *Variety*, December 8, 1976.

———. *Variety*, June 6, 1977.

———. *Variety*, October 14, 1977.

———. *Variety*, January 5, 1978.

———. *Variety*, October 19, 1979.

———. *Variety*, September 10, 1980.

———. Variety, December 16, 1981.

———. *Variety*, March 29, 1982.

———. *Variety*, May 17, 1982.

———. *Variety*, October 29, 1982.

———. *Variety*, April 13, 1984.

———. *Variety*, December 5, 1985.

———. *Variety*, May 14, 1986.

———. *Variety*, June 19, 1987.

———. *Variety*, July 19, 1988.

———. *Variety*, March 3, 1989.

———. *Variety*, July 5, 1989.

———. *Variety*, September 29, 1992.

———. *Variety*, October 13, 1992.

———. *Variety*, March 17, 1993.

———. *Variety*, July, 27, 1993.

———. *Variety*, March 1, 1995.

———. *Variety*, March 7, 1995.

———. *Variety*, August 30, 1995.

———. *Variety*, January 12, 1996.

———. *Variety*, December 16, 1996.

———. *Variety*, May 8, 1998.

———. *Variety*, July 16, 1998.

———. *Variety*, November 23, 2004.

———. "The Sound Was Inadequate." *Variety*, March 7, 1994.

Archibald, Lewis. "Jack Nicholson, an Edge of Darkness." *Aquarian*, November 30, 1983.

Ashton, Richard. "Hitting the Jackpot." *Daily Breeze*, May 1, 1998.

Associated Press, "Meet Mr. Nicholson: He Wants to Be King." *Philadelphia Inquirer*, March 31, 1974.

Atlas, Jacoba. "An InterView with Jack Nicholson." *Los Angeles Times*, August 13, 1971.

Atlas, Jacoba, and Marni Butterfield. "Odd Man In-Jack Nicholson," *Show*, May 1971.

Attanasio, Paul. "Jack Nicholson, Genuinely." *Washington Post*, June 14, 1985.

Bacon, James. "'Deeply Shocked' Declares Friend Jack Nicholson." *L.A. Herald Examiner*, February 1, 1978.

Bahrenburg, Bruce. "How to Be a Hollywood Star." *Newark Sunday News*, September 20, 1970.

Baker, Kathryn. "Heady Time for Jack Nicholson." *USA Today*, March 7, 1994.

Baker, Richard. "Jack Nicholson's Bizarre Family Secret." 1994.

Barton, David. "He Resembles Those Remarks." *L.A. Herald Examiner*, March 10, 1984.

———. "Jack's Rx for a Sunburn." *L.A. Herald Examiner*, May 12, 1984.

Beck, Marilyn. *Daily News (New York)*, January 28, 1981.

———. "Nicholson's Back in the News." *L.B. Press Telegram*, October 28, 1989.

Beck, Marilyn, and Stacy J. Smith. "Anspach Hopes She's Home Free after Years-Long Legal Dispute." *Daily News (New York)*, March 11, 1997.

———. "Jack Calls It a Year," *Daily News (New York)*, July 30, 1993.

———. "Jack's on Guard." *Daily News (New York)*, May 3, 1993.

———. "MacLaine Brings Peacock along for Sun City Show." *Daily News (New York)*, July 8, 1993.

———. "Next Anspach-Nicholson Chapter: 11." *L.A. Daily News (New York)*, June 12, 1996.

Bell, Arthur. Bell Tells. *Village Voice*, March 18, 1981.

Beverly Hills Independent. "The Manhattan Mood." June 11, 1980.

Bierman, Noah. "Can I Quote You on That, Mr. Nicholson?" *Variety*, June 27, 1994.

Billboard, "Jack Nicholson and Bobby McFerron," April 11, 1987.

Blerman, Noah. "Nicholson Horrifies at Confab." *Variety*, June 13, 1994.

Blume, Mary. "Best-Actor Nominee Nicholson Knows How to Play the Game." *Los Angeles Times*, April 4, 1971.

Bourne, Brendan. "Judge Lets Nicholson Off Hook in Car-Bashing." *New York Post*, May 3, 1994.

———. "Nicholson's 'In the Rough' Golf Swings." *New York Post*, February 18, 1994.

Bourne, Brendan, and Kate Perrotta. "Nicholson Crashes in Brand-New Mercedes." *New York Post,* July 9, 1999.

Bowles, Scott. "I Can Still Cause Trouble." *USA Today*, October 6, 2006.

Box Office, "Appearance by Stars Is Highlight of 'Easy Pieces' Vancouver Debut," November 23, 1970.

Breslin, Rosemary. "Jack Be Nimble, Jack Be Quick." *Daily News (New York)*, June 9, 1985.

Brill, Marius. "Talk of the Devil." *Sunday Times (London)*, July 21, 1996.

British Film Institute, "Sexy Jessica Was the Girl for Me Says Jack," 1981.

Brodie, John. "4 Make 'Blood' Pact with Nicholson, Fox." November 8, 1995.

———. "Searchlight Sips Rights to Wine." *Variety*, May 26, 1995.

Brooks, Richard. "You've Got to Be Joking, Jack." *Observer*, March 14, 1993.

Brozan, Nadine. "Chronicle" *New York Times*, May 7, 1994.

Burchill, Julie. "A Bit Long in the Tooth," *Sunday Times (London)*, August 28, 1994.

Burton, Tony. "Nicholson's 'Sister' Was His Mother." *Daily Mail*, March 2, 1994.

Busch, Anita. "Kinnear Near Deal of *Old Friends*." *Variety*, September 5, 1996.

———. "Nicholson Eyeing *Old Friends*." *Variety*, December 4, 1995.

———. "Nicholson Firms Pact to Join *Old Friends*." *Variety*, April 24, 1996.

———. "US 'Primary' to Roll in April." *Variety*, January 15, 1997.

Byrne, Bridget. "Jack Enthralls Festival Fans." *L.A. Herald Examiner*, 1975.

Cagin, Seth. "Tracking." *Soho Weekly News*, March 25, 1981.

Carr, Jay. "Nicholson at Peace—Not Such a Big Bad Wolf." *L.B. Press Telegram*, June 18, 1994.

Carroll, Kathleen. "Jack Nicholson, a Hard-Driving Drifter," *Daily News (New York)*, February 10, 1974.

———. "Neither Work nor Play Made Jack a Dull Boy," *Daily News (New York)*, September 21, 1975.

Cassavetes, John. "Maybe There Really Wasn't an America-Maybe It Was Only Frank Capra." *Variety*, October 1969.

Caulfield, Deborah. Morning Report. *Los Angeles Times*, November 4, 1987.

———. "Nicholson on the Matter of His Honor." *Los Angeles Times*, June 10, 1985.

Chaillet, Jean-Paul. "Wild Card." *Sunday Times (London)*, November 24, 1991.

Champlin, Charles. "Star and Director: Jack, Be Nimble." *Los Angeles Times*, July 9, 1989.

———. "Two Films with an Uncommon Actor." *Los Angeles Times*, July 20, 1975.

Changas, Estelle. "Carole Eastman," *Los Angeles Times,* May 2, 1971.

Chase, Chris. At the Movies. *New York Times*, February 5, 1982.

Christy, George. The Great Life. *Hollywood Reporter*, March 9, 1993.

———. The Great Life. *Hollywood Reporter*, March 8, 1994.

Cieply, Michael, and J. Bates. "Academy, Flush with Funds, Plans Film Museum." *Los Angeles Times*, February 3, 2004.

Citizen News, "Tintypes: Jack Nicholson," August 1974.

Clark, Dick. "Youth Should Have Its Day: Vast, Ready-Made Market Waits." *Variety*, October 1967.

Clein, Harry. "Jack Nicholson: An Irreverent Filmmaker Sounds Off on Motion Pictures, His Career, and the Labor Unions." *Entertainment World*, November 7, 1969.

Cox, Dan. "AFI Honors Nicholson." *Variety*, October 18, 1993.

Cushell, Garry. "Things Batman Should Know about Joker Jack." *Sun*, October 29, 1988.

Cushing, Caroline. "South to *The Border*." *L.A. Herald Examiner*, September 8, 1980.

Daily Mail, "£6m—The price of True Love for Jack Nicholson," May 1, 1992.

Daily Mail, "A Bevy of Hollywood Beauties?" March 5, 1994.

Daily Mail, "A Change as Good as Arrest for Joker Jack," March 2, 1994.

Daily Mail, "I Forgive, Says Driver in Clash with Nicholson," March 1994.

Daily Mail, "Jack and Anjelica Reunite to Set the Screen Alight," December 30, 1993.

Daily Mail, "Jack's Happy with a Small Role in *The Grandfather*," March 4, 1996.

Daily Mail, "No Joke as Nicholson Faces Prison," February 28, 1994.

Daily Mail, March 1, 1996.

Daily News (New York), "Coast Memos," September 20, 1971.

Daily News (New York), "Jack's All Right, Warren's Left," May 27, 1980.

Daily News (New York), "Maggie Confesses: "I Had Affair with Jack Nicholson," January 12, 1982.

Daily News (New York), "Nicholson: My Secret Dreams," June 1, 1986.

Daily News (New York), "Nicholson's Shopping Spree Here," January 31, 1979.

Daily News (New York), "Shootin' Some Hoops with Jack Nicholson," June 9, 1985.

Daily News (New York), January 13, 1986.

Daily News (New York), January 28, 1994.

Daily Telegraph, "Jack Joker," March, 7, 1998.

Daily Telegraph, "Holy Terror," August 15, 1998.

Daily Telegraph, "Nicholson Waffles . . ." August 28, 1994.

Dallas Times Herald, "Nicholson Purchase Helps Break Art Auction Record," May 20, 1983.

Dangaard, Colin. "Scary Jack Is Out to Get You." *London Sun*, 1981.

Davis, Victor. "Jack Heads for an Oscar via a Fountain." *Daily Express*, October 2, 1976.

———. "No Easy Ride to the Top." *Daily Express*, May 25, 1974.

———. "What Makes Jack Sexiest Man?" *Daily Mail*, March 7, 1994.

———. "Why Shining Megastar Jack Stayed in the Shade." *Daily Express*, 1980.

Dawes, Amy. "Nicholson's 'Two Jakes' Pushed Back until Spring." *Variety*, October 25, 1989.

Dawtrey, Adam. "Nicholson Uncorks Wine." *Variety*, May 19, 1995.

Dempster, Nigel. "Wolf at Door of Jack's Old Love." *Daily Mail*, October 9, 1995.

Dicker, Fredric, and Mark Stamey. "State Booze Bigs Bash Jack's Yule Toast." *New York Post*, December 8, 1997.

Dudar, Helen. "Fortune Caught Up." *New York Post*, June 21, 1975.

Ebert, Roger. "Jack of All Roles." *L.B. Press Telegram*, November 27, 1995.

Eller, Claudia. Dish. *Variety*, February 16, 1993.

———. "ICM Touting Nicholson-Nolte-Mancuso Project." *Variety*, February 2, 1993.

Entertainment Today, "Nicholson to Receive AFI Lifetime Achievement," October 22, 1993.

Evanfrook, John. "Miramax Is on Guard." *Variety*, October 28, 1993.

Evans, Gerard. "Producers Want Jack to Star in Easy Rider II." *Evening Star*, December 5, 1994.

Evening Standard, "Anjelica to Star with Ex-Love Jack," December 29, 1993.

Evening Standard, "Hollywood Tribute for Shy Jack," March 4, 1994.

Evening Standard, "Jack and the Infant Superman," March 19, 1971.

Evening Standard, "Jack Nicholson *As Good as It Gets*," March 12, 1998.

Evening Standard, "Jack the Lad, the Stone Age Rocker," June 7, 1995

Evening Standard, "New Love Child for Nicholson," August 17, 1994.

Farber, Stephen. "Jack Nicholson Comes to Terms with Middle Age." *New York Times*, 1983.

Farley, Ellen. "Oscar and Bankability." *Los Angeles Times*, April 9, 1988.

Ferrell, David. "The Lakers' Leading Man Always Knows His Lines." *Los Angeles Times*, June 8, 2004.

Fine, Marshall. "Jack Talk." *Journal News*, December 12, 2002.

Fink, Mitchell. "Happy Birthday, Jack." *L.A. Herald Examiner*, April 22, 1987.

———. "It's As Bad As It Gets for Nicholson Pooch." *Daily News (New York)*, July 9, 1999.

———. "The Joker Is Wild." *L.A. Herald Examiner*, October 26, 1989.

———. *L.A. Herald Examiner*, September 22, 1989.

Flatley, Guy. "Jack Nicholson—Down to the Very *Last Detail*." *New York Times*, February 10, 1974.

Fleming, Michael. Dish. *Variety*, March 31, 1998.

———. "Jack Nicholson Is Nearing *Mars*," *Variety*, February 2, 1996.

———. "Megabuck Star Deals Still Driving H'wood Machine." *Variety*, February 5, 1996.

Fleming, Michael, and Karen Freifeld. Inside New York. *Newsday*, April 28, 1989.

France, Louise. "My Friend Jack the Lad." *Times (London)*, May 15, 1998.

Freedman, Samuel G. "Defiant Nicholson . . ." *Sunday Telegraph* (London), November 11, 1991.

Friendly, David T. "*Two Jakes* on the Shelf Now." *Los Angeles Times*, May 9, 1985.

Froelich, Paula. "Jack-Axed Lara Puts the Moves on Bruce." *New York Post*, September 14, 2000.

Frook, John. "Farrow Ankles *Wolf*." *Variety*, March 23, 1993.

———. "Huston and Nicholson on Guard." *Variety*, December 28, 1993.

Gallagher, Tag. "Jack Nicholson, Easy Actor." *Village Voice*, June 9, 1975.

Galloway, Stephen. "Searchlight to Serve 'Wine' for Nicholson." *Hollywood Reporter*, May 26, 1995.

Ginsberg, Steven. "RKO Antes Up $25 Mil for Universal Pix." *Variety*, May 20, 1981.

Glasgow Herald, "Libel Damages for Jack Nicholson," May 11, 1984.

Goldstein, Patrick. "Close Encounters." *Los Angeles Times*, June 16, 1985.

———. "Forever an Original—If Not Forever Young." *Los Angeles Times*, February 12, 2003.

Goldstein, Richard. "Jack Nicholson: The American Hero Grows Up." *Village Voice*, June 21, 1976.

Goodman, Joan. "Jack the Lad Goes to the Devil." *Observer (London)*, October 4, 1987.

Gordon, George. "Nicholson Sued Over 'Iron Bar' Attack." *Daily Mail*, February 17, 1994.

———. "Playboy Nicholson Dumped by Woman Who Tamed Him." *Daily Mail*, September 1992.

———. "Waitress Makes Nicholson a Father Again." *Daily Mail*, August 18, 1994.

Graham, Caroline. "I Just Had To." *Sun*, March 18, 1995.

Grant, Lee. "John Belushi, All-Media Man." *Los Angeles Times*, May 31, 1978.

———. "Latest Rumor." *Los Angeles Times*, November 24, 1976.

Grant, Steve. "Jimmy Riddle." *Time Out (London)*, March 10–17, 1993.

Gray, Jim. "It's Not Cuckoo's Nest, but He Has a Great Seat." *Los Angeles Times*, January 4, 2003.

———. "The Winner for Best Sports Fan/Actor." *Los Angeles Times*, January 5, 2003.

Greco, Mike. "Strike Stalls 'Border' Film." *Los Angeles Times*, August 9, 1980.

Gross, Susanna. *Daily Mail*, March 7, 1994.

Guardian, "So You Think You Know about Jack Nicholson," March 14, 1998.

Guarino, Ann. "Nicholson's Future." *Daily News (New York)*, June 3, 1975.

Guart, Al. "Celebrity Con 'Artist' Gets 28 Months in Prison." *New York Post*, March 4, 1998.

Gussow, Mel. "Easy Actor's Road Was Hard Riding." *New York Times*, January 2, 1976.

Guttridge, Peter. "The Movie That Became a Monster." *Cinema*, 1991.

Haber, Joyce. "Brando, Nicholson." *Los Angeles Times*, June 10, 1975.

Hall, Allan. "Joker Hits £90m Jack Pot." *London Sun*, June 7, 1988.

Harmetz, Aljean. "Anjelica of the Hustons, Back in the Family Fold." June 27, 1986.

———. "The Joker Is Wild." *New York Times*, June 18, 1989.

Harvey, Alex, "Jack's the Lad for the Ladies." *London Sun*, August 24, 1981.

Harvey, Duston. "Boos for Jack Nicholson." *Morning Telegraph*, N.Y., August 4, 1971.

———. "Other Side of Success." *L.A. Herald Examiner*, July 27, 1971.

Harvey, Steve. "He Doesn't Need to Carry a Big Stick." *Los Angeles Times*, May 19, 1995.

———. "Only In L.A." *Los Angeles Times*, February 16, 1999.

Higgins, Bill. "Nicholson Nabs Globe Honor." *Variety*, November 6, 1998.

Higgins, Mike. "Vive la Nicholson." *Independent*, June 25, 1998.

Hinkley, David. "How to Be a Movie Star." *Daily News (New York)*, June 9, 1985.

Hinxman, Margaret. "I'm Acceptable." *Woman*, August 1971.

Hirschhorn, Clive. "The Trouble Jack Nicholson Has with Girls Like Suzy." *Sunday Express*, February 15, 1976.

Hiscock, John. "Why Nicholson Got Rid of Jack." *Daily Telegraph*, January 18, 2003.

Hollywood Reporter, "Clips: No Nicholson Charges," May 3, 1994.

Hollywood Reporter, "Film Shorts," October 5, 1998.

Hollywood Reporter, "Horrors! Nicholson's Day to Howl," June 13, 1994.

Hollywood Reporter, "In the State Courts," August 14, 1987.

Hollywood Reporter, "LAPD Salute Jack Nicholson," March 23, 1998.

Hollywood Reporter, "Legal Briefs," March 11, 1994.

Hollywood Reporter, "London," May 23, 1978.

Hollywood Reporter, "Man Sues, Says Nicholson Attacked Him," February 16, 1994.

Hollywood Reporter, "Nicholson Charged," March 1, 1994.

Hollywood Reporter, "Nicholson Guests," June 6, 1994.

Hollywood Reporter, "Nicholson Settles," March 14, 1994.

Hollywood Reporter, "Nicholson, Streisand, Lear Rally for President," December 17, 1998.

Hollywood Reporter, "Producer Circle Enters 1978 with $50 Mil in Production," December 28, 1977.

Hollywood Reporter, Rambling Reporter, November 22, 1985.

Hollywood Reporter, Rambling Reporter, February 24, 1989.

Hollywood Reporter, "RKO General Files Suit vs. Uni Studios," September 18, 1985.

Hollywood Reporter, "Shining," December 5, 1996.

Hollywood Reporter, "Tee Time," March 3, 1994.

Hollywood Reporter, July 11, 1978.

Hollywood Reporter, December 12, 1978.

Hollywood Reporter, March 22, 1979.

Hollywood Reporter, June 5, 1980.

Hollywood Reporter, March 1, 1983.

Hollywood Reporter, March 21, 1986.

Hollywood Reporter, March 18, 1994.

Hollywood Reporter, September 27, 1996.

Hollywood Reporter, December 4, 1996.

Hollywood Reporter, December 24, 1997.

Hollywood Reporter, February 11, 1998.

Hollywood Reporter, September 28, 1998.

Hollywood Reporter, August 5, 1999.

Honan, Corinna. "Jack Nicholson's Wild about His Girl and Prepares for the Patter of More Tiny Feet," *Daily Mail*, September 20, 1991.

Honeycut, Kirk. "AFI Honoring Nicholson for Shining Career," *Hollywood Reporter*, October 18, 1993.

———. "Nicholson's Wild Night Is a Good Time for All." *Hollywood Reporter*, March 7, 1994.

Howe, Desson. "The Heady Sunrise of Robert Towne." *Washington Post*, December 3, 1988.

Hurst, John. "Defense Rests in Trial of Miss Longet." *Los Angeles Times*, January 14, 1977.

Iley, Chrissy. "Relationship of the Week" *Times (London)*, June 23, 1995.

Jacobs, Jody. *Los Angeles Times*, July 28, 1975.

———. "Rock Dreams for Real at Adler's." *Los Angeles Times*, July 31, 1975.

Jacobs, Philip. "Revealed! The Incredible Story of Jack Nicholson's Past!" *Boston Herald*, May 15, 1983.

Jenour, Kenelm. "*The Shining* Won't Be Seen at Cannes Fest." *Hollywood Reporter*, May 13, 1980.

Johnson, Chip. "Actor Nicholson Charged after Attack on Car." *Los Angeles Times*, March 1, 1994.

Johnson, Richard. "Jack Jinxes Ex-Lover's Housepet." *New York Post*, January 12, 1998.

———. "Nicholson Gets a Lock on His Ex," *New York Post*, September 18, 1995.

———. "She Has Designs on Jack's Dough," *New York Post*, May 16, 2000.

Josie. *Sunday Woman*, December 2, 1979.

Julianelli, Janie. "Picking up the Pieces." *Women's Wear Daily*, September 23, 1970.

Kennedy, Dana. "Nicholson on Age, Acting and 'Being Jack.'" *New York Times*, September 22, 2002.

Kilday, Gregg. "Hedging Bets on 'Missouri' Deal." *Los Angeles Times*, August 9, 1976.

———. "Nicholson Corral." *Los Angeles Times*, May 9, 1977.

King, Andrea. "Nicholson, Nichols Close to Col Deal for Werewolf Film." *Hollywood Reporter*, October 25, 1991.

King, Susan. "Movie Trivia." *L.A. Herald Examiner*, July 2, 1989.

Kit, Zorianna. "Nicholson's Honor: Globes' DeMille Award." *Hollywood Reporter*, November 6, 1998.

Klady, Leonard. "AFI's Nicholson Fete an Evening of Shades." *Variety*, March 7, 1994.

———. "Jack Nicholson on Guard." *Variety*, March 26, 1993.

Kleid, Beth. "People Watch: The One Jake." *Los Angeles Times*, September 21, 1992.

Klein, Andy. "The Shades, the Grin, the Icon." *Variety*, January 15, 1999.

Knapp, Dan. "Jack Nicholson, the Bender of Film Boundaries." *Los Angeles Times*, August 8, 1971.

Krier, Beth Ann. "Confidence Sprouts in Hair Transplant." *Los Angeles Times*, October 13, 1976.

L.A. Herald Examiner, "Backstage Passes," November 11, 1988.

L.A. Herald Examiner, "Going to the Dogs," March 4, 1986.

L.A. Herald Examiner, "It's OK, Jack, Page 2 Will Wait 'til 2001 if It Has To," November 12, 1979.

L.A. Herald Examiner, "Jack 'n' Meryl," December 8, 1988.

L.A. Herald Examiner, "Jack of News Trade," December 12, 1987.

L.A. Herald Examiner, "Jack Puts a Dimmer on *The Shining*," May 12, 1980.

L.A. Herald Examiner, "No Joking Matter," June 30, 1988.

L.A. Herald Examiner, "Polanski Charged in Rape Here," March 12, 1977.

L.A. Herald Examiner, "Rumor Ruiner," August 24, 1989.

L.A. Herald Examiner, "Same to U-2," December 18, 1986.

L.A. Herald Examiner, "Say It Isn't So," May 17, 1989.

L.A. Herald Examiner, "Steep Scene," August 18, 1987.

L.A. Herald Examiner, "The Pack Joins Jack," March 5, 1988.

L.A. Herald Examiner, "Two Easy Pieces," September 10, 1980.

L.A. Herald Examiner, "Words to Live By," October 21, 1987.

L.A. Herald Examiner, July 23, 1975.

L.A. Herald Examiner, August 25, 1976.

L.A. Herald Examiner, February 26, 1979.

L.A. Herald Examiner, August 6, 1987.

L.A. Herald Examiner, March 24, 1989.

Landman, Beth. "Nicholson's Gonna Be a Daddy Again." *New York Post*, August 13, 1991.

Lardine, Bob. "Jack Nicholson: At Last an Oscar?" *New York Sunday News*, April 6, 1975.

———. "Jack Nicholson's Getting Crazier Every Day." *In The Know*, August 1975.

Lazar, Jerry. "Towne's Country." *Chicago Tribune*, December 4, 1988.

L.B. Press Telegram, "Movie Rated 4-F." 1993.

L.B. Press Telegram, "Nicholson Allegedly Golf-Clubs Car," February 24, 1994.

L.B. Press Telegram, "Nicholson Visits Venice," September 6, 1995.

L.B. Press Telegram, "People," August 14, 1991.

L.B. Press Telegram, "Stars Will Shine en Masse on Nicholson," February 22, 1994.

L.B. Press Telegram, "Time Marches On," April 26, 1993.

L.B. Press Telegram, "Tourney's Still On," March 3, 1994.

Levin, Myron. "Gift of Land by Nicholson Is Reported." *Los Angeles Times*, January 1, 1994.

Lewin, David. "Jack's the King." *Daily Mail*, October 29, 1985.

———. "Nicholson . . ." *Daily Mail*, February 27, 1984.

———. *Daily Mail*, August 8, 1989.

Lewis, Fiona. "Jack Nicholson: Both Sides of the Camera." *Los Angeles Times*, November 6, 1977.

London, Michael. "Three-Way Team Set up for *Chinatown* Sequel." *Los Angeles Times*, January 26, 1985.

Los Angeles Times, Cinefile, October 2, 1988.

Los Angeles Times, Cinefile, October 9, 1988.

Los Angeles Times, Cinefile July 16, 1989.

Los Angeles Times, Cinefile, October 22, 1989.

Los Angeles Times, "Fidel Knows Jack," Morning Report, July 17,1998.

Los Angeles Times, "First Off," Morning Report, March 20, 1989.

Los Angeles Times, "Jack's Latest Honor," November 6, 1998.

Los Angeles Times, "John Belushi, Man for All Media," 1977.

Los Angeles Times, "Landmark Status Sought for Road," August 19, 1995.

Los Angeles Times, "Listen," July 10, 1987.

Los Angeles Times, Morning Report, May 31, 1994.

Los Angeles Times, Morning Report, September 13, 1995.

Los Angeles Times, Morning Report, November 3, 1995.

Los Angeles Times, Morning Report, November 7, 1997.

Los Angeles Times, "Much in Demand," October 3, 1978.

Los Angeles Times, "Nicholson Gets Life," Morning Report, October 16, 1993.

Los Angeles Times, "Nicholson Settles," March 12, 1994.

Los Angeles Times, "Nicholson Settles Suit," May 1, 1984.

Los Angeles Times, "Nicholson Sought for Fingerprinting in Hashish Find," September 2, 1977.

Los Angeles Times, "The Cops Hope Jack Didn't Use the Club," March 3, 1994.

Los Angeles Times, "Three Not-So-Easy Pieces," October 27, 1991.

Los Angeles Times, "Unsafe Left Turn," Morning Report, July 10, 1999.

Los Angeles Times, July 18, 1976.

Los Angeles Times, April 7, 1978.

Los Angeles Times, April 27, 1978.

Los Angeles Times, May 25, 1979.

Los Angeles Times, July 13, 1979.

Los Angeles Times, October 2, 1979.

Los Angeles Times, April 25, 1989.

Los Angeles Times, December 4, 1996.

Macaulay, Sean. "Star of the Week." *Times (London)*, May 17, 2001.

MacIntyre, Ben. "Film Story Marine Found Murdered," *Times (London)*, April 6, 1994.

MacKenzie, Susie. "Dark Star." *Guardian,* August 28, 1994.

Mackie, Lindsay. "Nicholson, Hooked on Being Polite." *Glasgow Herald*, February 28, 1984.

Maddocks, Melvin. "Jack Nicholson: All-American Boy?" *Christian Science Monitor*, June 19, 1975.

Madigan, Nick. "Jack Nicholson Donates 60 Acres to Conservancy." *West L.A. Independent*, January 13, 1994.

Malcolm, Derek. "Forever Jack the Lad." *Guardian*, August 8, 1996.

———. "Jack Nicholson." *Guardian*, May 27, 1974.

Mann, Roderick. "For Nicholson, Fascination Still Rings with *Postman*." *Los Angeles Times*, March 15, 1981.

———. "Richardson: Mending an Evening." *Los Angeles Times*, January 12, 1982.

———. "Nicholson: Pendulum on Upswing Again." *Los Angeles Times*, February 21, 1982.

———. *Sunday Express London*, 1981.

Maychick, Diana. "Stalking the Seamy Underbelly." *New York Post*, June 13, 1985.

McCarthy, Todd. "Shining per-House Preem Figs Highest Ever, Says Warner." *Variety*, May 28, 1980.

McDonald, Peter. "Anjelica: My Dark Nights of the Soul over Nicholson." *Evening Standard*, January 6, 1998.

McLeud, Pauline. "Jack the Lad." *Daily Mirror*, March 5, 1984.

Milday, Gregg. "Jack's All Right." *L.A. Herald Examiner*, May 28, 1985.

The Mirror, "Near Miss for Nick," August 13, 1985.

Mitchell, Sean. "As Funny as It Gets?" *Los Angeles Times*, December 25, 1997.

Modderno, Craig. "Power Seats." *Los Angeles Times*, December 11, 1988.

Mrozek, Thom. "Arraignment Delayed for Jack Nicholson." *Los Angeles Times*, April 15, 1994.

———. "Nicholson Settles Case." *Los Angeles Times*, May 3, 1994.

———. "Prosecutors Will Fight Nicholson's Legal Move." *Los Angeles Times*, April 27, 1994.

MS London, "Jack the Lad," October 14, 1985.

National Enquirer, "I Love Jack Nicholson—He's So Zany," July 14, 1974.

New York Post, "Brady's Bunch," September 17, 1980.

New York Post, "Jack: Tables Turned," May 16, 1987.

New York Post, "Jack Turns Cheek to Celtic Fans," June 14, 1984.

New York Post, "Maggie Sequel: Jet Set Sex & Drugs," January 12, 1982.

New York Post, "Nicholson Stacks up in *Untouchable* Role," March 4, 1985.

New York Post, Susy, December 29, 1989.

New York Sunday News, August 22, 1971.

New York Times, "DeVito and Nicholson," May 31, 1991.

New York Times, "Every Picture Tells a Story," October 9, 1978.

New York Times, "Howling Jack Nicholson, a Wolf for All Seasons," June 12, 1994.

New York Times, "Nicholson Buys Rights to Book on Napoleon," July 17, 1984.

New York Times, "Nicholson Settles Suit over Drug-Use Report," May 5 1984.

New York Times, May 23, 1980.

New York Times, March 1, 1994.

New York Times, October 23, 1998.

Newsday, "Baby Booms," June 1, 1992.

Newsday, "Nicholson's Gift Sacked Happy Ending in Hollywood," June 25, 1990.

Newsday, "No Heartburn for Jack," March 19, 1986.

Newsweek, "A Lot of Jack to Go Around," November 6, 1989.

Osborne, Robert. Rambling Reporter, *Hollywood Reporter*, March 1, 1988.

The Outlook, "Nicholson Donates Land for Preserve," January 6, 1994.

The Outlook, "Nicholson Speaks Out on Clinton," January 30, 1998.

Owen, Michael. "Jack Nicholson." *Evening Standard*, May 24, 1974.

Parker, Jerry. "Nicholson." *Newsday*, June 25, 1975.

Parker, John. "Why Jack Was Dumped by His Rebecca." *Daily Mail*, September 18, 1992.

Pattarson, Dan. "Nicholson & Polanski at Strasberg." *Drama Logue*, June 3, 1977.

Peachment, Chris. "The Two Jacks." *Independent (London)*, November 17, 1991.

Pearson, Allison. "Jack the Lad Tells a New Bedtime Story," *Evening Standard*, December 11, 2002.

Pecchia, David. "The Movie Chart: Films Now Going into Production," *Los Angeles Times*, April 16, 1989.

Pendlebury, Richard, "Seven Days & Long Nights in the Life of Jack the Lad." *Daily Mail*, July 6, 1994.

Perry, George. "Leader of the Jack Pack." *Sunday Times (London)*, April 19, 1998.

Petrikin, Chris. "Backstage at the Golden Globes." *Variety*, January 26, 1998.

———. "Nicholson Eyeing MGM Pic *Julip*." *Variety*, January 9, 1998.

Pitman, Jack. "Subotsky Betting on Sword & Sorcery Fantasy for B.O. Bang." *Variety*, May 17, 1978.

Pollock, Dale. "20 Major WB Releases in Next Year." *Variety*, November 3, 1978.

———. "Company Favors Newcomer Types." May 1978.

————. "Towne: Toughing It Out to the Finish Line." *Los Angeles Times*, January 29, 1982.

Poole, Oliver. "My Lost Libido, by Jack . . . " *Daily Telegraph*, December 12, 2002.

Porter, Henry. "Why Jack Is as Good as It Gets." *Evening Standard*, March 9, 1998.

Pristin, Terry. "Hutton Wins $9.75 Million in MGM Suit." *Los Angeles Times*, February 26, 1989.

Pryor, Thomas M. "From the Studios of Universal City: Conglomerates." *Variety 36th Anniversary Edition*, October 1968–1969.

————. "Merger Mania, Lost Jobs, Classification." *Variety, 35th Anniversary Edition*, October 1967–1968.

————. "Room for Optimism, and More Change." *Variety*, October 1969.

Quinn, Martin. "Name of the Game: 'Blame Costs On Labor.'" *Variety, 34th Anniversary Edition*, October1966–1967.

Rafelson, Bob. "Jack Is Even Crazier Than You'd Think." *Guardian*, May 1, 1998.

Rainey, James. "Staples Center Puts a Price on Star Treatment." *Los Angeles Times*, November 19, 1998.

Rechtshaffen, Michael. "Can't Stand Still." *Hollywood Reporter*, January 19, 1999.

Reed, Rex. "The Man Who Walked Off with 'Easy Rider.'" *New York Times*, March, 1, 1970.

Reynolds, Mark. "Odd Couple." *Daily Mail*, March 3, 2001.

Roberts, Jerry. "Helmers Praise Nicholson's Knack for Nuance," *Variety*, January 15. 1999.

————. "The Pleasure of His Company." *Variety*, Jan 15, 1999.

Roberts, Steven V. "Film and Music Stars Raise $300,000 at a McGovern Concert." *New York Times*, April 17, 1972.

Robins, Wayne. "Nicholson: Still Going to Extremes." *Newsday*, June 14, 1985.

Rossell, Deac. "Riders' Silent Rage." *Philadelphia after Dark*, September 24, 1969.

Rush, George. "A Shining to Baby." *Daily News (New York)*, April 8, 1994.

Rush, George, Molloy, Joanna. "Happy 60th, Jack! It Won't Be an Easy Ride." *Daily News, (New York)*, April 18, 1997.

————. "Looks Like Cannes Is New Jack City." *Daily News (New York)*, May 24, 2002.

————. "Splendid Splinter on Road . . . " *Daily News (New York)*, February 20, 2001.

————. "The Tale That Sparked Jack's Battery Probe." *Daily News (New York)*, November 3, 1996.

Ryan, Ruth. "House That Jack Bought Now on Block." *Los Angeles Times*, November 12, 1998.

Safran, Don. "Producer Circle May Get Peck as TV Dodsworth." *Hollywood Reporter*, February 6, 1979.

Sapsted, David. "Actors's Generous Spirit Falls Foul of Licensing Laws." *Daily Telegraph,* December 19, 1998.

Shales, Tom. "Wrapping Up a Few Details," *Washington Post*, January 10, 1973.

Sheridan, Peter. "Yours Unfaithfully or Why Nicholson Lies to Some Ladies." *Daily Mail*, March 4, 1994.

Shin, Paul, and Michele McPhee. "Jack's Wild." *Daily News (New York)*, December 17, 1997.

Show Business, "Open Call for Young Jack Nicholson," January 7, 1987.

Silverman, Stephen M. "Jack Nicholson: The Rogue in Star's Clothing." *New York Post*, June 24, 1985.

Siskel, Gene. "For Them, the Fates Toss Only Losing Coins." *Chicago Tribune*, March 10, 1974.

————. "Terms of Fulfillment: Jack Nicholson Talks about His Career." *Chicago Tribune*, June 16, 1985.

Skolsky, Sidney. "Tintype: Nicholson Clicks." *Citizen News*, March 27, 1970.

Smith, Cecil. "The Unkindest Cuts of All." *Los Angeles Times*, February 20, 1976.

Smith, Julia Llewellyn. "Why America Adores Its Jack the Lad." *Times (London)*, March 15, 1994.

Smith, Liz. "*Batman's* Big Budget Battles." *Los Angeles Times*, August 14, 1991.

———. "Friendly Rivalry over Howard Hughes Role?" *L.A. Herald Examiner*, May 2, 1989.

———. "Jack, Anjelica and Sean." *Los Angeles Times*, December 28, 1993.

———. "Jack in Eruption." *Newsday*, March 11, 1998.

———. "Jack Nicholson." *Los Angeles Times*, June 28, 1991.

———. "Jack's All Fired up for Bob." *Los Angeles Times*, November 18, 2004.

———. "Nicholson Buys a Poisoned Napoleon." *Newsday*, July 19, 1984.

———. "Nicholson Shares the Secrets of His Success." *L.A. Herald Examiner*, August 18, 1989.

———. "Nicholson's the Nicest." *Daily News (New York)*, October 1974.

———. "Reconciliation Redux." *Daily News (New York)*, October 1, 1976.

———. *Los Angeles Times*, August 15, 1991.

———. *Los Angeles Times*, August 19, 1991.

———. *Los Angeles Times*, September 10, 1991.

———. *Los Angeles Times*, March 30, 1998.

Snow, Shauna. "Splitsville." *Los Angeles Times*, December 15, 1989.

South, John, M. Glynn, and C. Montgomery. "Jack Nicholson to Wed Longtime Love after Deathbed Vow to Her Dad, John Huston." *National Enquirer*, October 6, 1987.

Stall, Bill. "Roman Polanski Charged with Rape." *Los Angeles Times*, March 13, 1977.

Standard, "Actor Wins Drugs Libel Damages," May 10, 1984.

Stayton, Richard. "My Style." *L.A. Herald Examiner*, June 17, 1985.

Sterritt, David. "Jack Nicholson." *Christian Science Monitor*, March 31, 1976.

———. "Nicholson—Acting Is a Hard Trick." *L.A. Herald Examiner*, April 12, 1976.

Stewart, Jon. "Jack Nicholson Looks East." *Ramparts*, 1972.

Sun, "The Sun Pays Out to Jack Nicholson," May 1984.

Sunday Express (London), "Growing Old," March 18, 1984.

Sunday Express (London), "He May," May 15, 1980.

Sunday Telegraph, "Jack Nicholson, Larger?" August 22, 1999.

Sunday Times (London), "Devil of a Joker Is Laughing All the Way to the Bank," August 6, 1989.

Sunday Times London, "Jack Be Nimble," March 21, 1999.

Sunday Times (London), "King Lear," February 15, 1976.

Sunday Times (London), "Leading Role," July 12, 1998.

Sunday Times (London), "Talk of the Devil," July 21, 1996.

Taylor, Pauline. *Daily News*, April 3, 1977.

Taylor, Richard, and Barbara Sternig. "Jack Nicholson Gets Actress Pregnant & Won't Marry Her," *National Enquirer*, 1988.

Thomas, Gordan. "Sensual Jack, Understudy to the Devil." *Western Mail*, February 13, 1988.

Thomas, Kevin. "Nicholson Leaves Obscurity in Dust." *Los Angeles Times*, August 28, 1969.

Time Out, "Jack Nicholson," August 17, 1994.

Times (London), "Jack Nicholson, Trip to the Top," February 15, 1997.

Times (London), "Jack Nicholson Wins Libel Case," May 11, 1984.

Toepfer, Susan. "Jack the Ripper." *N.Y. Sunday News Magazine*, August, 24, 1980.

Travis, Neal. "Dave Makes Jack Gag." *New York Post*, March 29, 1995.

———. "Jack's Project." *New York Post*, March 9, 1978.

Tusher, Will. "Writers Dominate $23 Million Filmlog." *Hollywood Reporter*, July 22, 1974.

Ulmer, James. "Wolf-Man Nicholson Howls at Venice Fest." *Hollywood Reporter*, September 6, 1994.

USA Today, August 19, 1996.

USA Today, "Lifeline: Celeb Kudos," October 18, 1993.

USA Today, "Some People Now Get Therapy over the Phone," November 3, 1994.

Variety, "A Year in Show Biz: Day-by-Day," 1969.

Variety, "A Year in Show Biz: Day-by-Day," October 1965.

Variety, "A Year in Show Biz: Day-by-Day," *32nd Anniversary Edition*, October 1964–1965.

Variety, "A Year in Show Biz: Day-by-Day," *34th Anniversary Edition*, October 1966–1967.

Variety, "Anti-Establishment Becomes a Curriculum," April 28, 1971.

Variety, "Backstage Notes," March 24, 1998.

Variety, "Bicycling Editor Shears 'Shining' to Suit Kubrick," May 28, 1980.

Variety, "Biz Agents Cry: 'Remove IA Bug on Goin' South,'" October 18, 1978.

Variety, "Box Office News: As Good as Jack Gets," February 16, 1998.

Variety, "Cannes Castings," May 24, 1993.

Variety, "Cops Want Nicholson's Prints in Polanski Case," April 4, 1977.

Variety, "Down-to-Wire 'R' Allows Sun Ads on Kubrick's *Shining*," May, 21, 1980.

Variety, "Fire Guts Set of Kubrick 'Shining' $2,500,000 Cost," January 31, 1979.

Variety, Good Morning, January 15, 1993.

Variety, Good Morning, October 19, 1993.

Variety, "In the Hopper," April 21, 1997.

Variety, "Jack the Thumper," May 23, 1994.

Variety, Just for Variety, July 18, 1991.

Variety, Just for Variety, August 12, 1991.

Variety, Just for Variety, January 12, 1993.

Variety, Just for Variety, February 10, 1993.

Variety, Just for Variety, February 11, 1993.

Variety, Just for Variety, April 21, 1993.

Variety, Just for Variety, November 16, 1993.

Variety, Just for Variety, December 22, 1993.

Variety, Just for Variety, January 24, 1994.

Variety, Just for Variety, February 3, 1994.

Variety, Just for Variety, February 15, 1994.

Variety, Just for Variety, May 25, 1994.

Variety, Just for Variety, August 12, 1994.

Variety, "Nicholson at Nite," March 7, 1994.

Variety, "Nicholson Draws Majestic Blood," May 22, 1995

Variety, "Nicholson Feted at AFI Tribute," March 7, 1994.

Variety, "Nicholson in NY: End of 'Riot Fad' in U.S. Features," September 16, 1970.

Variety, "Nicholson Settles London Libel Action," May 11, 1984.

Variety, "Nicholson Sues NEC over Magazine Ad," November 19, 1986.

Variety, "Nicholson Suit Dropped," May 3, 1994.

Variety, "No Fingerprints Link Nicholson to Hash," April 20, 1977.

Variety, "Old Hands Rejoin Stevens for AFI Nicholson Tribute," February 25, 1994.

Variety, "Ordeal by Cameras for Roman Polanski," April 6, 1977.

Variety, "Pauline Kael Back at New Yorker," June 4, 1989.

Variety, "Pick Jack Nicholson for Mike Nichols Pic," April 29, 1970.

Variety, "R Tags Make Up Bulk of MPAA's Latest Ratings," May 20, 1980.

Variety, "Shining B.O. Drops after Strong Preem," June 4, 1980.

Variety, "The Border," July 18, 1980.

Variety, "The Horror, the Horror," April 1, 1993.

Variety, "Trailer Wars," August 3, 1992.

Variety, "U, Hemdale Sked Films with Same Title and Theme," April 16, 1979.

Variety, "What Have You Done For Me Lately . . . ," June 14, 1994.

Variety, "Who Is the Most Popular Star?" April 1, 1993.

Variety, 32nd Anniversary Edition. October 1964-1965.

Variety, June 8, 1979.

Variety, June 26, 1979.

Variety, July 16, 1979.

Variety, December 4, 1979.

Variety, March 7, 1980.

Variety, May 30, 1980.

Variety, June 20, 1980.

Variety, June 30, 1980.

Variety, July 18, 1980.

Variety, July 22, 1980.

Variety, September 3, 1980.

Variety, September 10, 1980.

Variety, May 27, 1981.

Variety, October 10, 1982.

Variety, February 4, 1983.

Variety, February 7, 1983.

Variety, March 8, 1983.

Variety, March 14, 1983.

Variety, April 13, 1983.

Variety, July 29, 1985.

Variety, August 18, 1985.

Variety, December 18, 1985.

Variety, March 20, 1986.

Variety, March 26, 1986.

Variety, September 9, 1987.

Variety, September 11, 1987.

Variety, April 8, 1988.

Variety, June 9, 1988.

Variety, August 29, 1988.

Variety, November 7, 1988.

Variety, March 5, 1991.

Variety, April 19, 1991.

Variety, August 12, 1991.

Variety, October 2, 1992.

Variety, March 1994.

Variety, April 25, 1995.

Variety, February 20, 1996.

Variety, April 29, 1996.

Vineberg, Steve. *Guardian*, May 13, 1988.

Vogel, Carol. "Secret Tips on Art for the Wealthy and Wary." *New York Times*, August 12, 1997.

Wade, Judy. "I'm a Porn Fan, Says Jack Nicholson." *Sun*, May 5, 1981.

Wadler, Joyce. "Boldface Names." *New York Times*, February 17, 2004.

Walker, Ander. "Million Dollar Men." *Evening Standard*, September 9, 1976.

Walker, Beverly. "Jack Can Handle the Truth," *Variety*, Jan 15, 1999.

Wall Street Journal, "Star Wars," January 25, 1984.

Weaver, Neal. "I Have the Blood of Kings in My Veins, Is My Point of View." *After Dark*, October 1969.

Wedman, Les. "Jack Nicholson Has His Film Work Cut Out for Him," *Los Angeles Times*, January 11, 1970.

Weiler, A. H. "Arf, Arf! It's Jack Nicholson." *New York Times*, August 8, 1971.

Weiner, Marci. Hollywood Beat, *Entertainment Today*, April 1, 1994.

Weinraur, Bernard. "Who's Afraid of the Big Bad Book Editor?" *New York Times*, June 12, 1994.

Weisberg, Lori. "Nicholson Uses Humor to Field Flak on New Film," *UCLA Daily Bruin*, May 21, 1976.

Western Mail, "Honest, and Sometimes Lovable, Jack," March 17, 1984.

Williams, Whitney. "New Look Is Growth, Curbs and Explosion of Nonviolence." *Variety, 35th Anniversary Edition*, October 1967–1968.

———. "Turbulent 12 Months: Labor Restive as Studios Slash Jobs, Majors Sue TV Nets." *Variety*, 1969.

Willows, Terry. "Jack the Lovable Lecher." *Evening Star*, March 3, 1986.

———. "Jack's Raring to Go Wild." *Daily Star*, February 8, 1982.

———. "The Cobra Casanova." *Evening Star*, 1981.

Wilson, Earl. "Angelica's No Fink." *New York Post*, May 19, 1977.

———. "He Won't Go Oscar-Hunting." *New York Post*, November 18, 1975.

———. "It Happened Last Night," *New York Post*, January 23, 1970.

———. "Jack, the Household Name." *New York Post*, June, 6, 1975.

———. "Nicholson an Abnormally Normal Actor." *L.A. Herald Examiner*, June 18, 1975.

Winsten, Archer. Rages and Outrages. *New York Post*, April 27, 1979.

———. Rages and Outrages. *New York Post*, May 6, 1974.

Woman's Wear Daily, "Cuckoo Love Story," March 24, 1976.

Woman's Wear Daily, "London Highlife," August 23, 1976.

Wood, Gaby. "The Two Jacks." *Observer*, January 17, 2003.

York, David. "Secrets of the Great Seducer." *Sunday Mirror*, April 15, 1984.

MAGAZINES

Allen, Ted. "The Women We Love . . . Helen Hunt." *Esquire*, August 1998.

Andrew, Geoff. "Grin Reaper." *Time Out*, March 11, 1998.

Barrett, Rona. "Jack Nicholson." *Rona Barrett's Gossip*, 1975.

Brantley, Ben. "Anjelica Huston Hots Up." *Vanity Fair*, July 1990.

Buck, Joan Juliet. "Anjelica Huston: A Born Knock-Out." *Vogue*, September 1985.

Burr, Ty. "Best Picture." *Entertainment Weekly Special*, March 1998.

———. "Tom Cruise: Today's Top Gun." *Entertainment Weekly*, Fall 1996.

Cahill, Tim. "Knocking Round the Nest." *Rolling Stone*, December 4, 1975.

Calhoun, John. "Labor Pains." *Theater Crafts International*, February 1993.

Carson, Tom. "Ten Things You Can't Say about the Movies." *Esquire*, April 1999.

Case, Brian. "Howlin' Jack." *Time Out*, August 17, 1993.

Chase, Chris. "Nicholson: The Legend That Jack Built." *Cosmopolitan*, February 1983.

Chatman, Seymour. "Antonioni in 1980." *Film Quarterly*, September 22, 1997.

Claire, Marie. "Sexy at 60? Warren." *Hollywood Report*, February 1997.

Collins, Nancy. "Jack the Wolf." *Vanity Fair*, April 1994.

———. "The Great Seducer: Jack Nicholson." *Rolling Stone*, March 29, 1984.

Davidson, Bill. "The Conquering Antihero." *New York Times Magazine*, October 12, 1975.

Davies, Hunter. "Great Film Jack, Now Let's Talk About You," *Interview*, 1992.

Davis, Ivor. "Can Jack Save Jake?" *Los Angeles Magazine*, 1989.

Darrach, Brad. "Jack Finds His Queen of Hearts." *People*, July 8, 1985.

———. "Jack Is Nimble, Jack Is Best, Jack Flies over the Cuckoo's Nest–En Route to an Oscar?" *People Weekly*, December 8, 1975.

———. "Liddy Poo, the New Girl In Jack's Life." *People*, 1994.

Davis, Sally O. "Jack Nicholson: Really Good at Being Evil." *Senior Life*, July 1989.

Demaris, Ovid. "Is Jack Nicholson Hiding Something?" *Parade*, January 1, 1984.

Denby, David. "Big Pictures." *New Yorker*, January 8, 2007.

DeVries, Hilary. "Jack Nicholson on Sex, Freedom, Money . . . " *FanFare*, December 20, 1992.

D. M. "It Must Be Witchcraft," *Vogue*, June 1986.

Ebert, Roger. "Jack's Back." *Marquee*, February 1984.

Entertainment Weekly. "I Don't Want People to Know What I'm Actually Like . . . " January 8, 1993.

Entertainment Weekly. "Spring Movie Previews." February 4, 2003.

Esquire. October 1997.

Esquire. "The Sound and the Fury." March 2004.

Fayard, Judy. "Happy Jack." *Life Magazine*, Feb 21, 1971.

Film Buff. "Nicholson." January 1975.

Filmmakers Newsletter. January 1976.

Fink, Mitchell. "A Few Bucks." *People*, October 21, 1991.

———. "Au Revoir, Jack?" *People*, November 25, 1991.

———. "Did an Old Flame Flicker?" *People*, July 15, 1996.

———. "Jack's Back and the LAPD's Got Him." *People*, May 6, 1996.

———. "Trouble in the House that Jack Bought." *People*, September 28, 1992.

Friend, Tad. "Don't Touch That Dial." *New Yorker*, May 22, 2006.

Fuller, Graham. "Anjelica Huston." *Interview*, February 1, 2000.

Fury, Kathleen D. "Jack Nicholson." *Ladies Home Journal*, April 1976.

Genesis. "Jack Nicholson Interview." February 1975.

Giles, Jeff. "About Jack." *Newsweek*, December 16, 2002.

Goldstein, Patrick. "Empire of the Setting Sun." *Los Angeles Magazine*, February 1, 1996.

Graham, Mike. "Jack Flies Out of a Troubled *Cuckoo's Nest*." *Today*, March 10, 1988.

Greenspan, Andrew. "An Interview with Jack Nicholson." *New York Arts Journal*, September-November 1977.

Grimes, Teresa. "The Chameleon Smile: A Series of Jack Nicholson Films." *New American Cinema*, December 1980.

Grobel, Lawrence. "Glory Days." *Movieline*, August 1993.

———. "Saul Bellow." *Playboy*, May 1997.

Grogan, David, and J. Greenwalt. *People*, February 1, 1993.

GQ. "And the Nominees in the Category of Free Footwear Are . . . " March 1999.

GQ. "The 1998 Overrated List." September 1998.

Halberstadt, Michele. "Cool Rider." *Premiere (France)*, January 1986.

Hammack, Marchelle. "Jack of Hearts." *Vanity Fair*, June 1994.

Harmetz, Aljean. "The Two Jacks." *New York Times Magazine*, September 9, 1989.

Harris, Kathryn. "Edgar in Hollywood," *Fortune*, April 15, 1996

Hedegaard, Erik. "A Singular Guy." *Rolling Stone*, October 5, 2006.

Hello. "Fun with Rebecca Broussard & Celebrity Friends . . . " September 17, 1974.

Hello. "Jack Nicholson." July 16, 1994.

Hello. "Jack Nicholson & Rebecca Broussard." August 6, 1994.

Hello, August 27, 1994.

Hendrickson, Matt. "Random Notes." *Rolling Stone*, February 5, 1998.

Hirschberg, Lynn. "Jack Nicholson." *Rolling Stone*, November 10, 1987.

Hobart, Christy. "Sea Voyager." *House & Garden*, August 2006.

Hoffer, Richard. "Banks Shot." *Sports Illustrated*, February 21, 1997.

Hunter, Derek. "The Nerve of Nicholson." *Movie News*, 1975.

Hutchins, Chris. "Just a Rose by Any Other Name." *Today*, February 2, 1988.

Janos, Leo. "Jack Nicholson: Bankable and Brilliant." *Cosmopolitan*, December 1976.

————. "The Star with the Killer Smile." *Time*, August 12, 1974.

J. B. "Nicholson." *Chicago Tribune Magazine*, 1980.

Kael, Pauline. The Current Cinema, *New Yorker*, June 9, 1980.

Kauffmann, Stanley. On Films. *New Republic*, May 3, 1993.

Kaylin, Lucy. "Jack Nicholson Has Never Been to an Orgy," *GQ*, January 1996.

Kelly, Ken. "Tales from Tosca." *San Francisco Focus*, April 1991.

Kilday, Gregg. "Jack Nicholson's Face Odysseys." *GQ*, March 1981.

Lahr, John. "Making it Real: How Mike Nichols Re-Created Comedy & Himself," *New Yorker*, February 21, 2000.

Leedham, Robert. "Rebel Rouser." *FanFare*, December 20, 1992.

Leigh, Danny. "Don't Fence Me In." *Sight & Sound*, May 2003.

Lewin, David. "Jack Nicholson." *US Magazine*, March 16, 1982.

Lynch, Lorrie. "Stars Get Scooped in Ice Cream Tale." *People*, September 12, 1986.

Markham-Smith, Ian. "Nicholson." *US Magazine*, April 9, 1984.

Martin, Jim. "So Cool, So Reichian," *Steamshovel Press*, Summer 1994.

Martin, Richard. "A Taste of Los Angeles." *Nation's Restaurant News*, September 22, 1997.

Marx, Arthur. "On His Own Terms." *Cigar Aficionado,* Summer 1995.

Masters, Kim. "It All Began at Paramount." *Vanity Fair*, April 2000.

Mehle, Aileen. *W*, December 1994.

Miller, Edwin. "No Ego in His Act." *Seventeen,* April 1976.

Miller, George. "Jack of All Trades," *Time Out*, May 18, 1988.

Miller, Samantha, R. Ellenson, and J. Jerome. "Jack Nicholson, Bio." *People*, December 16, 2002.

Modderno, Craig. "A Chat with Jack," *Hollywood Life*, November 2004.

News of the World Sunday Magazine. "You're All Right." October 24, 1985.

Newsweek. February 13, 1978.

Newsweek. December 5, 1983.

New York. "Anjelica and Jack: Cries and Whispers," February 7, 1994.

New York, "Fin de Smoking," April 10, 1995.

New York. "Jack to Jason: Fangs for the Yelp," April 26, 1993.

New York. "Movies," September 11, 1989.

Observer. "Jack the Lad Goes to the Devil," April 10, 1989.

Observer. "Werewolf in Wonderland," July 10, 1994.

Orecklin, Michele. "Can Bad Boys Be Good Citizens?" *Time Out*, March 14, 1998.

Palmer, Marlyn. "Jack the (Ex) Lad." *London Times Magazine*, December 28, 2002.

Peden, Lauren. "Jack Nicholson." *US Magazine*, February 1999.

People. "A Crash Course in Avoiding a Scene." August 2, 1999.

People. "A Fine Romance," December 26, 1994.

People. "A Photographer Covering . . . " June 23, 1997.

People. "Big Bunny." June 8, 1981.

People. "Bonofide Admirer," January 18, 1988.

People. "Dance Fever." May 27, 1996.

People. "Furthermore." February 18, 1980.

People. "Good to Go." February 2, 1998.

People. "Images." March 15, 1999.

People. "Jack's Clip Hanger." June 9, 1980.

People. "Joining the Club." December 6, 1993.

People. "Laud of the Rinks." February 9, 1998.

People. "Let the Good Times Roll." March 23, 1998.

People. "Lunacy." August 16, 1976.

People. "Mail." August 18, 1989.

People. "New Jack City." September 7, 1992.

People. "None Flew Over." July 5, 1976.

People. "Ranger Rover." December 16, 1996.

People. "Rights & Permissions." August 14. 1972.

People. "Room at the Top." May 17, 1993.

People. Star Tracks. July 20, 1998.

People. Star Tracks. September 11, 1995.

People. Star Tracks: "Charities." June 1, 1998.

People. Star Tracks: "Crazy Mountain High." May 21, 1984.

People. "Suffering by Comparison." August 18, 1997.

People. "The Dame." September 29, 1997.

People. "Uneasy Rider." July 26, 1999.

People. "Young Hollywood through the Decades." November 18, 1996.

People. May 22, 1976.

People. August 26, 1991.

People. November 15, 1993.

People. January 24, 1994.

People. May 16, 1994.

People. March 20, 1995.

People. May 1, 1995.

People. July 31, 1995.

People. September 16, 1996.

People. July 13, 1998.

People. February, 23, 1998.

Playboy. December 1979.

Playgirl. "Evans Advises Nicholson." August 1976.

Playgirl. "Jack Nicholson: 'I Don't Know Why I Do the Things I Do.'"

Playgirl. "We've Always." October 1981.

Playgirl. December 1979.

Playgirl. March 1980.

Renold, Evelyn. "The Entertainer." *Midwest Magazine*, March 28, 1976.

Renson, David. "Heidi Fleiss." *Playboy*, August 1996.

Ritz. "Jack Nicholson & Litchfield." June 1984.

Rinzler, Alan. "A Conversation with Jack Nicholson." *Rolling Stone*, April 29, 1971.

Rolling Stone. Correspondence. May 14, 1998.

Rolling Stone. "The Great Seducer." March 29, 1984.

Rosenbaum, Ron. "Acting: The Method and Mystique of Jack Nicholson." *New York Times Magazine*, July 13, 1986.

Sager, Mike. "Jack Nicholson, 66." *Esquire*, January 2004.

Schickel, Richard. "Time 100/ Most Influential Actors." *Time Magazine*, June 8, 1998.

Schiff, Stephen. "Jumping Jack," *Vanity Fair.* August 1986.

Schruers, Fred. "Gentleman Jack." *US Magazine*, July 1994.

———. "The Rolling Stone Interview: Jack Nicholson." *Rolling Stone,* August 14, 1986.

Scott, Walter. *Parade Magazine*, October 11, 1987.

Screen International. "News In Brief," October 27, 1995.

Screen International. "Sun to Pay Nicholson Damages," May 19, 1984.

Screen International. November 18, 1994.

Screen International. May 26, 1995.

Screen International. September 13, 1996.

Screen International. October 11, 1996.

Screen International. February 9, 1996.

Screen International. September 11, 1998.

Serwer, Andy. "Extreme Makeover." *Fortune,* May 29, 2006.

Sheff, David. "Playboy Interview: Jack Nicholson." *Playboy,* January, 2004.

Shepard, Alicia. "Celebrity Journalists." *American Journalism Review.* September 1997.

Show. "Odd Man In." May 1971.

Smith, Gale. "Sitting Ducks: The Jagloms." *Interview.* March 1979.

Smith, Gavin. "Mike Nichols." *Film Comment,* May 1, 1999.

Spy Magazine. May 1993.

Sragow, Michael. "Darkness at the Edge of Towne," *American Film,* February 1989.

———. "Director Tony Richardson on *The Border.*" *Rolling Stone,* April 1, 1982.

Svetkey, Benjamin. "Jack on Jack." *Entertainment Weekly,* January 3, 2003.

Swenson, Karen. "One More Look at 'On a Clear Day You Can See Forever.'" *Barbra Quarterly* no. 9, Summer 1982.

Szymanski, Michael, and P. Keogh. "Hoffa 'the Movie' Appears." *US Magazine,* February 1993.

Thomson, David. "Nicholson, King of Mulholland: He Just Wants to Make It Nice." *Playgirl,* April 1981.

Time. "Bio Pic," October 17, 1994.

Time. "Charged: Jack Nicholson." March 14, 1994.

Time. "Charges Dismissed." May 16, 1994.

Time. "Salaries." July 1, 1991.

Time. "The Reformation of a Rogue?" August 8, 1994.

Time. April 11, 1994.

Torgoff, Martin. "Jack Nicholson." *Interview,* August 1984.

Trebbe, Ann, and Karen Thomas. "Nicholson, Broussard May be Expecting No. 2." *USA Today,* August 14, 1991.

TV Guide. "What I Watch: Peter Fonda." August 13, 1994.

TV Guide. April 19, 1980.

TV Guide. October 2, 1993.

TV Guide. April 10, 1999.

US. "Jackie B. Good." October 12, 1998.

US. "One Shot." May 1998.

US. March 30, 1982.

Vance, Vick. "Jack Nicholson." *Les Gens,* 1988.

Vanity Fair. Letters to Editor: "Jumping Jack." June 1992.

Vanity Fair, "What's Up, Jack?" April 1984.

Ventura, Michael. "Jack Nicholson Interview #3001." *L.A. Weekly,* June 28, 1985.

Warhol, Andy. "Andy Warhol Listens to Jack Nicholson." *Interview.* December 1976.

Waterman, Ivan. "Baby Love Helps Jack." *Today,* June 28, 1994.

———. *Today,* August 7, 1989.

Wild, David. "Jack Nicholson," *Rolling Stone,* May 3, 2007.

Wilmington, Michael. "Jack Nicholson." *Playgirl,* August 1985.

Women's Wear Daily. "Wolfman Jack." March 10, 1994.

Woods, Vicki. "Jack Oozy." *Tattler,* June 1984.

W. August 14, 1981.

W. Suzy, March 1998.

W. Suzy, May 1998.

Wolf, William. "Jack Nicholson Can Do Anything, Can't He?" *Cue,* July 7, 1975.

PHOTO CREDITS

INDEX